AIX Version 4: System and Administration Guide

AIX Version 4: System and Administration Guide

by James W. DeRoest

McGraw-Hill

New York   San Francisco   Washington, D.C.   Auckland   Bogotá
Caracas   Lisbon   London   Madrid   Mexico City   Milan
Montreal   New Delhi   San Juan   Singapore
Sydney   Tokyo   Toronto

Library of Congress Cataloging-in-Publication Data

DeRoest, James W.
    AIX version 4 : system and administration guide /
James W. DeRoest
        p.   cm. — (J. Ranade workstation series)
    Includes index.
    ISBN 0-07-036688-8
    1. AIX (Computer file) 2. Operating systems (Computers) 3. IBM
RS/6000 Workstation.   I. Title.   II. Series.
QA76.76.063D4725   1997
005.4'32—dc21   97-6203
                                                                      CIP

McGraw-Hill

A Division of The McGraw·Hill Companies

ISBN 0-07-036688-8

*The sponsoring editor for this book was Judy Brief, the editing
supervisor was Marc Campbell, and the production supervisor was
Pamela A. Pelton. It was set in Century Schoolbook by North Market
Street Graphics.*

Printed and bound by R. R. Donnelley & Sons Company.

McGraw-Hill books are available at special quantity discounts to use as
premiums and sales promotions, or for use in corporate training programs. For more information, please write to the Director of Special
Sales, McGraw-Hill, 11 West 19th Street, New York, NY 10011. Or contact your local bookstore.

 This book is printed on recycled, acid-free paper containing
a minimum of 50% recycled, de-inked fiber.

This book is dedicated to my Dad and my Grandfather. They taught me that we all need faith, family, and hard work.

Contents

Preface   xxiii

Part 1   System Administration Tasks and Tools

Chapter 1. Introduction   3

1.1	System Administration	3
1.2	AIX and UNIX	4
1.3	AIX and OSF	4
1.4	System Administration Activities	6
	1.4.1 System Administration Tasks and Tools	7
	1.4.2 System Architecture	7
	1.4.3 System Installation and Operation	7
	1.4.4 System Configuration	7
	1.4.5 Network Configuration	7
	1.4.6 Network File Systems	7
	1.4.7 Distributed Services	8
	1.4.8 Managing Users and Resources	8
	1.4.9 System Recovery and Tuning	8
	1.4.10 Advanced Distributed Architectures	8

Chapter 2. InfoExplorer   9

2.1	AIX Help	9
2.2	InfoExplorer Overview	9
2.3	InfoExplorer Installation	10
	2.3.1 InfoExplorer on CD-ROM	10
	2.3.2 InfoExplorer on Fixed Disk	11
	2.3.3 InfoExplorer over NFS	12
2.4	Using InfoExplorer	12
	2.4.1 Hypertext Links	14
	2.4.2 Searching	14
	2.4.3 History and Bookmarks	15
	2.4.4 Note Facility	16
	2.4.5 Output	17

2.5	InfoExplorer and man	18
	2.5.1 Extracting Man Pages	18
	2.5.2 Man Page Format	19
2.6	Feedback	22
2.7	QwikInfo	22

Part 2   System Architecture

Chapter 3. POWER Architecture   25

3.1	Know Your RISC	25
3.2	POWER	26
3.3	POWER2	26
3.3	PowerPC	28
3.4	POWER Multiprocessor	29
	3.4.1 SMP	30
	3.4.2 SP	32
3.5	Compatibility	32

Chapter 4. AIX V4 Kernel   35

4.1	Multiprocessing Kernel	35
4.2	Kernel Architecture	35
	4.2.1 Threads	37
	4.2.2 Signals	37
	4.2.3 Locks	38
	4.2.4 Scheduling and Dispatching	39
	4.2.5 Overhead	40
4.3	POWER Multiprocessors	40
4.4	InfoExplorer Keywords	41
4.5	QwikInfo	41

Part 3   System Installation and Management

Chapter 5. System Management Tools   45

5.1	SMIT	45
5.2	Using SMIT	46
	5.2.1 SMIT Display	47
	5.2.2 SMIT Keys	48
	5.2.3 SMIT Help and Messages	49
	5.2.4 SMIT Log File	49
	5.2.5 SMIT Script File	51
	5.2.6 SMIT FastPaths	51
5.3	Customizing SMIT	52
5.4	Visual System Management	53
5.5	Distributed Systems Management	55
	5.5.1 DSMIT	56
	5.5.2 DME History	58
5.5	InfoExplorer Keywords	59
5.6	QwikInfo	59

Chapter 6. AIX Installation and Maintenance   61

6.1   Installation Considerations   61
6.2   Installation and Maintenance Planning   62
    6.2.1   Product Packaging   62
    6.2.2   Support Information   63
    6.2.3   Choosing an Installation Method   68
    6.2.4   Apply and Commit   68
    6.2.5   File System Expansion   69
    6.2.6   System State   69
    6.2.7   Upgrading Existing AIX Systems   70
6.3   Installing AIX   71
6.4   Installing Licensed Program Products   72
6.5   Installing Non-LPP Products   78
6.6   Applying Maintenance   78
6.7   Postinstallation and Maintenance Tasks   79
    6.7.1   Review Install/Update Status   79
    6.7.2   Restoring Your Environment   80
    6.7.3   Create New Bootable Media and Backups   80
6.8   Distributed Systems   82
    6.8.1   NFS Installation Support   82
    6.8.2   Creating a Reference System   82
    6.8.3   Network Install Manager   83
6.9   InfoExplorer Keywords   94
6.10   QwikInfo   95

Chapter 7. System Boot and Shutdown   97

7.1   AIX Boot Process   97
7.2   Booting the System   97
    7.2.1   Stand-alone Boot   98
7.3   Creating Bootable Media   99
    7.3.1   Configuring the Boot List   99
    7.3.2   Installing a Boot Image   100
    7.3.3   Creating Stand-alone Boot Media   100
7.4   Boot Sequence of Events   100
    7.4.1   Key Mode Switch Position   101
7.5   ROS Initialization   101
    7.5.1   Built-In Self Test—BIST   102
    7.5.2   Power-On Self Test—POST   103
    7.5.3   Initial Sequence Controller Test   103
    7.5.4   Core Sequence Controller Test   104
    7.5.5   IPL Controller Load Boot Image   104
7.6   Boot Kernel Configuration   105
    7.6.1   Phase 1   106
    7.6.2   Phase 2   109
    7.6.3   Phase 3   110
    7.6.4   Runtime   111
7.7   Stopping the System   112
7.8   Troubleshooting   112
7.9   InfoExplorer Keywords   113
7.10   QwikInfo   113

Part 4   System Configuration and Customizing

Chapter 8. Runtime Configuration   117

8.1   AIX Runtime   117
8.2   System Environments   117
    8.2.1   Time Settings   117
    8.2.2   Language Environment   118
    8.2.3   Characteristics of the Operating System   118
    8.2.4   Number of Licensed Users   121
    8.2.5   System Logs   121
    8.2.6   Dump Device   122
8.3   PTY   122
8.4   Console   123
8.5   InfoExplorer Keywords   123
8.6   QwikInfo   124

Chapter 9. Devices Configuration and the Object Data Manager   125

9.1   AIX Dynamic Device Configuration   125
9.2   ODM Overview   125
9.3   ODM Components   126
    9.3.1   ODM Database   126
    9.3.2   Objects and Object Classes   127
    9.3.3   Command and Library Interface   128
9.4   ODM Editor   128
9.5   Configuration Tables and the ODM   129
9.6   Device Configuration   131
9.7   Predefined and Customized Devices   132
9.8   Device States   134
9.9   Boot Devices   134
9.10 Small Computer System Interface   135
    9.10.1   SCSI-1 and SCSI-2   135
    9.10.2   Cables and Adapters   135
    9.10.3   Single-Ended and Differential SCSI   135
    9.10.4   SCSI Addressing   136
9.11 Updating the Product Topology Diskette   136
9.12 InfoExplorer Keywords   137
9.13 QwikInfo   137

Chapter 10. Tapes   139

10.1 Tape Characteristics   139
    10.1.1   Physical Characteristics   139
    10.1.2   Data Format   140
    10.1.3   Block Size   141
    10.1.4   Device Names   142
    10.1.5   Tape Positioning   143
    10.1.6   Permissions   144
10.2 Tape Tools   145

10.3   Public Domain Tape Tools   145
10.4   IBM Tape Devices and Characteristics   146
10.5   InfoExplorer Keywords   146
10.6   QwikInfo   147

Chapter 11. Disks and File Systems   149

11.1   Disk Evolution   149
11.2   Disk Hardware   150
       11.2.1   Serial Storage Architecture   150
       11.2.2   RAID   150
       11.2.3   Fixed Disk Architecture   151
11.3   Disk Installation   152
11.4   Logical Volume Manager   152
11.5   Configuring Volume Groups   154
       11.5.1   Quorum   156
       11.5.2   Root Volume Group—rootvg   157
11.6   Configuring Logical Volumes   157
       11.6.1   Logical Volume Types   158
       11.6.2   Logical Volume Size   158
       11.6.3   Interdisk Policy   158
       11.6.4   Intradisk Policy   159
       11.6.5   Mirrors   160
       11.6.6   Adding a Logical Volume   161
11.7   File Systems   161
       11.7.1   Super Block   161
       11.7.2   Inodes   163
       11.7.3   Data Blocks   164
       11.7.4   Fragments   164
       11.7.5   Compression   165
       11.7.6   Large Files and File Systems   166
       11.7.7   Virtual File System   166
       11.7.8   Journaled File System Configuration   167
       11.7.9   Mounting File Systems   170
       11.7.10 AIX Root Tree   171
       11.7.11 AIX V3 File System Compatability   172
11.8   Paging Space   173
11.9   Volume Maintenance   174
       11.9.1   Moving File Systems   175
       11.9.2   Moving Volume Groups   175
       11.9.3   Resizing File Systems   175
11.10 Troubleshooting   176
11.11 InfoExplorer Keywords   177
11.12 QwikInfo   178

Chapter 12. Terminals and Modems   179

12.1   AIX TTY   179
       12.1.1   AIX STREAMS Subsystem   179
12.2   Serial TTY Support   180
       12.2.1   Cabling   180
       12.2.2   Modem/DCE Wiring   181

12.2.3 TTY/DTE Wiring   181
12.2.4 Serial Cable Length   183
12.2.5 Port Addressing   184
12.3 AIX TTY Definition   184
12.3.1 Line Speed   185
12.3.2 Data Format   186
12.3.3 Terminal Type   186
12.3.4 Control Characters   188
12.3.5 Line Discipline   188
12.3.6 Login State   190
12.4 Modem Support   190
12.4.1 Line Signals   191
12.4.2 Problems   192
12.5 Low-Function Terminals   192
12.5.1 Keyboard   193
12.5.2 Display   194
12.5.3 Display Fonts   194
12.6 Console   196
12.6.1 Console Problems   197
12.7 Pseudo-TTY Devices   197
12.8 InfoExplorer Keywords   198
12.9 QwikInfo   198

Chapter 13. Printers   201

13.1 Printing Overview   201
13.2 Print Devices   204
13.2.1 Testing the Device and Driver   207
13.3 Print Queues   209
13.3.1 Local and Remote Queues   210
13.3.2 Backend Programs   210
13.3.3 Remote BSD and SYSV Support   211
13.3.4 Postscript Printing   212
13.3.5 Custom Backends   212
13.3.6 Customizing Banner Pages   212
13.4 Virtual Printers   214
13.5 Testing and Modifying Printer Configuration   214
13.6 qdaemon and /etc/qconfig   215
13.7 lpd Daemon   216
13.8 Administering Jobs and Queues   217
13.8.1 Starting and Stopping Queues and Printers   218
13.8.2 Listing Print Jobs   219
13.8.3 Changing Priority   219
13.8.4 Removing Print Jobs   220
13.9 ASCII Terminal Printers   220
13.9.1 Pass-Through Mode   221
13.10 X-station Printers   221
13.11 Desktop Print Sharing   222
13.12 InfoExplorer Keywords   222
13.13 QwikInfo   223

Part 5 Network Configuration and Customizing

Chapter 14. Network Architecture   227

  14.1 Internet History   227
      14.1.1 OSI Model   227
      14.1.2 ARPANET   228
      14.1.3 NSFNET   228
      14.1.4 CREN   229
      14.1.5 Future NET   229
  14.2 Wireless Networking   230
      14.2.1 History   230
      14.2.2 Cellular Service   230
      14.2.3 Packet Radio   231
      14.2.4 Mobile IP   231
      14.2.5 Wireless Systems   231
      14.2.6 Wireless Information   232
  14.3 AIX Networking   232

Chapter 15. TCP/IP   233

  15.1 TCP/IP   233
  15.2 TCP/IP Suite   233
  15.3 Planning   234
  15.4 Hardware Components   234
      15.4.1 Ethernet   235
      15.4.2 Token Ring   238
      15.4.3 Fiber Distributed Data Interface (FDDI)   239
      15.4.4 SLIP/PPP   241
      15.4.5 Serial Optical Channel Converter (SOCC)   242
      15.4.6 Asynchronous Transfer Mode (ATM)   243
  15.5 TCP/IP Software Configuration   244
  15.6 Addressing   244
      15.6.1 Hardware Address   244
      15.6.2 IP Address   244
      15.6.3 Domain Address   246
      15.6.4 Host Tables   246
      15.6.5 Domain Name Service   246
  15.7 Network Routing   251
      15.7.1 Static Routes   252
      15.7.2 Dynamic Routes   253
      15.7.3 Subnets   253
      15.7.4 Interface Configuration   254
  15.8 System Resource Controller   255
      15.8.1 TCP/IP Subsystem   255
      15.8.2 Master Daemon—Inetd   256
      15.8.3 Other Network Daemons   259
      15.8.4 Startup Configuration   260
  15.9 SLIP and PPP   260
      15.9.1 Dedicated SLIP   261
      15.9.2 Nondedicated SLIP   262
      15.9.3 PPP   263

15.10 Anonymous FTP   265
15.11 Security   266
       15.11.1 Network Trusted Computing Base   266
       15.11.2 Traditional Security Measures   267
       15.11.3 Security Information   268
15.12 Network Management   268
       15.12.1 AIX SNMP   269
15.13 Troubleshooting   270
       15.13.1 Sniffers   270
       15.13.2 AIX iptrace   270
       15.13.3 Interface Status   271
       15.13.4 Reachability   271
       15.13.5 Server Applications   271
       15.13.6 Name Service   272
       15.13.7 mbuf Allocation   272
15.14 Other TCP Performance Options   273
15.15 InfoExplorer Keywords   274
15.16 QwikInfo   275

Chapter 16. UUCP   277

16.1   UUCP Overview   277
16.2   Using UUCP   277
       16.2.1   UUCP Addressing   278
16.3   UUCP Configuration   278
       16.3.1   UUCP Login ID   279
       16.3.2   Host Name   279
       16.3.3   Directories and Permissions   279
       16.3.4   Configuration Tables   280
16.4   UUCP Daemons   286
16.5   Housekeeping and Logs   286
16.6   Hardware   287
16.7   UUCP Commands   287
16.8   Troubleshooting   288
16.9   InfoExplorer Keywords   288
16.10 QwikInfo   289

Chapter 17. System Network Architecture   291

17.1   Introduction to SNA   291
17.2   SNA Overview   291
17.3   AIX SNA Services/6000   293
       17.3.1   Physical Interface   294
       17.3.2   Defining the Network   294
       17.3.3   Starting and Stopping Services   295
17.4   SNA Security   296
17.5   Network Management   297
17.6   Troubleshooting   297
17.7   InfoExplorer Keywords   297
17.8   QwikInfo   298

Part 6   Networked File Systems

Chapter 18. Network File System   303

18.1   Virtual File Systems   303
18.2   Network File System   303
    18.2.1   Configuring NFS   304
18.3   NFS Server   305
    18.3.1   NFS Server Daemons   306
    18.3.2   Exporting Server File Systems   306
18.4   NFS Clients   307
    18.4.1   Importing File Systems   308
18.5   Secure NFS   309
    18.5.1   Yellow Pages   310
    18.5.2   YP Name Space   310
    18.5.3   YP File Classes   311
    18.5.4   YP Servers and Clients   311
    18.5.5   Public Key Authentication   312
    18.5.6   Starting YP (NIS) Services   313
    18.5.7   Automounter   313
18.6   Troubleshooting   314
18.7   Highly Available Servers   316
    18.7.1   High-Availability Network File System   317
    18.7.2   High-Availability Cluster Multiprocessor   318
18.8   High-Speed NFS   319
18.9   NFS V3   319
18.10 InfoExplorer Keywords   320
18.11 QwikInfo   320

Chapter 19. DCE Distributed File System   323

19.1   Distributed File System Overview   323
    19.1.1   Andrew File System   323
    19.1.2   Distributed File System   324
    19.1.3   Access Control   324
    19.1.4   File System Structure   325
    19.1.5   Local File System   326
    19.1.6   VFS Compatibility   327
19.2   DFS Components   327
19.3   Installation and Configuration   329
    19.3.1   System Control Machine   331
    19.3.2   Fileset Database Machine   332
    19.3.3   File Server   332
    19.3.4   Creating Aggregates and Filesets   333
    19.3.5   Exporting and Mounting Filesets   334
    19.3.6   Backup Database Machine   335
    19.3.7   Fileset Replicator   335
    19.3.8   Installation Verification   335
19.4   Operation and Administration   336
19.5   Starting DFS   337
19.6   Access Control Lists   338
19.7   Replication   338

19.8   DFS Backup   339
19.9   InfoExplorer Keywords   340
19.10   QwikInfo   340

Chapter 20. Desktop File Services   343

20.1   Samba   343
20.2   Installation and Configuration   343
        20.2.1   smb.conf   344
        20.2.2   Name Service   345
        20.2.3   Directory Shares   346
        20.2.4   Printer Shares   347
20.3   NFS and DFS Compatability   348
20.4   Samba Licensing   348
20.5   What about Macs?   349

Part 7   Distributed Services

Chapter 21. Electronic Mail   353

21.1   Mail System Overview   353
        21.1.1   Mail User Agents   353
        21.1.2   Mail Transport Agents   354
        21.1.3   Addressing and Headers   355
        21.1.4   How Mail Is Sent   356
21.2   Sendmail Configuration   356
        21.2.1   sendmail.cf   357
        21.2.2   sendmail.nl   360
        21.2.3   Aliases   361
        21.2.4   Mail Logs   362
21.3   Starting and Stopping sendmail   363
21.4   Debugging   363
21.5   Managing Mail Queues   365
21.6   POP and IMAP   366
        21.6.1   POP   367
        21.6.2   IMAP   367
        21.6.3   IMSP and ACAP   368
        21.6.4   Pine   368
21.7   InfoExplorer Keywords   370
21.8   QwikInfo   371

Chapter 22. News   373

22.1   Read All about It   373
22.2   News Resources   373
22.3   News Server   374
22.4   News Readers   375
22.5   Newsgroups   376
22.6   News Software Sites   377
22.7   QwikInfo   378

Chapter 23. World Wide Web   379

23.1   WWW Overview   379
    23.1.1   Web Servers   379
    23.1.2   Web Browsers   380
    23.1.3   Locating Servers   380
23.2   AIX V4 Bonus Pak   381
    23.2.1   Java   381
    23.2.2   Netscape Navigator   382
    23.2.3   Adobe Acrobat Reader   382
    23.2.4   Ultimedia Services   383
    23.2.5   Netscape Commerce Server   384
    23.2.6   IBM Internet Connection Secure Server   385
23.3   WWW Server Administration   385
    23.3.1   Access Control   386
    23.3.2   Site Structure   387
23.4   Creating HTML Documents   388
23.5   Java   390
23.6   JavaScript   391
23.7   Security   393
    23.7.1   PKCS   393
    23.7.2   SSL   394
    23.7.3   Certificates   394
    23.7.4   DCE/Kerberos   394
    23.7.5   GSSAPI   395
    23.7.6   LDAP   395
    23.7.7   IPSec   395

Chapter 24. X11 Administration   397

24.1   Windowed Systems   397
24.2   X11 Overview   397
24.3   AIXWindows Components   398
24.4   X11 and CDE   399
    24.4.1   Application Defaults   399
    24.4.2   Fonts   400
    24.4.3   Window Managers   402
    24.4.4   X-Windows Display Manager (xdm)   406
24.5   Common Desktop Environment   406
    24.5.1   CDE Overview   407
24.6   CDE Componets   408
    24.6.1   Login Manager   409
    24.6.2   Session Manager   410
    24.6.3   Front Panel   411
    24.6.4   Style Manager   411
    24.6.5   File and Application Managers   411
    24.6.6   Workspace Manager   412
    24.6.7   Help Manager   413
24.7   CDE Summary   414
24.8   IBM Xstation Administration   414
    24.8.1   Configuration and Boot   415
    24.8.2   AIX Xstation Manager Configuration   416

24.9   InfoExplorer Keywords   418
24.10   QwikInfo   418

Part 8   Managing Users and Resources

Chapter 25. Managing the User Environment   **423**

25.1   User Administration Policy   423
25.2   Physical Resources   424
        25.2.1   User File Systems   424
25.3   UID Space and Groups   425
        25.3.1   /etc/group and /etc/security/group   425
25.4   Resource Limits   427
        25.4.1   /etc/security/limits   427
25.5   User Account Access Rights   431
25.6   User Account Environment   431
        25.6.1   /etc/environment and /etc/profile   432
        25.6.2   /etc/security/environ   435
        25.6.3   /etc/security/login.cfg   438
25.7   Managing User Accounts   438
        25.7.1   Adding a User Account   438
        25.7.2   Updating User Accounts   439
        25.7.3   Removing User Accounts   441
        25.7.4   Restricting Access   442
25.8   Password Files   442
        25.8.1   /etc/passwd   442
        25.8.2   /etc/security/passwd   443
        25.8.3   /etc/security/user   443
25.9   InfoExplorer Keywords   444
25.10   QwikInfo   444

Chapter 26. Process Management   **447**

26.1   Process Overview   447
26.2   Process Attributes   447
        26.2.1   Displaying Process Attributes   448
        26.2.2   Process Identifiers   449
        26.2.3   Effective and Real UID and GID   449
        26.2.4   Controlling Terminal   450
        26.2.5   Resource Untilization and Priority   450
        26.2.6   Process State   451
26.3   Parent Child Inheritance   451
26.4   Controlling Processes   452
        26.4.1   Rules of Thumb   452
        26.4.2   Ignoring Hangup   454
26.5   Scheduled Processes (cron)   454
        26.5.1   crontab   455
        26.5.2   Ad Hoc Jobs   456
        26.5.3   Managing cron Activities   456
26.6   System Resource Controller   457
        26.6.1   SRC Components   457

26.7   InfoExplorer Keywords   459
26.8   QwikInfo   459

Chapter 27. System Accounting   461

27.1   Accounting Overview   461
27.2   Data Collection   462
       27.2.1   Connect Time   462
       27.2.2   Process Resource Usage   462
       27.2.3   Command Usage   462
       27.2.4   Disk Usage   462
       27.2.5   Print Usage   463
       27.2.6   Accounting Files   463
27.3   Accounting Configuration   463
       27.3.1   Setup Collection Files   463
       27.3.2   Identifying Shifts   464
       27.3.3   Disk Accounting (/etc/filesystems)   464
       27.3.4   Print Accounting (/etc/qconfig)   465
       27.3.5   Report Directories   465
       27.3.6   Crontab Entries   465
       27.3.7   Work Unit Fees   466
27.4   Accounting Commands   466
       27.4.1   Starting and Stopping Accounting   466
       27.4.2   Displaying Statistics   466
       27.4.3   Summary Reports   468
27.5   Periodic Housecleaning   469
27.6   InfoExplorer Keywords   469
27.7   QwikInfo   470

Part 9   Security

Chapter 28. Auditing and Security   473

28.1   Security Overview   473
28.2   Defining a Security Policy   474
28.3   Passwords   474
       28.3.1   Shadow Password Files   474
       28.3.2   Password Rules and Restrictions   475
       28.3.3   Resetting User Passwords   476
       28.3.4   Superuser Access   477
       28.3.5   Auditing Passwords   477
       28.3.6   Converting Password Files from Other Sources   478
28.4   Trusted Computing Base   478
       28.4.1   tcbck Command   478
       28.4.2   /etc/security/sysck.cfg   479
       28.4.3   Trusted Communication Path   480
28.5   Access Control   480
       28.5.1   Access Control Lists   481
28.6   Authentication Methods   482
       28.6.1   Authentication Tables   483
       28.6.2   Smart Card Authentication   485
       28.6.3   Kerberos—Trusted Third Party   485

28.7   Network Security   487
28.8   System Auditing   487
        28.8.1   Audit Logging   487
        28.8.2   Event Types   488
        28.8.3   Audit Configuration   489
28.9   Security Tools and Information   491
        28.9.1   virscan   491
        28.9.2   COPS   491
        28.9.3   Information Sources   492
28.10   InfoExplorer Keywords   492
28.11   QwikInfo   492

Chapter 29. Distributed Computing Environment   495

29.1   DCE Overview   495
        29.1.1   DCE RPC   496
        29.1.2   Cell Directory Service   496
        29.1.3   Security Service   498
        29.1.4   Distributed Time Service   498
        29.1.5   Threads   499
        29.1.6   Distributed File Service   499
        29.1.7   DCE Versions   499
29.2   AIX and DCE   500
29.3   DCE Planning   502
        29.3.1   Cell Topology   502
        29.3.2   Server Topology   503
        29.3.3   Principals and Security   504
        29.3.4   Test Cell   505
29.4   DCE Installation and Configuration   505
        29.4.1   Security Service   507
        29.4.2   Directory Service   507
        29.4.3   Distributed Time Service   507
        29.4.4   Clients and Servers   508
        29.4.5   Verifying DCE Configuration   509
29.5   DCE Implementation Considerations   511
29.6   InfoExplorer Keywords   513
29.7   QwikInfo   513

Part 10   System Recovery and Tuning

Chapter 30. Backup and Copy Utilities   517

30.1   System Backups   517
30.2   Backup Strategies   517
        30.2.1   What and When   518
        30.2.2   Mounted or Unmounted   518
        30.2.3   Sizing   518
        30.2.4   Full and Incremental Dumps   519
        30.2.5   Backup Schedules and Rotation   519
        30.2.6   Disaster Recovery and Validation   520
        30.2.7   Backup Media   520
30.3   Backing up a File System   521

30.4   Restoring Files and File Systems   521
30.5   Other Dump Utilities   521
30.6   Operating System Dumps   522
30.7   Network Backups   522
30.8   The Whole Nine Yards   523
30.9   InfoExplorer Keywords   523
30.10   QwikInfo   523

Chapter 31. System Monitoring and Tuning   525

31.1   Know Your Workload   525
31.2   AIX Operating System Characteristics   525
        31.2.1   CPU Scheduling   525
        31.2.2   Virtual Memory Management   526
        31.2.3   Disk I/O   528
        31.2.4   Network Performance   528
31.3   AIX Monitoring and Tuning Tools   531
        31.3.1   Traditional UNIX Tools   532
        31.3.2   AIX Specific Tools   533
        31.3.3   Graphical Performance and Monitoring Tools 534
        31.3.4   Public Domain Monitor Package   534
31.4   Additional Help and Documentation   535
31.5   InfoExplorer Keywords   535
31.6   QwikInfo   536

Chapter 32. Problem Analysis and Recovery   537

32.1   When Things Go Bump in the Night   537
32.2   Backups and Bootable Media   538
32.3   LED Status Information   539
32.4   System Memory Dumps   540
32.5   System Logs   542
32.6   AIX Kernel Structure   545
32.7   Using crash   546
32.8   Hardware Diagnostics   548
32.9   Calling for Help   548
32.10   InfoExplorer Keywords   551
32.11   QwikInfo   551

Part 11   Advanced Distributed Architectures

Chapter 33. Clustering   555

33.1   Cluster Overview   555
33.2   Rules of the Road   556
33.3   Hardware Topology   556
33.4   Single System Image   559
        33.4.1   Cluster Domain Name   559
        33.4.2   Common File System   560
        33.4.3   Scalable Password Service   561

33.4.4   Configuration and Installation Management   563
33.4.5   Cluster Batch Queuing   564
33.5   Summary   565

Chapter 34. Network Archiving   567

34.1   Storage Management   567
34.2   IEEE Mass Storage Reference Model   568
34.2.1   Components   568
34.2.2   Development History   569
34.3   ADSTAR Distributed Storage Manager (ADSM)   570
34.4   Unitree   570
34.5   High-Performance Storage System (HPSS)   571
34.6   Choosing a Storage Management System   572

Appendix   573

RS/6000 Welcome Center   574
IBM Austin   574
IBM Direct   574
AIX Customer Support   575
IBM Link   575
IBM Solution Developer Support   575
Team RS/6000   576
RS/Magazine   576
AIX FAQ   576
AIX Software Archive   576
Newsgroups and Mail Lists   577
City of AIX   577
Other Sites of Interest   577

Bibliography   579
Index   581

Preface

AIX V4: Systems and Administration describes the administration and management activities required to install, configure, and operate the AIX V4 operating system on a wide range of POWER, POWER2, and PowerPC platforms. This includes management of environments ranging from single-user workstations to symmetric multiprocessors to clusters of hundreds of nodes. This text focuses on the features and subsystems present in AIX Version 4. It does not address the AIX Version 3 environment but does point out differences where appropriate.

New Features in AIX V4

AIX has undergone significant changes since my previous text directed at AIX V3, *AIX RS/6000: System and Administration Guide*. The hardware base has expanded to include PowerPC and multiprocessor architectures. This has dictated that kernel and operating system services be enhanced to encompass a wide range of hardware platforms, support multiprocessor threaded execution, and scale to larger distributed environments. SP2 clusters with hundreds of nodes are commonplace in the business community as well as the scientific arena. Larger processor environments mean large problems; thus, the AIX V4 file system has been expanded to support file systems larger than the traditional 2GB UNIX file system.

In a sense, the network has become the computer. This mandates that new protocols and management functions exist to facilitate the nervous system connecting machines. AIX V4 now includes the Distributed Computing Environment (DCE) client in the base operating system packaging. DCE brings to AIX a scalable authentication and authorization infrastructure for building multivendor/multiarchitecture client/server applications. The DCE distributed file system enables data sharing across the network, honoring the access controls set in place by DCE.

AIX itself has been bundled into new packaging tailored to fit the roles played by client and server systems in this network-centric environment. New packing has been followed with enhanced installation support. The Network Installation Manager (NIM) facilitates centralized installation and maintenance activities to clusters of remote disk and diskless workstations.

The X/Open and OSF Common Desktop Environment (CDE) has replaced AIXWindows Desktop as the graphical user interface on AIX V4. CDE offers a desktop environment akin to what we have come to expect in the personal computer worlds of MS/Windows, OS/2 Warp, and Macintosh. You will also find the CDE environment present on other vendor UNIX offerings from SCO, DEC, Sun, and HP.

The World Wide Web, network commerce, and home access to the Internet are probably the biggest changes that have occurred in computing and networking since AIX V3 was first announced. Not to be left behind, IBM has packed popular Web support tools into the AIX V4 bonus pak. The bonus pak includes Netscape Navigator, Java, Adobe Acrobat, Ultimedia Services, Netscape Commerce Server, and IBM Internet Connection Secure Server: just about everything you could ask for in Web support. Point-to-point protocol (PPP) has also been added to the AIX V4 base to support dialup networking.

Who Should Read This Book

The text is intended as a base reference for both new and experienced AIX system administrators. Even though UNIX has taken on a larger role in the computing community, there are still those unacquainted with its features. There are also differences in vendor UNIX offerings that require architecture-specific texts such as this to assist those who are required to manage multivendor UNIX environments.

Subject matter is partitioned by function to facilitate quick access. Sections of keywords and Qwikinfo lists are provided at the end of many chapters to be used as pointers into the detailed documentation presented in the IBM hard copy manuals and InfoExplorer information bases.

The book culminates with a discussion of advanced clustering and mass storage technologies. These chapters include examples of these technologies and information on obtaining representative implementations.

An appendix is included that lists a number of network archive and information sites for acquiring additional information related to AIX and other technologies addressed in this text.

Acknowledgments

The knowledge I've pieced together for this work is based on the combined support and talents of computer professionals I have worked with over the years: specifically, the members of the University of Washington Computing & Communications organization. I've worked with many of these people for well over 10 years. We've seen and facilitated the evolution of the UW computing environment from the single-system mainframe era into the distributed network computer we all use today. It's not just our system anymore; it's everyone's systems working together as a single information service. I want to acknowledge the folks at *RS/Magazine* who have supported and encouraged my columns since the magazine's inception. I'd like to thank Jeff Jilg of IBM Austin AIX Development, who has kept me abreast of changes in the operating system while I completed this task. Finally, I'd like to recognize my local IBM representative, Tom Bilbro. Tom has been working with me and my group since the first RS/6000 showed up at our shop. He was quick to learn that we university types tend to do our own thing and don't always follow IBM's direction in computing. Most of all, Tom has been a good friend. He had the good sense to take a year-long sabbatical in the forests of Washington State away from all this technology. I wish I had the same good sense. I'm deeply envious!

James W. DeRoest, Jr.

AIX V4: System and
Administration

AIX Version 4: System and Administration Guide

System Administration Tasks and Tools

1

Introduction

1.1 System Administration

The UNIX operating system hasn't achieved the "drop it in and forget it" simplicity that makes MS-DOS, Windows, and Macintosh so popular with the masses. Until recently, UNIX primarily inhabited the dusty halls of research institutions and universities. In these environments, UNIX was used as a programmer's tool that could be built upon to meet the needs of the research community. It didn't have to be easy—it just had to be low-cost and provide standard common interfaces to support research collaboration and tool building. It is the open, standards-based face of UNIX that has brought it to the forefront of the movement toward open systems.

The proliferation of low-cost RISC processors has brought UNIX onto the desktop. The open systems and right sizing movements have brought UNIX into the commercial glass house. The time has come. UNIX has gotten a hair cut, put on a suit, and gone head to head with the legacy operating systems from desktop to big iron. Vendors and standards groups are scrambling to define and implement UNIX system management and administration tools to satisfy the needs of this diverse user base. Are they succeeding?

We are beginning to see some of the first offerings in the realm of UNIX system management. Many of these tools are taking a good deal of heat from the traditional UNIX system administrator crowd because of the new approaches and protocols being employed to manage stand-alone and distributed UNIX environments. Whether this is good or bad remains to be seen. The Open Software Foundation (OSF) struggled with its Distributed Management Environment (DME) technology in late 1993, yet it never saw the light of day. Tivoli, Hewlett-Packard, and others have taken up the challenge and are now offering a robust multivendor OS and network management tools. Are they interoperable? The sales glossies and CD demos certainly indicate that, not only are they interoperable, but they meet all the latest standards specifications. Remember standards? Everybody's got one. Rather than spending a great deal of time validating the standards issue, the best use of your time is to give each product a test drive and vote with hard-earned cash. Since you are reading this book, I can safely assume there is still some work to be done regarding development of the perfect systems management tool.

Like any multiuser operating system, UNIX requires special care to ensure that resources are distributed equitably among the user base and that these resources are secured from intrusion or failure. Our job as system administrators is to guarantee that these requirements are being met. How do we do it? Read on!

1.2   AIX and UNIX

Is AIX UNIX? It's certainly different in many respects from what might be coined legacy UNIX systems. What defines UNIX? Most vendor UNIX offerings including AIX pass the SVID tests, are POSIX compliant, and are X/Open certified. Does this make them UNIX? Before you answer that, remember: MVS, now OS/390, is X/Open certified. Most of the differences found in AIX are related to system administration. As you might expect, the system administrators are the most vocal when it comes to complaining or praising UNIX evolution. AIX offers a very solid mixture of BSD and SYSV features. Users from either environment will find it easy to make themselves at home. The measure of an operating system should be whether it provides an environment that assists rather than hinders your ability to do meaningful work. It must also be interoperable with other architectures. AIX holds up very well under this definition. Table 1.1 shows an approximate genealogy of UNIX development milestones and lineage of the AIX operating system.

As far as where UNIX is going, one can only hope that the vendor community is serious about maintaining a common UNIX look and feel. The Common Open Software Environment (COSE) alliance started by HP, Sun, IBM, SCO, USL, and Univel was a step in the right direction. There have been other vendor coalitions, and we have seen interfaces like the Common Desktop Environment (CDE) become a reality.

1.3   AIX and OSF

AIX commands and libraries were accepted by the OSF as the basis of the Application Environment Specification for the OSF/1 operating

TABLE 1.1   A Brief History of UNIX

Year	Event
1969	UNIX is born on the DEC PDP-7
1974	ACM publishes Thompson and Ritchie's paper on UNIX
1975	Bell Labs licenses UNIX to universities
1977	SCO and Interactive Systems founded
	BSD 1.0
1978	UNIX Version 7
	BSD 2.0
1979	Berkeley ARPAnet Contract
	BSD 3.0
1980	BSD 4.0
1981	SUN founded
1982	AT&T System III
	SUN becomes Sun Microsystems
1983	AT&T System V
	BSD 4.2
	Hewlett-Packard HP-UX
1984	AT&T System V.2
	DEC ULTRIX
	X/Open founded
1985	Sun NFS
	POSIX founded
1986	AT&T SYSV.3, Streams, RFS
	BSD 4.3
	IBM AIX RT PC
1987	AT&T SYSV.3.1
	IBM IX/370
1988	AT&T SYSV.3.2
	BSD 4.3 Tahoe
1989	AT&T SYSV.4
	IBM AIX/370 and AIX/PS2
	OSF founded
	OSF Motif
	UNIX International founded
	Internet Worm on November 2
	Sun SPARCstation
1990	BSD 4.3Reno
	IBM AIX RS/6000
	OSF/1
1991	IBM AIX/ESA
	Apple, IBM, Motorola Alliance
	Sun Solaris 1.0
1992	BSD 4.4
1993	IBM PowerPC
	IBM Scalable POWER Parallel SP/1
	AIX 3.2.5
1994	AIX V4.1
	SMP RS/6000 (J30, G30, R30)
1996	AIX V4.2

system. This was good news for the AIX user community in that they could expect to find the face of AIX on OSF/1 offerings and OS technologies spawned by the OSF efforts. Applications developed on AIX should port easily to OSF/1 certified operating systems (grain of salt here).

1.4   System Administration Activities

If you're new to UNIX system administration, you may be asking yourself just what does a system administrator do. Why, they're faster than a speeding bullet, able to leap tall buildings in a single bound, and they always know the best latte stands within walking distance! Seriously, UNIX system management involves a diverse set of skills that covers the gamut from system installation and configuration to end-user hand holding. A large glass-house UNIX environment might be managed by a group of administrators, each responsible for a particular subsystem. A researcher might only be grappling with a UNIX workstation on the desktop. Whether acting alone or as part of a team, administrators must have a general understanding of overall UNIX system management activities to ensure that their areas of responsibility seamlessly interoperate with all the subsystems that make up the UNIX operating system. Desktop or glass house, this responsibility often extends beyond the local system to the network and other vendor platforms that make up a distributed environment like the Internet.

The text is organized logically to reflect AIX administration themes and components, facilitating rapid location of the subject matter. Chapters are comprised of detailed subject descriptions, examples, and diagrams. Where appropriate, both the AIX System Management Interface Tool (SMIT) and command line options are presented. Command examples are flagged with the shell prompt character (#) to distinguish them from other bullets and to remind the reader that most configuration activities are performed with superuser privileges.

```
# command
```

Each chapter culminates with an InfoExplorer topic list for obtaining further information. InfoExplorer is the online manual interface for AIX and associated applications. This text is intended as a pointer to the more specific information provided in the AIX hard copy and InfoExplorer documents. It will also provide some insights based on practical experience with RISC System/6000 hardware and the AIX operating system.

1.4.1 System administration tasks and tools

Part 1 of this book overviews system administration responsibilities and identifies the base reference and management tools. Characteristics of the AIX help system InfoExplorer are described.

1.4.2 System architecture

The next part describes the RISC System/6000 hardware development history and architecture. An overview of the AIX kernel is provided to illustrate operating system principles that will assist you in understanding configuration and management issues presented in later chapters.

1.4.3 System installation and operation

Part 3 describes the AIX System Management Interface Tool (SMIT), which can be used to manage most aspects of the AIX operating system. Tips to tailor and streamline SMIT are provided to assist the reader in getting the most from SMIT. As you may have heard, "SMIT happens." The discussion then turns to the steps required to install and apply service to the AIX operating system in disk and nondisk systems. An overview of the RS/6000 boot process and operation follows.

1.4.4 System configuration

Once the operating system has been installed, it must be customized to meet the needs of the application environment. Part 4 describes the Object Data Manager (ODM) and how it is used to store and manage system configuration data. The steps involved to add disk drives, printers, terminals, and tape devices to the RS/6000 and AIX are then detailed.

1.4.5 Network configuration

These chapters describe how to make your system accessible from a number of network architectures and topologies. What tools and protocols are required to manage centrally a network of machines? Part 5 reveals all.

1.4.6 Network file systems

Network-based file systems provide the underlying architecture for sharing information in a distributed environment. These chapters outline a number of common file-system architectures, their features, and implementation requirements, including mechanisms for facilitating file sharing between UNIX and Windows systems.

1.4.7   Distributed services

Now that you have a machine and a network connection, how are you going to make use of them? Configuring E-mail, network news, Web servers/browsers, and X-Windows services are discussed. Web topics include tools for workgroup collaboration, secure servers, and the AIX bonus pak.

1.4.8   Managing users and resources

A great deal of system administrator time and energy is devoted to managing user accounts. This section outlines ways to streamline account management, reporting and maintaining system security. Part 8 concludes with a discussion of how DCE and Kerberos can be implemented to secure and authorize principals in large networked environments.

1.4.9   System recovery and tuning

What do you do when things go bump in the night? Part 9 shows you how to keep your RS/6000 running hot and lean. Backup strategies and policies are explained. System monitoring tools and problem analysis techniques are reviewed.

1.4.10   Advanced distributed architectures

This section looks at tools and techniques that can be employed to build a farm of networked RISC System/6000s functioning as a loosely coupled multiprocessor. Strategies for providing interactive, batch, parallel, and archive services in a clustered environment are described. This includes technologies for implementing a clustered topology as a single system image.

2

InfoExplorer

2.1 AIX Help

Help! It's often the first word uttered by a new AIX system administrator. You've invoked man to access help for a particular command. If you're very lucky, a man page will be displayed, but it may be followed by two or three more! Being intrigued rather than put off, you type man man and discover the existence of an information marvel called InfoExplorer (info). You're still feeling adventurous, so you type info and press RETURN. Just when you thought it was safe to go into the water!

One of the first hurdles for new AIX users is mastering the help system, confusion over documentation location and access mechanisms being the primary problem. The AIX InfoExplorer hypertext documentation system is a very powerful help search and retrieval tool. However, you'll have to improve your learning curve before you feel comfortable using the help system. It's too bad that you need so much help to learn and use help!

2.2 InfoExplorer Overview

InfoExplorer is implemented upon an extensive GUI for perusing online documentation. It is at its friendliest when used from an X11 display, but it may also be used from ASCII tty and pty connections. The documentation information bases include AIX and RS/6000 manual text and graphics, reference index, glossary, product related help files, and add-on databases like the AIX Technical Library of HOWTO and closed APAR documents. Hypertext links are used as fast paths between related documents, files, and programs. A public and private note facility supports annotation of documents. The user interface can be individually tailored to specify entry points, search criteria, and printing options. History trails and bookmarks further facilitate moving between documents.

2.3 InfoExplorer Installation

The InfoExplorer package is delivered as a part of one of the AIX run-time bundles (See Chap. 6 for more information on products, packages, and bundles). The executables, fonts, ispaths data, and NLS information bases are located in /usr/lpp/info (see Table 2.1). NLS Information bases (textual help documents by language) may reside either on CD-ROM or fixed disk. Locating the information bases on fixed disk will provide snappier access response but will require an additional 300 MB of disk space.

In multilanguage environments, more than one NLS information base set may be installed. Access to a given NLS information base is defined by the $LANG environment variable. Separate information bases are provided for each product. A product information base may provide an updated version of the /usr/lpp/info/data/ispaths file. The ispaths file contains the hypertext paths and links used to cross-reference data in the information bases. Care must be taken to make certain you are using the correct ispaths file for the information bases installed on your system.

2.3.1 InfoExplorer on CD-ROM

If disk space is at a premium, access the InfoExplorer information bases from the distribution CD-ROM. Note that the CD-ROM distribution of InfoExplorer information bases are a bit different than preinstalled versions on disk. Mount the InfoExplorer distribution CD-ROM as a cdrfs file system. The "Managing Topics" section regarding InfoExplorer suggests using a mount point directory named /infocd. If you follow this procedure, you can then invoke the supplied script linkinfocd to create the required ispaths links. If you don't want to add another mount entry in your root directory, it's possible to mount the info CD-ROM over the existing fixed disk path /usr/lpp/info/lib/$LANG. To do this:

TABLE 2.1   InfoExplorer Paths

/usr/lpp/info/bin	Executables for X11 and ASCII displays
/usr/lpp/info/data	ispaths files describing paths and links, public notes
/usr/lpp/info/dt	Desktop icons and config
/usr/lpp/info/lib/$LANG	Information databases (CD-ROM mount point)
$HOME/info	Private bookmarks and notes

```
# mount -v cdrfs -r/dev/cd0 /usr/lpp/info/lib/$LANG
# cd /usr/lpp/info/lib/$LANG
# ln -s ispaths /usr/lpp/info/data/ispaths
```

To have the InfoExplorer CD-ROM file system mounted at boot time,
add an entry for the cdrfs file system to /etc/filesystems
The following is an InfoExplorer CD-ROM /etc/filesystems entry:

```
/usr/lpp/info/lib/en_US:
dev                  = /dev/cd0
vfs                  = cdrfs
mount                = true
options              = ro
account              = false
```

For higher availability, copy selected information bases to fixed disk.
These information bases will be available should the CD-ROM cdrfs
file system not be mounted.

2.3.2   InfoExplorer on fixed disk

If you have disk space to spare, InfoExplorer response will be much
better if the information bases are stored on fixed disk. You can either
install the information bases during product installation or copy
selected information bases from CD-ROM. To copy selected information bases from CD-ROM to the fixed disk, mount the InfoExplorer distribution CD-ROM as a cdrfs file system on the temporary mount point
/mnt. Copy the selected information bases from the CD-ROM to the
corresponding /usr/lpp/info/lib/$LANG/<name> directories. Unmount
the CD-ROM cdrfs file system when copying has been completed.

```
# mount -v cdrfs -r /dev/cd0 /mnt
# ls -al /mnt/$LANG
```

Copy the desired databases from the CD-ROM to disk (examples:
nav, aix).

```
# cp /mnt/$LANG/nav/* /usr/lpp/info/lib/$LANG/aix41/nav
# cp /mnt/$LANG/cmds/* /usr/lpp/info/lib/$LANG/aix41/cmds
```

Unmount the CD-ROM.

```
# umount /mnt
```

If you decide to remove an information base from disk at a later date,
use the rm -r command to erase the information base subdirectory

from the /usr/lpp/info/lib/$LANG directory. For instance, to remove Pascal help, enter:

```
# rm -r /usr/lpp/info/lib/$LANG/pascal
```

2.3.3   InfoExplorer over NFS

If you want to share InfoExplorer information bases in a networked environment, export the /usr/lpp/info/lib/$LANG directory using NFS. Interactive response over NFS to information bases residing on the server's hard disk is a bit better than local CD-ROM response. You may wish to export selected information bases rather than the whole set. Add the information base directories to the NFS server's /etc/exports file and an /etc/filesystems mount entry on each client. For example:

```
/usr/lpp/info/lib/en_US -anon=0,ro,access=daisy.duck.com
```

is the proper syntax for a server command. For the client, enter:

```
/usr/lpp/info/lib/en_US:
dev        = /usr/lpp/info/lib/en_US
vfs        = nfs
nodename   = daffy.duck.com
mount      = true
type       = nfs
options    = ro,bg,soft,intr
account    = false
```

2.4   Using InfoExplorer

To start an InfoExplorer session, invoke the info command in X11-based environments or info -a for ASCII devices. InfoExplorer will display the default task selection window and an InfoExplorer overview window for first-time users. The default menu buttons allow you to select the InfoExplorer Topic & Task Index, List of Commands, List of Books, Programming Reference, History, List of Bookmarks, List of Notes, Path, or Search. The look and feel of InfoExplorer has changed somewhat in AIX 3.2.5 and later releases, as compared with earlier AIX releases. These differences are minor; thus, the information provided will be applicable to earlier versions.

```
# info          Start X11 interface

# info -a       Start ASCII interface
```

Access to alternate information bases like the AIX Technical Library are selected using info -l <name>.

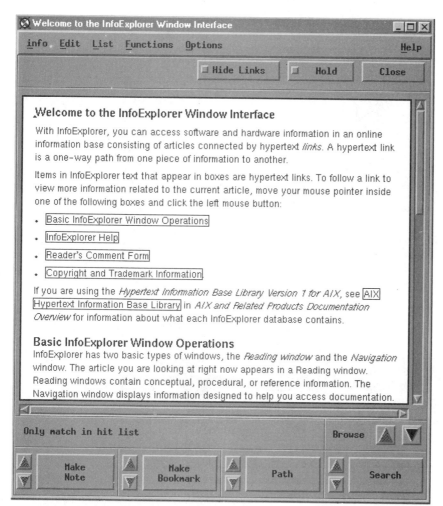

Figure 2.1   InfoExplorer welcome display.

info -l techlib   Select techlib information base

In the X11 environment, menu options and hot links are selected using the mouse point-and-click inteface. Scrollbars are used when text or option sets will not fit on one screen. Option boxes are provided to set notes and bookmarks quickly or move back and forth through the screen path. The initial entry-point window and other options may be customized after you become familiar with the system. Use the Options menu-bar field to set defaults and preferences.

Accessing InfoExplorer from an ASCII device requires the use of keys to negotiate your way around the system (see Table 2.2).

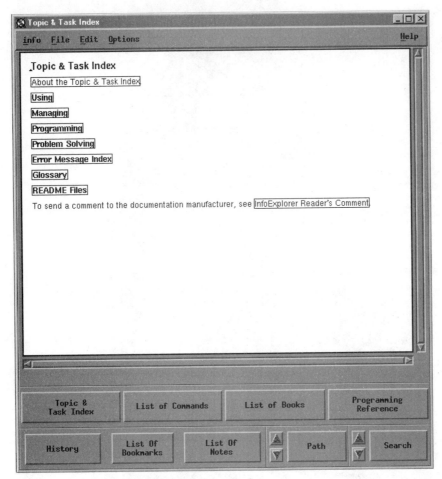

Figure 2.2   InfoExplorer topic and task index display.

2.4.1   Hypertext links

Along with menu selections, InfoExplorer allows you to jump between related documents, glossary definitions, and data files and invoke commands through the use of hypertext links. Hypertext links are identified within displayed text through highlighting. To activate a link, point and click the mouse button on the highlighted text in an X11 session, or TAB to the highlighted text and press ENTER in an ASCII session. Movement between links will be recorded in your session history file.

2.4.2   Searching

The InfoExplorer search facility helps you find information when you aren't quite certain what you are looking for. Simple and compound

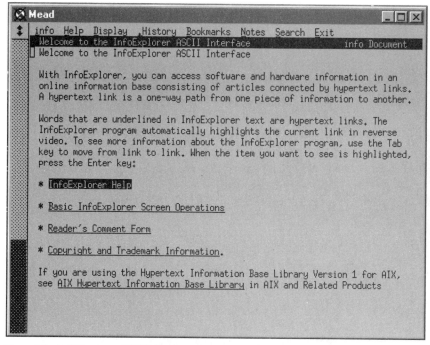

Figure 2.3   InfoExplorer ASCII display.

text searches are supported with wild card matching. A simple search involves a single short text string as a search argument. Compound searching supports boolean search semantics and allows you to define the scope of the search within the document. You may also limit the information bases included in the search to improve response.

Quick searches may be invoked from the command line using the info -h option.

```
# info -h <searchkey>
```

2.4.3   History and bookmarks

To facilitate moving around in an InfoExplorer session, InfoExplorer records the document and display path in a history file. New path information is appended to the file as you move about in the system. At any time, you may jump forward or backward by selecting the path option. History files may be saved, restored, and shared with other users.

Selected information may be marked for later reference using the bookmark facility. Bookmarks are stored in the $HOME/info directory and may be shared with other users by copying the bookmark files to the user's $HOME/info directory.

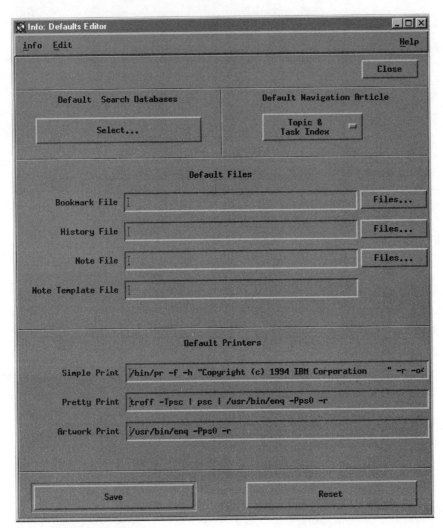

Figure 2.4   Preferences display.

2.4.4   Note facility

Just like writing in the margins of hardcopy manuals, InfoExplorer supports an annotation facility. Individual users may tag information-base text with private notes. Notes are stored in $HOME/info/notes. The note format may be customized to individual tastes.

Private notes may be added or collected from public notes by the system administrator. Public notes can be grouped together and made available to the entire user base using the /usr/lpp/info/bin/mergenote command. Specify the private notes files to be included in the public repository as a blank separated list on the command line. Public notes

TABLE 2.2 InfoExplorer ASCII Key Mapping

CTRL-N/PGDN	Page down
CTRL-P/PGUP	Page up
CTRL-W	Toggle reading and navigation
CTRL-F/TAB	Move to next hypertext link
CTRL-B	Move to previous hypertext link
CTRL-L	Refresh screen
LEFT ARROW	Move cursor one character left
RIGHT ARROW	Move cursor one character right
UP ARROW	Move cursor one character up
DOWN ARROW	Move cursor one character down
<	Move cursor 20 characters left
>	Move cursor 20 characters right
CTRL-O	Activate menu bar
ESC-ESC/CTRL-O	Close menu bar and move to text
SPACEBAR	Cycle through options in a ring
ENTER	Activate a link or selection

are stored in the /usr/lpp/info/data directory by default but can also be directed to other locations.

```
# /usr/lpp/info/bin/mergenote <-d directory-path> <note-list>
```

2.4.5 Output

Text from InfoExplorer information bases may be printed or cut and pasted into other documents. Users may customize default print options by defining any valid command and filter stream using shell I/O redirection. Two print selections are supported: Simple Printer and Pretty Print. The AIX V3.2 Artwork Printer is no longer an option in AIX V4.

```
troff -Tpsc | psc | enq -P <PrinterName>      Postscript stream
```

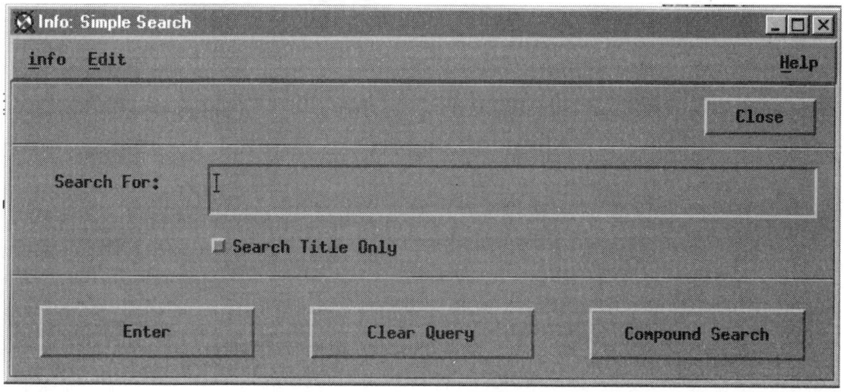

Figure 2.5 Simple search menu.

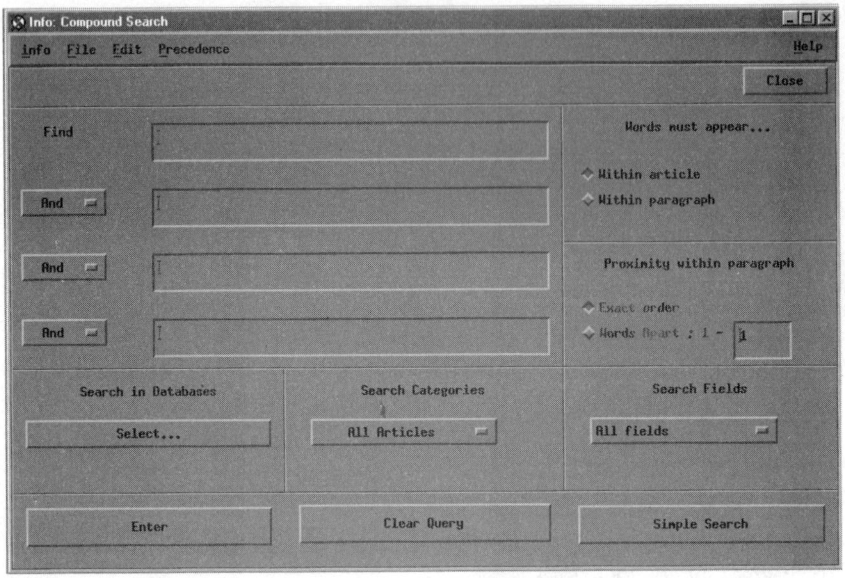

Figure 2.6 Compound search menu.

2.5 InfoExplorer and man

The man command has access to information stored in InfoExplorer databases. When invoked, man will first search /usr/man/cat? directories, then /usr/man/man?, and finally InfoExplorer data. The commands man and catman map man page sections 1, 2, and 8 to InfoExplorer commands documents, sections 2 and 3 to InfoExplorer subroutines documents, and sections 4, 5, and 7 to InfoExplorer files documents. You will need to periodically execute catman -w to keep the database for the apropos and whatis commands up to date.

```
# catman -w
```

2.5.1 Extracting man pages

AIX V3 provided a /usr/lpp/bos/bsdadm README file that assisted BSD system administrators in making the move to AIX. This file contained a script that could be used to extract the man sections stored in InfoExplorer and store them as flat files in the appropriate /usr/man/cat? subdirectories. There is nothing fancy about the script. Basically it runs the man command on each file and redirects the output to a temp file. The temp file is then moved to /usr/man/cat?. Here's the AIX V3 script, which you can modify to do essentially the same thing for AIX V4:

```
#!/bin/bsh
#
# usage: catman.sh "path" section
# stores AIXv3 man pages as flat text in appropriate
/usr/man/cat directory
#

PATH=/bin:/usr/bin:
NAMEPATH="/bin /usr/bin /usr/ucb"        # modify this to taste
SECTION="1"

if [ -n "$1" ] ; then
  NAMEPATH="$1"
fi
if [ -n "$2" ] ; then
    SECTION="$2"
fi
for p in "${NAMEPATH}" ; do
 for name in 'ls "${p}"' ; do
  if [ -x "${p}/${name}" ]; then
   if ( man "${SECTION}" "${name}" >/usr/tmp/"${name}" ) ;
   then
    mv /usr/tmp/"${name}"           /usr/man/cat"${SECTION}"/
    "${name}"."${SECTION}"
   fi
  fi
 done
done
```

To generate Section 2:

```
# mkdir /tmp/syscalls; cd /tmp/syscalls
# touch 'egrep '^[a-z]' /lib/syscalls.exp | awk '{ print $1
}'|tr'''2''
# catman.sh /tmp/syscalls 2
```

To generate section 8:

```
# mkdir /tmp/sysmaint; cd /tmp/sysmaint;
# (cd /etc; file * | grep executable | awk -F: '{ print $1 }'
) | xargs touch
# catman.sh /tmp/sysmaint 8
```

2.5.2   man page format

From time to time, you may need to add your own custom man page
information. This could be a help file explaining charging policies,

backup support, locally developed software, and so on. It's a good idea to keep local man pages separate from vendor-supplied help. This keeps them from getting stepped on during installation, maintenance, and upgrade activities. Commonly used location paths for local man pages are /usr/man/manl or /usr/local/man/man?. The $MANPATH environment variable can be set in /etc/environment to include your local man page path. Users may also use $MANPATH to support their own man directories.

```
Local man Page Repositories

/usr/man/manl
/usr/local/man/man?
/usr/local/cat/cat?
```

When creating new man pages, you can use an existing man page as a template. Try to stay within a common style so that your users know what to expect. Each man page should include a name section identifying the topic or command; a synopsys describing the command and argument options and format; a description section that describes the topic; an options section that details parameter and value information; and a section on known bugs. At the end of the man page, a "see also" section indicating related information and an optional author section identifying the author name and address can be considered.

The following is an example man page style:

```
mycommand(1)
NAME
     mycommand - Does just what I want to do.
SYNOPSYS
     mycommand [will|wont] work
     mycommand is always used as a last resort. It can
     be expected either to work or fail. mycommand
     contains no surprises at all.
OPTIONS
     will    Completes the work at hand.
     wont    Take a vacation.
BUGS
     mycommand is always error free!
SEE ALSO
     myprogram(1), myshell(1)
AUTHOR
     Me. Who did you think it was?
```

You can include nroff tags in the man page to control display format (see Table 2.3). After the tags are included, you can test them using nroff.

TABLE 2.3 Sample nroff Tags

.TH <name> <numw>	Man page name and section number
.SH <section>	Identifies a subsection
.B <text>	Bold or highlighted text
.I <test>	Italics text
.PP	Block out a paragraph
.TP <num>	Indent paragraph <num> spaces except first line

```
# nroff -man mycommand.1 | more
```

Here is a sample man page with tags inserted:

```
.TH mycommand 1

.SH NAME
mycommand \- Does just what I want to do.

.SH SYNOPSYS
mycommand [will|wont] work
.SH DESCRIPTION
.B mycommand
is always used as a last resort. It can
be expected either to work or fail.
.B mycommand
contains no surprises at all.

.SH OPTIONS
.TP 3
will
Completes the work at hand.
.TP 3
wont
Take a vacation.

.SH BUGS
.B mycommand
is always error free!

.SH SEE ALSO
myprogram(1), myshell(1)

.SH AUTHOR
.B Me.
Who did you think it was?
```

Remember to run the catman -w command periodically to keep the apropos and whatis data up to date. You might want to add it to roots crontab.

```
# catman -w
```

2.6 Feedback

The IBM Austin Information Design and Development group would like your feedback and comments concerning AIX documentation and the InfoExplorer help system and other AIX publications. An InfoExplorer Readers Comment Form is included as part of the system and is accessible from the Topic & Task Index. Follow the instructions on the form and return it to the indicated address. You can also E-mail comments to them at the following Internet address:

```
aix6kpub@austin.ibm.com
```

2.7 QwikInfo

- InfoExplorer

`/usr/lpp/info`	InfoExplorer product directory
`/usr/lpp/man/lib/$LANG`	Hypertext database directory (disk, CD-ROM, NFS)
`mount -v cdrfs -r /dev/cd0 /usr/lpp/info/lib/$LANG`	Mount info CD-ROM
`info`	Motifinterface
`info -a`	TTY interface

- man pages

`/usr/man/cat?`	Formatted text; search first
`/usr/man/man?`	nroff format; search second
`/usr/lpp/info/$LANG`	Hypertext; search third
`catman -w`	Update whatis database for apropos command

System Architecture

3

POWER Architecture

3.1 Know Your RISC

Periodically I find that I need to force my head above the mire of SPEC-mark and clock cycle ratings to do a quick level set of the system architectures that make up the various POWER products. Let's review where RISC systems have been, where they are now, and where they're going. With processor speeds doubling and tripling faster than I can read all the associated IBM announcement letters, it's difficult to keep perspective for planning purposes. Should I consider adding new microprocessor architectures along side older RISC systems in an integrated client/server environment? Are there compatibility issues to consider? Over the longer term, might it be beneficial to replace existing POWER systems with faster PowerPC processors now or migrate to more tightly coupled multiprocessor technology? This week's fast CPU may not include the I/O or network options I need for a particular application set. Technology trends may indicate that I need to rethink how the modules of an application are deployed. It may be the application that requires upgrading.

The only way to make decisions like these is to maintain a good understanding of the available system architectures and development directions. This advice goes for new as well as old equipment. Even if you have a big budget, don't dismiss older processor models or the used equipment market when planning for additional resources. In our shop, we call these older systems "light bulbs." They can be used for noncritical support services and easily replaced at low cost if they burn out. No maintenance contract required! Just keep a few on the shelf for when you need them. With this in mind, let's take a look at an overview and history of POWER architecture. I cringe at the thought of committing details of state-of-the-art POWER systems on the page. It most certainly will end up a fossil before the ink dries, even if I do make my copy deadline!

3.2   POWER

The first Reduced Instruction Set Computer (RISC) was developed in 1975 at IBM T. J. Watson Research Center as a spinoff of telephone switching research. The processor architecture, called 801, implemented a reduced instruction set of 120 instructions fused in hardware and executed one instruction per clock cycle. The IBM PC RT, first commercially available in 1986, was based on the 801 work. To improve performance, the 801 project team began working on methods that would process multiple instructions per clock cycle, reducing execution wait time during branch and memory operations. This work resulted in a second-generation, three-processor architecture dubbed AMERICA. The AMERICA effort was moved to the IBM Austin development lab in 1986. Austin evolved AMERICA into what was known as RIOS and finally into the architecture we know today as Performance Optimized with Enhanced RISC (POWER).

Like AMERICA, the POWER architecture married three independent functional units into a superscalar configuration with the ability to execute multiple instructions per clock cycle. This ability spawned a recoining of the RISC acronym by IBM to represent Reduced Instruction Set Cycles. The POWER instruction set had put on a little weight, increasing to 184 instructions; the change was probably in order. The POWER triprocessor complex of separate branch, integer, and floating-point units are fed via a four-word-wide I/O path from separate instruction and data caches, dispatching up to four instructions per clock cycle at 20 to 30 MHz (see Fig. 3.1). The superscaler pipeline implementation uses a branch prediction algorithm to minimize holes in the instruction stream that occur when a conditional branch is taken. Each branch requires that a new sequence of instructions be fetched from memory and loaded into the cache before processing continues. IBM began delivering the POWER RISC System/6000 product line in early 1990. You might still be running one of the early 200, 300, or 500-series systems. We still have one of the first beta-model 530s running production work. We may even have a few RTs around, too, but I'm not talking.

3.2   POWER2

The next phase in POWER architecture development incorporated additional integer and floating point units into a custom 8-chip design and was christened POWER2. The POWER2 architecture is based on the existing POWER instruction set for upward comparability. It also

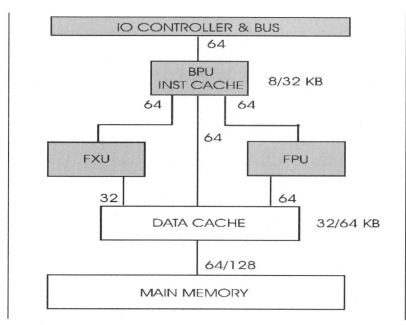

Figure 3.1 Power processor complex.

incorporates a set of new instructions that capitalize on the wider data paths, additional processors, and registers available in the new design. Using compound instructions like FMA (floating point multiply and add), the complex is capable of executing eight instructions per clock cycle at rates from 50 to 80 MHz. You and I both know it will be faster by the time you read this.

The 8-chip POWER2 complex (see Fig. 3.2) is housed in a multichip module (MCM) set that includes an instruction cache unit (ICU), fixed point unit (FXU), floating point unit (FPU), four data cache units (DCU), and a storage control unit (SCU). The ICU processes instructions stored in the instruction cache and dispatches non-ICU instructions to the FXU and FPU. The FXU and FPU each house two execution units that are responsible for doing all the numeric data crunching. The DCU manages the four-way, set-associative, dual-ported data cache to keep information moving in and out of the processor complex. The SCU arbitrates communications between the processors, memory, and SIO bus. This includes programmed I/O and DMA processing. Greater numbers of faster processors and wider paths mean you can consume data at a higher rate, so data cache sizes were increased to 128 or 256K, depending on configuration. The instruction cache is 32K. With a larger cache, it made sense to add a Level 2 (L2) cache to improve I/O performance between processor cache and memory. The L2 cache stores snapshots of recently used memory and ranges in size from 256K on smaller systems to 2 MB on big RISC System/6000s. IBM announced its POWER2 systems in the fall of 1993. Three different iterations of the architecture have since been introduced, directed at the specialized needs of the scientific and commercial markets.

3.3 PowerPC

In 1991, with the POWER2 work well underway, IBM began a joint development venture to consolidate the POWER architecture into a high-performance, low-cost, single-chip design that could be produced in high volume. The chip was to remain binary-compatible with other POWER architectures, support 64-bit extensions, and be multiprocessor-enabled. Target applications would include everything from PDAs and printers to personal computers and multiprocessor supercomputers. The PowerOpen development alliance of IBM, Motorola, and Apple Computer was announced in 1993, heralding the third generation of the POWER architecture, the PowerPC.

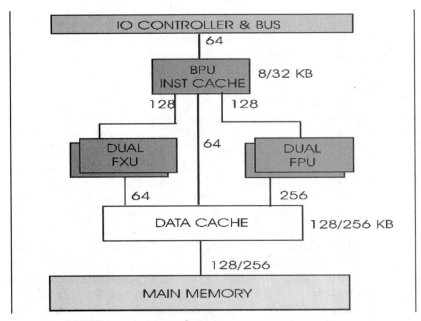

Figure 3.2   POWER2 processor complex.

The most notable feature of the PowerPC architecture is the extension to 64-bit addressing with dynamic switching to 32-bit mode for backward compatibility. Existing POWER binaries will execute on the PowerPC but will run slower until recompiled under the new instruction set. Complex POWER instructions were eliminated to simplify and streamline the instruction set. Additional single precision, cache management, and locking operations were added to utilize features better in the new chip architecture. The architecture can adapt to either big or little endian byte ordering to meet your particular OS preference. At the time of this writing, PowerPC processors are pushing clock speeds of 200 MHz, with plans for stepping up to 300 MHz in late 1997/early 1998. Microchannel, PCI, and ISA bus configurations are available depending on the model to fit home, commercial, and research computing environments.

PowerPC architecture is represented by a number of microprocessor configurations. At the low end, the PowerPC model 601 is based on a three-processor configuration similar to the original POWER implementation (see Fig. 3.3). The 601 is a bridge architecture that supports all but two of the nonprivileged POWER instructions. Products based on the 601 are targeted for the desktop PC and technical workstation markets. Hybrid controller microprocessors called the 602 and the 401 are directed at consumer graphics systems, PDAs, and printers. A low-power configuration that splits the 601's combined data and instruction cache into separate caches called the 603 is used in laptop computers like the Power Series ThinkPad (see Fig. 3.4). The 604 and 620 are the sports cars of the PowerPC line, directed at numerically intensive computing and multiprocessing. Additional fixed-point units, larger data and instruction caches, and an embedded secondary cache controller allow these processors to peak at five instructions per clock cycle (see Fig. 3.5). Although architecture and instruction sets vary a bit across the PowerPC processor line, a common hardware reference platform (CHRP) is defined to facilitate cross-platform software development. Yes, you can run the same code on any of the models with the exception that multiprocessor code may not run in uniprocessor mode.

3.4 POWER Multiprocessor

Now that I have the POWER architecture descriptions out of the way, it's time to focus on how they are used to support multiprocessor (MP) computing. In order for an operating system or application to capitalize on MP capability, there must be a way to synchronize execution between the processors and their use of system resources. Single instruction, multiple data (SIMD) architectures rely on a central processor to parcel out and conditionally control the execution of instructions on the individual processors in an MP complex. Multiple

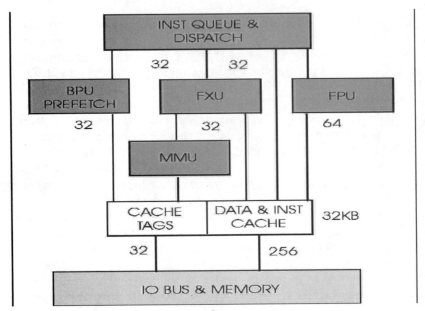

Figure 3.3   PowerPC 601 processor complex.

instruction, multiple data (MIMD) configurations allow each processor to execute its own instruction stream and relies on message passing or shared memory methods to synchronize execution. POWER MP architecture is based on the MIMD model and comes in two flavors: a tightly coupled symmetric MP represented by the RISC System/6000 J, G, and R series; and a loosely coupled, shared-nothing MP as implemented by the Scalable PowerParallel (SP) product line.

3.4.1   SMP

The RISC System/6000 J, G, and R40 architecture uses a 1.8-MB nonblocking crossbar switch to interconnect 2, 4, 6, or 8 PowerPC microprocessors to a globally shared memory resource and the I/O subsystem. The model 30 systems are based on the 601 processor. The model 40 uses 604 processors. Each processor has local memory as well as access to shared memory. Contention for system resources between the processors is managed by the AIX V4 MP kernel with the exception of memory. Cache and memory coherency between processors' executing applications must be managed by the individual applications. This eliminates complexity and overhead in the MP operating system implementation. There is a service processor in the product configuration that monitors the system, but it does not function like the control processor in a SIMD implementation.

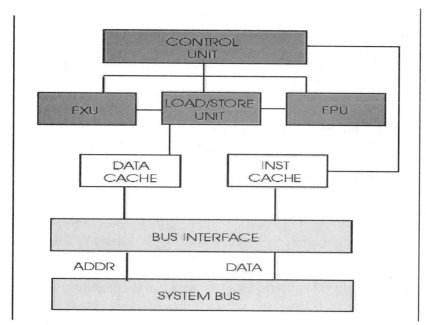

Figure 3.4   PowerPC 603 processor complex.

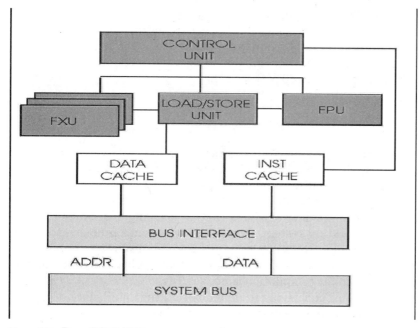

Figure 3.5   PowerPC 604/620 processor complex.

3.4.2   SP

The SP product line represents the other side of IBMs MP architectures. An SP complex is made up of 2 to 512 individual POWER, POWER2, or PowerPC nodes linked via a network fabric. Each processor has its own memory, IO adapters, and copy of the AIX operating system. Discounting network-shared disk, each SP node shares nothing with its associate nodes. Type 2 to 16 nodes make up an SP frame, and there may be a mixture of thin, wide, or high node types. Thin nodes are POWER2-based processors, focusing on memory and compute resources. Wide nodes are also POWER2 nodes but have additional microchannel expansion slots and disk bays to support file and peripheral services to the complex. Wide nodes support most of the available microchannel network and device adapters for connecting the SP to outside systems and disk and tape devices. High nodes are PowerPC 2- to 8-way 604-based symmetric MPs directed at transaction processing. Communication between nodes is facilitated by a network fabric best suited by the high performance switch (HPS).

The HPS implements an indirect cut-through switch architecture that reduces packet buffering requirements and limits communication deadlock problems. Message packets from each node contain routing information in the packet header and can be moved across multiple paths when traversing the switch to destination nodes. The HPS is made up of one switchboard per rack, connecting an 8-element adapter board in each node and providing a 16-way connection. One node in each frame may be configured as a switch-only node for interconnection with other SP frames. I/O rates across the switch will vary based on the protocol used. The hardware peak rate is 150 MB/sec for a uni-directional communication and 300 MB/sec bidirectional. Average real-world rates are in the 80 MB/sec range.

3.5   Compatibility

With all the chip, system, and instruction architectures available in the POWER product line, one might be worrying about application compatibility in a mixed environment. The good news is that older binaries will likely run on newer architectures. Exception software would include things like device drivers that have changed between releases of the AIX operating system. This should be less of a problem if all your boxes are running the same release. There is also a "qarch" option in the compiler that can be used to optimize an application for a particular architecture at compilation time (see Table 3.1).

I know it's difficult trying to remember all the details for one vendor architecture alone, so adopt a sliding window view of the computing

TABLE 3.1   Compiler "qarch"

-arch= pwr	POWER
-arch= pwr2	POWER2
-arch= com	PowerPC (default)
-arch= ppc	601 Bridge POWER—PowerPC (32-bit)

world. Keep a bit of the old, current, and future computing technologies in the back of your head. This will help you from repeating yesterday's purchasing and implementation mistakes or at least let you put a new twist on them. Hey, you have a big budget, so you can afford to fudge a little. Buy lots of real fast machines and no one will know the difference. At least IBM will love you.

**TABLE 3.2   RISC System/6000 Specifications
SPEC '92—IBM Direct 1994**

Model	Clock (MHz)	MFLOPS	SPECint	SPECfp
220	33	6.6	20.4	29.1
230	33	8.8	28.5	39.9
250	66 (601)	12.7	62.6	72.2
320	20			
320H	25			
340	33			
340H	42	18.8	48.1	83.3
350	42			
355	42	18.8	48.1	83.3
360	50	22.2	57.5	99.2
365	50	22.2	57.5	99.2
370	62	25.9	70.3	121.1
375	62	25.9	70.3	121.1
520	20	9.2	32.8	
520H	25			
530	20	15.4	46.1	
530H	33			
540	30	16.5	38.7	
550	42	18.8	48.1	83.3
560	50			
570	60	22.2	57.5	99.2
580	62	38.1	73.3	134.6
580H	55	101.1	97.6	203.9
590	66	130.4	117.0	242.4
730	25	15.4	46.1	
930	25			
950/950E	42			
970	50	36.7	117.0	
970B	50	31.0	58.8	108.9
980	62	42.1	126.2	
980B	62	38.1	73.3	134.6
990	71	140.3	126.0	260.4

TABLE 3.3   RISC System/6000 Specifications SPEC '95—IBM Direct 1996

Model	Clock (MHz)	MFLOPS	SPECint_base	SPECfp_base
43P	100/120/133	—/25.5/27.8	3.36/4.01/4.55	3.04/3.23/3.59
25T	66/80	12.7/15.1	1.69/2.03	2.23/2.58
41T/41W	80	20.1	2.03	2.58
42T/42W	120	22.4	3.75	3.37
3AT/3BT/3CT	59/67/67	49.7/55.1/133.6	2.71/3.09/3.2	6.81/7.24/8.75
250	66/80	12.7/15.1	1.69/2.03	2.23/2.58
E20	100/133	23.5	3.43	3.06
E30	133	23.1	4.56	3.34
F30	133	23.1	4.56	3.34
C10	80	20.3	2.37	2.97
C20	120	22.7	3.85	3.50
390	67	55.1	3.09	7.24
39H	67	133.6	3.2	8.75
G40	112			
590	66	131.8	3.19	9.69
591	77	156.0	3.67	11.2
59H	66	132.0	3.2	8.74
J40	66			
R20	66	132.0	3.2	8.74
R24	71.5	141.0	3.41	9.33
R40	112			

In closing this chapter, I leave you with Tables 3.2 and 3.3, which are performance charts gleaned from the pages of the IBM Direct RS/6000 Catalog two years apart. The SPEC ratings are SPEC '92 and SPEC '95 respectively. The MFLOP rating is DP. You should be able to use reference systems like the 250 (PowerPC) and 390 (POWER) in both tables to formulate a comparison between architectures and how they have changed over the years.

4

AIX V4 Kernel

4.1 Multiprocessing Kernel

Remember the good old days when the "process" was the indivisible dispatchable unit of work under AIX V3? Each process neatly lined up by priority in serial run queues awaiting a turn on the CPU. There were parent processes, children, grandchildren . . . each process generation spawning the next. All members of one big happy init family. Like most families, it was often difficult to get family members to talk to each other or share their belongings. When you did get them to communicate or share, everyone tried to talk or grab a resource at the same time. You had to get heavy-handed and resort to locks and semaphores to keep everyone in line. Process life could be difficult, but it was simple and understandable.

Then came AIX V4 multiprocessing. AIX developers decided to speed up the pace of life in process city. Rather than make all processes wait on just one CPU, they added the capability to dispatch across multiple CPUs. More CPUs mean that the work gets done faster. They also decided to break up the process structure into components called threads. Each thread is a dispatchable unit of work. Multiple threads can be executing simultaneously on multiple CPUs. These new features improved system throughput, but they didn't come without additional complexity and some overhead. The following discussion is directed at the new multiprocessing features in the AIX V4 kernel; however, many of these new features are also applied to uniprocessor configurations.

4.2 Kernel Architecture

The AIX kernel is fundamentally a System V.2 kernel. However, the SYSV architecture only represents AIX's roots, not its whole. The AIX kernel design includes a number of features and extensions that set it apart from other SYSV-based kernels. AIX V3 introduced most of these features when POWER architecture hit the marketplace in 1990. The AIX kernel is dynamically extensible, meaning that new device drivers and other system extensions can be added to a running system without requiring a kernel rebuild or system reboot. The AIX Virtual Memory Manager (VMM) surpasses most UNIX kernels with an address space of 4 petabytes indexed in 256-megabyte segments. VMM per-process address space is 4 gigabytes. Large per-process memory resources combined with memory mapped computational and file I/O reduces the limitations inherent in kernel architectures that rely on buffer cache for I/O. The kernel itself is pageable yet still supports real-time processing. Other AIX I/O subsystem enhancements include asynchronous I/O and I/O pacing to reduce wait time and improve overall throughput.

Along with large memory capacity, the AIX kernel can scale to supporting large numbers of running processes and open files. This feat is achieved by eliminating hard-coded tables size limits that are common in other UNIX kernels like MAXPROC. The addition of the Object Data Manager (ODM) eliminated a number of large device and configuration tables improving operating system access to configuration information and enabling dynamic system configuration updates. A new device can be plugged into a running system and made immediately available for use by updating ODM information with the cfgmgr command.

```
# cfgmgr     Update ODM information
```

The next big kernel enhancement came in AIX V4 with the introduction of multiprocessing support. Much of the task of instrumenting multiprocessing support in the AIX kernel was facilitated by the design of the AIX V3 kernel and the characteristics of the PowerPC architecture. The kernel in AIX V3 is preemptable. This means that the kernel can be interrupted at any time to service higher priority tasks, a feature important to MP support. However, some operations must remain atomic (i.e., they can't be interrupted) and are run with interrupts disabled. This type of operation can be problematic in an MP environment. New locking mechanisms were implemented to ensure that these atomic operations remained MP safe and MP efficient. Two special-purpose reserve instructions and the weakly ordered memory architecture of the PowerPC processor formed the basis of the new AIX V4 locking algorithms. Along with interrupt and locking enhancements, POSIX threads and plugable schedulers have been added to the AIX kernel to facilitate a new thread-based dispatch model for UP and MP based computing.

4.2.1 Threads

Threads provide the means of overlapping, multiplexing, and parallel-izing operations within a process. The process structure is separated into dispatchable components and global resources. Global resources remain a part of the common-process user and proc structures. Threads are peer entities and share global resources like address space. Thus, threads within a process don't require the overhead related to manag-ing shared memory spaces or semaphores common with traditional interprocess communication.

Along with the shared resources maintained in the process proc and user structures, each thread has corresponding thread-specific thread and uthread structures. These include stack, registers, and other kernel data. These structures make it unlikely that one misbe-having thread can corrupt the thread-specific structures of other threads. However, globally shared code sections called critical sec-tions can be corrupted if signal and update processing are not syn-chronized. Each processor has its own L1 and L2 cache hardware. Care must be taken to ensure that updates to code sections resident in more than one processor cache are validated and serialized. Cache coherency is an important consideration when designing thread-safe applications.

AIX V4 threads are based on the POSIX 1003.4a draft 7 model as implemented in OSF/1 libpthreads. Threads in AIX V4 are represented by user and kernel thread components. For every user thread, there is a corresponding kernel thread. Kernel threads may exist indepen-dently. This user-to-kernel thread mapping is known as the 1:1 thread model. The DCE pthreads implementation in AIX 3.2 was based on an N:1 thread model. DCE allowed multiple user threads to be mapped onto a single kernel thread. Like processes fork() and exec() call for cre-ating new processes, threads are created by invoking pthread_create() and pthread_atfork(). A process and its associated threads can be cloned using the forkall() routine.

4.2.2 Signals

Signals are defined at the process level but are handled at the thread level. Each thread has local signal mask. Synchronous signals are delivered to the thread that caused the exception. Asynchronous sig-nals like kill() are delivered to only one thread in a process. The signal will be delivered to a thread that has initiated a sigwait() for the par-ticular signal number or to a thread that does not have it blocked. Dis-abling signals at the process level to protect a critical code section in a thread may not work as expected in that the signal may be delivered to a thread executing on another processor.

4.2.3 Locks

Locks are the primary mechanism for synchronizing updates and protecting critical code sections. Note that the lock test and set operation itself is critical and must be protected from interrupts, thus the requirement for hybrid lock operations. Lock requests will block until the lock is available by either spinning or waiting. A spin lock will cause the thread to loop for a predetermined period until the lock is free. If the period time expires, then the requestor will sleep until the lock is released by the holder. A wait lock will sleep until the lock is available.

Two OSF lock types are implemented in AIX V4: simple locks and complex locks. Simple locks spin and are exclusive but may be preempted by higher priority requestors. Simple locks are combined with disabling of interrupts if initiated from an interrupt handler via the disable_lock() and unlock_enable() sequence. Complex locks are used to synchronize requests between a writer and multiple readers. Complex locks are wait locks, are not exclusive, and may be called recursively.

As previously mentioned, two special-purpose reserve instructions and the weakly ordered memory architecture of the PowerPC processor formed the basis of the new AIX V4 locking algorithms. Load and store operations are considered complete at address translation time to facilitate out-of-order instruction execution by the PowerPC's multiple execution units. Dependencies and cache misses automatically reorder instruction execution. Address compare at load and store time also ensure that correct instruction order is maintained. The load and store operations are implemented in the PowerPC as the lwarx and stwcx instructions. The lwarx instruction loads and reserves a word from memory, while stwcx stores a word if and only if a reservation is still present. Reservations are automatically removed if the address has been updated by another execution unit. These operations extrapolate easily to the locking paradigm required by MP topologies.

AIX V4 lock instrumentation is provided to maintain cache coherency between threads running on multiple processors. The lock state of the system can be queried using the lockstat command if this facility has been enabled by bosboot options. Since the AIX V4 kernel is aware of its UP versus MP run mode status, MP-specific lock requests are ignored in a UP environment to shorten code paths. Application developers may then write software exclusively for MP environments yet still be supported under UP configurations.

```
# bosboot -a -L      Create a boot image with MP lock support
# lockstat -a        Display system lock usage statistics
```

4.2.4 Scheduling and dispatching

It's probably obvious by now that changes to the AIX scheduler were required to support threads. As the dispatchable units of work, threads are assigned a priority from 0 to 127. Each level is represented by a run queue. The scheduler periodically scans the run queues and recalculates priority based on processor use history for those tasks not running at a fixed priority. Note that some functions that effect queue priority like nice still operate on the process as a whole rather than per individual thread.

The AIX dispatcher had to be changed to facilitate the way in which threads are allocated to available processors. The highest priority thread may not be the next one available to be dispatched due to processor binding. When a thread is bound to a processor, this is called processor affinity. The system experiences fewer cache misses if threads can be dispatched to the same processor on which they last ran. Conversely, overall processor untilization is improved if threads can be scheduled on any available processor. The AIX V4 dispatcher implements what has been termed opportunistic affinity. An attempt will be made to run a thread on the same processor on which it last ran if that processor is available. The bindprocessor() routine is available for those instances when a programmer would like to enforce processor affinity for a code section.

```
# bindprocessor <proc-id> <processor>    Bind process to processor
```

To grandfather like device drivers in processor-dependent software, processor binding or funneling was required to ensure that UP code sets remained bound to a single processor when running in MP mode. Logical processor IDs are used to identify each physical processor number starting with 0. Logical-to-physical processor mapping information is stored in the ODM. Use the cpu_state command to display logical-to-physical processor mapping or enable/disable individual processors on the system.

```
# cpu_state
```

ODM Name	Physical Number	Logical Number	Processor State
/proc0	0	0	Enabled
/proc1	1	1	Enabled
/proc2	2		Disabled
/proc3	3	2	Enabled

UP code sets are bound to the MP_MASTER processor /proc0. MP_MASTER designation is used to identify the default processor in a set rather than indicate any master/slave relationship. Selectable UP and MP kernel support is built into AIX V4, the only restriction being that a UP kernel will not execute on a multiprocessor like the R40. MP kernels will execute on uniprocessor models like the 43P. Separate UP and MP kernels are shipped as part of the BOS run time environment filesets. The bos.rte fileset contains common code to both UP and MP environments; bos.rte.mp contains MP only commands and the MP kernel.

`/usr/lib/boot/unix_up`	UP kernel
`/usr/lib/boot/unix_mp`	MP kernel

The bootinfo command can be used in early AIX V4 systems to determine if the platform is MP capable. Note that bootinfo is included but not supported in AIX V4.2 or later.

`# bootinfo -z`   Display MP capable

Along with general thread support, three new scheduling options are available, SCHED_RR, SCHED_FIFO and SCHED_OTHER. SCHED _RR enforces strict round-robin scheduling. SCHED_FIFO uses a fixed-priority, first in, first out ordering. SCHED_FIFO does not support preemption and is not time-sliced. A thread must either block or yield the processor when running under the SCHED_FIFO scheduler. The third option, SCHED_OTHER, represents the standard AIX scheduling algorithm where task priority degrades with CPU usage.

4.2.5 Overhead

The ability to dispatch work across multiple processors does not come without some overhead. An 8-way system isn't going to perform at eight times the throughput of a single processor of the same architecture. MP contention for kernel structures, longer instruction paths, spinning and waiting on locks, bus contention, and maintaining cache coherency all add to system overhead. When application threads are executing on different processors, they may be required to synchronize before further work can be accomplished. One task will have to wait on the other, adding to application overhead. The AIX V4 design goal was to keep increased MP overhead within 15 to 20 percent of UP throughput.

4.3 POWER Multiprocessors

A multiprocessing kernel isn't much good without a multiprocessor to run on. Sure, AIX V4 will execute in uniprocessor (UP) mode, but where's the fun in that? Multiprocessors come in many shades and sizes. In the world of Power architecture (Chap. 3), they come in basically two flavors: loosely coupled shared nothing multiprocessors (MP) and tightly coupled symmetric multiprocessors (SMP). The loosely coupled shared nothing variety is best represented by the SP2. The SP2 is made up of individual POWER CPUs linked together via a network fabric. Each processor has its own memory, I/O adapters, and copy of the operating system executing in UP mode. Discounting network-shared disk, each SP2 node is an individual RS/6000 uniprocessor sharing nothing with its associate nodes. For the sake of this definition, let's temporarily ignore the fact that an SP2 can also have SMP high nodes. The RS/6000 R40 is an example of a tightly coupled symmetric multiprocessor. Two to eight Power processors share a global memory space, I/O bus, adapters, and peripherals. Contention for these resources is synchronized by the AIX V4 kernel executing in MP mode.

4.4   InfoExplorer Keywords

MP	lockstat
SMP	scheduler
UP	dispatcher
threads	sysconfig
pthread	VMM
bootinfo	cfgmgr
bosboot	bindprocessor
cpu_state	

4.5   QwikInfo

# sysconfig	Add kernel extension
# cfgmgr	Update ODM device data
# bootinfo -z	Display MP capable
# bosboot -a -L	Create a boot image with MP lock support
# cpu_state	Display processor state and mapping
# lockstat -a	Display system lock usage statistics
# bindprocessor <proc-id> <processor>	Bind process to processor

System Installation and Management

5

System Management Tools

UNIX has a bad reputation when it comes to system management. Most of the traditional UNIX management tools are the products of necessity, built by frustrated system programmers. Historically, UNIX development efforts have focused on designing the building blocks that support this roll-your-own methodology, Perl and Tcl/Tk being cases in point.

In production enterprises, UNIX must conform to the management policies and practices that are the hallmarks of big-iron operating systems. Ad hoc tool development is not acceptable in many of these environments. A new breed of UNIX management tools are required that provide centralized control over distributed heterogeneous resources. The tools should also interoperate with the existing legacy tool sets. The Open Software Foundation (OSF) worked hard to define its Distributed Management Environment (DME) specification; unfortunately, DME did not achieve the wide acceptance of other OSF technologies like Motif or DCE.

Rather than wait for consensus on an overall platform-independent system administration strategy, many vendors began testing the waters with their own UNIX management tools. In general, most of these tools integrate graphical interfaces with traditional UNIX commands to streamline system installation, configuration, and management tasks.

5.1 SMIT

AIX's base system administration and management tool is called System Management Interface Tool (SMIT). SMIT is a complete administrator's tool box that may be used to perform system management activities like installing software, configuring devices, administering user accounts, performing system backups, and diagnosing problems. SMIT uses a menu-driven interface that streamlines and simplifies the complexity of many system management activities. SMIT does not inhibit or replace command-line access to system management; rather, it uses the same commands under the cover of the menu-driven interface. Not all possible command and argument combinations are available under SMIT. Command and parameter selection is based on the most common use to complete a given management task.

For novice administrators, SMIT simplifies system management through the use of task-oriented dialogs. New users can zero in on a particular task by stepping through SMIT's submenu hierarchy. Menu options for a specific task are identified with descriptive field titles and contextual help. Error checking routines validate argument type and range.

The advanced administrator may find that SMIT provides a faster interface to many management tasks. The SMIT script facility may be used to assist in creating complex administration scripts.

The choice is yours whether you elect to use SMIT to manage AIX. As you gain experience with SMIT and the AIX environment, you may find that you prefer to use SMIT for some management activities and the command line for others. Whether you love it or hate it, SMIT is here to stay.

5.2   Using SMIT

SMIT is started by executing the smit command from the command line. By default, SMIT will enter the top-level system management menu (see Fig. 5.1). To enter SMIT at a particular task submenu, supply the SMIT FastPath name as an argument.

```
# smit          Start SMIT at the top-level menu
# smit user     Start SMIT at the "user admin" submenu
```

SMIT allows you to take a test drive utilizing all of its features without making changes to the operating system. Invoke SMIT with the -X to kick the tires and get a feel for how it operates. SMIT will log the commands it would have executed in the $HOME/smit.script file.

```
# smit -X
```

You can also use the F6 key within SMIT to display the AIX command and arguments it will invoke before committing the update.

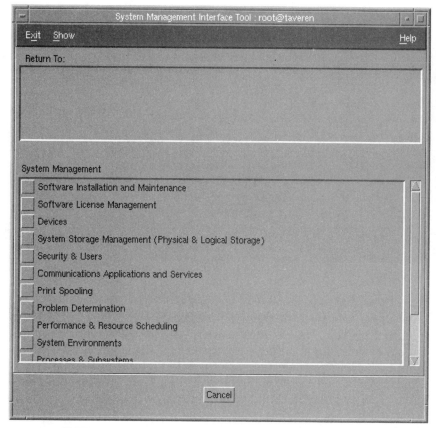

Figure 5.1 SMIT X11 Display.

5.2.1 SMIT display

SMIT provides both an ASCII and a Motif-based user interface. The Motif interface is invoked by default on an X11 managed display and employs a point-and-click feel. The Motif display enhances the operating environment through the use of buttons, slider bars, and submenu panels. The SMIT ASCII interface (see Fig. 5.2) is invoked using the smitty or smit -C commands.

```
# smit          SMIT X11 interface
# smitty        SMIT ASCII interface
# smit -C       SMIT ASCII interface
```

Each SMIT panel is divided into three parts. At the top of the panel, the task title and instructions appear. The middle of the screen con-

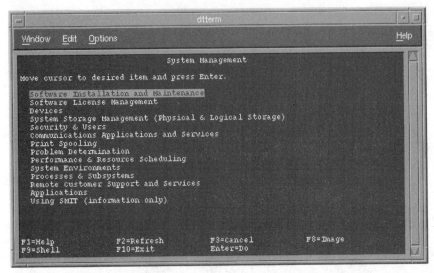

Figure 5.2   SMIT ASCII interface.

tains menu selections or input fields. Location in the set of fields is indicated by "top," "more," and "bottom." At the bottom of each panel, the set of valid function keys are listed in four columns. SMIT flags input field types and selection lists through the use of field mark characters and buttons displayed to the far left and right of the input fields. Table 5.1 shows the SMIT dialog symbols.

5.2.2   SMIT keys

To navigate between fields and options in a SMIT panel, use the TAB and arrow keys or the mouse. Input field values may be typed from the keyboard or in some cases selected from a list. The ENTER key invokes and commits the selection or task. SMIT also provides a set of function keys to display additional information, access the shell, or exit (see Table 5.2).

TABLE 5.1   SMIT Dialog Symbols

Symbol	Type
*	Entry is required
#	Numeric field
X	Hexadecimal field
/	File name field
+	List available (ASCII display only)
[]	Field delimiters (ASCII display only)
Arrow button	Fixed set of options (Motif display only)
List button	List of choices (Motif display only)

TABLE 5.2   SMIT Function Keys

Key	Action
F1	Help
F2	Refresh screen
F3	Cancel
F4	Display selection list
F5	Undo entry—reset to default
F6	Display command and args
F7	Edit or select
F8	Display FastPath name
F9	Shell escape
F10	Exit SMIT
ENTER	Execute
TAB/SHFT-TAB	Move between options

5.2.3   SMIT help and messages

SMIT help can be invoked from any menu by pressing the F1 key. The help and message text is located in /usr/lpp/smith/$LANG/. Note that the message catalog is a National Language (NLS) catalog and is thus dependent on the setting of the $LANG environment variable. An invalid or missing $LANG specification will result in missing or garbled help and message information.

5.2.4   SMIT log file

SMIT creates an audit log of each SMIT session in the user's $HOME directory named smit.log. The log file indicates the SMIT submenu path traversed during the session by object class ID, panel sequence number, title, and the FastPath name. Each new SMIT session is appended to the existing log file. Care must be taken to monitor the size of the log file over time. The location of the log file may be set using the smit -l <PathName> option. The level of logging verbosity may be increased using smit -vt.

```
# smit -l /tmp/smit.log -vt    Use /tmp to hold log file
```

For example, to add a 9-track tape drive, enter:

```
[Sep 07 1993, 13:29:36]
Starting SMIT
```

(Menu screen selected as FastPath)

```
id          = "__ROOT__"
id_seq_num = "0"
next_id     = "top_menu"
title       = "System Management"
```

(Menu screen selected)

```
FastPath   = "top_menu"
id_seq_num = "0"
next_id    = "top_menu"
title      = "System Management"
```

(Menu screen selected)

```
FastPath   = "dev"
id_seq_num = "020"
next_id    = "dev"
title      = "Devices"
```

(Menu screen selected)

```
FastPath   = "tape"
id_seq_num = "080"
next_id    = "tape"
title      = "Tape Drive"
```

(Selector screen selected)

```
FastPath   = "maktpe"
id         = "maktpe"
next_id    = "maktpe_"
title      = "Add a Tape Drive"
```

(Selector screen selected)

```
FastPath   = "maktpe"
id         = "maktpe_9trk_scsi"
next_id    = "maktpe_9trk_scsi_hdr"
title      = "Add a Tape Drive"
```

(Dialogue screen selected)

```
FastPath   = "maktpe"
id         = "maktpe_9trk_scsi_hdr"
title      = "Add a Tape Drive"
[Sep 07 1993, 13:29:50]
Command_to_Execute follows below:
>> mkdev -c tape -t '9trk' -s 'scsi' -p 'scsi1' -w '10'

[Sep 07 1993, 13:29:52]
Exiting SMIT
```

5.2.5 SMIT script file

Along with the log file, SMIT appends the AIX commands invoked during the session to a local $HOME/smit.script file. The script file information can be used to create complex management scripts or review the commands invoked during a previous session. For example, you might use SMIT to configure the first of a set of 64 TTY devices. Then edit the $HOME/smit.script file and, duplicating the mkdev command 62 times for the remaining devices, change each device name and attributes as required. The script file can be executed from the command line to complete the definition for the remaining devices. Use the smit -s <PathName> option to create a script file in a location other than your home directory.

```
# smit -s /tmp/smit.script    Create a script file in /tmp
```

To add the 9-track tape drive with SMIT script:

```
#
# [Sep 07 1993, 13:29:50]
#
mkdev -c tape -t '9trk' -s 'scsi' -p 'scsi1' -w '10'
#
# [Sep 16 1993, 17:35:00]
#
lslv #
#
# [Sep 16 1993, 17:35:10]
#
lsvg -o|lsvg -I -l
#
# [Sep 16 1993, 17:35:14]
#
lsvg -o|lsvg -I -l
#
# [Sep 16 1993, 17:35:49]
#
lslv hd3
```

5.2.6 SMIT FastPaths

SMIT allows you to bypass menu levels and enter a task directly through the use of a FastPath name (see Table 5.3). A FastPath name is an identifier for a particular SMIT panel. FastPath names are recorded as part of the $HOME/smit.log information. The FastPath name is included as an argument to the smit command to enter a task panel directly.

```
# smit nfs    Access SMIT NFS management
```

TABLE 5.3   Common SMIT FastPath Names

dev	Devices management
diag	Diagnostics
jfs	Journaled file system management
lvm	Logical volume manager management
nfs	NFS management
install	Software installs and maintenance
spooler	Print queue management
system	System management
tcpip	TCP/IP management
user	User administration

Remembering all the FastPath names and management commands can be a real bear. Fortunately, the AIX developers implemented an easy-to-remember rule for the FastPath and command names. A set of four prefixes—ls, mk, ch, and rm—are appended to a root task name in list, make, change, and remove operating system objects. For example, to make a TTY device, the FastPath or command name is mktty. This doesn't work all the time, but hey, it's better than nothing!

FastPath and Command Algorithm

Operation	`mk, ls, ch, rm`
Objects	dev, user, fs, vg, pv, tty, diskette, tape, etc.

5.3   Customizing SMIT

SMIT is comprised of a hierarchical set of menu panels, an NLS message catalog, a command interface, and a logging and scripting facility. These components are integrated to provide a seamless interface for managing the operating system and system resources.

Three types of SMIT display panels are used to manage the dialog between the user and management tasks: Menu, Selector, and Dialog. Menu panels display management task selections. Selector panels (see Table 5.4) present a range of values from which you must choose before proceeding with the management task. You may choose more than one. Dialog panels provide input fields for specifying command arguments and values.

SMIT panels, command link descriptions, option defaults, and attributes are stored as objects in the ODM database. SMIT object classes (see Table 5.5) reside in the /usr/lib/objrepos directory.

TABLE 5.4   SMIT Panel Types

Menu	List task options
Selector	Request additional input before proceeding
Dialog	Request values for command arguments and options

TABLE 5.5   SMIT Object Classes

sm_menu_opt	Menu titles and options
sm_name_hdr	Selector titles, attributes and links to other screens
sm_cmd_hdr	Dialog titles, base command, links
sm_cmd_opt	Defaults, input types, selector/dialog attributes

SMIT object classes may be manipulated using ODM commands just like any ODM object (Chap. 9). After becoming experienced with the ODM and SMIT architectures, you may use ODM commands to customize SMIT. SMIT object class names and object identifiers are listed in the SMIT log file when SMIT is invoked with the verbose trace -vt option.

```
# smit -vt    SMIT verbose tracing
```

To display an object class description associated with a SMIT object, identify the object class, identifier, and number from the log. Then use the odmshow or odmget commands to list the object description. Check to see that your $ODMDIR environment variable is referencing /usr/lib/objrepos.

```
# odmshow sm_menu_opt    Display SMIT menu object class
```

The command odmget can be used for retrieving an existing entry for modification or as a template for a new object. After updating the definition, delete the old entry with odmdelete and add the new object using odmadd. This is not something I would recommend unless you are very familiar with the ODM and SMIT. Always back up the existing object class information before making any modifications.

5.4   Visual System Management

For those of you who prefer a bit more flash in system management tools, then Visual System Management (VSM) is the tool for you. VSM is an object-oriented graphical user interface that allows you to perform system administration and management tasks under a mouse-driven, point-and-click drag-and-drop X-based desktop environment. It's intuitive to use, more colorful than SMIT and it keeps you from having to wallow in the muck of the AIX command line. Managed objects and associated tasks are displayed as icons on the X desktop (see Fig. 5.3). To perform an action, simply drag the desired object icon onto the task icon. If additional information is required, a VSM or SMIT dialog panel is displayed to accept configuration information.

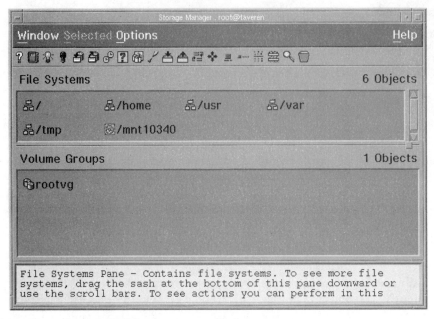

Figure 5.3 Example VSM storage manager display.

VSM Administration Applications

Software installation

Software maintenance

Device management

Print management

Storage management

User management

Date, time, job scheduling

VSM applications can be started from the AIX Common Desktop Environment (CDE) application manager System_Admin window (Fig. 5.4) or from the command line. Command line invocation supports standard X options like display and geometry.

VSM Commands

$ installm   Installation manager

$ xmaintm   Software maintenance

$ xdevicem   Device manager

$ xprintm   Print manager

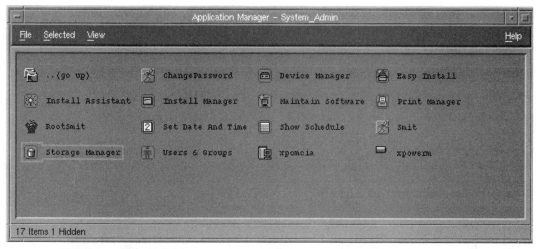

Figure 5.4 CDE System_Admin display.

$ xlvm   Storage manager

$ xuserm   User manager

$ xdat   Date, time, job manager

Your first experience with VSM will likely occur during AIX BOS installation. The VSM installation manager is displayed after BOS install is completed to assist you in configuring your AIX runtime environment (see Fig. 5.5). An entry is placed in the system's /etc/inittab file to invoke automatically the VSM install manager at boot time. This inittab entry is removed when you select Tasks Completed—Exit to AIX Login from the VSM front panel.

If you prefer to use the keyboard rather than having to reach for the mouse for each operation, the VSM interface supports key-mapped equivalents to mouse operation (see Table 5.6).

5.5 Distributed Systems Management

Distributed system management tools seem to come and go with the seasons. Distributed SMIT is available as part of IBM's system management products, which provided a SMIT interface for managing distributed UNIX platforms. References to DSMIT began to disappear after the announced merge of SystemView with Tivoli's Tivoli Management Environment (TME). As of this writing, I don't know whether this is good or bad. Both SystemView and TME provide very comprehensive network and systems management tool sets. I would only expect that the combined SystemView/TME architecture will meet the needs of

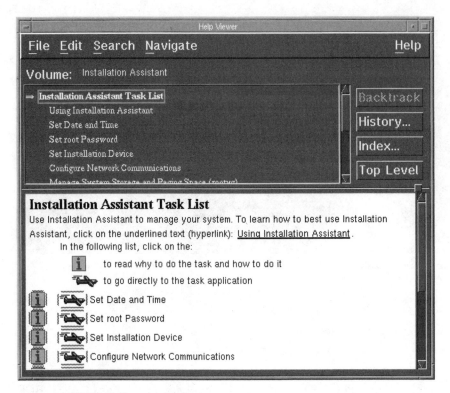

Figure 5.5   VSM install_assist display.

most distributed environments. All I can say is wait and see how this all comes out.

5.5.1   DSMIT

Distributed System Management Interface Tool (DSMIT) is installed as a separate product on AIX V3.2.5 and AIX V4. Functionally, it is the same as single-system SMIT but goes one step further in allowing remote management of a number of vendor UNIX products including:

- AIX 3.2.5, AIX V4
- Sun OS 4.1.3
- Solaris 2.3, Solaris 2.4
- HP-UX 9.0

As you might expect, DSMIT is broken up into clients (managed systems) and servers (managing systems). Machines managed by DSMIT

TABLE 5.6   VSM Key Definitions

SPACEBAR	Select object
SHFT-SPACEBAR	Multi-select objects
CTRL-/	Select all
CTRL-\	Deselect all
INSERT	Drop object on area
TAB	Move focus next area
SHFT-TAB	Move focus previous area
Arrow keys	Move focus in area
F1	Help
F2	Sort in area
F3	Find in area
F4	Filter in area
F5	Large icons
F6	Small icons
DELETE	Trash selected object
CTRL-BACKSPACE	Notebook selected object
ALT-F3	Lower window
ALT-F4	Close window
ALT-F5	Restore window
ALT-F6	Move next window
ALT-SHFT-F6	Move previous window
ALT-F7	Move
ALT-F8	Re-size window
ALT-F9	Minimize window
ALT-F10	Maximize window
ALT-TAB	Raise next window
ALT-SHFT-TAB	Raise previous window
ALT-ESC	Raise next window without moving focus
ALT-SHFT-ESC	Raise previous window without moving focus

are grouped into domains. Subsets of machines within a domain are called the working collective. The breakdown of systems and various configuration information is stored in the /usr/share/DSMIT directory.

DSMIT Configuration Files: /usr/share/DSMIT

domains	Client groups
dsmitos	Operating systems managed
clients	Managed hosts
security/v5srvtab	Principal key
security/admin.cfg	Administrator keys
security/managing.cfg	Managing systems keys
security/managed.cfg	Managed systems keys
security/dsmit.ptr	DSMIT config file server

As you might imagine, security in a distributed management environment is a critical issue. DSMIT uses MIT Kerberos V5 security services for authenticating DSMIT servers and clients. Commercial masking data facility (CMDF) and message authentication code (MAC) protocols are used to ensure data integrity and guard against message tamporing. The nice thing about this is that, as a system administrator, as soon as you have validated yourself to Kerberos, you don't need to log into each system you will be managing.

DSMIT allows you to select sets of systems for management functions. When an update is to be made, you can choose to send the command to all machines in the set at once (concurrent mode) or one at a time (sequential mode). You can bail out in the latter case if problems with an update are indicated. To make things easy or confusing (depends on your point of view), a shell environment variable can be set to indicate that DSMIT should be run when a user or administrator types SMIT.

SMIT=d   Invoke DSMIT instead of SMIT

This is about all I'm going to say about DSMIT, since my bets are being placed on a replacement from Tivoli. To give you some background on Tivoli's systems management technology, the following section describes the OSF's Distributed Management Environment (DME) specification. Tivoli was one of the principle technology providers for the DME specification.

5.5.2   DME History

The Open Software Foundation defined a management standard for distributed systems called the Distributed Management Environment (DME) in the early 1990s. The DME technology specification defines a uniform and consistent set of tools and services that may be used to manage both stand-alone and distributed heterogeneous systems, applications, and networks.

DME combines a select set of vendor management technologies into a consistent framework based on a three-tier model. The lowest tier supports single-host management activities. The second level provides cell naming and security management in distributed environments. The top level encompasses enterprise wide management via Motif based GUI interfaces. DME routines communicate with managed objects using DCE, SNMP, and OSI CMIP.

DME Technology Selections

IBM	Data Engine, System Resource Controller
MIT Project Athena	Palladium Print Services
Tivoli	WIzDOM Object Oriented Framework

Banyan	Network Logger
HP	Open View Network Management Server
	Software Distribution/Installation Utils
	Network License Manager
Groupe Bull	Consolidated Management API
Gradient	PC Ally and Client Lib for Net License Server
	PC Agent and Event Components

The DME Request For Technology (RFT) was first issued in July of 1990. After evaluation by OSF's Munich Development Office, a selection was made in September 1991. The selected technologies went through a period of integration testing, during which time code snapshots were made available to interested parties. DME license fees were set and the first code release was scheduled for the fourth quarter of 1993.

5.5 InfoExplorer Keywords

smit	odmdelete
smitty	VSM
smit.log	xinstallm
smit.script	xmaintm
NLS	xdevicem
LANG	xprintm
ODM	xlvm
odmshow	xuserm
odmget	xdat
odmadd	DSMIT

5.6 QwikInfo

- **SMIT**

`smit`	Motif interface
`smit -C, smitty`	TTY interface
`smit -X`	Inhibit updates, test drive SMIT
F6 key	Display command to be executed by SMIT
`smit <fast-path-name>`	Display SMIT submenu
`$HOME/smit.log`	SMIT transaction log

`$HOME/smit.script`	SMIT command log
`/usr/lib/objrepos/` `sm_xxxxxx`	SMIT ODM panel database
`DSMIT`	Distributed SMIT
`SMIT=d`	Invoke DSMIT instead of SMIT

- **VSM**

xinstallm	Installation manager
xmaintm	Software maintenance
xdevicem	Device manager
xprintm	Print manager
xlvm	Storage manager
xuserm	User manager
`$ xdat`	Date, time, job manager

AIX Installation and Maintenance

6.1 Installation Considerations

One thing that IBM is well known for is documentation. It's a close bet whether the Installation and Maintenance documentation you receive with each RISC system weighs more than the hardware. Although I have mixed feelings about the information provided in some of the IBM documentation, the *AIX Installation Guide Version 4.2, SC23-1924* is a first-rate document. It's easy to follow, it helps get the job done, and it exercises your upper body each time you pick it up.

Another thing IBM is known for is changing the maintenance procedures with each new release! IBM might claim otherwise, but I've been upgrading systems for a very long time and that has been my experience. Each time you install AIX, I recommend you follow the installation guide *carefully,* even when you feel like you can do it in your sleep. I can tell you from experience that cutting corners can have catastrophic results. Follow the install path that fits your environment and you'll keep surprises at a minimum. Rather than duplicate all the information contained in the install document, I'll concentrate on condensing the install process down to the general tasks. I'll also make a few suggestions to help keep your existing environment isolated from the install and maintenance process.

Along with maintenance procedure changes, compiler and binary format changes have occurred since the AIX V3 text was published. If you're running a mixed AIX V3 and AIX V4 environment, you'll want to keep this in mind. I recommend staying as close to the current release as is comfortable. This will get you the best support from IBM when questions or problems occur. I will concentrate on installation and maintenance function at the AIX V4.2 level, it being the most recent one I have personally used before penning this text. Most of the SMIT panels are similar to those used in earlier releases. The FastPath names have changed a bit since AIX V3.2.5. If you are running an older release of AIX, read this text while looking through a glass of water. If you're still uneasy, start at the top and proceed through the SMIT software maintenance submenus until you find what you're looking for.

6.2   Installation and Maintenance Planning

Installing a brand new operating system or application on a new computer is like painting on clean canvas. You're not encumbered with preserving or working within any existing paradigm. You have the freedom to plan your environment from scratch. Planning is the key word here. Operating-system and product-file-system configuration should not waste disk space. Implement a configuration that facilitates future product upgrades and maintenance tasks. Reserve disk space for non-rootvg volume groups to hold your user and local product file systems. If you are installing multiple machines, consider installing one system as a reference system that can then be cloned from a network install manager. Eliminate duplicate file system requirements for diskless, client-based shared product object trees (SPOT). Make use of the worksheets provided in the planning section of the installation guide. The planning sheets make a good reference set when you need to review your installation plan at some time in the future.

Installation Considerations

Installation media

Additional maintenance

BOS disk space

Licensed program product disk space

Paging space

/tmp space

Separate volume group for local user and product file systems

Reference system and network install manager

Network parameters

SPOT support for diskless clients

Preservation of configuration and data on existing systems

6.2.1   Product packaging

To simplify the installation and maintenance process and group products by intended service profile more accurately, a new packaging scheme was introduced in AIX V4. Software is grouped as products, packages, bundles, and filesets. At the lowest level, a fileset identifies software that provides a specific function. A fileset is the smallest installable and updatable unit for maintenance purposes. You'll get to know filesets very well. You tend to have to install them individually because the ones you want never seem to be included in the product set you've just installed (word of warning). Filesets that have been grouped to provide a common service set are called packages, like the collection of filesets that make up bos networking or DCE. Licensed products represent a collection of packages that are distributed as a set on installation media. Groups of packages, filesets, and associated maintenance that are combined for a specific service profile are called bundles. Examples would include client, server, or diagnostic profiles. You can create your own custom bundles using SMIT to capture a particular application level or to group filesets and packages the way you think they should have been grouped in the first place.

Fileset	Specific function software set
Package	Common function filesets
Licensed product	Distribution package sets
Bundle	Group of filesets, packages, and maintenance

6.2.2 Support information

Before jumping in with both feet, read any product-related README files. Contact IBM support representatives concerning the latest maintenance level and planning information for the release level being installed. Before you contact an IBM service representative or software manufacturer, make sure you have your AIX version and release numbers; your service modification level, machine serial number and model number; and your customer number. To identify the version and release numbers for an existing system, use the uname command. AIX 3.2.4 provides a new command for identifying the operating system level, oslevel. The </> characters indicate whether you are at a lower level (<), at a higher level (>), or on the same level as the one displayed (<>).

```
# uname -v -r
2 4
```

Note that uname will give the release level first, regardless of the argument order. Thus, 2 4 indicates V4 R2.

The command uname -m displays machine ID in the form xxyyyyyy mmss, which breaks down as follows:

xx	00 for RS/6000
yyyyyy	CPU ID
mm	Model identifier
ss	Submodel identifier

The command oslevel returns the AIX product level. Mine reads 4.2.0.0.

Your system maintenance level can be obtained from bos.rte history. Use the lslpp -h command to display the maintenance history and state.

```
# lslpp -h bos.rte      Short listing


Fileset       Level  Action  Status  Date   Time
-----------------------------------------------
Path: /usr/lib/objrepos
bos.rte
    4.2.0.0  COMMIT         COMPLETE  06/24/96  23:18:07
    4.2.0.1  COMMIT         COMPLETE  10/03/96  16:28:34


Path: /etc/objrepos
bos.rte
    4.2.0.0  COMMIT         COMPLETE  06/24/96  23:18:07Name

# lslpp -a -h bos.rte    Verbose listing


Fileset       Level  Action  Status  Date   Time
-----------------------------------------------
Path: /usr/lib/objrepos
bos.rte
    4.2.0.0  COMMIT         COMPLETE  06/24/96  23:18:07
    4.2.0.1  COMMIT         COMPLETE  10/03/96  16:28:34
    4.2.0.1  APPLY          COMPLETE  10/03/96  16:28:01


Path: /etc/objrepos
bos.rte
    4.2.0.0  COMMIT         COMPLETE  06/24/96  23:18:07
```

A quick snapshot of maintenance level and state can be obtained using the -L option to lslpp.

```
# lslpp -L bos.rte
Fileset       Level  State  Description
---------------------------------------
bos.rte       4.2.0.1  C  Base Operating System Runtime
```

```
State codes:
A -- Applied.
B -- Broken.
C -- Committed.
O -- Obsolete. (partially migrated to newer version)
? -- Inconsistent State...Run lppchk -v.
```

AIX V4.1 introduced a new maintenance strategy (I told ya so). Product updates are no longer distributed as program temporary fix (PTF) sets. Under AIX V4, the fix level of filesets are incremented until a new cumulative fileset maintenance or base level is available. Fileset levels are identified using the version.release.modification.fix numbering scheme; for example, 4.2.0.1 rather than the AIX V3 PTF level U493250. For pre-AIX V4 systems, look for the following PTF numbers in the lslpp output stream. It will give you an indication of the modification level of your system. The lslpp history command still works the same. It's just a bit less verbose than in AIX V3 (see Table 6.1).

For specific problem fixes, contact

IBM Support
1-800-237-5511

IBM AIX/6000 support offers a number of options for specialist assistance for installation, problem solving, and tuning. For general information, contact

AIX/6000 Support Family
40-B2-05
IBM Corporation
P.O. Box 9000
Roanoke, TX 76262-9989
1-800-CALL-AIX
1-800-IBM-4FAX
call-aix@vnet.ibm.com

You can review the problem and service the database yourself if you have network access to IBMLink or Support Line sites. If you don't

TABLE 6.1   AIX V3 Release Levels

PTF	Level
U493250	3.2.5
U420316	3.2.4
U411711	3.2.3 Extended
U409490	3.2.3
U403173	3.2.2
U401864 only	3.2.0 else 3.2.1

have network access to these sites, IBM provides periodic snapshots of the IBMLink question and service databases on CD-ROM. Order AIX Technical Library/6000 CDROM. See App. A for additional information on AIX help sites and archives on the Internet. A few key sources are listed below:

- Remote login

    ```
    # telnet IBMLink.advantis.com
    ```

- Web sites

    ```
    http://service.software.ibm.com/aixsupport
    http://www.ibmlink.ibm.com/
    http://www.austin.ibm.com/services/
    ```

You can download patches and fixes over the Internet using IBM's FixDist tool kit. FixDist is an FTP interface that allows users to select and retrieve maintenance from anonymous FTP servers at the service.software.ibm.com site. You can select maintenance by PTF and APAR numbers. FixDist will take care of ensuring that all requisite fixes are included in the set. A companion tool called TapeGen can then be used to stack the fixes onto a tape that can be read by SMIT. This is handy if you are maintaining a large number of machines that don't have access to a network install service. These tools are available via anonymous FTP from service.software.ibm.com in the /aix/tools/fixdist directory.

```
# ftp service.software.ibm.com
        login: anonymous
        password: your-email@address.com
        ftp> bin
        ftp> cd /aix/tools/fixdist
        ftp> get fd.tar.Z          (This is a FixDist tool.)
        ftp> get fixdist.ps.Z      (This is the PostScript user guide.)
        ftp> quit
```

After uncompressing and untarring FixDist into a directory on your workstation, you can invoke the tool by typing fixdistc for character mode or fixdistm for X display (see Fig. 6.1). Tailor FixDist to your site. Configuration information will be stored in $HOME/.fixdist_home/.fixdistcfg. Download a copy of the current fix database fddb. You can now search and select fixes from the database for downloading from the FTP fix server (see Fig. 6.2).

If you have access to a Usenet news service, check out the comp.unix.aix discussion and archives. The best help information comes from peers who are using AIX in the field. IBM support personnel and developers also watch these groups and may lend assistance.

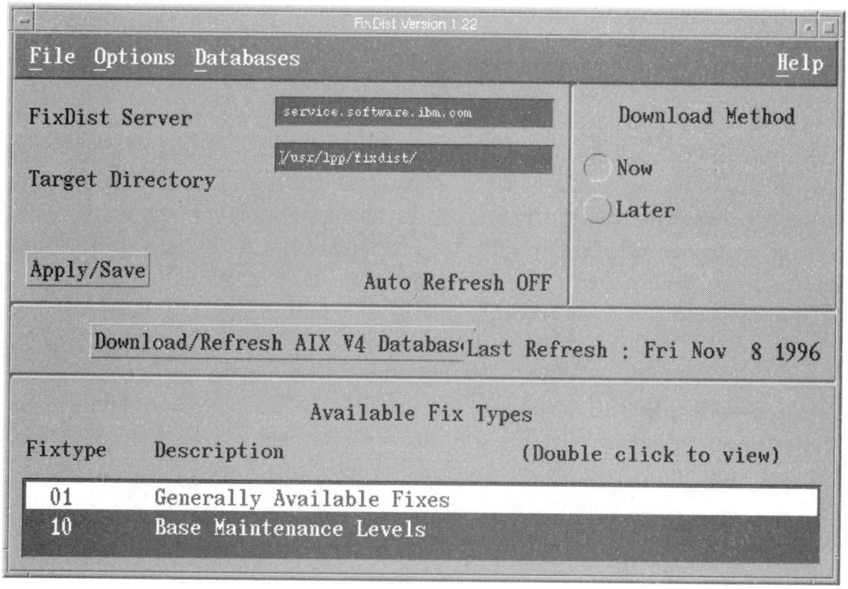

Figure 6.1   FixDist display.

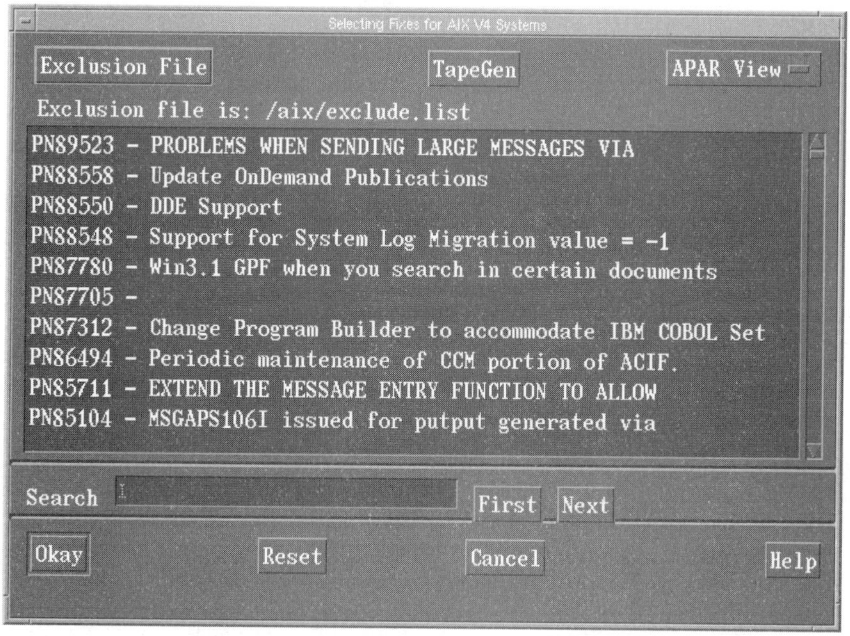

Figure 6.2   FixDist search and select.

6.2.3   Choosing an installation method

AIX can be installed using one of three methods: complete overwrite install, preservation install, or migration install. A complete overwrite install is used to install AIX on new computers or to overwrite a previous installation of the operating system. This option does not preserve any of the existing configuration. A preservation install will attempt to preserve existing user directories in the root volume group by only overwriting the /, /usr, /var, and /tmp file systems. As I will explain later in the chapter, a much safer strategy is to keep any user or local data in file systems that don't reside in the root volume group. Preservation install is the default when upgrading from an AIX V3.1 or AIX V4.2 base. The migration install option is used to retain the root volume group layout and system configuration files. This option can be used for systems installed at AIX V3.2 or newer releases of the operating system. If you have heavily customized your system, a migration install can give you the biggest headache in that it will selectively remove or move system components. Make certain you are intimately familiar with your existing installation before choosing to use a migration install.

6.2.4   Apply and commit

To commit or not to commit—that is the question.

Before installing new software or maintenance on an existing system, you need to have a backout strategy in the event that problems occur during or after the installation. The AIX default is to add new software and maintenance to the system using the APPLY option. This option keeps a history file and a backup copy of each object replaced by the software update. If you are not happy with the update, you can REJECT it and restore the previous version. When using SMIT to install software updates, use the "COMMIT software? no" option.

```
# installp -qa -d /inst.images -X all     APPLY updates
# installp -rB -X all                      REJECT updates
```

Once satisfied with the update, you can COMMIT the update to remove the backup copy of the previous version.

```
# installp -c -g -X all     COMMIT updates
```

The caveat of installing using the APPLY option is that additional disk space is required to hold the old version. This additional space is also difficult to reclaim once the new software is committed. If you don't have the disk space to spare, you may elect to install the update with COMMIT. This option will save on disk space, but it does not provide a simple backout mechanism. Make a full backup of your root file systems prior to installing with COMMIT. In the event of a problem, you can restore the backup.

```
# installp -qa -d /inst.images -c -N all     Install with COMMIT
```

In the event that you must remove a committed lpp, you can invoke the deinstall function of installp. This option will remove product files, associated maintenance, and vital product data (VPD) from the system regardless of the product installation state.

```
# installp -u     Remove software
```

6.2.5 File system expansion

To ensure that sufficient file system space is available, you can elect to have file system size automatically increased during the installation. Unfortunately this process tends to overallocate file system space, the result being wasted disk space at the end of the installation. Automatic file system expansion can also cause the installation to abort if the requested increment in logical partitions is not available. In most cases, you will be better off calculating the space required for the update and allocating the space manually. Remember you cannot easily shrink a file system once it is overallocated.

```
# installp -qa -d /inst.images -X all     Auto expansion
# installp -qa -d /inst.images all         No auto expansion
```

6.2.6 System state

When installing a new product release or maintenance, limit the activity on your system. For some products, this may only involve restricting access to the application being updated and stopping any related subsystems and subservers. Use the stopsrc command to shut down subsystems and subservers.

```
# stopsrc -g tcpip     Stop tcpip subsystem
```

When updating your operating system or a group of products, it is easier to reduce system activity by shutting down to maintenance mode. This will stop all subsystems and restrict access to the system other than from the system console.

```
# telinit M     Shutdown to maintenance mode
```

You can temporarily inhibit login access by creating a /etc/nologin file. The tsmlogin command will display the contents of the /etc/nologin file at each login attempt and then exit. For example:

```
Login access is temporarily inhibited due to system
maintenance activities. Please try again later.
```

6.2.7   Upgrading existing AIX systems

Installing an upgrade or maintenance to an existing AIX system is much easier if you have kept your user file systems and local product data on non-rootvg volume groups. Before installing the upgrade or maintenance, these volume groups may be exported, protecting them from update problems. Use:

```
# exportvg <VGname>
```

Once the update is complete, the volume groups can be imported back into the system. Use

```
# importvg <VGname>
```

You may also wish to save some configuration files like password files, auditing configuration, printing qconfig, and network tables. If you know the installation date of your last upgrade, you can use the find command to walk the rootvg file systems and log file names modified since the last upgrade date. Edit the log file and remove any unnecessary file names. The log file can then be easily converted into a script to copy the desired configuration files to a safe location or backup media. I would recommend doing this even if you will be doing a migration install.

```
# find /etc -mitime <Ndays> -print > save-config
# find /usr/lib -mitime <Ndays> -print >> save-config
```

Before initiating a preservation install, record the location, layout, and space on each of the physical volumes to be used by the install process. Begin by displaying the physical volume names.

```
# ipl_varyon -i

PVNAME    BOOT DEVICE   PVID                VOLUME GROUP ID
hdisk0    YES           000004065a4ad7ce    0000406042e9db9f
hdisk1    NO            000004065a4b372d    0000406042e9db9f
hdisk2    NO            00000444d7afade3    00004060db76b544
```

For each physical volume, display the location information.

```
# lsdev -C -l hdisk0
hdisk0 Available 00-08-00-00 670 MB SCSI Disk Drive
```

Use df and lsvg to total the used and free space making up the root file systems and the root volume group.

```
# df -v / /usr /tmp /var
```

Filesystem	Total KB	used	free	$used	iused	ifree	%iused	Mounted
/dev/hd4	32768	29796	2972	90$	1864	6328	22%	/
/dev/hd2	499712	456704	43008	91$	17438	107490	13%	/usr
/dev/hd3	323584	21068	302516	6$	103	81817	0%	/tmp
/dev/hd9var	1048576	227520	821056	21$	1635	260509	0%	/var

```
# lsvg rootvg
```

VOLUME GROUP:	rootvg	VG IDENTIFIER:	00001508fce80427
VG STATE:	active/complete	PP SIZE:	4 megabyte(s)
VG PERMISSION:	read/write	TOTAL Pps:	574 (2296 megabytes)
MAX Lvs:	256	FREE Pps:	60 (240 megabytes)
Lvs:	10	USED Pps:	514 (2056 megabytes)
OPEN Lvs:	9	QUORUM:	2
TOTAL Pvs:	2	VG DESCRIPTORS:	3
STALE Pvs:	0	STALE Pps	0
ACTIVE Pvs:	2	AUTO ON:	yes

6.3   Installing AIX

If you are installing a brand new RISC System/6000, parts of the basic operating system (BOS) and product runtime environments may be preinstalled on the system. Note that the preinstalled system does not represent the full product or maintenance set. You must complete the installation of the remaining products and maintenance before configuring the system for use.

If you will be using a serial attached TTY as the console, use the following settings on the TTY:

9600 bps

8,1,none

24×80 display

Auto LF off

Line wrap on

New line CR

Follow this nine-step list to install AIX:

1. Complete installation planning.
2. Turn on all attached devices.
3. Set the key switch (if present) in the SERVICE position.
4. Insert installation media or mksysb bootable tape.
5. Turn on system power.
6. Select console and install language when prompted.
7. When the "Welcome to Base Operating System Installation and Maintenance" screen is displayed, you must decide whether to proceed with installation defaults or to verify and/or modify settings before continuing. Enter 88 at any time to display help information. Installation modifications include:

Installation method	New and complete overwrite install.
	Preservation install.
	Migration install.
Primary language environment	
System settings	Install disk and file system sizing.
Trusted computing base	Turn on high-level system security. Note that this will disable functionality, and TCB cannot be removed without reinstallation of AIX.

8. Turn key (if present) to NORMAL position.
9. The system will reboot and the VSM install assistant screen will be displayed. The VSM panel (see Fig. 6.3) will assist you in finishing system configuration. This will include setting the date and time, setting the root password, and so on. The VSM panel won't be displayed at each system boot until you have selected "Tasks Completed—Exit to AIX Login" to signal that your configuration changes have been completed.

6.4 Installing Licensed Program Products

Installing Licensed Program Products (LPP) can be managed using the SMIT install FastPath or by using the installp command. It's much easier to do this with SMIT in that SMIT will remind you of all the options associated with performing an install or updates.

```
# installp -qa -d /inst.images -X all    APPLY updates
```

Products and maintenance will usually be installed into the LPP directory, /usr/lpp. A separate subdirectory is created for each product, package, and fileset.

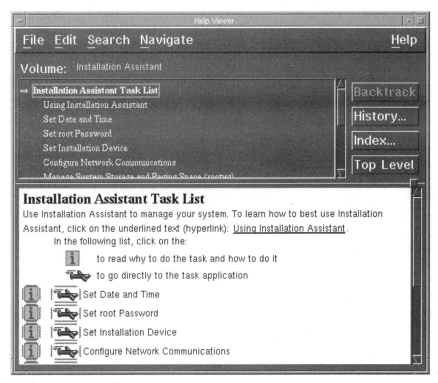

Figure 6.3   VSM install assistant.

```
# ls -aF /usr/lpp

./                          X11.help.En_US/
../                         X11.help.en_US/
Adobe/                      X11.info/
Java/                       X11.info.en_US/
Netscape.navigator/         X11.loc.En_US/
SLEUTH/                     X11.loc.en_US/
UMS/                        X11.man.en_US/
UMS.info.en_US/             X11.motif/
UMS.loc/                    X11.msg.En_US/
UMS.msg.en_US/              X11.msg.en_US/
Unicode/                    X11.vsm/
X11/                        X11.x_st_mgr/
X11.Dt/                     bos/
X11.adt/                    bos.acct/
X11.apps/                   bos.adt/
X11.base/                   bos.diag/
X11.compat/                 bos.dlc/
X11.fnt/                    bos.dosutil/
```

```
bos.games/                          devices.isa_sio.PNP0501/
bos.iconv/                          devices.isa_sio.PNP0700/
bos.ifor_ls/                        devices.isa_sio.PNP0E00/
bos.info.en_US/                     devices.isa_sio.PNP0F03/
bos.info.rte/                       devices.isa_sio.baud/
bos.loc.adt/                        devices.isa_sio.km/
bos.loc.com/                        devices.mca.8fc8/
bos.loc.iso/                        devices.msg.Ca_ES/
bos.lrn/                            devices.msg.De_DE/
bos.msg.Sv_SE/                      devices.msg.En_US/
bos.msg.ZH_CN/                      devices.msg.Es_ES/
bos.msg.Zh_TW/                      devices.msg.Fr_FR/
bos.msg.en_US/                      devices.msg.It_IT/
bos.net/                            devices.msg.Sv_SE/
bos.perf/                           devices.msg.ZH_CN/
bos.powermgt/                       devices.msg.Zh_TW/
bos.rcs/                            devices.msg.en_US/
bos.som/                            devices.pci.00100100/
bos.sysmgt/                         devices.pci.14101c00/
bos.terminfo/                       devices.pci.1c104ac2/
bos.txt/                            devices.pci.86808404/
bos.up/                             devices.pci.PNP0A00/
bosinst/                            devices.pcmcia.a4000200/
dce/                                devices.pcmcia.a4001e00/
dce.client/                         devices.pcmcia.ethernet/
dce.compat/                         devices.pcmcia.tokenring/
dce.dfs_server/                     devices.rs6ksmp.base/
dce.doc/                            devices.rspc.base/
dce.msg.en_US/                      devices.scsi.disk/
dce.pthreads/                       devices.scsi.tape/
dce.xdsxom/                         devices.sio.ktma/
dcedoc/                             devices.sys.PNP0A03/
devices.base/                       devices.sys.pci/
devices.common.IBM.disk/            devices.tty/
devices.common.IBM.ethe             diagnostics/
rnet/                               fddb/
devices.common.IBM.fda/             fixdist/
devices.common.IBM.ppa/             fonts/
devices.common.IBM.scsi/            gai/
devices.common.base/                https-us/
devices.common.rspcbase/            ifor_ls.client/
devices.graphics/                   ifor_ls.msg.en_US/
devices.isa.IBM0010/                ifor_ls.server/
devices.isa.PNP80CC/                info/
devices.isa_sio.IBM000E/            internet/
devices.isa_sio.IBM001C/            internet_server.base/
devices.isa_sio.PNP0303/            internet_server.msg.en_US/
devices.isa_sio.PNP0400/            internet_server.ps.en_US.u
```

```
p_n_running/                        ipfx.msg.pt_PT/
internet_server.security.us         ipfx.msg.sv_SE/
_secure/                            ipfx.msg.zh_CN/
inu_LOCK*                           ipfx.msg.zh_TW/
ipfx/                               ipfx.rte/
ipfx.msg.Da_DK/                     netscape/
ipfx.msg.De_DE/                     netscape.https-us/
ipfx.msg.En_GB/                     nfs/
ipfx.msg.En_US/                     printers/
ipfx.msg.Es_ES/                     printers.msg.Ca_ES/
ipfx.msg.Fi_FI/                     printers.msg.De_DE/
ipfx.msg.Fr_FR/                     printers.msg.En_US/
ipfx.msg.It_IT/                     printers.msg.Es_ES/
ipfx.msg.Ja_JP/                     printers.msg.Fr_FR/
ipfx.msg.Nl_NL/                     printers.msg.It_IT/
ipfx.msg.No_NO/                     printers.msg.Sv_SE/
ipfx.msg.Pt_PT/                     printers.msg.ZH_CN/
ipfx.msg.Sv_SE/                     printers.msg.Zh_TW/
ipfx.msg.da_DK/                     printers.msg.en_US/
ipfx.msg.de_DE/                     printers.rte/
ipfx.msg.en_GB/                     ptfload.log
ipfx.msg.en_US/                     save.config/
ipfx.msg.es_ES/                     smith/
ipfx.msg.fi_FI/                     som/
ipfx.msg.fr_FR/                     tapegen/
ipfx.msg.it_IT/                     x_st_mgr/
ipfx.msg.ja_JP/                     xlC/
ipfx.msg.ko_KR/                     xlC.cpp/
ipfx.msg.nl_NL/                     xlC.msg.en_US/
ipfx.msg.no_NO/                     xlC.rte/
```

The contents of the installation media may be reviewed by selecting "List Software and Related Information" from the SMIT Software Installation and Maintenance menu or executing installp with the -l option.

```
# installp -q -d /dev/cdrom -l

Fileset Name    Level    I/U Q Content
=======================================================
Adobe.acrobat   2.1.0.0  I N usr
# Adobe acrobat reader


Java.dev        1.0.0.0  I N usr
# DEVELOPMENT ENV for Sun's Java(tm) Programming Envir
```

```
Java.rte          1.0.0.0  I N usr
# RUNTIME ENVIRONMENT for Java

Java.samples      1.0.0.0  I N usr
# SAMPLES for Java

UMS.H_32x         2.1.4.0  I Y usr
# AIX Ultimedia Services H.32x Collaboration Support

UMS.demo          2.1.4.0  I Y usr,root
# AIX Ultimedia Services Demo

UMS.objects       2.1.4.0  I Y usr,root
# AIX Ultimedia Services

UMS.samples       2.1.4.0  I Y usr
# AIX Ultimedia Services Samples
```

In the event that one or more of the applications will be installed on multiple machines, you might want to copy the contents of the install media to disk for use with an install server. Select "Copy Software to Hard Disk for Future Installation" from the SMIT maintain_software menu and refer to Sec. 4.5.3 for details on configuring and using an install server. You may also use the bffcreate command to copy the software update to disk (see Fig. 6.4).

```
# bffcreate -qv -d'/dev/rmt0' -t'/inst.images' '-X' all
# smit maintain_software
```

To install *all* software and maintenance on the media, invoke SMIT with the install_all FastPath name. You will be prompted for the media type, and installation will proceed using default options. If you want to select other update options or install a subset of the updates on the media, start SMIT using the "install_latest" FastPath. Use the F4 key to list the products available on the media. Individual entries may be tagged using F7 (see Fig. 6.5).

```
# smit install_latest
```

In the previous section on installation planning, I discussed the pros and cons of installing with COMMIT and automatically extending the file system. The same arguments relate to product and maintenance updates. If you have extra disk space to play with, electing not to COMMIT and allowing file system extension will make the install smoother.

During the installation and update process, progress information is displayed by SMIT and installp. SMIT will log this information to the

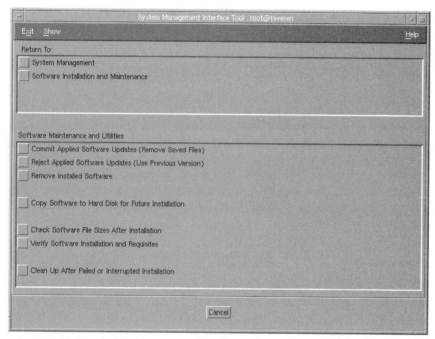

Figure 6.4   SMIT software maintenance and utilities panel.

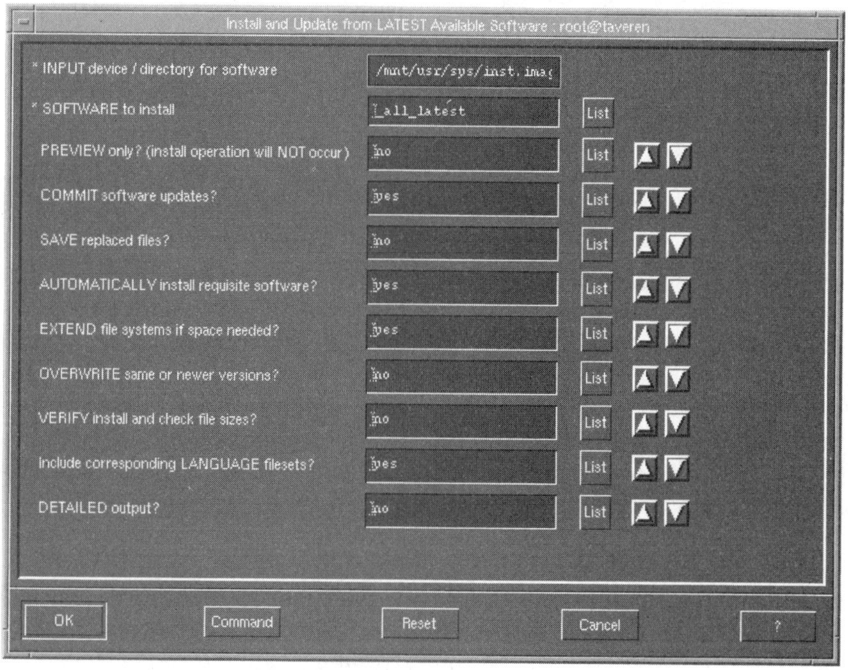

Figure 6.5   SMIT selective install panel.

smit.log file. You may wish to redirect output from the installp to a file if it was invoked from the command line. Once the install has completed, verify the status of the update (see Sec. 4.4 for details on product and maintenance installation status).

6.5 Installing Non-LPP Products

It's a good idea to keep local, public domain, and vendor products separate from BOS directories. This will ensure that they will not be clobbered by BOS upgrades and installations. A common practice is to create a local product file system called /usr/local. Within /usr/local, create subdirectories bin, lib, etc, and src. You can add these directories to the default command PATH and create symbolic links from BOS directories if required.

6.6 Applying Maintenance

The first and foremost rule of system maintenance: "If it isn't broken, don't fix it!" If only it was that easy! The AIX operating system and product set is made up of a large number of subsystems. Each subsystem contains hundreds or thousands of components. In this not-so-perfect world, problems will crop up in many of these objects. You have to decide which bugs will be tolerated and which ones must be fixed. Each new maintenance level that is applied to the system or subsystem will include a new set of gremlins. The trick is to find a maintenance level that provides stability for your environment and is within current maintenance levels supported by the vendor.

All the operating system and applications vendors are doing their best to drive product error rates down. This is a very difficult task that is complicated in shared-library environments. Think of the number of commands and subsystems that depend on libc.a! IBM has addressed the problems encountered with the old selective-fix strategy by packaging fixes by fileset into maintenance levels. In the selective-fix environment, it was difficult to collect all the prerequisite (prereq) and corequisite (coreq) fixes that represented a particular system snapshot. A prereq or coreq often involves a component not related to the problem being addressed. The unrelated component often requires other fixes. Components are duplicated many times in the fix set. You end up with a 50 megabyte fix tape to fix a small problem in csh.

The AIX V4 maintenance strategy packages prereq and coreq fixes by fileset. A fileset is the smallest updatable unit and represents a specific function. Maintenance levels are packaged and shipped at a frequency of 3 or 4 times a year. AIX V4 also provides a new installp options. Most notable are the flags -V, which adjusts the verbosity of status messages; -u, which provides deinstall capability for COM-MITED products; -L indicates which products are already installed; and -g, which automagically installs, commts, or rejects requisite software.

The rules for installing maintenance are the same as described in the previous section on installing program products. For distributed environments, you may wish to copy the maintenance set to disk for access from an install server. You might also choose to build a reference system image accessible from an network install server (see Sec. 4.5.3 for details).

Read the maintenance documentation carefully before beginning the update. A short description of maintenance levels or supplemental information on the media may be displayed from smit list_media or using installp with the -i or -A options.

```
# installp -iq -d /dev/rmt0 all     Display supplement information
# installp -qA /dev/rmt0 all        Display APAR information
```

6.7   Postinstallation and Maintenance Tasks

With the installation or maintenance process complete, there is still a bit of tidying up to be done before making the system available for use. A new installation requires that you set default system and environment variables. If you installed over an existing system, you will need to restore the previous environment. Product updates or maintenance will require testing before committing or rejecting the update. Finally, create new stand-alone media and take a fresh backup of the new system. A clean snapshot can be used as a reference point for installing additional machines or as a fallback should problems arise in the future.

6.7.1   Review install/update status

Review the status of software product and maintenance updates using "List All Applied but Not Committed Software" from the SMIT sinstallp menu or by invoking lslpp from the command line.

```
# lslpp -h bos.rte     Display lpp history

Fileset    Level  Action  Status  Date   Time
---------------------------------------------------
Path: /usr/lib/objrepos
bos.rte
    4.2.0.0  COMMIT      COMPLETE  06/24/96  23:18:07
    4.2.0.1  COMMIT      COMPLETE  10/03/96  16:28:34
```

```
Path: /etc/objrepos
bos.rte
  4.2.0.0  COMMIT    COMPLETE  06/24/96  23:18:07Name
```

LPP software can be in one of the following states:

APPLY   Fileset was being applied

COMMIT   Fileset was being committed

REJECT   Applied fileset was being rejected

DEINSTALL   Fileset was being removed from the system

CLEANUP   Fileset cleanup after failed apply or commit

In the event of problems with the update, invoke cleanup and reinstall. LPP cleanup can be executed from smit cleanup or via the installp -C option. Installations using SMIT or the installp command will normally perform any cleanup automatically in the event of a failure.

```
# installp -C <Fileset>    Clean up failed install
```

6.7.2   Restoring your environment

Setting default system environments is a final step for the installation paths described thus far. This involves setting or validating the default language, time zone, console type, number of licensed users, and number of virtual terminals (see Fig. 6.6). IBM has kindly provided a SMIT FastPath that addresses each of these variables. With root permissions, invoke SMIT system FastPath.

```
# smit system
```

In a networked environment, you will also need to set your network interface address and characteristics (see Part 5).

Set the root account password. The default installation does not provide a password for root. Need I say more?

Restore any configuration tables from the previous system, and reimport any volume groups exported as part of the preliminary installation planning.

```
# importvg <VGname>
```

6.7.3   Create new bootable
media and backups

Next make sure you have multiple copies of stand-alone bootable media that reflect the new system's install and maintenance level. Notice I said *multiple copies*. I must admit that I have been bitten more

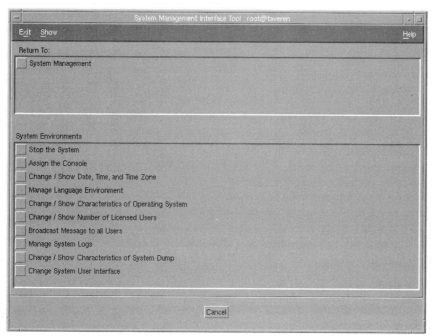

Figure 6.6 SMIT system configuration panel.

than once having only a single copy of some crucial bit of data. Create a backup image of the new rootvg on tape using the mksysb command. These tapes can be used to recover from a disk failure or be used to install additional machines. Begin by using the mkszfile command to create an /image.data file. This file contains descriptive information about the file systems in the rootvg. Edit this file so that it contains only those file systems you wish to include in your reference set. Use the following procedures to create the backup and bootable images. When booting from the standalone tape, the AIX Install/Maint shell is executed, which will guide you through the restoration process.

To create a backup copy:

1. # `mkszfile`   Create rootvg map
2. # `chdev -l rmt0 -a block_size=512`   Set correct block size
3. # `tctl -f /dev/rmt0 rewind`   Rewind tape
4. # `mksysb /dev/rmt0`   Create backup
5. # `chdev -l rmt0 -a block_size=<blocksize>`   Reset tape block size

To create bootable media:

1. # `cp /var/adm/ras/bosinst.data /bosinst.data`   Create bosinst.data
2. # `mkszfile`   Create rootvg map

3. # `chdev -l rmt0 -a block_size=512`   Set correct block size

4. # `tctl -f /dev/rmt0 rewind`   Rewind tape

5. # `bosboot -ad /dev/rmt0.1`   Create boot image

6. # `mkinsttape /dev/rmt0`   Create bos inst/maint

7. # `chdev -l rmt0 -a block_size=<blocksize>` Reset tape block size

Now is a good opportunity to move the /usr/sys/inst.images directory into a separate file system if you are installing from a disk image like /inst.images. The /usr file system is not a good target for present or future installation and maintenance activities. The inst.images subdirectory requires constant resizing to accommodate new install and maintenance images. Create a new JFS file system called /inst.images and move the current contents of /usr/sys/inst.images into the new directory. If you want to continue using the /usr/sys/inst.images path, use it as the mount point for the new installation and maintenance file system.

6.8   Distributed Systems

If installing or updating a single system isn't problem enough, think about repeating the process over and over again in a multisystem environment! In many cases, these systems represent both disk and nondisk configurations.

6.8.1   NFS installation support

In networked environments with existing AIX systems, copy product and maintenance images to a file system, /inst.images. NFS export this file system to each of the remote sites. This method requires repeating the installation process on each machine. It provides the capability of individually tailoring the update on each system.

6.8.2   Creating a reference system

To minimize the amount of time and work required to update multiple disk systems, create a single reference system image that can be cloned on each machine.

1. Update and tailor one system that represents your base configuration.

2. Invoke mkszfile to create a /image.data table.

3. Edit the /image.data file such that it contains only those file systems you want to include in your reference system image.

4. Invoke mksysb to create a bootable reference image.

In nonnetworked environments, direct mksysb output to portable media. If network access is available, direct the output image to a file system, /inst.images.

5. Create a network install manager in networked environments with NFS and TCP/IP support.

6.8.3 Network Install Manager

AIX V4 Network Install Manager (NIM) replaces the AIX V3 Diskless Workstation Manager (DWM) for administering diskless/dataless clients and standalone workstations. NIM facilitates central point management of software installation and maintenance across all AIX workstations participating in a distributed networked environment. NIM can also customize, boot, and run diagnostics remotely on each of the NIM-managed workstations. NIM is TCP/IP-based, using the BOOTP, TFTP, and NFS protocols to distribute boot images and software to each NIM client. NIM can be used over any network that supports the TCP/IP protocol and can support multiple network interface types on the central server.

A NIM environment is comprised of two system types: a NIM master and one or more NIM clients. A NIM master centrally orchestrates all the management functions for the NIM clients in the network. The master server must be a stand-alone AIX V4 workstation with sufficient storage resources to provide boot images and shared product object trees (SPOT) for all managed clients. The NIM master server must be installed with the AIX network and sysmgt filesets required for NIM operation. There is only one NIM master per set of clients. NIM clients may be any mixture of diskless, dataless and standalone workstations with network connectivity to the NIM master.

NIM supports three types of clients:

Stand-alone	Workstations with local copies of AIX and LPPs
Diskless	Network file systems, paging, and dump; bootstrap ROM for network boot
Dataless	Network file systems; local paging and dump; bootstrap ROM for network boot; better performance than diskless configuration

The AIX filesets that make up NIM support are bundled in bos.sysmgt. The bos.sysmgt.nim.master fileset is used to build the NIM master server. The bos.sysmgt.nim.client fileset is installed on each fo the standalone NIM clients. The fileset bos.sysmgt.nim.spot is used to create SPOT file systems for NIM diskless and dataless client types.

The NIM master stores information required to identify each managed client and network type as objects in an ODM database. This is where most of the difficulty comes in managing a NIM environment. Commands are supplied to list, update, and verify NIM ODM objects and relationships, but, in practice, fencing with the ODM is not quite as straightforward as working with human-readable tables. The NIM master must maintain relationships that link machine objects to network objects, network objects to network objects (routing), and machine objects to machine objects. Common NIM commands used to update and verify NIM ODM objects and relationships include nim, nimconfig, nimclient, and lsnim. My recommendation is that you use SMIT to configure and manage NIM. The SMIT panels do a much better job in reminding you of all the attributes that must be associated with NIM objects to ensure that proper object-to-object relationships are maintained. Go ahead and use lsnim to do a quick check of ODM contents, but use SMIT to do the rest. I'll use SMIT in the following treatment of setting up a NIM environment.

6.8.3.1 Creating a NIM master server. To create a NIM master server, begin by choosing a stand-alone workstation that has the network connectivity required by all the clients it will manage. It's also a good idea to add disk and file systems to the server as respositories for NIM resources. Begin by creating a /export and /tftpboot file systems that will be used to house NIM scripts and boot images. Network boot images are created in /tftpboot when a SPOT is created. Each boot image can be roughly 30 MB in size.

```
# smit crjfs
```

Or if you prefer the old-fashioned command-line way:

```
# crfs -v jfs -g rootvg -a size=8192 -m /export -A yes
# crfs -v jfs -g rootvg -a size=81920 -m /tftp -A yes
```

Mount the /export and /tftpboot file systems and create the following subdirectories:

```
# mount /tftpboot
# mount /export
# mkdir /export/nim
# mkdir /export/nim/scripts
```

Next install the bos.net.nfs, bos.sysmgt.nim.master, and bos.sysmgt.nim.spot filesets. It's possible to use another server to manage SPOTs and mount them via NFS on the NIM master, but this just adds another level of complexity to what can easily become a tangled web.

```
installp -a -g -X -d <dev> bos.net.nfs
installp -a -g -X -d <dev> bos.sysmgt.nim.master
installp -a -g -X -d <dev> bos.sysmgt.nim.spot
```

Now you're ready to activate and configure the NIM master by invoking SMIT nimconfig or the nimconfig command (see Fig. 6.7). This is primarily initiated by defining a master network object. You'll need to think of a network object name to associate with the network interface type and attribute information. Attributes will include things like cable type or ring speed. This operation will populate /export, create /etc/niminfo, and start the NIM nimesis daemon.

```
# smit nimconfig      Configure and start NIM master
```

As an exercise, invoke lsnim and lsnim -a master to verify what you have created. I've just created a monster!

```
# lsnim               List NIM-defined objects
# lsnim -a master     List master server info
```

Create any additional network interface objects on the master using the SMIT nim_mknet FastPath (see Fig. 6.8).

```
# smit nim_mknet      Create NIM network objects
```

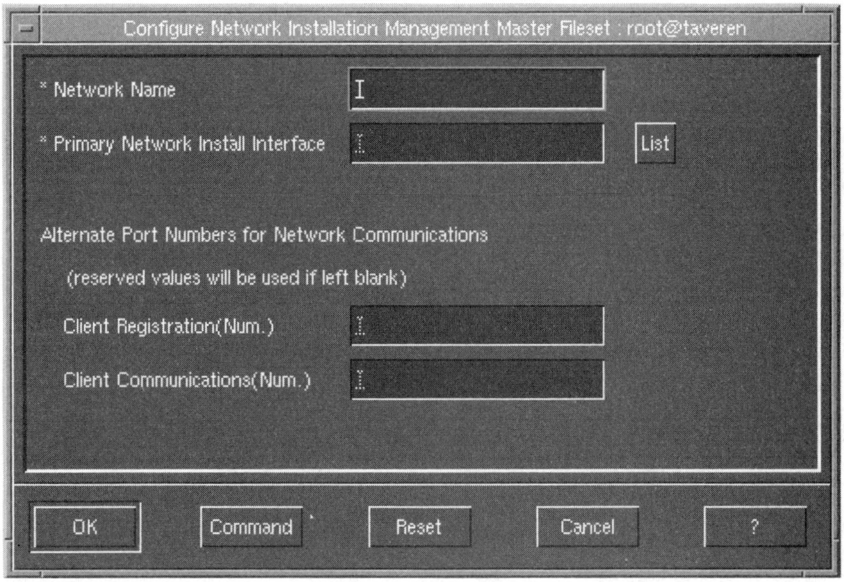

Figure 6.7 SMIT NIM master configuration.

If you will be traversing subnets between NIM master and clients, you will need to add routing information. Do this by invoking SMIT nim_mkroute. Remember to verify what you have created in each step using SMIT or lsnim.

```
# smit nim_mkroute    Define NIM network routes
```

If you're satisfied with your work thus far, then it's time to create resources for standalone client installation. This is accomplished by creating an lpp_source object. The object references filesets and packages that will be used to install standalone clients. The lpp_source object can reference either a file system like /usr/sys/inst.images or installation media like CD-ROM. At a minimum, lpp_source must include:

bos

bos.rte.up

bos.rte.mp

bos.diag

bos.net

bos.sysmgt

devices.all

bos.terminfo

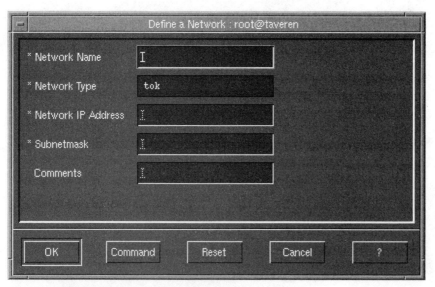

Figure 6.8   SMIT NIM network interface definition.

The contents of lpp_source is checked by NIM, which will update the simiges attribute to indicate that it is valid for installation. Note that you can elect to add other filesets to the minimum set (see Fig. 6.9). To create the lpp_source object, run SMIT nim_mkres (see Fig. 6.10).

```
# smit nim_mkres      Create lpp_source
```

Now create SPOTs to be used by bos_inst operations and for diskless and dataless workstations. A SPOT contains the bos runtime images required for NIM operation or system use. The SPOT may either be the /usr file system on the NIM master or an alternate subdirectory tree, /export. SPOT support for diskless and dataless clients must include the following:

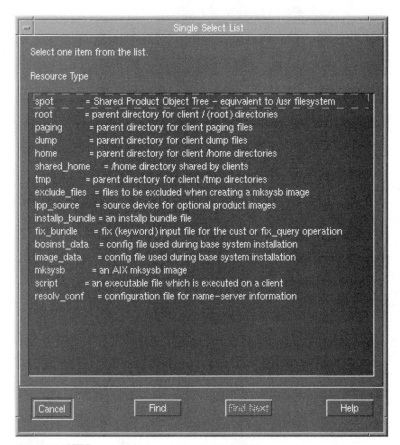

Figure 6.9   NIM manage resources.

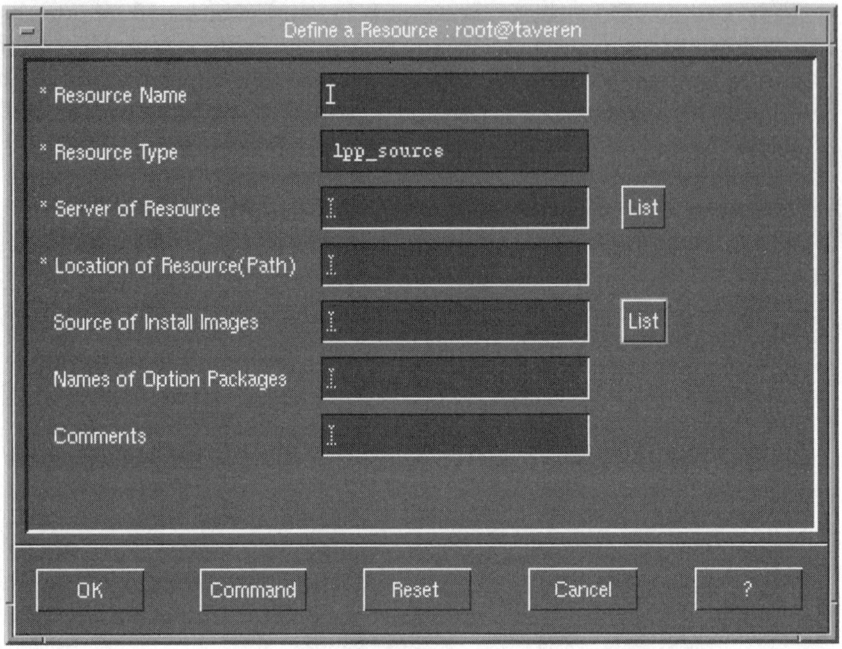

Figure 6.10   NIM create lpp_source resource.

root
dump   (diskless only)
paging   (diskless only)
home
resolv_conf
shared_home   (exported to all clients)
tmp

To create a SPOT, invoke SMIT nim_mkres and supply an object name, master server name, and directory path for the SPOT (see Fig. 6.11).

```
# smit nim_mkres      Create bos runtime resource
```

On standalone clients with an existing AIX installation, you can create the NIM bos runtime resource locally by invoking SMIT nim_alloc on the client.

```
# smit nim_alloc      Create bos_inst resource on client
```

6.8.3.2 Configuring NIM clients. NIM clients access the master server by loading boot image over network interface using BOOTP and TFTP.

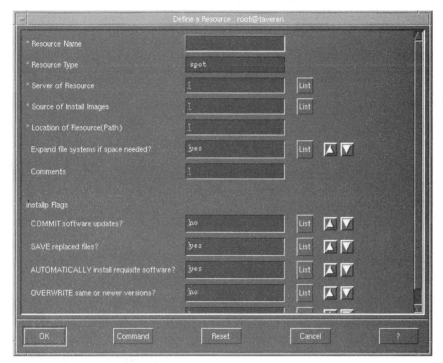

Figure 6.11   NIM SPOT runtime resource.

Some older microchannel systems don't support BOOTP in IPL ROM. To address this problem, you can create IPL ROM emulation media. Execute bootinfo -q <adapter> to verify whether IPL ROM emulation is required.

```
# bootinfo -q <NetworkAdapter>      Return 1 if no emulation required
```

If you need to build IPL ROM emulation media, you can do this using the bosboot command.

```
# bosboot -r /usr/lpp/bos.sysmgt/nim/methods/IPLROM.emulation
\ -d <DeviceName> -M both<<t>>
```

Each client must be identified on the NIM master using the hardware mac level address as an object. Use the following procedures to record the mac level address and to initiate a NIM boot by the given architecture type.

A. Diskless/Dataless Systems
1. Boot from CD-ROM.
2. Press F4 when logo screen appears.
3. Select "Select Boot Device."
4. Select "Configure 1st Boot Device."
5. Select "Network Adapter."
6. Select LAN interface for you workstation.
7. Press ENTER.
8. Press ESC.
9. Select "Utilities."
10. Select "Remote Initial Program Load Setup."
11. Select "Adapter Parameters," "View Parameters," and "Hardware Address."
12. Record hardware address to be added as a NIM object on the master.
13. Press ESC until "Network Parameters" shows.
14. Select "IP Parameters."
15. Enter client, server, gateway IP addresses, and subnet mask.
16. Press ESC until "System Management Services" shows.
17. Select "Select Boot Devices."
18. Select "Boot Other Device."
19. Select "Network Adapter."
20. Press ENTER to initiate BOOTP request
B. ISA Bus Systems
1. Boot from CD-ROM.
2. Press F4 when logo screen appears.
3. Select "Utilities."
4. Select "Remote Initial Program Load Setup."
5. Select "Adapter Parameters," "View Parameters," and "Hardware Address."
6. Record hardware mac address for NIM object.
7. Press ESC until "Network Parameters" shows.
8. Select "IP Parameters."
9. Enter client, server, gateway IP addresses, and subnet mask.
10. Press ESC until "System Management Services" appears.
11. Select "Select Boot Devices."
12. Select "Boot Other Device."
13. Select "Network Adapter."
14. Press ENTER to initiate BOOTP request.
C. UP Microchannel Systems
1. If required, insert IPL ROM emulation media.
2. Turn key to the secure position.
3. Turn on power.
4. Turn key to "service" when LED reads 200.
5. Press RESET.

6. Select "Select BOOT (Startup) Device."
7. Select network adapter and press ENTER.
8. Select "SET OR CHANGE NETWORK ADDRESSES."
9. Record hardware address for NIM object.
10. Enter client, server, gateway IP addresses, and subnet mask. Pad entries with zeroes. Leave IP addresses as "0" if the client and the master are on the same LAN.
11. Type 99 and Press ENTER to save.
12. Select "Exit Main Menu and Start System (BOOT)."
13. Follow instructions to turn key to normal position.
14. BOOTP request is initiated.

D. SMP Microchannel Systems

1. Turn key to "secure."
2. Turn on power.
3. Turn key to "service" when LED reads 200.
4. Press RESET.
5. Select "System Boot."
6. Select "Boot from Network."
7. Select "Select BOOT (Startup) Device."
8. Select netowrk adapter and press ENTER.
9. Select "SET OR CHANGE NETWORK ADDRESSES."
10. Enter client, server, gateway IP addresses, and subnet mask. Pad entries with zeroes. Leave IP addresses as "0" if the client and the master are on the same LAN.
11. Type 99 and Press ENTER to save.
12. Select "Exit Main Menu and Start System (BOOT)."
13. Follow instructions to turn key to normal position.
14. BOOTP request is initiated

Now that you have the network adapter mac address for each client, create objects for each client using SMIT nim_mkmac (see Fig. 6.12).

```
# smit nim_mkmac     Create client network object
```

Standalone clients require bos.sysmgt.nim.client be installed. You must also set "push permission" for the master with SMIT nim_perms. You might also elect to allocate bos_inst resources locally on the client.

```
installp -a -g -X -d <dev> bos.sysmgt.nim.client  Install nim.client
# smit nim_perms     Set master push permission
# smit nim_alloc     Create bos.inst resources
```

6.8.3.3 Installation using NIM. To initiate installation using NIM, first select the source for the installation. Valid sources include lpp_source, SPOT, or a mksysb image. To push an install from the master, invoke SMIT nim_mac_op and select the object name of the client. Next select

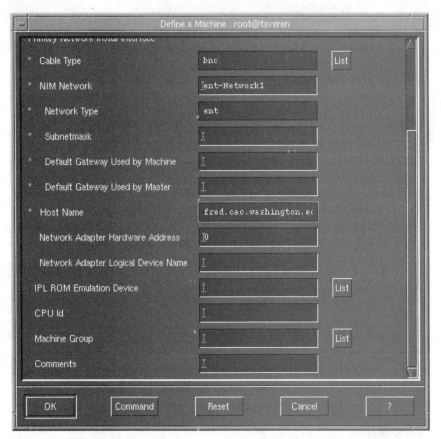

Figure 6.12   NIM create client object.

bos_inst to start a standalone install or dkls_init to initialize a diskless or dataless workstation. You can start an installation from a standalone client using SMIT nim_install. Once installation is complete, verify that things went well using nim_mac_op lppchk.

# smit nim_mac_op	Select client and resource
# smit bos_inst	Push install standalone client
# smit nim_install	Pull install from client
# smit dksl_init	Initialize diskless client
# smit nim_mac_opp lppchk	Verify installation

6.8.3.4   NIM utilities.   Just a few closing notes concerning NIM: First of all, you may have noted that it is a real pain having to create objects for every client you want to support with NIM. I don't have a quck solution for this, but you can install a group of clients concurrently by creating a NIM group object that identifies the set (see Fig. 6.13). Do this by invoking SMIT nim_mkgrp.

```
# smit nim_mkgrp       Create a NIM client group
```

Now that you've done all this work, you'll want to safeguard it by backing it up. A quick way to do this is to use SMIT nim_backup_db, which will create a tar archive of your configuration. Just to be safe, SMIT nim_restore_db puts it all back.

```
# smit nim_backup_db       Backup NIM configuration
# smit nim_restore_db       Restore NIM configuration
```

Use SMIT nim_client_op to do things like remotely rebooting a client or shutting a client down to maintenance mode for diagnostics. You won't get much excercise this way, but it saves on joint wear and tear.

```
# smit nim_client_op       Remotely operate a NIM client
```

Lastly, if you've really made a mess of things, you can punt by unconfiguring your master using the SMIT nim_unconfig. Hey, they didn't call the master NIM daemon *nimesis* for nothing!

```
# smit nim_unconfig       Unconfigure NIM master
```

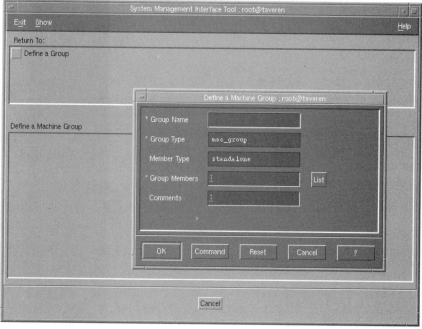

Figure 6.13   NIM create client group.

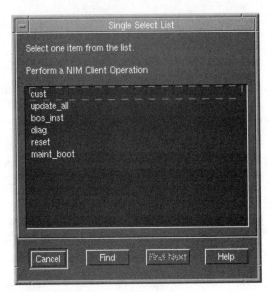

Figure 6.14   NIM remote client operations.

6.9   InfoExplorer Keywords

uname	find
oslevel	rootvg
lpp	lsvg
bos.rte	df
bundle	bosboot
fileset	mksysb
product package	mkszfile
lslpp	NIM
installp	SPOT
bffcreate	mkspot
stopsrc	bootp
startsrc	tftp
telinit	diskless
tsmlogin	lsspot
exportvg	nimesis
importvg	

6.10   QwikInfo

- Software Install/Maintenance

  Information and support:

1-800-CALL-AIX	
1-800-IBM-4FAX.	
1-800-237-5511	Problem support
IBMlink.advantis.com	Internet telnet IBMLink

  Maintenance level and history:

`oslevel`	AIX 3.2.4+ version and release level
`uname -v -r`	Display version and release level.
`lslpp -a -h <product>`	List maint history

  Packaging:

Fileset	Specific function software set
Package	Common function filesets
Licensed product	Distribution package sets
Bundle	Group of filesets, packages, maintenance

  Backup RootVG:

`mkszfile`	Create image.data file for mksysb
`mksysb /dev/rmt0<<t>>`	Backup RootVG to tape

  Maintenance installation:

`smit install`	Base install panel
`smit install_latest`	Selective install panel
`smit install_all`	Install ALL products
`bffcreate -qv -d <media> -f <disk-path>`	Copy maint to disk
`installp -qa -d <media-path> -X all`	APPLY updates
`installp -rB -d -X all`	REJECT updates
`installp -c -g -X all`	COMMIT updates
`Installp -u <fileset>`	DEINSTALL a fileset
`installp -C <fileset>`	CLEANUP failed install

- **NIM**

smit nimconfig	Configure and start NIM master
smit nim_mknet	Create NIM network objects
smit nim_mkroute	Define NIM network routes
smit nim_mkmac	Create client network object
smit nim_mkres	Create lpp_source
smit nim_alloc	Create bos.inst resources
lsnim	List nim defined objects
bootinfo -q	Check IPL ROM emulation
bosboot -r	Create IPL ROM media
smit nim_alloc	Create bos_inst resource on client
smit nim_perms	Set master push permission
smit nim_mac_op	Select client and resource
smit nim_mkgrp	Create a NIM client group
smit bos_inst	Push install standalone client
smit nim_install	Pull install from client
smit dksl_init	Initialize diskless client
smit nim_mac_opp lppchk	Verify installation
smit nim_backup_db	Backup NIM configuration
smit nim_restore_db	Restore NIM configuration
smit nim_client_op	Remotely operate a NIM client
smit nim_unconfig	Unconfigure NIM master

7

System Boot and Shutdown

7.1 AIX Boot Process

Each time you power up an RS/6000, a complex series of system check-out and initialization tasks are executed. The only outward sign of this activity is the play of numbers across the 3-digit LED display on the front panel of some POWER computers. This system startup process is what you might be familiar with on other UNIX systems as bootstrapping. Bootstrapping a POWER AIX system involves a hardware initialization phase followed by AIX kernel initialization. IBM refers to the hardware phase as *Read Only Storage Initial Program Load* (ROS IPL) or *Read Only Memory IPL* (ROM IPL). Sometimes you will hear it referred to as *ROS* or *ROM init*. I'm an old AIX hand, so I've already been conditioned to use *ROS* versus *ROM*. In the discussion that follows, you can interchange *ROM* for *ROS* if you find it confusing. You may find that the terms *IPL* and *boot* are often used interchangeably in many of the IBM documents. Since *IPL* conjures images of 370/390 MVS or VM architectures and *boot* is more common in UNIX circles, I'll tend to use boot in the remainder of the chapter. Old habits are hard to break!

Whatever it is called, it's important that the system administrator be familiar with the sequence of events that are taking place under the system unit cover at boot time. Understanding the system startup flow of control will assist you in diagnosing hardware and configuration problems when they occur. Notice that I said "when they occur!"

7.2 Booting the System

AIX on the RS/6000 may be started in one of three ways:

1. Normal boot

2. Stand-alone boot

3. Network boot

The normal boot is a boot from a local disk. The system is initialized with runtime kernel. Set the key mode switch in normal position (if present). The normal mode of operation is resumed.

The stand-alone boot is similar to the normal boot, but the system is brought up with a single-user maintenance, install, or diagnostic mode kernel. The system is booted from local disk, tape, or CD-ROM. Set the key mode switch to the service position (if present). This boot is used when installing software or performing maintenance or diagnostics (see Sec. 7.2.1).

With the network boot, the boot information and kernel are provided by a network-based file server. ROS broadcasts a boot request packet to locate a boot server. The reply packet from the server indicates how to load the boot image from the server. The boot kernel and file system are copied from the server via TFTP. Note that the network boot on older microchannel systems may require IPL ROM emulation (Sec. 6.8).

Once the boot kernel and file system are loaded, generally the same steps are followed in all three modes to initialize a runtime AIX kernel.

Assuming that the system is configured correctly, normal and network boot proceed with bringing AIX up to multiuser mode after power-on without additional intervention, the exception being boot for installation or maintenance purposes. The boot sequence of events is outlined in Sec. 7.4 and in detail later in the chapter.

7.2.1 Stand-alone boot

In the event of a system problem or when required for AIX installation or maintenance, you may need to start the system in Stand-Alone Mode. In stand-alone mode, the system is running the boot kernel and provides minimal access to the volume groups and file systems on disk. Booting the system in stand-alone mode will assist you in recovering corrupted system configuration files and file systems.

Here is the stand-alone boot procedure:

1. Set the system key in the service position (if present).

2. Insert a CD-ROM or tape containing a boot image and power on the system.

3. When prompted, select the console display.

4. Select "Start Maintenance Mode for System Recovery."

5. Select "Access a Root Volume Group."

6. Select the volume group number.

7. Select "Access This Volume Group and Start a Shell."

7.3 Creating Bootable Media

In order to boot AIX, a boot image or bootstrap kernel must be available on one or more boot devices specified by boot lists stored in nonvolatile system RAM. ROS boot code will attempt to access each device in the list until a valid boot device is found from which to load the boot image.

The boot device characteristics and the location and size of the boot image on the device are described by a boot record. The boot record may be added to the beginning of the boot image, or in the case of a disk device, the boot record is written to the first sector of the disk. The boot image and file system may or may not be compressed to save space and access speed.

7.3.1 Configuring the boot list

At system startup, the ROS boot code will attempt to access boot devices from a list of boot devices stored in nonvolatile RAM (nvram). The boot list can be tailored or recovered by invoking the bootlist command.
Examples:

```
# bootlist -m normal hdisk0 cd0 rmt0

# bootlist -m ent0 gateway=128.95.135.100\
       bserver=128.95.132.1 \
       client=128.95.135.10 cd0<<t>>
```

Separate lists are maintained for normal boot, service boot, and previous boot. Valid AIX V4 boot device types are listed in Table 7.1.

Device drivers for each of these device types are available in nvram. New device drivers may be loaded using the nvload command for custom boot configurations.

TABLE 7.1   Boot Device Types

Boot device	Medium
fdXX	Diskette
hdiskXX	Disk
cdXX	CD-ROM
rmtXX	Tape
entXX	Ethernet
tokXX	Token ring
fddiXX	FDDI

7.3.2 Installing a boot image

A boot image consists of a stripped kernel and skeleton root file system-tailored for the boot device and boot type (normal, service, or both). The kernel is stripped of symbols to reduce its resident size. The boot file system contains the device configuration tables, driver routines, and commands that will be required to gain access to the systems devices and file systems. To create a boot image for a particular boot device, use the bosboot command. The boot image type is specified by the -M normal,serv,both flag.

Examples:

```
# bosboot -a -d -M both /dev/hdisk0        Disk image
# bosboot -s -z -M both -d/dev/network     Compressed network
```

Just in case bosboot fails when creating a new boot image on the default boot device hdisk0, *don't* attempt to reboot the system. It's quite likely that the old boot image is corrupted, and it's no fun rebuilding a system from scratch. Attempt to determine the reason for the failure. Get it corrected and try again.

7.3.3 Creating stand-alone boot media

It should go without saying that a local boot device be configured as part of your standard boot list for maintenance purposes. Remember to keep multiple copies of the stand-alone boot media that reflect your AIX maintenance level. See Sec. 7.8, "Troubleshooting," for the stand-alone boot procedure.

To create bootable media:

1. `# cp /var/adm/ras/bosinst.data /bosinst.data`   Create bosinst.data
2. `# mkszfile`   Create rootvg map
3. `# chdev -1 rmt0 -a block_size=512`   Set correct block size
4. `# tctl -f/dev/rmt0 rewind`   Rewind tape
5. `# bosboot -ad /dev/rmt0.1`   Create boot image
6. `# mkinsttape /dev/rmt0`   Create bos inst/maint
7. `# chdev -1 rmt0 -a block_size=<block size>`   Reset tape block size

7.4 Boot Sequence of Events

In a nutshell, when the power switch is toggled to the on (1) position, the system startup begins by self-checking and initializing hardware. Once hardware has been reset, a boot device is located and a boot kernel and file system is loaded into memory. Peripheral devices and adapters are identified and enabled. Virtual memory support and the process scheduler are initialized. The root volume group is varied online and the root file systems checked and mounted. Runtime init is dispatched to complete system configuration, check and mount remaining file systems, and start the service daemons. Login processing is enabled, and the system is up and ready for use. Sounds simple!

In the following sections we will dissect each of the boot stages and explore them in more detail. I'll list the steps performed at each stage in the boot process and the 3-digit LED code displayed on some power systems that is associated with each major step being performed. If the computer you are using doesn't have an LED, then ignore the numbers listed in the text. You can use the LED indicators as road marks to assist you in following the boot process in real time. Being able to identify boot stages from the LED information will give you a better feel for when to start getting worried during system power-up!

The orchestration of steps conducted at boot time depend on hardware state, key mode switch setting, available boot devices, and the system reset count retained in memory from the previous run (see Fig. 7.1).

7.4.1   Key mode switch position

There are three selectable options for the front panel key mode switch on some POWER systems: "normal," "secure," and "service."

Normal position is used for standard AIX operation. The system will boot to multiuser mode and support user login. The RESET button is operational.

Secure position is used to inhibit rebooting a running system or starting a system that has been shutdown. The RESET button is not operational. This position secures changes in the run state of the system.

Service position is used when you want to run system diagnostics or bring the system up in stand-alone mode (see Sec. 7.8, "Troubleshooting," for more information on running system diagnostics).

As a precaution, keep one of the two keys supplied with the system unit and the other tucked away where you won't easily forget it. You can always get a replacement key and lock from IBM; however, turnaround time may be a problem for your users.

7.5   ROS Initialization

A ROS IPL is invoked when hardware events trigger a system reset. Normally this occurs when you turn the system on or press the RESET

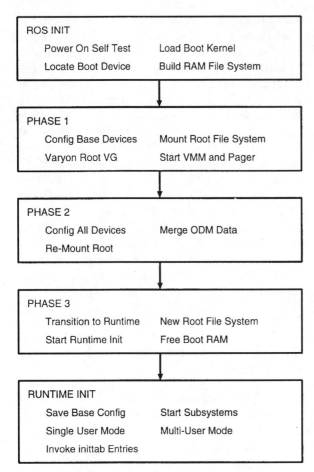

Figure 7.1   Boot block diagram.

button. Resets also occur in the event of a hardware failure or machine check (see Fig. 7.2).

One of two types of IPL are performed depending on the value of the system reset count: cold IPL and warm IPL.

Cold IPL   Reset count = 0 OCS BIST checkout, OK LED=100.

Warm IPL   Reset count = 1 BIST bypassed. ROS IPL.

7.5.1   Built-in self test—BIST

A cold IPL is started each time the computer is turned on. If the model is equipped with an On-Card Sequencer (OCS), the OCS performs a built-in self test (BIST) of the processor complex. The OCS fetches seed and signature patterns from ROM to test and validate each processor component. The seed pattern is sent to a common on-chip processor

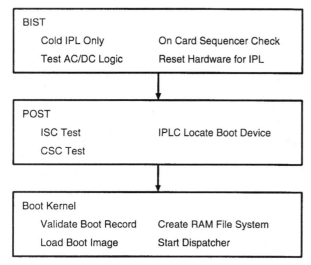

Figure 7.2   ROS initialization block diagram.

(COP) resident on each of the processor chips. Test results are compared with the signature data. BIST performs the following functions:

1. Initialize and test COPs and embedded chip memory

2. Test AC/DC logic

3. Initialize and reset hardware for ROS IPL

A warm IPL occurs when the RESET button is pressed on a running system or initiated via software control. For example, a warm IPL results when the reboot command is executed at runtime. The BIST phase is bypassed during a warm IPL. Processor memory, cache, and registers are reset, and the system branches to the warm IPL entry point in ROS.

7.5.2   Power-on self test—POST

At this point, the power-on self test (POST) code is executed. POST processing further verifies system components. There are three phases to POST processing: initial sequence controller (ISC) tests, core sequence controller (CSC) tests, and IPL controller (IPLC) boot device interrogation and kernel load.

7.5.3   Initial sequence controller test

ISC begins by performing a CRC check on system ROM. If an error is found, you may be able to refresh ROM by switching the key mode switch to the service position and rebooting. If the CRC still fails, it's time to place a call to IBM Service.

Next, ISC inspects the system check stop count stored in NVRAM. Under normal circumstances, the value is 0. A nonzero value indicates that some type of noncorrectable machine check has occurred. The system is halted, and the error code associated with the machine check is displayed on the front panel LED display.

Physical memory is interrogated and a bitmap built representing each 16K block of available memory in the system. This bitmap is stored in the IPL control block for later use (see /usr/include/sys/iplcb.h). The ISC verifies that 1 MB of contiguous memory is available for loading the boot image from a boot device.

1. Perform CRC on system ROM. Error LED = 211.
2. Inspect system check stop value in NVRAM.
   If nonzero, halt; LED = error code.
3. RAM POST—check physical memory.
4. Build and store memory bitmap in IPL control block.
5. Reserve 1 MB boot image area.

7.5.4 Core sequence controller test

ISC passes control to CSC, which completes POST testing. Routines stored in ROS are used by CSC to test and validate the operational presence of all devices required for successful booting of the system. CSC records the IDs of all devices and adapters discovered in the IPL control block.

1. Locate and validate boot devices.
2. Complete DMA, I/O, Interrupt, SCSI POSTs.
3. Recorded device information in IPL control block.

7.5.5 IPL controller load boot image

IPLC takes control and begins looking for a boot device and path from which to load an IPL record and boot image. The boot device list is read from NVRAM corresponding to the boot type, and each device in the list is polled in turn until a valid boot record is found. If the selection process fails, IPLC will enter a boot list rebuild/retry loop in an attempt to locate a valid boot device. The front panel LED alternates between 229 and 223 for each iteration of the retry loop. If the NVRAM boot list is invalid, then the system default boot list is used.

Once the boot device is located, the system validates the IPL record. The IPL record describes the media characteristics and the location, length, and entry points of the boot kernel code and file system (see /usr/include/sys/bootrecord.h). IPLC loads the boot record into memory and makes it part of the IPL control block. From the information contained in the boot record, IPLC begins loading the boot kernel into the one-megabyte memory area reserved by the ISC.

If the reserved memory space is exhausted during kernel loading, noncontiguous memory may be used if the fragmentation flag is set in the boot record. If fragmentation is disallowed, then IPLC aborts and tries the next device in the bootlist. Upon load completion, interrupts are disabled and control is passed to the boot kernel along with a pointer to the IPL control block. ROS initialization complete.

1. Retrieve boot device list from NVRAM.

2. Locate boot device from list.

3. Load and validate boot record.

4. Load boot image into reserved 1 MB RAM.

5. Pass control to boot kernel.

7.6   Boot Kernel Configuration

We're still a long way from user and process scheduling at this point. The object data manager (ODM) has yet to be configured, there is no logical volume manager (LVM) support, and the scheduler and pager services are not available.

The newly loaded boot kernel determines the type of RS/6000 it is running on and saves base custom vital product data (VPD) for subsequent ODM configuration. A list of free memory is built based on the bitmap created earlier by the ISC. The kernel uses a section of this memory space to create a RAM disk /dev/ram0, which will be used to support the RAM file system data read from the boot device. The RAM file system contains the programs and file system structures required to support the remainder of kernel initialization. A prototype template defines which files will make up the RAM file system based on the boot device type. These templates are used by the mkfs command when creating the boot file system.

disk.proto	Disk template
diskette.proto	Diskette template
tape.proto	Tape template
net.proto	Network template
cdrom.proto	CD-ROM template

Virtual memory manager (VMM) services are next on the list. Structures for page device, page frame, repage, and hash tables are created.

These tables will be used by the VMM to track and allocate virtual memory for each process in the running system. Translation Look-aside buffers (TLB) and kernel stack areas are allocated.

Address translation is enabled. The RS/6000 uses 32-bit effective addresses in conjunction with a segment address to designate virtual memory locations. The most significant 4 bits of the effective address is used to index into one of sixteen memory segment registers. The indexed 24-bit segment address is then concatenated with the remaining 28 bits of the effective address to create a 52-bit virtual address. Each segment represents 256 MB of virtual memory. The RS/6000 hardware supports 2^{24} segments per register.

The I/O subsystem is started after VMM initialization is completed. First-level interrupts are enabled for attached devices and adapters. On microchannel systems, input/output channel controller (IOCC) support and the planar I/O address space is initialized. The IOCC provides the I/O pipe between the microchannel bus and the planar CPU complex.

The process table is allocated and the remaining kernel structures and services defined in init_tbl are set up. The system dispatcher is invoked as pid(0), and process table entries for init and wait are defined. Default exception handlers are set. The dispatcher is now ready to begin process scheduling. From here on, the dispatcher is referred to as the scheduler.

The scheduler maintains fair-share allocation of CPU resources by periodically scanning the process table and recomputing process CPU priorities and time slices. The scheduler also maintains repage history in order to manage thrashing conditions. Thrashing and repaging occur when memory has been overallocated, forcing processes to refetch pages required for execution each time they are dispatched. Thus, the term *thrashing* is used to describe this rapid page-in/page-out process. When the system repage rate exceeds 30 pages/second, the scheduler temporarily suspends processes to reduce thrashing.

1. Save base VPD.

2. Create /dev/ram0 and RAM file system.

3. Initialize VMM.

4. Initialize I/O subsystem.

5. Setup kernel tables and structures.

6. Start the dispatcher/scheduler.

7.6.1   Phase 1

The boot init image is loaded by the scheduler as pid(1) from /usr/lib/boot/ssh in the RAM file system. This heralds the beginning of Phase 1 (see Fig. 7.3). Phase 1 is also referred to as base device configuration

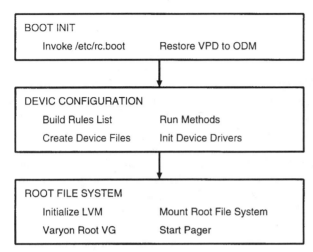

Figure 7.3 Phase 1 block diagram.

phase. boot init starts by forking a shell and invoking the /etc/rc.boot script with an argument value of 1. Base device customization information is restored by invoking restbase to build the object data manager (ODM) /etc/objrepos database. cfgmgr is executed, and the Config_Rules object class is queried for all configuration rules with a phase value of 1. The bootmask for each rule is checked to see if the rule is to be included for this boot type. Custom configuration rule sequences can be defined by manipulating the bootmask for each rule or method. See /usr/include/sys/cfgdb.h for more information.

```
# cfgmgr -m <mask>     Run rules with specified mask
```

Bootmask*	Bits
DISK_BOOT	0×0001
TAPE_BOOT	0×0002
DISKETTE_BOOT	0×0004
CDROM_BOOT	0×0008
NETWORK_BOOT	0×0010
PHASE0_BOOT.	0×0020

A list of Phase 1 rules is established and sorted by sequence number. cfgmgr invokes each method using odm_run_method() to establish

---

* Bootmask 0 always run.

device state information in the ODM. Predefined methods are located in /usr/lib/methods.

Device states	Status
Defined	Device listed in the custom DB; not configured or available
Undefined	Not represented in the custom DB
Available	Configured and available for use
Stopped	Configured but not available for use

The defsys method establishes the top-level system object sys0. cfgmgr forks a child process for each dependent method until all devices are configured. ODM Custom Device (CuDv) and Custom Attribute (CuAt) status entries are updated and the associated methods run. These methods define device special files and install device drivers. Each device is initialized by sysconfig() and the device switch table updated by a call to devswadd(). Microcode is downloaded to the device if required and VPD information updated.

It's worth noting that you may experience problems with third-party SCSI disks when the cfgscsi method is run. cfgscsi attempts to start SCIOSTART and query SCIOINQU for each device identified at each SCSI ID/logical unit number (LUN) location. Devices identify themselves via a 5-byte header and optional vendor data. Disk device methods attempt to spin up each disk and query the physical volume ID (PVID) associated with the disk. This can cause problems for external disk devices that may have already spun up and results in a ghost device defined with no PVID at the same SCSI-ID and LUN. The old PVID definition is left in the defined state. Each PVID in a logical volume group must be set to the available state before the volume group can be varied online. You can usually fix this problem by removing the ghost PVID entry and rebooting the system after powering the disks off and on.

Phase 1 completes by initializing the logical volume manager (LVM). The LVM is defined as a pseudodevice in the ODM. The LVM device driver, lvdd, interfaces to the SCSI device driver, hscsidd, to provide logical disk volumes.

Method list	
Start method invocation	LED 538
cfgsys (system, memory, and I/O planar)	LED 813
cfgbus (micro channel bus)	LED 520
cfgscsi (SCSI adapters/devices)	LED 869
deflvm (logical volume manager)	LED 591
Complete methods	LED 539
Phase 1 complete	LED 512

Phase 1 completes by varying the root volume group (rootvg) online. The root file systems are checked and mounted. At this point, root (/) is mounted over /mnt. The pager is started via swapon.

Here is the procedure for Phase 1:

1. Invoke boot init as pid(1).
2. Invoke /etc/rc.boot 1.
3. Invoke restbase to restore VPD to ODM.
4. Build Phase 1 config rules list.
5. Run Phase 1 methods, planar, MCA, SCSI, etc.
6. Create device special files, device drivers, etc.
7. Initialize LVM.
8. Vary rootvg.
9. Check and mount root file systems.
10. Start pager.

7.6.2   Phase 2

Control is returned to boot init, which restarts the /etc/rc.boot script with an argument value of 2 to begin Phase 2 (see Fig. 7.4). The volume group map, device special files, and ODM object classes created during Phase 1 are merged into the real root file system. Hardware VPD information is deleted from the user-customized ODM entries. Devices not configured in Phase 1 are configured. After all device configuration information has been updated in the root file system, the root file system is remounted as / over the boot file system, and newroot is invoked.

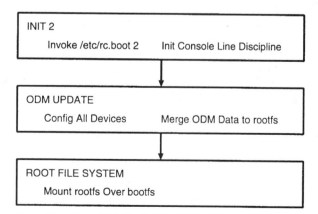

Figure 7.4   Phase 2 block diagram.

Here is the procedure for Phase 2:

1. Invoke /etc/rc.boot 2, LED=551, with init.

2. Initialize console line discipline.

3. Merge RAM ODM and device files into rootfs.

4. Configure any devices not configured by Phase 1.

5. Remount rootfs over bootfs, LED=517.

6. Complete Phase 2, LED=553.

7.6.3   Phase 3

Phase 3 (see Fig. 7.5) marks the transition from boot init to runtime init or Phase 2 service mode. Service mode is entered when the key switch is set in the service position. All running processes except the scheduler and boot init are killed. After all of its children exit, boot init exits and becomes a zombie process. The scheduler discovers that pid(1) has exited and invokes newroot. newroot releases the RAM file system, remounts the virtual root file system, and invokes proc1restart(), which starts /etc/init as pid(1). boot init has now been replaced by runtime init.

Here is the procedure for Phase 3:

1. Kill all running processes.

2. Exit boot init.

3. Invoke newroot with scheduler.

4. Free old RAM file system.

5. Point at real rootfs with VFS.

6. Invoke runtime init with proc1restart.

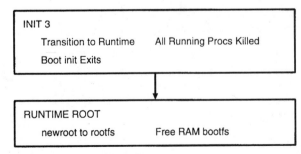

Figure 7.5   Phase 3 block diagram.

7.6.4 Runtime

Runtime init (see Fig. 7.6) begins by setting the init state to single user mode. It examines entries in /etc/inittab and invokes /sbin/rc.boot 3. The /tmp file system is checked and mounted. cfgmgr is invoked based on the key mode switch setting. If the key position is set to "normal," cfgmgr runs Phase 3 rules. If the key position is set to "service," cfgmgr runs Phase 2 rules. Phase 1 methods are rerun. The console pseudo-device is configured and assigned. savebase is executed to save custom ODM entries to NVRAM for subsequent system boots. If the key mode switch is in the service position, then system diagnostic pretest is run. If the key is in the normal position, the remaining single user mode /etc/inittab entries are run. srcmstr is started, which in turn invokes subsystems defined in /etc/inittab. The init state is set to 2 and the system transitions to multiuser mode. Login processing is now available to your user base. The system's up! Start hacking!

Runtime follows this procedure:

1. Set init state for a single user.

2. Invoke /etc/inittab entries.

3. Start /sbin/rc.boot 3.

4. Start fsck and mount/tmp.

5. Invoke cfgmgr:

   Phase 2 if key=normal

   Phase 3 if key=service

6. Phase 1 rules rerun.

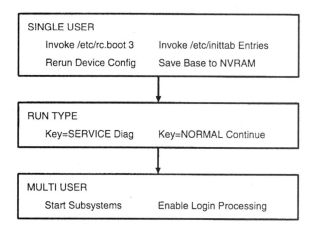

Figure 7.6   Runtime block diagram.

7. Config and assign console pseudodevice:

/dev/hft0   LED=c32

/dev/tty0   LED=c33

8. Invoke savebase to save custom settings to NVRAM.

9. If key=service, invoke diagnostics; if key=normal, complete /etc/inittab entries.

10. Set init state to multiuser.

11. Start srcmstr and subsystems.

12. Enable login processing.

7.7   Stopping the System

Like all things in life, runtime must occasionally come to an end. In this event, you can use the shutdown or reboot commands to bring services and the system off-line gracefully.

The shutdown command supports a number of flags to control how the system is to be brought down. By default, it will warn users, wait one minute, terminate active processes, sync the file systems, and halt the CPU. You may indicate that the system is to be immediately restarted after shutdown by using the -r flag or by invoking the reboot command.

`# shutdown -m +5`	Shut system down to single user in 5 minutes
`# shutdown -r`	Shut down and reboot
`# shutdown now`	Shut down immediately
`# shutdown -k`	Abort shutdown procedures

7.8   Troubleshooting

The RS/6000 is very good about checking its hardware during the built-in self-test (BIST) at power-up time. Keeping track of the LED information during system power-up will assist you in debugging hardware problems. If you suspect hardware problems or the system won't boot, use the RS/6000 diagnostic programs to assist in determining the failure. The diagnostic programs may be run in stand-alone mode or in concurrent mode with AIX online using the diag command. For concurrent mode operation, as superuser enter the diag command and follow the menu instructions. Stand-alone mode is similar to booting from tape or CD-ROM as described above.

1. Set system key in service position (if present).

2. Insert a CD-ROM disc or a tape containing a boot image and power on the system.

3. When prompted, select the console display.

4. Select "Start Maintenance Mode for System Recovery."

5. Select "Access Advanced Maintenance Mode Functions."

7.9   InfoExplorer Keywords

bootlist	reboot
bosboot	shutdown
mkboot	nvram
restbase	mkboot
savebase	diag

7.10   QwikInfo

- System boot

`bootlist`	Set boot device list
`bosboot`	Create new boot image
`/etc/rc.boot`	Boot phases
`/etc/inittab`	Subsystem startup

- System shutdown

`shutdown now`	Shut down immediately
`shutdown -m`	Shut down to single user
`shutdown -k`	Abort shutdown
`reboot`	Shut down and restart
`telinit`	Set system run level

- Stand-alone boot (see procedure in Sec. 7.8)

System Configuration and Customizing

## Chapter 8

Runtime Configuration

8.1 AIX Runtime

Here's a short and sweet chapter on defining your runtime settings. Most of this can be done from one SMIT environment screen. The reason that I'm making it a separate chapter is that, more often than not, administrators forget to take care of this chore after completing an install or upgrade. It's just too tempting to select "Tasks Completed—Exit to AIX" at the end of a long day of installs. A week later, we're standing around scratching our heads trying to figure out why we can't run just one more process or that there seems to be only two active licenses on the system.

The other reason for making this a separate chapter is that most of the coarse level system tuning can be done from these screens. Things like setting maximum I/O buffers and pacing. In a mixed work-load environment, a small change in some of these numbers can make a big difference in system throughput.

8.2 System Environments

To get to the SMIT catchall runtime settings panel (see Fig. 8.1), use the FastPath system. Kind of intuitive, isn't it?

```
# smit system
```

8.2.1 Time settings

Two easy settings that should have been handled at the end of the installation process are time and language settings (see Fig. 8.2). Aha! Now you know why the date/time stamps in the mail headers have been off by a few time zones. You can set the correct date and time zone by invoking SMIT chtz. Not as obvious as the last FastPath.

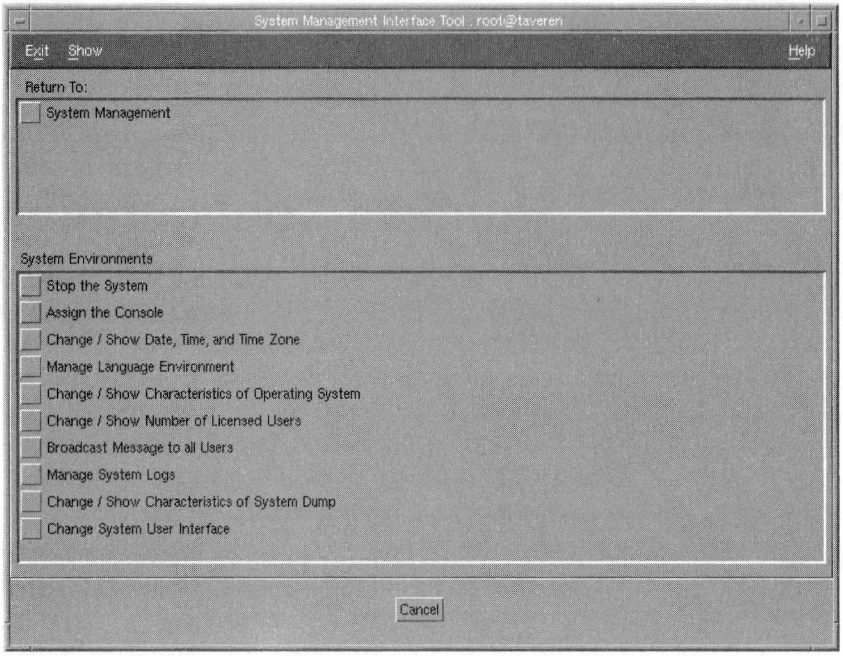

Figure 8.1   SMIT system environments panel.

```
# smit chtz
```

8.2.2   Language environment

Most likely you got the correct language set during installation, but did you know that you can add other languages to the set? AIX will allow you to configure a hierarchy of language environments (see Fig. 8.3). This may be helpful in multilingual communities. You can also use SMIT to translate messages and flat files into a new base language.

```
# smit mlang
```

8.2.3   Characteristics of the operating system

This is an ominous-sounding section and rightly so. From just one panel in SMIT (see Fig. 8.4), you can alter AIX kernel characteristics that hit most of the critical subsystems like the virtual memory manager, the scheduler, and the dispatcher. It's a great screen for wreaking havoc on a system. Open the AIX Pandora's box by using the SMIT FastPath chgsys.

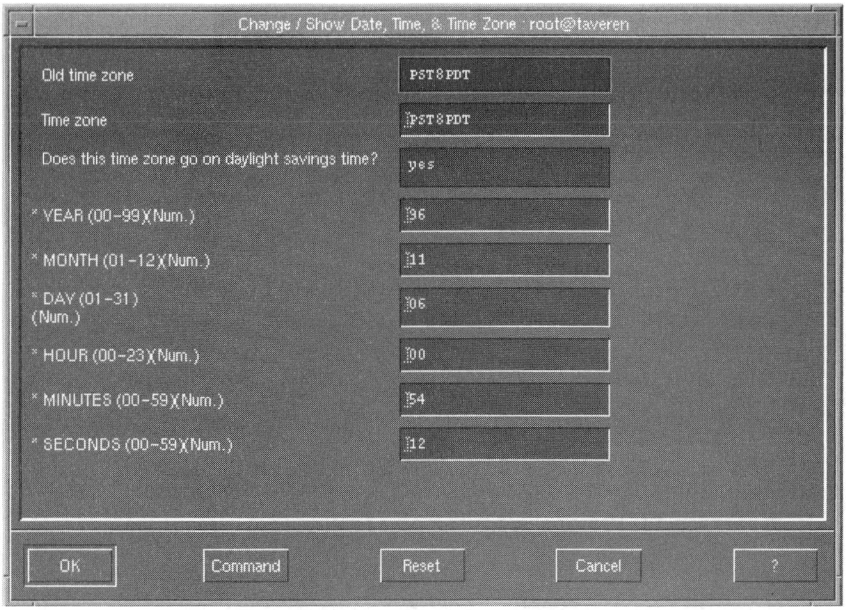

Figure 8.2 SMIT date time panel.

```
# smit chgsys
```

The first entry in the panel is for the maximum number of processes allowed per user. Maybe this is why you can't start one more process. There are tradeoffs in making this parameter too large or too small. Making it too large can cause you grief during situations when you have a runaway process that is forking new copies of itself. It seems

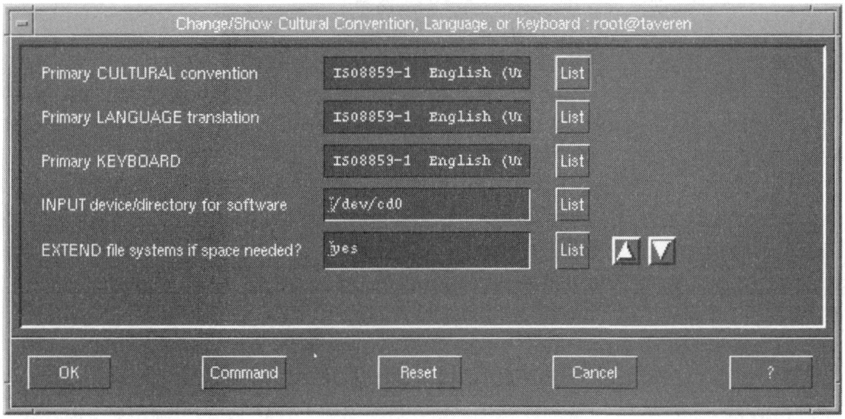

Figure 8.3 SMIT language environment panel.

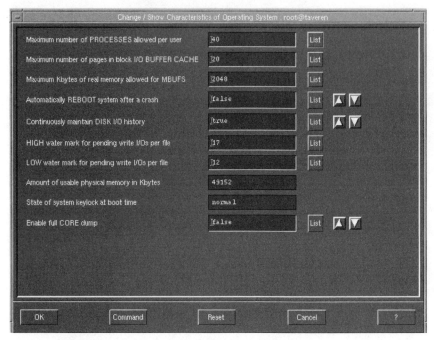

Figure 8.4 SMIT "characteristics of the operating system" panel.

like every year we get a new batch of programmers who like to try out a tight fork() and exec() loop. Setting the maximum number of processes too low means frustration when you try to start that one process too many.

Next in the list is the maximum number of pages in block I/O buffer cache. This setting is used as a buffer for I/O to block special files. Basically, it mimics a BSD or SYSV buffer cache. It's not heavily used by the system and takes away from real memory.

The next entry controls the amount of real memory that can be pinned for network MBUFS. Again this is another parameter that takes away from real memory. Use the netstat -m command to see if you are running out of MBUFS before making it larger.

You might want to set the switch for automatically rebooting the system after a crash to "true" for systems that are left unattended in order to maintain system availability.

If you regularly use the iostat command to check statistics on disk I/O rates, you will want to leave this active. It's not that much overhead, but you could elect to turn it off until you want to do I/O monitoring.

The next two entries control the high and low water marks that control pending I/Os. These parameters can have a dramatic effect on system throughput and are primarily geared toward the type of work being done by the machine. When a process writing to a file hits its high-water mark for pending I/Os, that process is suspended until the I/O queue drops to or below the low-water mark. This can keep big database load processes from holding out a user trying to open an E-mail inbox. Conversely, you could set these to favor a big writer to speed up building a large file.

Skipping to the last entry, "Enable full CORE dump" may be important when debugging applications where you need to see memory locations outside of kernel structures and space. Note that if you enable this, you're going to need a dump device that can hold a dump of the whole memory space.

8.2.4 Number of licensed users

Back to the "System Environments" panel. Select "Change/Show Number of Licensed Users" or run SMIT chlicense to alter the number of licensed users (see Fig. 8.5). The default is a two-user license and no floating licenses. This might be another reason why you can't start one more instance of an application. Hmmm.

```
# smit chlicense
```

8.2.5 System logs

The system error log (ErrLog) is a very nice facility when it comes to tracking system hardware and applications problems. Unfortunately, it is one of the most ignored features in AIX. Without active housecleaning, the error log /var/adm/ras/errlog is usually missing the critical history information that leads up to a system problem. The log should be monitored regularly to scan for intermittent system problems. The companion Alog screens are used to control logs produced by the alog command. This command is used in conjunction with other command output piped to the alog standard input.

```
# smit logs
```

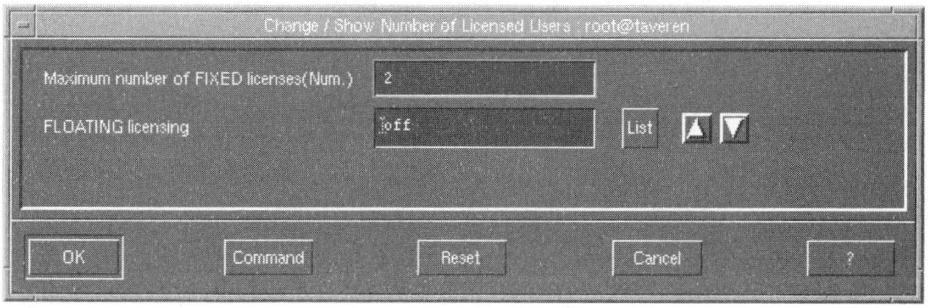

Figure 8.5 SMIT licensed users panel.

8.2.6 Dump device

Like the log screens, the "Characteristics of System Dump" menu (see Fig. 8.6) is critical to managing problem information. The system dump devices need regular maintenance to clear out old system dumps to make sure that space is available to support dumps being used for a current system problem. Access the SMIT dump menu with the dump FastPath.

```
# smit dump
```

8.3 PTY

Unlike its predecessor AIX V3, AT&T-style pseudo-TTYs (PTYs) are not allocated automatically under AIX V4. The number of PTYs must be specified for both AT&T- and BSD-style devices (see Fig. 8.7). This is the likely cause of not being able to start additional X11 applications. Change the number of PTYs using the SMIT chgpty FastPath.

```
# smit chgpty
```

Figure 8.6 SMIT system dump panel.

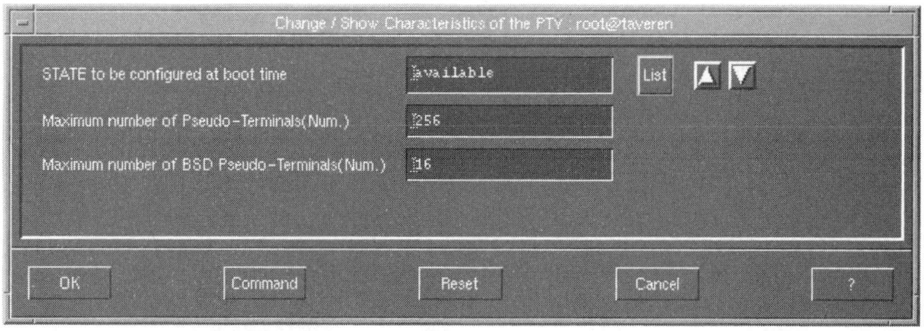

Figure 8.7 SMIT PTY panel.

8.4 Console

This last section is directed to setting the system console device (see Fig. 8.8). Sure, it worked fine during installation when you had a terminal plugged into the serial port. Then you unplugged the tube without resetting console support. You don't need to have a terminal plugged into an RS/6000 for operation, but you may want to direct console output to another device or file. You can do this from the SMIT chcons and swcons FastPaths.

```
# smit chcons
```

8.5 InfoExplorer Keywords

time	console
dump	license
errlog	locale
pty	NLS

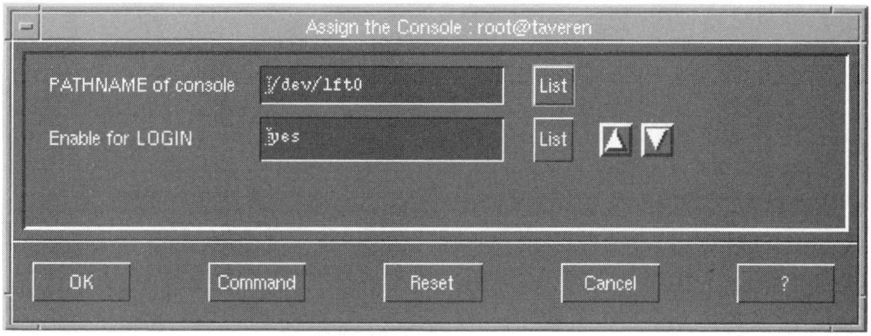

Figure 8.8 SMIT console panel.

8.6   QwikInfo

`smit system`	System runtime settings
`smit chgsys`	System characteristics
`smit chlicense`	Change licensed users
`smit chtz`	Change time zone
`smit mlang`	Change language environment
`smit logs`	Change system log settings
`smit dump`	Manage dump devices
`smit chgpty`	Change number of PTYs
`smit chgcons`	Set systems console

Devices Configuration and the Object Data Manager

9.1 AIX Dynamic Device Configuration

Unlike many traditional UNIX systems, AIX supports dynamic device configuration and management. In many cases, you can connect external devices to a running system, configure the device attributes, and begin using the new device. No kernel rebuild! No system reboot! How this works is that AIX allows dynamic kernel extensions and device driver installation to a running kernel and dynamic device configuration through the object data manager (ODM). If you spend much time with AIX, it's essential that you develop a good understanding of ODM structure and operation. Since device management and the ODM are so tightly coupled, it makes sense to begin the discussion on devices by outlining the functional characteristics of the ODM.

9.2 ODM Overview

In the beginning, there were UNIX system configuration tables. They were sent forth to the BSD and SYSV masses, bringing all into a common fold of administration. But lo, workstations multiplied and prospered. Configuration tables became large and unwieldy. Out of this mire of table-parsing, a new doctrine was prophesied that would reduce the waiting and gnashing of teeth during login processing and password updates. It was called dbm and it was good. dbm routines reduced large configuration tables into a database of key-content pairs. Items in a database are retrieved in one or two file I/Os, while dbm databases are represented as an index file, *.dir, and a data file, *.pag. A common example of a dbm database is the password passwd.dir and passwd.pag file.

IBM decided to take the dbm doctrine one step further by introducing a hierarchical object-oriented database for configuration data called the object data manager (ODM). The ODM centralizes a number of the standard configuration tables into a single management structure with update validation. AIX commands and kernel routines access ODM objects using SQL-like semantics.

9.3   ODM Components

The ODM is comprised of a database of object classes based on a simple UNIX file access method. The database is managed using a library of routines and commands. Information is stored as objects within an object class. Each object is associated with a set of attributes associated with the object class definition.

9.3.1   ODM database

Object classes are implemented as standard UNIX files in a directory that represents the ODM database. AIX V4 uses two default ODM directories: /etc/objrepos and /usr/lib/objrepos. The ODMDIR environment variable defines the directory path used as the default ODM database directory. The default ODMDIR path is set to /etc/objrepos by the /etc/environment file. ODMDIR may be manipulated to designate custom application databases.

/etc/objrepos   Default object class directory

CdiagAtt	DSMOptions.vc	PdiagTask	SwservAt.vc	product.vc
CdiagAtt.vc	DSMenu	PdiagTask.vc	TMInput	sm_cmd_hdr
CdiagDev	FRUB	PdAt	config_lock	sm_cmd_hdr.vc
Config_Rules	FRUs	PdAt.vc	errnotify	sm_cmd_opt
CuAt	InetServ	PdCn	history	sm_cmd_opt.vc
CuAt.vc	MenuGoal	PdDv	history.vc	sm_menu_opt
CuDep	PdiagAtt	PdDv.vc	inventory	sm_menu_opt.vc
CuDv	PdiagAtt.vc	SRCnotify	inventory.vc	sm_name_hdr
CuDvDr	PdiagDev	SRCodmlock	lpp	sm_name_hdr.vc
CuVPD	PdiagDev.vc	SRCsubsvr	lpp.vc	
DAVars	PdiagRes	SRCsubsys	lvm_lock	
DSMOptions	PdiagRes.vc	SwservAt	product	

/usr/lib/objrepos   Additional AIX V4 directory

CC	KEYBOARD.vc	PDiagTask.vc	fix_lock	sm_cmd_hdr.vc
CC.vc	MESSAGES	PdAt	history	sm_cmd_opt
DSMOptions	MESSAGES.vc	PdAt.vc	history.vc	sm_cmd_opt.vc
DSMOptions.vc	PdiagAtt	PdCn	inventory	sm_menu_opt

DSMenu	PdiagAtt.vc	PdDv	inventory.vc	sm_menu_opt.vc
FONT	PdiagDev	PdDv.vc	lpp	sm_name_hdr
FONT.vc	PdiagDev.vc	XINPUT	lpp.vc	sm_name_hdr.vc
GAI	PdiagRes	XINPUT.vc	product	
GAI.vc	PdiagRes.vc	fix	product.vc	
KEYBOARD	PDiagTask	f	ix.vc	sm_cmd_hdr

9.3.2 Objects and object classes

ODM objects are the data items that make up object classes. Object attributes are mapped to a C language structure that represents the object class definition. The object class definition describes the descriptor-value pairs that make up an object. Object classes may be relationally joined to other object classes using a special link descriptor.

Initially the object class definition is constructed as an ASCII text file identified by the .cre extension. This description file is read by the odmcreate command to create the object class. The result is an empty object class and a .h header file that may be used by application programs to populate and manipulate members in the object class. As an example, consider the generic attributes of an inventory object class for a music store.

```
class Inventory {
char item[20];
char description[80];
char color[20];
short unit_number;
char manufacturer[20];
long quantity;
long unit_price;
method order_more;
}
```

```
# odmcreate inventory.cre     Create an object class called inventory
```

For the inventory object member:

```
Inventory:
item          = "Drum Sticks"
description   = "Rudimental drum sticks, plastic tip."
color         = "black"
unit_number   = 293
manufacturer  = "Prehistoric Logs"
quantity      = 20
unit_price    = 2050
order_more    = /usr/local/bin/check_inventory
```

The object class definition may specify a method descriptor (see Table 9.1). The method defines a program that is to be invoked by the odm_run_method routine. The method updates the state of the object. In the example, the method would check the inventory and change state when the inventory was exhausted. Each object in the object class may specify a unique method program. Methods are represented as null-terminated 255-character strings. The ampersand (&) may be appended to the method for asynchronous execution.

9.3.3 Command and library interface

Users and applications manipulate ODM data via commands and library routines. The odme ODM editor is no longer available in AIX V4. The list of commands and library routines in Table 9.2 will give you a feeling for types of operations permitted on ODM data.

9.4 ODM Editor

As I mentioned in the previous section, the odme editor is no longer available in AIX V4. This is a sad situation. The ODM is one of the most difficult subsystems to manage in AIX. IBM may hope that it is fool-proof, but the reality is that it is not! When objects and their associated attributes and methods become corrupt, it is next to impossible to correct them using ODM commands. I would hope that IBM development would see fit to provide a similar visual interface to the ODM in the future. While we wait, I will go ahead and briefly discuss the AIX V3 odme to give you a feel for what the tool can do. It was often the last-resort tool to correct problem ODM configuration objects.

Whether you use the standard ODM commands or a tool like odme, you have to understand the object attributes and relationships. I repeat, do not try this unless you are very familiar with the object class relationships! Use odme or the ODM command set from an account without write permissions for the object classes you would like to browse to ensure that ODM integrity is maintained. Begin by selecting the object class name of interest. You may then display and manipulate information in the selected class.

TABLE 9.1 ODM Descriptors

short	2-byte short integer
long	4-byte long integer
char	Fixed-length null-terminated string
vchar	Variable-length null-terminated string
binary	Arbitrary bit string
link	Link to another object class
method	Fork and exec child command or program

TABLE 9.2　ODM Commands and Library Routines

Library routine	Command	Use
odm_set_path		Set ODM database location (ODMDIR represents a shell environment variable)
	restbase	Retrieve customized objects from boot image and store in ODM
	savebase	Store ODM-customized objects in boot image
	odmdrop	Remove an object class
	odmshow	Display object class definition
odm_create_class	odmcreate	Create empty object class with associated C headers for applications
odm_add_obj	odmadd	Add an object to an object class
odm_change_obj	odmchange	Modify object attributes
odm_rm_obj	odmdelete	Delete object from an object class
odm_get_obj	odmget	Retrieve an object in odmadd format
odm_get_by_id		Retrieve an object by its ID
odm_rm_by_id		Remove an object by its ID
odm_get_first		Retrieve first object that matches criteria
odm_get_next		Retrieve next object that matches criteria
odm_get_list		Retrieve a list of objects that match criteria
odm_free_list		Free memory allocated for odm_get_list
odm_run_method		Execute method associated with an object
odm_close_class		Close object class
odm_err_msg		Retrieve error message string
odm_lock		Lock object for update
odm_unlock		Unlock object
odm_initialize		Initialize ODM session
odm_terminate		Terminate an ODM session

As an exercise, set the ODMDIR environment variable to point to a subdirectory in your $HOME directory. Use an editor (see Fig. 9.1) to create a sample object class and invoke odmcreate to build the new object class. Use odme (see Fig. 9.2) and the commands listed in the previous section to manipulate data in the test object class.

```
# odme
```

Set the default object class type and then select "Retrieve/Edit Objects."

9.5　Configuration Tables and the ODM

To support traditional UNIX administration techniques, some ODM information is mirrored in traditional UNIX configuration tables. Care must be taken to make certain that ODM information is kept synchronized with configuration table contents. ODM and table synchronization is performed automatically if updates are introduced using SMIT. In some cases, you can edit the standard configuration file and invoke synchronization commands to incorporate the updates into the ODM.

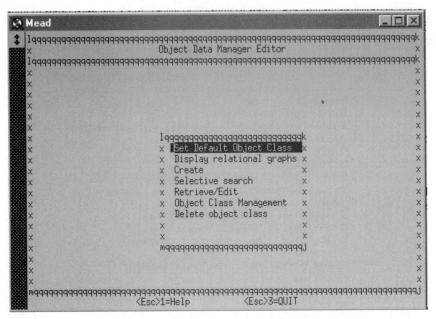

Figure 9.1   Object data manager editor.

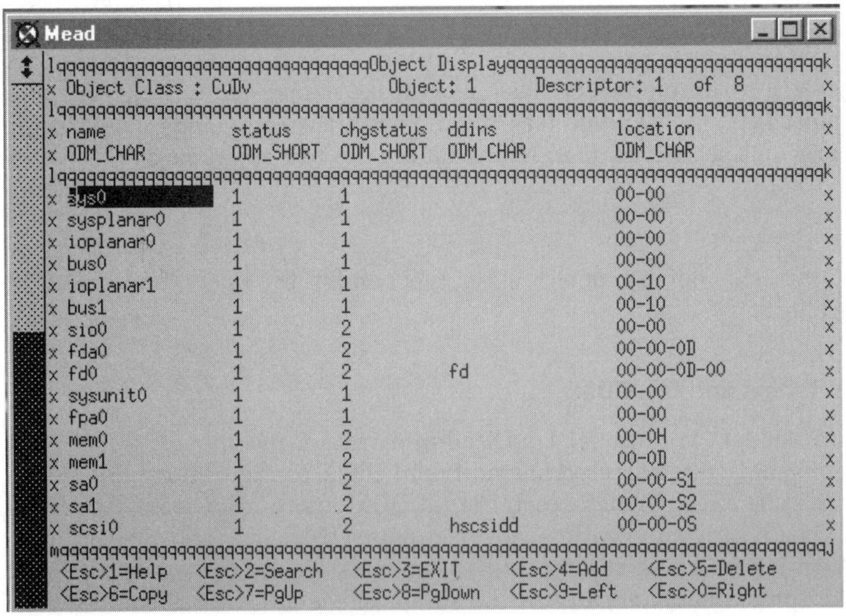

Figure 9.2   Sample odme panel.

9.6   Device Configuration

Device interface definitions and configuration attributes are stored as objects in the ODM database. Each time the system is booted, the cfgmgr command walks the I/O bus and identifies all devices present on the system. Device location and type information is stored in the ODM, and the associated configuration rules and initialization methods are run to make the devices available for use (Chap. 7).

cfgmgr can also be invoked on a running system from the SMIT devices menus or by executing cfgmgr, mkdev, chdev, or rmdev from the command line. The same dynamic device configuration activities preformed at boot time are invoked while the system is up and available for use. This feature allows you to make new devices available without requiring a system reboot (see Fig. 9.3).

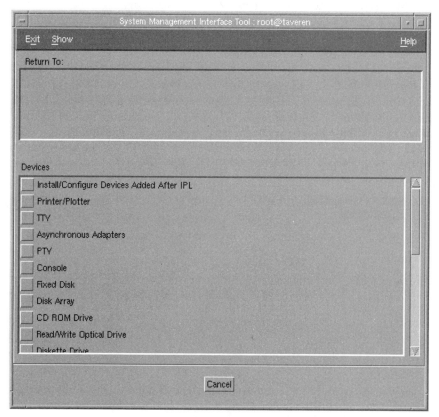

Figure 9.3   SMIT devices panel.

```
# smit devices

# mkdev -1 tty0              Add a TTY device

# lsdev -C -s scsi -H        List existing scsi devices

# chdev -1 rmt0 -a block_size=0   Change tape block size

# lsattr -D -1 rmt0          List tape attributes

# rmdev -1 rmt0 -d           Remove a tape device

# cfgmgr                     Update ODM and kernel
```

9.7   Predefined and Customized Devices

Device configuration information is separated into predefined and customized object classes. Predefined object class information represents default configuration information for all devices supported by AIX. Customized object classes represent the devices actually present on the system.

/etc/objrepos/Pdxxx   ODM predefined devices/attributes
   PdAt   PdCn   PdDv

/etc/objrepos/Cuxxx   ODM customized devices/attributes
   CuAt   CuDep   CuDv   CuDvDr   CuVPD

Device object classes are linked hierarchically into subclasses. For example, 7207 and 3490E tape devices represent subclasses under the tape object class. The tape object class in turn is a subclass of the scsi object class. This hierarchy enforces configuration relationships.

Parent object class information must be configured before child subclass configuration.

Parent object class information may not be modified if child subclasses exist.

Parent object classes may not be removed if child subclasses exist.

A special object class, predefined connections (PdCn), defines the hierarchy of device classes and subclasses. Device attributes are maintained as separate attribute object classes. See Table 9.3 for a sampling of AIX object classes.

You can display object class definitions using the odmshow command.

```
# odmshow <ObjectClassName>
```

Tables 9.4 through 9.7, representing the predefined and customized device and attribute descriptors, will give you some idea as to how device information is represented and linked.

TABLE 9.3   Sampling of AIX Object Classes

PdDv	Predefined devices supported by AIX
PdAt	Predefined device attributes
PdCn	Predefined device subclass connections
CuDv	Customized devices attached to the system
CuDvDr	Customized device drivers
CuAt	Customized device attributes
CuDep	Custom device dependencies
CuVPD	Customized vital product data
Config_Rules	Configuration rule sets

TABLE 9.4   PdDv Descriptors

type	Device type
class	Device class
subclass	Device subclass
prefix	Prefix name
devid	Device id
base	Base device flag
has_vpd	VPD flag
detectable	Device detectable flag
chgstatus	Change status flag
bus_ext	Bus extender
fru	FRU flag
led	LED value
setno	Set number
msgno	Message number
catalog	Catalog number
DvDr	Device driver name
Define	Define method
Configure	Configure method
Change	Change method
Unconfigure	Unconfigure method
Undefine	Undefine method
Start	Start method
Stop	Stop method
inventory_only	Inventory only flag
uniquetype	Unique type

TABLE 9.5   PdAt Descriptors

uniquetype	Unique type
attribute	Attribute name
deflt	Default value
values	Attribute values
width	Width
type	Type flags
generic	Generic flags
rep	Representative flags
nls_index	NLS index

TABLE 9.6   CuDv Descriptors

name	Device name
status	Device status flag
chgstatus	Change status flag
ddins	Device driver instance
location	Location code
parent	Parent device
connwhere	Where connected
PdDvLn	Link to predefined device

TABLE 9.7   CuAt Descriptors

name	Device name
attribute	Attribute name
value	Attribute value
type	Attribute type
generic	Generic flags
rep	Representative flags
nls_index	NLS index

9.8   Device States

The cfgmgr routine is responsible for updating custom device information using the configuration rule sets. cfgmgr invokes the method specified for each attached device and updates the devices state. After the device method is complete, the device is set to one of three states: defined, stopped, or available.

Device States

Defined	Device defined but not available for use
Stopped	Device configured but not available
Available	Device configured and available

9.9   Boot Devices

A small ODM database representing device configuration information is maintained as part of the AIX boot images. This information can be updated from the master ODM database using the savebase command. Likewise, ODM information from the boot image can be restored to the master ODM database by invoking the restbase command (Chap. 7).

# savebase	Save master ODM custom device data to the boot image
# restbase	Restore custom ODM data from the boot image to the master ODM database

9.10   Small Computer System Interface

The most common device interface for the RISC System/6000 is the small computer system interface (SCSI). The SCSI standard defines a generic interface and command protocol that will support most device types. Devices are attached in a daisy-chain fashion to the host adapter. The total chain length cannot exceed the distance maximum for the adapter type.

9.10.1   SCSI-1 and SCSI-2

The RISC System/6000 supports both SCSI-1 and SCSI-2 adapters and devices. Both SCSI-1 and SCSI-2 devices may be mixed on either adapter type; however, throughput to the device will be limited to SCSI-1 speeds. The cfgmgr queries the device type during SCSI device configuration and records the SCSI type. This eliminates the need for device drivers to continually query the SCSI type to determine if extended SCSI-2 commands are supported. SCSI-1 support provides transfer rates up to 4 megabytes per second. The SCSI-2 "Fast SCSI" mode extends synchronous transfer rates to 10 megabytes per second. SCSI-2 signal control is also two to three times faster than SCSI-1.

9.10.2   Cables and adapters

The SCSI-2 cable uses the same pin assignments as the SCSI-1 adapter. The only difference is that, on the adapter end, the SCSI-2 adapter only has 50 pins like the integrated SCSI cable. If you are sharing a SCSI string between two machines, use IBM pass-through-terminator (PTT) cables between the first device and the adapter on each end of the shared string. Device to device connections can use standard SCSI cables.

9.10.3   Single-ended and differential SCSI

Single-ended SCSI connections have a combined distance limitation of 6 meters. The logic level of each wire is based on the voltage difference with a common ground. Differential SCSI connections can run up to 25 meters. Logic levels on differential connections are based on the potential difference between two signal wires.

Single-ended connections can be a real problem with some RS/6000-9XX systems. The SCSI cable management arm in early 9XX racks eat up approximately 4.75 meters of the total 6-meter cable length. A single-ended SCSI to differential SCSI adapter can be used to get around the problem.

9.10.4 SCSI addressing

Each SCSI string supports eight addresses (0–7) that must be divided up between the devices and the adapter. Some device controllers support multiple devices from a single SCSI ID using logical unit numbers (LUN). In most cases, you are only going to have seven addresses that may be assigned to seven devices on the chain. The SCSI adapter requires one of the addresses, normally SCSI ID 7. Arbitration on a SCSI chain begins with the high address numbers, so better reponse is provided to devices with larger SCSI IDs. Device SCSI IDs are commonly selectable via jumpers or from a selector wheel on the device frame or housing.

The SCSI address format is:

AB   Two-digit SCSI address where *A* represents the SCSI ID and *B* represents the logical unit number

Devices are identified by a location code. Verify that the location code matches the actual hardware slot and interface using the lsdev command.

The device location codes are as follows:

AA-BB-CC-DD

where   *AA* = Drawer Location or Planar
BB = I/O Bus and slot
CC = Adapter Connector Number
DD = SCSI ID or Port Number

9.11 Updating the Product Topology Diskette

It's a good idea to update the topology diskette supplied with your system each time you add a new device. These diskettes are used by IBM service and support representatives to keep a record of your system configuration. These are especially helpful for sites that have a number of machines. After updating the diskette, send a copy to IBM hardware support using the mailer and address label supplied with the update diskette.

Here is the topology update procedure:

1. Shut down the system.

2. Set the key switch to the service position.

3. Boot the system.

4. At the "Diagnostics Operating Instructions" display, press ENTER.

5. At the "Function Selection" menu, select the "Service Aid" option.

6. At the "Service Aids Selection" menu, select the "Product Topology" options.

7. Follow the instructions displayed. When prompted, "Do you have any update diskettes that have not been loaded?" answer yes and insert the Product Topology Update diskette. Follow the instructions to update the Product Topology System diskette. If the "EC and MES Updates" screen is displayed, select the PF key to commit updates.

8. Repeatedly press PF3 to exit all diagnostics menus.

9. Reset the key switch to the normal position.

10. Reboot the system.

9.12   InfoExplorer Keywords

dbm	mkdev
ODM	chdev
ODMDIR	rmdev
odmcreate	savebase
method	restbase
odme	SCSI
cfgmgr	

9.13   QwikInfo

- Object data manager

`/etc/objrepos`	ODM database directory
`/usr/lib/objrepos`	ODM database directory
`export ODMDIR=<path>`	Set ODM database path

- Devices

`cfgmgr`	Add devices after IPL
`lsdev, mkdev, chgdev, rmdev`	Manage devices

10

Tapes

10.1 Tape Characteristics

Magnetic tape, due to its large storage capacity, low cost, and long storage life (usually in excess of 2 years), has been the secondary storage medium of choice for many years. The RISC System/6000 supports QIC ¼-inch, 4-mm, 8-mm, 9-track, and 18-track drives.

Before we look at the attributes of the individual device types and tape formats, it will be helpful to do a level set concerning general tape characteristics. An understanding of how data is represented on the media will assist you in making better use of the resource.

10.1.1 Physical characteristics

The earliest use of magnetic tape was in the German magnetophon. This device used a plastic tape doped with iron oxide. Later, the United States experimented with paper tape coated with iron oxide. This was followed by acetate and finally polymer-based tape. The thickness of the oxide coating, particle density, and particle distribution on the tape surface determines the signal strength that may be encoded. A thicker and denser oxide layer improves the signal strength but reduces high-frequency response for audio tape. If the layer is too thin, print through may occur. Print through is the transfer of recorded magnetic signal between tape layers on the reel. Tape thickness and base substrate also determine transport friction, media durability, and shelf life. Data-grade tape employs a thicker and denser oxide coating than standard audiotape and is usually more expensive. This is changing somewhat with digital audio tape (DAT). The same is true for data and video 8-mm tape. Good quality videotape will work in your RISC System/6000 tape drive, but I wouldn't recommend it! I learned the hard way!

Over the last few years we have also seen improvements in mechanical transport and head technologies. Helical-scan heads are replacing fixed-head configurations for digital recording (see Fig. 10.1). Helical-scan heads spin as the tape moves across the head surface. This reduces the transport speed requirements for the tape moving from spindle to spindle. Data is written diagonally across the tape surface. This will be an important point to remember when we talk about block sizes later in the next section.

10.1.2   Data format

Data is recorded on tape in blocks. Each block of data is separated from the next by an inter-record gap. Files on a tape are delimited by tape marks or file marks. A tape mark indicates the beginning of tape (BOT). Two tape marks in succession indicate the end of tape (EOT). BOT may also be followed by a special file called a tape label. The label indicates the volume name, size, and sequence number in a multivolume set.

Blocks are either fixed or variable in length (see Fig. 10.2). Fixed-block format means that data is read and written in chunks that are all the same size. The amount of data read and written to the media must be done in multiples of the block size. Variable-block format leaves it up to the application to determine the length of each block of data. A request to read more data than is available in the next tape block will

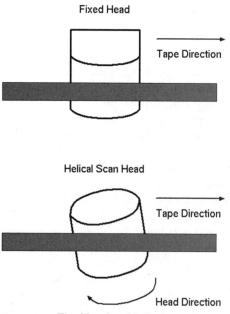

Figure 10.1   Fixed head and helical scan head.

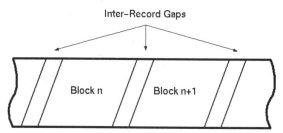

Inter-Record Gaps

Block n   Block n+1

Figure 10.2   Tape block and gap format.

result in a short read when using variable format. This feature is useful for commands like dd that will support short reads, but it is detrimental to less forgiving commands like tar, cpio, backup, and restore. The good news is that, when using variable block size, the dd command can be employed with an excessive block size to buffer input to tar, cpio, backup, and restore.

```
# dd if=/dev/rmt0.1 ibs=64k obs=512  | restore -xvB
# dd if=/dev/rmt0.1 ibs=64k obs=5120 | tar -xvBf-
# dd if=/dev/rmt0.1 ibs=64k obs=5120 | cpio -ivB
```

10.1.3   Block size

Block size is an important consideration and will effect the total media capacity and the time required to read or write data on the device. Larger block sizes reduce the number of inter-record gaps and make better use of the tape. The block size should also reflect the physical block size written by the device. For example, an 8-mm tape drive writes 1024 bytes per block diagonally across the width of the tape. If the block size defined to AIX for the device is fixed at 512-byte blocks, then the device will write out 512 bytes of data and pad the remaining 512 bytes in the physical 1024-byte block. This effectively reduces the media capacity by half. When variable-length blocks are defined in AIX for the example 8-mm device, block sizes larger than 1024 will fill each physical block on the tape. If the block size used by the application is not a multiple of 1024, then the last physical block written will be padded.

Block size is application dependent. Selecting the wrong block size can inhibit the ability to read AIX distribution and backup media, and cause portability problems. IBM uses a default block size of 512 bytes for product distribution media. You must also use a block size of 512 bytes for backups of the root volume group. If you do not use a block size of 512, the installation and restore programs will abort with the error message

```
/dev/rmt0: archive not in backup format
```

You can change the default block size defined to AIX for a tape device using the chdev command. Remember that this does not alter the physical block size used by the device!

```
# chdev -1 rmt0 -a "block_size=0"          Variable block size
# chdev -1 rmt0 -a "block_size=512"        Fixed 512-byte block size
# chdev -1 rmt0 -a "block_size=1024"       Fixed 1024-byte block size
```

If portability is an issue, you will want to define a default block size of 0, which indicates a variable block size. Byte ordering and ASCII/EBCDIC conversion can be handled by the conv option to the dd command.

```
# dd if=/dev/rmt0 conv=swab                Swap byte pairs
# dd if=/dev/rmt0 conv=ascii               Convert EBCDIC
                                           to ASCII
# dd if=/dev/rmt0 ibs=512 obs=1024 conv=sync   Pad blocks
```

Table 10.1 provides a few hints when using tar to move data from an RS/6000 to one of the listed vendor types.

10.1.4   Device names

Along with the block size, you must also be aware of the implicit tape ioctl operations associated with the device special file names. Device special file names are associated with a unique major number that identifies the tape device driver location in the device switch table A per-device unique minor number identifies entry points in the tape device driver that correspond to various density and tape control operations. If you are familiar with other UNIX tape systems, you know that nearly everyone uses his or her own scheme for naming device special files. Table 10.2 represents the AIX V3 default device names and the corresponding control operations and density.

The high and low density values are dependent upon the device. Consult the vendor documentation concerning the device characteristics. The mode numbers in Table 10.3 identify the density for the particular IBM device.

TABLE 10.1   RS/6000 Tape Conversions Using tar

DEC	OK. Check for compatible tape type/density.
Sun	Sun uses 512-byte blocks by default.
	On RS/6000, set block size to 512 or use dd
	conv=sync to pad blocks when reading Sun tapes
HP	OK. Check for compatible tape type/density.
SGI	Swap byte pairs using dd conv=swab.

TABLE 10.2   Tape Device Name Implicit Options

File name	Rewind on close	Retension on open	Density
/dev/rmt*	Yes	No	High
/dev/rmt*.1	No	No	High
/dev/rmt*.2	Yes	Yes	High
/dev/rmt*.3	No	Yes	High
/dev/rmt*.4	Yes	No	Low
/dev/rmt*.5	No	No	Low
/dev/rmt*.6	Yes	Yes	Low
/dev/rmt*.7	No	Yes	Low

Make sure you take a close look at the rmt man page information on how BOT, EOF, and EOT are handled for both reading and writing. You may be in for a surprise if you do not select the correct device name for your applications requirements. This can be especially true for EOT handling on 9-track tape drives. UNIX generally does not sense EOT before reaching it. Improper tape positioning at EOT can cause the application to run the tape off the end of the reel. You will make few friends in the operations staff if you do this very often.

10.1.5   Tape positioning

The tape device driver supports a somewhat standard set of ioctl operations used to control tape positioning. These operations can be invoked

TABLE 10.3   IBM Density Modes

Mode number	Description
140	8-mm, 5-GB compression mode
20	8-mm, 2.3-GB mode
0	8-mm, 5-GB compression mode
15	7207-12 QIC-120
16	7207-12 QIC-150
17	7207-12 QIC-525
21	7207-12 QIC-1000
0	7207-12 QIC-1000
15	7207-11 QIC-120
16	7207-11 QIC-150
17	7207-11 QIC-525
0	7207-11 QIC-525
15	7207-01 QIC-120
16	7207-01 QIC-150
0	7207-01 QIC-150
3	9-track 6250 bpi
2	9-track 1600 bpi
0	Sensed tape density

from the local command line, remotely, or within a program. Local and remote positioning is handled by the tctl and rmt commands, respectively. If you are familiar with the mt command on other UNIX platforms, you can link mt to tctl, as their operations are similar. rmt is used in conjunction with rcmd or rexec.

```
# tctl -f/dev/rmt0 rewind
```

For remote operation, be aware that AIX ioctl call numbers don't necessarily map one-for-one with those on the remote system (see Table 10.4). You can fix the mapping problem by creating a wrapper for rmt to remap the command line parameters to those in use by the remote system.

Be aware of where you are during tape operations. After each program read() or write() operation, the tape head is positioned at the beginning of the next block or the beginning of blank space. Tape marks are treated exactly like a file, so they must be accounted for when skipping from file to file on a tape.

10.1.6   Permissions

Restricting access to tape devices tends to be a problem on many UNIX systems. The device special files are commonly set "rw" by the world. In the absence of additional tape allocation software, you can easily create your own drive reservation application using the following algorithm:

1. Check for a free device (absence of device lock files). If all devices are in use, exit. If not, continue.

2. Fork and spawn a new shell. Wait until process exit to release device.

3. Create lock file for selected device.

4. Set permissions and ownership to requester.

TABLE 10.4   AIX to UNIX ioctl Mapping

AIX	ioctl number	Remote	ioctl number	Comment
STOFFL	5	MTOFFL	6	Rewind unload tape
STREW	6	MTREW	5	Rewind tape
STERASE	7	MTERASE	9	Erase tape
STRETEN	8	MTRETEN	8	Retension tape
STWEOF	10	MTWEOF	0	Write end-of-file marker
STFSF	11	MTFSF	1	Forward space file
STRSF	12	MTBSF	2	Back space file
STFSR	13	MTFSR	3	Forward space record
STRSR	14	MTBSR	4	Back space record
N/A	N/A	MTNOP	7	NO-OP
N/A	N/A	MTEOM	10	End-of-media
N/A	N/A	MTNBSF	11	Back space to BOF

The following are the default device permissions:

```
# ls -al /dev/rmt*

crw-rw-rw-  1 root   system  22,  0 Aug 23 12:54 /dev/rmt0
crw-rw-rw-  1 root   system  22,  1 Aug 23 12:54 /dev/rmt0.1
crw-rw-rw-  1 root   system  22,  2 Aug 23 12:54 /dev/rmt0.2
crw-rw-rw-  1 root   system  22,  3 Aug 23 12:54 /dev/rmt0.3
crw-rw-rw-  1 root   system  22,  4 Aug 23 12:54 /dev/rmt0.4
crw-rw-rw-  1 root   system  22,  5 Aug 23 12:54 /dev/rmt0.5
crw-rw-rw-  1 root   system  22,  6 Aug 23 12:54 /dev/rmt0.6
crw-rw-rw-  1 root   system  22,  7 Aug 23 12:54 /dev/rmt0.7
```

10.2   Tape Tools

AIX provides a limited set of tape utilities. The following set of commands supports tape manipulation.

dd	Read/write variable block sizes and perform data conversion
tcopy	Display tape directory or copy tape to tape
tapechk	Verify QIC tapes for errors
tar, cpio, backup/restore	Archive; may use tape as a medium.

10.3   Public Domain Tape Tools

Due to the absence of tape allocation mechanisms, label support, and tape librarians in UNIX, a number of vendor and public domain tape handling applications have been developed. Vendor packages change faster than the publication life of this book, so I encourage you to refer to advertisements and reviews in publications like *RS/Magazine*. I found the following set of public domain tools after spending a few minutes searching the Web for "tape." No warranty or guarantees implied!

ansitape	Read and write ANSI and IBM standard labels in ASCII and EBCDIC. Read multivolume tapes. Requires ioctl command changes like rmt on AIX. comp.unix.sources archive v08i099.
cmstape	Process IBM VM/CMS TAPE DUMP format. comp.unix.sources archive v07i008.
copytape	Tape-to-tape copy program. comp.unix.sources archive v10i099
dectp	Map and read a DEC ANSI labeled tape.
exatoc	Manipulate a table of contents on the beginning of an 8-mm tape.
ibmtape	Read IBM standard labeled tape.

magtapetools	Package of tape tools supporting interrogation of tape contents, tape copy, reading random blocks, and reading/writing ANSI labels.
rmtlib2	Library and generic rmt.h file supporting remote tape operations from a program similar to rmt. comp.unix.sources archive v18i109
tapemap	Map a tape. Reports min/max blocksize and block count for each file on the tape.
tprobe	Tape copy package. comp.sources.3b1 archive volume02
with	Tape device reservation with operator messages.

10.4   IBM Tape Devices and Characteristics

Table 10.5 lists IBM tape device characteristics. For third-party devices, see documents in pub/oemhw, available via anonymous ftp from ibminet.awdpa.ibm.com.

Figuring out QIC tape portability characteristics is an art unto itself. Table 10.6, for IBM 7207 models, is based on data put together by Brian Murphy from IBM development. Brian's original information is available from comp.unix.aix archives, May 1993.

10.5   InfoExplorer Keywords

dd	ioctl
tar	tctl
cpio	mt
backup	rcmd
restore	rexec
rmt	

TABLE 10.5   IBM Tape Device Characteristics

Model	Format	Max capacity	Max transfer rate	Interface
7207-01	QIC	150 MB	90 KB/sec	SE SCSI
7207-11	QIC	525 MB	200 KB/sec	SE SCSI
7207-12	QIC	1.2 GB	300 KB/sec	SE SCSI
7206	4-mm	4.0 GB	732 KB/sec	SE SCSI
7208-1	8-mm	2.3 GB	245 KB/sec	SE SCSI
7208-2*	8-mm	2.3 GB	245 KB/sec	DF SCSI
7208-11	8-mm	10.0 GB	500 KB/sec	SE SCSI
7208-12*	8-mm	10.0 GB	500 KB/sec	DF SCSI
½ inch	9-track	180 MB	768 KB/sec	SE SCSI
3480/3490	18-track	2.4 GB	3 MB/sec	370 channel
3490E	18-track	2.4 GB	3 MB/sec	DF SCSI

* AS/400 Compatible.

TABLE 10.6   IBM 7207 QIC Tape Compatibility

Read compatibility

	QIC-24	QIC-120	QIC-150	QIC-525	QIC-1000
DC300XLP	01,11,12				
DC600A	01,11,12	01,11,12			
DC6150	01,11,12	01,11,12	01,11,12		
DC6250	01,11,12	01,11,12	01,11,12		
DC6037	01,11,12	01,11,12	01,11,12		
DC6320	01,11,12	01,11,12	01,11,12	11,12	
DC6525	01,11,12	01,11,12	01,11,12	11,12	
DC6080	01,11,12	01,11,12	01,11,12	11,12	
DC9100				12	
DC9120				12	

Write compatibility

	QIC-24	QIC-120	QIC-150	QIC-525	QIC-1000
DC300XLP					
DC600A	01				
DC6150	01,11,12	01,11,12			
DC6250	01,11,12	01,11,12			
DC6037	01,11,12	01,11,12			
DC6320	01,11,12	01,11,12	11,12		
DC6525	01,11,12	01,11,12	11,12		
DC6080	01,11,12	01,11,12	11,12		
DC9100				12	
DC9120				12	

Column numbers represent 7207 model. DC300XLP and DC600A tapes are not recommended and may cause head damage. DC9135, DC9164, DC9200, DC9210 tapes are not supported.

10.6   QwikInfo

`chdev -1 <device> -a block_size=NNN`	Set block size:
where *NNN* = 0	Variable block size for compatibility
512	Backup/install block size
1024	Efficient block size for 8-mm devices
`tar, cpio, backup`	Archive commands
`dd`	Implement data dump tool, conversion, reblocking
`tcopy`	Copy tape to tape
`tctl`	Control tape device

11

Disks and File Systems

11.1 Disk Evolution

Are your file systems half full or are they half empty? It doesn't matter how much disk space you throw into a system. They are always half full and growing fast! With multimedia tools becoming commonplace, it's not unusual to see large numbers of audio and video files where minimum sizes are well over a megabyte. It won't be long before multimedia electronic mail will be shipping these multimegabyte files all over the network. If you aren't already thinking in terms of multigigabyte personal computer and workstation storage, then you are not going to be ready for the storm. A full-blown AIX BOS installation requires one-third of a gigabyte just for the operating system. The InfoExplorer information bases can eat up another third of a gigabyte. Remember when 10-MB hard files on an IBM PC/XT seemed like more storage than you could ever use? What all this means is that you better get comfortable installing new disks and managing file systems.

The new file system enhancements in AIX V4 will provide a little extra data breathing room. The new logical volume and file system capabilities in AIX V4 have been overshadowed by all attention directed at AIX V4 multiprocessing. This is unfortunate because these new features may well be a better reason for many AIX V3 customers to upgrade their systems to the next release (my opinion). New file system options in version 4 include Berkeley Unix-style file system fragments, variable inode allocation, compression, file system sizes larger than 2 GB, and logical volume striping. Some of these features, although new to AIX, have been available for some time in the Berkeley Unix fast file system and under other operating systems like MS-DOS. The bottom line is that by using AIX V4, you can save on disk space and provide additional file-system capabilities without buying new hardware.

11.2   Disk Hardware

Workstation and personal computer disk drives have primarily been either an integrated drive electronics (IDE) drive or a small computer system interface (SCSI) drive. IDE drives integrate all the controller functions into the disk housing. SCSI drives also integrate controller function in the disk assembly but require a more complex adapter card on the I/O bus. The RISC System/6000 supports internal SCSI disks as well as microchannel or PCI adapters (depending on model) for attaching external single ended, differential, fast, narrow, wide SCSI, and SCSI-2 disk devices.

11.2.1   Serial storage architecture

A more recent option for connecting disk devices is IBM's serial storage architecture (SSA). SSA uses a loop configuration for connecting devices to one or more RS/6000 computers. The loop architecure is akin to token ring or dual-ring FDDI in that the loop can be broken and traffic will be rerouted using the remaining link. It provides fault tolerance in the machine to device connection that is not available with SCSI or IDE-type attachment. There is also no bus arbitration protocol like that required in SCSI configurations. SSA supports concurrent full duplex 80 MB/sec I/O between the host and disk device. This capability is called spatial reuse.

11.2.2   RAID

A redundant array of independent disks (RAID) brings additional fault tolerance into storage support through the use of data mirroring and striping technologies. In addition to data fault tolerance and availability, RAID can maximize read I/O performance by spreading access across multiple disk devices. Essentially, RAID is a group of drives (strip or mirror set) that are linked by a special-purpose bus, processor, and cache memory structure to distribute file data across all the drives in the set. The type of mirroring or striping performed is designated by the RAID level 0–5 (see Table 11.1). RAID level 0 is used to strip data across disks without any parity recovery support. RAID level 1 is what we have come to know as mirroring. All the data for a file is duplicated on two separate disks or logical volumes. RAID level 2 is a technique originally patented by Thinking Machines, Inc. In a RAID 2 configuration, data is bit- or byte-striped across multiple drives along with parity information that can be used to reconstruct the data on any individual driver in the event of a failure. Like RAID 2, RAID level 3 synchronously stripes data across drives but uses a single drive to store the parity information for the stripe set. RAID level 4 stripes data like RAID levels 2 and 3 and records parity. It differs from the other two in that data can be read asynchro-

TABLE 11.1   RAID Levels

RAID 0	Striped data, no parity
RAID 1	Mirrored data
RAID 2	Striped data with parity
RAID 3	Striped data with parity drive
RAID 4	Striped data with parity and asynchronous read access
RAID 5	Striped data with striped parity

nously across the drives in the stripe set, improving concurrent read access. Writes must occur synchronously, so an I/O is not complete until all drives in the set have been updated. RAID level 5 is similar to the previous three with the exception of parity data. Parity is striped across the drive set to eliminate the problem created if a single parity drive should fail. Higher RAID levels are somewhat vendor-dependent architectures and include capabilities like recovery of two simultaneous drive failures and splitting the host-device I/O dependency using a memory cache. This latter capability improves I/O in that the host only writes to memory and does not have to wait for the synchronized drive write to complete.

11.2.3   Fixed disk architecture

The disks themselves are multiple platters stacked like records on a hub (see Fig. 11.1). Each platter is coated with a magnetic substrate. One or more electromagnetic heads may be moved back and forth across a platter from outer edge to inner edge. The heads react to the polarization of the magnetic particles formatted in circular tracks around the surface of the platter. The heads are positioned on the platters by a disk controller circuit which receives its instructions from the operating system.

Most disks come preformatted with a bad-sector map allocated. If you have to format a disk, invoke the diag command or reboot the sys-

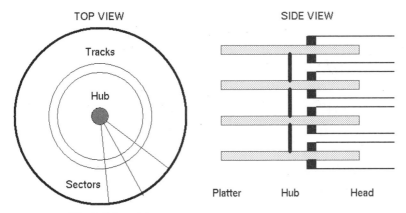

Figure 11.1   Fixed disk architecture.

tem in single-user maintenance mode. From the diag function selection, select "Task Selection" followed by "Media Format" and "Media Certify." Note that the diag command is not available on all platforms.

```
# diag
```

Function selection

   Task selection (Diagnostics, Advanced diagnostics, Service aids, etc.)

      Format media

      Certify media

Formatted space on the disk is made up of sectors or blocks. The sector size will vary with make and model and may be either fixed or variable. Tracks are made up of sectors aligned in circles on each platter. Stacked tracks on the platters make up a cylinder.

11.3   Disk Installation

To add a new SCSI disk to the system, plug the disk onto one of the SCSI adapters on the back of the system unit. This is best done with the system powered down, but it can be done online if you are *very careful*. Multiple SCSI devices may be daisy-chained off a single SCSI adapter. Each disk must represent a unique SCSI ID and logical unit number (LUN) in the chain. The SCSI ID is jumper or switch selectable on the drive assembly or casing. SCSI IDs range from 0 through 7, with 7 usually assigned to the adapter. When the system is booted, the new disk is automatically identified and recorded in ROS and the ODM database. You can update device information online by invoking cfgmgr or using the mkdev command. The new disk is assigned the next available hdisk<nn> label.

```
# mkdev -c disk -s scsi -t osdisk -p scsi2 -a pv=yes
# SMIT cfgmgr
```

Use the diag command (not available on some platforms) to verify that the system can access the new device.

```
# diag
```

11.4   Logical Volume Manager

The physical disk is now available for partitioning. A partition is a section of disk space that can be used for file systems or paging space. Legacy UNIX systems restrict partitions to contiguous space on a single disk. AIX uses the concept of logical volumes as indirection to physical space. A logical volume is represented by a mapping of contiguous logical partitions to discontiguous physical partitions residing on one or more physical disks. Each physical disk may contain up to 1016 physical partitions ranging in size from 1 to 256 megabytes in powers of 2. The default physical partition size is 4 megabytes. One to three physical partitions may be mapped to a logical partition. Logical volumes are allocated from logical partitions within a Logical Volume Group (LVG). Each LVG is made up of 1 to 32 physical disks. Partition mapping, volume management, and interfaces are implemented through a pseudo-device driver and manager called the logical volume manager or LVM (see Figs. 11.2 and 11.3).

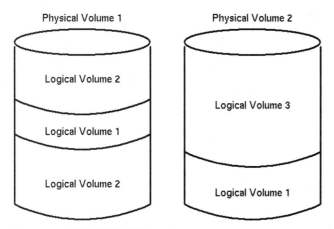

Figure 11.2 PV to VG to LV mapping.

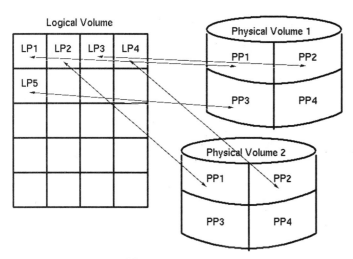

Figure 11.3 LV to LP to PP mapping.

Using the abstraction of logical to physical partition mapping, AIX is able to dynamically increase the size of volume groups, logical volumes, and ultimately file systems without service interruption! Prior to LVM support, you had to back up a file system to disk or tape, destroy it, rebuild it with the new allocation sizes, and restore the backup. LVM allows you to manage disk space online dynamically rather than requiring hours of file system downtime.

Tailoring the logical partition mapping allows you to optimize file system placement. Busy file systems should be located in the center of the physical disk and spread across multiple physical disks. The LVM also supports mirroring, making duplicate copies of a logical volume available for concurrent read access. Mirroring also improves data availability.

AIX V4 LVM supports RAID 0 striping. As you may already know, striping is a mechanism that allows you to distribute a file or file system's data blocks evenly across multiple disks to improve I/O performance. Striping is specified when you create a logical volume. There are a few restrictions when using striped volumes. Physical partitions must be allocated evenly between the disks included in the stripe set. You can't combine other LV features like mirroring with striping, and you can't move a striped LV after creation. Do your homework up front before settling on a striped configuration. You won't be able to change it as easily as standard AIX LVs.

Logical volume services are also a part of the Open Software Foundation's OSF/1 operating system. Although the implementation is different, the conceptual services are very similar.

11.5   Configuring Volume Groups

In order for a new disk to be made available to the logical volume manager (LVM), it must be designated a physical volume and assigned a physical volume identifier (PVID) and label. The PVID is a sixteen-digit hexadecimal number.

```
# chdev -l hdisk<n> -a -pv=yes
```

You can list physical disks on your system using lsdev.

```
# lsdev -C -c disk

hdisk0 Available 00-00-0S-00 1.2 GB SCSI Disk Drive (in 2.4
  GB Disk Unit)
hdisk1 Available 00-00-0S-10 1.2 GB SCSI Disk Drive (in 2.4
  GB Disk Unit)
hdisk2 Available 00-04-00-30 Other SCSI Disk Drive
```

```
hdisk3 Available 00-04-00-40 Other SCSI Disk Drive
hdisk4 Available 00-04-00-50 Other SCSI Disk Drive
hdisk5 Available 00-04-00-00 Other SCSI Disk Drive
hdisk6 Available 00-04-00-10 Other SCSI Disk Drive
hdisk7 Available 00-04-00-20 Other SCSI Disk Drive
```

To list the PVIDs associated with these disks, use the lspv command.

```
# lspv

hdisk0 000008870001c7e1 rootvg
hdisk1 00001508fce5bbea rootvg
hdisk2 00004060c388efc4 vg00
hdisk3 000015082c6e92df vg00
hdisk4 0000150837cc1a85 vg01
hdisk5 000015082c28f5c7 vg01
hdisk6 000015082c2931f5 vg01
hdisk7 000015082c296d8f vg01
```

To add the new disk to a new or existing volume group, use SMIT (see Fig. 11.4) or the mkvg and extendvg commands.

```
# mkvg -f -y vg10 hdisk10 hdisk11
```
Create a volume group vg10 using physical disks 10 and 11

```
# extendvg -f rootvg hdisk8
```
Add disk 8 to the rootvg volume group

```
# smit mkvg
```

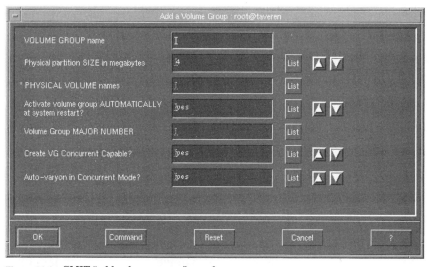

Figure 11.4 SMIT "add volume group" panel.

A volume group identifier (VGID) is assigned to each volume group. The VGID is a sixteen-digit hexadecimal number. Each VGID in the system is represented by an entry in the /etc/vg directory.

```
# ls /etc/vg
./                      vg0000150837CC1FBA     vg00001508CECC7A4C
../                     vg000015084549417D     vg00001508EA5D85C7
lvdd_kmid               vg000015084549F2C6     vg00001508EA5DEB29
vg0000150837CAEE45      vg00001508AC04C232     vg00001508EA5F84DA
vg0000150837CB78DD      vg00001508CA7846C0     vg00001508FCE80427
```

To display the configuration of the existing volume groups on your system, use the lsvg command.

```
# lsvg                  List volume groups
  rootvg
  vg01
  vg02
  vg03

# lsvg -p rootvg    List physical volumes in the root volume group

  rootvg:
  PV_NAME  PV STATE  TOTAL Pps  FREE Pps  FREE DISTRIBUTION
  hdisk0   active    287        17        00..12..04..01..00
  hdisk1   active    287        43        00..17..00..00..26
```

11.5.1 Quorum

Each physical volume in the volume group is marked with a volume group descriptor area (VGDA) and a volume group status area (VGSA). The VGDA contains identifiers for all logical and physical volumes and partitions that make up the volume group. The VGSA is a bitmap used to indicate which physical partitions on the disk are stale and require synched update.

When a volume group is activated using the varyonvg command or SMIT, the LVM verifies that it has access to at least 51 percent of the VGDA and VGSA copies before going online. This majority is called a Quorum and is required by the LVM to ensure data integrity. Any physical volume not available is reported. The system administrator must decide whether to continue if a device is not accessible. If a majority quorum is not established for the volume group, it is not activated.

```
# varyonvg <VGname>
```

You can take a volume group off-line using the varyoffvg command or via SMIT. Note that all access to logical volumes in the volume group must be terminated. Any file systems located in the volume group must be unmounted, and any paging space must not be active.

```
# varyoffvg <VGname>
# smit varyoffvg
```

To remove or replace physical volumes in a volume group for maintenance purposes, use SMIT or the chpv command.

```
# chpv -vr <Pvname>      Remove disk from VG
# chpv -va <Pvname>      Replace disk in VG
```

An entire volume group may be moved as a unit from one system to another. Use SMIT or the exportvg and importvg commands to export a volume group from the old system and import it on to the new system. The volume group must first be deactivated before attempting to export it from the system.

When the volume group is exported, all references to it are removed from the system tables. When the volume group is imported on the new system all device table, special file, and /etc/filesystem entries are added automatically. You can export and import a volume group on the same system to resynchronize the VGDA and ODM information.

```
# exportvg <VGname>
# importvg <VGname> <PVname>
```

11.5.2   Root volume group—rootvg

A special VG called rootvg is used by AIX for the operating system's root file systems and the default paging areas. It's a good idea to use separate volume groups for user and local application file systems. This way you can export and import these volume groups before and after operating system upgrades. Each AIX BOS intallation destroys all or part of rootvg.

11.6   Configuring Logical Volumes

To make use of the disk space available in a volume group, you will need to create a logical volume. Logical volumes are analogous to partitions on other UNIX systems but provide some significant enhancements. The structure and features provided by logical volumes should be well understood before proceeding with allocating space for file systems or paging areas. In other words, you should be able to determine the following:

Logical volume type

Size in logical partitions

Interdisk partition layout

Write scheduling policy

Intradisk partition layout

Will it be mirrored?

Will it be striped?

11.6.1 Logical volume types

The LVM basically manages all logical volume types the same way. A logical volume may warrant special consideration when defining some of the other attributes. For example, you may wish to locate paging logical volumes in the center of the disks to reduce head movement. There are five logical volume types used by AIX:

File system	Holds file system data and metadata
Log	Holds JFS metadata update log
Paging	Paging areas
Boot logical volume	Boot block and RAM file system code
Dump area	Holds panic dumps

11.6.2 Logical volume size

When you create a new logical volume or add space to an existing logical volume, you will be working in logical partition units. If you accepted the default 4-megabyte partition size, then a 512-megabyte logical volume will require 128 logical partitions. Define a maximum number of logical partitions that will be used for the logical volume. This value limits the size a file system may grow within the logical volume. If additional file system space is required at a later date, the maximum limit may be increased.

You may notice that, when you add up the number of partitions represented by the physical volumes in a volume group, you have lost somewhere between 7 to 10 percent of the total formatted space. This is due to space overhead required by the LVM to manage the volume group. Remember the VGDA and VGSA structures described in the previous sections?

11.6.3 Interdisk policy

The interdisk layout policy determines the range of physical disks that may be used to allocate partitions for the logical volume. The interdisk policy may be either minimum or maximum, along with a range limit governing the number of physical disks that may be used.

Minimum   Provides highest availability. All partitions are allocated on a single physical volume. For mirrored logical volumes, the first copy will be allocated on a single physical disk. The second copy can be allocated across multiple physical volumes up to the range limit unless the "strict" option is selected.

Maximum   Provides the best performance. Each logical partition in the logical volume will be allocated sequentially across up to the range limit of physical volumes. If one of the physical disks fails, then the entire logical volume is unavailable.

11.6.4 Intradisk policy

The intradisk layout policy (see Fig. 11.5) defines where partitions will be allocated within a physical disk. One of five regions may be selected: inner edge, inner middle, center, middle, and outer edge. Inner edge and outer edge have the slowest seek times. Average seek times decrease toward the center of the disk.

Use the lsvg command to display the layout of existing logical volumes and the number of free partitions.

```
# lsvg rootvg
```

Disk Allocation Policy

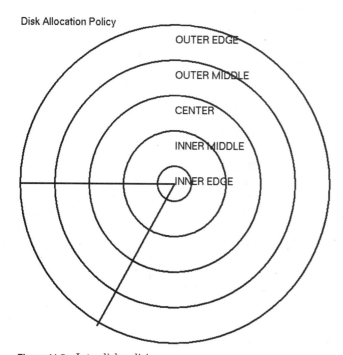

Figure 11.5 Intradisk policies.

```
VOLUME GROUP:    rootvg          VG IDENTIFIER:    00000707b47ff02b
VG STATE:        active          PP SIZE:          4 megabyte(s)
VG PERMISSION:   read/write      TOTAL Pps:        480 (1920 megabytes)
MAX Lvs:         256             FREE Pps:         267 (1068 megabytes)
Lvs:             9               USED Pps:         213 (852 megabytes)
OPEN Lvs:        8               QUORUM:           2
TOTAL Pvs:       1               VG DESCRIPTORS:   2
STALE Pvs:       0               STALE Pps         0
ACTIVE Pvs:      1               AUTO ON:          yes
Concurrent:      Non-Capable     Auto-Concurrent:  Disabled
VG Mode:         Non-Concurrent
```

```
# lsvg -1 rootvg
```

```
rootvg:
LV NAME    TYPE     LPs    Pps    Pvs    LV STATE        MOUNT POINT
hd6        paging   68     68     1      open/syncd      N/A
hd5        boot     2      2      1      closed/syncd    /blv
lv01       jfs      49     49     1      open/syncd      /usr/local
hd8        jfslog   1      1      1      open/syncd      N/A
hd4        jfs      25     25     1      open/syncd      /
hd2        jfs      44     44     1      open/syncd      /usr
hd1        jfs      8      8      1      open/syncd      /home
hd3        jfs      8      8      1      open/syncd      /tmp
hd9var     jfs      8      8      1      open/syncd      /var
```

11.6.5 Mirrors

For high-access file systems, mirrors provide a mechanism that improves availability (a copy of the primary logical volume is maintained) and access time (multiple paths to the data). You may choose to keep two mirrored copies in environments that require higher levels of availability and fault tolerance.

When reading a mirrored logical volume, if the primary path is busy, the read can be satisfied by the mirror. Writes are sequential to logical volumes confined to a single physical disk. If mirrors occupy more than one physical disk, write scheduling can be either sequential or parallel.

Sequential writes	Writes are ordered in the sequence that they occur. Each write operation is scheduled sequentially to each copy and returns when both updates are completed.
Parallel writes	Writes are scheduled across the multiple disks at the same time. The write returns after the longest write completes.

Mirrors can be created when the logical volume is created by requesting more than one copy. To mirror an existing logical volume, use the SMIT FastPath mklvcopy (see Fig. 11.6).

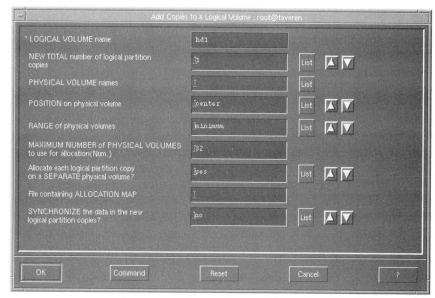

Figure 11.6   SMIT "mirror logical volume" panel.

```
# smit mklvcopy lv01     Start SMIT and select logical volume to be
                         mirrored
```

11.6.6   Adding a logical volume

After selecting the volume placement characteristics for the new logical volume, you can create it using the SMIT FastPath mklv (see Fig. 11.7).

```
# smit mklv
```

11.7   File Systems

The most common use of logical volumes is to contain file systems. A file system is the structure that supports a UNIX directory and file tree. A file system tree begins with the root directory at the top, with subdirectory branches proceeding down from the root. Each directory level in the tree may contain files and directories. The primary structures that make up the file system are the super block, inodes, and data blocks.

11.7.1   Super block

The super block describes the overall structure of the file system within the logical volume. It contains the file system name, the size, the pointer to the inode and free block lists, and so on. The super block is used to keep track of the file system state during operation. Super

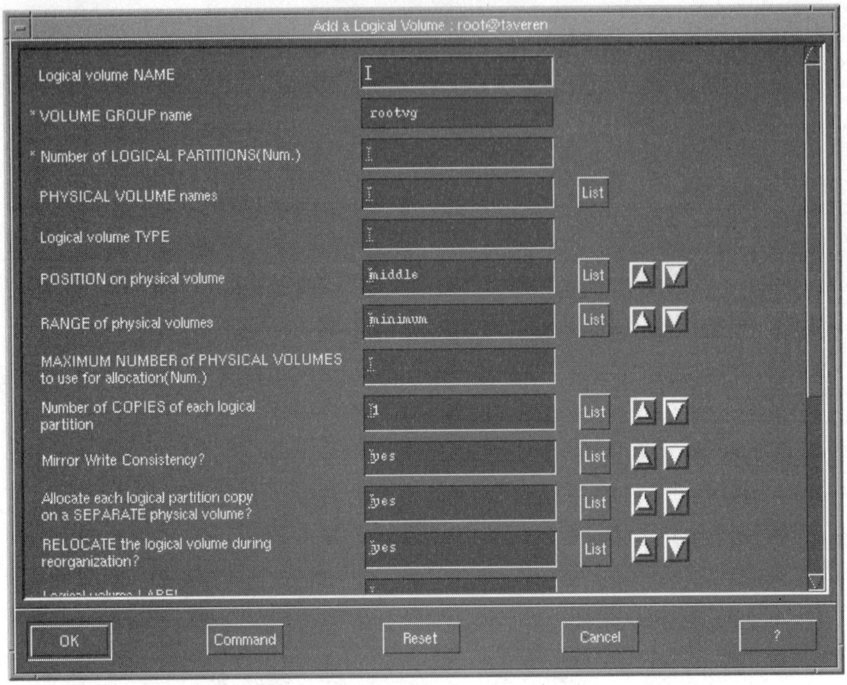

Figure 11.7 SMIT "add logical volume" panel.

block information is also used to verify the integrity of the file system as part of the boot process and in the event of a failure.

Each directory and file in the file system is represented by an inode. The inode can be thought of as an index entry. Each inode is sequentially numbered from 1 up to the maximum number of inodes defined for the file system. The inode identifies the attributes of the file or directory it represents:

File mode

File type

Owning UID and GID

Date and time stamps

Number of links

Pointer to data blocks

Size in bytes

Size in blocks

11.7.2 Inodes

The number of inodes created for file systems are based on the size of the file system. The native AIX V4 JFS file system permits limited control over the number of inodes allocated. This means more wasted space for file systems that will contain a small number of very large files; for example, databases. The numbers of inodes allocated is no longer directly fixed to the number of file system blocks allocated. The number of inodes to be created is controlled using the "Number of Bytes Per Inode" (NBPI) option at file system creation time. This value allocates one inode per number of file system bytes as specified by NBPI. The NBPI value is a multiple power of 2 ranging from 512 to 16,384. To reduce the number of inodes for a file system, select a large NBPI value. For more inodes, pick a small value. Note that you can't change the NBPI value for an existing file system. This isn't quite as flexible as one might like in that there is a small range of values for NBPI, but it is an improvement over the fixed AIX V3 NBPI value of 4096.

You can list the inode numbers associated with files and directories using the -i flag to the ls command.

```
# ls -ailF

total 1088
18 drwx------   13 deroest   system   1024   Aug 23 15:03 ./
 2 drwxr-xr-x   10 bin       bin       512   May 07 13:19 ../
25 -rwx------    1 deroest   system     27   Jan 11 1993 .forward*
21 -rwxr-x---    1 deroest   system   1499   Dec 23 1992 .kshrc*
24 -rwxr-x---    1 deroest   system    315   Nov 20 1992 .login*
```

Information for a particular inode can be displayed using the istat command.

```
# istat 25 /dev/hd1

Inode 25 on device 10/8 File
Protection:      rwx------
Owner:           4084(deroest)      Group: 0(system)
Link count:      1       Length 27 bytes

Last updated:    Tue Apr 20 08:15:50 1993
Last modified:   Mon Jan 11 14:01:24 1993
Last accessed:   Fri Aug 20 00:00:39 1993

Block pointers (hexadecimal):
25     0     0     0     0     0     0     0
```

To find the file name associated with the inode number, use the -inum flag with the find command.

```
# find /home -xdev -inum 25 -print
/home/deroest/.forward
```

11.7.3 Data blocks

Data blocks are used to store the actual file data in the file system. Each inode contains 13 data block address slots. The first eight address slots point at the first eight file data blocks of the file. The ninth address points to an incore inode structure. The disk inode information is copied to this structure when the file is opened. The tenth through thirteenth addresses point to indirect data blocks, which are used to address data blocks for large files. Each indirect block supports 1024 addresses. Because file addressing is restricted to 32 bits, third-level indirection is not used.

11.7.4 Fragments

AIX V4 JFS introduces BSD-like disk fragmentation. Fragments are small file system blocks based on a division of a power of 2 of the full 4K block size. The fragment size is defined at file system creation time and may take a value of 512 bytes, 1K, 2K and 4K (default). Individual file systems may have different fragment sizes specified. Fragment sizes are specified on a per-file-system basis. You can define small fragment sizes for file systems that support small files and larger fragment sizes for those with large files. Fragments provide a means for using the unallocated space left in partially filled 4K blocks.

There are some restrictions and a downside, too, when using fragments. First of all, fragments are only supported in inode direct blocks. JFS inodes have eight direct block addresses. The ninth is used for indirect addressing. The upper nibble of an inode direct block address is used to store the fragment ratio for the block. Thus fragments are only supported for file sizes up to 32K. Files that are larger than 32K use the full 4K block sizes. Note that large files do not use fragments for the first 32K and full block sizes for the remainder. Also, you may have already guessed that by using small fragment sizes you increase the fragmentation of your overall file system space. To address this, AIX V4.1 delivers a new utility, defragfs, to defrag file systems.

```
# defragfs /usr          Defragment /usr file system
# defragfs -r /usr        Report /usr fragment state
```

```
statistics before running defragfs:
number of free fragments 43107
number of allocated fragments 199581
number of free spaces shorter than a block 0
number of free fragments in short free spaces 0

statistics after running defragfs
number of free spaces shorter than a block 0
number of free fragments in short free spaces 0

other statistics:
number of fragments moved 2285
number of logical blocks moved 2285
number of allocation attempts 635
number of exact matches 136
```

Eliot Lim, a programmer on the staff here at University of Washington, did a profile analysis of "generic" user file systems on our multi-user UNIX systems. The file systems contained user mail folders, shell scripts, C programs, data files, and the like. He found that roughly 40 percent of the files in a file system were 512 bytes or less. You can easily see that, for these file systems, we would save a great deal of space by using fragment sizes smaller than 4K.

11.7.5 Compression

It's nice to see that UNIX is catching up with mature operating systems like MS-DOS when it comes to disk management utilities. I know, MS-DOS isn't an operating system. AIX V4 JFS now supports file compression and decompression. JFS compression is an installable BOS fileset option. Again, compression support is selected on a per-file-system basis at file system create time. AIX applies compression at the logical block level rather than at the file level. This improves random I/O performance in that the entire file does not have to be decompressed. Compression is also only applied to regular files and long symbolic links.

Space allocation can be a problem for compressed file systems. It is always difficult to tell how much space will be required by a file after compression. To avoid overallocation problems, AIX allocates the full block requirement for the uncompressed file. The assumption being that after compression the file won't be larger than the original.

AIX V4 uses the Lempel-Ziv (LZ) algorithm for data compression ("A Universal Algorithm for Sequential Data Compression," *IEEE Transactions on Information Theory,* May 1970). This algorithm can achieve compression rates as high as 50 percent. IBM benchmarks on a 601 processor have demonstrated compression rates of 1.2 MB/sec and decompression rates of 6 MB/sec. The algorithm requires 50 cycles per byte to compress and 10 cycles per byte to decompress. The design of the JFS compression system also provides a means for replacing the LZ algorithm with other compression algorithms to fit custom data types.

11.7.6   Large files and file systems

AIX supports file systems larger than 2 GB. This is good news to many sites. However, this does not mean that *files* larger the 2 GB are supported. Large files are coming; be patient! 64-bit integer support in the AIX compiler has led the way to 64-bit file table byte offsets. A new offset type, offset_t, is used with a new system call, llseek, to access the larger file system space. Corresponding changes in the device driver are also required to reach beyond 2 GB. This makes the theoretical offset limit for AIX 1 terabyte. Unfortunately, limitations in other kernel and JFS data structures limit maximum file system size to 256 GB. As of this writing, the IBM tested and supported limit is 64 GB. We have used 24 GB file systems successfully on our RAID devices with the thanks and appreciation of our research faculty.

11.7.7   Virtual file system

AIX V3 supplies a generic file system interface called the Virtual File System (VFS) that permits it to support a number of file system types. VFS is an abstraction of the underlying physical file system mount structure, inodes, and operations.

The underlying physical file system is represented in VFS by a generic mount structure and an array of operations permitted on the physical file system called vfsops. VFS uses a paired abstraction of vnodes and gnodes to reference the underlying file system inode structures. One or more vnode structures reference a gnode that is linked to the real inode. VFS operates on the underlying inodes using vnode operations called vnodeops. VFS-supported file system types are defined in /etc/vfs:

```
%defaultvfs   jfs    nfs
#
cdrfs  5    none                          none
jfs    3    none                          /sbin/helpers/v3fshelper
dfs    7    /sbin/helpers/dfsmnthelper    none
nfs    2    /sbin/helpers/nfsmnthelp none  remote
sfs    16   none                          none
```

11.7.8   Journaled file system configuration

The native file system in AIX is a log-based file system called the Journalized File System (JFS). Log-based file systems like JFS improve recovery by maintaining a circular update log. In the event of a failure, the JFS log is replayed to recover the file system state. Log recovery of a file system is completed several orders of magnitude faster than a full fsck walk of a file system. AIX provides the fsck to assist in disaster recovery; however, it is not invoked as part of the standard boot procedure.

When a JFS file system is created, a log logical volume is also created if it does not already exist. A log logical volume can support several file systems within a volume group.

Create or update a JFS file system using the SMIT fast path or the crfs and chfs commands (see Fig. 11.8). A new JFS file system may be created in an existing empty logical volume, or a new logical volume will be built to hold the new file system. Be careful when specifying the size of the file system! File system blocks are 512 bytes in size. The general rule of thumb is:

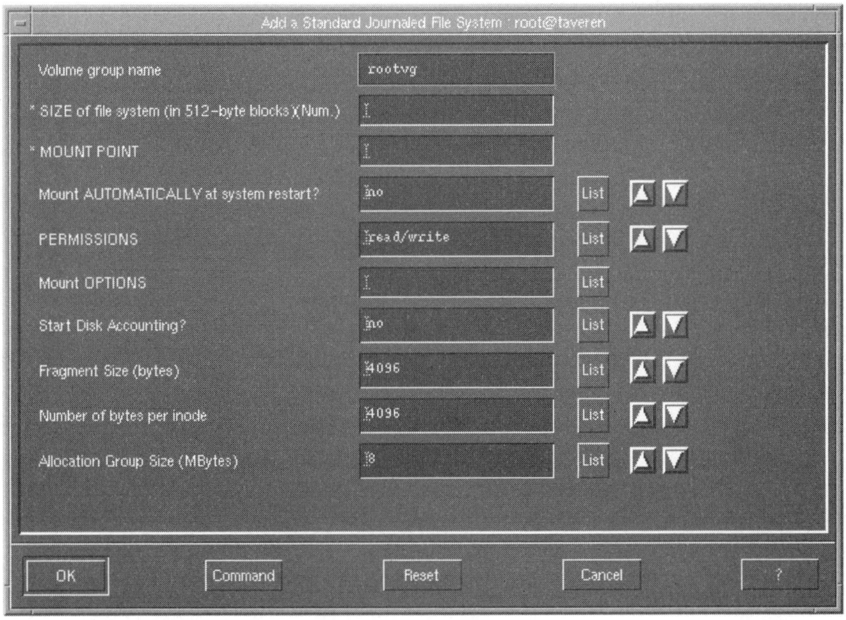

Figure 11.8   SMIT "add journaled file system" panel.

Block size	Action
512	Updating new or existing file system size
1024	AIX commands that report file system use
512–4096	AIX fragment sizes
4096*	Managing logical partitions for logical volumes

If it was any clearer than this, it wouldn't be UNIX, and it sure wouldn't be AIX.

```
# crfs -v jfs -g uservgl -m /u4 -a size=1048576
SMIT crjfs
```

The file system attributes are recorded in the ODM custom databases and the /etc/filesystem file. You may want to edit the /etc/filesystems entry for the new file system to implement accounting or disk quotas:

```
/:
    dev       = /dev/hd4
    vfs       = jfs
    log       = /dev/hd8
    mount     = automatic
    check     = false
    type      = bootfs
    vol       = root
    free      = true

/home:
    dev       = /dev/hd1
    vfs       = jfs
    log       = /dev/hd8
    mount     = true
    check     = true
    vol       = /home
    account   = true
    free      = false
    quota     = userquota

/usr:
    dev       = /dev/hd2
    vfs       = jfs
    log       = /dev/hd8
    mount     = automatic
    check     = false
```

---

* Default logical partition size.

```
type      = bootfs
vol       = /usr
free      = false

/var:
   dev       = /dev/hd9var
   vfs       = jfs
   log       = /dev/hd8
   mount     = automatic
   check     = false
   type      = bootfs
   vol       = /var
   free      = false

/tmp:
   dev       = /dev/hd3
   vfs       = jfs
   log       = /dev/hd8
   mount     = automatic
   check     = false
   vol       = /tmp
   free      = false

/mnt:
   dev       = /dev/hd7
   vol       = "spare"
   mount     = false
   check     = false
   free      = false
   vfs       = jfs
   log       = /dev/hd8

/usr/lpp/info/En_US:
   dev       = /usr/lpp/info/En_US
   vfs       = nfs
   nodename  = fracio.geo.meca.com
   mount     = true
   type      = nfs
   options   = ro,bg,hard,intr
   account   = false
```

You may remove a file system using the rmfs command

```
# rmfs /n5      Remove file system /n5
```

or SMIT.

```
# smit rmjfs
```

11.7.9 Mounting file systems

File system data is made accessible by mounting the file system on a mount point. The mount point is a directory in a previously mounted file system like the root file system. You might think that this is a chicken-and-egg problem; however, the boot procedure handles the special case of mounting the root file system. The mount point is usually an empty directory, but that is not a requirement. If you mount a file system over a populated directory, the previous subdirectory tree is not harmed, but it is no longer accessible until the file system has been unmounted.

File systems may be mounted or unmounted with the mount and umount commands

```
# mount /dev/hd5 /n5      Mount /dev/hd5 on /n5
# umount /n6              Unmount file system /n6
```

or by using SMIT (see Fig. 11.9).

```
# smit mountfs
```

You cannot unmount a file system that is busy. A file system is busy if any application has a file or directory open. This can be caused by an executing process or a user whose current directory path is within the file system. Use tools like fuser and the public domain lsof commands to identify which processes and users have files open.

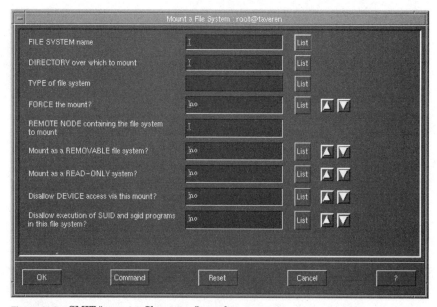

Figure 11.9 SMIT "mount a file system" panel.

```
# fuser -u /dev/hd1     AIX open file lister

/dev/hd1: 32605c(deroest) 43100c(deroest) 47029(root)

# lsof /dev/hd1         Public domain open file lister

COMMAND  PID     USER     FD   TYPE DEVICE      SIZE/OFF INODE/NAME
ksh      32605   deroest  cwd  VDIR 10, 8 1536  18 /home (/dev/hd1)
aixterm  43100   deroest  cwd  VDIR 10, 8 1536  18 /home (/dev/hd1)
ksh      47029   root     63u  VREG 10, 8 2678  78 /home (/dev/hd1)
```

Specify which file systems are to be mounted automatically at boot time by adding the mount=automatic or mount=true parameters for each file system stanza in the /etc/filesystems.

File systems may also be identified as a group by adding a type=<name> parameter for the group in /etc/filesystems. The group name can then be used to mount or unmount all the file systems in the group from a single command.

```
# mount -t nfs     Mount all file systems in /etc/filesystems with type=nfs
```

To display the currently mounted file systems and their state, use the df and mount commands.

```
# df -v

Filesystem   Total KB  used    free    %used  iused  ifree   %iused  Mounted on
/dev/hd4     32768     21876   10892   66%    1239   6953    15%     /
/dev/hd2     499712    456776  42936   91%    17440  107488  13%     /usr
/dev/hd9var  1048576   235524  813052  22%    1687   260457  0%      /var
/dev/hd3     323584    19260   304324  5%     101    81819   0%      /tmp
/dev/hd1     135168    74824   60344   55%    236    33556   0%      /home

# mount

node   mounted        mounted over   fvs   date           options
----   -----------    ------------   ---   ------------    ----------------
       /dev/hd4       /              jfs   Aug 23 12:53   rw,log=/dev/hd8
       /dev/hd2       /usr           jfs   Aug 23 12:53   rw,log=/dev/hd8
       /dev/hd9var    /var           jfs   Aug 23 12:53   rw,log=/dev/hd8
       /dev/hd3       /tmp           jfs   Aug 23 12:53   rw,log=/dev/hd8
       /dev/hd1       /home          jfs   Aug 23 12:55   rw,log=/dev/hd8
```

11.7.10   AIX root tree

The root file system tree was reorganized with version 3.2 of AIX. This was done to organize the data types in the root file system tree to facilitate mounting and maintenance. It also improves compatibility with root trees available on other UNIX platforms. For backward compatability sake, AIX 3.2 incorporates symbolic links emulating the old 3.1 root file system tree.

The AIX 3.2 root file system tree groups operating-system files into the following structure:

AIX 3.2	AIX 3.1 Link	Description
/		Root mount point and superuser shell files
/etc		Machine dependent configuration files
/usr		Shared executables and files
/usr/bin	/bin	
/usr/lib	/lib	
/usr/sbin		
/sbin		Executables and files needed to boot and mount /usr
/dev		Device special files
/tmp		Temporary work files
/var		Machine dependent logs and spool files
/home	/u	User home directories
/export		Server files exported to remote clients

11.7.11   AIX V3 file system compatibility

A number of new parameters have been added to the JFS and LV administration command sets to support the new file system features in AIX V4. Most of these additions show up in mkfs, crfs, lsfs, mklv, and lslv. The output display formats have been modified to include information like fragment size and compression status. If you are concerned with compatibility with other AIX V3.5 systems in your shop, then use the default values for the command parameters. This will result in the creation of an AIX V3.5 file system that can be exported and imported on an AIX V3.5 system. If you wish to migrate an AIX V3.5 file system into AIX V4 format, it will require a backup, file system deletion, and recreation. There are no tools to do this automatically.

As for application compatibility, if you work with file system structures at the highest levels, you'll be fine, assuming you do nothing more esoteric than your standard open, read, write, and close operations. If you like to fiddle at the file system and device structure directly, then you're going to have to modify your existing applications. Many on disk and kernel structures have changed to support the new format. This includes the super block, incore inode, and disk inode structures. The new structure fields and formats indicate the fragment size, inode value (NBPI), status of compression, and file system version. You will most certainly bump up against these changes if you do any disk quota manipulation. A carry bit has been added to the dqblk structure to account for partial fragments. It goes without saying that the quota files themselves are not compatible from AIX V3.5 to AIX V4.

11.8 Paging Space

Paging (swap) space is used by AIX to support virtual memory services. When free memory becomes low or exhausted, AIX moves data pages from primary storage to the paging areas based on a least-recently-used algorithm. A threshold is maintained for virtual memory usage by the operating system. When the threshold is exceeded, a SIGDANGER signal is sent to all processes. If a second threshold, called the kill level, is exceeded, then the operating system sends SIGKILL signals to the biggest memory offenders. This process continues until memory utilization falls below the threshold levels.

In order to keep this kind of trouble from occurring, you need to make sure that sufficient paging space is available. How much is going to depend on your system use profile. What are the average working set sizes required by your work load? Multiuser systems running a number of processes with large working sets may require two or more times the available real memory as paging space. A single-user workstation can get away with far less depending on available real memory and disk. Paging space is allocated as paging logical volumes. You can split up paging space as separate logical volumes on separate physical disks to improve paging performance. Try to limit paging partitions to one per physical disk.

Paging logical volumes can be managed using SMIT (see Fig. 11.10) or the mkps, chps, and rmps commands. Note that you must deactivate

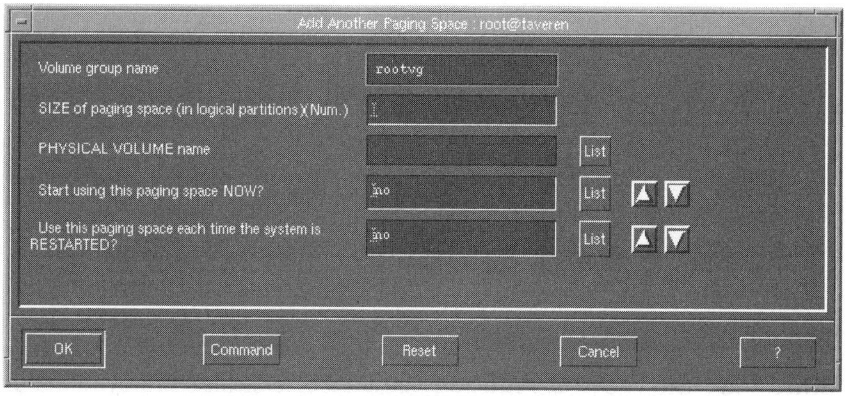

Figure 11.10 SMIT "add paging space" panel.

a paging logical volume and reboot the system before you can remove it. You may increase paging logical volumes while they are active.

# mkps	Add a new paging area
# chps	Increase the size of a paging area
# rmps	Remove a paging area

In SMIT, type

```
# smit mkps
```

New paging areas may be activated with the system up using SMIT or the swapon command.

```
# swapon -a
```

Paging areas that are activated by a swapon -a are identified in the /etc/swapspaces file.

```
hd6:
    dev = /dev/hd6

hd61:
    dev = /dev/hd61

paging00:
    dev = /dev/paging00
```

To display the current allocated paging logical volumes, use the lsps command.

```
# lsps -a
```

Page Space	Physical Volume	Volume Group	Size	%Used	Active	Auto	Type
paging00	hdisk2	fujivg	400MB	29	yes	yes	lv
hd61	hdisk1	rootvg	40MB	61	.yes	yes	lv
hd6	hdisk0	rootvg	40MB	73	yes	yes	lv

Occasionally, stale pages from processes are left on the paging logical volumes. To clean up paging space, use the slibclean command.

| # slibclean | Clean up paging space |

11.9   Volume Maintenance

Other than the cases of reducing the size of existing file systems or paging areas, the AIX LVM and JFS systems make disk management a breeze. It's the "other than" cases that still require a bit of work.

11.9.1   Moving file systems

File systems may be moved within a machine provided there is sufficient free disk space. If you are short on disk space, follow the procedure as described in Sec. 11.9.3 concerning resizing file systems. To migrate the file system logical volume to a new location, use the migratepv command or the SMIT pv FastPath.

1. Use lslv to identify the current logical volume location and produce a physical disk map.

2. Use the migratepv -l command to move the logical volume to its new location.

11.9.2   Moving volume groups

You can also move a volume group from one system to another using the exportvg and importvg commands or the SMIT vg FastPath.

1. Unmount all the file systems and deactivate any paging areas contained in the volume group to be moved.

2. Export the volume group using exportvg.

3. Move the physical disks containing the volume group to the new system.

4. Import the volume group on the new system using importvg. All table references will be updated automatically.

5. Mount the file systems and active paging space on the new system.

11.9.3   Resizing file systems

Increasing the size of a file system, logical volume, or volume group can be done on the fly with SMIT as described in the previous sections. To decrease the size of a file system requires doing things the old-fashioned way: back up the file system, recreate it, and restore the backup. It gets even trickier if you are resizing one of the operating-system file systems like /usr. Let's use /usr as an example since it's a worst-case scenario. Note that, in step 1, if you will be using tape as a backup device, you must make sure that the block size is set to 512.

1. Set the tape device block size to 512.

   ```
   # chdev -l rmt0 -a block=512 -T
   ```

2. Export any non-rootvg volume groups. Makes for peace of mind.

   ```
   # exportvg <VGname>
   ```

3. Invoke mkszfile to create an image.data map of the current file system attributes.

   ```
   # mkszfile
   ```

4. Create a rootvg backup using mksysb.

   ```
   # mksysb /dev/rmt0
   ```

5. Reboot the system from stand-alone media.

6. Choose "Change/Show Installation Settings and Install" from the "Welcome to Base Operating System Installation and Maintenance" menu.

7. Toggle the "Shrink File Systems" selection to "yes." You will then be prompted to select a new size. Note that changing the file system size will override the map created in step 3. *Make sure you leave enough space to restore your backup image!*

8. Insert the mksysb backup media and select "Continue with choices indicated above."

9. Reboot the system after the restore is complete and import the non-rootvg file systems that were exported in step 1.

   ```
   # importvg <VGname>
   ```

10. Reset to the tape device blocksize back to its previous setting.

    ```
    # chdev -1 rmt0 -a block=<size> -T
    ```

11.10   Troubleshooting

Troubleshooting disk hardware, LVM, and file system problems usually require intimate knowledge of the event history leading to the problem. For hardware problems:

- Check error log
- Check cabling
- Check SCSI terminator
- Check SCSI ID jumpers or switch settings
- Run diagnostics

Some versions of AIX had problems with SCSI disks that auto-spinup when powered on. AIX likes to request spinup as part of identifying the device. Disable the hardware auto-spinup if available.

For LVM-related problems, try resynchronizing the ODM and configuration table entries by exporting the problem volume group followed by an import. You can narrow down the problem area by using lslv to display logical volume attributes and maps.

If a file system has become corrupted, take the file system off-line and run the fsck command. fsck will walk the file system structures and identify problem entries or chains. In an emergency situation (no backups), you can use the file system debugger to modify super block and inode entries. Do not try this one unless you are very familiar with these structures.

Occasionally a volume-group-related ODM update may abort leaving the volume group locked. To unlock a volume group, issue a getlvodm/putlvodm sequence using the volume group name as an argument.

```
# putlvodm -K 'getlvodm -v rootvg'    Unlock rootvg
```

11.11 InfoExplorer Keywords

diag	vnodes
cfgmgr	inode
mkdev	/etc/filesystem
PVID	JFS
VGID	fsck
lspv	crfs
mkvg	rmfs
extendvg	mount
lsvg	umount
varyonvg	fuser
varyoffvg	df
chpv	mkps
exportvg	rmps
importvg	chps
rootvg	/etc/swapspaces
mklvcopy	swapon
mklv	lsps
mirgratepv	slibclean
getlvodm	mkszfile
putlvodm	defragfs
istat	mksysb
find	compression
/etc/vfs	fragment
gnodes	

11.12   QwikInfo

- **Disk**

`cfgmgr`	Configure disks added after IPL
`diag`	Diagnostic routines

- **Volume groups**

`mkdev -l <hdisk?> -a -pv=yes`	Create a PVID
`mkvg -f -y <VGname> <hdisk? hdisk?>`	Create a VG
`lsvg`	List VG
`extendvg -f <VGname> <hdisk>`	Add to a VG
`varonvg/varyoff <Vgname>`	VG online/off-line
`importvg/exportvg <VGname> <hdisk?>`	Import/export VG
`putlvodm -K 'getlvodm -v <Vgname>'`	Unlock a VG

- **Logical volumes**

`smit mklv`	Create LV
`lslv`	List LV

- **Journaled File System**

`smit crjfs`	Create JFS
`/etc/filesystems`	File system attributes
`mount, umount`	Mount/unmount file system
`fuser, lsof`	Locate open files
`defragfs`	Defragment a file system

- **Paging Space**

`smit mkps`	Create page space
`lsps -a`	List page space
`swapon -a`	Activate all page space
`/etc/swapspaces`	Paging space table

12

Terminals and Modems

12.1 AIX TTY

We've come a long way from the days when the term *TTY* referred to a real teletype device. I remember the satisfaction of finally leaving the card punches behind and getting access to the teletype lab in my undergraduate days. *TTY* is now loosely used to describe everything from serial cathode ray terminals (CRT) to software-driven pseudo-TTY (PTY) devices. The attributes and configuration options associated with these devices quite often overlap. In many cases, the terminology used to describe these attributes are holdovers from the teletype days. Add to this mix vendor enhancements and you end up with what can be a fairly confusing configuration and management task.

12.1.1 AIX STREAMS subsystem

AIX V4 comes with a whole new TTY subsystem called STREAMS. The architecture originally surfaced in UNIX System V and was later adopted by the OSF. The STREAMS implementation in AIX V4 is SVID 3 compliant and OSF thread safe. What STREAMS brings to AIX is a modular I/O pipe between devices and applications. On the device end of the pipe, the STREAMS driver represents either a real hardware device driver or a software pseudo-device driver. At the opposite end of the pipe, the STREAMS head module links to the user process. Layered in between the head and driver end points are STREAMS modules that manipulate the data passing through the pipe. Protocol stacks can be implemented in real time using the STREAMS architecture by deploying modules that architect the protocol between the network device and application. STREAMS drivers and modules are identified and configured in /etc/pse.conf:

```
#
# PSE Configuration File
#
# format:
#
#        attribute filename [argument [node [minors...]]]
#           [# comment]
#
#                    attribute:    d(river),m(odule),s(tandard),+
#                                  (multi-configure)
#                    filename:     pathname to extension, relative to
#                                  /usr/lib/drivers/pse
#                    argument:     optional argument passed to
#                                  extension's config routine
#                    node:·        alternate node to create (default
#                                  is /dev/filename)
#                    minors:       list of minors to create (nodes
#                                  are strcat(node,minor))
#
#
# PSE drivers and modules
#
d+    stddev echo /dev/echo      # what-u-write-is-what-u-read
d+    stddev nuls /dev/nuls      # streams version of /dev/null
d     spx                        # streams "pipe multiplexor"
m     sc                         # streams config list (scls)
                                      module
m     stdmod tioc                # streams nop tioc module
```

12.2   Serial TTY Support

One might think that a well-seasoned specification like RS-232D wouldn't still be causing so much grief. I know that a good deal of my gray hair has come from sweating over a soldering iron and a breakout box in the wee hours of the morning trying to get those old TTY and modem connections up and running on the new box in town.

Serial connections have always been a cost-effective way of providing console support for UNIX systems. Modem support on UNIX has waned until the recent demand for dial-up Internet services using PPP and SLIP.

12.2.1   Cabling

First comes cabling. Common RS-232C interfaces use DB25 or DB9 male and female connectors. Signal direction and the wiring configuration at each end of the cable depend on whether you are connecting to a Data Terminal Equipment (DTE) or Data Communication Equipment (DCE) device. DTE devices are usually workstations or terminals. DCE devices are most often modems (modulator/demodulator) devices used for dial-up service. Only a subset of the EIA-CCITT definition signals (see Table 12.1) are used in most instances.

Vintage RS/6000's are equipped with 10-pin Modu S1 and S2 ports on the back of the system unit. These are similar to the serial interface found on the IBM RT/PC. These interfaces require a 10-pin-Modu-to-DB25 adapter, PN#59F3740 (see Fig. 12.1). Newer RS/6000s provide standard DB25 interfaces.

12.2.2 Modem/DCE wiring

AIX assumes a DCE (modem) interface by default (see Fig. 12.2). Modem connections have to see DCD. If carrier is lost on the line, they *must* hang up the connection. There are many horror stories of modems not hanging up the line on a long distance call, resulting in phone bills larger than the national debt. Keep this in mind when wiring up a modem cable.

12.2.3 TTY/DTE wiring

A DTE device, like a TTY or printer, will require a null modem cable or adapter. IBM calls this a Terminal/Printer Interposer. A null modem cable basically connects the transmit line from one end of the connection to the receive line on the other and vice versa to support DTE to DTE communication (see Fig. 12.3). You may also need to wire hardware flow control lines as well.

Most terminals don't use RTS/CTS handshake signals, although this is not a hard and fast rule. There are some vendors that require an

TABLE 12.1 EIA CCITT Interface Signals

DB25	DB9	Abbrev	Name	Direction
1		FG	Frame Ground	
2	3	TxD	Transmit Data	DTE → DCE
3	2	RxD	Receive Data	DTE ← DCE
4	7	RTS	Request To Send	DTE → DCE
5	8	CTS	Clear To Send	DTE ← DCE
6	6	DSR	Data Set Ready	DTE ← DCE
7	5	SG	Signal Ground	
8	1	DCD	Data Carrier Detect	DTE ← DCE
20	4	DTR	Data Terminal Ready	DTE → DCE
22	9	RI	Ring Indicator	DTE ← DCE

Positive voltage = 0, Space
Negative voltage = 1, Mark

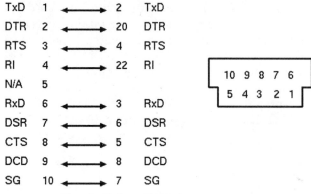

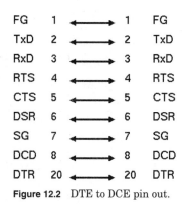

TxD	1	←→	2	TxD
DTR	2	←→	20	DTR
RTS	3	←→	4	RTS
RI	4	←→	22	RI
N/A	5			
RxD	6	←→	3	RxD
DSR	7	←→	6	DSR
CTS	8	←→	5	CTS
DCD	9	←→	8	DCD
SG	10	←→	7	SG

Figure 12.1   Ten-pin Modu to DB25 pin out.

FG	1	←→	1	FG
TxD	2	←→	2	TxD
RxD	3	←→	3	RxD
RTS	4	←→	4	RTS
CTS	5	←→	5	CTS
DSR	6	←→	6	DSR
SG	7	←→	7	SG
DCD	8	←→	8	DCD
DTR	20	←→	20	DTR

Figure 12.2   DTE to DCE pin out.

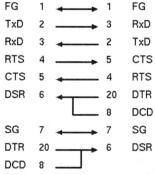

FG	1	←→	1	FG
TxD	2	⟶	3	RxD
RxD	3	⟵	2	TxD
RTS	4	⟶	5	CTS
CTS	5	⟵	4	RTS
DSR	6	⟵	20	DTR
			8	DCD
SG	7	←→	7	SG
DTR	20	⟶	6	DSR
DCD	8			

Figure 12.3   DTE to DTE null modem pin out.

RTS/CTS handshake to jump-start connections before commencing data flow. DSR and RI are only useful for modem connections. AIX assumes a DCE port by default. This means the host will expect to see DCD go high (+12 v), before it will start sending data. For a terminal connection, the DTE-to-DTE pin-out configuration in Fig. 12.3 will satisfy the DCE DCD/DSR condition by raising these lines when the terminal exerts DTR.

You can reduce the number of signal lines required by using soft carrier. *Soft carrier* is a term referring to software pretending that DCD is present. To use soft carrier, you can add clocal to the stty settings defined for the port via SMIT. We will look at SMIT definitions a little later. Using soft carrier, you should be able to run your terminal with the wiring configuration shown in Fig. 12.4.

For twisted pair wiring, use one pair for data send and one pair for data receive. The second wire in each pair should be connected to ground. This will compensate for voltage spikes on the line. For a safe connection, the shield should be connected to frame ground on one end only. If your terminal type requires an RTS/CTS handshake to jump-start the connection, bridge the RTS/CTS together on the device end. This configuration works very well with RJ11/RJ45 to DB25/DB9 modular connectors. These modular connectors can then be used with factory terminated RJ11/RJ45 flat cables. This type of connection will allow you move things around quickly and easily by unplugging the cable from the adapter without having to remove adapter screws.

12.2.4 Serial cable length

How far can these cables be run? According to EIA-232D, cables should not exceed a length of 200 feet, providing they do not exceed a load of 2500 pF (pico-Farads). The lower the capacitance, the longer the cable. The length is also somewhat dependent on baud rate. As standards tend to be on the conservative side, in practice you can run cables much farther than 200 feet. I've run cables over 500 feet, but if you're nervous about playing fast and loose with standards, you can use a short-haul modem or mux to boost the signals.

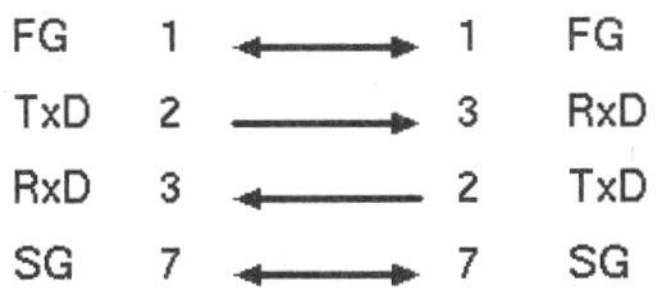

```
FG    1  ◄────────►  1   FG
TxD   2  ─────────►  3   RxD
RxD   3  ◄─────────  2   TxD
SG    7  ◄────────►  7   SG
```

Figure 12.4 Four-wire TTY pin out.

12.2.5 Port addressing

You may notice some ambiguity concerning port and adapter names. The first planar serial port marked S1 is referred to as location 00-00-S1-00, parent adapter sa0, and port number s1. The second serial port labeled S2 follows as location 00-00-S2-00, parent adapter sa1, and port number s2.

TTY location addressing is as follows:

AA.BB.CC.DD

where   AA = Planar, drawer, or expansion and slot number
         BB = Bus and slot number
         CC = Adapter connector number
         DD = Port number

12.3 AIX TTY Definition

Now that the device is cabled and connected to the system unit, define the TTY device characteristics to the operating system. AIX TTY device attributes are stored as ODM objects. The type of information is similar to what you may be used to seeing in the BSD /etc/ttys, /etc/ttytype, and /etc/gettytab files, or the SYSV /etc/inittab, /etc/gettydefs, and /etc/gettytab files. Like SYSV, AIX sets the initial boot state of each TTY in /etc/inittab.

To define or modify TTY attributes, invoke SMIT or use the mkdev command. Considering the number of parameters that must be defined, it will be easier to use SMIT.

If you are adding or updating a large number of devices, add one device via SMIT and then use the $HOME/smit.script file as a boilerplate shell script for defining the remaining devices. Edit the smit.script file and look for the mkdev line used to configure the first device. Remove any old commands and text from previous SMIT runs. Duplicate the mkdev line and update the address information for each new device. Save the file and execute it to configure the remaining devices. This approach is quite useful when configuring terminal servers and concentrators. For best results, make sure the device is powered up during configuration.

```
# smit maktty
# mkdev <options>
```

When updating an existing TTY port, use the SMIT FastPath chgtty. The configuration menu contains the same parameter list as maktty with the exception that the existing port number and location are displayed.

```
# smit chgtty
```

The SMIT menu will display the list of TTY attributes that must be customized for the device type (see Fig. 12.5).

You will need to supply the default line speed, data format, terminal type, control characters, line discipline, and login state. SMIT fills in the fields with default information which will assist you in determining the type and format of the data to be supplied.

12.3.1   Line speed

Line speed is also called baud rate. This is the bits-per-second bandwidth between devices across the wire. Setting this entry is usually straightforward in cases where a single data rate is specified for the device. It gets a little trickier when you want to support multiple data rates for dial-in connections. Supporting multiple data rates is called autobaud. Autobauding allows the port to cycle through a range of baud rates on a time-slice basis or when control break is received on the line. Each data rate is tried until the line speed matches that of the connecting device.

To get autobauding working on the RISC System 6000, enter the desired baud rates separated by commas into the baud rate field. Note that they can be entered in any order. Set the time before advancing to

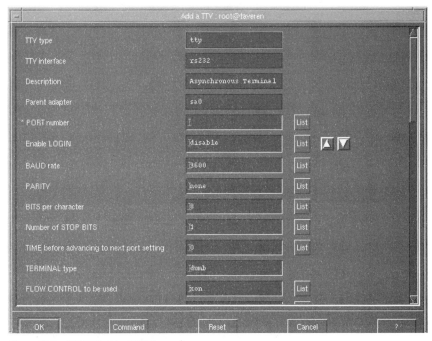

Figure 12.5   SMIT "add a TTY" panel.

next port setting to the number of seconds to wait before cycling to the next baud rate in the list. If the user does not enter a login ID before the time slice expires or sends a control break (ESC), then the next baud rate in the list is tried. The system will continue to cycle through the list until the list is exhausted or the user successfully logs in. If the cycle time is set to 0, manual control breaks are required to cycle through the list.

```
BAUD rate [9600, 19200, 38400]
TIME before advancing to next port setting [6]
```

12.3.2   Data format

When characters are sent across the wire, they are framed into sequences of bits, which enables the hardware and software to validate the data. Each frame is constructed of the data bits followed by a number of stop bits and parity. The most common selections are

```
PARITY                [none]   [even]
BITS per character    [8]      [7]
Number of STOP BITS   [1]      [2]
```

There are also a number of compression and error checking protocols that may be used to send more data across the wire. These techniques are handled by the hardware and do not require configuring into the operating system.

12.3.3   Terminal type

If it is known that a particular terminal type will always be using the port, you may define the terminal name in the terminal type field. The name used must match an entry in the SYSV terminfo and optionally in the BSD termcap files. Each of these files define the attribute character strings that are used by AIX to initialize and control terminal attributes.

For modem connections, you may not know the terminal types that will be connecting to the system. I recommend selecting a terminal type of dumb in this instance. This informs AIX to use very rudimentary terminal control when the connection is established. Use the tset command in the .profile, .login, or shell .rc scripts to query the terminal type after the user logs onto the system. tset can negotiate most of the common terminal types connecting to your system. In the case that it is baffled, it will prompt the user to enter the terminal type and may also be configured to supply a default suggested type.

After terminal type negotiation is complete, login stores the type in the TERM environment variable for use by the various shells and commands.

The following example can be used in a .profile or .login script to prompt the user for a terminal type and suggest a default of vt100 if nothing is entered.

```
tset -m 'dumb:?vt100'
```

AIX interacts with your terminal type based on the characteristics defined in the /usr/lib/terminfo files. Entries in the terminfo are identified by file name descriptors for various vendor terminal devices. Field attributes for a particular terminal type describe the special character sequences used to initialize the terminal, highlight or underline text on the screen, identify function keys, and so on.

The terminfo definitions for each terminal type are stored in binary form. Each terminal file is located in a subdirectory under /usr/lib/terminfo based on the first character of the file name.

Terminfo binaries are compiled from source code definition files by using the tic command. The terminfo source may also be extracted from the binary file by using a public domain program like untic or infocmp. Source code for the distribution terminal types is provided in /usr/lib/terminfo. Source files are identified by a .ti suffix in the file name.

The following is a sample terminfo source:

```
vt102|vt100p|vt100p-nam|dec-vt100p|dec vt100p,
am, mir, xenl, xon, cols#80, lines#24, vt#3,
bel=^G, blink=\E[5m$<2>, bold=\E[1m$<2>,
clear=\E[;H\E[2J$<50>, cr=\r, csr=\E[%i%p1%d;%p2%dr,
cub1=\b, cud1=\n, cuf1=\E[C,
cup=\E[%i%p1%d;%p2%dH$<10>, cuu1=\E[A, dch1=\E[P,
dl1=\E[M, ed=\E[J$<50>, el=\E[K$<3>, home=\E[H, ht=\t,
il1=\E[L, ind=\n, is2=\E[1;24r\E[24;1H, kbs=\b,
kcub1=\EOD, kcud1=\EOB, kcuf1=\EOC, kcuu1=\EOA,
kf1=\EOP, kf2=\EOQ, kf3=\EOR, kf4=\EOS, rc=\E8,
rev=\E[7m$<2>, rf=/usr/lib/tabset/vt100, ri=\EM,
rmir=\E[41, rmkx=\E[?11\E>, rmso=\E[m, rmul=\E[m,
rs2=\E>\E[?31\E[?41\E[?51\E[?7h\E[?8h, sc=\E7,
sgr0=\E[m$<2>, smir=\E[4h, smkx=\E[?1h\E=, smso=\E[7m,
smul=\E[4m,
```

AIX also supplies a rudimentary /etc/termcap file for use with BSD applications. You can also convert termcap definitions into terminfo source using the captoinfo program. The majority of the termcap attribute identifiers map to terminfo identifiers; however, there are some exceptions.

The following is a sample termcap source:

```
vt102|vt100p|vt100p-nam|dec-vt100p|dec vt100p:\
    :am:al=\E[L:b1=^G:bs:cd=50\E[J:ce=3\E[K:cl=50\E[;H\E[2J:\
    :cm=10\E[%i%d;%dH:co#80:cr=^M:cs=\E[%i%d;%dr:dc=\E[P:\
    :dl=\E[M:do=^J:ei=\E[4l:ho=\E[H:im=\E[4h:is=\E[1;24r\E[24;1H:\
    :k1=\EOP:k2=\EOQ:k3=\EOR:k4=\EOS:kb=^H:kd=\EOB:ke=\E[?11\E>:\
    :kl=\EOD:kr=\EOC:ks=\E[?1h\E=:ku=\EOA:le=^H:li#24:\
    :md=2\E[1m:mr=2\E[7m;mb=2\E[5m:me=2\E[m:mi:\
    :nd=\E[C:nl=^J:pt:rc=\E8:rf=/usr/lib/tabset/vt100:\
    :rs=\E>\E[?3l\E[?4l\E[?5l\E[?7h\E[?8h:\
    :sc=\E7:se=\E[m:so=\E[7m:sr=\EM:ta=^I:ue=\E[m:\
    :up=\E[A:us=\E[4m:vt#3:xn:
```

12.3.4 Control characters

The AIX TTY device drivers intercept a set of input control characters defined by the termio interface that force execution of various ioctl routines. These routines do things like start and stop screen display, edit characters in the terminal input buffer, and the like. You are probably familiar with using CTRL-C to interrupt execution of a process, CNTRL-Z to suspend a process, and CTRL-H to erase characters on the command line. These are examples of the interaction the termio control characters and the device drivers. In most cases you will want to take the default character set presented by SMIT. These characters can always be overridden on an individual basis from the command line or from login scripts using the sttv command. The stty command allows you to tailor termio behavior for your session. I'll explain stty further in the following section on line discipline.

# stty -a	Display current termio setting
# stty erase ^?	Define CTRL-? as erase

12.3.5 Line discipline

You will need to define the default runtime and login line discipline options for each TTY port being configured. The login options are those in effect when a connection is made and during login processing. The runtime options are those that control terminal I/O processing after login is completed unless overridden by stty in the login scripts or from the command line (see Table 12.2). In most cases, you can accept the defaults provided by SMIT.

Like the control characters described above, the line discipline options control how TTY I/O processing is handled. Options are set and queried using the stty command. Unlike AIX V3 that supported multiple line discipline types via a stack including POSIX, ATT, and Berkeley, AIX V4 supports a single comprehensive POSIX streams framework. A number

TABLE 12.2 stty Attributes

Option	Runtime/Login	Description
hupcl	R,L	Hang up on close
cread	R,L	Enable receiver
clocal	R	Local line no modem ctl
ignbrk	R	Ignore break
brkint	R	Signal INTR on break
ignpar	R	Ignore parity errors
parmrk	R	Mark parity errors
inpck	R	Input parity checking
istrip	R	Input strip to 7 bits
inlcr	R	Map NL to CR character
igncr	R	Ignore CR
icrnl	R	Map CR to NL character
iuclc	R	Input map upper to lower case
imaxbel	R	Echo bell on input full
isig	R	Check for INTR and QUIT characters
icanon	R	Canonical input with line editing
xcase	R	Canonical upper/lower case
echo	R	Echo input characters
echoe	R,L	Echo erase character
echok	R	Echo NL and KILL character
echonl	R	Echo NL character
noflsh	R	Disable queue flushing
tostop	R	Send SIGTTOU on bg write
echoctl	R	Echo control characters
echoprt	R	Echo ERASE/WERASE chars if ECHO
echoke	R	Echo KILL by erase
flusho	R	Flush output
pending	R	Reprint pending input
iexten	R	Recognize other function data
opost	R	Process output options
olcuc	R	Output map lower to upper case
onlcr	R	Map NL to CRNL
onocr	R	No CR output at column 0
onlret	R	NL performs CR function
ofill	R	Use fill chars for delay
ofdel	R	Fill chars is DEL
tab3	R	Horizontal tab style
cs8	L	Character size 8 bits
Ixany	L	Any char restart output queue
ixon	L	START/STOP handshaking on output queue
ixoff	L	START/STOP handshaking on input queue

of the stty and stack management options are no longer needed and have been removed from the system.

```
[disp, add, del, get] [att, berk, bsd, diag]
```
stty options removed in AIX V4

AIX V3 nl semantics have also changed. Under AIX V4, icrnl, CR to NL mapping occurs when nl is set and disabled for -nl.

12.3.6 Login state

The Enable LOGIN parameter indicates how connections are established to the TTY port after system boot is completed. Use LOGIN state to restrict the port to incoming, outgoing, or bidirectional data traffic. This parameter is very important when setting up lines for modem support. LOGIN state values include ENABLE, DISABLE, SHARE, and DELAY.

ENABLE   Use for direct attach TTY or dial-in-only modem support. AIX starts a getty process for each enabled port. The getty process locks the port for exclusive use. An incoming connection negotiates line speed and raises DCD. Upon detecting DCD, getty presents a login herald on the connection. The connecting system may now login to AIX.

DISABLE   Use for dial-out-only support. No getty process is started and the port is available for dial-out applications like kermit, ATE, and so on.

SHARE   Use for bidirectional support. AIX starts a getty -u on the port, a routine that does not lock the port until it sees the DCD signal go high. The port may be locked and opened for use by other processes. When DCD is present but the port has been locked and in use by another application, the getty process associated with the port loops, attempting to lock. If the port has not been locked, getty will lock the port and present a login herald on the line when DCD is asserted.

DELAY   Similar to SHARE. A getty -r is started on the line. Rather than relying on the DCD signal to indicate a connection request, getty waits for a character on the input buffer before locking the port and presenting the login herald. The port is available to other processes when not locked for use by getty.

The initial TTY state for each port is defined in /etc/inittab. The inittab format is not what you may be familiar with in SYSV UNIX, yet the information supplied is similar.

The following is a sample /etc/inittab entry:

```
Format: Identifier:run level:Action:Command

tty1:2:off:/etc/getty /dev/tty1    Disable tty1 at multi-user.
tty2:2:on:/etc/getty /dev/tty2     Enable tty2 at multi-user.
```

12.4 Modem Support

In the previous sections describing TTY configurations, options associated with DCE devices have been discussed. However, modems require special attention.

12.4.1 Line signals

Most modems come from the factory with settings that assume connection to a personal computer. The idea is to either strap signals high or ignore them altogether to make life easier for the novice PC user. Unfortunately these settings can cause real grief to UNIX systems. Dial-up connections will require that modem be set for auto-answer. For Hayes-compatible modems, auto-answer is enabled by setting the S0 flag to value greater than zero. You will also need to set the TTY port status to "enabled," "shared," or "delay."

ATS0=3   Answer incoming calls on the third ring

If the port state is set to "enabled" or "shared," the getty process will present a login herald when DCD is raised due to modem carrier detection on the wire. The modem should also hang up and drop DCD when remote carrier disappears. This interaction requires that the modem DCD signal follows the presence of the remote carrier.

AT&C1   DCD signal follows remote carrier

If DCD is strapped high on the modem and command echoing is set, this configuration *will* cause a getty race condition when the port is enabled. The getty process sees DCD, so it locks the port and asserts the login herald. The modem echoes back the login herald, which is interpreted as an invalid login attempt; thus, getty respawns and a new login herald is asserted. The modem echos it back. You get the picture? Make certain that DCD follows carrier as described above, and if your applications don't require command echoing, disable it!

ATE0   Don't echo modem command strings

For you UNIX old-timers that still like to use tip, you will need to have the modem always assert DCD. If you intend to use the line for both dial-in and dial-out connections, send the AT&C0 command string to the modem when you intend to use tip.

Modem response strings can also cause problems if they are not set to local only. The "ring" status sent to the port when an incoming call is detected will be echoed back to the modem. The modem thinks that it has received a command, so it dutifully hangs up on the incoming call.

ATQ1   Disable command response strings

You want the modem to enable auto-answer and be ready to accept commands when the RS/6000 presents the DTR signal on open(). When DTR drops on close(), the modem should hang up and reset to accept new connections.

AT&D3   Hang up at DTR drop and reload default parameters

Making certain that DCD and DTR handshaking is working correctly will reduce the possibility of an unforgettably high phone bill.

In most cases you will want to use hardware handshaking for modem connections. For example, XON/XOFF flow control characters will confuse UUCP checksumming.

12.4.2 Problems

To debug or test TTY ports, connect the tty device and enable the port. You should see the login herald displayed on the screen. If the login herald is not displayed, check the cable connections and wiring. If you have a break-out box, add it to the cabling between the device and RS/6000. These devices make it much easier to validate signal connections.

If the characters displayed are garbled, validate that the parity and bit definitions for the TTY device are correct. Parity and bits per character may also be a problem if the login herald is displayed but input characters are not recognized.

For modem lines, you could try playing with ate or kermit, but these applications require a whole level of configuration in themselves. I recommend using the simpler cu program. Disable the line if it isn't already disabled. Add the following stanza to the /lib/uucp/Devices file for the serial port you are using. In the example, I'll assume /dev/tty0, a Hayes modem, and a 19200-baud line speed.

```
Direct tty0 - Any direct
ACU tty0 -19200 hayes \D
```

After adding the port to /lib/uucp/Devices, you should be able to connect to the modem using the cu command. Once connected, you can begin sending commands to the modem.

```
# cu -1 /dev/tty0 -b19200
```

If you have problems, add the -d flag to the cu command to start a diagnostic trace on the connection. If you can't connect, then check the cabling and signals with a break-out box. If characters are garbled, check the line speed, parity, data, and stop bits.

A low-function terminal (LFT) is a pseudo-terminal device that emulates a TTY on a graphics display. Some commands only effect HFT (like chkbd and chsound).

12.5 Low Function Terminals

STREAMS-based low function terminal (LFT) subsystem has replaced the high function terminal device support available in AIX V3. The

LFT subsystems provide a simple serial 25×80 ASCII TTY interface to support system installation, boot, and diagnostics functions. Only one color, one font, and one keyboard table are supported for LFT devices. LFT provides most of the functionality of the HFT driver, but there are exceptions. There is no virtual terminal support under LFT. HFT monitor mode and HFT specific commands and ioctls have been removed. The keyboard is the only valid input device for LFT. The AIXwindows subsystem can be used to support additional devices like mouses, tablets, and dials. AIXwindows is also used to fully exploit graphics hardware capabilities.

HFT Commands Removed in AIX V4

chcolor

chcursor

chhwkbd (supported by keyboard device driver)

chkeymap

chnumvt

chsound

gm

lscolor

lsscreen

mkkbd

open

swkbd

HFT Commands Changed in AIX V4

chdisp	New format
chfont	Requires reboot
chkbd	Requires reboot
lsdisp	New format
lsfont	New format
lskbd	New format
mkfont	Requires reboot

12.5.1 Keyboard

You must define a keyboard map for the type of locally attached keyboard in use on the RS/6000. The keyboard map reflects the location and function of each key on the keyboard. AIX supports three keyboard types: 101-Key Keyboard, 102-Key Keyboard, and the 106-Key Keyboard. The keyboard map is a table that defines the ASCII character string transmitted by each key. The keyboard map tables are located in the /usr/lib/nls/loc directory. Entries in the keyboard map table are configurable as required by custom applications. Source files for each keyboard map table are located in the /usr/lib/nls/loc directory and are identified by the .src suffix.

To create or modify a keyboard map, edit the source file as required and execute the genxlt command to compile the code set. See the InfoExplorer document or man page for the genxlt command for a description of the format of the code set source files.

```
# genxlt < codeset.src > codset.new
```

Keyboard maps are associated with the locale in use. The locale defines the language and code set in use (see Table 12.3). Multibyte code sets are not supported for HFT devices. To display the keyboard maps available, use the lskbd command. Note that many of the commands associated with HFT configuration must be entered from the HFT primary device.

```
# lskbd
```

The current software keyboard map = /usr/lib/nsl/loc/en_US.lftkeymap.

You can also use the setmaps command to set, display, and debug terminal and code set maps. AIX supplied terminal maps are located in the /usr/lib/nls/termap directory.

```
# setmaps              Display current map and code set
# setmaps -t tty-map   Set TTY map
# setmaps -s code-map  Set code set map
```

12.5.2 Display

The RS/6000 supports a number of natively attached displays and graphics adapters. There are some common parameters that may be tailored that span most of these devices. These include the display fonts, color palette for color displays, and cursor shape. You will have to refer to the installation instructions for configuration options specific to the device. Graphics capabilities under AIX V4 are supported under AIXwindows. I can't keep up with IBM development fast enough to list all the options here!

12.5.3 Display fonts

Display fonts are as religious an issue as favorite editors and operating systems. The available HFT fonts are located in /usr/lpp/fonts. You can get a list of the available fonts using the lsfont command.

TABLE 12.3   AIX Locale and Code Sets

Locale	Language	Code set
Da_DK	Danish, Denmark	IBM-850
da_DK	Danish, Denmark	ISO8859-1
De_CH	German, Switzerland	IBM-850
de_CH	German, Switzerland	ISO8859-1
De_DE	German, Germany	IBM-850
de_DE	German, Germany	ISO8859-1
el_GR	Greek, Greece	ISO8859-7
En_GB	English, Great Britain	IBM-850
en_GB	English, Great Britain	ISO8859-1
En_US	English, United States	IBM-850
en_US	English, United States	ISO8859-1
Es_ES	Spanish, Spain	IBM-850
es_ES	Spanish, Spain	ISO8859-1
Fi_FI	Finnish, Finland	IBM-850
fi_FI	Finnish, Finland	ISO8859-1
Fr_BE	French, Belgium	IBM-850
fr_BE	French, Belgium	ISO8859-1
Fr_CA	French, Canada	IBM-850
fr_CA	French, Canada	ISO8859-1
Fr_FR	French, France	IBM-850
fr_FR	French, France	ISO8859-1
Fr_CH	French, Switzerland	IBM-850
fr_CH	French, Switzerland	ISO8859-1
Is_IS	Icelandic, Iceland	IBM-850
is_IS	Icelandic, Iceland	ISO8859-1
It_IT	Italian, Italy	IBM-850
it_IT	Italian, Italy	ISO8859-1
Ja_JP	Japanese, Japan	IBM-932
ja_JP	Japanese, Japan	IBM-eucJP
Nl_BE	Dutch, Belgium	IBM-850
nl_BE	Dutch, Belgium	ISO8859-1
Nl_NL	Dutch, Netherlands	IBM-850
nl_NL	Dutch, Netherlands	ISO8859-1
No_NO	Norwegian, Norway	IBM-850
no_NO	Norwegian, Norway	ISO8859-1
Pt_PT	Portuguese, Portugal	IBM-850
pt_PT	Portuguese, Portugal	ISO8859-1
Sv_SE	Swedish, Sweden	IBM-850
sv_SE	Swedish, Sweden	ISO8859-1
tr_TR	Turkish, Turkey	ISO8859-9.

```
# lsfont

    FONT    FILE            GLYPH   FONT
    ID      NAME            SIZE    ENCODING
    ====    ============    ====    ==========
    0       Erg22.iso1.snf  12x30   ISO8850-1
    1       Erg11.iso1.snf  8x15    ISO8859-1
```

You may define a default font palette that consists of up to 8 alternate font identifiers. Available font alternates are identified by a number ranging from 0 through 8. To make a new font available, use the mkfont -n command.

```
# mkfont -n fontname.path
```

To list all the font identifiers available in the current font palette, use the chfont -l command (see Fig. 12.6).

```
# chfont -l
```

You may switch between alternates by invoking chfont -a.

```
# chfont -a5     Switch display font to alternate number 5
```

You may also set the display fonts and font palette using SMIT.

```
# smit chfont
```

12.6 Console

In most cases the system console will either be the primary display or TTY0. You can redirect console output to another device or file using the chcons and swcons commands. Using a file for console output is helpful when you are administering a large number of machines that may or may not have actual terminals attached to them. The chcons command sets the console path for the next system boot. The swcons command redirects console output for the current session.

```
# chcons pathname     Switch output on next boot
# swcons pathname     Switch output now
```

To check the current console path, use lscons

```
# lscons
/dev/lft0
```

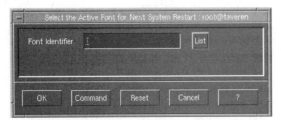

Figure 12.6 SMIT chfont display.

12.6.1 Console problems

If you are running a system without an attached console or sharing a console between systems, make certain that you have the termio option clocal defined for the device. This inhibits console output from blocking if the device is not available. You might end up with multiple srcmstr daemons running if console output is blocked. This situation tends to confuse the srcmstr as the current state of any subsystem it is controlling. Bad news!

In some instances, a TTY device can become hung, or can no longer display output. If the TTY device is also the system console, this can be a real nuisance. In many instances, you can free a hung TTY by writing to /dev/lft[n], directing the stty command sequence to the device, or using the tput command.

Examples:

```
# echo "Open Sez-A-Me"> /dev/lft0
# stty sane
# tput -Tlft clear > /dev/lft0
```

Note that there may be a delay before the commands take effect.

12.7 Pseudo-TTY Devices

A PTY device is represented by a pair of character device drivers in a master/slave pair that implement a pseudo-TTY connection. The master/slave pair may be operating on different systems in a network or on the same computer. The master, /dev/pty, side of the connection sends and receives data like a user at a real TTY. The slave, /dev/tty, side of the connection provides the standard terminal interface to applications like login shells.

AIX implements two PTY interfaces, AT&T and BSD. The AT&T PTY type is opened as /dev/ptc. The operating system allocates both the master PTY and slave TTY devices, which eliminates the need for the application program to test both sides of a PTY connection to determine if it is in use (see Appendix B for sample C code to allocate a PTY pair). AIX V4 differs from AIX V3 in that the number of PTY devices must be preallocated using SMIT chgpty. Under AIX V3, AT&T PTYs were allocated automatically, and the maximum was governed by system resources like the open file table size. The default number of AT&T style PTYs in AIX V4 is 256.

AT&T PTY Naming Convention

/dev/ptc   Master clone driver

/dev/pts/[n]   Slave

BSD-style PTYs are available for use with traditional BSD applications. Like the AT&T PTYs, they must be preallocated using SMIT chgpty (see Fig. 12.7). Default number of BSD-style PTYs is 16. You may create additional BSD PTYs manually using chdev.

BSD PTY Naming Convention

/dev/pty[p-zA-Z][0-f] Master

/dev/tty[p-zA-Z][0-f] Slave

```
# smit chgpty
```

12.8   InfoExplorer Keywords

mkdev	ate
maktty	cu
chgtty	uucp
terminfo	genxlt
termcap	lskbd
tset	setmaps
TERM	mkfont
tic	lsfont
untic	chfont
infocmp	chcons
captoinfo	swcons
stty	srcmstr
getty	lft
/etc/inittab	tput
tip	PTY/pty

12.9   QwikInfo

Serial port settings:

```
smit maktty                 Create TTY port
smit chgtty                 Modify TTY port
cu -l /dev/tty0 -b19200     Test modem port
```

Line states set by /etc/inittab entry:

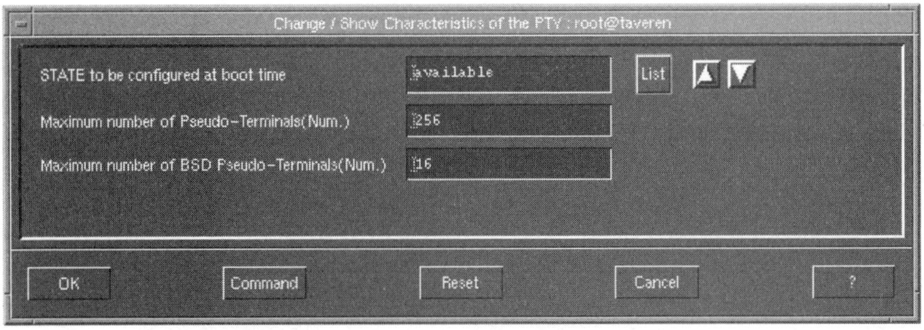

Figure 12.7 SMIT change PTY display.

ENABLE	getty running on port and login herald presented
DISABLE	No getty running on port, dedicated dial out
SHARE	getty -u running on port with no lock; wait for DCD high, then lock and present login herald
DELAY	getty -r running on port; wait for characters on input buffer before presenting login herald

Defining terminal type and attributes:

/usr/lib/terminfo	SYSV TTY database
tic, untic, infocmp	Manage terminfo src
tset -m 'dumb:?vt100'	Query TTY type
/etc/termcap	BSD TTY database
captoinfo	termcap to terminfo src

Line discipline:

stty -a	Display port attributes

LFT devices:

setmaps	Display/set keyboard map and code set
smit chfont	Display/set font set
tput -Tlft clear > /dev/lft[n]	Unlock hung LFT
lscons, chcons, swcons	Console path

PTY devices:

/dev/ptc	Auto alloc AT&T PTYs
smit chgpty	Set number PTYs

13

Printers

13.1 Printing Overview

The AIX printing subsystem provides a rich set of commands and configuration options that go far beyond the printing facilities offered by many other UNIX implementations. If you are familiar with the traditional BSD or SYSV printing environments, you will find that the AIX printing subsystem is not only interoperable with these environments, but that it also involves some significant differences. The printing subsystem in AIX is comprised of approximately forty commands designed to meet the demands of the distributed printing technologies found in most networked work groups. Most of these commands are provided to support compatibility at the user interface level with BSD, SYSV, and older versions of AIX. Users familiar with BSD printing commands will be able to use the same commands and options when printing files on an AIX system. The same holds true for SYSV commands. What's even better is that AIX also provides one command that will do most everything the other forty can do.

At the systems administration level, AIX V4 greatly simplifies the complex printing architecture present in AIX V3. Adding a printer and queue under AIX V3 was a four-step process. You first defined the printer, followed by a queue, queue device, and virtual printer. The architecture does provides valuable flexibility in configuring large complex spooling environments; however, it requires a bit of a learning curve for systems managers.

General spooling configuration has been reduced to two steps in AIX V4. You define a printer that represents the print device attached to the system. Next add a print queue to hold files waiting to be output to the device. If this isn't simple enough, you can use the Visual System Manager (VSM) Print Manager (see Fig. 13.1) to define print-

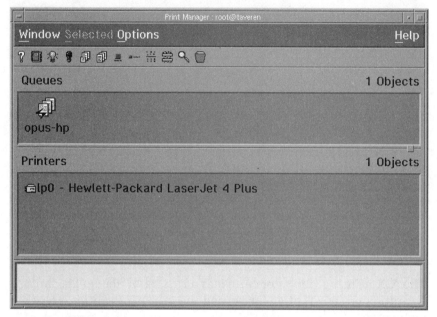

Figure 13.1   VSM print manager.

ers and print queues using a graphical drag-and-drop interface from the AIX CDE desktop. I will say that I found it easier to define a printer and print queue using SMIT. I always worry about assumptions being made by a warm-and-fuzzy software interface. I'm not saying you should hand-code the interface in assembly language and microcode. I just like to have a good idea up front as to what I have defined. At the spooling daemon level, the AIX V4 architecture is much the same as in AIX V3. What has changed is the administration interface. Virtual printers and queue devices are still there—they are just hidden by the administration interface. This can be a bit confusing in itself. Go figure!

AIX V3 Printing Administration

Print device	Device driver and hardware interface
Queue device	Holding area for files waiting to be printed on the associated print device
Queue	Holding area for files waiting for delivery to another queue or queue device
Virtual printer	Logical abstraction of queue and device based on data stream format

AIX V4 Printing Administration

Print device   Device driver and hardware interface

Print queue   Holding area for files waiting to be printed on a local
                      print device

The normal life cycle of a file in the AIX printing subsystem begins when a user or application submits the file for printing with a specified queue name. When the files priority in the queue brings it to the top of the list of waiting jobs, the qdaemon determines the next step in processing based on queue definition stanzas in the /etc/qconfig file. The device and backend entries in the queue stanza indicate how the file is to be filtered and passed to a either a local printer or transfered to a remote site. If the destination is a remote printer, the file is routed over the network to an lpd daemon for further handling. For more information, see Fig. 13.2.

It is the system administrator's responsibility to tailor the stanzas in /etc/qconfig to apply the appropriate filtering and routing to jobs in the queuing subsystem to ensure that they arrive at their destinations with the appropriate attributes for printing. This must be done in a way that hides the complexities of the underlying processing and interfaces from the end users.

Here is a reading of the /etc/qconfig stanzas:

```
lp:
        discipline = fcfs
        up = TRUE
        device = dlp0
```

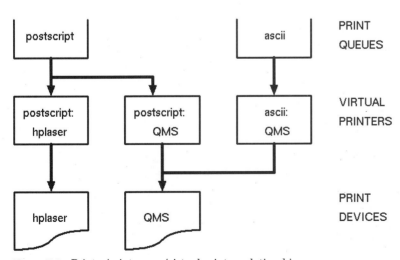

Figure 13.2   Printer/print queue/virtual printer relationship.

```
dlp0:
        file = /dev/lp0
        header = never
        trailer = never
        access = write
        feed = never
        backend = /usr/lib/lpd/piobe
```

The following sections will cover the steps required to configure printers and print queues. Although these procedures will involve tailoring the subsystem interfaces using SMIT, the corresponding stanzas in /etc/qconfig are generated automatically by SMIT. You may find that once you have become familiar with the overall process and the format of the qconfig stanzas, you may wish edit the /etc/qconfig file directly and avoid using the SMIT panels. I would recommend that you avoid doing this initially until you feel comfortable with the interaction of all the components in the printing subsystem.

13.2   Print Devices

Local printer and plotter devices managed by AIX will usually be attached to a serial RS-232/RS-422 port or parallel port. Access to networked print devices is handled by the remote queuing facilities that will be discussed in a later section. The RS/6000 system planar provides both serial and parallel interfaces. You may also use multiport serial adapters available from IBM and third-party vendors for connecting additional devices. The planar female DB25 parallel port may require the use of a DB25 to Centronics adapter cable to connect the device to the system. Older RS/6000 systems require a 10-pin MODU to DB25 or DB9 adapter. The pinout diagrams in Fig. 13.3 describe the serial DB25 interface for the planar connection and the RJ45 to DB25 interface used by the IBM multiport concentrators. Note that the RS/6000 expects to see CTS high when the printer is powered up. You can force the CTS signal high by connecting CTS and RTS on the computer side of the interface if the printer does not supply CTS.

Next review your printer's hardware manual carefully concerning the attributes of the device interface and printing characteristics. These include things like number of bits per character, parity bits, signal handshaking, lines per page, special control codes, and so on. This information will be required to tailor the AIX device driver configuration for the device. Make sure that the device is connected to the system and powered up before beginning the device configuration process. Use the SMIT FastPath mkprt to begin device driver customization (see Fig. 13.4).

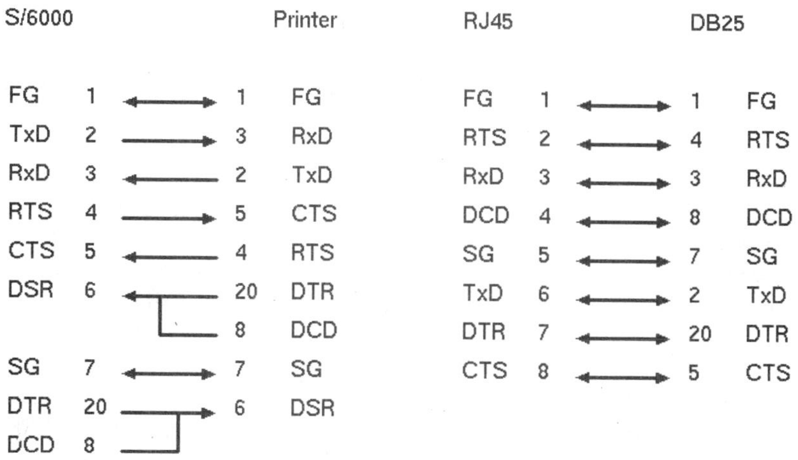

S/6000   Printer   RJ45   DB25

FG	1	→	1	FG
TxD	2	→	3	RxD
RxD	3	←	2	TxD
RTS	4	→	5	CTS
CTS	5	←	4	RTS
DSR	6	←	20	DTR
			8	DCD
SG	7	↔	7	SG
DTR	20	→	6	DSR
DCD	8			

FG	1	↔	1	FG
RTS	2	↔	4	RTS
RxD	3	↔	3	RxD
DCD	4	↔	8	DCD
SG	5	↔	7	SG
TxD	6	↔	2	TxD
DTR	7	↔	20	DTR
CTS	8	↔	5	CTS

Figure 13.3 Serial cable pin out diagram.

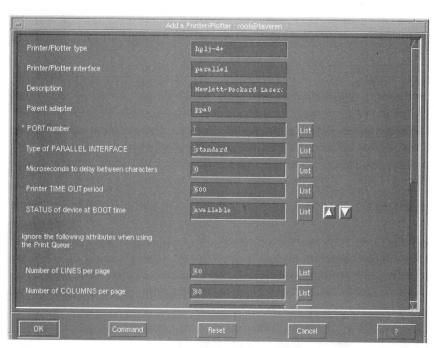

Figure 13.4 SMIT "add printer" panel.

```
# SMIT mkprt
```

Select the SMIT option Add a Printer/Plotter. SMIT will display a set of preconfigured driver selections for various IBM and vendor printers and plotters (see Fig. 13.5). If the device type you are using is not displayed, then select from the options "Other parallel printer or Other serial printer." If the printer you are adding emulates one of the IBM-supplied devices, it may be easier to select one of these entries if you are not certain of the correct device characteristics required for the driver definition. I have always found that there are less headaches involved if you can make one of the standard configurations work. You can always go back later and customize it to meet your requirements.

Note that printer backends are packaged separately in AIX V4 from the spooler. The spooler and commands are included in bos.rte. Printer backends are packaged as printers.rte. Each printer type is also a separate fileset printers.[PrinterType].rte. If the printer's filesets have not been installed when you select a printer type, SMIT will automagically invoke the installp process. This is nice, except it will install *all* of the printers.[PrinterType].rte filesets whether you want them or not!

SMIT will now prompt you for the type of interface you are using (see Fig. 13.6). The screen options displayed will depend on the type of interfaces supported by the previously selected printer model. For

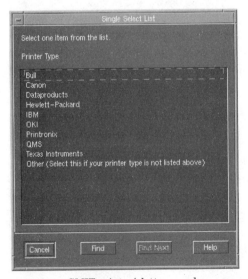

Figure 13.5   SMIT printer/plotter panel.

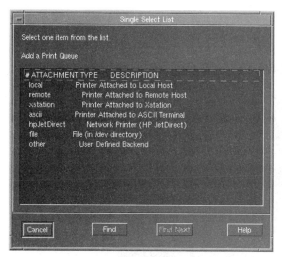

Figure 13.6   SMIT printer/plotter interface panel.

example, a preconfigured entry for a parallel printer will not prompt you for a selection of serial port options like bits per character, parity, and number of start/stop bits. If a serial port is selected, SMIT may further prompt you for parent adapter and port number.

After you have selected the interface type, the real work begins. SMIT will display the panel of driver options supported by the chosen device type. The device driver configuration will determine how the input data stream is interpreted and whether carriage control information is to be generated and/or passed through to the device. For example, a form feed control character can be generated automatically by the device driver and sent to the printer when the input line count exceeds the number specified by "Number of Lines per page" and if "Send Form Feeds" is enabled. Remember that you can get into confusing situations when you have a printer jumpered for generating auto-form-feeds at the desired number of lines and the device driver configured to do the same. Most of the options are self-explanatory but must be mapped closely to the printer's hardware settings and capabilities (see Fig. 13.7).

13.2.1   Testing the device and driver

Once you have completed the device driver configuration, you may test the interface by sending a file directly to the printer, bypassing handling by the queuing system. This can be done using an application like the cat command to direct a file to the device special file name for the printer.

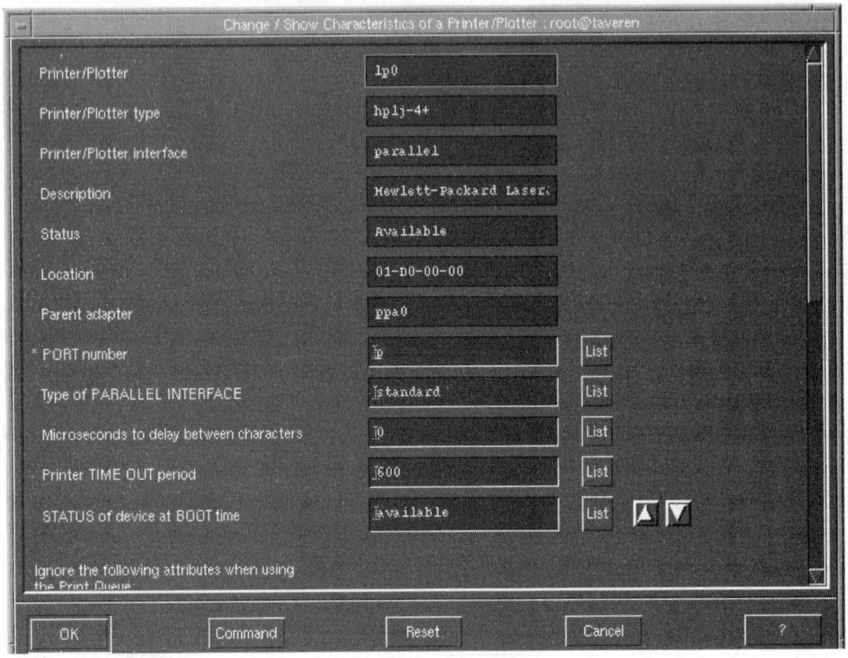

Figure 13.7 SMIT "show/change printer/plotter" panel.

```
# cat [FileName] > /dev/lp0
```

If you want to disable the translation done by the device driver to test the printer hardware interface and settings, use the splp command to enable transparent access to the printer.

```
# splp -p + /dev/lp0           Enable transparent access
# cat[FileName] > /dev/lp0     Direct file to the interface
# splp -p ! /dev/lp0           Enable driver translation
```

Another useful tool for testing the device driver and interface is the lptest command. lptest will produce a ripple pattern of characters that can be directed to the device special file name. You can control the number of columns and lines produced with options on the command line. This is useful when testing line wrap handling and the generation of auto-form feeds.

```
lptest[Columns] [Lines] > /dev/lp0
```

Modifications to the printer device driver may be made via SMIT chgprt. If you have upgraded a system from AIX V3 to AIX V4, note that printer device names have changed. In most instances, you can prefix the printer name with ibm. For example a 4207-2 device becomes ibm4207-2. The device name change may cause problems! Take, for example, the following AIX V3 to AIX V4 print device name changes:

AIX V3 Name	*AIX V4 Name*
4207-2	ibm4207-2
7272	ibm7372

```
# smit chgprt
```

The SMIT panel options are similar to the driver options listed when you initially added the device. You may also update device options from the command line using splp. If no options are included on the command line, then the current driver settings are displayed. /dev/lp0 is used as a default if no device name is specified.

```
# splp

device = /dev/lp0 (+ yes ! no)
CURRENT FORMATTING PARAMETERS (ignored by qprt, lpr, and lp
commands)
Note: -p + causes the other formatting parameters to be
      ignored.
-p ! pass-through?              -c + send carriage returns?
-l 66 page length (lines)       -n + send line feeds?
-w 80 page width (columns)      -r + carriage rtn after
                                     line feed?
-I 0 indentation (columns)      -t ! suppress tab
                                     expansion?
-W ! wrap long lines?           -b + send backspaces?
-C ! convert to upper case?     -f + send form feeds?
CURRENT ERROR PROCESSING PARAMETERS
-T 600 timeout value (seconds)  -e ! return on error?
```

13.3 Print Queues

Print queues are somewhat like teller lines at the bank. Each file waits its turn in line for the next available printer or queue. Just like preferred customer and short transaction tellers, you may define custom scheduling disciplines for high priority and quick job queues. When defining your print queuing topology and scheduling decisions, it will be important to understand the difference between a queue and a queue device. Basically, a queue device holds files for dispatching to local device drivers, whereas as a queue may dispatch to yet another queue or queue device. The procedures for creating both queue types are the same with the exception of the destination as defined by the "file=" stanza. To create a queue, use the SMIT FastPath command mkque.

```
# smit mkpq
```

13.3.1 Local and remote queues

AIX supports both local and remote printer queues. Local queues are used to feed printers directly attached to the local machine, whereas remote queues are local holding tanks for files that are to be transferred over the network to a remote machine. Although both queue types are functionally equivalent, they are configured and handled differently by the queuing subsystem. Common configuration options for local and remote queues require that you supply a queue name, activation state at system boot time, a scheduling discipline, and accounting options. The scheduling discipline defines the priority a job has in relation to other jobs in the queue. Most commonly these are either "shortest job next" (SJN) or "first come first serve" (FCFS). The accounting options will be covered in the chapter on AIX Accounting. You may also specify that the queue is the system default if no queue name is specified on the command line when a job is submitted for printing (see Fig. 13.8).

13.3.2 Backend programs

The primary differences in how files in local and remote queues are handled, are governed by the backend program invoked by the qdaemon for each job in the queue. The backend program is responsible for housekeeping chores, data filtering and conversion, and dispatching the file to

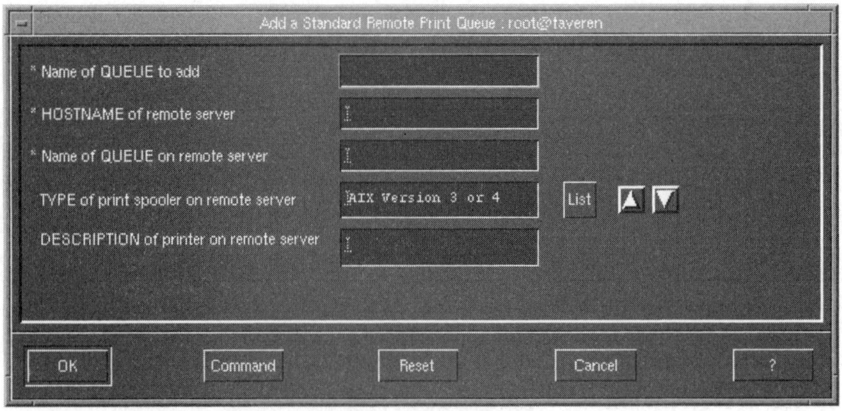

Figure 13.8   Add remote print queue.

its destination. For local queues, the backend program is usually piobe, and for remote queues, the rembak program is used. It is also possible to include your own program or shell script as a backend program for custom applications. A simple batch-scheduling system may be implemented, using the print queuing system to control the dispatching of batch jobs. Backend programs may be used to execute shell scripts submitted by a user with preconfigured resource limits. The queuing system will govern the number of batch jobs executing on the system and delineate priorities based on the scheduling disciplines used.

The default local queue backend, /usr/lpd/piobe, creates a pipe line of filters for converting data formats. The output from the filter stream is directed to the printer with header and trailer pages as specified by the configuration options. Whether the configuration defines a queue, queue device, or custom queue will depend on the values supplied for the backend, file, and access stanzas. In the case of a queue device, the output file is normally the device special file name of the printer. If the queue will be used to dispatch files to other local queues, then the name of the destination queue can be used. For custom applications, you can control the access permissions the backend program has to the output file. Normally, access will be defined as write-only or read/write.

Remote queues are processed by a /usr/lpd/rembak. The rembak backend program creates an lpd control file for each print job that will be passed along with the data file to a remote lpd daemon. These control files contain tag information that specifies the data stream type, origin information, and handling options as specified when the user submitted the job for printing. When configuring the remote queue entry in SMIT, you will need to specify the remote host's domain name and remote queue name. You will also need to specify the short and long filter names to be used to filter the status information passed by remote lpd systems.

13.3.3   Remote BSD and SYSV support

The AIX printing subsystem will interoperate with BSD and SYSV print spooling systems. Many of the standard BSD and SYSV commands are available in AIX to allow users to easily move back and forth between systems in a heterogeneous environment. They don't have to use different commands on each system. As a system administrator, you will find that the AIX printing subsystem is much closer to SYSV than to BSD in the way it handles remote printing. Many of the lpd control file tags supported in the BSD environment are not available in AIX. When print jobs are inbound from a remote BSD system, AIX will ignore these unsupported control file tags. The control file tags used by AIX and SYSV are the same in most cases. Use the bsdshort and bsdlong filter names for remote status queries for BSD systems. Use attshort and attlong for SYSV status information (see Table 13.1).

TABLE 13.1   Queue Status Filters

aixshort	Default AIX short filter
attshort	AT&T short filter
bsdshort	BSD short filter
aix2short	RT short filter
aixlong	Default AIX long filter
attlong	AT&T long filter
bsdlong	BSD long filter
aix2long	RT long filter

13.3.4 Postscript printing

AIX provides support for postscript printing through the use of the Adobe TranScript utilities. These utilities are also available in source code from AT&T as part of the AT&T Tool Kit. These utilities are primarily filters that may be used as backends to convert from ASCII, troff, plot, and Diablo into postscript (see Table 13.2). Postscript header and trailer programs for banner pages are located in the /usr/lpd/pio/burst directory.

13.3.5 Custom backends

You may wish to use your own custom shell scripts and programs as queue backends. If your backend application requires access to variables and data handled by the qdaemon, there is a library of routines supplied in /usr/lib/libqb.a that will allow you to communicate with the elements of the queuing system. Normally your backend program should write to standard out. qdaemon will open and lock the output file specified in the file parameter in the qconfig stanza for you. For a complete list of the routines supported in /usr/lib/libqb.a, see InfoExplorer *Understanding Backend Routines in libqb.a*.

13.3.6 Customizing banner pages

If you will be using header and/or trailer pages for a local queue, you can customize their format to match those used by other systems in your environment. The format templates for burst pages are stored in

TABLE 13.2   Code Conversion

TranScript Utility	Conversion
escript	ASCII to postscript
psc, psdit, psroff	troff to postscript
psplot	plot to postscript
ps630	Diablo to postscript

the /usr/lpd/pio/burst directory. For each format template, a file name prefix of H is used to indicate header definitions and T for trailers. There are sample definitions provided for ASCII, plotter, and postscript banners. The templates consist of program, text, and variable sections. Variables are prefixed with a percent sign (%) (see Table 13.3).

The following is an example of an H.ascii banner:

```
*#######################################################*
* EXAMPLE H.ascii Banner
*#######################################################*
*****************************************************************
%t %T
%p %P
%q %Q
%h %H
%s %S
%d =====> %D <=====
*****************************************************************
%a
%A
*****************************************************************
```

You may wish to add your own custom banner definitions to this directory. Use one of the existing header or trailer pages as a template. You can update the associated queue entry via the SMIT FastPath command chpq. You may find it much easier to simply edit the appropriate printer field in the /usr/sbin/pio/custom file and build a new memory image of the definition for use by piobe. The memory image is built by /usr/lpd/pio/etc/piodigest. The memory images are kept as colon files in the directory /usr/lpd/pio/ddi. Since the piodigest options are a little verbose, you can quickly create a new colon file by executing /usr/sbin/lsvirprt without any attribute options for the given queue or virtual printer name.

```
# /usr/sbin/lsvirprt -d lp0
```

TABLE 13.3   Banner Template Variables

%A	Formatting flag values
%D	Banner user name
%H	Machine name
%P	Time printed
%Q	Time queued
%S	Submitting user name
%T	Title
%%	Escape for percent sign

Remember to conserve paper. Only use burst pages when they are needed. You may also specify that a single header and/or trailer page will be used for all of a particular user's queued files by grouping. Encourage your users to recycle and keep recycle bins near your printers and plotters.

13.4   Virtual Printers

Virtual printers allow you to direct print jobs to particular queue devices based on the data stream format of the file. A virtual printer name represents a logical view of the queue, queue device, and printers associated with a print job based on its attributes. When you configure a virtual printer you will supply all three of these components. To create a virtual printer, use the SMIT mkvirprt FastPath.

```
smit mkvirprt
```

13.5   Testing and Modifying Printer Configuration

You may test your virtual printer, queue, queue device, and print device combinations with the same tools used when testing the hardware interface and driver. Simply use the virtual printer, queue, or queue device name when using the /usr/bin/cat or /usr/bin/lptest commands.

```
# cat[FileName] > lp
# lptest[Columns] [Lines] > lp
```

It goes without saying that you must verify the operation of the AIX printing subsystem in the same way your end users will interoperate with it. Develop a short suite of print commands and options based on the environments used by your user community to validate the subsystem any time you have made any changes. Depending on your user base, you may need to test all of the AIX, BSD, and SYSV commands.

When you need to display or modify your configuration, it is helpful to remember that AIX uses a two-character command and SMIT FastPath prefix scheme with the unique suffixes that represent virtual printers (virprt), print queues (pq), and print devices (prt). These prefixes are usually mk to add, ls to list, ch to change, and rm to remove a component. For example, the FastPath names to make, list, modify, and remove a print queue are mkpq, lspq, chpq, and rmpq, respectively. This is not always the case, but you may find it a helpful rule that will reduce the time you spend in InfoExplorer. In some cases, you will have to remove the entry and then readd it to make the desired modification.

13.6 qdaemon and /etc/qconfig

The AIX printing subsystem is managed by the master print daemon, /etc/qdaemon. qdaemon is started, refreshed, or stopped similar to other subsystems under AIX with the startsrc, refresh, and stopsrc commands.

```
# startsrc -s qdaemon      Start the qdaemon
# refresh -s qdaemon       Build new /etc/qconfig.bin
# stopsrc -s qdaemon       Stop the qdaemon
```

qdaemon is automatically started and stopped during system boot and shutdown when the init state changes as specified in /etc/inittab.

```
qdaemon:2:wait:/usr/bin/startsrc -s qdaemon
```

qdaemon reads the queuing system configuration from a binary copy of the /etc/qconfig file called /etc/qconfig.bin. The binary copy is automatically created by /usr/lib/lpd/digest when qdaemon is started or refreshed.

Once you have become familiar with the process of configuring the queuing subsystem, you may find it tedious using the SMIT FastPath menus. You can make your modifications by modifying the stanzas in /etc/qconfig with a standard editor. After you have made your changes, refresh qdaemon to bring them into production. Remember that for new printers and plotters you will also need to create the associated device special files.

The following is an example of /etc/qconfig:

```
*
* PRINTER QUEUEING SYSTEM CONFIGURATION FILE
*
* /etc/qconfig
*
* Local Queue Device
*
lp:
    discipline = fcfs
    up = TRUE
    device = dlp0
dlp0:
    file = /dev/lp0
    header = never
    trailer = never
    access = write
    backend = /usr/lib/lpd/piobe
```

```
*
* Remote BSD Queue
*
rp:
   host = daffy.acme.com
   s_statfilter = /usr/lpd/bsdshort
   l_statfilter = /usr/lpd/bsdlong
   rq = applelaser
   device = drp0

drp0:
   backend = /usr/lpd/rembak
*
* PostScript Queue to Convert ASCII
*
ps:
   device = dps
   discipline = fcfs

dps:
   backend = /usr/bin/enscript
   file = lp
*
* Batch Queue for Running Shell Scripts
*
bsh:
   device = bshdev
discipline = fcfs
bshdev:
   backend = /usr/bin/sh
*
* Custom Queue Backend
*
alw:
   device = dalw
   up = TRUE
dalw:
   file = /dev/null
   backend = /usr/local/etc/lpd2prt
```

13.7 lpd Daemon

Inbound print requests from a TCP/IP based network are managed by the /usr/sbin/lpd daemon. The lpd daemon manages incoming job requests from the network and deposits them into the appropriate queues for subsequent processing by qdaemon. Like qdaemon, the lpd daemon is a subsystem that can be started as part of system boot and shutdown processing by adding it to /etc/inittab, or as required from the command line. The /var/spool/lpd/stat/pid file contains the PID of the currently running lpd daemon.

```
# startsrc -s lpd      Start lpd daemon
# stopsrc -s lpd       Stop lpd daemon
```

To control which remote systems may communicate with lpd and access your local queues, you must add the host name of each remote system into the /etc/hosts.lpd file. A single plus (+) character in the hosts.lpd file indicates that any remote system may have access to your local queues.

The following is an example of /etc/hosts.lpd:

```
#
# /etc/hosts.lpd
#
# This file defines which foreign hosts are permitted to remotely
# print on your host. To allow a user from another host to print
# on your host, that foreign hostname must be in this file
#
daffy.acme.com
judy.acme.com
star.acme.com
```

Communication with remote lpd daemons is handled by the writesrv subsystem. If you have trouble communicating with a remote system that is responding to other network services, make certain that the writesrv subsystem is running and that it is listening to a socket.

```
# lssrc -s writesrv            Verify subsystem operative
# ps aux | grep writesrv       Verify process is running
# netstat -a | grep writesrv   Verify socket connection
```

13.8 Administering Jobs and Queues

Now that you have the print queuing subsystem configured, the real fun begins. This might be analogous to opening a new freeway. You are going to need to define policies as to how the system is to be used and provide tools for your traffic cops to keep things flowing smoothly.

Queue management and administration tasks in AIX can be handled by one magical command, /usr/bin/enq. AIX does provide wrapper programs for enq that may be easier to remember, but in most cases they use the same options. Once you have a handle on the option set, it will likely be easier to use enq. If you are familiar with the BSD or

SYSV print management commands, you may use these in the AIX environment to provide uniformity in a heterogeneous environment. For the sake of this discussion, we will focus on enq and its wrapper counterparts. For the weak of heart, you can perform these functions using SMIT. The basic administration responsibilities for the queuing subsystem include starting and stopping access, listing queue jobs and status, promoting jobs in a queue, and removing jobs from a queue. The enq command and its associated wrapper programs may focus the action of each of these tasks to all jobs or queues, specific queues, specific users, or specific jobs using the options listed in Table 13.4.

13.8.1 Starting and stopping queues and printers

From time to time, you may find you will have to stop a queue due to a device malfunction or to let a backlog of jobs clear out before accepting additional print requests. Use qadm or the enq command to manipulate the availability of a queue or device. Note that these commands have no effect on remote queues. To stop qdaemon from sending more jobs to a queue and let the currently queued jobs print use:

```
# qadm -D[Printer]
# enq -D[Printer]
```

To keep qdaemon from queuing more jobs and to kill the currently printing jobs, use:

```
# qadm -K[Printer]
# enq -K[Printer]
```

To bring the queue and printer back online, use:

```
# qadm -U [Printer]
# enq -U[Printer]
```

TABLE 13.4   enq Options

Option	Focus
–A	All queues
–P printer	Specific printer
–u user	Specific user
–# number	Specific job
#L	Long format output
–j	Report job number

13.8.2   Listing print jobs

In order to manipulate jobs in the queuing subsystem or to review their status you will need to display the contents of each queue. This is done using the qchk, qstatus, and enq commands. The display format of each is similar. To list the print jobs in all queues, enter one of the commands:

```
# qchk -A
# qstatus -A
# enq -A
```

To list the jobs queued to a particular printer, use:

```
# qchk -P[Printer]
# qstatus -P[Printer]
# enq -A[Printer]
```

```
Queue   Dev   Status   Job   Files         User   PP   Blks   Cp   Rnk
-----   ---   ------   ---   ----------    ----   --   ----   --   ---
lp0     lp0   DOWN
              QUEUED   35    smit.script   root   40          1    1
              QUEUED   36    payroll.rpt   izar   20          1    2
```

The display will list the jobs by queue and device, status, job number, file name, submitting user, percent printed, size in blocks, copy count, and priority. You will use the information listed in these fields to manipulate the jobs in the queue. The status field provides feedback on the state of the queue, device, and current jobs (see Table 13.5).

13.8.3   Changing priority

There are times when special circumstances require that you change the priority of jobs in a queue overriding the default queuing discipline. It may be that you want to defer printing a large job, or an impa-

TABLE 13.5   Printer State

Status	State
READY	Printer accepting print requests
DOWN	Printer is offline
UNKNOWN	Printer state is unknown
OPR_WAIT	Printer waiting operator response
DEV_WAIT	Printer not ready
RUNNING	Print job being queued or printing
QUEUED	Print job is ready for printing

tient user is leaning over your shoulder with that "I needed this yesterday" look. To change the standing of a job in the queue, use the qpri or enq commands. To move a job up in priority, give it a higher number. You cannot change the priority of jobs in a remote queue. Once the priority is changed, you should see the position related to other jobs in the queue change by the value in the rank field.

```
# qpri -P[Printer] -#[JobNumber] -a[Priority]
# enq -P[Printer] -#[JobNumber] -a[Priority]
```

13.8.4   Removing print jobs

To remove a print job from a queue use the qcan or enq commands. If the job you wish to remove is printing, you will first have to stop the printer before removing the job.

```
# qcan -P[Printer] -x[JobNumber]
# enq -P[Printer] -x[JobNumber]
```

If circumstances require that you remove all jobs in a queue, use the -X flag.

```
# qcan -P[Printer] -X
# enq -P[Printer] -X
```

13.9   ASCII Terminal Printers

Many ASCII terminals support an auxiliary serial port or parallel port for screen print and printing from connected computers. Routing a print job from the remote computer to the auxiliary port on the terminal requires the sending of a special sequence of characters before and after the print job to enable and disable connection to the terminals auxiliary serial or parallel port. The particular control character sequences are terminal specific and may be configured in the terminfo database entry for the given terminal type. Consult your terminal documentation for the specific sequence. Some terminals also include the capability to temporarily ignore control character sequences to support sending non-ASCII data to a printer. Note that this requires that the data stream *not* contain the transparent mode on/off character sequence. The transparent mode on/off sequence can be included with the AUX port on/off sequence in terminfo.

terminfo AUX Print Variables

mc5=[ctl char sequence]   AUX print on
mc4=[ctl char sequence]   AUX print off

To configure a serial TTY printer:

1. Configure TTY port information.
2. Update AUX port on/off control sequence for TTY type in terminfo.
3. Create a virtual printer and print queue for the ASCII type using smit mkpq or the /usr/lib/lpd/pio/piomkpq command.

Dial-up modem ports may be supporting a number of different terminal types. In order to identify the printer terminfo data for a dialup printer connection, set the PIOTERM environment variable to identify the terminfo terminal type.

```
$ set PIOTERM=[Terminal-Type]; export PIOTERM
```

13.9.1 Pass-through mode

A number of public-domain applications exist that will send vt100 auxiliary port sequences to a remote terminal or terminal emulation program. Most of these programs use the following algorithm:

1. Save the TTY state.
2. Set the TTY to raw mode.
3. Send the start aux sequence.
4. Send the file.
5. Send the stop aux sequence.
6. Restore the TTY state.

Many terminal emulation packages for personal computers support vt100 pass-through mode sequences. These include kermit for direct connect and dial-up access and NCSA telnet for TCP/IP.

13.10 X Station Printers

AIX supports printing to printers attached to IBM X Stations. You may also be able to support printing to other vendor X terminals using either lpd or the pass-through mode printing technique described for ASCII terminals. When using the IBM X Station Manager, define an X-station-attached printer to the queuing subsystem with the mkvirprt command.

```
# smit mkvirprt
```

Select option 2, "Printer or Plotter Attached to Xstation," from the SMIT menu and supply the X station name.

You will be asked to supply the interface type, X station model, printer baud rate, parity, bits per character, start/stop bits, and printer model. This is quite similar to the procedure for adding a standard locally attached printer. Refer to the previous sections on print devices and queue devices and queues.

The backend program used for IBM X-station printing is /usr/lpp/ x_st_mgr/bin/lpx. The stanza generated by SMIT for the /etc/qconfig file should look like the following entry:

```
*
* Xstation Queue Device
*
xceed:
    discipline = sjn
    up = TRUE
    device = dxceed

dxceed:
    file = false
    header = never
    trailer = never
    backend = lpx xceed -s 19200,n,8,1
```

13.11   Desktop Print Sharing

The AIX queuing system can interoperate with desktop printers managed under MS/Windows and MacOS using software like Samba and CAP. See Chap. 20 for details.

13.12   InfoExplorer Keywords

qdaemon	rembak	lssrc
/etc/qconfig	piobe	netstat
lpd	/lib/libqb.a	enq
mkprt	/usr/lpd/pio/burst	qadm
cat	lsvirprt	qchk
splp	mkvirprt	qstatus
lptest	startsrc	qpri
chgprt	refresh	qcan
mkpq	stopsrc	

13.13 QwikInfo

`/etc/qconfig`	Printer definitions
`smit mkprt`	Create new printer
`splp =p + /dev/lp0`	Transparent access
`splp -p ! /dev/lp0`	Enable translation
`cat <FileName> > /dev/lp0`	Test the interface
`lptest <Columns><Lines> > /dev/lp0`	Print test pattern
`startsrc -s qdaemon`	Start qdaemon
`/etc/qconfig`	Printer definitions
`bsdlong bsdshort`	lpd control file support
`piobe`	Local print backend
`startsrc -s lpd`	Start lpd remote print
`rembak`	Remote print backend
`/usr/lpd/pio/burst`	Banner pages
`lsvirprt -d lp0`	Create new colon file
`smit mkvirprt`	Create virtual printer
`enq <options>`	Admin print subsystem
`stty-lion`	64-pt concentrator print

Network Configuration and Customizing

14

Network Architecture

14.1 Internet History

Network technologies took form and began to appear in the late 1960s. Much of what was available at the time was housed in research labs and based on many different design models. It was recognized early on that differing network models would ultimately result in road blocks to information sharing. Standards organizations came into being to address the problem of interoperability and formulate a common network model. The Open Systems Interconnect (OSI) model was proposed by the International Standards Organization (ISO) and adopted as the basis for the majority network development over the last 30 years.

14.1.1 OSI model

The OSI model is a layered protocol abstraction that is delimited as seven functional interfaces. At the bottom layer, the model defines the hardware interface for transferring data as signals on the physical medium. Higher levels of the protocol specify packet definition, routing, data integrity, and connection authentication. At the highest levels, data formats and user interfaces are defined:

Layer	Name	Description
7	Application	User interface and services
6	Presentation	Application data transformations
5	Session	Connection authentication
4	Transport	End-to-end data ordering
3	Network	Routing and reporting mechanisms
2	Data	Packet format, integrity, and address definition
1	Physical	Physical hardware specification

A unit of data in the model is based on the packet or in newer protocols, the cell. Packets are variable length, whereas cells are fixed length. Each is made up of a header and data component. Depending upon the protocol and layer, header information identifies the type, address, sequence number, and checksum. Each layer in the OSI stack adds or subtracts headers to facilitate end-to-end delivery of the information.

14.1.2   ARPANET

Around the same time that the OSI model was being formulated, the Defense Advanced Research Project Agency (DARPA) funded a project to build a national network connecting government and university research labs. The ARPANET was built using an early point-to-point protocol called the Network Control Program (NCP) and packet-switching minicomputers running a protocol called 1822. This topology was replaced in the early 1980s with the CCITT X.25 packet-switching protocol and a new protocol developed by Bolt, Baranek, and Newman (BBN) called Transmission Control Protocol/Internet Protocol (TCP/IP). The TCP/IP suite was bundled into BSD UNIX 4.2 and, due to popularity and widespread use, became the de facto standard for internetworking.

Internet protocol definitions are based on a request for comment (RFC) process. Draft RFCs are presented to the Internet Activity Board for review. RFC draft status is documented quarterly in the IAB Official Protocol Standards. RFC documents are available from a number of sites electronically via anonymous FTP.

Network bandwidth and security problems quickly overcame the rapidly growing ARPANET community. In the late 1980s, the ARPANET was divided into the Defense Research Internet (DRI) and the National Science Foundation Network (NSFNET). DRI took with it the military research labs from the original ARPANET, leaving the NSFNET to provide wider communication support to universities and other research organizations.

14.1.3   NSFNET

The National Science Foundation (NSF) funded a phased migration from the ARPANET into a new three-level hierarchical topology. A national backbone would interconnect regional networks. The regional networks provide access to the NSFNET backbone to universities and organizations residing in their areas of service. NSFNET bandwidth has migrated from T1 to T3 service in most locations. NSFNET long-distance circuits are provided by MCI and interconnected using IBM-developed nodal switching systems (NSS). Early NSSs were based on nine IBM RTs, which have since been replaced by a single RS/6000, from whence came the early nickname for the NSS, "nine small systems." NSFNET is managed and operated by Merit, Inc.

14.1.4 CREN

While the evolution of the Internet was taking place, two other popular university-based networks converged to form the Corporation for Research and Education Network (CREN), these being the Computer Science Network (CSNET) and the Because It's Time Network (BIT-NET). These networks were originally based on dial-up/X.25 and NJE/BISYNC connections, respectively. CREN is moving toward an IP topology similar to NSFNET. A first step has involved encapsulating NJE in IP for the existing BITNET sites. It's worth mentioning CREN because of the role it played in popularizing network use and the role it will likely play with NSFNET in the future of large-scale networking.

14.1.5 Future NET

With the transformation of NSFNET into a commercial network there is a race going on involving the telcos, cable companies, computer vendors, and the entertainment industry to bring full multimedia services into your living room or workplace. Television, computer gaming, and internetworking are evolving into a new species of home entertainment.

The telcos have the switching equipment but until recently lacked bandwidth from the curb into your home or office. This is changing with new technologies like asymmetric digital subscriber line (ADSL) expected to deliver 1.5 to 9 Mb/sec over the plain old telephone service (POTS) you already have in your home. Cable companies have the bandwidth but lack the switching infrastructure. Cable modems will compete with ADSL and other technologies for the consumer dollar. The computer and entertainment industries hold the applications and products of interest to the home community. Businesses and research sites hold vast data archives. The result is cross industry collaborations and partnerships in an attempt to bring all the pieces together to provide a full-function entertainment and information service.

Concern over available Internet backbone bandwidth has caused a number of regional and corporate Intranets to spring up. These networks are built using dedicated physical layer links to ensure bandwidth availability for corporate business, education, or other information exchanges. Intranets may be connected to the Internet backbone using a firewall or gateway to restrict traffic flows.

14.2   Wireless Networking

If over crowding on the Internet backbone weren't bad enough, what about dealing with mobile and wireless systems? Cellular modems are available in the market for your laptop. Many airplanes support data links from the air phones located on the back of each seat. It's getting to the point that you can't even walk across the hall without carrying your personal digital assistant (PDA) with an infrared link to your workstation or central system. As a matter of fact, I'm sitting on a flight to Australia while I write this text.

14.2.1   History

Radio is the most common transport for long distance wireless connections. The first wireless telegraph system was developed by Guglielmo Marconi in 1895. The first transatlantic telegraph transmission using Marconi's equipment was sent in 1901. By 1915, AT&T had begun testing a radio telephone service. It was a bit expensive for the time at $75.00 per 3-minute call. As radio became popular, problems arose due to the lack of channels in the low-frequency band. Telephone services require a channel for each caller, and a full duplex connection requires double the bandwidth.

14.2.2   Cellular service

To address the bandwidth problem, a scheme was developed to geographically partition the use of radio bandwidth used for telephone service. A partition, called a cell, is serviced by a base station that supports a fixed number of concurrent connections between mobile telephone units. Each cell is geographically distant enough from its neighbors such that frequencies used by one cell could be reused by another. This system becomes very complex when mobile units roam across cell boundaries. Tracking is facilitated by assigning an International Mobile Station Identity (IMSI) to each mobile telephone unit and maintaining location information in a database.

This cellular technology was known in the late 1940s but was not actually tested until the 1960s by Bell Labs in their Advanced Radio Telephone Service (ARTS) and Advanced Mobile telePhone System (AMPS). The AMPS and ARTS systems were put into commercial service in late 1970. In 1983, the FCC merged them into one standard. Competing and incompatible standards were also developed by various countries. Radio waves don't respect commercial or international boundaries; thus, a common cellular standard is required. The group special mobile or global system of mobile communications (GSM) system was developed in 1982 to address cellular interoperability.

14.2.3   Packet radio

In the mid 1960s, packet radio technology was developed for ARPANET. Packet radio uses a terminal node controller (TNC) to packetize a message for transmission via radio waves. The TNC can be thought of as similar to a modem in the telephone system. A TNC can support speeds from 300 bps to 56 kbps, depending on the frequency band and modulation used. Tetherless Access has a spread spectrum technology that has a raw data speed of 160 kbs. Range between stations can be limited; however, intermediate stations can be used to retransmit for long-distance communications. A number of packet protocols are supported via packet radio including TCPIP, X.25, and ROSE (an X.25 derivative).

14.2.4   Mobile IP

Although one can easily use a cellular modem to call a remote internet provider, it is desirable to support subnet and media roaming in the IP world. The Mobile IP group of the Internet Engineering Task Force (IETF) is chartered to develop or adopt the technologies and protocols that would support this type of IP roaming. Analogous to cellular systems, Mobile IP tracks mobile nodes by their home address in a home-agent registry. When a node is roaming away from its home subnet, an in-care-of-address is bound to the home address by a foreign agent. This binding is used to route traffic to the roaming node through the us of IP encapsulation—that is, encapsulating an IP packet within an IP packet. Although this design sounds simple enough, there are additional complexities in determining with how registration occurs, how home agents and foreign agents announce themselves, how mobile node authentication is realized, and how routing may be optimized using mobile route caches. If you are interested in the gory details, take a look at the drafts on the IETF Web page.

14.2.5   Wireless systems

Most wireless systems, whether radio or infrared, employ substations to route wireless traffic through wired networks. For example the Xerox PARC Ubiquitous Computing Project uses infrared transceivers to interconnect palmtops and display panels to standard networked environments. Infrared connections work well over short distances and are best suited to departmental and classroom computing within a building. The University of Washington has a wireless project based on the Xerox PARC model called "Wit." Don't ask me what *Wit* stands for. Wit builds on the wireless-to-wired model through an application programming interface that enables development of partitioned applications. Partitioned applications are those that can be separated into mobile and stationary components. Partioning provides a means for taking advantage of the features offered by the wireless and wired components of a LAN.

For longer-haul environments, the Ricochet system from Metricom uses radio receivers mounted on light poles or buildings to provide a campus-wide solution. A Ricochet system has been under evaluation at the University of California at Santa Cruz. The test environment connected academic buildings with two residence halls. Those evaluating the system used cellular modems at rates that varied from 14.4 kbs to 34 kbs, depending on traffic.

14.2.6   Wireless information

There are a large number of mobile and wireless computing projects under way. I don't have the space or the time to include them all here. I apologize to all of you who deserve the mention. Please take the time to browse some of the mobile computing Web pages on the Internet. Terri Watson's page is a good place to start. It contains links to a number of archives, product, and project pages that will give you a better feel for what is possible or near-possible for wireless systems. The Mobile Computing Bibliography has a query system that is also an excellent tool for mining the mobile data stores.

```
http://snapple.cs.washington.edu:600/mobile/mobile_www.html
```

I once read an article by Ray Bradbury concerning the social and personal aspects of mobile computing. Ray stressed that it is important to spend time in introspection. His fear was that mobile computing was taking away these opportunities. For example, long air flights provide us time to consider our situation in life while gazing at the cloudscape from a window seat. I would agree with Ray that the lure of "getting ahead in cyberspace" needs to be put into prospective with the rest of what life has to offer. Go for a walk in the woods and leave the laptop at home! When you do have to work, take advantage of mobility and work in the park or on the beach. Wireless systems have cut the tether to our office, so work in a setting that promotes your creativity. Just don't do it all the time! Even Spock leaves his tricorder at home from time to time.

14.3   AIX Networking

In the following chapters, we will review some of the dominant UNIX networking protocols that make the Internet and Intranets. These include TCP/IP, UUCP, and SNA. This discussion will be followed by application layer protocols required in supporting network file systems, client/server software, security, and network management.

15

TCP/IP

15.1 TCP/IP

The Transmission Control Protocol/Internet Protocol (TCP/IP), a mouthful, to say the least, is the fundamental glue that makes up most of what we call the Internet. TCP/IP is in fact two protocols, as its name suggests. Both protocols make up the software conduit that allows two systems to communicate over network hardware.

15.2 TCP/IP Suite

It's difficult to get a one-to-one mapping between the TCP/IP and OSI models. TCP/IP bundles much of the functionality defined in the OSI model into a smaller number of layers. Rather than attempt to define a TCP/IP to OSI mapping, it will be pertinent to this discussion to present a model of the TCP/IP suite (see Fig. 15.1).

The physical layer represents a conglomeration of hardware interfaces and protocols that interoperate via the conduit defined in the upper layers. These interfaces employ a wide range of data speeds and physical architectures.

The Internetwork layer combines the OSI data link layer and a portion of the OSI network layer. The layer is comprised of two protocols, Internet Protocol (IP) and Internet Control Message Protocol (ICMP). IP and ICMP are connectionless datagram protocols that provide the basic data buckets and control in the network.

The transport layer defines two protocols, Transmission Control Protocol (TCP) and User Datagram Protocol (UDP). TCP ensures a reliable ordered transport, whereas UDP service is unreliable and does not ensure delivery. It has been shown that TCP reliability operations cause a significant bottleneck in network throughput on fast processors and

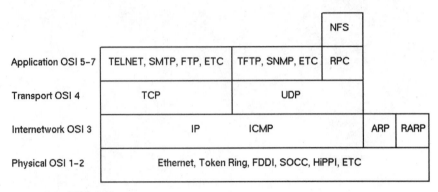

Figure 15.1   TCP stack.

networks. The conjecture is that the current network transports are significantly cleaner than those around when the protocol was defined. TCP checksum processing ties up host cycles that could be better used elsewhere. Newer network interface hardware is moving TCP processing into the interface and off of the host processor to improve throughput.

The application layer in the TCP/IP suite, like the OSI model, implements the user interface. Client/Server protocols are most often defined at the application layer. Common application-level services include Telnet, File Transfer Protocol (FTP), Simple Mail Transfer Protocol (SMTP), Network File System (NFS), and the X11 Window System.

15.3 Planning

Whether you are new to TCP/IP or sport a fair number of stars on your wizard's hat, installing or upgrading your network infrastructure will require some careful planning and plenty of homework. If you aren't considering the implications of the multimedia boom in your bandwidth calculations, then you probably need to increase them by an order of magnitude. Once you turn on the information faucet, your users won't be able to get enough! Have you thought about how you are going to back up all those low-cost multigigabyte disks populating your workstations? How about telecommuting capability? Fortunately, gateway configurations will allow you to mix and match components to meet most of your connection and bandwidth needs. Notice that I did say *most!*

15.4 Hardware Components

The RISC System/6000 supports the gamut of traditional hardware interfaces as well as newer high-speed adapters approaching gigabit-per-second transfer rates. In the following sections I'll outline the attributes of each of the more common network interfaces along with cabling and support hardware. This will include Ethernet, Token Ring, FDDI, SOCC, Serial, and ATM. Other high-speed options like high performance parallel interface (HiPPI) and Fiber Channel Standard are available for AIX, and I would direct you to IBM's Web page for information regarding these technologies and current support.

15.4.1 Ethernet

Ethernet was developed in the early 1980s by Xerox and represents the largest TCP/IP install base due to its low cost (likely being challeged by dial IP). It is a broadcast-based protocol that uses collision detection and avoidance to regulate network traffic. The Carrier Sense Multiple Access/Collision Detection (CSMA/CD) protocol allows any system to start a conversation on the wire but requires it to back off and wait a pseudorandom period of time if it detects that it has interrupted an existing conversation. The wait-before-retry interval is bounded by a multiple of 51.2 microseconds; 51.2 microseconds is the time it takes to transmit a 512-bit packet.

The ether exists on a segment of cable terminated at each end. The segment terminators absorb signals inhibiting reflections from either end of the wire. Computers and other peripheral equipment are connected to the segment using a tap and transceiver. Cable segments are bridged together into larger networks using repeaters.

The most common Ethernet implementation runs at 10 megabits per second. In reality it will only sustain around 1 megabit per second. One hundred megabit Ethernet is available for the RS/6000 and 1 gigabit Ethernet is just around the corner. As of this writing, the standards process is just settling out for 100 megabit Ethernet specification, even though a number of products are already available on the market. One hundred megabit Ethernet will likely replace FDDI due to its low cost. One gigabit Ethernet will certainly give ATM networking a run for the money, although ATM may still win out for long-haul links and where charging per packet is an issue (Telcos).

Ethernet segments are commonly constructed from coaxial or category-5 twisted pair cable. The choice of cable will depend on the environment and dictate the cost. As you might expect, twisted pair is the cheapest and easiest media to install and manage. Newer media options like optical fiber, digital radio, digital microwave, or satellite links may be used between segments to span almost any distance you might have in mind (see Table 15.1).

A transceiver is used to connect the computer adapter to the ethernet segment (see Fig. 15.2). Internal transceivers located on the adapter

TABLE 15.1   Common 10-Megabit Ethernet Media

Type	Medium	Cable	Maximum segment length	Nodes/segment	Topology
10BASE5	Thickwire*	RG 11	500 m	100	Bus
10BASE2	Thinwire†	RG 58	185 m	30	Bus
10BASET	Twisted pair	24 AWG	100 m	16	Star

* Transceivers 2.3 m apart and segment lengths multiples of 23.4 m.
† Transceivers .5 m apart.

card attach to the ethernet segment using a T tap or an RJ-45 plug (10BaseT). External transceivers are powered from the segment itself and attach to the adapter via a drop cable. Drop cables may be constructed using shielded twisted pair or optical fiber, depending on distance requirements. Multiport transceivers may be used to connect multiple machines to a segment using one tap.

RJ-45 10BaseT Pin-Out

Pair	Pin
1 (orange)	1 and 2
2 (green)	3 and 6
3 (blue)	4 and 5
4 (brown)	7 and 8

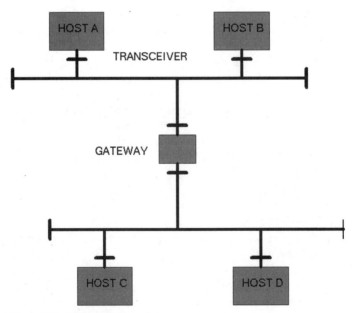

Figure 15.2   Ethernet network.

Drop Cable DB15 Pin-Out

Version 1,2	Pin	IEEE 802.3
Shield (Ground) *	1	Not connected
Collision (+)	2	Collision (+)
Transmit (+)	3	Transmit (+)
Reserved	4	Logic reference (ground)[†]
Receive (+)	5	Receive (+)
Power return	6	Power return
Reserved	7	Not connected
Reserved	8	Not connected
Collision (−)	9	Collision (−)
Transmit (−)	10	Transmit (−)
Reserved	11	Not connected
Receive (−)	12	Receive (−)
Power	13	Power
Reserved	14	Not connected
Reserved	15	Not connected

Configure your Ethernet adapter (see Fig. 15.3) via the SMIT chgenet FastPath. You may want to increase the value of the TRANSMIT buffer. The value represents a queue of buffers for outgoing packets. Values may range from 20 to 150.

```
# smit chgenet
```

Expanding the size of an Ethernet network beyond a single segment requires the use of active devices to recondition packets and to isolate and route traffic. These tasks are performed by repeaters, bridges, and routers, respectively. Repeaters are used to connect segments separated by distance. Remote repeaters are used in pairs and connected together via optical fiber. Repeaters retime and retransmit packets from one segment to the next. Bridges reconstitute packets similar to repeaters. In addition, they learn the addresses of the machines on each side of the bridge and eventually determine whether to pass traffic from one side to the other based on the addresses of the sender and receiver. Routers determine which segment a particular packet must take to reach its destination. Routers exchange data concerning who their neighbors are to create a picture of the network topology.

---

* Version 1,2 shields attached to pin 1 and hood.
† IEEE 802.3 inner shield attached to pin 4, outer shield attached to casing.

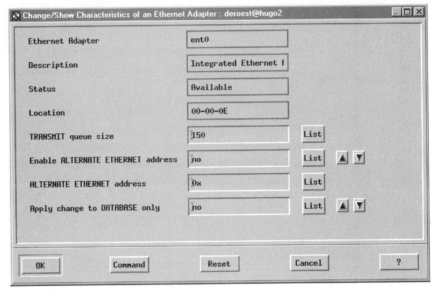

Figure 15.3   SMIT Ethernet adapter panel.

15.4.2   Token ring

Token ring networks provide a little bit better throughput than standard Ethernet. It was originally developed by IBM and later adopted by the IEEE as specification 802.5. Token ring protocol uses a token passing mechanism to regulate traffic on the ring. A particular workstation on the ring must gain control of a token before it can transmit data onto the ring. While data is being transmitted on the ring, a token is not available to other stations. A dual ring topology will provide a degree of fault tolerance. If the ring is broken the dual paths are used to form a new ring. Token ring supports either 4- or 16-megabit-per-second bandwidth. At the high-end token ring can sustain around 12 megabits per second throughput.

Each computer in the ring is configured with an adapter card. The adapter is connected to a multistation access unit (MAU) with an adapter cable. A MAU is a concentrator that supports up to 8-station ports along with a ring-in and ring-out port to interconnect other MAUs. Like Ethernet, repeaters are used to extend distances between MAUs by retiming and retransmitting packets. A repeater may be integrated into a MAU making it an active MAU. MAUs local to the work space can be rack mounted in a wiring closet. A number of cable options are available to fit most environmental, cost, distance, and speed requirements (see Table 15.2).

TABLE 15.2   Token Ring Media

Type 1	22 AWG	2 shielded pairs
Type 2	22 AWG	2 shielded, 4 unshielded pairs
Type 3	24 AWG	1 unshielded pair
Type 5		Solid core optical fiber
Type 6	26 AWG	2 stranded shielded pairs
Type 8	26 AWG	2 parallel shielded pairs
Type 9	26 AWG	2 solid conductor shielded pairs

A star ring topology can be built from a central ring with one or more MAU devices. Dual pair cables connect each MAU to the ring and represent the lobes of the star. For Type 1 cable, lobe lengths can be no more than 100 m with a maximum of 260 stations on the main ring. Type 3 cable, being unshielded, allows no more than 45 m for each lobe unless active MAUs are used to boost distance. A maximum of 72 stations may be attached to a Type 3 main ring (see Fig. 15.4).

Ring traffic control is distributed between all active stations. Each station receives a token or data frame from its nearest neighbor. If the station is not the intended recipient, it retransmits the frame back onto the ring to the next station on the ring (see Fig. 15.5).

```
# smit chgtok
```

15.4.3   Fiber distributed data interface (FDDI)

Fiber distributed data interface (FDDI), ANSI X3T9.5, is a token-passing protocol similar to token ring but implemented using optical fiber rings. FDDI and its copper-based cousin, Copper Distributed Data Interface (CDDI), support data rates at 100 megabits per second. FDDI was designed to be implemented as a network backbone. It has been

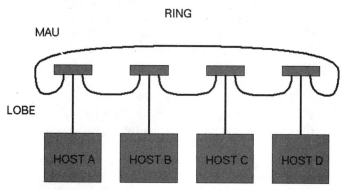

Figure 15.4   Token ring network.

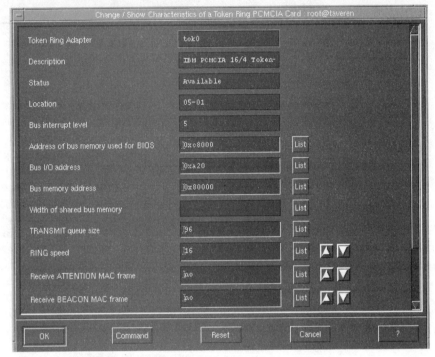

Figure 15.5 SMIT token ring adapter panel.

slow to gain acceptance due to high per-node cost. Although FDDI provides significant bandwidth improvements over standard Ethernet and token ring, it is thought to be too little, too late, when compared with other emerging technologies.

FDDI, like token ring, operates with distributed control over all stations connected to the ring. Each station receives token or data frames from one neighbor and, if not the recipient, passes them on to the next neighbor. The media access control (MAC) layer of the FDDI specification supports tailoring of the token handling time to reflect the data types generally transmitted over the ring. Low-time values provide better interactive response, whereas high values are better for moving large block data.

The RS/6000 supports both single-ring and dual-ring topologies. A single-attach station (SAS) is used for single ring configurations. The dual-attach station (DAS) adapter provides the ability to support a primary and secondary ring topology. In this configuration, the secondary ring supports traffic flow in the opposite direction from the primary ring. This allows a failover ring to be formed in the event that the ring is segmented. Note that the secondary ring is available for fault tolerance only and may not be used as a separate network.

It is recommended that 62.5/125-micron multimode optical fiber be used for each ring. You can get away with using other popular fiber sizes as long as you keep signal loss to a minimum. FDDI concentrators may be connected as lobes in a star ring topology. Fiber distribution panels can be located in wiring closets similar to token-ring MAUs (see Fig. 15.6).

```
# smit chgfddi
```

15.4.4 SLIP/PPP

AIX V4 supports TCP/IP over dial-up lines using serial line internet protocol (SLIP) and point-to-point protocol (PPP). The hardware employed by these protocols uses standard serial ports, modems, and switched lines (see Chap. 12). SLIP is a very simple protocol for framing IP packets on a serial line. It does not support packet addressing or type fields, data compression, or reliability. Only one protocol may be supported on a link at a time. SLIP links must be started manually.

PPP goes further than SLIP by including a link control protocol (LCP) for link control and a set of network control protocols (NCP) to support multiple protocols at a time.

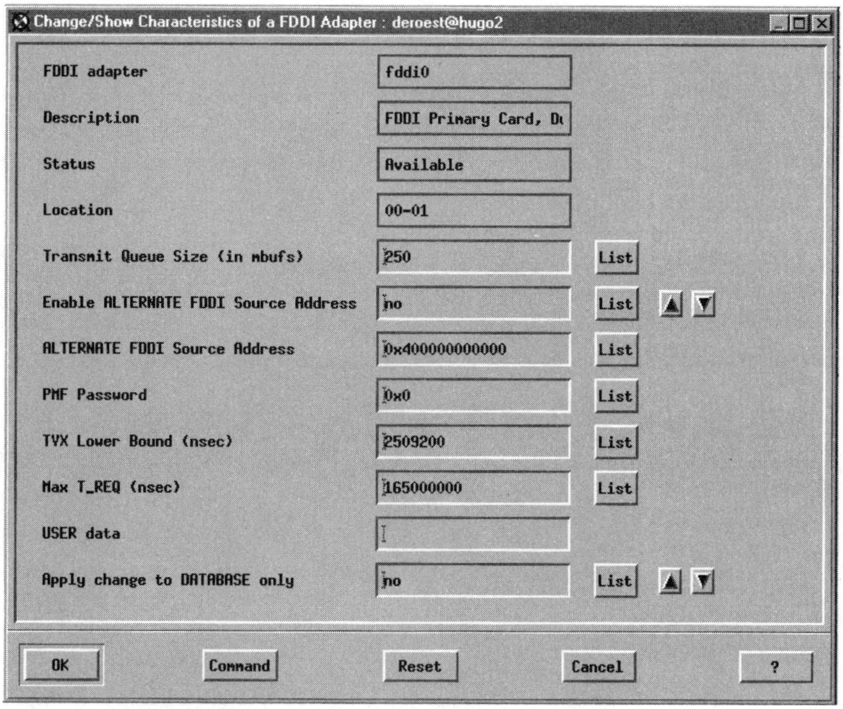

Figure 15.6 SMIT FDDI adapter panel.

To set up a serial port for SLIP/PPP, use SMIT mktty (see Fig. 15.7). In most instances, you will want to use link speeds at or above 9600 bits per second. If the serial port will be used for dial out only set the LOGIN state to DISABLE. For dial-in support, use ENABLE. For dial-in and dial-out, use SHARE.

```
# smit mktty
```

15.4.5 Serial optical channel converter (SOCC)

IBM supplied a proprietary fiber pipe on older RISC System/6000 called the Serial Optical Channel Converter (SOCC). Although the device is not an IBM strategic direction for networking, it does provide a high-speed option for interconnecting RISC System/6000s. SOCC adapters have two half-duplex fiber channels, each operating at 220 megabits per second. The adapters are connected directly to the planar, enabling fast data paths to system memory by bypassing the microchannel bus. The architecture can sustain speeds at 18 megabytes per second in native mode. TCP and UDP are supported at slower rates due to packet processing overhead in the central CPU. SOCC is a

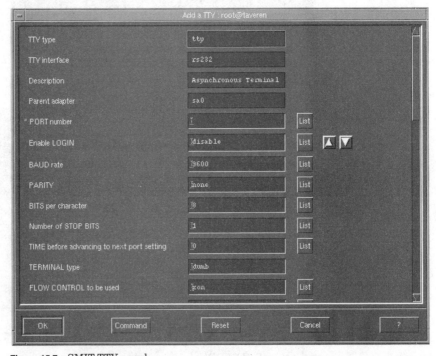

Figure 15.7 SMIT TTY panel.

point-to-point architecture. Network Computing Systems markets a DX switch that may be used to interconnect SOCC adapters in a star topology (see Fig. 15.8). It also provides gateway adapters for Ethernet, token ring, FDDI, HIPPI, and Hyperchannel.

```
# smit opschange
```

15.4.6 Asynchronous Transfer Mode (ATM)

Asynchronous Transfer Mode (ATM) is a full duplex cell-switching protocol that supports end-to-end connections between participating ATM components. ATM systems segment TCP/IP packets (called protocol data units or PDUs in ATM) into 53-byte cells for transmission over the ATM network. Each cell identifies the source and next hop in a pair of header fields called the virtual path identifier (VPI) and the virtual

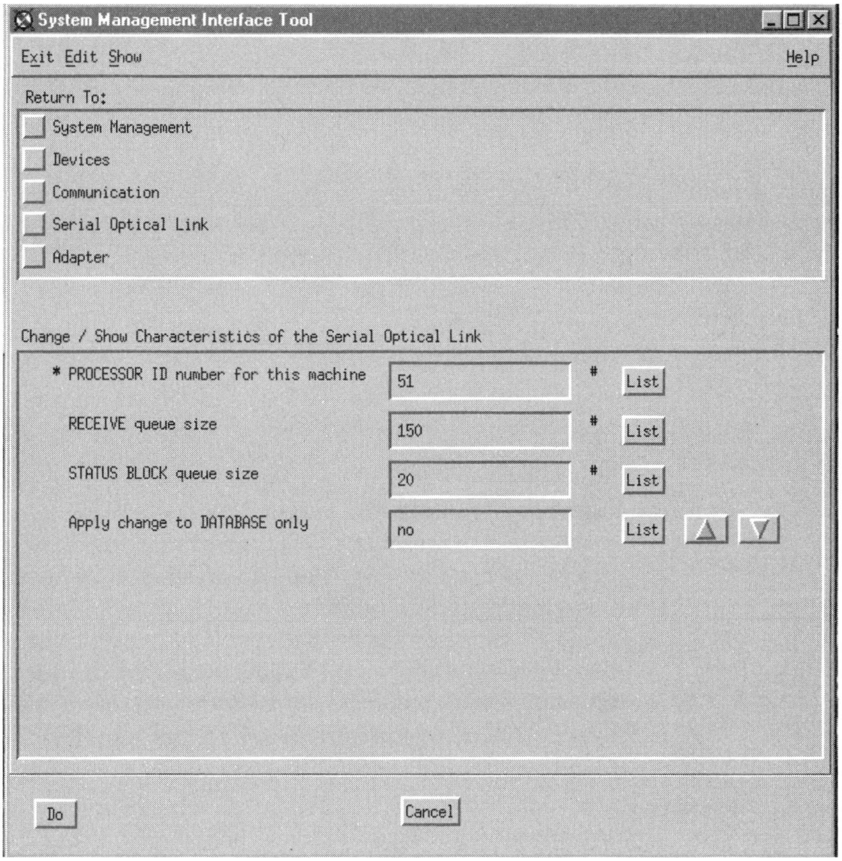

Figure 15.8 SMIT SOCC panel.

channel identifier (VCI). The aggregate of VPI:VCI sets that define the path between the source and recipient, define the virtual circuit. ATM switches bundle together cells that share the same next hop destination. Cells are reassembled into a PDU at the receiving end of the virtual circuit. RFC 1577 defines the specification for supporting TCP/IP over ATM.

AIX V4 supports ATM adapters running at 25, 100, and 155 megabits per second over single- or multi-mode fiber to an ATM switch. Up to 1024 switched or permanent virtual circuits are supported per adapter. Multiple adapters can be tied together using switches with multi-gigabit switched backplanes. Switch-to-switch communication is handled using one or more adapters running at 155 and 622 megabits per second.

15.5   TCP/IP Software Configuration

Under AIX V4 TCP/IP configuration, tables have been decoupled from the ODM. This was accomplished by removing the InetServ object class from the ODM and the associated inetimp and inetexp commands. Keeping the ODM information and configuration tables in synch was a major point of confusion on older AIX V3 systems. In the discussion and examples that follow, you may either update the TCP/IP subsystem tables directly or use SMIT to make configuration changes.

15.6   Addressing

Each computer in the network must be known by a unique identifier. TCP/IP uses three levels of addressing: hardware address, IP number, and domain name.

15.6.1   Hardware address

Manufacturers encode a unique hardware address into each adapter that they produce. You might think that this should satisfy network uniqueness, so why the three levels? Using Ethernet as an example, the hardware address of an interface is a 48-bit number. The first 24 bits identify the manufacturer. The second 24 bits are assigned sequentially to represent each Ethernet adapter produced by the manufacturer. This number is all that is required to identify machines at the physical network layer. These numbers are a bit hard to remember, even when represented in hexadecimal.

15.6.2   IP address

A unique IP address is assigned by the network administrator to represent each computer in the network. The IP address abstracts the hardware address to a more general use. At this address level, we aren't concerned with the adapter interface type used on a particular machine. The IP address format is common across the network.

An IP address is a 32-bit number represented as 4 octets. Each octet is a number in the range of 0 through 255, 255.255.255.255. The address is split into two parts at octet boundaries, representing a network address and a host address on that network. The network and host portions represent address classes. There are three address classes: class A, class B, and class C. See *RFC 1166—Internet Numbers* for a complete description of IP address definition.

IP Address Classes

Class	Address	Hosts
A	N.H.H.H	16M*
B	N.N.H.H	64K*
C	N.N.N.H	254*

N = network address; H = host address.
* Numbers 0, 127, 255 are reserved.

Address classes are assigned to organizations depending on the number of machines they project attaching to the network. If the organization represents a number of departments, it may want to request a class A or class B address. This will allow the group to assign class B or class C network addresses respectively to each of the departments. The departments may then assign and administer the host addresses available within the network address class.

An example class C network address of "128.99.233" will allow the administrator to assign host addresses in the range of "128.99.233.1" through "128.99.233.254". Numbers 0, 127, and 255 are reserved. The number 0 is used to represent an octet unknown to the local host. The number 127 indicates a loopback or local host address. The number 255 is used for broadcast.

Since IP numbers must be unique on the Internet, they are administered by a central authority. InterNIC, the Internet Network Information Center, is a cooperative of the National Science Foundation, Network Solutions, Inc. and AT&T. You can obtain the necessary forms to register your site from InterNIC. Return the completed forms to hostmaster@internic.net. Most internet service providers (ISP) can assist you in obtaining IP addresses and registering your domain with InterNIC. See the InterNIC Web site for information on registries outside the United States.

InterNIC Registration Services
P.O. Box 1656
Herndon, VA 22070
USA
(703) 742-4777

hostmaster@internic.net   (registration)
http://rs.internic.net   (Web site)
rs.internic.net   (FTP site for forms)

Even if you don't initially intend to connect to the Internet, it is a good idea to have the NIC assign you an address class. The address set assigned will be recorded for your use and will not be assigned to any other organization. You may administer numbers within the class. Later on, if you connect to the Internet, it will eliminate the possibility of having to renumber all your host addresses due to address collisions with other sites.

15.6.3   Domain address

Although IP addresses uniquely identify computers on the network, they are not easily remembered. This brings us to the third level in the addressing hierarchy, domain address.

The simple solution is to map host names to the associated IP numbers. These host tables are installed on each machine in the network and provide a directory for host name to IP number address resolution. This works for small networks but immediately breaks down as we scale up to large numbers of systems. Mapping host names to IP numbers is subject to the same scaling problems encountered when mapping given names to phone numbers in a large city. There are far too many name collisions and the phone book is too large for timely incorporation and distribution of updates.

15.6.4   Host tables

For small networks, the simplest address resolution method is to record the host name to IP number of all the machines in the network in a table. The table is then distributed to each machine in the network. This method is implemented by the /etc/hosts file, as in the following example:

```
#
# IP Number Host Names
#
127.0.0.1 localhost
128.95.135.13 daffy
128.95.135.24 louie
128.95.142.30 huey
140.27.133.4  donald
```

15.6.5   Domain name service

To address the scaling problem, a hierarchical name space methodology was adopted for the Internet community that enforces uniqueness and supports timely distribution of updates. This name space system is a client/server protocol called BIND domain name service (DNS).

Computers and organizations in DNS are identified by a domain name. A domain name is a name tuple delimited by dots that represents the administrative hierarchy of the name space of which it is a member. Domain names are usually represented in two to four levels (see Fig. 15.9). Note that there is no implied mapping of subdomains to IP number octets!

Domain Names

Format   hostname.subdomain.subdomain.topdomain

Examples   dingo.bornes.com   vnet.ibm.com

For large networks, the DNS provides a more efficient and distributed name management and resolution. In the DNS hierarchy, upper-level domains (see Table 15.3) need only record the names of the next lower level in the tree along with the IP numbers of the name servers that resolve addresses for that level. A name-resolving protocol called BIND is used to recursively query name servers until a domain name is resolved to an IP number. All name servers must know the addresses of the top-level Internet name servers. This system supports local management of the name space and ensures timely information to the network at large.

Name service for an organization or department is handled by two servers, a primary and a secondary name service daemon, named. You don't need to run named on each machine in your network. The named daemon obtains local configuration information from a local startup file and table. It caches query data it has received from remote name servers to reduce network traffic. The cached data is time-dependent and is flushed periodically.

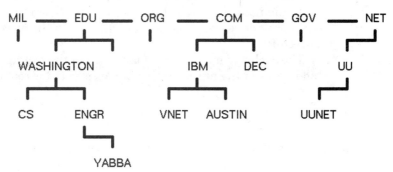

Figure 15.9 Sample internet domain subtrees.

TABLE 15.3 Top Level Domains

EDU	Education
GOV	Government
MIL	Military
ORG	Organizations
COM	Commercial
NET	Other Networks
Country code	Two character international identifier

At initialization time, the named daemon reads /etc/named.boot to determine if it is a primary or secondary server, default domain, zone of authority, and configuration table path. See the following examples:

```
; /etc/named.boot primary
;
directory /etc                                          ; named table path
domain    foo.bar.org                                   ; default domain
cache         .                   named.ca              ; cache file
primary   foo.bar.org             primary/named.data    ; host info
primary   0.0.127.in-addr.arpa    primary/named.rev     ; reverse info


; /etc/named.boot secondary
;
directory /etc                                          ; named table path
domain    foo.bar.org                                   ; default domain
cache         .                   named.ca              ; cache file
secondary foo.bar.org server1     secondary/named.data  ; host info
primary   0.0.127.in-addr.arpa    primary/named.rev     ; reverse info
```

The secondary server will contact the primary server (server1 in the sample) and request a zone transfer of host and reverse pointer information. It will cache local copies of this data in secondary (named.data named.rev) files. This cached data will allow the secondary server to obtain zone information at startup when the primary server cannot be contacted.

Once named has identified the configuration path, it reads the cache file named.ca, the host data file primary/named.data, and the reverse data file named.rev to obtain the remainder of the configuration data. IBM provides sample configuration tables in the /usr/lpp/tcpip/samples directory.

The cache prime file, (/etc/named.ca in the example), defines the IP addresses of the authoritative name servers for root domains:

```
;
; root cache
;
; Initial cache data for root domain servers.
;
```

```
                              999999    IN    NS    NS.INTERNIC.NET.
                              999999    IN    NS    NS.NIC.DDN.MIL.
                              999999    IN    NS    KAVA.NISC.SRI.COM.
                              999999    IN    NS    AOS.BRL.MIL.
                              999999    IN    NS    C.NYSER.NET.
                              999999    IN    NS    TERP.UMD.EDU.
                              999999    IN    NS    NS.NASA.GOV.
                              999999    IN    NS    NIC.NORDU.NET.
;
; Prep the cache (hotwire the addresses). Order does not matter
;
NS.INTERNIC.NET.      999999    IN    A    198.41.0.4
NS.NIC.DDN.MIL.       999999    IN    A    192.112.36.4
KAVA.NISC.SRI.COM.    999999    IN    A    192.33.33.24
AOS.BRL.MIL.          999999    IN    A    192.5.25.82
AOS.BRL.MIL.          999999    IN    A    128.63.4.82
AOS.BRL.MIL.          999999    IN    A    26.3.0.29
C.NYSER.NET.          999999    IN    A    192.33.4.12
TERP.UMD.EDU.         999999    IN    A    128.8.10.90
NS.NASA.GOV.          999999    IN    A    128.102.16.10
NS.NASA.GOV.          999999    IN    A    192.52.195.10
NIC.NORDU.NET.        999999    IN    A    192.36.148.17
```

The host data file, primary/foo, identifies table version number, cache refresh and expire times, query retry time, and host to IP number identification data for zone foo. The reverse file, named.rev, is used to supply IP number to host name mapping. Sample awk scripts are supplied to create named.data and named.rev from existing /etc/hosts tables.

```
# hosts.awk /etc/hosts > /etc/named.data
# addrs.awk /etc/hosts > /etc/named.rev
```

Information in the files are represented as fields. The fields, in order, are, NAME, Time To Live (TTL), CLASS, TYPE, and Resource Data (RDATA). The NAME field identifies the host name associated with the following data. The TTL field indicates the longevity of the information in seconds. The CLASS field indicates the protocol type, which in our case is IN, indicating the Internet. The TYPE and RDATA fields identify descriptive information for the associated NAME. The type of data is based on a set of predefined record types called resource records (RR) (see Table 15.4).

The following displays the contents of named.data:

```
; named.data
;.
```

TABLE 15.4 **Resource Records**

Type	Description
A	IP address of the site
CNAME	Canonical name—other alias names
HINFO	Descriptive host information for the site
MX	Preferred mail handler for the site
NS	Identifies authoritative name server
PTR	Pointer to another part of the name space
SOA	Start of zone of authority
WKS	Well-known services supported at this site

```
; OWNER  TTL       CLASS              TYPE RDATA
;
$ORIGIN foo.bar.org.
@                     IN  SOA server1.foo.bar.org.
(1.1                                 ; serial number for updates
        3600                         ; refresh time seconds
        600                          ; retry time seconds
        3600000                      ; expire time seconds
        86400                        ; minimum
)
;
; Name Servers
;
        99999999  IN  NS             server1.foo.bar.org.
        99999999  IN  NS             server2.foo.bar.org.
server1           IN  A              123.145.100.1
server2           IN  A              123.145.100.2
;
; Host Names
;
daffy             IN  A              128.145.100.13
                  IN  HINFO          "RS/6000-530, AIX 3.2"
                  IN  UINFO          "Jeff Jones, 123-4567"
                  IN  MX             10 mailserver.foo.bar.org
;
donald            IN  A              128.145.100.30
                  IN  HINFO          "DEC Alpha, OSF1"
                  IN  UINFO          "Jenny Smith, 123-6789"
                  IN  MX             10 mailserver.foo.bar.org
```

Here is named.rev:

```
; named.rev
;
; OWNER  TTL       CLASS              TYPE RDATA
;
@         IN        SOA                server1.foo.bar.org.
(                   1.1                ; serial number for updates
```

```
        3600                        ; refresh time seconds
        600                         ; retry time seconds
        3600000                     ; expire time seconds
        86400                       ; minimum
  )
  ;
  ; Name Servers
  ;
        99999999  IN  NS            server1.foo.bar.org.
        99999999  IN  NS            server2.foo.bar.org.
  1               IN  PTR           server1.foo.bar.org.
  2               IN  PTR           server2.foo.bar.org.
  ;
  ; Host Names
  ;
  13              IN  PTR           daffy.foo.bar.org.
  30              IN  PTR           donald.foo.bar.org.
```

The daemon named may also be run as a "caching only" server. In the caching only mode, the server does not supply any preconfigured host data. It only gains data by querying other name servers.

Each machine in the organization that will be using name service must have an /etc/resolv.conf file that identifies the default domain name and a list of name servers. When resolving a name to an IP address, a query is sent to the first name server in the list. If the time-out period expires before an answer is received, then the second-name server is tried.

Here is /etc/resolv.conf:

```
; /etc/resolv.conf
;
domain      foo.bar.org      ; default domain
nameserver  123.145.100.1    ; name server1
nameserver  123.145.100.2    ; name server2
```

15.7 Network Routing

It's not enough to know someone's name in the network. In order to send messages to people, you also have to know where they are and how to get there. Just like the interstate highway system, in order to navigate a network, we rely on information provided by third parties concerning which path to take at each junction. This is called routing.

In the previous discussion on hardware, I talked about how routers and gateways exchange network topology information based on each device's view of its own particular neighborhood. It is this information that we are trusting when we embark on journeys through the network. These devices use a number of tried and true protocols to derive their view of the network at large (see Table 15.5). These protocols are based on algorithms that maintain hop count metrics or compute spanning trees to determine the best route through the network jungle.

Routing information may be determined dynamically by querying the routers for a path from point A to point B or by the use of static routes configured by the system administrator. Static routes work fairly well for small networks, but as with the name space, they break down as the network size gets large.

15.7.1 Static routes

Static routes are set with the route command. In most cases, a default route is set for all instances to a knowledgable local router. Additional static routes may be set for networks and individual hosts. Static routing information is normally set as part of the systems tcpip startup procedures. It may be set via SMIT, or by editing the /etc/rc.tcpip startup script. When adding a static route, specify the type of route (network or host), IP address of the destination, IP address of the router, and the number of hops.

Static Routes

/etc/route -f	Flush all routes
/etc/route add default 123.145.100.10	Default route
/etc/route add net 123.145.50.0 123.145.50.100	Route to a net
/etc/route add host 123.145.40.2 123.145.40.33	Route to a host

You may query defined routes using the netstat -rn command. The -r indicates that netstat is to report routes, and the -n flag specifies not to use name service to determine names. This is much faster and will keep netstat from hanging when there are routing problems that inhibit access to name service.

```
# netstat -rn

Routing tables
Destination    Gateway    Flags    Refcnt Use    Interface
```

TABLE 15.5 Routing Protocols

EGP	External gateway protocol
RIP	Routing information protocol
IGRP	Internal gateway routing protocol
Hello	Initial "fuzzball" NFSnet protocol
OSPF	Open-shortest-path-first protocol

```
Netmasks:
255.0.0
255.255.255

Route Tree for Protocol Family 2:
(root node)
default     128.95.135.100   UG   266   71180277   en0
127         127.0.0.1        U    7     3991       lo0
128.95.135  128.95.135.13    U    191   42439693   en0
```

15.7.2 Dynamic routes

Collecting and/or broadcasting dynamic routing information is the job of the routed and gated daemons. The routed daemon understands the RIP protocol. RIP bases routing data on hop counts. A site with a hop count larger than 16 is deemed unreachable. The gated daemon understands RIP, EGP, and Hello protocols. EGP also responds to simple network monitoring protocol (SNMP) queries. The routed and gated daemons use information configured in the /etc/gateways table to identify other network gateways with which to exchange information. If RIP protocol is used, known networks are also listed in the /etc/networks table. Unless you are setting up a network router, you will want to use routed in query-only mode to learn routes from the active routers in the network. When used, the routed or gated daemons are started with the tcpip subsystem. You may enable them using SMIT or by editing the /etc/rc.net startup script.

/etc/routed -q	Query-only mode
/etc/routed -s	Announce routes
/etc/routed -t	Trace packets
# startsrc -s gated	Start gated daemon

This is a listing of /etc/networks:

```
loop 127 loopback
ethernet 123.145.100
```

Here is /etc/gateways:

```
net FOOnet  gateway server1  metric 0 active
```

15.7.3 Subnets

Subnets are mechanisms that allow an organization with many internal networks to hide the internal structure and routing and announce a single network address to the outside world. A subnet mask is used to mask out a portion of the host half of an IP address to be used for routing. Most commonly this is done by using a class B address known to the outside world and masking the third octet as subnet numbers.

When a machine within the organization wants to send a packet to another system, it applies the subnet mask to the destination address to see if the address is on the local network or if it must send it to a router for delivery.

The subnet mask is a four-octet number that indicates which bits in the address are to be masked as the network and subnet portion of the address. The low-order bits of the mask designate the host portion of the address.

```
netmask 0xfffffff0    14 hosts per subnet (0 and 15 excluded)
netmask 0xfffffff8    6 hosts per subnet (0 and 7 excluded)
```

15.7.4 Interface configuration

To begin using the network, the adapter interface must be configured with the local machine IP address, subnet mask, and broadcast address. The interface may be configured using SMIT (see Fig. 15.10) or by adding an ifconfig entry in the /etc/rc.net startup script. The same

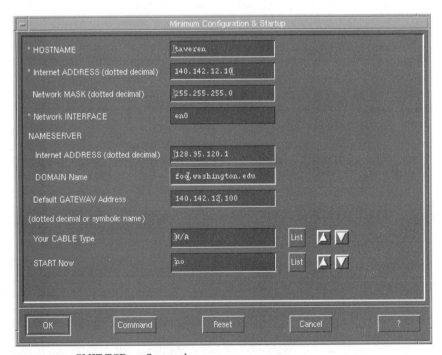

Figure 15.10 SMIT TCP config panel.

command can be used to change the addresses or masks of an adapter, should you need to make changes to the network configuration.

```
# smit mktcpip
```

The adapter interface can be brought up and down for maintenance or testing using SMIT or from the command line using the ifconfig command. Note that this will interrupt service to tcpip daemons.

```
# ifconfig en0 up        Start Ethernet interface
# ifconfig tk0 down      Stop token ring interface
```

The following are the ifconfig parameters:

```
ifconfig en0 123.145.100.18 netmask 0xffffff00 broadcast
123.145.100.255
```

15.8 System Resource Controller

The system resource controller (SRC) is a facility that allows the system administrator to manage easily a group of associated daemons and services as a single entity called a subsystem. Each of the daemons or services belonging to a subsystem are known as subservers. Subsystems that are related in function can be combined as a subsystem group. SRC administration commands allow the system administrator to start, stop, refresh, and trace subsystem groups, subsystems, and subservers as a unit, thus eliminating the complexity of dealing with each component individually.

Here is a list of SRC commands:

startsrc/stopsrc [–g] [–s] <subsystem>	Start/stop a group or subsystem
refresh [–g] [–s] <subsystem>	Refresh a group or subsystem
traceon/traceoff [–g] [–s] <subsystem>	Turn trace on or off
lssrc [–l] [–s] <subsystem>	List subsystem status

The SRC system master daemon, /etc/srcmstr, is started at boot time by an entry in /etc/inittab. Subsystems are also started by entries in /etc/inittab using the startsrc command.

15.8.1 TCP/IP subsystem

TCP/IP runs as a subsystem under AIX. This means that it is under the control of the system resource controller (SRC). The associated daemons that make up the TCP/IP subsystem are known as subservers. Daemons controlled by the master TCP/IP daemon inetd, like ftpd, are known as subservers. All services associated with TCP/IP may be started or stopped using the SRC startsrc and stopsrc commands.

```
# startsrc -g tcpip     Start tcpip services
# stopsrc -g tcpip      Stop tcpip services
```

Further configuration of the TCP/IP subsystem can be completed from the menu bullets listed on the SMIT configtcp panel (see Fig. 15.11). The following sections describe these tables and subservers in detail.

```
# smit configtcp     Customize TCP/IP subsystem
```

15.8.2 Master daemon—inetd

Rather than running some of the TCP/IP service daemons continuously, they can be started when a request is made for the service and shut down when the service has been completed. This capability is supported by the inetd daemon.

Configuration for inetd is located in the /etc/inetd.conf and /etc/services tables. Entries in the /etc/inetd.conf file indicate the service name and startup information. The /etc/service file lists the service name,

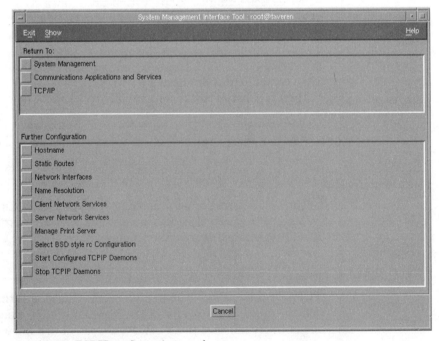

Figure 15.11 TCP/IP configuration panel.

whether it uses TCP and/or UDP protocols, and the well-known port number associated with the service. Anytime updates are made to either of these tables, you will need to refresh inetd. This can be done with SRC refresh command or by sending a hangup signal to the inetd process. Note that some daemons require that the portmap daemon be running. The inetd tables are no longer stored in the ODM. The ODM InetServ object class and associated commands inetimp and inetexp have been removed from AIX V4.

```
# refresh inetd
# kill -HUP <inetd-pid>
```

Here is a listing of /etc/inetd.conf:

```
# inted.conf
#
# service socket protocol wait/ user server server program
# name    type            nowait program  arguments
#
echo      stream tcp      nowait  root internal
echo      dgram  udp      wait    root internal
discard   stream tcp      nowait  root internal
discard   dgram  udp      wait    root internal
daytime   stream tcp      nowait  root internal
daytime   dgram  udp      wait    root internal
chargen   stream tcp      nowait  root internal
chargen   dgram  udp      wait    root internal
ftp       stream tcp      nowait  root /etc/ftpd ftpd
telnet    stream tcp      nowait  root /etc/telnetd telnetd
time      stream tcp      nowait  root internal
time      dgram  udp      wait    root internal
bootps    dgram  udp      wait    root /etc/bootpd bootpd
tftp      dgram  udp      wait    nobody /etc/tftpd tftpd -n
finger    stream tcp      nowait  nobody /etc/fingerd fingerd
exec      stream tcp      nowait  root /etc/rexecd rexecd
login     stream tcp      nowait  root /etc/rlogind rlogind
shell     stream tcp      nowait  root /etc/rshd rshd
talk      dgram  udp      wait    root /etc/talkd talkd
ntalk     dgram  udp      wait    root /etc/talkd talkd
uucp      stream tcp      nowait  root /etc/uucpd uucpd
comsat    dgram  udp      wait    root /etc/comsat comsat
```

The /etc/services file represents the mapping of service name to associated well-known ports:

```
#
# Network well known services
```

```
#
# Service    Port/Protocol Aliases
#
echo         7/tcp
echo         7/udp
discard      9/tcp     sink null
discard      9/udp     sink null
systat       11/tcp    users
daytime      13/tcp
daytime      13/udp
netstat      15/tcp
qotd         17/tcp    quote
chargen      19/tcp    ttytst source
chargen      19/udp    ttytst source
ftp-data     20/tcp
ftp          21/tcp
telnet       23/tcp
smtp         25/tcp    mail
time         37/tcp    timserver
time         37/udp    timserver
rlp          39/udp    resource    # resource location
nameserver   42/udp    name        # IEN 116
whois        43/tcp    nicname
domain       53/tcp    nameserver  # name-domain server
domain       53/udp    nameserver
mtp          57/tcp                # deprecated
bootps       67/udp                # bootp server port
bootpc       68/udp                # bootp client port
tftp         69/udp
rje          77/tcp    netrje
finger       79/tcp
link         87/tcp    ttylink
supdup       95/tcp
hostnames    101/tcp   hostname    # usually from sri-nic
iso_tsap     102/tcp
x400         103/tcp
x400-snd     104/tcp
csnet-ns     105/tcp
pop          109/tcp   postoffice
sunrpc       111/tcp
sunrpc       111/udp
auth         113/tcp   authentication
sftp         115/tcp
uucp-path    117/tcp
nntp         119/tcp   readnews untp
ntp          123/tcp
ntp          123/udp               # network time protocol (exp)
NeWS         144/tcp
snmp         161/udp               # snmp request port
```

```
snmp-trap    162/udp                   # snmp monitor trap port
mux          199/tcp                   # snmpd smux port
src          200/udp                   # System Resource controller
exec         512/tcp
login        513/tcp
who          513/udp   whod
shell        514/tcp   cmd             # no passwords used
syslog       514/udp
printer      515/tcp   spooler         # line printer spooler
talk         517/udp
ntalk        518/udp
efs          520/tcp                   # for LucasFilm
route        520/udp   router routed
timed        525/udp   timeserver
tempo        526/tcp   newdate
courier      530/tcp   rpc
conference   531/tcp   chat
netnews      532/tcp   readnews
netwall      533/udp                   # for emergency broadcasts
uucp         540/tcp   uucpd           # uucp daemon
new-rwho     550/udp
remotefs     556/tcp   rfs_server rfs      # remote filesystem
rmonitor     560/udp
monitor      561/udp
```

Table 15.6 represents a selection of servers that may be managed by inetd. The list is not exhaustive, but it does represent some of the more common applications.

15.8.3   Other network daemons

Not all TCP/IP service daemons (see Table 15.7 for a list) run under control of inetd. You may also choose to run an inetd subserver as a

TABLE 15.6   Inetd Subserver Daemons

ftpd	File transfer daemon for ftp
telnetd	Network login daemon for telnet
rlogind	Network remote login for rlogin
rshd	Remote shell daemon for rsh
rexecd	Remote command execution daemon
sendmail*	Network mail daemon
talkd	Network chat daemon for talk
comsat	Announce incoming mail
fingerd	Display user information for finger
tftpd	Trivial file transfer daemon for tftp
uucpd	TCP/IP to UUCP gateway
bootpd	Support bootp requests
nimesis	AIX network installation manager

   * Sendmail may run as a subserver of inetd or as a standalone subsystem.

TABLE 15.7   TCP/IP Subsystem Daemons

inetd	Master TCP/IP daemon; listens to ports and launches associated subserver daemon
gated*	Routing daemon supports RIP, EGP, and Hello
routed*	Routing daemon supporting RIP
named	Domain name service daemon
iptrace	Packet tracing support
rwhod	List logged in users on subnet systems
timed	Network time server
syslogd	Log daemon for network services

* Make certain that these two daemons are not running at the same time.

stand-alone daemon to service high-traffic loads. This eliminates the overhead involved in restarting the daemon for each service request. Start stand-alone service daemons using an entry in /etc/inittab or from a local rc.local file.

15.8.4   Startup configuration

The TCP/IP subsystem is normally started at system boot via an entry in /etc/inittab. The subsystem /etc/rc.net and /etc/rc.tcpip configuration files contain entries to enable the network interface, set the host name, set the default route, start inetd, and so on. If you want to start tcpip sans SRC and the ODM, comment out the entries in /etc/rc.net following the text "Part I—Configuration using the data in the ODM database." Remove the comments from the section labeled "Part II—Traditional Configuration" and tailor the host name, network interface, and default routes per your installation. For example:

```
#################################################################
# Part II - Traditional Configuration.
#################################################################
#
/bin/hostname lorrie.foo.bar.org        >>$LOGFILE 2>&1
/usr/sbin/ifconfig en0 inet 'hostname' up >>$LOGFILE 2>&1
/usr/sbin/route add default 123.145.100.10 >>$LOGFILE 2>&1
```

15.9   SLIP and PPP

The AIX V4 supports dial up TCP/IP via serial line internet protocol (SLIP) and point-to-point protocol (PPP). The following discussion assumes that a TTY port has been configured for dialing in and out as described in Sec. 15.4.4. Note that standard TCP/IP addressing and routing specifications apply to SLIP and PPP. In the following discussion concerning SLIP support, the configuration requirements have been split up into those used for dedicated SLIP links and those used for ad hoc SLIPLOGIN connections.

15.9.1 Dedicated SLIP

A dedicated SLIP link is a connection between two systems with the same IP and domain addresses. Since this type of link is not being used by multiple systems and users, the infrastructure to support it is not as complex. The AIX slattach command is executed to establish a SLIP link for both client and server connections. Command options include the TTY device to be used, line speed, and a Hayes-type dial string that will be used to establish the SLIP login session. The dial string is modem-dependent and will be set for either dial-out or auto-answer for incoming connections. The format of the dial string is the same as is used by UUCP. For example:

```
"" ATZ OK ATDT123-4567 CONNECT""
```

1. `""`   Null from modem
2. `ATZ`   Send reset to modem
3. `OK`   Response from modem
4. `ATDT...`   Send dial command to modem
5. `CONNECT`   Connection string
6. `""`   Done

For either the client or server side of a SLIP link, configure the interface addresses by invoking the SMIT mkinet FastPath and select "Add a Serial Line INTERNET Network Interface" (see Fig. 15.12).

```
# smit mkinet
```

You can also load the SLIP driver into the kernel and control the interface characteristics from the command line using the strload and ifconfig commands. Make sure you also add domain names for each IP address to be used in the appropriate name service tables.

```
ifconfig sl[n] [options]              Set SLIP interface characteristics
strinfo -m | grep "\'slip\'"          Check if SLIP kernel estension is
                                      loaded
strload -m /usr/lib/drivers/slip      Load SLIP kernel extension
```

On the system that will receive incoming connections, start SLIP using the slattach command with the TTY option. The system will now listen on this TTY port for SLIP requests.

```
# slattach tty[n]
```

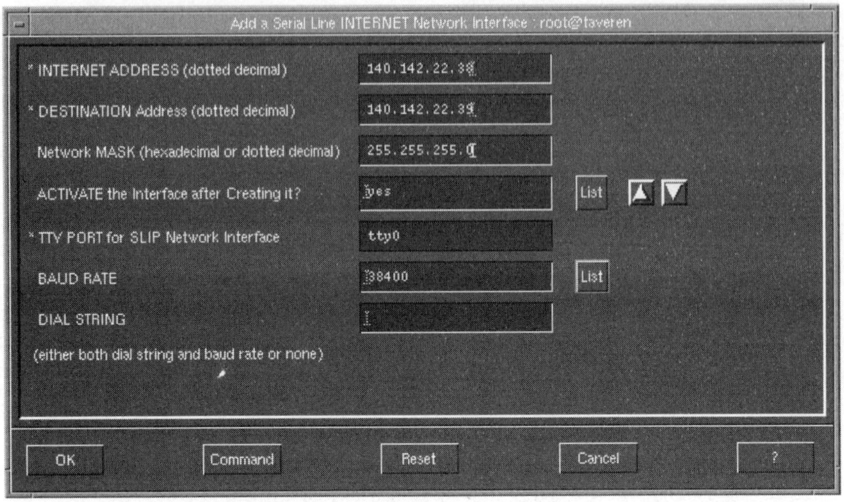

Figure 15.12   SMIT "configure SLIP interface" panel.

On the client dial-out system, start slattach. Note that you may include the baud rate and dial string on the command line.

```
# slattach tty[n] 19200 "" ATZ OK ATDT123-4567 CONNECT""
```

Once connected, you can control the SLIP interface using ifconfig.

```
# ifconfig sl0     Query sl0 interface
```

```
sl0: flags=30<POINTOPOINT,NOTRAILERS>
          inet 140.142.22.38 --> 140.142.22.39 netmask
          0xffffff00
```

To disable a SLIP connection, send a hangup (HUP) signal to the slattach process. Do not use -9 (KILL), as this may cause system panics.

15.9.2 Nondedicated SLIP

A SLIPLOGIN configuration is used for adhoc SLIP connections on interfaces which may be shared between multiple users. This type of link may also support different IP and domain address pairs for each user.

On the server side (dial in support) create AIX user accounts for each dial in user with the shell /usr/sbin/sliplogin. You'll either have to login to each of these accounts and reset the password or remove the ADM-CHG flag from /etc/security/passwords to remove the prompt for password change at first login.

Next edit the /etc/slip.hosts file to set the IP addresses to be used by each user connection. You will also need to add domain names for each IP address in the appropriate name service files. For example:

```
# format: user    server-slip-ip  caller-slip-ip hex subnet mask  options
          fred        7.9.8.1         7.9.8.2        0xffffff00      normal
          fred        7.9.8.3         7.9.8.4        0xffffff00      normal
          Jenny       7.9.8.1         7.9.8.2        0xffffff00      normal
```

Update /etc/uucp/devices to include the options for the dialup connection. This entry can be shared by both SLIP and UUCP.

```
Direct tty0 - 19200 direct
```

Make sure that the /etc/slip.login and /etc/slip.logout files exist and that the kernel extension is loaded.

`ifconfig sl[n] [options]`	Set SLIP interface characteristics
`strinfo -m | grep "\'slip\'"`	Check if SLIP kernel extension is loaded
`strload -m /usr/lib/drivers/slip`	Load SLIP kernel extension

On the client side of a connection, you will need to add IP and domain addresses to your name resolution tables and update the TTY options in /etc/uucp/Devices as described above. Use the slipcall command to start the connection.

```
$ slipcall [number] [tty] [baud] [user name] [password]
```

15.9.3 PPP

Point-to-point protocol (PPP) became available in AIX V4.1.4. PPP goes beyond the simple encapsulation protocol used by SLIP. The link control protocol (LCP) used in PPP can encapsulate and multiplex multiprotocol datagrams. PPP also provides additional session negotiation options, link-level error detection, compression, and authentication.

PPP is a subsystem managed by the system resource controller. The primary PPP control daemon pppcontrold is started as a subserver and is responsible for loading the PPP kernel extensions. One pppattachd subserver is started for each PPP connection. pppattachd binds the PPP and TTY STREAM. Configuration information for the PPP subsystem is stored in the /etc/ppp directory.

To configure the PPP subsystem, begin by invoking the SMIT ppp FastPath. The first step will be to configure LCP (see Fig. 15.13). You will need to choose a subsystem name for LCP. This can be any text string. It is not related to any TCP name service entry. Next define the maximum number of server (inbound connections), client (outbound connections), and demand (sessions started when network traffic detected) connections to be supported by LCP. You can throttle the mixture of server, client, and demand connections by the maximum number of IP interfaces and asynchronous hdlc attachments defined for the subsystem.

```
# smit ppplcp
```

Once the LCP subsystem is defined, you will need to set the IP addresses to be used when PPP connections are established. Invoke the SMIT FastPath pppip (see Fig. 15.14). Identify the local machines IP address, the base IP number for assigned addresses, the number of addresses to be assigned and the subnet mask.

```
# smit pppip
```

If you chose to use authentication for establishing connections, invoke the SMIT ppppap or pppchap FastPath (see Fig. 15.15). Add each user,

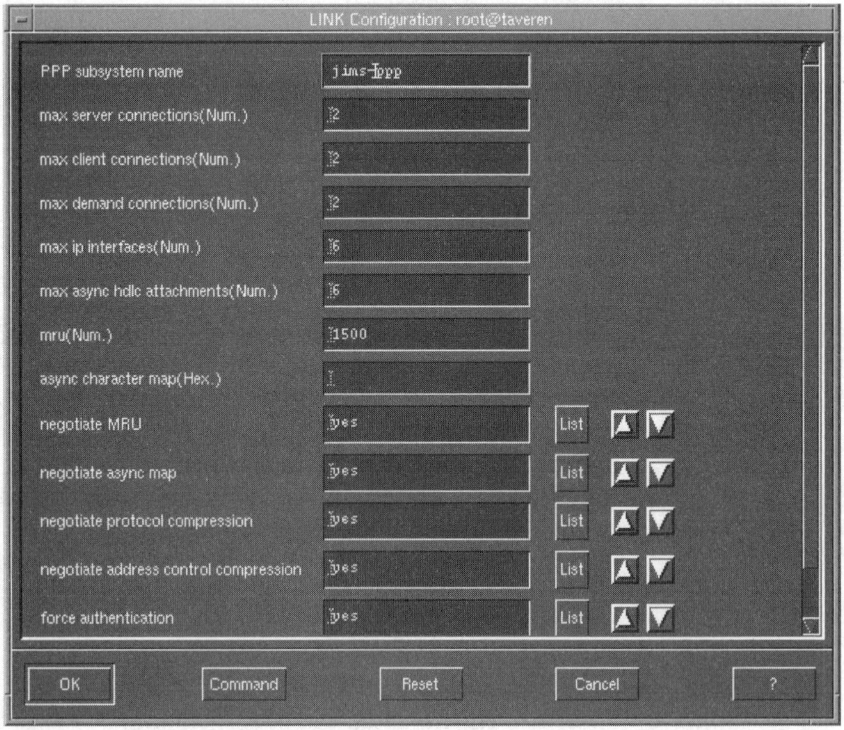

Figure 15.13   LCP configuration panel.

Figure 15.14   PPP IP address configuration panel.

machine, and password that will be allowed to establish a PPP connection. These values are stored in clear text in the /etc/ppp/ppp-secrets file. Verify that permissions restrict access to this file.

```
# smit ppppap
```

When configuration has been completed, you can start the PPP subsystem using SMIT or the startsrc command.

```
# startsrc -s ppp      Start PPP subsystem
```

To start a client PPP connection, use the pppdial command. Example client session ChatFiles (sign-on scripts) are available in the /etc/ppp directory. ChatFile format follows the conventions used for UUCP.

```
# pppdial -f [ChatFile]
```

15.10   Anonymous FTP

Anonymous FTP is a common service available on the Internet that provides public access to repositories of public domain applications and

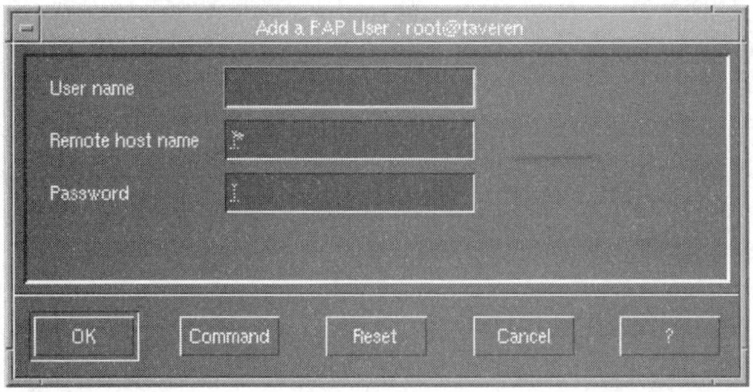

Figure 15.15   PPP authentication panel.

TABLE 15.8   Anonymous FTP Directory Permissions

~ftp	ftp	555
~ftp/bin	root	555
~ftp/bin/ls	root	111
~ftp/etc	root	555
~ftp/etc/passwd	root	444
~ftp/etc/group	root	444
~ftp/etc/pub	ftp	77*

* Write access will allow incoming data. You may wish to create a special directory under ~ftp/pub for incoming data.

information. Care must be taken when configuring an anonymous FTP server since you are granting a level of access to your system without password protection. You want to limit the commands and the directory paths that are accessible.

Create an account (FTP) and directory path to be used for anonymous FTP. The ftpd daemon provides a level of protection by invoking chroot(2) to set the root directory to the directory owned by the FTP account, effectively hiding anything outside that path. Create bin, etc, and pub subdirectories in the FTP account home directory. Copy the ls command to the bin subdirectory. Install edited copies of /etc/passwd and /etc/group in the etc subdirectory. These files should only contain root, daemon, and FTP accounts. Install software and documents you wish to make available in the pub directory. See Table 15.8 for more information.

A replacement ftpd server that provides additional options for anonymous FTP is available from wuarchive.wustl.edu.

15.11   Security

Network security is often viewed as a contradiction of terms. It is certainly true that you increase exposure to unauthorized access when you permit any outside access to your computing resource. Packet sniffers are publicly available, allowing users to watch all the data traversing the wires. Wire taps for broadcast networks like Ethernet are easily installed. A workstation in the hands of a hacker can impersonate trusted addresses. The tradeoffs between exposure and additional service must be weighed carefully. Network security is not really the oxymoron that the joke implies. You have the ability to implement security measures, however as you tighten down the locks, you may lose services and ease of use.

15.11.1   Network trusted computing base

AIX supports a set of access control and auditing facilities called the trusted computing base (TCB). The TCB system also encompasses network support and is known as network trusted computing base (NTCB). Along with TCB user authentication mechanisms, NTCB supplies connection authentication, secure session, auditing of network configuration files and events, and an enhanced security TCP/IP operation mode.

Connection authentication is provided by defining which remote host addresses are allowed to connect to the local system. Security levels may be defined for each network interface to limit the activities that may take place over a given interface.

Secure sessions are enforced through the use of trusted path, trusted shell (tsh), and secure attention key (SAK). The trusted path and shell limit the applications that may make use of a terminal session. The SAK establishes the environment necessary for a secure session.

The AIX auditing system records changes in permissions, modification times, checksums, and network events.

A full set of security features may be enabled using the securetcpip command. securetcpip disables untrusted commands and restricts access to interfaces that are not configured at specified security levels. The Berkeley r-commands rsh, rcp, rlogin, and rsh are disabled along with tftp. The ftp, telnet, and rexec commands provide additional security checking. Once the securetcpip command is invoked, the tcpip lpp must be reinstalled to restore standard operation. Interface security levels are based on the IP security option described in RFC 1038.

15.11.2 Traditional security measures

There are some less drastic measures you can take to secure your environment. The first is the judicious use of .rhosts and /etc/hosts.equiv files. Using these files allow use of the Berkeley r-commands without requiring a password. This eliminates passwords sent in the clear over the Net and limit the damage that may be done with PTY sniffer programs. It is true that if these files are compromised they can present a nasty security hole. Care must be taken when implementing their use. Basically these files list the hosts and user names that are allowed to execute r-commands without a password.

Connection authentication can be implemented on a service-by-service basis by implementing a wrapper program for inetd. The wrapper program validates and logs the connecting system's address based on an access table. The tcpd program available via anonymous FTP from cert.org is an example of this type of application. The tcpd system controls access by service class as well as individual service.

Another authentication mechanism gaining popularity is based on an encrypted ticket-granting algorithm authorizing timed access to a service. Tickets are granted by a secure trusted third party. Both the client and server must have the ticket authentication interface incorporated into their respective source code. The Kerberos authentication system follows this schema and is being implemented by most vendors. Kerberos is also the authentication system used by OSF technologies.

15.11.3   Security information

The Computer Emergency Response Team (CERT) based at Carnegie Mellon University tracks and disseminates vendor security information. CERT regularly posts information to the comp.security.announce Usenet group. They also support an anonymous FTP site containing security-related documents. Another Usenet security-related discussion group is alt.security.general. You may contact CERT at:

CERT Coordination Center
Software Engineering Institute
Carnegie Mellon University
Pittsburgh, Pennsylvania 15213-3890
24-hour hotline: (412) 268-7090
E-mail: cert@cert.org
anonymous FTP: cert.org
Web: http://www.cert.org/

15.12   Network Management

Implementing and maintaining a smooth-running TCP/IP network requires a similar network of individuals who plan, administer, operate, and troubleshoot the components that make up the system. There are far more models for the assignment of bodies and responsibilities for the people-side of network management than the number of protocols to be managed. Thus, I won't talk about that here. However, to make any management structure work you need good data collection and alert tools.

A great deal of standards work has gone into defining the structure and identification of management information (SMI—RFC 1155), the management information base (MIB—RFC 1156), and the simple network monitor protocol (SNMP—RFC 1157). SNMP has been recommended by the Internet Activities Board (IAB) as a short-term network management tool, while the ISO common management information protocol (CMIP) and the CMIP over TCP/IP (CMOT) protocols are investigated.

SNMP is a protocol used to communicate network element (NE) statistics and control information to network management stations (NMS). The NMS clients may set or query variable information collected by a NE. Asynchronous traps may be generated by a NE and delivered to a NMS client. The standard defines communication based on UDP. Variable types are grouped as objects. RFC 1213 provides a complete list of MIB objects and variable descriptions.

15.12.1 AIX SNMP

AIX V3 provides both SNMP client and agent functions. The client snmpinfo application supports SNMP get, next, and set functions. The AIX SNMP agent snmpd supports MIB-II groups: system, interface, at, ip, icmp, tcp, udp, egp, transmission, and snmp. An API is provided for application access to MIB data and alerts. MIB variables are stored in the /etc/mib.defs and /etc/mib_desc files. MIB objects are managed using the mosy command. Refer to RFC 1213 for a complete list of MIB-II groups.

Configuration data for the snmpd agent is specified in the /etc/snmpd.conf file. Configuration information includes the path and size of the log file, MIB views, access permissions, traps, and snmpd parameters. Well-known port numbers for snmpd network access must be defined in /etc/services. For instance:

```
snpd /etc/services ports

snmp        161/upd
snmp-trap   162/udp
smux        199/tcp


/etc/snmpd.conf

# smpd.conf
#
# Log attributes
  logging    file=/usr/tmp/snmpd/log      enabled
  logging    size=0                        level=0
#
# MIB views
#
# View name is an arbitrary three integer identifier
#
# view     <view name>    <MIB list>
  view     1.15.7      system
  view     1.15.6      interfaces
#
# Who has access to agent MIB information
#
# Community names defined in /etc/community
#
# community <name> <address> <netmask> <permission> <view name>
```

```
       community public
       community private    daffy    255.255.255.0 readWrite 1.15.7
  #
  # traps to catch
  #
  # trap mask:    fe block no traps
  #            7e block coldStart trap
  #            be block warmStart trap  .
  #            3e Block both coldStart and warmStart traps
  #
  # trap    <community name>    <address>    <view name>    <mask>
    trap    public             daffy        1.15.7         fe
  #
  # snmpd parameters
  #
    snmpd maxpacket=1024 querytimeout=120 smuxtimeout=60
    smux    1.3.6.1.4.1.2.3.1.2.1.2    gated_password    #gated
```

The snmpd daemon can be started and stopped as a subsystem using the SRC startsrc and stopsrc commands or via SMIT. It can also be started with the tcpip subsystem.

```
# startsrc -s snmpd      Start snmpd
# stopsrc -s snmpd       Stop snmpd
```

15.13   Troubleshooting

When Murphy said, "If something can go wrong, it will go wrong," he must have been talking about computer networks! Distributed systems magnify the complexity of stand-alone systems by orders of magnitude. Unfortunately, there isn't much in the way of integrated tools to assist the administrator in troubleshooting problems.

15.13.1   Sniffers

Probably the best tool to have handy for medium to larger networks is a sniffer. A sniffer is a custom computer that attaches to the network to analyze packet traffic. These systems are compact so they can be taken anywhere and are tuned to keep up with packet rates. Packet types can be filtered and logged to provide statistics over time. For the budget minded, there are packages available for workstations and PCs that provide many of the same functions.

15.13.2   AIX iptrace

If portability isn't a problem, the AIX iptrace and ipreport commands do a very good job at collecting IP traffic traces. The iptrace command supports options to record traffic by protocol, host, port, and interface. Protocol types must be defined in the /etc/protocols file. Output from iptrace is recorded in a file that can later be formatted into a report using the ipreport command.

```
# iptrace /tmp/trace.data
# ipreport /tmp/trace.data /tmp/trace.report
```

15.13.3   Interface status

The netstat command can be used to display interface statistics and connection status for a given workstation or host. An interval flag may be used to record snapshots over time. Useful netstat flags include:

-i   Summary packet rates and errors by interface

-a   Display active connection status

-r   Display routing table information

-m   Display mbuf allocation and usage

15.13.4   Reachability

When you want to check reachability, the ping command is a useful tool. ping sends ICMP echo requests to a remote site. Statistics are gathered and displayed based on the round trip time and dropped packets. In most cases, reachability problems will be related to routing information or netmask.

```
# ping foo.bar.com

PING foo.bar.com (130.111.58.1): 56 data bytes
64 bytes from 130.111.58.1: icmp_seq=0 ttl=252 time=8 ms
64 bytes from 130.111.58.1: icmp_seq=1 ttl=252 time=3 ms
64 bytes from 130.111.58.1: icmp_seq=2 ttl=252 time=8 ms
64 bytes from 130.111.58.1: icmp_seq=3 ttl=252 time=5 ms
--- foo.bar.com ping statistics ---
4 packets transmitted, 4 packets received, 0% packet loss
round-trip min/avg/max = 3/5/8 ms
```

15.13.5   Server applications

The telnet command can be used to validate the operation of a server application that is listening on a particular port number. Use the port number option with telnet to connect to the remote port. Once you have connected, you can interactively initiate a dialog with the application.

```
# telnet daffy.foo.bar.org 25        Telnet to smtp port
```

15.13.6   Name service

To validate the operation of your name servers, use the nslookup command. nslookup can be directed at individual name servers and request specific resource record information. It also supports specifying the query type to use.

```
# nslookup
> daffy.foo.bar.org
Server: <default.server>
Address: 121.91.130.1

Non-authoritative answer:
Name: daffy.foo.bar.org
Address: 121.91.135.14
```

15.13.7   mbuf allocation

Large networked multiuser or application server systems often run into the problem of exhausting network buffers called mbufs. mbuf structures are used to store data moving between the network and the operating system. Under older versions of UNIX, when you hit the mbuf wall, you had to increase a kernel parameter for mbufs and/or mbclusters, rebuild the kernel, and reboot. This is real bad news for your uptime statistics. AIX provides an mbuf management facility that dynamically controls the allocation and use of mbufs and mbclusters. The default allocation is based on a low to medium packet rate and is somewhat dependent on the number of adapters. The kernel mbuf management service netm controls the minimum and maximum available free space in the pools and the maximum amount of memory that may be used for the pools. Note that the mbuf and mbcluster pools are pinned in memory. netm increases the pool sizes as network load increases. The mbcluster pool is reduced as load decreases; however, the mbuf pool is never decreased. Each mbuf is 256 bytes in size and each mbcluster is 4096 bytes.

You don't want to overcommit or undercommit memory to mbuf pools. What you need to do is monitor your packet rates under normal loads and adjust the mbuf parameters at boot time to pin as much memory as you will need and no more. Use the netstat -m command to determine if you are running out of mbufs. Then use the no command to set the maximum size of the mbuf pool thewall.

```
# netstat -m               Check mbuf use
# no -o thewall=[value]    Set max mbuf pool size
```

15.14   Other TCP Performance Options

The network options or no command is used to set most of the tunable parameters pertaining to your TCPIP environment. These include things like buffer sizes, packet time to live, and retransmit values. Use no -a to query the current values. Then set the specific parameter value using no -o [parameter]=[value]. Note that a number of the parameter names have changed in AIX V4.

```
no -a      Query TCPIP network option settings

thewall = 8192
sb_max = 65536
somaxconn = 1024
net_malloc_police = 0
rto_low = 1
rto_high = 64
rto_limit = 7
rto_length = 13
arptab_bsiz = 7
arptab_nb = 25
tcp_ndebug = 100
ifsize = 8
arpqsize = 1
strmsgsz = 0
strctlsz = 1024
nstrpush = 8
strthresh = 85
psetimers = 20
psebufcalls = 20
strturncnt = 15
pseintrstack = 12288
lowthresh = 90
medthresh = 95
subnetsarelocal = 1
maxttl = 255
ipfragttl = 60
ipsendredirects = 1
ipforwarding = 0
udp_ttl = 30
tcp_ttl = 60
arpt_killc = 20
tcp_sendspace = 16384
tcp_recvspace = 16384
udp_sendspace = 9216
udp_recvspace = 41600
rfc1122addrchk = 0
```

```
nonlocsrcroute = 0
tcp_keepintvl = 150
tcp_keepidle = 14400
bcastping = 0
udpcksum = 1
tcp_mssdflt = 512
icmpaddressmask = 0
tcp_keepinit = 150
ie5_old_multicast_mapping = 0
rfc1323 = 0
ipqmaxlen = 100
directed_broadcast = 1<<t>>
```

no -o [parameter]=[value]   Set TCPIP network option

15.15   InfoExplorer Keywords

TCPIP	lssrc
chgenet	srcmstr
chgtok	/etc/inittab
opschange	inetd
chgfddi	/etc/inetd.conf
named	/etc/services
awk	portmap
/etc/hosts	ftpd
/etc/resolv.conf	telnetd
route	rlogind
netstat	rshd
routed	rexecd
gated	talkd
/etc/gateways	sendmail
/etc/networks	comsat
/etc/rc.net	fingerd
ifconfig	tftpd
startsrc	bootpd
refresh	uucpd
traceon	SLIP
traceoff	slattach

sliplogin   snmpd

slipcall   SNMP

PPP   mosy

pppcontrold   /etc/snmpd.conf

pppattachd   iptrace

pppdial   ipreport

chroot   /etc/protocols

securetcpip   ping

/etc/hosts.equiv   nslookup

tcpd

15.16 QuikInfo

Network adapters:

`smit chgenet, chgtok, chgfddi, opschange, mktty`	Adptr config Fast-Paths
`smit mkinet, ppp`	SLIP and PPP FastPaths
`ifconfig`	Config interface

Addressing:

`/etc/hosts`	Static host table
`/etc/resolv.conf`	Name servers for address resolution
`/etc/named.boot`	Name server config
`/etc/named.ca`	Root name server cache
`/etc/named.data`	Address listing
`/etc/named.rev`	Reverse pointer listing
`nslookup`	Query name server info

Network routes:

`route`	Administer routes
`netstat -rn`	List defined routes
`routed`	Routing daemon (RIP)
`gated`	Routing daemon (RIP, EGP, Hello)
`/etc/gateways`	Known gateways
`/etc/networks`	Known networks

Services:

`/etc/services`	Well-known ports
`/etc/inetd.conf`	Inetd subservers

TCPIP group subsystem:

`/etc/rc.net`	TCPIP startup config
`startsrc -g tcpip`	Start all tcpip subsystems
`startsrc -s inetd`	Start master internet

Debugging:

`iptrace`	Start packet trace
`ipreport`	Format trace output
`netstat`	Network statistics
`ping`	Check reachability

Security:

Network Trusted Computing Base	Secure TCP
CERT Coordination Center	
E-mail: cert@cert.org	
cops	Security checkout package

16

UUCP

16.1 UUCP Overview

The UNIX to UNIX Copy Program (UUCP) is almost as old as UNIX itself. It was originally developed by Mike Lesk at Bell Labs around the mid 70s. In the early 80s, it was rewheeled by Peter Honeyman, David Nowitz, and Brian Redman and became HoneyDanBer UUCP. UUCP is a simple mechanism that supports remote command execution, file, and E-mail transfer between consenting systems over dialup and LAN connections. AIX knows UUCP as the basic networking utilities (BNU), which are based on the HoneyDanBer version of UUCP. BNU services are part of BOS Extensions.

UUCP provides an ideal avenue for downloading Usenet news or providing Internet E-mail access when you don't want to support a continuous connection to the Internet. Connections may be established from the local site to trusted remote sites within restricted operation parameters. UUCP uses a store and forward mechanism to communicate with sites beyond immediate neighbors. Files are transferred from one machine to the next using hop addressing and host tables. The downside of the store and forward nature of UUCP is the extra administration complexity involved in maintaining the host tables.

16.2 Using UUCP

A user invokes a UUCP command to transfer a file to a remote site. A work file containing address and control information, and a copy of the file to be transferred are created in the spool directory. The uucico daemon is started—this looks up the name of the first host hop in the /usr/lib/uucp/Systems file. The Systems file entry identifies a connection device that uucico matches to an entry in the /usr/lib/uucp/Devices file.

With the connection information in hand, uucico attempts to contact the remote system. The connection involves logging in to the uucp account on the remote system. Passwords to remote sites are maintained in the local Systems file. A successful login starts uucico on the remote system. The two uucico daemons communicate as a master-slave pair. If permitted by the remote system, the local uucico daemon transfers any files destined for the remote site. The remote site, if permitted, may use the connection to transfer files destined for the local site. The connection is dropped once transfers are complete.

In the event that a connection could not be established or transfer was aborted, the transfer request remains in the uucp spool. Periodically the uusched daemon may be spawned by cron to attempt to deliver any queued requests.

16.2.1   UUCP addressing

UUCP addresses specify each machine name (hop) in the path from the local to the remote destination. The hop path is read from left to right and terminates with the recipient user name. Each name in the path is delimited by an exclamation point (!).

hop1!hop2!hop3!user

daffy!beaver!jeffries

16.3   UUCP Configuration

UUCP operation requires that connection information for neighboring remote sites is configured into a set of local tables, and that this information is coordinated with these neighboring UUCP sites. The easiest way to coordinate access with the UUCP community is by joining UUNET. UUNET originally provided access to other UUCP sites and gateways to networks like the Internet and Bitnet. UUNET has now expanded to providing a full suite of Internet services, one of which is UUCP. A small connection and use charge is required that provides access to a large number of network services and topology coordination. For more information on UUNET, contact:

UUNET Technologies Inc.
3060 Williams Drive
Fairfax, Virginia 22031-4648
1-800-488-6383
(703) 206-5600
Fax: (703) 206-5601
uunet!info, info@uu.net
Web: http://www.uu.net/
Internet anonymous FTP site: ftp.uu.net

16.3.1 UUCP login ID

As indicated in Sec. 16.1.2, each system participating in the network must supply access to an account for UUCP connection. The AIX BNU installation process creates a uucp account with UID 5, GID 5, home directory /usr/spool/uucppublic, and login shell /usr/lib/uucp/uucico. This account is used to schedule uucp activities on the system.

```
uucp:!:5:5:unix to unix
copy:/usr/spool/uucppublic:/usr/lib/uucp/uucico
```

To reduce the possibility that a remote site could modify local UUCP configuration tables, create nonprivileged accounts for remote access. Each additional account should be a member of the uucp group GID 5. Notify the remote site system administrators concerning the account name and password that should be used when connecting to your system.

16.3.2 Host name

Select a host name that identifies your system to the network. If the number of machines in your network is small, the task is trivial. AIX BNU supports host names up to eight characters. If you will be connecting to a large network like UUNET, you will need to coordinate the selection of a host name such that it does not collide with other names in the name space. You can query the local host name with the uuname command.

```
# uuname -1
```

16.3.3 Directories and permissions

Special attention should be devoted to verifying the command, configuration files, and spool permissions defined for UUCP. BNU makes use of four directories:

/usr/bin	User commands
/usr/lib/uucp	Configuration files and daemons; symbolic link to /etc/uucp for configuration files and /usr/sbin/uucp for daemons and administrative commands
/usr/spool/uucp	Logs and daemon workspace
/usr/spool/uucppublic	User directories and uucp home

All UUCP files and directories other than those owned by users in /usr/spool/uucppublic should be owner and group UUCP. Special permissions are as follows:

`/usr/lib/uucp`	0755	UUCP directory
`uucp/System`	0400	Remote sites and passwords
`uucp/uucico`	4755	Master UUCP daemon
`uucp/uusched`	4755	Schedule daemon
`uucp/uuxqt`	4755	Command execution daemon
`uucp/{cmds,scripts}`	0755	Support commands
`uucp/{files}`	0640	Other configuration files
`/usr/spool/uucp/{subdirs}`	0755	Log and work directories
`/usr/spool/uucppublic`	0777	Public access

Use the uucheck command to validate directory ownership and permissions.

```
# uucheck
```

16.3.4 Configuration tables

UUCP makes use of five configuration tables: Systems, Devices, Permissions, Dialers, and Dialcodes.

Systems	Who you will talk to
Devices	What interfaces are available for connections
Permissions	Permissions supported for each remote system
Dialers	Modem handshaking and negotiation
Dialcodes	Phone numbers

You can build a functioning UUCP system by modifying the first three and accepting the defaults from the Dialers table. The tables may be edited manually or through the use of the /usr/lib/uucp/uucpadm command. uucpadm is a menu-driven utility that allows you to configure table stanzas similar to SMIT (see Fig. 16.1).

```
# /usr/lib/uucp/uucpadm
```

16.3.4.1 /usr/lib/uucp/Systems. The Systems table defines who you will talk to. Because the Systems file contains passwords for remote systems, special care must be taken to make certain that it is not accessible by unauthorized users. Each remote system is represented by a stanza that defines:

System name

Times when connections are allowed

Link type

Link speed

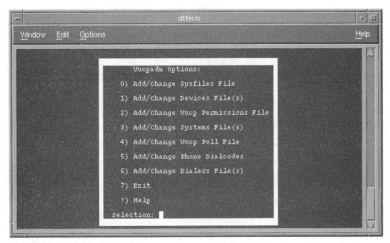

Figure 16.1 uucpadm panel.

Phone number

Login handshaking, user name and password

System names may be represented more than once. Additional entries represent alternate communication links. When a connection is requested, uucico will try each entry in turn, attempting to establish the connection.

The Times field represents the days of the week and the 24-hour clock representation of the times when connections are supported. Inversely, time intervals outside those represented inhibit connection attempts. Weekdays are represented with the following character codes: Mo, Tu, We, Th, Fr, Sa, Su, Wk, and Any. A connection retry interval in minutes may be specified following the time intervals separated by a semicolon. Default retry time is 5 minutes. For example:

`Wk2300-0800,SaSu`	Weekdays between 11 PM and 8 AM; anytime on Saturday and Sunday
`Any`	Access allowed anytime
`Wk0800-1700;5`	Weekdays from 8 AM to 5 PM with a 5-minute retry interval

The Type field represents any device type identified in the Devices file and a conversation protocol (see Table 16.1). The default protocol is "g." Device types are as follows:

TABLE 16.1   Conversation Protocol

g	Used for modem connections. Provides packetizing and checksum functions.
t	Assumes error-free channel. No packetizing or checksums.
e	Use for direct BNU connections. Not reliable for modem connections.

ACU	Modem
Direct	Direct serial link
TCP	TCP/IP connection

The Class field defines the line speed in bits per second. If the line supports any line speed, use the keyword "Any."

The Phone field specifies the full phone number for a dialup connection. If the entry represents a prefix number that is used in multiple entries, an alphabetic abbreviation may be substituted to represent an entry in the Dialcodes file. An example dialcodes prefix is as follows:

```
local5648 "local" Dialcodes 9=354
```

The Login field is a short handshaking script that represents the login negotiation for connecting to the remote system. It is a graphic representation of the send and receive character streams that would be used if you were logging in interactively. (Special characters perform special functions—see Table 16.2.) The remote site sends `login:` and the local site responds with the user name. The remote site sends `password:` and so on. It is sufficient to list only enough of the prompt strings to make them recognizable. An example Login script may read:

```
""\r\d\r login:--login: uucp word: Zx&za01
```

System entries may read:

```
goofy Any ACU    2400    -    ""\r\d\r in:--in: uucp word: qrs
venus Any TCP    -       -    in:--in: rudy word: 1jx733z
```

16.3.4.2 /usr/lib/uucp/Devices. The Devices file defines the connection device types that are available on the system. They are identified by a

TABLE 16.2   Login Script Special Characters

" " or \N	Expect null string
EOT	Send end of transmission
BREAK, @, or \k	Send a break signal
\b	Backspace
\c	Suppress new line
\d	Delay one second
\E	Start echo checking
\e	Turn off echo checking
\p	Pause for .25 to .5 seconds
\n	New line
\r	Carriage return
\ooo	Octal digits
\\	Back slash

Type string, followed by Line, Line2, Class, and Dialer Tokens. Note that the second Line2 field is a holdover from the old days when modems and dialers were separate devices (see Table 16.3).

The Type field is commonly:

ACU   Modem

Direct   Direct-connect serial link

TCP   TCP/IP connection

The Line and Line2 parameters identify the ports used by the connection, such as tty1. For a TCP connection, use a hyphen (-) character as a placeholder.

The Class field matches the speed parameters specified in the Systems file. It can either be a value representing bits per second or the multispeed parameter Any.

The Dialer Token field represents the name of a modem type listed in the Dialers file. It may be followed by a flag indicating where an associated phone number is located. The \D flag indicates the phone number is specified in the Systems file. The \T flag specifies the Dialcodes file as the source for the phone number. For TCP/IP connections, use the parameter TCP. For direct connections, specify direct. For instance:

```
ACU     tty1   -   1200 hayes \D
Direct  tty2   -   9600 direct
TCP     -      -   -    TCP
```

16.3.4.3 /usr/lib/uucp/Permissions. The Permissions file specifies the privileges available to each UUCP login account or machine name. Each entry in the Permissions file specifies the account name, the send/receive permissions, and the commands that are allowed for execution. Be very careful not to include setuid shell scripts as part of the command list. In general, setuid shell scripts are not a good idea anywhere. Note that these permissions do not affect access to non-UUCP login accounts. A user at a remote site may access a non-UUCP login account using ct, cu, or tip and obtain the full set of permissions and command paths available to the account.

Permissions file stanzas are represented as parameter=value pairs. Permissions parameters are as follows:

TABLE 16.3   Devices Fields

Type	Device type identifier
Line	Port
Line2	Second port for 801 dialer
Class	Line speed
Dialer Tokens	Modem identifier

■ Entry:

`LOGNAME=<LoginID:LoginID…Options>`	UUCP account stanza
`MACHINE=<MachineName:MachineName…Options>`	System stanza
`MACHINE=OTHER <Options>`	Generic system stanza

■ Options:

`REQUEST=<yes/no>`	Request to transfer
`SENDFILES=<yes/no>`	File transfer allowed
`READ=<PathName:PathName…>`	Read paths
`NOREAD=<PathName:PathName…>`	Read exception paths
`WRITE=<PathName:PathName…>`	Write paths
`NOWRITE=<PathName:PathName…>`	Write exception paths
`COMMANDS=<Command:Command:…>`	Commands allowed
`COMMANDS=ALL`	All commands allowed
`VALIDATE=<Name:Name>`	Used with COMMANDS=ALL
`CALLBACK=<yes/no>`	Callback required

Once configured, you can validate the format of the Permissions file using the uucheck command.

```
# uucheck
```

The following is an example Permissions entry:

```
LOGNAME=vase \
    VALIDATE=jose \
    REQUEST=yes \
    SENDFILES=yes \
    READ=/u1/jose \
    WRITE=/u1/jose \
    COMMANDS=ls:who

MACHINE=goofy \
    REQUEST=yes \
    SENDFILES=yes \
    COMMANDS=ALL
```

UUCP maintains a log of connection attempts by sites not listed in the Permissions file. Unauthorized connection attempts are logged by the remote.unknown script in the /usr/spool/uucp/.Admin/Foreign file.

16.3.4.4 /usr/lib/uucp/Dialers. In most cases, you can accept the default Dialers file as distributed with AIX BNU. The Dialers file defines the attributes and command strings required to initialize various modem types. Each modem entry in the file is represented by a name, dial-tone and wait characteristics, and initialization and connection sequence. Add entries to this file when you are using a modem type that is not listed. The default Dialers file is set up as follows:

```
#  UUCP Dialers
#
# Execute /usr/lib/uucp/uucpadm for on-line uucp configuration help
#.
hayes  =,-,  ""\dAT\r\c OK \pATDT\T\r\c CONNECT
penril =W-P ""\d > s\p9\c )-W\p\r\ds\p9\c-) y\c : \E\DP > 9\c OK
ventel =&-% "" \r\p \r\p-\r\p-$ <K\D%%\r>\c ONLINE!
rixon  =&-% "" \r\p \r\p-\r\p-$ <K\D%%\r>\c ONLINE!
vadic  =K-K "" \005\p *-\005\p-*\005\p-* D\p BER? \E\D\e \r\c LINE
micom        ""       "".\s\c NAME? \D\r\c GO
#
TCP
direct
```

See Table 16.4 for a listing of the special characters used in the Dialers file.

16.3.4.5 /usr/lib/uucp/Dialcodes. The Dialcodes file is basically a phone prefix directory for UUCP. Each prefix number is represented by an alphabetic identifier. The identifiers are used as shorthand for phone numbers in the Systems file. Dial tone (=) and pause (-) characters may be used as required in the prefix number.

TABLE 16.4 Dialers Special Characters

=	Wait for dial tone
-	Pause
" "	Null no wait
\d	Delay one second
\r	Carriage return
\c	New line
\p	Pause .25 to .5 seconds
\T	Send telephone number

The following chart shows Dialcodes format:

Identifier	Prefix Number
local	9=356
oregon	9-1503

16.4 UUCP Daemons

AIX BNU support is managed by four daemons:

uucico	Master daemon responsible for connection and transfer control
uusched	Schedule UUCP requests
uuxqt	Execute command requests from remote sites
uucpd	Support UUCP over TCP/IP

The UUCP master daemon uucico establishes connections and transfers files created by the uucp and uux commands. Transfer requests are spooled to the /usr/spool/uucp/<SystemName> directory. uucico records transfer activities and status to the /usr/spool/uucp/.Log/uucico file. The uucico daemon is invoked by uucp, uux, and uusched. It can also be invoked from the command line to debug connections. The uusched daemon is started periodically by cron using the uudemon.hour command. uusched locates files queued in the /usr/spool/uucp/<SystemName> directory and invokes uucico to attempt delivery. Each request type is identified by a prefix character, C.* (command files); D.* (data files), and E.* (execute files).

uuxqt is invoked periodically like uusched by cron. It scans the /usr/spool/uucp/<SystemName> directory for execution requests from remote systems. The remote execution requests are identified by the X.* prefix.

UUCP over TCP/IP connections are established by the uucpd daemon. uucpd runs as a subserver invoked by inetd. The server uses reserved port number 540, which must be configured in /etc/services. A typical uucpd entry reads:

```
uucp    540/tcp    uucpd
```

16.5 Housekeeping and Logs

UUCP requires periodic housekeeping to ensure a smooth running facility. The chores include periodically running uusched and uuxqt to handle queued requests and clean up log and work files. These types of activities are handled by cron. The following uucp crontab is supplied as part of the default AIX BNU configuration and can be enabled to take care of UUCP housekeeping chores. To enable cron support, edit the crontab and remove the comments from the schedule lines. Adjust the times per your environment.

```
#
# UUCP Crontab - Housekeeping Chores.
#
20,50 **** /bin/bsh -c "/usr/lib/uucp/uudemon.poll > /dev/null"
25,55 **** /bin/bsh -c "/usr/lib/uucp/uudemon.hour > /dev/null"
45 23 *** /bin/bsh -c "/usr/lib/uucp/uudemon.cleanu > /dev/null"
48 8,12,16 *** /bin/bsh -c "/usr/lib/uucp/uudemon.admin > /dev/null"
```

Like most other AIX systems, BNU creates a number of log files that periodically need to be closed and archived. Log files are compacted and cycled by the uudemon.cleanu command. The uudemon.cleanu utility is configured in the default uucp crontab.

16.6   Hardware

UUCP connections are supported over serial links and TCP/IP as described in the previous sections. Refer to Chap. 12 and Chap. 15, respectively, for detailed descriptions concerning serial and TCP/IP based interfaces.

16.7   UUCP Commands

It's helpful to understand the command set that makes up a service. The combination of user and administrator commands can provide insights into how the service can be used and enhanced.

Cvt	Convert non-BNU UUCP files to BNU
uucheck	Validate Permissions file
uuname	List host names from Systems file
uucpadm	Tailor configuration files
uuclean **or** uucleanup	Clean spool directories
uukick	Establish connection with debug support
uulog	Display log information
uupoll	Poll a remote site
uuq	Display scheduled job queue
uusnap	Display status
uustat	Display statistics
uutry	Establish a debug connection overriding retry limits
uucp	Transfer a file to a remote site
uux	Execute a command on a remote site

uuencode	Encode a binary file for text transfer
uudecode	Decode a uuencoded file
ct, cu, tip	Establish connection to a remote site
uusend	Send a file to a remote site
uuto	Copy a file to a remote site

16.8 Troubleshooting

Testing a new or problem connection can be done using uucico or uutry. The uucico debug flag -x<num> will display a connection trace. You control the verbosity of the trace by specifying a <num> value from 1 to 9:

```
# uucico -r1 -x9 -sgoofy

  conn(goofy)
  Device type goofy wanted
  getto ret 6
  expect: ("")
  got it
  sendthem (^MDELAY^M)
  expect: (login:)
  timed out
  Call Failed: LOGIN FAILED
  conversation complete: Status FAILED
```

You can use this feedback to validate your entry in the Systems file for the particular site. You can also use a simple connection command like cu to validate that your link is operational. See Chap. 9 for information on testing serial links.

Use the uucheck command to validate file permissions and configurations defined in the Permissions file. Use uulog to display connection histories.

16.9 InfoExplorer Keywords

UUCP	/usr/lib/uucp/uucico	uucp
uucico	uuname	uux
/usr/lib/uucp/Systems	uucheck	uuxqt
/usr/lib/uucp/Devices	uucpadm	uucpd
uusched	/usr/lib/uucp/Permissions	inetd
cron	/usr/lib/uucp/Dialers	uutry
/usr/spool/uucppublic	/usr/lib/uucp/Dialcodes	cu

16.10   QwikInfo

Addressing:

host1!host2!user   UUCP store and forward hop addressing
                                 format

Tables:

/usr/lib/uucp   Configurations files
/usr/spool/uucppublic   Public spool directory
/usr/spool/uucp   Logs and workspace
/usr/lib/uucp/System   Host table
/usr/lib/uucp/Devices   Network interfaces
/usr/lib/uucp/Dialcodes   Phone numbers
/usr/lib/uucp/Dialers   Modem control and logon handshaking
/usr/lib/uucp/Permissions   UUCP login privileges

Daemons:

uucico   Master UUCP daemon
uusched   UUCP scheduler daemon
uuxqt   Execute a command
uucpadm   UUCP configuration tool
uucpd   UUCP over TCP

Commands:

See Sec. 16.7.

System Network Architecture

17.1 Introduction to SNA

System Network Architecture (SNA) is a layered proprietary network architecture developed by IBM for interconnecting systems. To fully address SNA configuration and operation requires an understanding of a large set of SNA program and hardware components spanning a number of operating system environments. This subject is beyond the scope of this book. The following discussion will concentrate on how the RISC System/6000 can be incorporated into the SNA environment and the services it provides. To provide a level set for those new to SNA, I'll begin by defining basic SNA lingo along with a diagram of a logical SNA network.

17.2 SNA Overview

Each system participating in a SNA network (see Fig. 17.1) is known as a node. Nodes are interconnected to other nodes via links. Nodes are classified based on the services they provide as either a boundary node or peripheral node. Boundary nodes manage routing and address translation for the global network. Peripheral nodes have a local view of the network and support limited routing and addressing capability. They rely on the boundary nodes to hide the structure of the global network. Nodes are also further broken down into types based on the interfaces they support.

Each node contains a set of resources called network addressable units (NAU). A NAU can be either a physical unit (PU), logical unit (LU), or control point (CP). A PU controls real physical resources like links, storage, and I/O hardware.

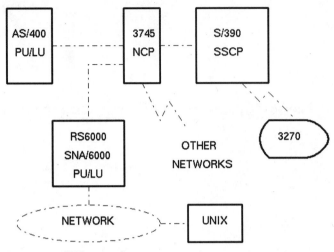

Figure 17.1 SNA network.

PU Type 2.1	Peripheral node with limited addressing and routing control. Provides multiple links and multiple LU sessions.
PU Type 4.5	Boundary node providing address translation and routing control. PU type 5 contains the domain SSCP.

An LU provides transparent network access to the end user. An end user LU is either a program or device.

LU Type 0	Primary and secondary LU support via API access for point-of-sale devices.
LU Type 1	LU support for input/output devices (printers, punches, storage devices, console).
LU Type 2	LU emulation of 3270 data streams.
LU Type 3	LU emulation of 3270 printer streams.
LU Type 6.2	Advanced program-to-program communication (APPC) between LUs on a peer-to-peer basis versus primary-to-secondary.

A CP manages a node. A master CP called the system services control point (SSCP) manages all the nodes defined within its domain. Multiple SSCPs may exist on a network, interconnecting their domains in a peer-to-peer relationship. Like nodes, NAUs are also broken down into types based on their characteristics and legacy.

Information exchange between NAUs on remote nodes involves creating paths at each layer of the protocol. At the physical layer, an attachment must be started in either outgoing call or incoming listen mode. The attachment represents the hardware and driver programs that interface the node to the network.

A connection is created between the nodes. The connection describes the network path between the nodes. This includes the attachments, addresses, and application descriptions.

A session must be established between the two NAUs. Sessions are long-lived paths that may be used serially by a number of applications.

At the top level, the LUs coordinate information transfer via a conversation. A resource ID (rid) is returned when a conversation is started to identify the conversation. A conversation description clearly identifies the send and receive application roles (see Fig. 17.2).

17.3 AIX SNA Services/6000

The RISC System/6000 can be incorporated into a SNA network through the facilities provided by the AIX SNA Services/6000 licensed program product. AIX SNA Services/6000 implements a set of programs, C library routines, device drivers, and configuration files that provide LU and PU application transaction support. AIX SNA Services/6000 does *not* provide PU type 4 or 5 boundary node support.

SNA services run as subsystems under the system resource controller (SRC). The SNA system resource manager (SRM) interacts with SRC to coordinate LU sessions and conversations. SRM is responsible for starting and stopping connections and sessions and maintains secure conversations.

Applications access SNA network services via a set of library routines that interact with a multiplexed device driver, /dev/sna. The library routines resident in /lib/libsna.a manage network interaction and data flow work through the equivalent AIX operating system calls. AIX standard I/O library calls are supported by the SNA device driver. This allows applications and standard AIX commands to interact with SNA network services just like any I/O device. A connection identifier name may be used as an extension to the /dev/sna device special file name to indicate the remote service to be used with the application.

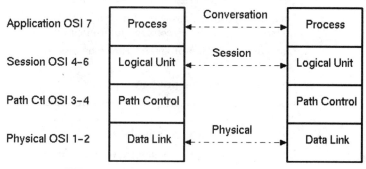

Figure 17.2 SNA stack.

```
# cat file-name > /dev/sna/<connection-identifier>
```

17.3.1   Physical interface

AIX SNA Services/6000 supports Ethernet (standard and IEEE 802.3), token ring, X.25, and synchronous data link control (SDLC) protocols. SDLC is a synchronous packet protocol that supports serial data over switched and nonswitched point-to-point and multipoint links. SDLC protocol is available for EIA232D, EIA422A, X.21, V.25, and V.35 physical links. SNA and TCP/IP may coexist on a single Ethernet or token ring adapter.

17.3.2   Defining the network

SNA configuration data is defined via SMIT and stored as structured objects in a database. Access to configuration profiles is controlled via subroutine calls to a data manager. Under AIX 3.1, profile information is located in /usr/lpp/sna/objrepos. In keeping with the file system tree restructuring in AIX 3.2, the profiles have been moved to /etc/objrepos/sna. Profiles describe the characteristics and attributes of all network interactions. They are as follows:

SNA	Defines attributes and environment of SNA, SRM, and SRC
Attachment	Defines network link characteristics. May be referred to by multiple connection profiles. Related hierarchically to lower-level control point, logical link, and physical link profiles.
Control Point	Describes local PU. May be referred to by multiple attachment profiles.
Logical Link	Defines the protocol used by an attachment.
LU Address Reg	Generic LU addresses.
Physical Link	Defines physical interface hardware type.
Connection	Defines characteristics of the network link.
Local LU	Local LU definition associated with a TPN. May be referred to by multiple connection profiles.
TPN List	Lists all transaction programs that may access a connection.
TPN	Defines a transaction program.
RTPN List	Lists all remote transaction programs that may access a connection.
RTPN	Define remote transaction program.
Mode List	List all mode rule profiles associated with a connection.
Mode	Defines a rule set that governs interaction on a connection.

You may have noted that the profile descriptions indicate that they are related hierarchically (see Fig. 17.3). When defining a new service, configure the associated profiles from the bottom level of the profile to the top. This will make configuration procedures easier, since higher level protocols refer to lower level names. Select a connection name for the service and use it to name the other related profiles. SMIT will append profile specific suffixes to this name.

After installing AIX SNA Services/6000, you will be prompted to configure your network interfaces along with the local and remote applications that will communicate over the link. The configuration information is applied by completing the profiles associated with each level of the service. Since some of this information is defined by remote sites and the domain SSCP, you will want to collect this data before running the initial configuration. Sample profile forms are supplied in *AIX Communication Concepts and Procedures, Vol. 2, GC23-2203* in the section titled "AIX SNA Services Customization Forms." The peu command is used to create the profiles that are verified by the verifysna command. These are invoked automatically by the installation procedures but may also be invoked later if required.

17.3.3 Starting and stopping services

AIX SNA Services/6000 may be started at each boot by editing the /etc/rc.sna script and uncommenting the SRC startsrc -s sna command.

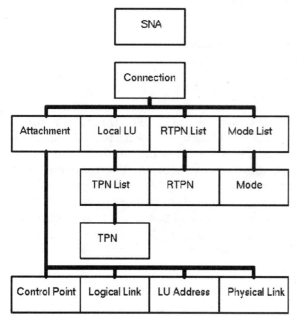

Figure 17.3 Profile hierarchy.

You may also start the sna daemon manually or via SMIT.

```
# startsrc -s sna
```

Attachments and connections may also be started with the SRC startsrc command. These can be started as needed or as part of the boot procedures by incorporating them in /etc/rc.sna. The type and name are included as arguments to startsrc.

```
# startsrc -t attachment -o name
# startsrc -t connection -o name
```

Once started, the resource state may be listed as active, inactive, or pending. The active state indicates that the resource is available for use. The inactive state indicates that the intended device is not available. If the server has received the start request but has not completed startup processing, then the state is pending.

SNA services may be stopped using the SRC stopsrc command or via SMIT. Three types of stops are supported as selected by the associated stopsrc flag: normal, forced, or cancel. A normal shutdown waits for application activity to complete. A forced shutdown does not wait for application completion but informs the remote stations that the link is being dropped. The cancel stop is similar to the forced one, but no notification is sent. Stopping attachments and connections require the specification of the type and the name.

```
# stopsrc -s name      Normal shutdown
# stopsrc -f name      Forced shutdown
# stopsrc -c name      Cancel shutdown
```

17.4   SNA Security

Secure communications on the network are enabled through the use of two passwords: a Communication Authority Password and a BIND Password. If the configuration profile database is not secured, then a communication authority password is not required. The communication authority password is required on secured systems to change configuration profiles. You may set the communication authority password using the mksnapw command from the command line or via SMIT. To change the password, use the chsnapw command or SMIT. To remove the password, set the security level to "unsecured" and use rmsnapw or SMIT.

```
# mksnapw
# chsnapw
# rmsnapw
```

BIND passwords may be required for LU 6.2 sessions. You specify the password when configuring the profile for the LU. The password is requested from the remote system when a connection is requested. You can generate cryptic BIND passwords using the Security Keys facility. This can be done via SMIT or using the genkeys command. You specify the encryption phrase and number of keys as arguments.

```
# genkey -n <number> <encryption phrase>
```

The BIND password may be updated via SMIT or using the chsnaobj command.

```
# chsnaobj -t connection -u lu6.2 -v no <name>
```

17.5 Network Management

SNA network management procedures are implemented and operated from NetView, NWays, or Tivoli Management Environment (TME) running on the domain SSCP. The RISC System/6000 can be configured to pass topology and alert information from attached networks and local applications to the central NetView manager on the SSCP. This is implemented using an SSCP-PU connection between the SSCP NetView and an AIX network manager application.

Network management applications have been a moving target over the life time of AIX. Initially, AIX Network Manager/6000 was used to manage SNMP information on TCP/IP-based networks. This product has been replaced by NetView/6000 Entry for networks up to 32 SNMP agents. SystemView NetView/6000 V2 is used for networks larger than 32 SNMP agents. The NetView/6000 Entry manager provides all the necessary communication support to interchange data with the central SSCP. The SystemView NetView/6000 V2 manager requires both SNA Services/6000 and AIX NetView Service Point to communicate with the central SSCP. Now NetView is being incorporated into NWays and TME. See Chap. 15 concerning SNMP.

17.6 Troubleshooting

Since SNA resources are initiated by SRC, you can display limited status information using the SRC lssrc command or via SMIT.

```
# lssrc -l -s sna                      Display general link status
# lssrc -l -t connection -o name       Display connection status
# lssrc -l -t attachment -o name       Display attachment status
```

SNA links may also be traced using the trace facility. Specify the trace level and associated name to the traceson and tracesoff commands. Flags and options are similar to the lssrc command. Use trcrpt to generate a report. As always, tracing can also be managed from SMIT. Trace output is located in /usr/lpp/sna for AIX 3.1 and /var/sna for AIX 3.2.

```
# traceson -l -t type -o name      Start a trace
# tracesoff -t type -o name        Stop a trace
# trcrpt /var/sna/name             Generate a report
```

API level traces may be managed using the trace and trcstop commands or using SMIT. Reports are generated using trcrpt.

```
# trace -a -j 271      Start an API trace
# trcstop              Stop an API trace
# trcrpt -d 271        Generate a report
```

SNA events and errors are logged to an internal error log called /usr/lpp/sna/snalog.* under AIX 3.1 and /var/sna/snalog.* at AIX 3.2. You can interrogate the error log using your favorite pager. Remember to periodically clear the log using errclear.

```
# more /var/sna/snalog.*      Display log entries
```

17.7   InfoExplorer Keywords

/lib/libsna.a	rmsnapw
/dev/sna	genkeys
SNA	chsnaobj
SSCP	lssrc
LU	startsrc
PU	traceson
peu	tracesoff
verifysna	trcrpt
/etc/rc.sna	trace
mksnapw	trcstop
chsnapw	snalog

17.8   QwikInfo

/lib/libsna.a	SNA C I/O library
/dev/sna	SNA multiplexed device
peu	Create SNA profiles

`verifysna`	Verify profiles
`startsrc -s sna`	Start SNA subsystem
`startsrc -t attachement -o <name>`	Start SNA attachment
`startsrc -t connection -o <name>`	Start SNA connection
`mksnapw, chsnapw, rmsnapw`	Connection authority pw
`genken`	Gen encryption key
`chsnaobj`	Update SNA config

Networked File Systems

18

Network File System

18.1 Virtual File Systems

Distributed file systems are made possible by generalizing UNIX file system data structures to provide a common interface to various underlying file system architectures. This open interface is called a virtual file system (VFS). Early work by Bell Labs used this VFS abstraction to develop their remote file system. Later on Sun Microsystems decided to move the interface abstraction down to the file level to better facilitate a common operation interface. File system architectures supported by VFS are represented in the /etc/vfs file:

```
%defaultvfs jfs                         nfs
cdrfs  5    none                        none
jfs    3    none                        /sbin/helpers/v3fshelper
dfs    7    /sbin/helpers/dfsmnthelper  none
nfs    2    /sbin/helpers/nfsmnthelp    none    remote
sfs    16   none                        none
```

In core VFS structures, allow the kernel to operate on various local file system architectures. VFS structures also provide a switch point for determining local or remote file system operations. The general mount structure for a virtual file system contains an array of operation types supported on the underlying file system. This array is called vsops. Likewise, a VFS inode abstraction called vnodes contains an array of inode operation types called vnodeops. A gnode structure is used to map inodes and vnodes.

18.2 Network File System

To support remote file system operations, a facility is required to trap and reroute file system operations from one machine to another. This must include support for file system operations between machines with different architectures and operating systems. A method is needed to map data formats from one architecture to another. Sun developed a remote procedure call (RPC) mechanism that allows a remote machine to execute functions on behalf of the local system and return the results to the originating process. Sun also provided an external data representation (XDR) language that is used to communicate data formats between machines. These specifications along with VFS semantics became the basis of Sun's Network File System (NFS) (Fig. 18.1). NFS is based on a client/server architecture that enables applications to seamlessly interoperate with files and directories shared between networked machines without regard to their locale. Sun later placed this architecture in the public domain, and it became a defacto standard for distributed file systems.

18.2.1 Configuring NFS

NFS is managed as a subsystem by the AIX srcmstr. Thus, NFS subserver daemons may be started or stopped as a group using the startsrc and stopsrc commands. NFS operation may also be managed from the SMIT nfs submenus (see Fig. 18.2).

```
# startsrc -g nfs      Start NFS subsystem
# stopsrc -g nfs       Stop NFS subsystem
```

NFS startup options and daemons are configured in the /etc/rc.nfs script. The script begins by starting the NFS block I/O biod daemons. If

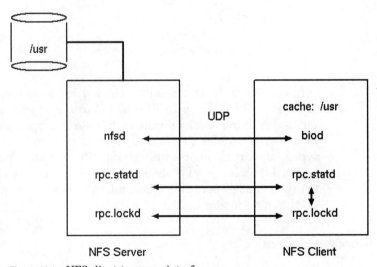

Figure 18.1   NFS client-to-server interface.

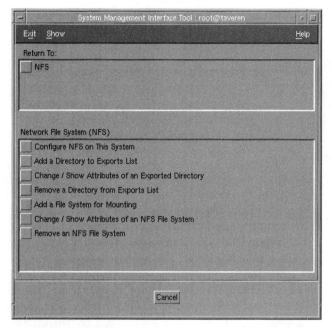

Figure 18.2 SMIT NFS support panel.

the /etc/exports file exists, it is exported using exportfs -a followed by nfsd and rpc.mountd startup. The script finishes up by starting the rpc.statd and rpc.lockd daemons. The /etc/rc.nfs script also contains entries for starting NIS and HANFS subsystems and subservers.

NFS may be made the default remote file system type by defining it as the defaultvfs in /etc/vfs. Uncomment the following lines in the /etc/vfs table.

```
%defaultvfs jfs nfs
nfs 2 /etc/helpers/nfsmnthelp none remote
```

18.3   NFS Server

The NFS server is designed as a stateless system. This eliminates the need to support recovery operations in the event of a server or client failure. It turns out that this is not entirely true. NFS uses UDP as a transport, and we all know that UDP does not guarantee packet delivery or packet order. To overcome the deficiencies of UDP, NFS servers must maintain a volatile cache of recent RCP handshaking state to avoid duplicate, out-of-order, or lost I/O operation packets. This also means that the server must keep track of who it is talking to. To keep the nfsd daemon stateless, additional daemons are used to track machine connections, RPC status, and file locks. IBM's high availability network file system (HANFS) makes use of the volatile cache state and lock daemon information to support backup NFS servers.

To ensure file integrity, NFS servers use a write-through cache, forcing file updates immediately to disk. Data integrity is maintained for the sake of performance. Asynchronous write support is available in some architectures to improve read performance when data integrity is not an issue.

18.3.1 NFS server daemons

NFS servers rely on a number of daemons to manage distributed filesystem services. I/O requests from multiple clients are multiplexed through a configurable number of nfsd and biod daemons. The nfsd daemons manage file I/O operations, and the biod daemons control block I/O services. The actual number of nfsd and biod daemons required is based on the client load the server is expected to support. The default configuration starts eight nfsd daemons and six biod daemons.

Being that NFS is RPC-based, the NFS servers must register themselves with the portmap daemon. The portmap daemon maintains the available set of RPC applications on a particular machine. Each application is represented as a tuple of application name, version, and port number. Servers register their application data with the portmap daemon. Client applications query the portmap daemon to learn the port number associated with a known server application name and version. portmap listens to a well-known port number listed in /etc/services, thus avoiding the "chicken and egg" problem of determining what portmap's port number is.

The rpc.mountd daemon is used by the server to manage and track client mount requests. Recent RPC operations between clients and servers are cached by the rpc.statd daemon. SYSV advisory file and record locking is supported by the server's rpc.lockd daemon.

The NFS server daemons are as follows:

nfsd	NFS server daemon
biod	NFS block I/O daemon
portmap	RPC program to port manager
rpc.mountd	NFS mount manager
rpc.statd	RPC status manager
rpc.lockd	NFS lock manager

18.3.2 Exporting server file systems

Each file system or directory available for remote mounting is identified by an entry in the server's /etc/exports file. Along with the direc-

tory path name, the /etc/exports entry controls which machine names
are allowed root permissions and write access. If NFS root access is not
enabled for a remote NFS client, the root UID of the server is mapped
to a default UID of –2 (4294967294), user name nobody. This restricts
access against the super user UID on a remote machine.

The /etc/exports is a flat ASCII text file that may be edited or maintained via the SMIT mknfsexp FastPath (see Fig. 18.3). Updates to the
/etc/exports file must be made known to the server daemons. Update
notification is achieved by invoking the /usr/sbin/exportfs command.

The following is an example of /etc/exports:

```
/usr/lpp/info/En_US -ro,access=alph,lisa
/home -rw,root=alph,access=alph,lisa,armada

# /usr/sbin/exportfs -a

# smit mknfsexp
```

18.4   NFS Clients

To improve performance, the NFS clients implement client-side data
caching. This requires that some level of cache consistency be main-

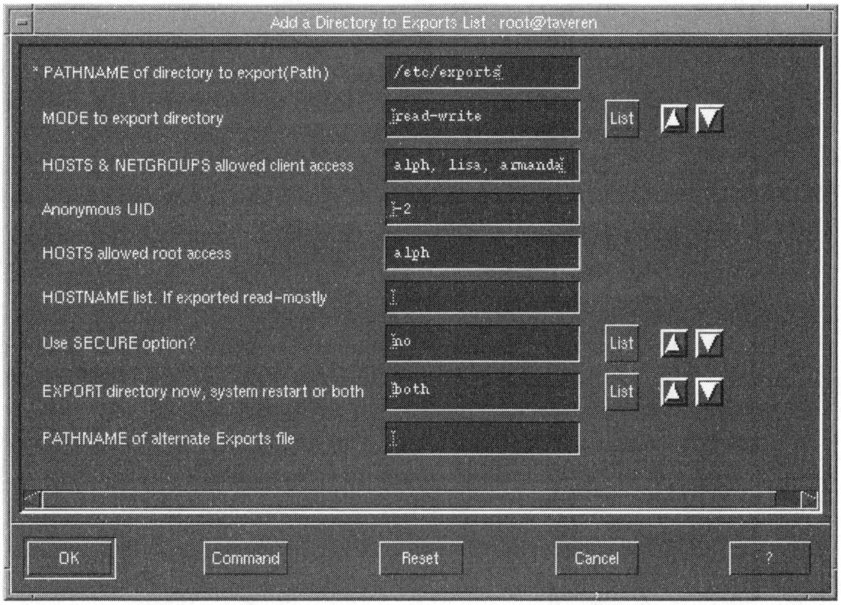

Figure 18.3   SMIT NFS exports panel.

tained between multiple NFS clients and the server. A time stamp expiration mechanism is used to allow the clients to update cache information when it becomes stale.

Each client runs multiple copies of the NFS biod block I/O daemon. Clients also run the portmap daemon. portmap is queried to identify RPC services and bind port connections to NFS servers.

NFS RPC mechanisms allow clients to block applications in the event of a server failure. I/O operations continue when access to the server is restored. A retry limit is provided such that client applications do not wait forever in the case of long-term server failures. Sun also added hard- and soft-mount options so that a client could be interrupted when server access is blocked. There are two NFS client daemons:

biod   NFS block I/O daemon

portmap   RPC program to port manager

18.4.1 Importing file systems

Client NFS file system definitions are configured as stanzas in the /etc/filesystems file. The stanza is similar to a local file system definition with the addition of the remote owning site name listed in the node-name= parameter. The dev= parameter defines the directory path on the remote machine to be mounted. /etc/filesystems entries may be edited directly or managed using the SMIT mknfsmnt FastPath (see Fig. 18.4).

```
# smit mknfsmnt
```

The following is an example of /etc/filesystems NFS stanza:

```
/usr/spool/news/nn/NN:
        dev          = /news/nn/NN
        vfs          = nfs
        nodename     = news
        mount        = true
        type         = nfs
        options      = ro,bg,soft,intr,nosuid
        account      = false
```

The type=nfs parameter may be added to the stanza definitions to identify NFS file systems as a group. This way, they can be mounted or unmounted as a group using the -t option of the mount and umount commands.

```
# mount -t nfs
# umount -t nfs
```

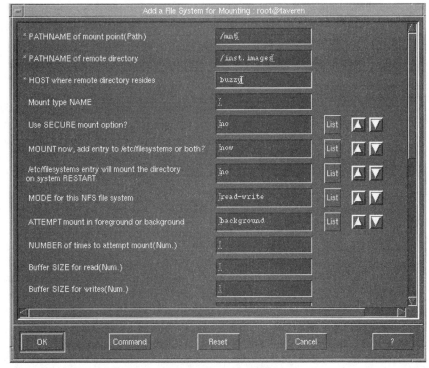

Figure 18.4   SMIT NFS mount panel.

18.5   Secure NFS

NFS suffers from a few security holes. These security problems are primarily due to collisions in the UID and GID name space and the lack of authentication in the RPC. For example, UID 1234 might be user "sleepy" on one machine and user "tulip" on another. If the file system with sleepy's home directory is NFS-mounted on tulip's machine, then tulip will have owner permissions over sleepy's files.

To solve these problems, Sun implemented a distributed file management and authentication system called yellow pages (YP) or network information system (NIS). AIX provides secure NFS services using the Sun YP management tools. Since the YP prefix is used for most NIS commands and daemons, I'll use YP when referring to secure NFS tools in the following sections. Yellow pages is the older and probably better-known terminology.

AIX also supports access control lists (ACL) over NFS. This feature is an addon function to the RPC and does not alter NFS protocol. AIX ACL support is only available to AIX V3 NFS clients.

18.5.1 Yellow pages

The yellow pages system uses a master server and one or more slave servers to distribute a common set of system configuration files to a collection of client machines under the jurisdiction of the YP domain. Each file in the distribution set is converted into ndbm database format and stored as a YP map file in the server /var/yp/<DomainName> directory. YP maps are created from text files using the makedbm command. The maps are then distributed using the yppush command. A common ndbm Makefile, /var/yp/Makefile, is used to create YP maps. Collectively, the YP map files make up the YP database as created by the ypmake command. A YP database may be transferred to another domain using the ypxfr command.

18.5.2 YP name space

The YP domain name and the set of participating machine names are defined using the /bin/domainname command. The domain defines the area of administrative control available to the servers.

```
# /bin/domainname <DomainName>
```

YP Netgroups define collections of machines that are identified for special configuration and administration requirements. A Netgroup does not necessarily correspond to a particular domain. It might be that a subset of machines in the domain are configured with a different /etc/hosts.equiv file from the rest of the domain. The Netgroup definition file, /etc/netgroups, identifies each Netgroup name followed by participant tuples. Each tuple is enclosed in parenthesis and identifies the machine, user, and domain name of the Netgroup participant.

The format for /etc/netgroups is as follows:

```
netgroupname1    (host,user,domain) (host,user,domain)...
netgroupname2    (host,user,domain) (host,user,domain)...
```

Users within domains and groups are identified by a Net name. A Net name is a concatenation of the operating system name, user name, and Internet domain name. Net names are maintained in the /var/yp/<DomainName>/netid.byname YP map. The following example provides the format (Operating system name.user name@domain name):

```
unix.janice@fido.net
```

Net names incorporate the primary host name entry from the /etc/hosts table. Sites that use domain name service must also have /etc/hosts tables available that match name service entries.

18.5.3 YP file classes

The YP versions of the distribution files for the domain use the same format as their local system counterparts. What differs is how they are used. Three classes of files govern the behavior of client machines in the YP domain: local, global, and optional. Local files override YP copies of the same information. For example, the local /etc/passwd file takes precedence over /var/yp/yppasswd. Global files override their local counterparts. Examples would include files like /etc/hosts and /etc/networks. Optional files override local copies if the local copy contains a netgroup identifier or the magic YP plus character. The plus prefix to a table entry indicates that the YP equivalent information should be used.

All the distribution files may be updated on the master server and then pushed to the slave servers and clients. Local client updates are possible in some instances through the use of YP update commands. For example, the YP version of the passwd file yppasswd can update global password information if the user changes the password using the yppasswd command.

18.5.4 YP servers and clients

To create a YP master server, YP slave server, or YP client, invoke the SMIT FastPaths mkmaster (Fig. 18.5), mkslave (Fig. 18.6), or mkclient, respectively. Servers may be initialized by invoking ypinit from the command line.

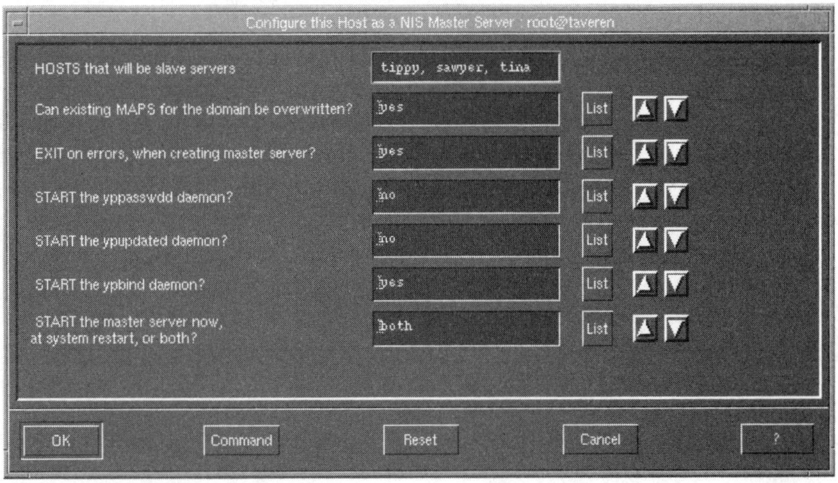

Figure 18.5 SMIT NIS master server panel.

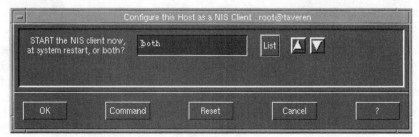

Figure 18.6 SMIT NIS client panel.

```
# smit mkmaster    # ypinit -m     Initialize a master
# smit mkmaster    # ypinit -s     Initialize a slave
# smit mkclient                    Initialize a client
```

18.5.5 Public key authentication

NFS authentication is implemented through the use of DES public key services. Each user in the YP domain must have his own public and private encryption key entries in the /etc/publickey file. The system administrator defines new user entries in the file via the newkey command. Users update their public keys using the chkey command. The /etc/publickey file is then YP-mapped to /var/yp/publickey.byname. Users' entries are identified in the files by their Net names.

```
# newkey -u username          Create user public key entry
# newkey -h hostname          Create root public key entry
# cd /var/yp; make publickey  Build YP publickey.byname
```

The keyserv daemon encrypts the public keys and stores them as private keys in the /etc/keystore file. A separate file, /etc/.rootkey, is used to hold the superuser private key. This avoids problems when private keys are wiped clean during a system reboot following a crash. To initialize the keyserv server, invoke the SMIT mkkeyserv FastPath (see Fig. 18.7) or the /usr/etc/yp/mkkeyserv command.

```
# smit mkkeyserv
# /usr/etc/yp/mkkeyserv -B
```

The keylogin command is used to decrypt a user's secret key, which is stored by the keyserv server for secure RPC operations. keylogin can be added to the default system login profile. A keyserv entry is required to access file systems flagged with the -secure option in /etc/exports and /etc/filesystems. Note that this mechanism requires synchronized

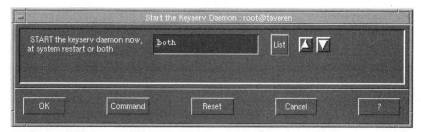

Figure 18.7 SMIT mkkeyserv panel.

clocks between participating machines. System time is used to create and expire keys stored in the server. The default secure NFS expiration is 30 minutes.

18.5.6 Starting YP (NIS) services

Like NFS, YP is managed as a subsystem under AIX. YP daemons are started using the SRC startsrc and stopsrc commands. The /etc/rc.nfs script contains code to start up YP services before bringing up NFS.

```
# startsrc -g yp      Start yellow pages
# stopsrc -g yp       Stop yellow pages
```

The YP daemons are as follows:

ypserv   YP server daemon
ypbind   YP server binding manager
yppasswdd   YP passwd update daemon
ypupdated   YP map update invoked by inetd
keyserv   Public key server daemon
portmap   RPC program to port manager

18.5.7 Automounter

The automount daemon can be run in a large YP network to simplify NFS file system access. The automount daemon will automatically mount a file system whenever a file or directory in the file system is opened. Files and directories associated with an automount file system are kept in a YP map. Automount forks child processes that appear as NFS clients that monitor file systems based on the information in the maps. The daemons umount file systems that have not been accessed in the last 5 minutes. The master automount map file is auto.master.

```
/usr/sbin/automount      Automount daemon
```

18.6   Troubleshooting

Complex distributed services like NFS and NIS present a real debugging puzzle when things run amok! Based on the symptoms and error messages associated with the problem, begin examining each component of the system. Refer to Chap. 15 for details on debugging network problems.

Begin troubleshooting problems by listing and verifying the current set of client mounts known to the server. The client mount list is recorded in /etc/rmtab and is displayed using the showmount command.

```
# showmount -a

asimov:/usr/local/gnu
asimov:/usr/local/bin
asimov:/usr/local/lib
softy:/n0
softy:/n1
```

The showmount command can also be used to verify the list of exported directories as recorded in the /etc/xtab file. This information should match up with the entries in /etc/exports. If the data doesn't match, invoke exportfs -a to refresh /etc/xtab.

```
# showmount -e

/usr/lpp/info/En_US  alph, lisa
/n1                  softy
/n0                  softy
/usr/local/gnu       asimov
/usr/local/lib       asimov
/usr/local/bin       asimov
```

NFS I/O statistics can be reset and displayed using the nfsstat command. Statistics include the number and success of RPC and NFS calls for both servers and clients. Check to see if you have a high number of time-outs and retransmissions. You may need to increase the number of nfsd and biod daemons on the server and client. We have some NFS servers with over 100 nfsd daemons to keep up with traffic.

```
# /usr/sbin/nfsstat
```

Server rpc:

```
calls       badcalls    nullrecv    badlen    xdrcall
10341661    0           0           0         0
```

```
Server nfs:
calls       badcalls
8492917     0
null      getattr     setattr    root      lookup       readlink  read
0 0%      821190 9%   23522 0%   0 0%      4641837 54%  2884 0%   932979 10%
wrcache   write       create     remove    rename       link      symlink
0 0%      608394 7%   15528 0%   13485 0%  4400 0%      940 0%    2059 0%
mkdir     rmdir       readdir    fsstat
832 0%    592 0%      996294 11% 427981 5%


Client rpc:
calls       badcalls    retrans     badxid      timeout     wait      newcred
329686      13          1255        73          1249        0         0


Client nfs:
calls       badcalls    nclget      nclsleep
304494      7           304494      0
null      getattr     setattr    root      lookup       readlink  read
0 0%      55533 18%   54 0%      0 0%      96869 31%    213 0%    100873 33%
wrcache   write       create     remove    rename       link      symlink
0 0%      53 0%       36 0%      27 0%     19 0%        0 0%      9 0%
mkdir     rmdir       readdir    fsstat
2 0%      0 0%        35008 11%  15798 5%
```

RPC errors like "Application Not Registered" are related to the portmap daemon. Check to see that the portmap daemon is running on both the local and remote system. You can also verify the application, version, protocol, and port data maintained by local and remote portmap daemons using the rpcinfo command.

```
# rpcinfo -p daffy

program   vers    proto    port
100000    2       tcp      111       portmapper
100000    2       udp      111       portmapper
100001    1       udp      1060      rstatd
100001    2       udp      1060      rstatd
100001    3       udp      1060      rstatd
100012    1       udp      1061      sprayd
100003    2       udp      2049      nfs
100005    1       udp      810       mountd
100005    1       tcp      812       mountd
100024    1       udp      824       status
100024    1       tcp      826       status
300082    1       udp      829
300082    1       tcp      831
```

```
100021       1       tcp       906         nlockmgr
100021       1       udp       908         nlockmgr
100021       3       tcp       911         nlockmgr
100021       3       udp       913         nlockmgr
100020       1       udp       916         llockmgr
100020       1       tcp       918         llockmgr
100021       2       tcp       921         nlockmgr
300049       1       udp       681
300049       1       tcp       683
```

Verify that the srcmstr daemon is aware of the current NFS and NIS subsystems and subservers states. Erratic behavior will occur if the SRC environment is out of sorts. Subsystem and subserver states can be displayed using the lssrc command.

```
# lssrc -g nfs

Subsystem       Group       PID         Status
biod            nfs         8417        active
nfsd            nfs         13324       active
rpc.mountd      nfs         15908       active
rpc.statd       nfs         12851       active
rpc.lockd       nfs         18499       active
```

Since small deltas in Client/Server response times can add up quickly for large NFS environments, you may want to closely monitor traffic between systems. You can easily collect statistics with network sniffers or by using a public domain package like nfswatch.

18.7   Highly Available Servers

Those of you who have been dealing with IBM for any number of years have surely heard of "Reliability, Availability, and Serviceability" (RAS). To remain competitive in the glass house environments, UNIX must provide the same 7-by-24 availability that has been the hallmark of operating systems like MVS. The proliferation of X stations and disk-less workstations in departmental computing environments, means that there are a whole lot of folks out there who are depending on those RS/6000 servers to be ready whenever they are.

Like everyone else, I hate any system interruptions. Whenever a system or service drops out of sight, I want that service back as quickly as possible. The sooner it is back up and running, the happier I am going to be. A highly available system should be able to survive a single point of failure and impose only the minimum required delay while service recovery transitions occur.

18.7.1 High-availability network file system

One of the problems with NFS is that when the NFS server goes down, so do all your applications and diskless workstations that were depending on the server's file systems. A high-availability network file system (HANFS) provides an extension to standard NFS services that allows a second RS/6000 to act as a backup NFS server should the primary NFS server fail. HANFS can be configured such that each RS/6000 may be acting as primary NFS servers for distinct file systems while acting as backup servers for the other, the primary requirement being that they share physical connections to external SCSI disks and additional network adapters (see Fig. 18.8). Note that the shared disks volume groups are only online to the primary NFS server and that internal disks are not supported.

HANFS makes use of the server's RPC cache information along with the journaled file system (JFS) logs to enable NFS server recovery on the backup system. The primary server's NFS RPC cache information is recorded in the JFS logs and is read by the backup server to reconstruct the cache.

During normal operation, the HANFS servers periodically exchange alive messages. When the primary NFS server fails, the backup server takes over the volume groups and checks their consistency. It rebuilds the duplicate cache from the information stored in the JFS logs and begins impersonating the failed server's network IP address. NFS locks are then resynchronized by stopping the rpc.lockd daemon from accepting new locks while the rpc.statd daemon requests all NFS clients to reclaim their locks. After a grace period, the rpc.lockd daemon begins to accept new lock requests. Other than the notification to reclaim file system locks, remote NFS clients only experience a short delay while server recovery procedures are completed. Recovery time

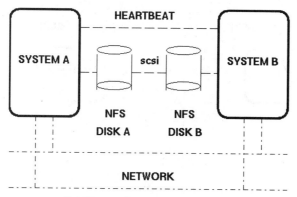

Figure 18.8 HANFS interface diagram.

after a server failure is somewhere in the neighborhood of 30 to 300 seconds.

HANFS also supports the automatic reintegration of the primary server once the problem failure has been rectified and the system is back online. Basically the procedure described in the previous paragraph is reversed and the servers go back to doing their old jobs. Note that no changes to standard NFS client software is required to make use of HANFS services. HANFS will work fine with your Sun, HP, DEC, and other standard (grain of salt here) NFS clients and servers.

18.7.2 High-availability cluster multiprocessor

The high-availability cluster multiprocessor (HACMP) goes beyond HANFS by providing configurable recovery and restart capabilities for critical applications on the backup server during a system failure. HACMP is essentially a small cluster of up to eight loosely coupled RS/6000s (see Fig. 18.9), each of which may be custom-tailored to support application specific recovery procedures in the event of a failure on the primary server.

HACMP/6000 operates in one of three modes. A mode-1 operation involves using the RS/6000s as an idle standby system. The standby system will take over support of the shared SCSI devices and network services in the event of the primary systems failure. A mode-2 operation permits independent use of all RS/6000s connected in the cluster. All systems are running independent workloads as well as acting as a

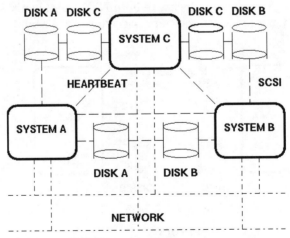

Figure 18.9 HACMP interface diagram.

backup server for each other. Should any part of the system fail, critical applications and devices may be recovered and restarted on the surviving system. You will take a performance hit on the survivor due to increased load. Mode-3 operation will allow concurrent shared-disk access by the same application running on all processors as well as prove the same backup recovery facilities in modes 1 and 2. Applications developed to make use of mode-3 operation will remain available during recovery and restart processing.

18.8   High-Speed NFS

There are several bottlenecks that contribute to slow NFS throughput. You begin with limited network bandwidth. At only 10 megabits per second, a moderately loaded Ethernet can cause significant delays for NFS traffic. The 10-ms wait for collision detection and avoidance in Ethernet is also significant overhead for frequent low-cost NFS operations. NFS server CPU cycles and memory must be shared between all operating system components. Network processing, file system buffering and control, kernel scheduling, and other OS daemons are all competing for the same resources. Finally, device interfaces are not optimized for network file system serving. NFS synchronous disk writes will block other NFS traffic on the device. This all adds up to *slow* NFS response. Hardware solutions generally involve higher-speed network adapters like FDDI, ATM, or FCS. Accelerator cards that implement TCP/IP and/or NFS on the adapter are available from a number of vendors. Hybrid NFS servers like the Auspex that combine network acceleration with high speed cached storage are also an option.

18.9   NFS V3

Future releases of AIX should include NFS Version 3. This new version of NFS is still based on the stateless design employed by NFS V2. This means that existing V2 clients will still interoperate with V3 servers. The same mounting and locking protocols are used. The change is that you can elect to use TCP rather than UDP to improve connection security and packet reliability. You can also use 64-bit addressing for interacting with file sizes larger than 4 GB. Performance improvements include use of larger block sizes for networks like FDDI, FCS, and HIPPI, and asynchronous write and commit semantics. Other improvements include a server weak cache consistency model to better facilitate client side data caching.

18.10 InfoExplorer Keywords

/etc/vfs	stopsrc	/etc/networks
jfs	exportfs	/etc/hosts
cdrfs	portmap	mkmaster
nfsmnthelp	/etc/services	mkslave
inode	mknfsexp	mkclient
vnodes	mount	ypinit
gnode	umount	/etc/publickey
NFS	ndbm	newkey
srcmstr	NIS	chkey
/etc/exports	YP	keyserv
nfsd	makedbm	/etc/keystore
biod	yppush	/etc/.rootkey
rpc.mountd	ypmake	mkkeyserv
rpc.statd	ypxfr	keylogin
rpc.lockd	domainname	showmount
defaultvfs	netgroup	nfsstat
HANFS	/etc/netgroups	rpcinfo
startsrc	yppasswd	

18.11 QwikInfo

Tables:

/etc/exports	Exported file systems
/etc/filesystems	File system mount information
/etc/vfs	File system type information

Daemons:

startsrc -g nfs	Start nfs subsystem
nfsd	Server I/O mux daemons
biod	Client I/O mux daemons
rpc.lockd	File lock daemon
rpc.statd	Status daemon
rpc.mountd	Track mount requests
portmap	RPC port mapping daemon

NIS/yellow pages:

`startsrc -g yp`	Start YP services
`/var/yp/Makefile`	Create YP maps
`domainname`	Define hosts in YP domain
`/etc/netgroups`	Collection of hosts for administrative purposes
`/var/yp`	YP maps
`/var/yp/yppasswd`	YP password file
`smit mkmaster, ypinit -m`	Make YP master server
`ypinit -s`	Initialize YP slave
`smit mkclient`	Make YP client
`keyserv`	YP encryption daemon
`/etc/keystore`	Private key file
`/etc/.rootkey`	Root private key
`/usr/etc/yp/mkkeyserv`	Initialize keyserv

Debugging:

`showmount`	Display client mounts
`nfsstat`	NFS statistics
`rpcinfo`	RPC port accessibility

19

DCE Distributed File System

19.1 Distributed File System Overview

In the late 1980s, the Open Software Foundation (OSF) went looking for a network-based file system architecture that overcame some of the limitations inherent in Sun NFS. The file system had to be statefull to support access control and locking better in a distributed environment. Improvements in caching, replication, and cloning were desired to improve performance and availability. A centrally managed directory structure was needed to enforce a common file system view between participating systems yet not restrict flexibility and access. All of these are features exhibited by the Andrew File System (AFS) architecture. So, the OSF selected AFS V4 from Transarc Corporation as the basis for its Distributed Computing Environment (DCE) Distributed File System (DFS) technology. Whew—too many acronyms this early in a chapter!

Conceptually, DFS is enhanced AFS. The major differences involve the tight integration of DFS with the other DCE services, and the underlying DCE local file system (LFS). DFS requires a larger number of support daemons than are normally used with AFS and far more than NFS. Users who are familiar with AFS will be able to adapt to the DFS semantics easily. System administrators will require a little more homework in order to configure and activate all the DCE services on which DFS depends, as well as manage the DFS environment itself. My intent in this chapter is to provide a cursory overview of AIX DFS. Proper treatment of the subjects of AIX DFS and AIX DCE easily requires an entire book unto itself. I hope to at least get you started. First a bit of history.

19.1.1 Andrew file system

In order to impose additional levels of authentication and administration and to improve the scalability of NFS, Carnegie Mellon University developed the Andrew File System (AFS). AFS, now a product of Transarc Corporation, uses a remote procedure call mechanism called RX to support client/server interactions. AFS uses the Kerberos V4 authentication system to validate client access to remote file systems. AFS introduces the notion of a cell, which defines the administrative domain over file systems in the shared space. A consistent view of the shared file system space is provided using a common root tree, /afs. Subtrees for each cell follow the root using the cell name /afs/cellname/. Note that no restriction is placed on mount points or naming under NFS. AFS cells are identified by a database called CellServDB.

AFS security is further enhanced through the use of Access Control Lists (ACL). ACLs extend the standard UNIX file permissions to provide a finer degree of granularity on access rights. AFS uses the first 4 UNIX permission bits to define read, lookup, insert, write, delete, lock, and administer (rliwdka) permissions. Note that AFS ACLs only apply to the directory levels of a file system. AFS also uses a UserList to define access rights and mapping. Users gain access to the AFS shared file space via the klog command, which grants them a Kerberos ticket for access. They can release their rights via the unlog command. Under AFS, the standard path can no longer be used to access files on the server.

Another important enhancement for distributed file systems is that AFS separates the logical file system structure from the disk blocks used to contain the file system. AFS volumes may contain one or many file system hierarchies. The volumes are made up of partitions that are collections of disk blocks identified by the special name, vicepnn, n=a,b,c,.... AFS also improves client cache consistency using a callback mechanism to invalidate data blocks that have been modified. Release level file system replication is also supported by AFS.

19.1.2 Distributed file system

DFS takes the features offered by AFS and marries them to the other OSF DCE services that comprise a tightly integrated client/server computing environment. DFS relies on other DCE services to coordinate communication, access control, and synchronization. These services include the DCE remote procedure call (RPC), DCE security service, DCE global and cell directory service, and DCE distributed time service. These DCE servers must be configured and started before you can begin working with DFS (Chap. 29).

19.1.3 Access control

Access control is delegated by administrative domains called DCE cells. Principals in a cell authenticate themselves via the DCE security service based on MIT Kerberos V5. Unfortunately AFS Kerberos V4 security service and the DCE Kerberos V5 based security service are not interoperable making migration from AFS to DFS a bit of a chore. ACLs are used in DFS, and they apply to both directories and files. DFS modifies the standard UNIX file permission bits to support, read, write, execute, control, insert, and delete (rwxcid) permissions. The UNIX permission bits reflect the ACL permissions when viewed with standard commands like ls. DFS users are identified uniquely and globally to the DCE environment such that problems with UID and GID collisions are eliminated.

19.1.4 File system structure

DFS shared file system trees are also similar to AFS in that a common root is identified with the next lower level delimited by cell name. The DFS shared root is named /... and cell subdirectories follow as /.../cell-name/. "/.:" and "/:" are shorthand strings to indicate the local cell. Clients only need mount root "/..." level DFS space to access all filesets exported by DFS file servers in the cell space.

Path Name Comparison

AIX	DFS
/u/deroest/.kshrc	/.:/u/deroest/.kshrc
	/.../[CellName]/u/deroest/.kshrc

A DFS file system mount point is similar in concept to a UNIX file system or NFS mount point. However, rather than using a directory as the mount point, DFS uses an object as the mount interface. To mount a DFS filesystem use the fts crmount command.

```
# fts crmount -dir [PathName] -fileset [FilesetName | FilesetID]
```

As an end user, you won't be able to tell the difference between a mount point directory and a mount point object. Use the fts lsmount command to see if a directory serves as an access to the mount point.

```
# fts lsmount -dir /.:/u/deroest
```

DFS is a cached file system. Frequently accessed files and directories are cached on the client either in memory or on disk. Client cache consistency is maintained via a token-passing mechanism complete with callback for synchronizing shared access to file metadata. DFS servers control the rights to file access tokens that must be acquired by a client before modifying data. DFS also supports both scheduled and release (manual) file system replication.

Under AIX V4 and DCE 2.1, you can also export an AIX CD-ROM file system from a DFS file server. The exported CD-ROM file system can be mounted into the DFS file space and accessed from DFS client machines. In addition, DFS supports file system sizes greater than 2 GB.

19.1.5   Local file system

In order to gain the full benefit of DFS services and take advantage of access control lists, you must use the DCE local file system (LFS) as the underlying physical file system for DFS. The LFS architecture is comprised of aggregates that are analogous to UNIX disk partitions and filesets, which are collections of related files and directories. LFS directories are called containers, which hold other containers (subdirectories) and LFS objects, better known as files.

LFS is a log-based file system similar to the AIX journaled file system (JFS). All file system metadata updates are grouped and logged as atomic transactions. Groups of transactions against a single object are also grouped into an equivalence class to facilitate recovery. The transaction equivalence class ensures that either all or none of the updates will be applied during system recovery.

DFS filesets may be moved between LFS aggregates while maintaining online access via a procedure called fileset cloning. Space must be available in the partition to build a copy of the fileset. The cloned fileset is marked "read only" and kept up to date via copy-on-write procedures until the move is complete. Filesets may also be replicated. Think of this as somewhat like cloning between computers over a network. Cloning and replication along with logging and dynamic aggregate sizing provide a highly available file system architecture that is quite easy to administer (see Fig. 19.1).

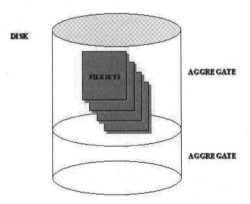

Figure 19.1   DFS aggregates and filesets.

Here is a comparison of LFS and non-LFS:

FS	Non-LFS (JFS)
rw/ro/backup filesets	rw filesets
Multiple filesets/aggregate	Single fileset/aggregate (only 1 fileset in a JFS)
DCE ACLs	

19.1.6 VFS compatibility

Any virtual file system (VFS) that has been enhanced to support DCE VFS+ can be exported by DFS file servers. DFS also provides an NFS protocol exporter to provide DFS file system access to NFS clients. An NFS client may have difficulty working with DFS ACLs in the exported file system since it does not have a way to get a DCE context. What you have to do is set default ACLs that cause a slight security exposure:

```
# acl_edit /.:/[PathName] -m any_other:rwxcid
# acl_edit /.:/[PathName] -ic -m any_other:rwxcid
# acl_edit /.:/[PathName] -io -m any_other:rwxcid
# acl_edit /.:/[PathName]/[EachFile] -m any_other:rwxcid
```

The NFS/DFS authenticating gateway maintains DCE credentials on behalf of NFS clients to satisfy ACL permission restrictions. To use the authenticating gateway, install the dce.dfsnfs.rte fileset. Note that I'm talking AIX installation fileset versus a DFS fileset. DFS, AFS, and NFS may also be used independently on a DFS file server. Given these capabilities, you should be able to easily integrate DCE DFS into existing NFS and AFS environments.

19.2 DFS Components

I've already mentioned that DFS requires a number of servers for coordinating file system activities in a cell. These servers can be distributed and in some cases replicated across a number of machines, or they can be run on a single computer. I would not recommend the latter unless you are running a very small cell. The gaggle of DFS servers include:

- The system control machine (SCM) is responsible for housing and distributing the administration lists. These lists determine which principals (users and machines) can issue requests to the DFS servers. The group of servers managed by the SCM is called its domain. The SCM must be configured before any of the other DFS servers. Administrative lists managed by the SCM are stored in /opt/dcelocal/var/dfs, which is a link to /var/dce/dfs under AIX V4. Two server processes are run on the SCM: bosserver and upserver. The bosserver process is the basic overseer server, which runs on all DFS machines. The upserver distributes administration lists to other DFS machines.

- The binary distribution machine distributes /usr/lpp/dce/bin executables to other server machines in the cell of the same architecture (CPU/OS). The binary distribution machine runs the same upserver process as used by the SCM. In this case, the upserver distributes the DFS binaries. You can also use the binary distribution machine to distribute non-DFS binaries.

- The DFS fileset database machine (FLDB) runs the flserver process, which is responsible for maintaining information on all filesets available in a cell. All DFS file servers must register their filesets with the FLDB. The FLDB maps pathnames to the associated file server and make this information available to DFS clients. Since the FLDB is essentially a directory name server, it is a good idea to run multiple FLDB systems. Implement an odd number of FLDB servers since the machines vote to see who will be primary and who will be secondary. Primary servers are RW. Secondaries are RO copies. I know . . . what happens if one of the servers is down and there is an even number? The author leaves this as an exercise for the reader hint: weighting). Like the other servers, the FLDB also runs the bosserver and upclient.

- The file server machine runs the fileset exporter fxd, which makes filesets available to DFS clients. AIX filesets can include LFS, non-LFS, and CD-ROM types. Along with fxd, the file server also runs the fileset server ftserver, directory and security process dfsbind, and upclient to receive administration lists and binaries. Principals and groups with fileset authority are listed in the admin.ft admin list. A token manager is associated with each file server to track access to metadata. A special server called a private file server can be run by a workstation user who would like to export his or her own filesets. This is handled independent of the SCM.

- The fileset replicator machine manages fileset replication in a domain. It is primarily responsible for handling scheduled replication. Replicas improve availability of critical filesets in a domain.

- The backup database machine (BDM) manages the dump schedules of all the fileset families requiring backup services. The backup database machine interacts with the Tape Coordinators to access dump devices. This is a critical resource, so you should run more than one BDM. The bakserver process is responsible for maintaining backup information on the BDM. You guessed it: There is a bosserver and an upclient.

- The tape coordinator machine (TCM) controls physically attached dump devices and makes them available for use by the BDM. The TCM may actually run on the same computer as a BDM. This would save you a bosserver and an upclient, for instance.

- DFS clients access filesets exported by the DFS file servers. A client contacts the FLDB to find the DFS file server that is exporting the desired fileset. Each client runs a copy of dfsd, which manages the cache on the client and synchronizes the cache against the DFS file servers. A client also runs the dfsbind process, which interacts with the DCE cell directory service, security service, and FLDB to resolve path names to file servers.

- Aggregates are similar to UNIX partitions. Each aggregate can contain multiple filesets. Aggregates under AIX are logical volumes that have been formatted as a DCE LFS using the newaggr command.

- Filesets are collections of related files and directories administered as a unit under DCE/DFS. DCE quotas are applied at the fileset level. Each fileset is identified by a fileset ID number and fileset name. The fileset ID number is two positive integers separated by two commas. Quotas in DFS are applied at the fileset level in 1K increments. Filesets are either RW, RO, or backup. A backup fileset is a clone (snapshot) of an active fileset used for backup purposes.

- The local file system (LFS) is a log-based file system that supports all the features available under DFS. This includes DCE ACLs, replication, quotas, and multiple filesets per aggregate.

19.3 Installation and Configuration

Most of the following discussion assumes that you have already installed DCE base services. If you haven't already taken care of this, refer to Chap. 29. At a minimum, you will need a DCE cell directory server, a DCE security server, and three distributed time servers. Each DFS client or server must also be configured as a DCE client or server. The message "Cannot configure DFS components until a CDS clerk (cds_cl) is configured" is the first clue that DCE is not working.

I will note that one of the first things you will want to do when installing DCE and DFS is to create a separate file system for /var/dce in a non-rootvg volume group. Nearly everything that DCE services create is stored in the /var/dce directory. For DFS, the big hitter will be on-disk cache. Creating a separate /var/dce will cut down on grumbling later on when you start running out of space in rootvg. This should preferably be done before you install DCE or any components. The IBM texts recommend making /var/dce 30 MB. If you are running other DCE services on this machine, you should make it twice that size and monitor it carefully for possible expansion. You will regularly need to clean out expired credentials and audit files from this file system, so consider adding these tasks to cron.

Along with DCE client support, you will need to install one or more of the following AIX DFS packages:

dce.client	DCE Client
dce.dfs_server	DFS Servers
dce.dfsnfs	DFS/NFS Authenticating Exporter
dce.doc	Online Documentation
dce.edfs	Enhanced DFS Services

After installing the required DCE and DFS filesets, you can use SMIT to configure the base DFS servers by invoking the mkdcesrv FastPath. Command line tools are available for administering DFS (Sec. 19.4); however, I would recommend using SMIT until you are comfortable with the environment. The majority of the AIX online documentation concerning DFS is directed at SMIT help (see Fig. 19.2).

```
# smit dfsjfs      Export JFS under DFS
# smit dfscdrom    Export CD-ROM under DFS
```

If you have done your DCE homework (Chap. 29), a number of the fields in the SMIT DFS configuration screens will already be filled in. These should include:

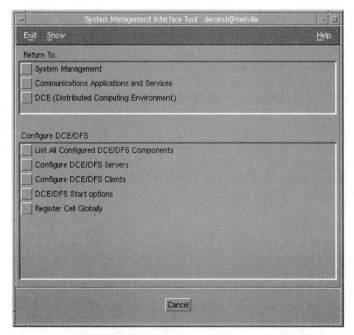

Figure 19.2   SMIT DFS administration panel.

- Cell name
- Security server
- CDS server (if in a separate network)
- Cell administrator's account
- LAN profile

You will also be prompted for the DCE cell administrator's password from time to time as you configure each service. This should have been set when you installed and configured the base DCE services. If you don't know the cell administrator's password, don't ask me!

19.3.1   System control machine

The first thing to do is configure one or more SCMs. Each SCM will control an individual domain in the cell. Select DFS (distributed file service) system control machine from the SMIT DFS configuration menu or use the FastPath mkdfsscm. After verifying the cell services settings are correct, select "OK" and supply the cell_admin password when prompted. See Fig. 19.3.

```
# smit mkdfsscm       SMIT FastPath
# mkdfs dfs_scm       Command line
```

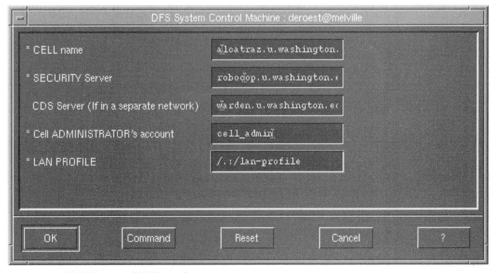

Figure 19.3   SMIT "create SCM" panel.

19.3.2   Fileset database machine

Now configure one or more FLDB systems for your cell. Multiple FLDBs will improve availability and share the workload of client requests. Select DFS fileset database machine from the SMIT DFS menu or use the mkdfsfldb FastPath. You'll run the same routine of verifying the cell profile data and supply the cell_admin password when prompted. See Fig. 19.4.

```
# smit mkdfsfldb                              SMIT FastPath
# mkdfs -s /.:/hosts/[SCMName] dfs_fldb      Command line
```

19.3.3   File server

One or more DFS file servers will be required to export DFS aggregates and filesets. Choose the DFS file server machine option from the SMIT menu or use the FastPath mkdfssrv. Verify the cell profile and supply the cell_admin password when prompted. This process will start the DFS file server daemons, but at this point you don't have anything to export. You will need to create the root.dfs LFS fileset (see Fig. 19.5).

```
# smit mkdfssrv                              SMIT FastPath
# mkdfs -s /.:/hosts/[SCMName] dfs_srv       Command line
```

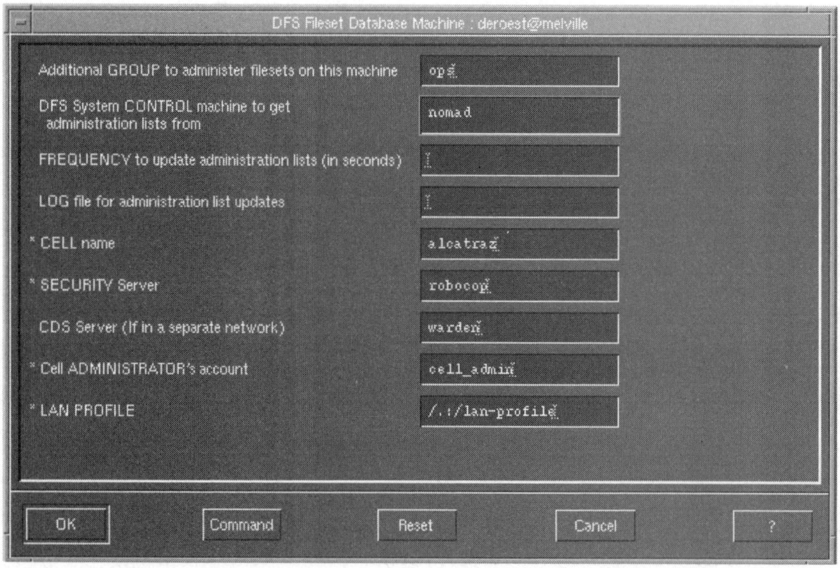

Figure 19.4   SMIT "create FLDB" Panel.

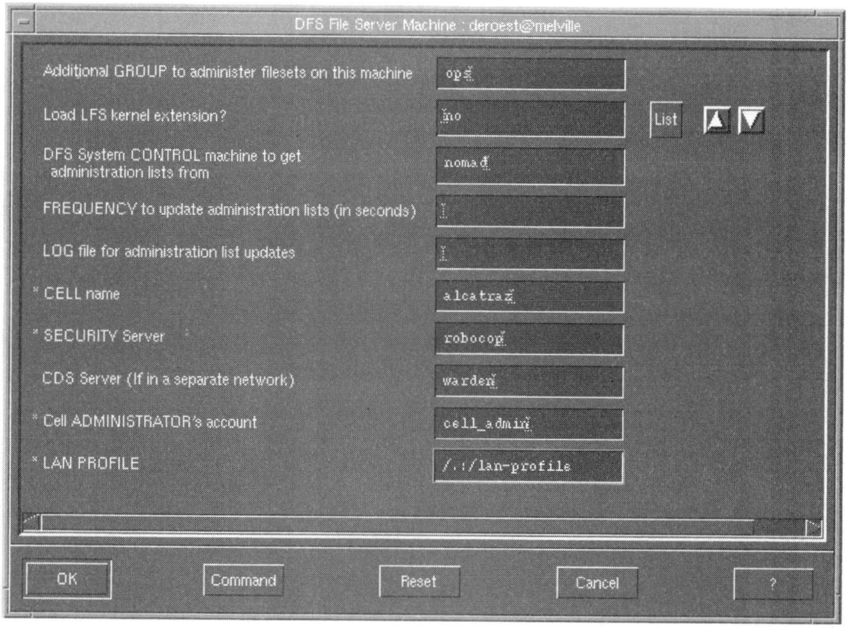

Figure 19.5   SMIT "create file server" panel.

19.3.4 Creating aggregates and filesets

Create an aggregate logical volume to hold the LFS filesets. It's probably easiest to use SMIT to do the whole process. If you decide you want to use the newaggr command line option, remember that you will need to create a logical volume device first to map to the aggregate. If you set the logical volume type to lfs within SMIT, the aggregate creation will be handled for you. You might also want to tune the aggregate blocksize to match the intended use of the file system. For example, use a small blocksize for file systems that will hold many small files.

```
# smit mklv                SMIT FastPath
# newaggr -aggregate /dev/[LVName] -blocksize 8192 \
-fragsize 1024 -overwrite   Command line
```

Now you are ready to create filesets in the aggregate. The first fileset that must be created is the root fileset named root.dfs. The fileset name is entered in the fileset field on the SMIT menu and can be any text string with the exception of the root fileset. You will also need to specify a mount point for the fileset. In the case of the root fileset, this is automatically set to /.:/fs. Once the fileset is created, an entry is placed in /opt/dcelocal/var/dfs/dfstab (see Fig. 19.6).

```
# smit dfslfs                                    SMIT FastPath
# mkdfslfs -f [LFSName] -m [MountPoint] \        Command line
        -n [AggregateName] -d [LVDevice]

# fts create -ftname [FilesetName] -aggregate [AggregateName]
```

19.3.5 Exporting and mounting filesets

You can export newly created aggregates and filesets either from the SMIT dfslfs panel or with the dfsexport command. Along with making the aggregate and/or fileset available to clients, these commands will also register the exporter in the FLDB. Note that exporting an aggregate makes all the filesets it contains available to clients. Once a fileset has been exported, it can be mounted using fts crmount.

```
# dfsexport -aggregate [AggregateName]    Export an aggregate
# fts crmount -dir [PathName] -fileset     Mount fileset
  [FilesetID]
```

The default permissions for a fileset are rwx------(700). You may wish to modify these permissions using acl_edit after mounting. Also verify that the fileset quota is sufficient. Check and set the fileset quota with fts lsquota and fts setquota, respectively.

```
# acl_edit [PathName] -m [Permissions]     Set ACL
# fts lsquota -dir [PathName] -fileset     Check quota
  [FilesetID]
# fts setquota -dir [PathName] -fileset    Set quota
  [FilesetID] -size [KB]
```

AIX V4 supports exporting JFS and CD-ROM filesystems. This can be done using the SMIT FastPaths dfsjfs and dfscdrom.

```
# smit dfsjfs      Export JFS under DFS
# smit dfscdrom    Export CD-ROM under DFS
```

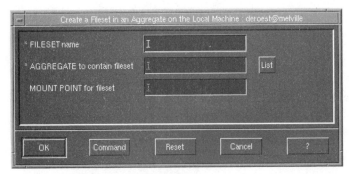

Figure 19.6 SMIT "create fileset" panel.

19.3.6 Backup database machine

To perform periodic DFS backups, create one or more DFS backup database machines. You can select the option for DFS backup database machine from the DCE/DFS configuration menu or invoke the SMIT mkdfsbkdb FastPath. After completing the SMIT information and option execution, the system will be configured to run the bakserver process. See Fig. 19.7.

```
# smit mkdfsbkdb
```

19.3.7 Fileset replicator

```
# smit mkdfsrepsrv
```

Click on "DFS Fileset Replication Server Machine" on the SMIT DFS menu. SMIT will request the cell_admin password. This is all that is required to start the replication server on the system.

19.3.8 Installation verification

After completing configuration of the DFS service machines, verify the configuration from each participating system. First look at the /etc/mkdce.data file to list the DFS services being run on the particular machine.

```
# cat /etc/mkdce.data
```

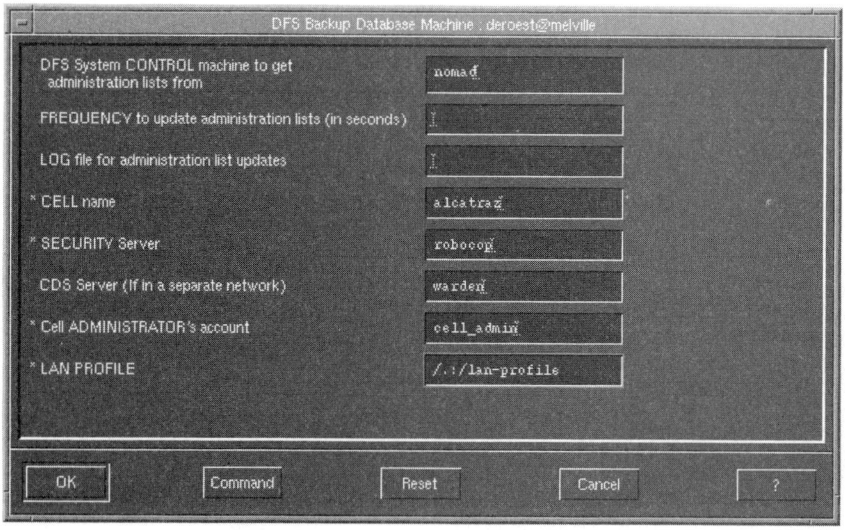

Figure 19.7 SMIT "create BDM" panel.

```
cds_cl       COMPLETE   CDS Clerk
cds_srv      COMPLETE   Initial CDS Server
dfs_cl       COMPLETE   DFS Client Machine
dts_local    COMPLETE   Local DTS Server
rpc          COMPLETE   RPC Endpoint Mapper
sec_cl       COMPLETE   Security Client
cec_srv      COMPLETE   Security Server
```

Next, verify aggregates, filesets, and exports. Check the dfstab for aggregates residing on the machine. Use dfsexport to list filesets exported from the machine.

```
# cat /opt/dcelocal/dfs/dfstab

# blkdev          aggname     aggtype    aggid    [UFS fsid]
/dev/lfsrootlv    lfsroot     lfs        1
dfsexport

dfsexport: dfs_domain#root,lfs, 1, 0,,1
dfsexport: dfs_domain#dfs1,lfs, 2, 0,,4
```

Use fts lsfldb to verify that all filesets and servers are listed in the FLDB.

```
fts lsfldb

root.dfs
  readWrite    ID 0,,1 valid
  readOnly     ID 0,,2 invalid
  backup       ID 0,,3 invalid
number of sites: 1
  server              flags aggr siteAge principal  owner
  et-home.u.washingt  RW    /dfs/root 0:00:00 hosts/neruda  <nil>
user.d1
  readWrite  ID 0,,4 valid
  readOnly   ID 0,,5 invalid
  backup     ID 0,,6 invalid
number of sites: 1
  server flags aggr  siteAge principal  owner
  et-home.u.washingt RW  /dfs/dfs1 0:00:00 hosts/neruda <nil>
-------------------------------
Total FLDB entries that were successfully enumerated: 2 (0 failed;
0 wrong aggr type)
```

19.4 Operation and Administration

We've already covered a number of the commands used to administer DFS. Each of the DFS commands supports enough options and parameters that the permutations and combinations are well beyond what I can cover in a single chapter. What I will do is give a list of the base commands and the procedure for obtaining help. In most instances, you can invoke the command name with the help [option] string for a brief listing of available options.

`# CommandName help [option]`   Display command help

DFS Administration Commands

`mkdfs`	Create DFS components
`rmdfs`	Remove DFS components
`lsdfs`	List DFS components
`bak`	Manage backup system
`bos`	Bosserver access
`cm`	Cache manager control
`dfsexport`	Export aggregates and filesets
`fts`	Manage filesets
`growaggr`	Expand aggregates
`newaggr`	Create aggregates
`salvage`	Check LSF integrity
`scout`	Monitor exporters

19.5   Starting DFS

To set your DFS services startup configuration, invoke the SMIT Fast-Path mkdceitab. You will be prompted to select the DCE and DFS servers to start followed by a panel asking whether to start the servers now, at the next restart, or at both. SMIT will take care of updating your /etc/inittab and /etc/rc.dce files (see Fig. 19.8).

`# smit mkdceitab`   Start DFS services

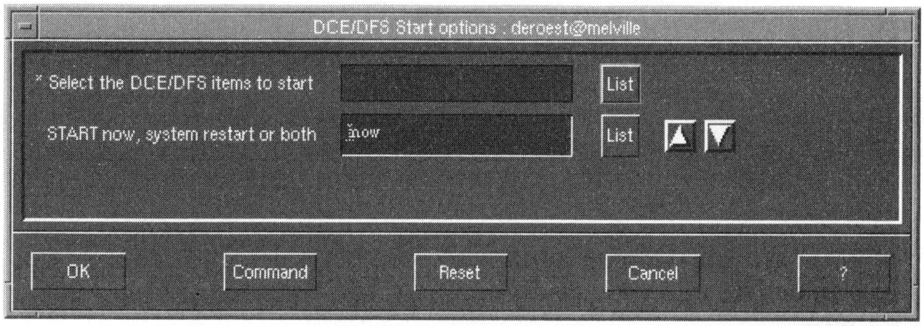

Figure 19.8   SMIT "start DFS" panel.

19.6   Access Control Lists

Just a few words about DCE ACLs: They work a bit differently than what you may expect from dealing with standard UNIX permissions. ACLs are applied to containers and objects. DFS containers are directories that contain objects (files) or other containers. By default, directories and files inherit the container ACL of the directory under which they reside. You can set specific ACLs for users, groups, and others using the acl_edit command. ACLs are very nice in that they can be set up by the owning user. You as a system administrator only have to worry about system default ACLs that are required to ensure general security. Remember that ACLs only apply to LFS filesets.

ACLs are associated with object types mask_obj, user_obj, group_obj, and other_obj. The mask_obj entry is used to filter the maximum set of permissions that can be granted by object types. Note that it cannot be used to increase or extend permissions (see Tables 19.1 and 19.2).

```
$ acl_edit [PathName] -m [ACLs]      Modify ACLs
$ acl_edit [PathName] -1             List ACLs
```

19.7   Replication

DFS replication is a handy tool for managing common file system trees across a number of machines when availability requirements won't allow network mounting. A replicated fileset should be a group of files that aren't modified often. Good candidates for replication include operating system commands and application binaries. Replicas are created from a RW master copy. Each replica fileset is RO. Replicas are updated either at scheduled intervals or at manually called release. To create a replica, begin by setting the replication information and site list on the machine with the master copy of the fileset.

```
# fts setrepinfo [-release | -scheduled]    Source replica type
# fts addsite                               Source sitelist update
```

On the target machine(s), first create an aggregate large enough to hold the replica and update the site list.

TABLE 19.1   ACL Permissions

r	(read)
w	(write)
x	(execute)
c	(control ACL)
i	(insert, meaningless for files)
d	(delete, meaningless for files)

TABLE 19.2 ACL Types

user_obj	The user who owns the object
user	The user "username" from the local cell
foreign_user	The user "username" from the foreign cell "cell_name"
group_obj	Members of the group who own the object
group	The group "group_name" from the local cell
foreign_group	The group "group_name" from the foreign cell "cell_name"
other_obj	Users from the local cell who do not match any preceding entries
foreign_other	Users from the foreign cell "cell_name" who do not match any of the preceding entries
any_other	Users from any foreign cell who do not match any of the preceding entries
mask_obj	Mask for maximum permissions that can be set, except for group_obj and other _obj

The any_other entry is used for users who are not authenticated to the local cell.

fts addsite   Client sitelist update

If you chose scheduled replication, then the fileset will be replicated at the interval you indicated. For release replicas, you can manually start replication using the fts release option.

fts release   Manual replication

Note that replication improves availability by making multiple copies of a fileset available to clients. The client cache manager will select RO replicas when acquiring a mount point unless RW is specified.

19.8 DFS Backup

DFS has its own backup system that keeps track of tapes, dump dates, backup sets, and other types of fileset recovery information. You can't perform dumps using standard UNIX dump commands due to DFS specific metadata like ACLs. A non-LFS fileset mounted on the local system can be backed up using standard UNIX tools, since non-LFS filesets don't have ACLs. Note that you can use standard UNIX tools in a DFS environment to create archives like tar and cpio; however, no ACL information is stored in the archive.

The DFS dump process begins by taking a snapshot of an active file system called a clone. The clone is not a copy of the data, but rather a set of pointers to the data blocks that made up the file system at the time the clone was made. Users may continue to actively use the file system while the clone is traversed for backup purposes. This eliminates the problem of backing up an active file system where an inode may be invalid due to updates in progress.

fts clone -fileset [FilesetID]   Clone a fileset
bak dump -family [FilesetFamily] -tcid [DevID]   Start a dump

The bak command is used to configure, dump, and track dump status. DFS backup supports both full and incremental dumps. The DFS bak command is another one of the commands that is best left to more extensive documentation concerning its vast number of options (see Table 19.3).

19.9   InfoExplorer Keywords

DFS	newaggr
ACL	salvage
fileset	scount
aggregates	cell
LFS	DCE
quota	replication
lsquota	clone
dfsexport	fxd
fts	flserver
bak	ftserver
mkdfs	upserver
rmdfs	upclient
lsdfs	admin.ft
bosserver	bakserver
cm	dfsd
growaggr	

19.10   QwikInfo

Directories:

`"/.../[CellName]"`	Cell root level
`"/.:"`	
`"/:"`	
`/var/dce, /opt/dcelocal`	Config file, cache, logs, etc.
`/etc/mkdce.data`	Configured components
`/usr/lpp/dce`	DCE product set

TABLE 19.3   DFS bak Options

addump	Add dump schedule
addftentry	Add new fileset entry
addftfamily	Create a new fileset family
addhost	Add host to configuration database
apropos	Search by help text
deletedump	Delete a dump from the database
dump	Start dump
dumpinfo	View information about the most recent backups
ftinfo	Display a dump history for a fileset
help	Get help on commands
jobs	List running jobs
kill	Kill running job
labeltape	Label tape
lsdumps	List dump levels
lsftfamiies	List fileset families
lshosts	List hosts in configuration database
quit	Leave the program
readlabel	Read label on tape
restoredb	Restore bak database from tape
restoredisk	Restore aggregate
restoreft	Restore fileset
restoreftfamily	Restore a dump set
rmdump	Delete dump schedule
rmftentry	Delete fileset sub-entry
rmftfamily	Delete fileset family
rmhost	Delete host from configuration database
savedb	Copy bak database to tape
scantape	List filesets on tape
setexp	Set/clear expiration date for dump
status	Get tape coordinator status
verifydb	Check the integrity of bak database

Components:

SCM	System control machine
FLDB	Fileset database machine
FS	File server
FR	Fileset replicator
BDM	Backup database machine
TCM	Tape coordinator machine
LFS	DFS local file system
Aggregate	Similar to UNIX partition
Fileset	Group of related files
ACL	Access control list

Configuration:

smit mkdce	Set up DCE base
smit mkdfsscm	Create SCM
smit mkdfsfldb	Create FLDB
smit mkdfssrv	Create file server
smit dfslfs	Create LFS
smit mkdfsbkdb	Create BDM
smit mkdfsrepsrv	Create fileset replicator
smit mkdceitab	Start DCE/DFS

File system management:

fts crmount	Create a mount point
fts lsmount	List mounts
dfsexport	Export a file system
smit dfsjfs	Export JFS under DFS
smit dfscdrom	Export CD-ROM under DFS
bak	Back up file families
fts clone	Create a clone for backup
acl_edit	Modify ACLs

20

Desktop File Services

20.1 Samba

Interested in introducing your UNIX file system and print resources to Windows and OS/2 desktops? Maybe you're already sharing resources in the Windows environment using Windows or LAN Manager network servers. Why not swing your UNIX resource servers into step with the Windows servers? Get them all dancing together to the same tune. What tune, you ask? The Samba!

Samba is a Portuguese word meaning "a rhythm and a dance." It's derived from a term from the West African Bantu language: *semba,* meaning "to pray or invoke the spirits of ancestors." As a Bantu verb, *semba* means "to cry" or "to have the blues." In Brazil, a *samba* is a woman who is a sacred dancer. Depending on how your distributed services are working, maybe the "to cry" and "have the blues" definitions are applicable. If this rings true, then maybe it's time to start dancing to the beat of Andrew Tridgell's Samba.

Samba, in computer terms, is a suite of software programs that provides a NetBIOS interface to UNIX managed file systems and printers under session message block protocol (SMB). SMB is the protocol used by LAN Manager, Windows, and OS/2 to support distributed NetBIOS services referred to as shares. Samba implements SMB over TCP, so you can use your existing TCP/IP network infrastructure without adding gateway hardware (RFC 1001 and RFC 1002). From your desktop, Samba resources appear just like other Windows network devices (see Fig. 20.1). No special client-side software is required. It even works over dialup PPP connections.

20.2 Installation and Configuration

Samba installation is straightforward. Download and untar the distribution file into a temporary directory. Carefully study the README,

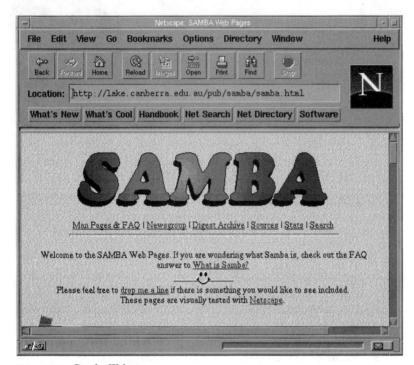

Figure 20.1 Samba Web page.

INSTALL.txt, and smbd.8 documents. Tailor the Makefile template to identify your OS type and the path particulars for where you want the distribution to be installed on your system. Next invoke the make command and follow step 2 in the INSTALL.txt document. It will direct you to obtain the required stimulants to get you through the Samba configuration process. It's really not that bad, but if you did your homework and looked closely at the smbd.8 man page, you'll have noticed that there are a vast number of configuration options available to tailor the service to meet the intricate rhythms of most distributed desktop computing environments.

20.2.1 smb.conf

Configuration work is focused on the smb.conf file. This file is similar to other UNIX config files in that it is stanza-based. It begins with a global section to set system-wide defaults, followed by stanzas for specific directory and printer shares (see examples 20.2 and 20.3). Variable substitution and wild card capabilities are provided using a set of "%" macros. Macros are very useful in cutting down on size and complexity of your configuration file. Once your smb.conf configuration is completed, you are ready to begin teaching your systems to dance the Samba.

Before letting your servers start doing the happy-feet dance, there are a few things of which you should be aware concerning Samba resource consumption on your server. Isn't there always! One smbd daemon is spawned for each user connection. A master smbd daemon can be run at system startup time, or it can be added to the /etc/inetd.conf file and invoked by inetd when referenced. In general, each smbd process is about 800 KB in size, but they may grow due to cache utilization. Some clients have nasty habits like not closing files to free up cache pages on the smbd server. Large numbers of open files and large directories mean large cache size on the server. You can limit smbd caching by modifying parameters in the local.h header file prior to building the Samba source code. This file includes knobs for controlling maximum cache size, maximum number of open files, maximum number of connections, and so on. See Table 20.1 for a list of Samba components.

20.2.2   Name service

Clients locate servers using the server name and standard DNS host name to IP address mapping provided either from name service or an /etc/hosts file. If you want to be able to browse share servers from your desktop client GUI, you will also need to run WINS name service. This can be accomplished by running the Samba nmbd WINS name server on your server and configuring an LMHOSTS file. The LMHOSTS format is similar to /etc/hosts in that it maps IP addresses to share server names (Example 20.1). A third parameter can be used with each address name pair to control preloading the server name and domain assignment. Problems with name service are among the most common bugs when trying to locate a share from a desktop client. Test your name service configuration using nmblookup.

```
# nmblookup -d2 '*'
```

TABLE 20.1   Samba Components

smb.conf	Configuration file
smbd	SMB server
smbclient	UNIX ftp-like SMB client
smbrun	smbd interface to invoke external programs
smbstatus	Check current connections
smbtar	Backup shares script
testprns	Test printer config
testparms	Test config file params
nmbd	Name server
nmblookup	Name service tool
smbpasswd	Set Samba password
addtosmbpass	Batch update Samba password

Note that some clients have problems with names larger than 8 characters, mixed-case names, or names with embedded spaces. Non-browsable servers can be accessed by directly supplying the server and share names. For example:

```
net use H: \\server\resource
```

You might wish to make a server nonbrowsable for security or privacy reasons.

Example 20.1   Sample LMHOSTS

```
0.0.0.0          mygroup      # local net group
122.95.23.255    aliengrp     # other net group
122.95.22.123    alienapp     # other app server
```

20.2.3   Directory shares

Shared UNIX directories appear as network drives to the desktop. They are assigned a drive letter when mounted and referenced like any other desktop drive. Configuration options are available to map or ignore long UNIX file names, hide files, and support DOS hidden file attributes. Access permissions are implemented as a mixture of UNIX, DOS, and Samba controls. UNIX permissions override all other parameters. To access a file on the server, a user must have an account on the server to enable UNIX file permissions. The account does not require a login shell. When accessing a server and share, the user must supply an account name and password. You may also elect to use Samba managed passwords. If you elect to use the same passwords on both your desktops and servers, you should be aware that there are some vulnerabilities in Windows password security. The Samba server may also be susceptible to brute force password attacks.

Samba provides a large number of parameters to control access and sharing. Restrictions may be placed at the network, host, group, and individual user levels through the use of access lists. You may also force the identity of a user to set specific ownership rights. Options to set file creation masks, restrict access to read only, and inhibit descending directory trees are available. Take a look at the stanzas in Example 20.2. The sample stanzas will give you a general idea on how granular access controls might be implemented.

Example 20.2   smb.conf File Share

```
[global]
  browseable = no
```

```
         public = no
         writable = no
         create mask = 0700

    [homes]
         comment = Home Directories
         browseable = no
         read only = no
         hosts allow = .only.our.org

    [apps]
         comment = Shared Applications
         path = /usr/local/bin
         public = yes
         writable = no
         printable = no

    [janeproj]
         comment = Jane's Project Directory
         path = /usr/local/jane
         valid users = jane bill jan
         public = no
         writable = yes
         create mask = 0750
```

20.2.4 Printer shares

Printer sharing is set up much the same way as directory sharing concerning permissions and access control (Example 20.3). When a file is printed from the desktop, Samba print services copies the file to a writable spool area on the server and invokes the server's print queuing system. Make sure that the spool has the correct directory permissions set. You will also need to identify the UNIX queuing type in smb.conf using the printing = option. Supported spooling systems include those found in Table 20.2.

You can also indicate a specific command to be invoked for processing print files using the command = option. Use a fully qualified path name as the parameter value. This option can be used to spool files to other UNIX services like batch systems.

TABLE 20.2   Samba Print Queue Types

printing = bsd	lpr based printing
printing = sysv	lp based printing
printing = aix	AIX spooling
printing = hpux	HP spooling

Example 20.3   smb.conf Printers

```
[global]
    printing = aix
    load printers = yes

[printers]
    path = /tmp
    browseable = yes
    writable = no
    printable = yes

[bobsprn]
    comment = Bob's Printer
    path = /home/bob
    valid users = bob
    public = no
    browseable = no
    printable = yes
    writable = no
```

20.3   NFS and DFS Compatibility

You might experience directory corruption exposure if you use Samba to share directories that are mounted on the server via NFS. I have done this successfully from both AIX and OSF/1 Samba servers, but I have heard of cases where editing can result in zero-length files. If you decide to try this, you're on your own. Note also that there is limited support for DCE DFS in Samba under AIX, OSF/1 and HP/UX. Samba supports per-instance DCE authentication and access to DFS filesets. It doesn't support DCE thread-safe signals. This means you can't use sighup to refresh an smbd server to read a new smb.conf file or trap sigbus or sigsegv exceptions.

20.4   Samba Licensing

Samba is available free of charge per the terms of the GNU general public license. Platforms include AIX, A/UX, BSDI, DGUX, HP/UX, Linux, NeXT OS, OSF/1 SCO, SGI, Sinix, Solaris, SunOS, SYSV, Ultrix, and others. If it remotely looks like UNIX, then somebody has probably done a Samba port. Novell has released a Samba port to Netware that is shipped as part of the migration CD. Samba enjoys a fairly extensive grassroots support group ready to assist new users and trade tips and tricks. An excellent Web page maintained by Paul Blackman (see Table 20.3) includes all the documentation you might require. The page also

TABLE 20.3   SAMBA and CAP Archives

Samba	`http://lake.canberra.edu.au/pub/samba/samba.html`
	`http://lake.canberra.edu.au/samba/docs/samba.faq.html`
	`http://www.c2.org/hackmsoft/`
	`ftp://nimbus.anu.edu.au/pub/samba`
	`ftp://sunsite.unc.edu/pub/Linux/Network/Samba/`
	`comp.protocols.smb`
	`http://www.thursby.com/davespd.html`

CAP	`http://paella.med.yale.edu:80/tpics/CAP.html`
	`http://www.astro.new.edu/lentz/mac/faqs/source/cap.html`
	`ftp://gatekeeper.dec.com/pub/net/appletalk/cap/`

includes profiles of sites that are successfully using Samba. The profile information includes a description of the site's Samba configuration, experiences, and wish lists. Sound like a tune you could dance to?

20.5   What About Macs?

A SMB client for Macintosh is now available called "Dave" from Thursby Software Systems, Inc. (see Table 20.3). To provide file and print sharing similar to Samba, you might want to take a look at the Columbia Appletalk Package (CAP) by Charlie Kim and Bill Schilit (see Table 20.3). CAP supports AppleShare compatible file service and LaserWriter spooling from UNIX servers. Platforms include AIX, A/UX, Dynix, HPUX, IRIX, NeXT OS, SunOS, and various flavors of BSD UNIX. CAP requires the use of an IPTalk capable gateway like the Cayman GatorBox or Cisco router.

I've barely brushed the surface of the capabilities provided by Samba. The best way to see what it can do is to try it out yourself. You should be able to get a test system up and running with minimal effort. Time to get up and dance. Everybody Samba!

Distributed Services

21

Electronic Mail

21.1 Mail System Overview

With mixed feelings I write this chapter on configuring and managing electronic mail. The reason being that electronic mail is addictive! Don't try to tell me it's not. It's one of those things that, once you have it, you can't live without it. Everyday my mail box receives close to a hundred mail files. I find myself sneaking an E-mail fix throughout the day, in the evenings, on weekends, after church! I feel like I'm pushing an uncontrolled substance!

Seriously, electronic mail provides avenues of collaboration that are changing the way we do business, conduct research, and interact with each other. Electronic mail is informal. People who have never been introduced feel at ease to discuss almost any topic via electronic mail. The impromptu nature of electronic mail seems to allow people to express their views and feelings honestly. Sometimes beyond their better judgement.

It's our duty as administrators to support this kind of interaction. After all, information sharing is what this industry is all about. With a little feeding and care, the electronic mail system can be a controlled substance that is good for everyone.

The electronic mail or E-mail system is conceptually if not physically divided into two components: the user agent (UA) and the mail transport agent (MTA).

`/bin/mail` or `/usr/ucb/mail`	User agent
`/usr/sbin/sendmail`	Mail transfer agent

21.1.1 Mail user agents

The mail user agent provides the user interface to the mail system. The UA presents incoming mail to the user for reading and archiving. Editor facilities for composing, forwarding, or replying are managed by the UA. A great deal of "human factors" research is being invested in UA design. Sure, make it even more addictive!

The ATT and BSD mail programs provide all the basic elements of a good UA. No frills but they get the job done. For naive users, these probably aren't good UAs to use. Full-screen, menu-oriented UAs like elm or pine are probably a better choice. Being that this is an administrator's text, I won't spend time on the pros and cons of the various UAs. It's a religious issue best left to the practitioners. Since I am employed by the University of Washington, I will at least say that you can obtain a copy of Pine via anonymous ftp from ftphost.cac.washington.edu. You can find elm and other user-friendly UAs from a number of ftp sites on the network. Use the Web to find the ftp site nearest you (see Appendix A).

In the following sections, where reference is made to a UA, assume basic ATT or BSD mail functionality and options.

The system administrator is responsible for setting the default UA configuration options. The default options are defined in the /usr/lib/.Mail.rc file. Each user may override the global defaults by resetting the options in a local $HOME/.mailrc file.

The following is a configuration file for UA:

```
# /usr/lib/Mail.rc
#
# Options
#
set ask askcc dot save keep crt
#
# Don't display the following header lines
#
ignore Received Message-Id Resent-Message-Id
ignore Status Mail-From Return-Path Via
```

21.1.2 Mail transport agents

The MTA is responsible for receiving and delivering mail. At a minimum, the MTA must be able to accept mail from UAs and the network, decipher addresses, and deliver the message to a local user mailbox or to a remote MTA. Better MTAs will be able to detect E-mail loops, route a single mail message for multiple recipients at the same site, support privacy, and route problem mail to a site postmaster. Common MTAs include BSD sendmail, mmdf, smail, and mhs. In the following sections, I will discuss sendmail configuration and administration.

21.1.3   Addressing and headers

In order for a mail message to traverse from user A to user B, an addressing mechanism that is understood by the MTAs must be used. From the discussion in Chap. 15 concerning the domain name space, you might think that this is a simple issue. However, E-mail gateways to other networks involving other addressing protocols can make address resolution problem as hard as artificial intelligence.

The most common UNIX mail formats involve Internet domain addressing and UUCP addressing.

```
user@domain-address          Internet address
host1!…!destination!user     UUCP address
```

Two types of mail headers are attached to each mail message that defines the attributes of the message. The simple mail transfer protocol (SMTP RFC 821) provides a command syntax that MTAs use to negotiate mail transfer from one MTA to the next.

The following example contains a SMTP header:

```
HELLO daffy.foo.bar.edu            Introduce yourself to the MTA
MAIL From: raphael@park.foo.edu    Indicate the originator
RCPT To: rachael@lite.house.com    Announce the recipients
DATA                               Supply the data of the E-mail
                                   message
QUIT                               Exit
```

The second type of mail header is the RFC 822 header. It is used by both the MTA and UA. The RFC 822 header identifies the path the mail message has traveled, date, originator, recipients, subject, and so on.

```
Received: from mailer.foo.edu
      by lite.house.com id AA03037;
      Sun, 10 Nov 96 15:07 PST
Received: from park.foo.edu
      by mailer.foo.edu id aa12242;
      Sun, 10 Nov 96 15:01 PST
Date: Sun, 10 Nov 96 14:59:10 PST
From: raphael@park.foo.edu
To: rachael@lite.house.com
Subject: Meeting Wednesday

Rachael:

Can we meet on Wednesday to discuss mailer
configuration for the department workstations?

Raphael
```

The ordering of the received lines indicates the MTA path that the mail message has traveled. This path can be used to debug routing problems and loops.

21.1.4   How mail is sent

When a user composes a mail message, the UA attaches a header envelope to the message separated by a blank line. The UA then hands the message off to the sendmail MTA. A new sendmail daemon is forked to process the new message. Sendmail passes each of the addresses associated with the mail message through address translation rule sets. The rule sets parse the address line and determines if the message destination is local or remote. If the message is destined for a remote site, name service may be queried to determine if a preferred mail exchange site is requested for the remote site (Name service MX record). If the remote site is running a sendmail MTA, the message is transferred to the remote site using the SMTP protocol described above. At the remote site, sendmail runs the addresses through the rule sets again to determine if the recipient is local or remote. If the recipient is local, the headers are rewritten and the message is spooled to the recipients mail inbox.

21.2   Sendmail Configuration

The sendmail MTA is probably the most common MTA in use. Unfortunately, it is one of the most difficult to configure. Sendmail was originally written by Eric Allman at the University of California at Berkeley at a time when mail traffic was sparser than what we experience today. It is to Eric's credit that sendmail has proven to be general enough to evolve with the traffic requirements. Sendmail has gone through many changes since its initial inception and as a result has become quite complex. Successfully configuring a sendmail.cf file can certainly be considered one of the rites of passage to UNIX wizardom.

Sendmail Data Files

`/etc/sendmail.cf`	Sendmail configuration file
`/etc/sendmail.cfDB`	Compiled sendmail configuration file
`/etc/sendmail.nl`	Sendmail national language rules
`/etc/sendmail.nlDB`	Compiled national language rules
`/etc/aliases`	Mail aliases
`/etc/aliases{DB, DB.pg}`	Compiled alias file
`/etc/sendmail.pid`	PID of sendmail daemon
`/etc/sendmail.st`	Mail statistics

NOTE: These files are accessed via symbolic links from /usr/lib.

21.2.1   sendmail.cf

The sendmail configuration file /etc/sendmail.cf contains the majority of the options and rules required by sendmail to deliver E-mail. The sendmail.cf file maintains three sets of configuration data:

Options, variables, and parameters

Address rewriting rule sets

Mailer identification and delivery

The best way to start configuring a new sendmail.cf file is to obtain a copy of one that works. AIX V4 supplies a boiler plate sendmail.cf file that can be used with minimal changes if your E-mail environment is not complex. By complex I mean that you have a number of mail gateways to other networks or a hierarchy of MTAs. You can tailor the sendmail.cf file using your favorite editor. AIX V3 had a nice tool for configuring sendmail.cf called /usr/lib/edconfig. edconfig provided a menu-oriented approach to editing sendmail.cf components. For those of you new to sendmail, it focused your attention on the option being changed. It's easy to get confused when working with the whole file in an editor. The problem was that the edconfig command could become confused with custom sendmail.cf files. Likely the reason for its demise.

Commands and definitions begin in column 1 in the sendmail.cf file. Comments begin with a number sign (#). Blank lines are ignored. Due to the number of special characters used, you need to be careful when adding address types like DECNETS "::" node delimiters. A set of predefined character symbols are used to indicate the definition of new symbols, classes, options, macros, or rules. Using a dollar sign ($) with a macro or variable name indicates the value of the variable or macro. A question mark (?) indicates a boolean test. In the following discussion, I'll define the symbols used in each section of the sendmail.cf file and provide an example.

21.2.1.1   Options and definitions section.
The first section of the sendmail.cf file identifies the runtime options and variables. These include definition of the host or domain name, the status of name service mail exchange support, message precedence, and so on. Option symbols are as follows.

"D" defines a symbol from text or a built-in variable.

```
DSfoo.bar.com
```
                         Define subdomain as variable S.

"C" defines a class from a list.

```
CFhost1 host2 host3
```
                         Define a host list as variable F.

"F" defines a class from a file.

`FF/usr/local/lib/hosts`   Obtain list F from hosts file.

"H" defines header formats.

`D?P?Return-Path: <$g>`   Define return-path format.

"O" sets sendmail runtime options.

`OA/etc/aliases`   Define alias file path.

`OK ALL`   Support all nameservice mail exchange
                                records and host table lookups.

"T" sets trusted users.

`Tusername1 username2`   These users may invoke sendmail and
                                masquerade as other users.

"P" sets message precedence.

`priority=100`   Indicate delivery priority if
                                precedence:header field is found. Negative
`junk=100`   numbers do not return mail on error.

21.2.1.2   Address rules.   The address rewriting rules are where the
wizards are separated from the apprentices. The sendmail daemon
uses the rule sets to parse the address lines from the mail header to
determine how the mail message should be delivered.

Each rule set is made up of three parts: left-hand side (LHS), right-
hand side (RHS), and optional comment (C). Each part is separated by
a tab. In general, if an address matches the LHS rule, then the RHS
rule is applied to the address. The rule sets are applied in order until
a failure occurs. Any number of rule sets can be defined (see Tables
21.1 and 21.2).

To deliver a mail message, the rule sets must resolve to a (mailer,
host, user) tuple.

TABLE 21.1   Default sendmail.cf Rule Sets

Rule set	Description
3	Applied first and is responsible for canonicalizing the address to internal form.
2	Rewrites recipient address.
1	Rewrites sender address.
0	Applied last and determines delivery. Address must be resolved to a (mailer, host, user) tuple.
4	Final rewrite of canonical internal form to external form.

TABLE 21.2   Rule Set Symbols

	LHS tokens
$*	Match 0 or more tokens
$+	Match 1 or more tokens
$-	Match exactly 1 token.
$=X	Match any token in class X.
$~X	Match any token not in X.
	RHS tokens
$n	Use token n from LHS.
$>n	Call rule set n.
$#mailer	Resolve to mailer.
$@host	Specify host to mailer.
$:user	Specify user to mailer.
$[host$]	Get host from resolver.
$@	Terminate rule set.
$:	Terminate current rule.

The following example shows a rule set of a seven-parses domain string:

```
S7
#Domain addressing (up to 6 level)
R$+@$-.$-.$-.$-.$-.$-.$-    @$2.$3.$4.$5.$6.$7
R$+@$-.$-.$-.$-.$-.$-       @$2.$3.$4.$5.$6
R$+@$-.$-.$-.$-             @$2.$3.$4.$5
R$+@$-.$-.$-                @$2.$3.$4
R$+@$-.$-                   @$2.$3
R$+@$-                      @$2
```

21.2.1.3 Mailer delivery. The last section of the sendmail.cf file identifies the mailers to be used to deliver the mail message. Each mailer is identified by a name, a program used to transfer the messages to the mailer, the set of program flags, the send and receive rules, and the argument set. The mailer identification format is as follows:

```
M<mailer> P=<prog> F=<flags> S=<send-rule> F=<receive-rule>
A=<arguments>
```

The following is an example of local and X.400 RFC 987 mailer definition:

```
Mlocal, P=/bin/bellmail, F=lsDFMmn, S=10, R=20, A=mail $u

M987gateway, P=/usr/lpp/osimf/etc/x400mailer, F=sBFMhulmnSC,
S=15, R=25,
    A=gateway -f/etc/x400gw.cfg $f$u
```

Sendmail accesses configuration file information from a compiled version of the /etc/sendmail.cf table. To compile a new version of the database, use the sendmail -bz flag.

```
# /usr/lib/sendmail -bz     Compile a new sendmail.cf database
```

21.2.2   sendmail.nl

The AIX-supplied sendmail daemon also obtains national language rule sets from the /etc/sendmail.nl file. The national languages rules are regular expressions that may be used to identify country names or country codes to support language translation. If the country is identified in the list of National Language Support (NLS) code sets, the message is converted to the correct code set.

Here is a listing of the AIX-supplied /etc/sendmail.nl:

```
# aix_sccsid[]="com/cmd/send/sendmail.nl;
#
# COMPONENT_NAME: CMDSEND sendmail.nl
#
# FUNCTIONS:
#
# ORIGINS: 10 26 27
#
# (C) COPYRIGHT International Business Machines Corp. 1985, 1989
# All Rights Reserved
# Licensed Materials - Property of IBM
#
# US Government Users Restricted Rights - Use, duplication or
# disclosure restricted by GSA ADP Schedule Contract with IBM Corp.
#
# Created: 03/24/89, INTERACTIVE Systems Corporation
#
#####################################################################
#
# This file contains lists of regular expressions which are
# compared against the destination address when sending out
# mail to other systems. Each comma-separated list is preceded
# by either "NLS:" or "8859:". Addresses which match an item
# in these lists will have the body of the mail item encoded
# as either NLS escape sequences or ISO 8859/1 characters,
# respectively.
#
# Before each address is compared with these lists it is passed
# through ruleset 7, which normally strips the user information
# from uucp-style addresses and route and user information from
```

```
# domain-style addresses.
#
# The following example lists shows how this file might look:
#
# #list the nls compatible systems
# NLS:     ^@.*madrid\.,
#          ^@rome,
#          ^@.*italy\.europe$,
#          !nagasaki!$,
#          lisbon!,
#          munich,
#          berlin
#
# #list the ISO-8859 compatible systems
# 8859:    .*vienna!$,
#          ^@bangkok\.thailand,
#          ^@tangiers,
#          ^@kinshasa
#
# Note that all dots "." in an address must be escaped with
# a backslash "\". All standard regular expression rules apply.
# Several of the above examples are not recommended for actual
# use but are shown to give some idea of the flexibility that
# is allowed. For example, the first example "madrid" will match
# any domain-style address which has this name as a subdomain.
# A more likely example of this type is "italy.europe" which will
# match all domains that are in that sub-domain. The examples
# "munich" and "berlin" are not recommended forms either since they
# will match a variety of addresses.
#
# This file must be compiled using the "-bn" option before sendmail
# can use it. It is recommended that this file be tested against
# common addresses using the "-br" option to verify that addresses
# are being interpreted correctly.
#
#####################################################################
```

21.2.3 Aliases

The sendmail alias database provides a mechanism for forwarding mail to one or more users when mail is addressed to the alias name. In particular, you will want to setup aliases for the site postmaster and MAILER-DAEMON IDs. The postmaster account is a standard used by the network at large for requesting mail help and information for a site. The MAILER-DAEMON account is used by sendmail to route problem mail.

Here is an example of /etc/aliases:

```
##
# Aliases in this file will NOT be expanded in the header from
# Mail, but WILL be visible over networks or from /bin/mail.
#
#      >>>>>>>>> The program "sendmail-bi" must be run after
#      >>NOTE>> updating this file before any changes
#      >>>>>>>>> show through to sendmail.
##
#
# Alias for mailer daemon
MAILER-DAEMON:root
#
# The Following alias is required by the new mail protocol, RFC 822
postmaster:root
#
# Aliases to handle mail to msgs and news
msgs: "|/usr/ucb/msgs -s"
nobody: "|cat>/dev/null"
#
# Alias for uucp maintenance
uucplist:root
#
### These are local aliases ###
trouble:        root
root:           deroest
```

Sendmail accesses alias information from a dbm version of the /etc/aliases table. To compile a new version of the /etc/aliases table, use /usr/lib/sendmail -bi.

```
# /usr/lib/sendmail -bi      Create new alias database
```

21.2.4 Mail logs

It's a good idea to keep logs of sendmail activity. They are very helpful in diagnosing problems, identifying slow mail loops, and sleuthing connections from remote sites. Sendmail logs activities using syslogd. The default log file location per /etc/syslog.conf is the /var/spool/mqueue/ syslog file.

Here is a sample excerpt from syslog

```
Aug 9 13:19:01 daffy sendmail[146022]: AA146022:
  message-id=<9308092018.AA05836 @mx1.cac.washington.edu>
Aug 9 13:19:01 daffy sendmail[146022]: AA146022:
  from=<MAILER@UWAVM.U.WASHINGTON.EDU>, size=1731, class=0,
  received from mx1.cac.washington.edu (140.142.32.1)
Aug 9 13:19:02 daffy sendmail[51047]: AA146022:
  to=<deroest@daffy.cac.washington.edu>, delay=00:00:02, stat=Sent
```

Because the log file tends to grow rapidly, you need to periodically close it and archive it. This procedure can be handled via cron and the /usr/lib/smdemon.cleanu script. The script closes the syslog file and copies it to a log.<n> file for archiving. The default root crontab contains an entry for smdemon.cleanu. However, it is commented out. Remove the comment and replace the crontab to activate log file clean-up:

```
45 23 * * * ulimit 5000; /usr/lib/smdemon.cleanu > /dev/null
```

21.3   Starting and Stopping Sendmail

Sendmail is invoked as a subsystem from the /etc/rc.tcpip script. The AIX sendmail automatically compiles the /etc/aliases and /etc/send-mail.cf files when it is started. If you are running a non-IBM-supplied sendmail, you may need to force a compile of these files as part of the startup.

```
# /usr/lib/sendmail -bi      Compile /etc/aliases
# /usr/lib/sendmail -bz      Compile /etc/sendmail.cf
# /usr/lib/sendmail -bn      Compile /etc/sendmail.nl
```

You can also use the /usr/lib/sendmail-bi command to compile the alias file. If you update any of the configuration information while sendmail is running, compile the files and refresh the sendmail subsystem by issuing an SRC refresh command or sending the daemon a SIGHUP.

```
# refresh -s sendmail
# kill -1 'cat /etc/sendmail.pid'
```

The basic startup flags for sendmail should invoke sendmail as a daemon and specify the time in minutes between mail queue scans for postponed messages. These flags are -bd and -q<time>.

```
# /usr/lib/sendmail -bd -q30m      Start and scan mail queue every
                                   30 minutes
```

To stop the sendmail daemon, use the SRC stopsrc command or send a SIGABORT to the daemon.

```
# stopsrc -s sendmail
# kill -6 'cat /etc/sendmail.pid'
```

21.4   Debugging

The simplest way to test sendmail is to use the -v verbose flag with /usr/bin/mail. It provides feedback on the interaction between MTAs.

```
# /usr/bin/mail -v bart@krusty.fun.com
Subject: help
Sideshow Bob did it!
bart…setsender: uid/gid = 4084/0
bart@krusty.fun.com… Connecting to krusty.fun.com.tcp…
bart@krusty.fun.com… Connecting to krusty.fun.com (tcp)…
220 krusty.fun.com Sendmail 5.65/Revision: 2.28
      ready at Mon, 9 Aug 93 12:40:42 -0700
>>> HELO mobius.bank.org
250 krusty.fun.com Hello mobius.bank.org, pleased to meet you
>>> MAIL From:<doogie@mobius.bank.org>
250 <doogie@mobius.bank.org>… Sender ok
>>> RCPT To:<bart@krusty.fun.com>
250 <bart@krusty.fun.com>… Recipient ok
>>> DATA
354 Enter mail, end with "." on a line by itself
>>> .
250 Ok
>>> QUIT
221 krusty.fun.com closing connection
bart@krusty.fun.com… Sent
```

Test rule sets by invoking sendmail with the -bt flag. Sendmail will prompt for the rule sets to be invoked and the desired address. Separate each rule set number with a comma.

```
# /usr/lib/sendmail -bt -C/usr/lib/sendmail.cf
ADDRESS TEST MODE
Enter <ruleset> <address>
> 2,4,0 deroest@washington.edu
rewrite: ruleset 2 input: "deroest" "@" "washington" "." "edu"
rewrite: ruleset 2 returns: "deroest" "@" "washington" "." "edu"
rewrite: ruleset 4 input: "deroest" "@" "washington" "." "edu"
rewrite: ruleset 4 returns: "deroest" "@" "washington" "." "edu"
rewrite: ruleset 0 input: "deroest" "@" "washington" "." "edu"
rewrite: ruleset 0 returns: "^V" "local" "^X" "deroest" "@" "daffy"
>
```

The sendmail command supports a number of debugging and trace levels. They can be activated using the startup option -d<nn>.<mm>, where <nn> and <mm> define the debug and trace levels. You'll want to redirect the output to a file, as it can be *very* verbose. The IBM AIX sendmail daemon only supports a value of 21.<mm>, where <mm> can be any positive integer. If you are running a current copy of sendmail, refer to the source code for debug and trace values.

```
# /usr/lib/sendmail -bd -q30m -d20.1
```

Check the logs, mail queue, and stats files periodically for stalled mail or loops. You can list the pending delivery queue using the mailq command.

```
# mailq

Mail Queue (1 request)
--QID-- --Size-- -----Q-Time----- -----------Sender/Recipient-----------
AA49872 (no control file)
```

Files in the mail queue are identified by a QID. The first character of the QID designates the type of queue file:

d   Message data file
l   Lock file
n   Backup file
q   Control file
t   Temp file
x   Transcript file

The /etc/sendmail.st file can be checked using the /usr/lib/mailstats command.

```
# mailstats

Mailer    msgs_from    bytes_from    msgs_to    bytes_to
local     123          8450          57         2780
```

To reset mail statistics, invoke mailstats with the -z flag.

```
# mailstats -z
```

21.5 Managing Mail Queues

As administrators, it's our responsibility to inform users when mail arrives and pester them to get rid of old unwanted mail. Since the latter is a difficult job at best, I'll start with the easy one of informing users when mail arrives.

The comsat daemon, when prompted by sendmail, informs users that new mail is waiting. This feature is supported by the MAIL and MAILMSG variables defined in the default /etc/profile.

```
MAIL=/var/spool/mail/$LOGNAME          Path to incoming mail
MAILMSG="[YOU HAVE NEW MAIL]"          Mail waiting message
```

The comsat daemon must also be defined in /etc/inetd.conf.

```
comsat dgram upd wait root /etc/comsat comsat
```

It's also a good idea to inform users when mail is waiting at login time. This can be accomplished by checking the mail from the default login scripts for each shell. See Chap. 25 for details on setting up system-wide default login scripts.

Here is a sample login mail check:

```
#! /bin/sh
#
if [ -s "$MAIL" ]
        then echo "$MAILMSG"
fi
```

Without being heavy-handed with your user community, it is difficult to encourage users to keep up with incoming mail. The best policy is to use regular reminders and track queue usage using disk utilization commands like du.

```
# du -s /var/spool/mail        Disk usage for mail queue
# du -s /var/spool/mail/*      Mail queue usage by user
```

21.6 POP and IMAP

I find myself regularly using more than a dozen systems each day. Moving from machine to machine has become an integrated part of my daily routine. Workstation at home. Laptop for travel. PDA for meetings. Workstation and distributed servers for work. You might say I'm an information-age junkie. Aren't we all?

One problem the distributed environment poses is collocating the data used by an application that resides on any or all of the systems you regularly use. Prime examples include electronic mail and network news. Many sites have news feeds and mail delivered to one or more centrally administered servers. For electronic mail, this configuration facilitates removing host names from a user's mail address, making it easier to move between systems. If you access these servers from a number of different computers, you can easily end up with a proliferation of folders, address books, and .newsrc files. None of these files will represent the full state of your current news or mail activities.

As an illustration, let's assume you read your favorite news group, alt.sex.gummy-bears, from a news client located on a workstation in your office. The .newsrc file on your office workstation is updated to reflect the articles you have read. Later in the day, you access the same news server using a news client from your home PC. The .newsrc file on your home PC is out of date with the one on your office workstation, so you end up seeing the same articles you read earlier in the day when you should have been working. Electronic mail complicates this scenario even further. Mail user agents may populate folders and address books on all the systems from which they are accessed. You can fix this problem by always reading your mail and news from a single client system. What you lose is the additional fault tolerance, distribution control, and ease of access provided by a truly distributed client environment.

21.6.1 POP

One of the oldest and best-known solutions to the distributed mail problem is post office protocol (POP). POP clients connect to a POP server, which is the repository for incoming mail. The client downloads the entire contents of the user's inbox to the client machine. The inbox is then processed on the local client. POP works very well for those users who run from a single client over a fast connection. If you operate from a number of clients, then you still have the problem of scattering your inbox folders between machines. POP uses a password for authentication, although newer implementations make use of Kerberos security services. You shouldn't have any difficulty in locating public domain, shareware, and vendor POP implementations for just about any operating system. This includes both POP clients and servers. POP support is included in later releases of AIX V4.2.

21.6.2 IMAP

Internet message access protocol (IMAP) was designed as a follow-on to POP to address the issues of shared access, resource localization, and low-bandwidth connections to a remote mail server. IMAP is a client/server protocol similar to NNTP. The IMAP protocol is used by a mail user agent to transfer mail header information or individual mail messages between the client and the server. Destination folders may reside on either the local client or mail server. This makes IMAP ideal for low-bandwidth connections like dialup access. IMAP can be used to transfer complete mailboxes from a server to a client to mimic POP services. Other IMAP facilities include searching mailboxes for text strings, accessing news servers, and managing MIME attachements (multipurpose internet mail extensions). MIME is used to attach multimedia files to a mail message using a 7-bit encoding of 8-bit data. IMAP news support provides a means for integrating user mail and news interfaces under a single client. The IMAP API library called the C-client is used to integrate IMAP support into existing mail user agents. IMAP server and C-client software is available from the University of Washington. IMAP based mail user agents may be obtained from a number of public and vendor sources. IBM has stated that IMAP will be available in AIX V4. A number of Web browser and desktop mail vendors are adding the IMAP protocol to their E-mail suites, most notably the introduction of IMAP in Netscape Communicator 4.0.

21.6.3 IMSP and ACAP

A number of projects are underway to enhance and augment IMAP. The Internet message support protocol (IMSP) enhances the IMAP command set to manage centrally address books in a fashion similar to IMAP managed mail folders. IMSP authentication and use of access control lists (ACLs) enable sharing of address books and folders between a group of individuals. The IMSP environment authentication is performed by either password or Kerberos. Resources within an IMSP environment are not only identified by type and owner; they are also identified by server. This provides a means for distributing user mailboxes between a number of servers to scale mail service for very large numbers of users.

Application configuration access protocol (ACAP) is a new version of the original IMSP protocol. It is directed at the problem of mobility on the Internet. How do you maintain a consistent environment configuration as you move from workstation to workstation? ACAP is independent of the IMAP protocol, so it can be adapted for environments not directly related to electronic mail support. It basically allows a client to send and receive configuration information from an application server.

21.6.4 Pine

IMAP solves the problem of centralizing the processing of mailboxes accessed from multiple distributed mail clients. IMSP extends the IMAP protocol to include administration of address books and clustering multiple IMAP servers. A complete solution requires a friendly IMAP-based user agent that is available for most popular operating systems. Enter the Pine mail user agent developed by the Computing & Communications group at the University of Washington. Pine is available for most UNIX systems, DOS, MS Windows, and VMS. More platforms are in the works. Pine is being used in more than 30 countries around the world. Over 3 million copies of the Pine release 3.89 information document have been retrieved from the archive site at the UW.

Pine provides a simple hot-keyed menu interface for processing both local-delivered and IMAP-managed mailboxes (see Fig. 21.1). Local

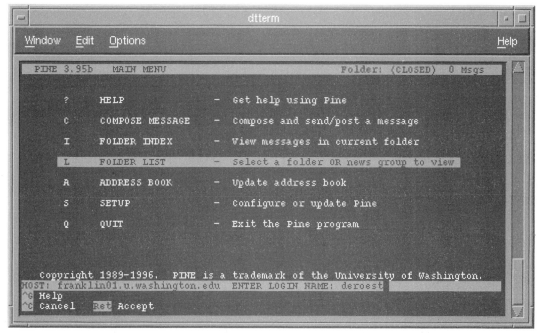

Figure 21.1   Pine main menu.

mail queue support allows Pine to work in non-IMAP environments like other popular mail user agents. Onscreen message management keeps you informed of the arrival of new mail and system warnings without interrupting work in progress. The Pine menu hierarchy includes address book management, mail and news folder lists (see **Fig.**

Figure 21.2   Pine inbox list.

Figure 21.3   Pine message composition.

21.2), sorted message indexes, message composition, and configuration. Online help is available everywhere in the system. Message composition is facilitated through the use of a basic editing tool called Pico and an integrated spelling checker (see Fig. 21.3).

Although Pine's goal is to provide a basic "meat and potatoes" interface to electronic mail processing, it also includes a number of sophisticated facilities for power users. Choose your own text editor and spell checker. Custom-sort message indexes. Tag messages for batch operation. Tailor message header display. Manage MIME attachments. These are just a few of the advanced features available in Pine. Local and global Pine session defaults are to be specified in setup files.

21.7   InforExplorer Keywords

/usr/lib/.Mail.rc mail	cron
.mailrc	/usr/lib/smdemon.cleanu
sendmail	mailq
mmdf	mailstats
smail	comsat
mhs	MAIL
/etc/sendmail.cf	MAILMSG
/etc/aliases	/etc/profile
/etc/sendmail.nl	/etc/inetd.conf
postmaster	inetd
/etc/syslog.conf	du
syslogd	

21.8 QwikInfo

Mail user agent:

`/bin/mail` **or** `/usr/ucb/mail`	User agent
`/usr/lib/Mail.rc`	Global options
`/home/$USER/.mailrc`	User options

Mail transfer agent:

`/usr/sbin/sendmail`	Mail transfer agent
`/etc/sendmail.cf`	Sendmail configuration
`/etc/sendmail.cfDB`	Compiled sendmail.cf
`/etc/sendmail.nl`	Sendmail NLS rules
`/etc/sendmail.nlDB`	Compiled NLS rules
`/etc/aliases`	Mail aliases
`/etc/aliasesDB`	Compiled alias file
`/etc/sendmail.pid`	PID of sendmail daemon
`/etc/sendmail.st`	Mail statistics
`/var/spool/mail/$USER`	Incoming mail
`/var/spool/mqueue`	Queued mail

Mail subsystem:

`sendmail -bi`	Build new alias DB
`sendmail -bz`	Build new sendmail DB
`sendmail -bn`	Build new NLS DB
`sendmail -bd -q30m`	Start sendmail
`mailq`	List queued mail
`mailstats`	List mail statistics

Debugging:

`mail -v <user@address>`	Verify delivery
`telnet <host> 25`	Telnet to SMTP port
`sendmail -bt -C/usr/lib/sendmail.cf`	Test rewrite rule sets
`sendmail -d20.1`	Run sendmail in debug
`/var/spool/mqueue/syslog`	Sendmail log

22

News

22.1 Read All About It

Usenet News is a network-based bulletin board system that reaches hundreds of thousands of users via Internet and UUCP connections. Users interact in electronic discussion groups called newsgroups using interfaces called news readers. The news reader clients present an interface that resembles electronic mail user agents. Usenet topics range from serious research discussions to humor, hobbies, politics, and just about anything else you can think of. News is another one of those addictive network services. Providing news service is a carrot that will assist in getting the hard-sell folks to use your computers. However, "Once you giveth, you canst taketh away!"

22.2 News Resources

Any system on the network can host a bulletin board and accept or provide news feeds with other interested sites. Depending on the feeds a site is willing to accept, a news server can receive tens of megabytes of news information a day. Dedicated spool space is required to house news data. Control over who you accept feeds from, the newsgroups you will accept, and expiration policies for old news allow you to manage the disk resources required. It is a good idea to house news in a file system of its own.

Network bandwidth is another important consideration. Sites receiving news feeds via dialup UUCP connections will want to run transfers during off hours and implement high-speed modems with data compression.

For very active news sites, the news server will require sufficient memory and CPU to support the connection daemons and search processing resources required by news reader connections. Using server software that supports threaded searches will reduce search CPU requirements.

22.3   News Server

The news server machine receives and transmits news feeds and accepts client connections using the network news transfer protocol (NNTP). The NNTP protocol is described in RFC977 along with the general overview of how network news functions. NNTP represents a basic protocol that supports a limited set of commands and responses allowing for the selection and identification of news groups and articles (see Table 22.1). The protocol is similar to that employed by the simple mail transfer protocol (SMTP) of electronic mail.

There are a number of news software packages available via anonymous ftp. Packages like nntp and inn provide the server support for reader/poster clients, transfer clients for newsfeeds, and administration tools for controlling resource utilization. Software like dnntp allows you to scale and partition your news service. News server daemons can be run stand-alone, or they can be invoked by inetd. The choice will depend on the traffic levels to be supported. The server forks a daemon for each client connection, this daemon maintains the dialog for news articles located in /var/spool/news. Note that most of the server software comes as a base package and a large number of patches. Make sure you get the whole set of patches when installing a particular release.

Servers can restrict client access and posting by identifying trusted sites in the /usr/lib/news/nntp.access file. Trusted sites are identified by address, access rights, posts allowed, and newsgroups. A host address may be either the host name, domain name, network name, or IP

TABLE 22.1   NNTP Commands

ARTICLE BODY HEAD	Return news article, body, or header
STAT	Set current article pointer
GROUP	Return first and last group article numbers
LIST	Return list of newsgroups
HELP	Return command summary
IHAVE	Identify article number to server
LAST	Set article pointer to previous article
NEWGROUPS	New groups created since date and time
NEWNEWS	List of message IDs of new articles
NEXT	Set article pointer to next article
POST	Request posting to a group
QUIT	End connection with server
SLAVE	Connect to a slave server

address. Wild cards are supported using the asterisk (*) character. Negation is implemented using the exclamation point (!) character.

```
/usr/lib/news/nntp.access

#
# Example nntp server access file
#
# Address           Access   Post    Newsgroups

default             xfer     no
ibm-competator      read     post    !comp.UNIX.aix
daffy               no       no
*.whatsamata.edu    no       no
128.239.2.110       read     no
```

Although these packages provide their own NNTP protocol support under the nntpxmit program, additional software like nntplink can be incorporated to improve performance and provide time-based news updates.

Your best bet is to take a look at all the server packages and pick one that represents your site's requirements. Be sure to review the documentation supplied with the server software carefully. Other server sites with which you interact are depending on the coordination of feeds. Subscribe to the administration and new user newsgroups for additional information. Here is a list of news-related newsgroups:

news.sysadmin

news.software.b

news.software.nntp

news.software.readers

news.newsites

news.announce.newusers

news.announce.newgroups

22.4 News Readers

Like cars on the highways, there are a number of news reader packages to choose from. Most sites end up supporting more than one news reader. Many Web browsers and E-mail clients include news readers (see Table 22.2). "Different strokes for different folks!"

The news readers are responsible for user interaction with the newsgroups. They perform functions like newsgroup subscription, archiv-

TABLE 22.2 News Readers

rn	Read News
trn	Threaded Read News
xrn	X11 Read News
nn	No News is Good News
tin	Threaded Internet News
gnus	Gnu Emacs News Macros
pine	Email User Agent with News Support
NewsGrazer	Macintosh News Reader
Netscape	Web Browser With News Reader

ing, searching, reading, and posting. Each user's news interaction state is kept in a $HOME/.newsrc file. The .newsrc file indicates which groups a user has subscribed and the identification number of the last article read.

```
$HOME/.newsrc

alt.activism! 1-27300
alt.angst! 1-2052
alt.aquaria! 1-12683
alt.atheism! 1-28722
alt.bbs! 1-10369
alt.beer! 1-5058
alt.books.technical! 1-953
alt.brother-jed! 1-1075
alt.callahans! 1-19131
alt.cd-rom! 1-2789
alt.co-ops! 1-464
alt.cobol! 1-781,785-786
alt.config! 1-8285


* it goes on and on and on *
```

Some news readers incorporate their own posting software, yet there are posting packages that may be added that provide additional features and improved header checking. In general, the posting software validates the news header, appends a user-supplied .signature file, and transfers the file to the news server.

22.5 Newsgroups

The last time I looked at my .newsrc file, there were 2,380 different newsgroups. Mind you, I don't subscribe to them all. On the average, I have noticed about five new news groups coming online each day. Sites may add local groups as they see fit. Network-wide groups must go through a balloting procedure before the group becomes public. Many electronic mail discussion lists are forwarded into newsgroups. A number of the Bitnet Listserv discussions are represented in newsgroups under the bit.listserv classification (see Table 22.3).

Newsgroups that are related to AIX and UNIX administration are listed below. You likely won't be able to follow them regularly, but they are worth checking out.

comp.unix.aix	AIX and RS/6000 discussion
comp.unix.wizards	UNIX wizards Q&A
comp.unix.sources	Public domain sources
comp.unix.large	Large and distributed UNIX systems
comp.unix.osf.misc	OSF general discussion
comp.unix.osf.osf1	OSF/1 discussion
bit.listserv.aix-1	Bitnet AIX E-mail discussion
bit.listserv.sp1-1	Bitnet POWER Parallel SP1 discussion
bit.listserv.11-1	Load Leveler batch discussion
bit.listserv.power-pc	POWER PC discussion
bit.listserv.dqs-1	Distributed Queuing System discussion

22.6   News Software Sites

The AIX public domain software repository at UCLA has both source and binary news server and news reader packages. See Appendix A for information on obtaining software from public servers.

TABLE 22.3   Newsgroup Classifications

alt	Alternative topics
bionet	Genetics and biology topics
bit.listserv	Bitnet Listserv discussion topics
biz	Vendor topics
clari	Newspaper
comp	Computer-related topics
gnu	Gnu freeware topics
k12	Elementary and secondary education topics
misc	Miscellaneous topics
news	Usenet administration and use
rec	Recreation topics
sci	Scientific topics
soc	Social topics
talk	General topics
vmsnet	VMS topics
*	Various local groups

22.7   QwikInfo

`nntp`	News daemon
`nntpxmit, nntplink`	News transfer
`/var/spool/news`	News spool
`/usr/lib/news/nntp.access`	Restrict nntp access
`rn, trn, xrn, nn, tin, gnus`	News readers
`$HOME/.newsrc`	Newsgroup state

World Wide Web

23.1 WWW Overview

It's time to hitch your wagon and set forth on the information superhighway. Setup a homestead and join the global village. Seek your fame
and fortune in the wide open spaces of the Internet. Words from the
annals of yesteryear! There is a new frontier out there. It's called the
World Wide Web (WWW or Web). Like any new community under development, what it will become and its intrinsic value will depend on how
it is organized and how we as users participate. How do you participate?
It's very easy. Just install the AIX V4 bonus pak. It provides a number
of options for making your foray onto the Web. Before delving into the
bonus pak, I'll digress a bit and provide a level set for those readers who
are not familiar with what the World Wide Web project is all about.

The WWW project was initiated by the Centre Europeen de la
Recherche Nucleaire (CERN). The initiative was to address the complex nature of accessing the various information sources available on
the Internet and to provide a means for distributing hypermedia. The
design preserves the distributed nature of these services, yet provides
a common user interface. Think of it as one-stop-shop software for all
your Internet needs. The goal is achieved by building client and server
software based on the hypertext transport protocol (HTTP). Separating
the protocol from the data, HTTP servers can interface with existing
text-based information servers like FTP, WAIS, News, and Gopher.
HTTP also provides the mechanism for distributing hypertext documents, graphics, video, and sound.

23.1.1 Web servers

Hypertext information is made available to the network via an httpd
server. The server's job is to provide a common access interface to

multimedia data and common Internet services. It does this via a combination of the HTTP protocol and hypertext markup language (HTML). HTML data pages residing on the server are transmitted to Web clients via HTTP. Tags within a page invoke links to other HTML objects and multimedia files residing on any server available on the Web. You guessed it! It works just like hot links in InfoExplorer. Web servers are also responsible for maintaining access control to secured information and negotiating secure channels with Web clients. A Web server can act as a firewall between the Internet and local LAN by functioning as a proxy server. A proxy server makes connections to the outside world on behalf of a user rather than using a direct connection from the user's workstation. Proxy servers can also improve performance by storing frequently accessed data on the local server.

23.1.2 Web browsers

On the client end of a Web connection, software called a browser presents Web hypermedia to the end user. The browser communicates with a Web server via HTTP, downloads hypermedia data from the server, and interprets the HTML for rendering the data at the user's workstation. To access new information referenced in a document, you simply click on or tab to a highlighted HTML link field. This causes the browser to surf the network for the server that will deliver the desired information.

Special tags within an HTML file can indicate a media MIME type that directs the browser to invoke a local application for presenting the data type. For example, an mpg MIME type could automatically invoke the meg-play program to display a compressed movie. Applications invoked via MIME types are called helper applications and can be configured by the end user. Browsers also keep logs of visited sites and host lists of favorite locations. Newer browser architectures are incorporating other Internet services like electronic mail and network news. To secure access to information, browsers negotiate with servers to form secure channels.

I should mention that in instances where you don't have a graphical display, there are character-only browsers that can be used to surf the Web. One of the most popular is Lynx, developed by the University of Kansas. You can obtain a copy of Lynx via anonymous ftp to:

```
ftp2.cc.ukans.edu pub/lynx
```

23.1.3 Locating servers

Services on the Web are located using a uniform resource locator (URL). URLs identify the service type, the server site, and document path name (see Table 23.1). URLs can be imbedded in HTML tags within a document or announced via Web directory and search servers like Yahoo and AltaVista. Web software packages called robots or spiders search server sites for URL information and use it to create subject indexes. As you might expect, these robots can put significant load on servers and the network. Be a good citizen and register your service URL with a directory provider rather than wait for them to find you.

23.2   AIX V4 Bonus Pak

IBM has made it easy for you to get started with the World Wide Web under AIX V4 by delivering a number of Web servers, browsers, and helper applications in the AIX V4 bonus pak. The bonus pak is a means for delivering IBM and non-IBM products not directly related to AIX base services that will enhance the AIX environment. They are packaged on separate media and can be installed individually using the standard AIX smit install procedures described in Chap. 6. The AIX V4.2 bonus pak includes:

Java V1.0

Netscape Navigator V2.01 or V3.0

Adobe Acrobat Reader V2.1

Ultimedia Services for AIX V2.1.4

Netscape Commerce Server V1.12

IBM Internet Connection Secure Server for AIX V4.0.2

Along with bonus pak release notes, a separate README file is included with each product.

23.2.1   Java

Java is an object-oriented technology developed by Sun that allows a Web server to deliver a small architecture-independent application called an applet over the network to a browser for execution on the client workstation. This allows Web developers to deliver an applica-

---

TABLE 23.1   Uniform Resource Locators

```
<access-method>://
file://domain.name/path
ftp://domain.name/path
http://domain.name:port/path
news:group
telnet://domain.name
```

tion for rendering their data without worrying whether the client already has the appropriate helper installed. Architecture independence means that the application does not have to be compiled into a separate copy for every workstation type on the network. Client-side Java interpreters take care of mapping Java metacone to the local architecture. The AIX Java Developers Kit V1.0 was ported by IBM's Hersley England Center of Competency for Development. The Java bonus pak product includes:

Appletviewer

Java Compiler

Debugger

Java Interpreter

Documentation Tool

Java Runtime Libraries

Java Object Classes

Sample Applets

`/usr/lpp/Java`   Java directory

23.2.2   Netscape Navigator

Next in this pack of goodies is Netscape Navigator. Besides being the king-of-the-hill Web browser, Navigator also includes features like a built-in JavaScript, MIME compliant POP E-mail client, and a news reader. An incline viewer capability allows helper applications like Real Audio, QuickTime VR, and Adobe Acrobat to be rendered within the browser rather than starting a separate application window. Browse the Web, read news, catch up on your E-mail, all from one interface. For secure connections, Navigator V3.0 supports the Secure Socket Layer (SSL) and Secure HTTP protocols (see Fig. 23.1).

`/usr/lpp/Netscape.Navigator`   Netscape Navigator directory

23.2.3   Adobe Acrobat reader

The Acrobat reader is a tool that can be used either stand-alone or as a browser helper for displaying Adobe portable document format (PDF) files. PDF is a nice interchange format for documents that contain text and graphics in that the documents can be manipulated and edited with other tools. This is something that is not easily done with Postscript files. The Acrobat reader can convert PDF files to Postscript. Adobe Acrobat Weblink browser plug-in can be used to set links within

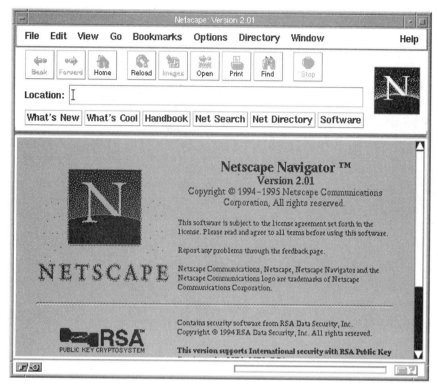

Figure 23.1 Netscape Navigator 2.01.

PDF files to other PDF or hypertext files. You'll appreciate the Acrobat reader the next time you access the U.S. IRS home page. PDF is a favorite for Tax Forms (see Fig. 23.2).

`/usr/lpp/Adobe`   Adobe Acrobat directory

23.2.4 Ultimedia services

You may be familiar with the Ultimedia products from earlier AIX and OS/2 releases. Basically, Ultimedia provides the multimedia drivers and interfaces for creating, delivering, and rendering graphics, video, and sound under AIX and OS/2. Version 2.1.4 supports encoding and playback of MEG-1 video. Supported graphics formats include TIFF, GIF, JPEG, and Kodak PhotoCD. MIDI and speech navigation/dictation functions are provided by Ultimedia audio applications. Video conferencing and broadcast over the network is available using the UMSTV and UMSRadio applets (see Figs. 23.3 and 23.4).

`/usr/lpp/UMS`   Ultimedia services directory

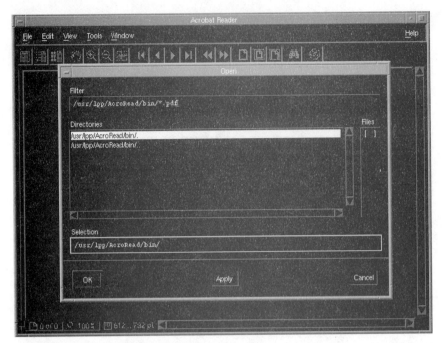

Figure 23.2   Adobe Acrobat.

Figure 23.3   UMS CD player.

23.2.5   Netscape Commerce Server

You've got a Web browser and a set of multimedia helper applications, so how about a Web server? The bonus pak has two. First there is the Netscape Commerce Server. The Commerce includes all the features required for publishing and delivering multimedia data on the Web. It also includes advanced security features that facilitate secure business

Figure 23.4   UMS MPEG player.

transactions. These include SSL, encryption, and user/server authentication. The Commerce Server uses X.509 certificates for secure transactions. These certificates are digitally signed and must be obtained
from a registered certificate authority.

`/usr/lpp/https-us`	Netscape Commerce Server Directory—United States
`/usr/lpp/https`	Netscape Commerce Server Directory—outside the United States

23.2.6   IBM Internet Connection Secure Server

If your server preference is blue, then try out the Internet Connection
Secure Server. Like the Netscape Commerce Server, this Web server
has been architected to support secure business transactions over the
Web. Proxy support allows you to use the Connection Server as a Web
firewall between your internal LANs and the Internet. Proxy caching
also improves access to popular pages referenced by users in your organization.

`/usr/lpp/internet/server_root`	Internet Connection Secure Server directory

23.3   WWW Server Administration

Whether you choose to run one of the bonus pak httpd servers or one of
the public domain servers, there are some administration rules of the
road that will make your life easier and your service a little more
secure. Most implementations use a master server httpd that is started
and run as a daemon as part of your system startup. Make sure that
httpd does not run with root permissions. I'll say more about this later.

Configuration files for the service are layered out in a directory structure similar to the following:

WWW Server Directory Structure

`./htdocs`	Your HTML files
`./cgi-bin`	CGI scripts
`./logs`	Logs and statistics
`./admin    ./conf`	Configuration files and binaries

23.3.1   Access control

The Netscape Commerce Server and IBM Internet Connection Secure Server are a bit more esoteric than most httpd implementations. Generally, WWW servers are administered in a similar fashion. There are usually three files that set the default configurations for your server: httpd.conf, srm.conf, and access.conf. The httpd.conf file sets the configuration for your httpd server. It determines the server name, which port it listens on, the default user and group for the server, location of log files, and who the Webmaster is. This file controls how the world identifies and accesses your server. The srm.conf defines the directory structure that is seen by users accessing your server. The access.conf file defines the access permissions for your directory structure. More specifically, it sets the permission options that can be set in per-directory .htaccess files. These files are the first line of defense for your server.

`httpd.conf`	httpd configuration
`srm.conf`	Viewable directory space
`access.conf`	Access control defaults
`.htaccess`	Per-directory access control

Use these files to set the minimum viewable directory space and access rights for your server. Consider setting execute-only permissions on directories to make the unreadable. Users then have to know the file names contained in them before they can retrieve them. You can also set access permissions by user, group, and domain and require passwords before granting access. As described earlier, the access.conf file is used to set default access control. To set specific permissions within a directory, place a .htaccess file in the directory. For example, if you wish to restrict access to only those hosts in a particular domain, use the permissions in Example 23.1.

Example 23.1   Access by Domain

```
<Limit GET>
order deny,allow
```

```
deny from all
allow from .u.washington.edu
</Limit>
```

To restrict access to a particular group or user and require a password, replace the allow and deny keywords with "require" followed by the user name list or group name. In Example 23.2, the group uw-students must use a password to access files in the directory. You probably guessed that the .htpasswd and .htgroup files house passwords and group lists.

Example 23.2   Access by Group and Password

```
AuthUserFile/[Your-Passwd-File-Path]/.htpasswd
AuthGroupFile/[Your-Group-File-Path]/.htgroup
AuthName ByPassword
AuthType Basic
<Limit GET>
require group uw-students
</Limit>
```

The .htgroup file specifies the group name followed by a colon and the list of users who are members of the group. The .htpasswd file is populated with user names and passwords by using the htpasswd command.

```
# htpasswd-c/[your-passwd-file-path]/.htpasswd [username]
```

If you will be using CGI scripts on your server, remember to make certain that your server does not run with root permissions. CGI scripts run under the permissions of the server and thus may present an avenue for a security breach. If you allow the use of CGI scripts on a server that supports multiple user pages, you might want to consider using a wrapper that sets the CGI permissions to that of the owning user before execution.

Keep access logs and save them on a periodic basis. This will assist you in tracking access problems and allow you to collect statistics on your site.

23.3.2 Site structure

Before you begin populating your ./htdocs directory with HTML files, take some time to design your directory structure and set some naming conventions. Try to group files by type within a directory and minimize the directory depth. This will make it much easier later on when you have hundreds or thousands of files to manage.

If you will be supporting an ongoing development effort, separate your development and production page areas. You can use a staging mechanism to move test pages into production. This will minimize the exposure of pages being changed while they are being accessed.

Use relative path names in your HTML files. This will facilitate moving the files to other directories or changing the server root directory path.

Finally, if you want people to see your creations, make sure you publicize your site in popular directory servers. Most servers provide a means for registering your site with the service. Make sure you identify the Webmaster for your site on your home page for user feedback.

23.4   Creating HTML Documents

How do you make your data available to the Web? Begin by creating a hypertext document as the focal point to your service. This document, called a home page, can be created using a standard editor. The format, links, and programmatic characteristics of the document are specified using hypertext markup language (HTML). HTML tags are special ASCII character sequences that are embedded within the text of the document. HTML tags take on one of three basic forms:

```
<tag-name> text </tag-name>
<tag-name attribute-name=args> text </tag-name>
<tag-name>
```

HTML tags are not case sensitive; thus, <TITLE> is equivalent to <title>. A sampling of HTML tags are listed in Table 23.2.

A basic HTML document will have a title, one or more headings, text paragraphs, and optionally programmatic interfaces like links, lists, images, or input/output fields. The title field identifies the purpose of the document and is usually displayed separate from the document by most browsers. This means you will want to echo the title information using a heading within the document body. Six levels of heading fields are available. Text within the document is contained by paragraph tags. If you want custom formatting within a paragraph, you must use additional tags to honor the formatting. Generally, line breaks and spacing are ignored.

It's very easy to build and test HTML documents. Create a document using an editor of choice and save it with a file extension .html. The .html extension is a convention rather than a requirement. Use the Open Local or Open File option of browsers like Netscape or Mosaic to display the document on the screen. Repeat the process until the document has been refined to meet your expectations. It's a good idea to review your document with a couple of different browsers to validate that it has a

TABLE 23.2   Sample HTML Tags

	Start field	End field
Title	`<TITLE>`	`</TITLE>`
First-level head	`<H1>`	`</H1>`
Paragraph	`<P>`	
Line breaks	` `	
Preformatted text	`<PRE>`	`</PRE>`
Anchor/link	`<A HREF=pathname>`	`</A>`
Lists:		
Numbered	`<OL>`	`</OL>`
Unnumbered	`<UL>`	`</UL>`
Entry	`<LI>`	`</LI>`
Definition list	`<DL`	`</DL>`
Term entry	`<DT>`	`</DT>`
Definition entry	`<DD>`	`</DD>`
Image	`<IMG SRC=image-url>`	
Text style:		
Bold	`<B>`	`</B>`
Italic	`<I>`	`</I>`
Typewriter	`<TT>`	`</TT>`

common look and feel. You can make things even easier by using one of the WYSIWYG HTML editors or toolsets. These tools will validate and/or display HTML information during the edit process. The Open Software Foundation (OSF) is currently evaluating HTML toolsets.

HTML offers a far richer set of capabilities than I have briefly outlined here. Take a look at one of the many online HTML guides like NCSA's *HTML Beginners Guide.* You can also get a number of ideas by using the View Source option from a browser to display the source listing of an existing HTML page that looks interesting.

Example 23.3   Sample Home Page   The following is HTML code for a typical home page, jim.html. To view the page as displayed in a browser window, see Fig. 23.5.

```
<HTML>
<TITLE>Jim's World Home Page</TITLE>
<BODY BACKGROUND="./images/temple.jpg">
    <H1>Jim's World</H1>
    <H2>Jim's World</H2>
    <H3>Jim's World</H3>
    <IMG SRC=husky.gif> Welcome to my abode.
    <BR>
    Take a look around but <I>don't stay too long.</I>
    <P>
    <B>Please send</B><A HREF=address.html>money!<A>
    <P>
</BODY>
</HTML>
```

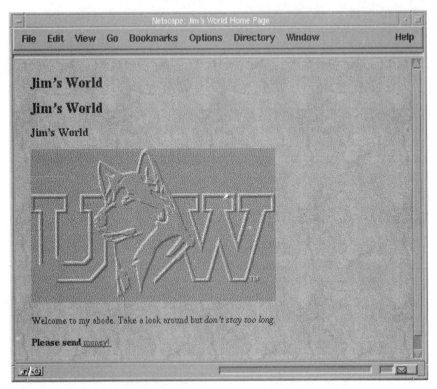

Figure 23.5   jim.html home page.

Remember to think about style when creating your document. There are literally thousands of home pages on the Web, all competing for attention. What will it take to get your page noticed? Surf the Web and take a close look at what others have done. What do you find attractive about a particular home page? You can use these ideas along with recommendations from HTML style guides to build a document style the fits your needs. Once you have chosen a particular style, stick with it! You can also collect buttons, bars, and other widgets from network archives to spruce up your documents.

23.5   Java

Java, originally called "Oak," was developed by a group at Sun Microsystems. Although similar to C++, it is not a retrofit of the C++ language. The original Sun development effort had intended to be based on C++, but the language was abandoned and the Java language was architected as a replacement. Java was designed from the ground up to meet the requirements of portable distributed realtime application environments. Features promoting distributed operations like garbage collection and threads were added. C++ staples like address manipulation (pointers) and multiple inheritance were stripped away in deference to security and simplicity. Other security features were instrumented to inhibit writing to client disks and accessing non-home URLs. It turned out to be a natural for World Wide Web applications. A word about security: Remember that Java applets are interpreted on the client machine, so security is a major concern. You might remember a bytecode problem with the Java Development Kit (JDK) versions 1.0 and 1.0.1 as reported in the March 26, 1996, *Wall Street Journal* ("Researchers Find Big Security Flaw in Java Language" by Don Clark; see also CERT Advisory CA-96.07). The problem was that a malicious applet could create and execute low-level machine instructions on the client computer. Patches were released for both the JDK and Netscape versions 2.0 and 2.01. The moral of the story is that you should keep close tabs on security. After all, you are allowing unknown and potentially untrusted applications to be automatically downloaded and run on your machine each time you connect to a Java-enhanced Web page.

Here is the Java applet development sequence:

1. Java source
2. Java compiler
3. Platform-neutral bytecode
4. Platform specific interpreter

I'm not going to delve into Java programming. There are a number of excellent books and online tutorials that will do a much better job than I could do here. The AIX V4 bonus pak delivers everything you need to begin cranking out applets. Once you have built a Java applet, you can reference it from your Web page using the APPLET HTML tag (Example 23.4). Pre-Java Web browsers will ignore this tag.

Example 23.4   HTML APPLET Tag

```
<APPLET CODEBASE="http://homeURL/path"
        CODE=appletName.class HEIGHT=value, WIDTH=value>
<PARAM NAME=param1Name VALUE=param1Value>
<PARAM NAME=param2Name VALUE=param2Value>
    ...
<PARAM NAME=paramNName VALUE=paramNValue>
</APPLET>
```

23.6   JavaScript

JavaScript, code-named "Mocha" and later "LiveScript" by Netscape, is concise interpreted script language that provides a subset of Java capabilities. JavaScript supports a smaller number of types, these being numeric, boolean, and string types. You can't do animations, but this can be solved using alternatives like GIF89. As I mentioned previously, JavaScript can be used for quick prototyping of applications that can later be implemented in compiled Java bytecode. However, don't underestimate the power of using JavaScript itself for production Web applications.

JavaScript can be wholly embedded in an HTML document using the SCRIPT tag (Example 23.5). It does not require JDK for development, only a Java-aware browser. For pre-Java-period browsers, you need to hide the script in order to keep from confusing the browser. You can hide JavaScript by using the tags shown in Example 23.6. Again, the reader is referred to the books and online tutorials for more information on JavaScript programming.

Example 23.5   JavaScript

```
<HTML>
<TITLE> JavaScript Example</TITLE>
<SCRIPT LANGUAGE="JavaScript">
    function hello Web() {
            document.write('Hello World Wide Web')
     }
</SCRIPT>
<BODY>
    ...HTML STUFF...
<SCRIPT>
    helloWeb()
</SCRIPT>
</BODY>
</HTML>
```

Example 23.6   Hiding JavaScript for Old Browsers

```
<SCRIPT LANGUAGE="JavaScript">
<!-- [Start hiding.]
document.write('Hello World Wide Web')
//[Stop hiding.]
</SCRIPT>
```

In a Web environment, Java-aware browsers act as middleware between applets and the user. These browsers include a number of predefined classes and objects that you can reference to obtain details about the page, history, and referenced URLs. Predefined classes include:

Window	Window properties (multiple for frames)
Location	Current URL properties
History	Visited URL properties
Document	Current document properties

When building your Java or JavaScript-enhanced Web page, try to keep in mind how the page is loaded by the browser. If you are referencing multiple applets, try to keep them small. Sequence the load of the page to keep your audience entertained while applets are being transferred to the client. This is especially important for slow modem connections. Netscape Navigator loads a page sequentially. The recommendation here is to locate your JavaScript entries in the top section of your HTML document. This will limit interruptions when the user clicks on the page before the script has completed loading.

23.7 Security

Use a Web browser as a general purpose interface to distributed applications carries along some significant baggage regarding access control requirements. This means that the browser has to support the authentication and authorization mechanism employed by each service you make available. Limiting the access scope to an enterprise intranet could require interactions with security systems including MVS RACF, UNIX, MS-Windows NT, Novell NetWare, DCE, Kerberos, Web certificates, and various database authentication schemes. Obviously some common security protocols will have to be employed to make this type of interaction a reality. The following is a list of technologies being used in a number of Web browsers and servers.

23.7.1 PKCS

Any authentication system you consider is going to require some level of encryption. It should be a given that the encryption algorithms follow the public key cryptography standard (PKCS). PKCS defines a set of standards for public key data encryption and interoperability. The latter is due to the fact that there are a number of encryption algorithms included in the standard. PKCS also describes methods for key exchange, hashing algorithms, and digital signatures. PKCS is issued by RSA in cooperation with a consortium of other interested industry parties. RSA is named after Ronald Rivest, Adi Shamir, and Len Adleman, inventors of the public key cryptosystem.

23.7.2 SSL

With encryption in mind, you next need a protocol for setting up a secure and reliable communication pipe between client and server. Netscape developed the secure sockets layer (SSL) to address this requirement for its browser and server products. The protocol has since been made available for free use and version 3 is currently represented by an Internet Engineering Task Force (IETF) draft. SSL is implemented in two layers. The lower level SSL record protocol is used to encapsulate a higher level protocol like the SSL handshake used to negotiate encryption type. SSL is currently the most widely used security technology on the Web.

23.7.3 Certificates

Now that we have a secure communication path, we need a way to authenticate the parties represented in the session. This is commonly done by binding an encryption key to a principle via a data structure that has been validated by a trusted third party. These data structures are called certificates and are issued and digitally signed by a certificate authority representing the trusted third party in transaction. The certificate authority is an entity that has issued some policy statement to ensure confidence and trust.

Certificates have time-based validity lifetimes. The idea is to limit the period of time that a certificate can be used for a session. You might also like to revoke a certificate before its lifetime has expired. This is handled via certificate revocation list profiles. All this is explained in detail in the IETF draft "Internet Public Key Infrastructure X.509—Certificate and Certificate Revocation List." The X.509 standard (CCITT X.509, ISO 9594-8) was originally published in 1988 as part of the CCITT X.500 directory services specification. It has been revised a couple of times, worked over in Privacy Enhanced Mail (PEM) and is now in version 3 of the IETF draft.

23.7.4 DCE/Kerberos

When looking at authentication and authorization systems, one must consider interoperation with DCE and Kerberos. DCE and Kerberos use a security server and ticket granting system somewhat akin to the certificate environment described above. Kerberos is developed by MIT as a network authentication system for distributed services. Kerberos version 5 (RFC 1510) was adopted by the Open Software Foundation (OSF) as the authentication technology to be implemented in DCE. DCE goes beyond Kerberos in providing authorization information as well as authenticating principals. DCE also uses its own RPC system for communicating between principals and servers. A Web service based on DCE has been architected by the OSF. The DCE Web service provides compatibility with SSL using a secure gateway technology.

23.7.5   GSSAPI

The last section discussing DCE Web and SSL hints at some of the security interoperability problems that exist in the standards arena. As I discussed in the introduction, this problem is exasperated when proprietary authentication systems are added to the picture. As with the DCE Web and SSL architectures, the problem can be eliminated using gateways. Software designers are quick to point out that a good API is the key to bridging between a number of different architectures. The Generic Security Services API (GSSAPI RFC 1508) provides the glue to link dissimilar authentication mechanisms. GSSAPI is a small library of routines to support generic authentication, key exchange, and encryption context between principals. It is independent of the underlying security and application protocol. The current description of the API can be found in IETF draft GSS V2-03.

23.7.6   LDAP

Most distributed security services use directory servers to identify and locate principals in the system. The DCE X.500 directory service is one of the most robust, but it is cumbersome to use. A pared-down version of X.500 was drafted as the lightweight directory access protocol (LDAP RFC 1777). LDAP provides access to online directory servers or X.500 backend servers without all the overhead associated with full X.500 implementations. The most widely used version of LDAP was implemented by the University of Michigan. LDAP is being adopted by Netscape, IBM, and many other vendors for use in Web-based applications.

23.7.7   IPSec

In the previous sections, I have focused on higher level protocols concerned with network authentication. I would be remiss if I didn't at least mention that the same security issues are also being addressed at the IP level. IPSec (RFCs 1825-1829) defines protocols for implementing key exchange, header authentication, and encryption (encapsulated security payload or ESP) using IP.

X11 Administration

24.1 Windowed Systems

Single-window ASCII displays are quickly becoming computing relics of the past. It won't be long before the only place you'll find them is in the museum next to the card reader and paper tape punch. Still have your card decks, huh? Don't fret. You can probably find some neat *Better Homes & Gardens* articles on the Net that tell you how to fold them into intricate Christmas wreaths.

TTYs have been pushed aside for windowed graphical displays. There just isn't much in the way of cool character-only applications or ASCII art these days. Everyone wants a cool bitmap background, movies, and sound. Once you have windows, you just can't live without them.

AIX V4's hot new window engine from X/Open and the OSF is the common desktop environment (CDE). CDE is an X11-based desktop system that seamlessly combines window management and desktop tools via a graphical API. CDE replaces the AIXWindows Desktop from earlier releases of AIX. You'll find CDE on other vendor UNIX offerings like Digital UNIX, HP-UX, and Solaris. Before getting too deep in CDE, let's take a look at the nuts and bolts that make it tie it together: AIXWindows, a.k.a. the MIT X11 Windows system. Understanding X11 fundaments is essential to understanding the more complex CDE system. You knew there would be a price to pay for that snazzy CDE desktop!

24.2 X11 Overview

The X-Windows System was developed by a group of vendors and researchers at MIT collectively known as the X-Consortium. The consortium was formed in January of 1988 to build upon the windowing system developed by the MIT Computer Science department and MIT Project Athena. Consortium membership is open to any organization as either an affiliate or member at large. For more information contact:

MIT X Consortium
Laboratory for Computer Science
545 Technology Square
Cambridge, MA 02139

X-Windows uses what is intuitively a reverse client/server mechanism for managing the desktop. Graphical widget and toolkit libraries are linked by applications and then used to manipulate networked or locally attached displays via remote procedure calls. The reason I call this reverse client/server setup is that, in the X environment, the clients are commonly the remote entities that are communicating with the local X server, which controls the local display. The X-Consortium code is freely available and will build on most UNIX architectures, even AIX.

24.3 AIXWindows Components

The fundemental components of the X11 environment include: the X-server, which controls the display; a window manager, which manages objects on the display and integrates the mouse and keyboard; a font library for displaying pretty text strings; widget libraries for adding things like buttons and pointers; and a set of X-clients that gives you everything from bouncing balls to graphical editors. The names of the basic X-components are as follows:

X	Server controlling a local display device
mwm	Motif window manager; one of many that assist in managing the screen environment
aixterm, xterm	Emulated terminal connection to a system using masterslave PTY devices
xrdb	Manage X resources like color map, font paths, and client attributes
xdm	X display manager primarily used with X-Stations

AIXWindows 2D is included and installed with the AIX V4 base operating system. It is built from the MIT X11R5 code base and comprises all the fundemental X-components listed previously, including an extensive X-client and library set. X11R4 fonts and commands have been removed from the current release of AIXWindows. Support for legacy X-applications is still available via X11R3 and X11R4 compatibility libraries.

AIXWindows filesets are identified by the X11. prefix in the /usr/lpp directory (see Table 24.1). Links are provided from the standard MIT directory locations to the various subdirectories in /usr/lpp (see Table 24.2).

24.4 X11 and CDE

The following sections describe X11 functionality as it pertains to supporting CDE. This information is provided in order to build a foundation for understanding the CDE environment for those system administrators unfamiliar with X11 administration. Although basic X11 functionality is still provided by AIXWindows, CDE is the primary X11 environment under AIX V4 and will be the focus of this chapter. MIT X11R5 applications and libraries can be built and installed to supplement or replace AIXWindows and CDE so as to implement a standard X11 environment. However, I would not advise this, as it may cause problems for a number of AIX support applications that rely on AIXWindows and CDE. For those readers interested in vanilla X11 support, I would direct them to one of the plethora of MIT X11 administration texts. I would recommend the *X-Window System* texts by O'Reilly & Associates.

24.4.1 Application defaults

A word concerning X11 resource default files: CDE brings its own session initialization files that define X-startup parameters and resources. These files replace .xinitrc and System.xinitrc functionality. X11 application default resource files are still used by CDE. These

TABLE 24.1 AIXWindows Base Filesets

X11	AIXWindows
X11.Dt	Common desktop environment
X11.adt	Application development tools
X11.apps	AIXWindows additional applications
X11.base	AIXWindows Runtime
X11.compat	AIXWindows X11 compatability libraries
X11.fnt	AIXWindows fonts
X11.motif	Motif
X11.info	InfoExplorer
X11.help	CDE help
X11.man	Man pages
X11.x_st_mgr	X-station manager
X11.vsm	Visual system manager

TABLE 24.2 **AIXWindows Paths**

X11	AIXWindows	Contents
/usr/bin/X11	/usr/lpp/X11/bin	Executables
/usr/lib/X11	/usr/lpp/X11/lib/X11	Libraries and defaults
/usr/lib/<Xlibs>	/usr/lpp/X11/lib/X11	Tool and widget libraries
/usr/include/X11	/usr/lpp/X11/include/X11	Include files and bitmaps
/usr/lib/X11/fonts	/usr/lpp/X11/lib/X11/fonts	X-fonts

files are located in the /usr/lib/X11/app-defaults and /usr/lib/X11/app-custom directories. These files can be tailored to set system default resources for each X application. X11 resources include things like foreground and background colors, fonts, and behavior.

/usr/lib/X11/app-defaults   Application resource defaults

/usr/lib/X11/app-custom   Custom resource defaults

24.4.2 Fonts

Default AIXWindows fonts are located in the /usr/lpp/X11/lib/X11/fonts directory. A symbolic link is provided so that they may be accessed using the standard X11 font path, /usr/lib/X11/fonts. Bitmap distribution format (*.bdf) and server normal format (*.snf) are X11R4 format fonts. The AIXWindows X11R5 distribution uses the portable compiled font (*.pcf) format. The pcf fonts take up less space and are readable across different machine architectures. The conversion program bdftopcf can be used to interchange formats.

Each of the /usr/lib/X11/fonts subdirectories contain two index files: fonts.dir and fonts.alias, both of which are referenced by X-clients and servers to locate particular font files. These index files are built by invoking the mkfontdir command.

To create font directories:

cd /usr/lib/X11/fonts/misc

mkfontdir   Create fonts.dir and fonts.alias

The fonts.dir maps the compressed font file to the logical name. The fonts.alias file is used to reference long logical font names using a short alias. The logical font name is created from the font attributes, which include: foundary, font family, weight, slant, width, style, pixels, points, horizontal dpi, vertical dpi, spacing, average width, owner, and code set. Here is an example of logical name mapping in fonts.dir:

Font File	Logical Name
7x13.pcf.Z	-misc-fixed-medium-r-normal--13-120-75-75-c-70-iso8859-1
7x14.pcf.Z	-misc-fixed-medium-r-normal--14-130-75-75-c-70-iso8859-1
clR8x12.pcf.Z	-schumacher-clean-medium-r-normal--12-120-75-75-c-80-iso8859-1
6x9.pcf.Z	-misc-fixed-medium-r-normal--9-90-75-75-c-60-iso8859-1
clR8x13.pcf.Z	-schumacher-clean-medium-r-normal--13-130-75-75-c-80-iso8859-1
clR8x10.pcf.Z	-schumacher-clean-medium-r-normal--10-100-75-75-c-80-iso8859-1
5x7.pcf.Z	-misc-fixed-medium-r-normal--7-70-75-75-c-50-iso8859-1
clR8x16.pcf.Z	-schumacher-clean-medium-r-normal--16-160-75-75-c-80-iso8859-1
clR8x14.pcf.Z	-schumacher-clean-medium-r-normal--14-140-75-75-c-80-iso8859-1
clR8x8.pcf.Z	-schumacher-clean-medium-r-normal--8-80-75-75-c-80-iso8859-1
5x8.pcf.Z	-misc-fixed-medium-r-normal--8-80-75-75-c-50-iso8859-1
clR9x15.pcf.Z	-schumacher-clean-medium-r-normal--15-150-75-75-c-90-iso8859-1
clR6x8.pcf.Z	-schumacher-clean-medium-r-normal--8-80-75-75-c-60-iso8859-1
clR5x6.pcf.Z	-schumacher-clean-medium-r-normal--6-60-75-75-c-50-iso8859-1
clR7x8.pcf.Z	-schumacher-clean-medium-r-normal--8-80-75-75-c70-iso8859-1
clR4x6.pcf.Z	-schumacher-clean-medium-r-normal--6-60-75-75-c-40-iso8859-1
clR5x8.pcf.Z	-schumacher-clean-medium-r-normal--8-80-75-75-c-50-iso8859-1
clR6x6.pcf.Z	-schumacher-clean-medium-r-normal--6-60-75-75-c-60-iso8859-1
12x24rk.pcf.Z	-sony-fixed-medium-r-normal--24-170-100-100-c-120-jisx0201.1976-0
7x13B.pcf.Z	-misc-fixed-bold-r-normal--13-120-75-75-c-70-iso8859-1
7x14B.pcf.Z	-misc-fixed-bold-r-normal--14-130-75-75-c-70-iso8859-1
clR6x12.pcf.Z	-schumacher-clean-medium-r-normal--12-120-75-75-c-60-iso8859-1
clR6x13.pcf.Z	-schumacher-clean-medium-r-normal--13-130-75-75-c-60-iso8859-1
clR6x10.pcf.Z	-schumacher-clean-medium-r-normal--10-100-75-75-c-60-iso8859-1
clR7x12.pcf.Z	-schumacher-clean-medium-r-normal--12-120-75-75-c-70-iso8859-1
clR7x10.pcf.Z	-schumacher-clean-medium-r-normal--10-100-75-75-c-70-iso8859-1

The following example shows alias mapping in fonts.alias:

Alias	Logical Name
fixed	-misc-fixed-medium-r-semicondensed--13-120-75-75-c-60-iso8859-1

```
variable    -*-helvetica-bold-r-normal-*-*-120-*-*-*-*-iso8859-1
5x7         -misc-fixed-medium-r-normal--7-70-75-75-c-50-iso8859-1
5x8         -misc-fixed-medium-r-normal--8-80-75-75-c-50-iso8859-1
6x9         -misc-fixed-medium-r-normal--9-90-75-75-c-60-iso8859-1
6x10        -misc-fixed-medium-r-normal--10-100-75-75-c-60-iso8859-1
6x12        -misc-fixed-medium-r-semicondensed--12-110-75-75-c-60-
            iso8859-1
6x13        -misc-fixed-medium-r-semicondensed--13-120-75-75-c-60-
            iso8859-1
6x13bold    -misc-fixed-bold-r-semicondensed--13-120-75-75-c-60-iso8859-1
7x13        -misc-fixed-medium-r-normal--13-120-75-75-c-70-iso8859-1
7x13bold    -misc-fixed-bold-r-normal--13-120-75-75-c-70-iso8859-1
7x14        -misc-fixed-medium-r-normal--14-130-75-75-c-70-iso8859-1
7x14bold    -misc-fixed-bold-r-normal--14-130-75-75-c-70-iso8859-1
8x13        -misc-fixed-medium-r-normal--13-120-75-75-c-80-iso8859-1
8x13bold    -misc-fixed-bold-r-normal--13-120-75-75-c-80-iso8859-1
8x16        -sony-fixed-medium-r-normal--16-120-100-100-c-80-iso8859-1
9x15        -misc-fixed-medium-r-normal--15-140-75-75-c-90-iso8859-1
9x15bold    -misc-fixed-bold-r-normal--15-140-75-75-c-90-iso8859-1
10x20       -misc-fixed-medium-r-normal--20-200-75-75-c-100-iso8859-1
12x24       -sony-fixed-medium-r-normal--24-170-100-100-c-120-iso8859-1
nil2        -misc-nil-medium-r-normal--2-20-75-75-c-10-misc-fontspecific
heb6x13     -misc-fixed-medium-r-semicondensed--13-120-75-75-c-60-
            iso8859-8
heb8x13     -misc-fixed-medium-r-normal--13-120-75-75-c-80-iso8859-8
a14         -misc-fixed-medium-r-normal--14-*-*-*-*-*-iso8859-1
olcursor    "-sun-open look cursor-----12-120-75-75-p-160-
            sunolcursor-1"
olglyph-10  "-sun-open look glyph-----10-100-75-75-p-101-sunolglyph-1"
olglyph-12  "-sun-open look glyph-----12-120-75-75-p-113-sunolglyph-1"
olglyph-14  "-sun-open look glyph-----14-140-75-75-p-128-sunolglyph-1"
olglyph-19  "-sun-open look glyph-----19-190-75-75-p-154-sunolglyph-1"
```

24.4.3   Window managers

What does a window manager do for you? As the name implies, you use a window manager to dynamically arrange the layout of windows and objects on your display. It stylizes frame and title decoration, imparting a common look and feel to all the objects displayed. It is the window manager that allows you to click and drag objects on the screen, shuffle windows up and down, and customize pulldown menus. Without a window manager, you don't have any way to manipulate or move overlapping objects or alter their size. It is quite easy to see just how much you depend on your window manager by trying to run your X-environment without using one.

Although I won't cover each of the window managers in the following list, it is worthwhile listing a few of them to give you a feel for the variety that are available. I will briefly cover the Motif and OPEN LOOK window managers, as these are fundamental to CDE window management. I will include examples of startup files that use a format similar to that used in CDE.

24.4.3.1 Configuration. The window manager is usually started last in your X-startup configuration file. It may either be started in foreground or background depending on the particular window manager. Starting the window manager last allows you to configure your environment such that you can exit the X-server when you exit the window manager. If you start your X-session with the xinit or startx commands, then the window manager is usually the last entry in your .xinitrc file. If you are using xdm, then it will be last in your .xsession file.

Window managers, like all well-behaved X-clients, provide a mechanism to allow users to customize the appearance, interaction, and behavior via resource files. A startup rc configuration file used in conjunction with the X-resource information defined in the .Xdefaults file can be modified to tailor the window manager to meet your needs. For the purpose of limiting the scope of this discussion, I will focus on the startup rc configuration files. If you are interested in the options supported in .Xdefaults, these are listed in the man page for the particular window manager.

The configuration file will generally allow you to define actions and menus, which are bound to a mouse button or key for activation. Although formats do differ for each window manager, they tend to follow the following format:

LABEL/TITLE, FUNCTION	Define menus and actions
KEY/BUTTON, CONTEXT, FUNCTION	Bind keys/buttons to actions

The context describes where the button or key action is active. For example, you may want to use a button to display a menu only when the cursor is on the root window. Window manager functions are called by defining the f.function-name in the configuration file entry. Common function names are found in Table 24.3.

24.4.3.2 Motif. The motif window manager (mwm) is the window manager most of us are familiar with ala previous releases of AIXWindows. The Motif window manager was the first technology to hit the streets from the Open Software Foundation. Its 3-D look and feel is based on the development work done by Hewlett-Packard and Microsoft. It is quite similar in look and feel to the Microsoft Presentation Manager and Microsoft Windows. The default configuration file used by mwm is /usr/lib/X11/system.mwmrc. Your local copy is called

TABLE 24.3 Window Manager Functions

f.exec	Start a command or shell script
f.kill	Kill the selected client
f.menu	Display a menu
f.title	Display a menu title
f.separator	Display a separator bar in menus
f.raise	Bring client to the front
f.resize	Resize a client
f.move	Move a client
f.minimize	Reduce the client to an icon
f.maximize	Restore icon to an open client
f.restart	Restart the window manager

.mwmrc. In the example that follows, I have defined a primary menu called RootMenu that will be displayed when button 1 on the mouse or the SHIFT-ESC key sequence is pressed with the cursor on the root window. I can also restart or quit mwm from the menu, or select a submenu called Applications. From the Applications menu, I can start an AIX PC simulator window.

```
# SAMPLE .mwmrc

# Menus and Functions

Menu RootMenu
{
        "Root Menu"    f.title
        no-label       f.separator
        "Appls"        f.menu Applications
        "Restart…"     f.restart
        "Exit mwm"     f.quit_mwm
}


Menu Applications
{
        "Applications"    f.title
        no-label          f.separator
        "Dos Window"      f.exec "pcsim -dmode v &"
}

# Key and Button Bindings

Keys DefaultKeyBindings
{
        Shift<Key>Escape root    f.menu RootMenu
}

Buttons DefaultButtonBindings
```

```
{
        <Btn1Down>    root    f.menu RootMenu
}
```

CDE workplace manager resources are essentially mwm resources, so a short example is in order. I have specified the use of the icon box, defined menus to use black lettering on a light blue background, and set rom14 as my default font.

```
# Sample .Xdefaults Mwm Resources


Mwm*useIconBox: true
Mwm*menu*foreground: black
Mwm*menu*background: lightblue
Mwm*fontList: rom14
```

24.4.3.3 OPEN LOOK. Next on the list of window managers is Motif's rival, the OPEN LOOK Window Manager or olwm. olwm was developed by Sun Microsystems and AT&T. Like the Motif window manager, OPEN LOOK window manager resources are compatible with the CDE Workspace Manager. OPEN LOOK tends to dictate much of the look and feel provided by the window manager, and thus has a very simple configuration file, .olwmmenu, for defining menus. One nice aspect of OPEN LOOK is its ability to pin a menu to the display. This means you don't have to hold the mouse button down to keep the menu displayed on the screen. The example configuration file defines a menu called root menu with a subtitle WINDOWS that will allow the user to start an xterm or tn3270 connection to a remote host and query the uptime information for a system using the rsh command.

```
# Sample .olwmmenu

TITLE       "root menu"
"Clients"   MENU
TITLE           "WINDOWS"
TITLE           "XTERM"
            "milton" "xterm -display $DISPLAY -sb -tn xterms
                -title milton &"
TITLE           "TN3270"
            "oly" "xterm -display $DISPLAY -title oly -e
                tn3270 oly &"
TITLE           "UPTIME"
            "byron" "rsh byron uptime &"
END

"Exit"      EXIT
```

24.4.4   X-Windows Display Manager (XDM)

Authentication is important in any distributed client/server environment. In the X11 world, the X-Windows Display Manager (XDM) provides a protocol for user-based access control to X11-managed displays. An unfortunate common practice in many X11 environments is to use the xhost command to restrict access to a display. xhost only authenticates at the host level. This means that anyone on a time-shared host that has been permitted via xhost has access to your X11 server. xdm uses an access control mechanism called a MIT-MAGIC-COOKIE, which is secured by file access permission. xdm writes a random number code (the magic cookie) into your $HOME/.Xauthority file and shares this number with your X11 server. X11 clients must then authenticate themselves to the server by presenting this code when connecting to the server. This magic cookie is shared with the other machines in the network using the xauth command. X11R5 added two more authentication protocols called XDM-AUTHORIZATION-1 and SUN-DES-1, respectively. Both protocols are based on the data encryption standard (DES). The current AIXWindows CDE release is interoperable with XDM at the X11R4 level.

24.5   Common Desktop Environment

What makes desktop operating systems like MS Windows, MacOS, and OS 2 so popular with the computing masses? Answers to this question might include: They run on low-cost personal computers, there are vast numbers of applications for them, they have multimedia capability, and they readily lend themselves to gaming. I would argue that their well-thought-out graphical user interface is closer to the mark. People like software that is intuitive and has a common look and feel across all the applications they use. Nobody enjoys spending time reading manuals. All of us want to be able to install an application and begin using it immediately. This means that each application must behave and interact with the user in ways that are already familiar. This capability can only be realized if the operating environment provides application interface specifications that can easily be incorporated into new software products, enabling them to exhibit similar traits even if developed by different vendors. As an operating system developer, the only path to successfully implementing common look and feel in your product is either through a specification agreement between the software vendors and customers or by carrying a big enough commercial stick to make everyone do things your way. Shame on you for assuming I had any particular operating system vendor in mind regarding that last statement.

In the UNIX world, many of us have designed and architected our own windowed desktop environments using the X11 windows system. This approach can be moderately successful when confined to centrally administered workgroups or departments. All bets are off as soon as you cross organizational boundaries or begin adding too many different vendor software packages. X11-based specifications like the Open Software Foundations (OSF) and Motif have tried to bring about some interface commonality by providing a platform-independent window manager and widget set, yet they still fall short of the standard set by the personal computer world.

To address these issues, a group of vendors got together at Uniforum in 1993 and formed the Common Open Software Environment (COSE). The COSE initiative proposed to assist in the development of open systems standards through technology sharing between the member vendors. The focus of much of the COSE effort centered around user interface infrastructure. This eventually led to a set of specifications called the Common Desktop Environment (CDE) based on windowing and object technologies from Hewlett-Packard, IBM, OSF, Novell, and SunSoft (see Table 24.4). CDE has since been added to X/Open branding for open systems and has been adopted by the reformed OSF.

24.5.1 CDE overview

CDE is a graphical desktop environment that provides a common user interface across vendor UNIX systems. To the end user, CDE's appearance and operational characteristics are very similar to the OS2, MS Windows, and Macintosh desktops. It includes all the goodies one has come to expect in the personal computer world: point and click, drag and drop, application launcher, file manager, automatic data interchange, productivity tools, session save. The CDE API allows application developers to use these features to better integrate their software into the "face" of the desktop.

Why is CDE important to us as systems administrators? For those of us living in an AIX world, CDE is the desktop environment in AIX V4 replacing the AIXWindows Desktop (XDT). Don't fret if you have already done extensive work configuring XDT. IBM has provided a nice little tool called xdt2cde to convert your XDT objects and icons into

TABLE 24.4   CDE Technologies

Visual User Environment desktop (HP)
Common User Access model and Workplace Shell (IBM)
Motif (OSF)
OPEN LOOK, DeskSet (SunSoft)
UnixWare clients/desktop manager (Novell USL)

CDE equivalents. You will also find CDE on other popular UNIX platforms like HP-UX, Solaris, SCO UNIX, and USL UNIX. The CDE promise is that it provides us with a common user environment that can be managed and administered uniformly across vendor platforms, and users will learn to use and expect this environment as they move between workstations just as they do in the personal computer world. The downside is that CDE configuration is a bit complex from an administrator's viewpoint. CDE entails a larger number of tables, directories, and daemons than a traditional X11 environment. But this is why they pay us the big bucks, right? This complexity is somewhat due to the additional features that CDE brings to the UNIX desktop. The trick is to become familiar with the CDE servers and associated directory structure. Table formats are for the most part similar to their X11 counterparts.

xdt2cde   Convert XDT Objects to CDE

24.6   CDE Components

CDE is a conglomeration of interoperating services that creates a uniform desktop persona (see Table 24.5). A login manager presents an xlogin-like login window on your desktop and authenticates your identity. A session manager then restores your last running application and window environment to your display. Workplace manager facilitates the manipulation of multiple desktops and manages your window and menu layout. The style manager provides the means for tailoring fonts, color, and wallpaper for each workplace. File, Application, and Help managers make up the interface to the UNIX file system, commands, and application set. These tools are accessed using the front panel launcher. If you're familiar with the OS2 launch pad, you'll feel right at home.

CDE components are tailored using a set of tables that live in three directory locations: /usr/dt, /etc/dt, and $HOME/.dt (see Table 24.6). The /usr/dt directory contains the distribution executables, libraries, and

TABLE 24.5   CDE Components

Login manager	Authenticate and initiate desktop
Session manager	Maintain desktop look between sessions
Front panel	User interface and launcher
Style manager	Customize desktop
Workplace manager	Window manager
File manager	GUI to view and manipulate file objects
Application manager	Application repository and management
Help manager	Hypertext help system

system-wide configuration tables that make up CDE. Custom system-wide default tables are stored in /etc/dt. Per user configuration, tables and session snapshots are stored in the user's home directory, $HOME/.dt. Access precedence is $HOME/.dt, followed by /etc/dt, and lastly /usr/dt. The CDE files and tables located in these directories can be configured to display a different desktop for each client or group in your organization. For example, you can include tools, icons, and applications that are pertinent to the work profile for particular departments or users. In the following paragraphs, refer to Table 24.7 for the directory path names of the referenced CDE configuration files.

24.6.1   Login manager

The login manager is, in a sense, the master CDE daemon. It is responsible for authenticating and starting each CDE session. Its design is based on the X11R4 version of XDM. Like XDM, the login manager /usr/dt/bin/dtlogin listens for incoming requests on the XDMCP port. As of this writing, AIX only supports direct-mode XDMCP. Upon startup, dtlogin scans the Xservers file to determine how login screens are to be generated for the various requesting display types such as a local console. A separate dtlogin process is spawned by the master daemon for each request to manage the associated display. CDE served displays are identified in the Xservers file by domain name.

```
Display-name:0 [Class] [foreign, local]
```

The displays dtlogin process invokes the CDE Xsession script to set up the desktop environment and resources. Note that dtlogin processing does not reference the user's .login and .profile. Shell environment settings normally handled by these files must be specified in the user's $HOME/.dtprofile.

The master dtlogin daemon can be enabled for automatic startup at system boot time using SMIT (see Fig. 24.1) or via the command line using the dtconfig command. You can also start, stop, or reset dtlogin manually. If you want to start the desktop without enabling dtlogin support, invoke the Xsession script as an argument to xinit.

```
# smit dtconfig      Configure using SMIT
```

TABLE 24.6   CDE Directories

/usr/dt	Executable and default configurations
/etc/dt	Locally customized versions of /usr/dt configuration
$HOME/.dt	User local configuration

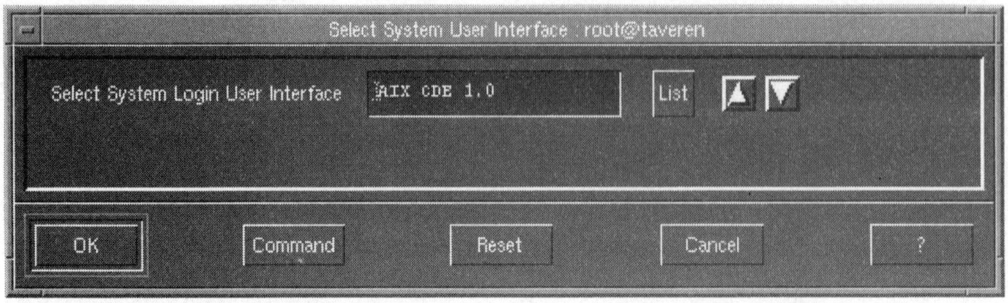

Figure 24.1   SMIT D+ configuration panel.

To start and stop CDE login services:

# dtconfig -e	Enable CDE
# dtconfig -d	Disable CDE
# /usr/dt/bin/dtlogin -daemon	Manual CDE start
# kill -term 'cat/var/dt/Xpid'	Manual CDE stop
# kill -HUP 'cat/var/dt/Xpid'	Reset CDE (re-read config tables)
$ xinit /etc/dt/Xsession	Start desktop without dtlogin

24.6.2   Session manager

The CDE session manager is responsible for setting up the user's desktop environment after login processing has completed. The session manager can either restore the user's initial desktop configuration (called the home session) or a snapshot of the running desktop saved by the session manager during the last logout (called the current session). This startup option is configurable by the user and can be set to select automatically either home or current, depending upon the display type. When the current session option is used, any application running at the time of last logout can be restarted if it stores the startup command and options in the XA_WM_COMMAND property of the application's top-level window. The environment and resources for home and current desktop sessions are stored in the user's $HOME/.dt/sessions directory. Users may also elect to have the session manager execute applications and scripts at login and logout times by placing the command strings in the sesionetc and sesionexit files.

As you might expect, an environment snapshot or application startup script may become corrupted, inhibiting the session manager from successfully restoring the desktop. When this occurs, you can start a CDE single window session from the login window that will allow you to correct the problem. After login, check for error messages recorded during the failed startup in the CDE errorlog.

24.6.3 Front panel

Now that login processing has completed and desktop resources have been restored, the CDE front panel will be displayed on the screen. The front panel is basically an application launcher that looks and behaves similar to the OS/2 Warp launch pad (see Fig. 24.2). Clicking on icons displayed on the front panel will expand selection drawers, open menus, and start applications. Like other CDE services, the front panel display can be personalized to support particular application sets and user preferences. Attributes that make up the front panel are stored in database files identified by a .fp suffix and stored in the CDE types subdirectories. Alternate types directories can be specified by storing the path information in shell environment variables (see Table 24.7).

Along with launching other CDE tools and UNIX applications, the CDE front panel also provides an interface to the printing subsystem. Clicking on the printer icon slides out a drawer that allows you to access the print manager and default printers. Default printers can be set for each user using the dtprintegrate command to specify the printer, queue, and icon. Once a printer and queue are identified, the printer can be accessed by clicking on the printer icon.

```
$ dtprintegrate -p [Printer-Name] -I [Icon] -d [Queue-Name]
```

24.6.4 Style manager

The CDE style manager's job is to make your life easier when customizing your desktop. It can be started from the front panel and provides a nice GUI interface to doing things like setting colors, fonts, wallpaper, keyboard layout, screen savers, and configuring window manager options. It greatly simplifies tailoring X-resources. The style manager is also used to set your login session preferences for the session manager. Style manager resources are stored in the Dtstyle file (see Fig. 24.3).

24.6.5 File and application managers

The CDE file and application managers (see Figs. 24.4 and 24.5) work jointly to provide a graphical interface to the UNIX file system. These tools assist you in navigating directories, managing files, and accessing

Figure 24.2   Front panel.

TABLE 24.7   CDE Environment Variables

```
DTDATABASESEARCHPATH
DTAPPSEARCHPATH
DTHELPSEARCHPATH
DTICONSEARCHPATH
DTICONBMSEARCHPATH
DTMANSEARCHPATH
```

applications using a file-and-folder, point-and-click paradigm just like MS Windows and MacOS. Files and applications are represented and manipulated as objects. This means that each object has an associated name, type, and behavior. Type and behavior attributes can include executable paths, passed parameters, prompts, and associated files. Object linking via type and behavior is how the file and application managers work together. For example, a C language source file can be branded with a type that would automatically invoke the xlC compiler when it is clicked on from the file manager. CDE object capability also extends to drag and drop behavior and associating particular icons by object type. File and application manager attributes are stored in databases identified by the .dt suffix in the CDE types directories.

24.6.6   Workspace manager

Windows, menus, and key bindings on the desktop are managed by the CDE workspace manager Dtwm. The workspace manager design is based on the Motif Window Manager (mwm). It also supports OPEN LOOK resources (mapped to Motif). Configuration syntax for Dtwm is very similar to mwm. You can convert your mwm resource files over to Dtwm by changing Mwm* references to Dtwm* and verifying that any resource path names are correct for the new environment. Dtwm resources are stored in .dtwmrc.

For those of you who aren't satisfied with just one desktop environment, the workspace manager also provides a multiple virtual desktop capability. Each virtual desktop can have its own associated style attributes and bindings. The virtual workspaces are accessed using the CDE front panel. Resources associated with each virtual workspace

Figure 24.3   Style manager.

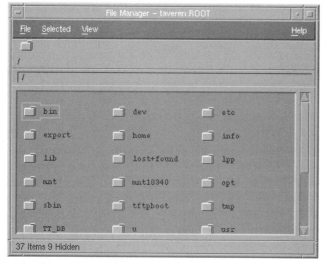

Figure 24.4   File manager.

are stored in the .dtwmrc file. A workspace may also be assigned to a URL that stores an imagemap. Areas on the imagemap can be clicked to initiate other Web transactions. Web integration in CDE includes the ability to drag and drop between Web page objects and the CDE file and application managers.

24.6.7   Help manager

The CDE help manager provides a help and documentation environment similar to InfoExplorer. It is hypertext-based, so it supports all the document attribute and link behavior you are familiar with using

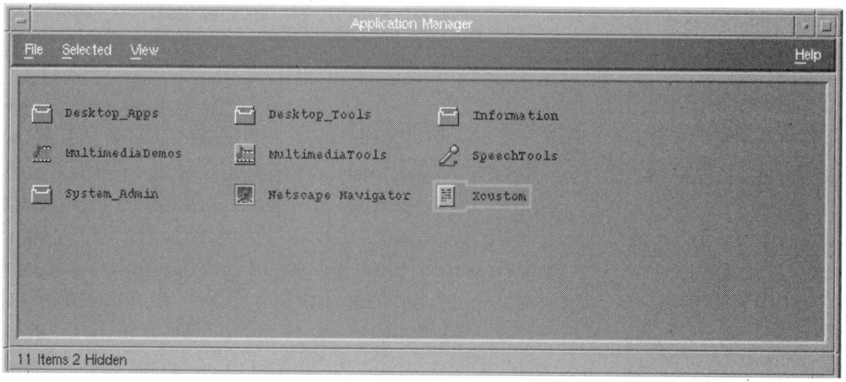

Figure 24.5   Application manager.

the AIX info system. Information is organized in a hierarchy by volume and subtopic. You navigate documents using index and search tools. The key here is that this system behaves just like you have come to expect from other desktop help interfaces. Nothing new, just comfortable intuitive operation.

24.7 CDE Summary

My initial response to CDE was a bit like my first exposure to SMIT. I wasn't buying the idea that it might actually be a useful tool. But, also like my experiences with SMIT, I have found that over time I'm beginning to use it more often than not. I've been surprised how the face of CDE has been consistent across the vendor implementations I've tried. Like many sites, we're already intrenched in our own X-desktop configuration, so any attempt to use CDE is going to be an uphill battle. What we need to make a good argument for migrating to CDE is continued support and commitment from the vendor community. We still need a bit more time to get used to the idea of a standard common UNIX desktop. Then there is the shifting paradigm to personal computer platform to consider. If your organization is new to the idea of UNIX desktops, then by all means give CDE a try. It's an off-the-shelf desktop environment and will certainly save you many headaches from trying to garner a design consensus for rolling your own. For more information on CDE configuration, see Table 24.8.

24.8 IBM Xstation Administration

Xstations provide an effective alternative to providing fully equipped disk workstations as platforms for X-Windows. Using one or more workstations as servers, Xstations provides all the functionality of a complete X-Windows-based workstation. Xstations also reduces much of the administration headaches for both the system administrator and end user.

Most environments support a number of different vendor Xstations and would like to manage them as a group from central servers under xdm. At EPROM level +1.5 for the Xstation 120 and using the IBM Xstation Manager at version 1.3 or above, all models of the IBM Xstation can be supported alongside the rest of your Xstation menagerie with xdm. You can also obtain boot server code from Advanced Graphics Engineering (AGE), which will allow the use of UNIX systems other than a RS/6000 or PS/2 as a boot server. Take a look at the IBM Red Book, *IBM Xstation 120/130,* GG24-3695 for more details. This book is a little dated; however, most of the information is still relevant.

TABLE 24.8   CDE Executables and Configuration Files

Login manager	
`/[usr/dt/bin, etc/dt]/Xservers`	Login display by type
`/usr/dt/bin/dtlogin`	Display manager (xdm like)
`/usr/dt/bin/dtgreet`	Display login screen
`/usr/dt/bin/dthello`	Display welcome message
`/etc/dt/app-defaults/$LANG/Dthello`	Welcome message
`/[usr/dt/bin, etc/dt]/Xsession`	Session configuration scripts
`/[etc, usr]/dt/config/Xsession.d`	Startup script directories
`/[usr, etc]/dt/config/Xconfig`	Specify X-resource files
`/[usr/dt/bin, etc/dt, $HOME/.dt]/Xresources`	X11 resource definitions
`/usr/dt/config/sys.dtprofile`	.dtprofile template
`$HOME/.dtprofile`	User startup environment

Session manager	
`$HOME/.dt/sessions/<current,home>/dt.resources`	X-resources
`$HOME/.dt/sessions/<current,home>/dt.session`	Running applications
`$HOME/.dt/sessions/<current,home>/dt.settings`	Desktop custom
`$HOME/.dt/sessions/<current,home>/dtxxxxx`	Application state
`$HOME/.dt/sessions/sesionetc`	Run after startup
`$HOME/.dt/sessions/sesionexit`	Run at logout
`$HOME/.dt/errorlog`	Error messages

Front panel file application-type databases	
`/[usr/dt, etc/dt, $HOME/.dt]/appconfig/types/$LANG` `$HOME/.dt/types`	CDE-type databases

Style manager	
`/etc/dt/appl-defaults/$LANG/Dstyle`	Application resources

Workspace manager	

`/[usr, etc]/dt/config/$LANG/sys.dtwmrc`
`$HOME/.dt/dtwmrc`
`/[usr, etc]/dt/app-defaults/$LANG/Dtwm`
`$HOME/.dt/Dtwm`
	Workspace resources

24.8.1   Configuration and boot

When you flip on the power switch, the Xstation performs a power-on self-test (POST). Once POST is passed, it will optionally direct or broadcast a bootp request packet in an attempt to find a boot server. Once contact is made, the information received determines the IP addresses of the Xstation and the server and the name of the boot configuration file. Since this information can be configured into the Xstation, you may opt to bypass the bootp step for normal operation. To configure address information into the Xstation, access the network configuration menu by pressing the F12 key after POST has completed. These configuration screens allow you to set the IP address information for the terminal, server, and gateway, and disable the bootp process. Similar information may be configured for token ring connections. The model 130, 150, and 160 also support IP over a serial link using SLIP. To configure the model 130, 150, and 160 for a serial TTY connection, press the F11 key after POST has completed.

Once the boot server has been contacted, the Xstation will tftp a copy of the boot file /usr/lpp/x_st_mgr/bin/bootfile from the server. The boot file and configuration file downloaded inform the Xstation which fonts, keymap, rgb database, and server code should be requested from the server. During the bootp and tftp steps, the Xstation display provides some diagnostic information concerning the terminal/server packet exchanges. The two lines of interest are:

```
BOOTP    0000 0000 0000 0000
TFTP     0000 0000 0000 0000 0000
```

The first group of numbers indicates the number of packets sent from the Xstation. The second group indicates the number of packets received from the server. The third group is the count of bad packets received. The fourth group displays the number of timeouts that have occurred. The fifth group on the TFTP line displays the final error code for the transaction. You may access further diagnostic and test information by simultaneously pressing CTRL-BREAK after POST has completed.

24.8.2 AIX Xstation Manager configuration

The AIX Xstation Manager program product provides the boot services for IBM Xstations. As I mentioned earlier, you may also get the Xoftware product from Age Logic, Inc., if you wish to provide boot support from other than a RS/6000 or PS/2. Once the Xstation Manager is installed, verify that its services are defined in the following tables:

- /etc/rc.tcpip

    ```
    /usr/lpp/x_st_mgr/bin/x_st_mgrd -b\
    /usr/lpp/x_st_mgr/bin/x_st_mgrd.cf -s x_st_mg
    ```

- /etc/services

    ```
    bootps 67/udp #bootp server port
    bootpc 68/udp #bootp client port
    x_st_mgrd 7000/tcp #ibm X terminal
    ```

- /etc/inetd.conf

    ```
    bootps dgram udp wait root/etc/bootpd bootpd /etc/bootptab
    ```

You may then define your network type, boot file, and boot file directory via the Xstation selection from the SMIT Devices menu. You may also specify whether the server is a primary or secondary server. It is a good idea to support two boot servers if possible. The Xstations may then be configured to try each server in sequence at startup time.

```
smit x_config     Configure Xstation Manager
```

The following is the Xstation Manager config file x_st_mgrd.cf:

```
xam.foo.edu DISPLAY=xam.foo.edu:0; export DISPLAY;\
XSTATION=xam.foo.edu; export XSTATION;\
LANG=En_US; export LANG;\
/usr/lpp/x_st_mgr/bin/pclient\
-p /usr/lpp/X11/defaults/xmodmap/En_US\
-l keyboard\
-s 5\
-m /usr/lpp/X11/bin/xmodmap\
-a "/usr/lpp/X11/bin/aixterm -fn Rom14 -geometry 80x25+0+0\
-W -e/usr/lpp/x_st_mgr/bin/login"
```

Here is the Xstation Manager boot file:

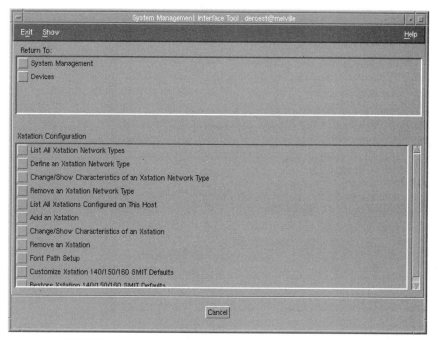

Figure 24.6 SMIT Xstation configuration panel.

```
/usr/lpp/x_st_mgr/nls/keymap
/usr/lpp/x_st_mgr/nls/msg
/usr/lpp/x_st_mgr/bin/x11xor3.out
/usr/lib/X11/fonts,/usr/lib/X11/fonts/ibm850
/usr/lpp/x_st_mgr/bin/rgb.txt
```

Once you have defined your network type, you may define each of the Xstations being supported. You need to identify each Xstation's network type, the hardware address of the adapter, whether xdm services will be used, and the initial application to be started. You may also define local printer support for Xstations equipped with printers via the SMIT printer/plotter menu.

24.9 InfoExplorer Keywords

AIXWindows	/etc/services
mwm	XDMCP
xinit	.Xsession
X11	xhost
xdm	xauth
X	bdftopcf
xterm	mkfontdir
aixterm	CDE
xbiff	xdt2cde
xrdb	dtprintegrate
bootp	Dtwm
tftp	dtconfig
x_st_mgrd	dtlogin
/etc/inetd.conf	

24.10 QwikInfo

AIXWindows, X11 components:

`/usr/bin/X11`	X11 programs
`/usr/lib/X11/fonts`	Font directory
`/usr/lib/X11/app-defaults`	Application defaults
`/usr/lib`	X11 libraries
`/usr/lpp/X11`	AIXWindows
`/usr/lpp/X11/Xamples`	Samples and contribs

Clients and server:

X	X-server
xdm	X-display manager
$HOME/.Xauthority	xdm magic cookie
mwm	Motif window manager
mwmrc	Mwm configuration
aixterm, xterm	X-terminal emulator
.Xsession	xdm startup file
mkfontdir	Fonts directory and alias files created

CDE directories:

/usr/dt	Default configurations
/etc/dt	Local custom defaults
$HOME/.dt	User local configuration

CDE components:

Login manager	XDM-like login
Session manager	Snapshot session management
Front panel	Application launcher
Style manager	Desktop customization
Workspace manager	Multiple workspaces management
File manager	GUI file system interface
Application manager	GUI application interface

CDE applications:

dtlogin	Login manager daemon
dtconfig	CDE started and stopped
Dtwm	CDE window manager
xdt2cde	XDT objects converted to CDE
dtprintegrate	CDE printer support

AIX Xstation Manager/6000:

/usr/lpp/x_st_mgr	AIX Xstation Manager
x_st_mgrd	Xstation daemon

Managing Users and Resources

25

Managing the User Environment

25.1 User Administration Policy

User is a four-letter word! If you administer multiuser systems and haven't taken care to define default environment policies or streamline account management, there are likely many other four-letter words in your vocabulary. A large user base can dominate a system administrator's time with trivial tasks like adding and expiring accounts, setting passwords, juggling home directories, fixing UID collisions . . . the list goes on and on, and so do the requests. Just remember that it's users that keep us employed!

The default environment policies can be thought of as a contract for basic services and resources. Whether it is formally stated or implied, your user base assumes some level of support. There will be less confusion for both your users and user support communities if the basic rules of the road are formally stated and documented. A simple way to disseminate this type of information is to make it available as a man page or help file. You can also provide a default policy statement as a msg file that is displayed the first time a user logs in to the system.

First you need to define what the policies are and how they will be implemented. What are the requirements for establishing an account? What basic resources are provided with an account? What does the default shell environment look like? How long does an account last?

Resource Policies

Physical resources

Resource limits

Account access rights

Account environment

25.2   Physical Resources

Let's start out by making sure we don't promise more than we can deliver. What are the workload characteristics of your user base? How much disk, tape, memory, and CPU resources will be required to support your expected total number of users and the expected concurrent user sessions? In an existing environment, you can construct a fairly good profile by sifting through old accounting information. It's also worthwhile to benchmark your application mix. Push the system to the limit. Stress the CPU, paging, and I/O subsystems. This will give you a feel for what to expect during spikes in load.

25.2.1   User file systems

After you have determined the resource level you can offer, structure the physical resources such that they can be managed easily under software control. Begin by segregating user home directory file systems from the rest of the operating system. This isolates these file systems from operating system upgrades and maintenance. Set up user file systems on different physical disks and volume groups. This will facilitate moving them between machines if circumstances require. Use a naming convention for user file-system mount points that are easy to remember and easy to identify. A possible method would be to use the /u<number> scheme on AIX. In a distributed or clustered environment you might use the first character of the machine name that owns the file system followed by an integer. Don't make them too long!

To reduce the impact of managing user home directories in multiple user file systems, use symbolic links to link the top-level user directories in each file system to a common /home directory. No matter where a particular user's home directory physically resides, it can be accessed via the /home/<user name> path. Specify the symbolic link path name for the home directory field in the /etc/passwd file. This will allow you to move user directories around in your user file systems to balance utilization without requiring each user to learn a new home directory path.

```
# ln -s /u6/stimpy /home/stimpy
stimpy:!:1234:30:Stimpson Cat:/home/stimpy:/bin/ksh
```

You will also need to size your user file systems. If large files are not heavily used, then multiple small file systems may be preferred. Small file systems (less than 1 GB) reduce backup and restore times. They can be easily moved and will partition your user community such that a file system catastrophe won't effect your entire user base.

25.3   UID Space and Groups

User account names are in fact a matter of human convenience in identifying users under UNIX. The AIX operating system identifies a particular user by an unsigned long integer called the UID. The UID is mapped to the user name in the /etc/passwd file. UIDs are used on other UNIX systems but may be represented under other integer formats. Traditionally, the UID space was limited to 32 K, but this has proved to be too small for large time-sharing UNIX systems.

It's a good idea to segregate your user UID space from the UIDs used by system daemons' administrative accounts. This simplifies the task of identifying privileged accounts for accounting and security applications. Pick a number like 1,000 to define the bottom of your user UID space for allocation. In a distributed environment where users may have accounts on different systems, or if you are using Network File System (NFS), you will want to ensure that UIDs are unique across systems. By *unique* I mean that if user "stimpy" is UID 1234 on host-A then the same UID is reserved for stimpy on any other system. Ownership and permission problems can arise if the same UID represents different users in distributed environments. Remember, the operating system identifies users by UID.

While you define your UID space, its also a good idea to plan your Group ID (GID) space. Groups provide a coarse mechanism for sharing information between users. In Chap. 28, file and directory permissions are described that permit read, write, and execute permissions for world, group, and owner. AIX and other UNIXs assume a limited group set to implement access privileges. What needs to be decided is whether you want to implement other GID sets for specific workgroups or collaborators. If your user base is small, this can be done relatively easily. For large numbers of users, managing GID sets can be a big chore.

AIX provides a much better solution to sharing information through access control lists (ACLs). ACLs supply a finer granularity of control and user management. ACLs will be discussed in Chap. 28. Note that JFS ACLs are not the same as DFS ACLs (Chap. 19).

25.3.1   /etc/group and/etc/security/group

GID mapping is maintained in the /etc/group and /etc/security/group files. The /etc/group file lists each group name and GID followed by the list of members. The /etc/security/group file contains a stanza for each group name in the /etc/group file and indicates whether the group may be administered by users other than root and identifies the administrators by user name. Groups and their associated attributes are managed via SMIT or from a series of group management commands.

mkgroup	Create a new group
chgroup	Change group attributes
lsgroup	List groups and attributes
chgrpmem	Change administrators or members of a group
setgroups	Reset the current groups set for a user
newgrp	Set the group ID for session
rmgroup	Remove a group

Now for a few examples. The first uses /etc/group; the second, /etc/security/group.

```
system:!:0:root,ops
daemon:!:1:
bin:!:2:root,bin
sys:!:3:root,bin,sys
adm:!:4:bin,adm,kenm,root
uucp:!:5:uucp
mail:!:6:
security:!:7:root
cron:!:8:root
staff:!:10:root,ren,stimpy,daffy,huey,dewey
user:!:30:luge,acadmus,gwyneira,bungi

system:
    admin = true
daemon:
    admin = true
bin:
    admin = true
sys:
    admin = true
adm:
    admin = true
uucp:
    admin = true
mail:
    admin = true
security:
    admin = true
cron:
    admin = true
staff:
    admin = false
    adms = ren,stimpy
user:
    admin = false
```

25.4   Resource Limits

How much of the pie are you going to give each user? How you do make sure each user gets no more than his or her fair share? Profiling the application mix with estimated concurrent users will give you some ballpark figures. AIX provides the capability to enforce limits on each user's slice of the available system resources through operating system controls. Limits can be defined for CPU, memory, and disk utilization on a per-process basis. The total number of concurrent processes per user is capped by the kernel configuration parameter. Aggregate file system usage can be governed through activating disk quotas at user and group levels.

25.4.1   /etc/security/limits

The kernel manages per-process limits using the setrlimit(), getrlimit(), and vlimit() system calls. Each process has an associated rlimit structure that indicates soft and hard ceilings for each resource type. The rlimit structure is defined in /usr/include/sys/resource.h. Default and resource limits for the system and users are specified in the /etc/security/limits file. Each user defined to the system is represented by a stanza identified by user name. System defaults are active for each user that does not have an overriding parameter under the user's stanza. When a process exceeds one of the specified limits, it is killed.

```
/etc/security/limits
*
* Sizes are in multiples of 512 byte blocks, CPU time is in seconds
*
* fsize      - soft file size in blocks
* core       - soft core file size in blocks
* cpu        - soft per process CPU time limit in seconds
* data       - soft data segment size in blocks
* stack      - soft stack segment size in blocks
* rss        - soft real memory usage in blocks
* fsize_hard - hard file size in blocks
* core_hard  - hard core file size in blocks
* cpu_hard   - hard per process CPU time limit in seconds
* data_hard  - hard data segment size in blocks
* stack_hard - hard stack segment size in blocks
* rss_hard   - hard real memory usage in blocks
*
* The following table contains the default hard values if the
* hard values are not explicitly defined:
*
```

```
* Attribute      Value
* ==========      ==========
* fsize_hard     set to fsize
* cpu_hard       set to cpu
* core_hard      -1
* data_hard      -1
* stack_hard     -1
* rss_hard       -1
*
* NOTE: A value of -1 implies "unlimited"
*

default:
        fsize = 2097151
        core = 2048
        cpu = -1
        data = 262144
        rss = 65536
        stack = 65536


root:

daemon:

bin:

sys:

adm:

uucp:

guest:

nobody:

lpd:

stimpy:
        fsize_hard = 10240
        cpu_hard = 3600

nuucp:
```

The kernel limits the maximum number of processes per user as specified by the kernel configuration parameter maxuproc. The default value of 40 indicates that up to 40 processes may be running concurrently for a given user. The value may not be exceeded by logging into the system multiple times. The maxuproc value may be altered via SMIT or with the chdev command (see Fig. 25.1).

```
# chgdev -1 sys0 -a maxuproc=80

# smit chgsys
```

Disk quotas limit the maximum number of blocks a user or group may consume on participating file systems. The AIX implementation of disk quotas is based on BSD quotas. User and group quota limits are set by the system administrator using the edquota command. Quota limits for disk blocks and inodes are specified by three parameters: soft limit, hard.limit, and grace period.

The value of the soft limit indicates at what point the user or group begins receiving warnings that the soft limit has been exceeded and that the hard limit is being approached. Warnings are delivered at login time and at each close that exceeds the specified limit. The hard limit specifies at what point the user or group will no longer be able to allocate additional disk space or inodes. The grace period defines a period of time that the user or group has to reduce utilization below the

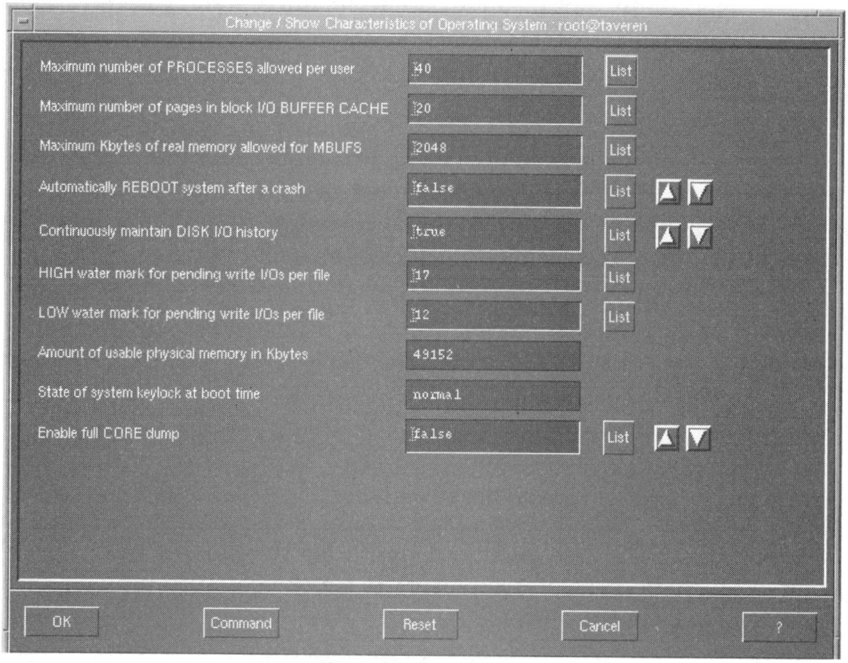

Figure 25.1 SMIT characteristics of the operating system panel.

soft limit value. If utilization is not reduced before the grace period expires, the soft limit is enforced as a hard limit.

To implement disk quotas on a file system, edit the stanza entry in /etc/filesystems associated with file system name. Add the parameter quota=<userquota>,<groupquota> to the stanza. The userquota and groupquota values indicate the quota types to be enforced. The quota limits for each user or group are recorded in files in the top-level directory named quota.user and quota.group, respectively. You may override these file names with your own by including userquota=<pathname> and groupquota=<pathname> parameters in the file-system stanza.

```
/etc/filesystems

/u1:
    dev = /dev/lv43
    vfs = jfs
    log = /dev/loglv00
    mount = true
    check = true
    options = rw
    quota = userquota
    userquota = /u1/user.quota
```

If the quota limit files do not exist on the file system, you can create them using touch.

```
# touch/u1/quota.user
```

Use the edquota command to create a user quota for one of the users on the system. These values will be used as a template for setting the limits for other users on the system. The edquota command will invoke the default editor and display the quota values for update.

```
# edquota stimpy

Quotas for user stimpy:
/u1: blocks in use: 50, limits (soft = 80, hard = 100)
        inodes in use: 11, limits (soft = 120, hard 150)
/u2: blocks in use: 0, limits (soft = 80, hard = 100)
        inodes in use: 0, limits (soft = 120, hard 150)
```

After setting the soft and hard limits for the default user, invoke edquota -p <default-user><new-user> to set the default limits for each additional user in the system.

```
# edquota -p stimpy ren
```

Enable the quota system by executing the quotaon command. As part of the nightly system housekeeping, update the information in the quota files by running the quotacheck command. You can use the -a flag to indicate all quota file systems. The following are quota update commands:

```
# quotaoff -a
# quotacheck -a
# quotaon -a
```

The quota limits for a user or a summary can be displayed using the quota and repquota commands, respectively.

```
# quota ren

Disk quotas for user ren (uid 4084):
Filesystem blocks quota limit grace files quota limit grace
/u1         11836* 5120  6144  none  363   1000  2000

# repquota
```

		Block	limits			File	limits	
User	used	soft	hard	grace	used	soft	hard	grace
root	--	31448	0	0	700	0	0	
bin	--	57700	0	0	2037	0	0	
sys	--	4	0	0	1	0	0	
news	--	4	0	0	1	0	0	
bilbro	--	16	0	0	4	0	0	

25.5 User Account Access Rights

Who gets an account and how long can they keep it? Access and expiration policies might not seem like a big deal for small workgroups; however, the less ambiguity, the better. There are also legal implications that can be avoided if these policies are formalized and made public. Expiring and cleaning up accounts on large user base systems can be automated easily if expiration policies are clearly defined. AIX provides a mechanism for expiring accounts and performing the cleanup housekeeping. By providing both facilities, AIX allows you to implement grace periods between when an account expires and when it is actually removed from the system. This can be incorporated into a last use policy. Chapter 28 covers expiration procedures.

25.6 User Account Environment

What face will the system present to new users? As system administrator, you are charged with setting up the default environment for each new account. You want to maintain some level of control over environment parameters, yet you want to allow users the freedom of tailoring their own work space. Shells, editors, terminal definitions, and the like are religious issues best left to the faithful! You can't keep everyone from shooting themselves in the foot. You also don't want to open the floodgates to more shell environments than you can support. You can provide a simple, modular login environment that simplifies recovery for the adventurous user when shell experimentation goes awry.

Begin by defining the default environment variables that will be set for all users. Environment variables are name=value pairs that are read by shells and commands to set values or determine behavior. For example, the environment variable EDITOR indicates what editor is to be invoked by applications like mail or rn. Environment variables may be command or shell specific, and they may be modified by the end user. See Table 25.1.

25.6.1   /etc/environment and /etc/profile

AIX provides two files that are used to set default environment variables for the system. The /etc/environment file contains default variables set for each process by the exec() system calls. The /etc/profile file contains the set of environment variables and commands that will be invoked when a user logs into the system. The contents of these files are read before local shell startup files and they are best kept non-shell-specific. The AIX-supplied /etc/environment and /etc/profile files provide a good boiler plate for tailoring your own defaults.

TABLE 25.1   Common Environment Variables

PATH	List of directory paths to search for commands and files
LIBPATH	List of library paths to search for binding
PAGER	Default full-screen pager
EDITOR	Default editor
TZ	Time zone
TERM	Terminal type
MAIL	Incoming mail path
MAILMSG	Message text prompt when new mail arrives
LANG	Locale name in effect for NLS
LOCPATH	Directory containing locale file
NLSPATH	Full path to NLS catalogs
USER	User name (csh)
LOGNAME	User name
TNESC	Telnet escape key sequence
HOME	Home directory path

Here is a listing of System /etc/environment:

```
# @(#)18   1.21 src/bos/etc/environment/environment, cmdsh, bos420,
          9613T 5/13/94
15:09:03
# IMB_PROLOG_BEGIN_TAG
# This is an automatically generated prolog.
#
# bos420 src/bos/etc/environment/environment
#
# Licensed Materials - Property of IBM
#
# (C) COPYRIGHT International Business Machines Corp. 1989,1994
# All Rights Reserved
#
# US Government Users Restricted Rights - Use, duplication or
# disclosure restricted by GSA ADP Schedule Contract with IBM Corp.
#
# IBM_PROLOG_END_TAG
#
# COMPONENT_NAME: (CMDSH) Shell related commands
#
# ORIGINS: 27
#
# (C) COPYRIGHT International Business Machines Corp. 1989, 1994
# All Rights Reserved
# Licensed Materials - Property of IBM
#
# US Government Users Restricted Rights - Use, duplication or
# disclosure restricted by GSA ADP Schedule Contract with IBM Corp.
#
##################################################################
# System wide environment file. This file should only contain
#   1. comment lines which have a # in the first column,
#   2. blank lines, and
#   3. Lines in the form name=value.
#
# WARNING: This file is only for establishing environment variables.
#     Execution of commands from this file or any lines other
#     than specified above may cause failure of the initialization
#       process.
#
# Searching the current directory last is usually a BIG time saver.
# If/usr/ucb is at the beginning of the PATH the BSD version of
# commands will be found.
#
PATH=/usr/bin:/etc:/usr/sbin:/usr/ucb:/usr/bin/X11:/sbin:/usr/local/bin
```

```
TZ=PST8PDT
LANG=en_US
LOCPATH=/usr/lib/nls/loc
NLSPATH=/usr/lib/nls/msg/%L/%N:/usr/lib/nls/msg/%L/%N.cat
LC_FASTMSG=true


# ODM routines use ODMDIR to determine which objects to operate on
# the default is /etc/objrepos - this is where the device objects
# reside, which are required for hardware configuration


ODMDIR=/etc/objrepos
```

The following shows /etc/profile:

```
# @(#)27   1.20 src/bos/etc/profile/profile, cmdsh, bos420, 9613T
         8/9/94 12:01:38
# IBM_PROLOG_BEGIN_TAG
# This is an automatically generated prolog.
#
# bos420 src/bos/etc/profile/profile
#
# Licensed Materials - Property of IBM
#
# (C) COPYRIGHT International Business Machines Corp. 1989,1994
# All Rights Reserved
#
# US Government Users Restricted Rights - Use, duplication or
# disclosure restricted by GSA ADP Schedule Contract with IBM Corp.
#
# IBM_PROLOG_END_TAG
#
# COMPONENT_NAME: (CMDSH) Shell related commands
#
# FUNCTIONS:
#
# ORIGINS: 3,26,27
#
# (C) COPYRIGHT International Business Machines Corp. 1989, 1994
# All Rights Reserved
# Licensed Materials - Property of IBM
#
# US Government Users Restricted Rights - Use, duplication or
# disclosure restricted by GSA ADP Schedule Contract with IBM Corp.
#
##############################################################################
```

```
# System wide profile. All variables set here may be overridden by
# a user's personal .profile file in their $HOME directory. However,
# all commands here will be executed at login regardless.

trap "" 1 2 3
readonly LOGNAME

# Automatic logout, include in export line if uncommented
# TMOUT=120

# The MAILMSG will be printed by the shell every MAILCHECK seconds
# (default 600) if there is mail in the MAIL system mailbox.
MAIL=/usr/spool/mail/$LOGNAME
MAILMSG="[YOU HAVE NEW MAIL]"

# If termdef command returns terminal type (i.e. a non NULL value),
# set TERM to the returned value, else set TERM to default lft.
TERM_DEFAULT=lft
TERM='termdef'
TERM=${TERM:-$TERM_DEFAULT}

# If LC_MESSAGES is set to "C@lft" and TERM is not set to "lft",
# unset LC_MESSAGES.
if [ "$LC_MESSAGES"="C@lft"-a "$TERM"!="lft"]
then
        unset LC_MESSAGES
fi

export LOGNAME MAIL MAILMSG TERM

trap 1 2 3
```

25.6.2   /etc/security/environ

Individual user environment variables may also be defined in the /etc/security/environ file. This file contains a stanza for each user in the system identified by user name followed by a list of environment variables and the associated value. The environment variable=value pairs are separated by commas. Those variables specified as usrenv are set at login. To protect environment variables from being reset by unprivileged applications, use the sysenv specification.

The following example shows an /etc/security/environ stanza:

```
stimpy:
    usrenv = "TNESC=35,PAGER=/bin/more,EDITOR=/bin/vi"
    sysenv = "HOME=/home/stimpy"
```

Next, define the default shell and shell environment variables. The default shell and startup files are set by the /usr/lib/security/mkuser.sys script and /usr/lib/security/mkuser.default file. The mkuser.sys script reads the mkuser.default file and creates the home directory, sets permissions, and copies the default shell startup file from /etc/security into the new home directory. The mkuser.sys script is invoked each time the mkuser command is executed by SMIT or from the command line to add a new account.

```
/usr/lib/security/mkuser.default

user:
      pgrp = staff
      groups = staff
      shell = /usr/in/ksh
      home = /home/$USER

admin:
      pgrp = system
      groups = system
      shell = /usr/bin/ksh
      home = /home/$USER
```

The shell startup files are as follows:

sh	.profile
ksh	.profile, .kshrc (if indicated by ENV)
csh, tcsh	.login, .cshrc, .logout

The default behavior of mkuser.sys is to copy a complete shell startup file into the user's home directory. This can be a problem should you decide to change some part of the default shell environment later on. You will need to incorporate the change into each user's startup files without destroying any customizations added by the user.

A simple solution is to create a skeleton shell startup file that contains a single line that sources or invokes a read-only system default shell startup file. The skeleton file is copied to the user's home directory at account creation time. Users may append lines to their local copy of the skeleton file, which overrides or adds to the environment variables, commands, and aliases specified in the system default startup file. The system administrator maintains the shell environment data in the system defaults files. Default startup would include things like displaying the message-of-the-day file /etc/motd or invoke the msgs command to display system update information at login time. Skeleton and associated system defaults startup files are created for each supported shell. The skeleton shell files should be available for copy should a user decide to change his or her default shell.

The following is an example of skeleton and system csh startup files:

```
# /usr/local/skel/.cshrc
#
# Skeleton .cshrc file copied to the users home
# directory at account creation.
#
# Source system csh defaults
#
source /usr/local/lib/std.cshrc
#
# Local user changes are added after this line.

# /usr/local/skel/.login
#
# Skeleton .login file copied to the users home
# directory at account creation.
#
# Source system csh defaults
#
source /usr/local/lib/std.login
#
# Local user changes are added after this line.

# /usr/local/lib/std.cshrc
#
# System default csh startup environment. (read only)
#
if!($?prompt) goto NOPROMPT
set prompt = "_'hostname'%"
set history = 30
set savehist = 30
alias a alias
alias h history
unmask 022
NOPROMPT:

# /usr/local/lib/std.login .
#
set ignoreeof
setenv PATH
"/usr/local/bin:/usr/bin/X11:/usr/ucb:/usr/bin:/bin:"
setenv EXINIT "set shell=/bin/csh"
stty dec crt
stty -tabs ff1
setenv TNESC 35
msgs -f
```

You can further break the system startup file hierarchy down to support a startup file that sets the PATH environment for all shells. That way, modifications to the search path only involve updating one file. You might also want to separate aliases from environment variables or TTY settings.

Depending on the shell, you will also need to be aware of how the startup files are handled by other commands. For example, the remote shell command rsh does not invoke $HOME/.login for csh users. Thus, important csh environment information should be maintained in the std.cshrc file rather than the std.login file.

25.6.3   /etc/security/login.cfg

Even with simple schemes like this, many of us don't want to have to support every shell that might be built by a user. You can restrict the shells supported on the system by specifying the shell path in the /etc/security/login.cfg file. Edit the usw: stanza and list the path name of each supported shell separated by commas after the shell= parameter.

The following shells are supported by /etc/security/login.cfg:

```
usw:
   shells =/bin/sh,/bin/bsh,/bin/csh,/bin/ksh,/bin/tsh,/usr/bin/sh,
        /usr/bin/bsh,/usr/bin/csh,/usr/bin/ksh,/usr/bin/tsh,
        /usr/mbin/sh,/usr/mbin/bsh,/usr/mbin/csh,/usr/mbin/ksh,
        /usr/mbin/tsh,/usr/local/bin/tcsh
```

The /etc/security/login.cfg file also defines the default login heralds, alternate authorization programs, and password profile. Stanzas associated with these facilities will be discussed in Chap. 28.

25.7   Managing User Accounts

System administrators can't escape the ongoing stream of account management requests that come from an active user community. The good news is that AIX automates the task of adding, updating, and removing user accounts by providing a set of tools that take care of updating all the appropriate tables and file systems. It's still not perfect, but it beats doing it by hand!

25.7.1   Adding a user account

To add a new user to the system, execute the mkuser command either from the command line or using SMIT. Due to the number of parameters involved, I suggest using SMIT unless you are accepting system defaults. In the event that you are adding a large number of users, you can add the first using SMIT, then duplicate the mkuser command in the smit.script file for each subsequent account to be created. See Fig. 25.2.

Figure 25.2   mkuser fields.

```
# smit mkuser
```

For most general user accounts, you can select a user name and accept the supplied defaults. Table 25.2 lists the option fields available for configuring account resources. There have been some changes in AIX V4, specifically password controls and resource hard and soft limits.

See Chap. 28 for more information concerning primary and secondary authentication methods as well as password support.

25.7.2   Updating user accounts

You can modify existing user accounts by invoking the chuser command from the command line or via SMIT. In most cases, only a small number of fields are changed, so using chuser from the command line does not involve a large number of arguments. You may also update system account tables directly with an editor in some cases. Care should be taken that stanza format and permissions are not compromised.

```
# smit chuser
```

You can list the current set of attributes defined for a user using the lsuser command.

TABLE 25.2   mkuser Fields

UserNAME	Up to eight characters; no uppercase or special characters
User ID	Unique integer; may need to be altered if you are using unique UIDs across multiple systems
ADMINISTRATIVE user	Administrative privileges
PRIMARY group	Default group at login
Group SET	Other group membership
ADMINISTRATIVE groups	User is an administrator of these groups
Another user can SU TO USER?	True/false
SU GROUPS	Groups that may issue the su commnd
HOME directory	Home directory path /u/<user name>
Initial PROGRAM	Login shell program
User INFORMATION	User full name, phone, etc. for GECOS field in /etc/passwd file
EXPIRATION date	Account will expire on this date
Is this user ACCOUNT LOCKED?	Is the user restricted from logging in?
User can LOGIN REMOTELY?	Can the user use rlogin to access the system?
Allowed LOGIN TIMES	Restrict access to these times
Number of FAILED LOGINS before user account is locked	Number of failed login attempts
Login AUTHENTICATION GRAMMAR	Authentication method
Valid TTYs	TTY ports that may be used to login to this UID
Days to WARN USER before	Number days to warn user with message at login. password expires
Password CHECK METHODS	Rules for validating proper passwords
Password DICTIONARY FILES	Word dictionaries used to validate password
NUMBER OF PASSWORDS before reuse.	How many passwords before reuse
WEEKS before password reuse	How long before reuse
Weeks between password EXPIRATION and LOCKOUT	How long after expiration before restricting access
Password MAX AGE	Maximum time before requiring a password change
Password MIN AGE	Minimum time before a password can be changed
Password MIN LENGTH	How short can a password be
Password MIN ALPHA	Minimum number of alphabetic characters
Password MIN OTHER	Minimum number of non-alpha characters
Password MAX REPEATED	Maximum repeated characters allowed
Password MIN DIFFERENT	Minimum number of different chars required
Password REGISTRY	Authentication mechanism
Soft FILE size	Soft resource limits changeable by user
Soft CPU time	
Soft DATA segment	
Soft STACK size	
Soft CORE file size	
Soft physical MEMORY	
Hard FILE size	Hard resource limits for the user
Hard CPU time	
Hard DATA segment	
Hard STACK size	
Hard CORE file size	
Hard physical MEMORY	
File creation MASK	Default umask for the user
AUDIT Classes	Audit classes representing this UID
TRUSTED PATH	Trusted path status
PRIMARY authentication method	Authentication program used to validate this user to the system; default SYSTEM represents standard user name and password
SECONDARY authentication method	Secondary authentication program; if it fails, it does not deny access

```
# lsuser stimpy
stimpy id=4084 pgrp=system groups=system,security home=/home/deroest
shell=/bin/ksh
login=true su=true rlogin=true daemon=true admin=true sugroups=ALL
admgroups=system
tpath=nosak ttys=ALL expires=0 auth1=SYSTEM auth2=NONE umask=22
SYSTEM=compat
logintimes= loginretries=0 pwdwarntime=0 account_locked=false minage=0
maxage=0
maxexpired=-1 minalpha=0 minother=0 mindiff=0 maxrepeats=8 minlen=0
histexpire=0
histsize=0 pwdchecks= dictionlist= dce_export=false fsize=2097151 cpu=-1
data=262144
stack=65536 core=2048 rss=65536 time_last_login=843748941
time_last_unsuccessful_login=839838086 tty_last_login=/dev/pts/1
tty_last_unsuccessful_login=/dev/dtlogin/_0
host_last_login=mead2.u.washington.edu
host_last_unsuccessful_login=taveren unsuccessful_login_count=0
```

25.7.3 Removing user accounts

To remove users from the system, use the rmuser command. It can be invoked from the command line or using SMIT (see Fig. 25.3). The rmuser command takes care of removing the user from the system tables and deleting the home directory from the file system. You also have the option of retaining user data in the /etc/security/passwd file.

```
# rmuser -p stimpy
# smit rmuser
```

To automate the process of removing accounts from the system, you can use cron to run a nightly process that looks for expired accounts and invokes rmuser. See Chap. 26 concerning using cron.

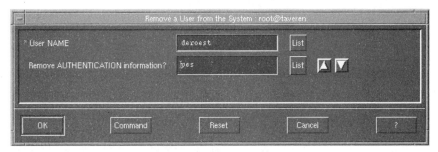

Figure 25.3 SMIT "remove user" panel.

25.7.4 Restricting access

If it is required to restrict access to the system for a particular user, you may deny access from a number of mechanisms depending on the situation. Login access can be restricted by setting the LOGIN User and User can RLOGIN fields to false. You may also restrict access by resetting the date in the EXPIRATION field. If you wish to send the user an informative message concerning account status, create a script or program to write the message to stdout and add the program name to the Initial PROGRAM field for the user. After the user supplies a user name and password at login time, the message is displayed and the user is logged off. Use the chuser command to enable the desired level of access restriction.

25.8 Password Files

All the information injected by the AIX account management tools end up as entries in a number of account support tables. I have discussed the structure that some of these files provide in the the previous sections. There are three other files that are primarily responsible for identifying an account to the operating system and application set. These are the /etc/passwd, /etc/security/passwd, and /etc/security/user files.

25.8.1 /etc/passwd

The /etc/passwd file uses the standard password file format available on most UNIX systems, the only exception being the use of a shadow password file. Shadow password support removes the encrypted password from the world-readable /etc/passwd file and places it into another file with restricted access. A place holder, the exclamation point (!), is inserted into the password field in /etc/passwd. Each field in the /etc/passwd file is separated by a colon:

```
USER NAME:!:UID:GID:GECOS:HOME DIRECTORY:SHELL
root:!:0:0:System Overseer:/:/bin/ksh
daemon:!:1:1::/etc:
bin:!:2:2::/bin:
sys:!:3:3::/usr/sys:
adm:!:4:4::/usr/adm:
uucp:!:5:5::/usr/lib/uucp:
stimpy:!:4084:30:Stimpson Cat:/u1/stimpy:/bin/ksh
```

AIX commands and applications that must resolve user information query /etc/passwd through the use of library calls like getpwnam(). Parsing large password files can cause significant delays in command response time. To improve response time, AIX supports building a structured dbm database from the /etc/passwd information. The mkpasswd command reads /etc/passwd and creates a keyed directory file, /etc/passwd.dir, and a data file, /etc/passwd.pag. Password dbm support is not required, but it is provided as an option for sites with large user communities.

```
# mkpasswd /etc/passwd
```
Create new passwd dbm database

25.8.2 /etc/security/passwd

Shadow password support is provided by the /etc/security/passwd file. Each user account is represented by a user name stanza. The stanza contains the encrypted password, time of last update, and the update flag. The update flag contains either the null value or one of the following:

ADMIN	Only root may change this password.
ADMCHG	A member of the security group reset this password so it must be changed at next login.
NO_CHECK	None of restrictions set in the /etc/security/login.cfg file are enforced for this account.

Here is an example /etc/security/passwd stanza:

```
stimpy:
        password = dWe3asfZpuoJ6
        lastupdate = 722287867
        flags = NO_CHECK
```

25.8.3 /etc/security/user

The /etc/security/user file contains the extended attributes defined for the user. Each user is identified by a user name stanza followed by each attribute and value. A default attribute set follows the header comments in the file. Each user entry may override a default attribute by specifying a local value. See the following example:

```
default:
        admin = false
        login = true
        su = true
        daemon = true
        rlogin = true
        sugroups = ALL
        ttys = ALL
        auth1 = SYSTEM
        auth2 = NONE
        tpath = nosak
        umask = 022
        expires = 0
```

```
stimpy:
        login = false
        rlogin = false
```

25.9   InfoExplorer Keywords

msg	touch
/etc/passwd	quotaon
/etc/group	quotacheck
/etc/security/passwd	repquota
/etc/security/group	/etc/environment
mkgroup	/etc/profile
chgroup	/etc/security/environ
lsgroup	/etc/security/mkuser.sys
chgrpmem	/etc/security/mkuser.default mkuser
setgroups	/etc/motd
newgrp	msgs
rmgroup	/etc/security/login.cfg
/etc/security/limits	su
rlimit	chuser
edquota	rmuser
/etc/filesystems	cron
quota	mkpasswd
groupquota	/etc/security/user
userquota	

25.10   QwikInfo

Passwords:

/etc/security/passwd	Secure passwd entries
/etc/passwd	Unsecure passwd entries
/etc/passwd.{pag dir}	DBM passwd files
mkpasswd	Create DBM files

Groups:

/etc/group	Group numbers and lists
/etc/security/group	Group configuration

`mkgroup, chgroup, lsgoup`	Manage groups
`chgrpmem`	Change administrators or members of a group
`setgroups`	Reset the current groups set for a user
`newgrp`	Set the group ID for session

System defaults:

`/etc/security/limits`	Resource limits
`/etc/security/user`	User authorization and configuration
`/etc/security/login.cfg`	System authorization, heralds, and shells
`chgdev -1 sys0 -a <attribute>`	Set kernel attributes
`smit chgsys`	Set kernel attributes

Disk quotas:

`/[file-system]/quota.user`	User quota/file system
`/[file-system]/quota.group`	Group quota/file system
`/etc/filesystems`	Set quota attributes
`edquota`	Edit user quota limits
`quotaon/quotaoff`	Enable/disable quotas
`quotacheck`	Set quotas/file system
`quota, repquota`	Report quota, usage

User environment:

`/etc/environment`	System environ defaults
`/etc/profile`	System login defaults
`/etc/security/environ`	User environ defaults
`/usr/lib/security/mkuser.defualt`	User environ defaults
`/usr/lib/security/mkuser.sys`	System environ defaults
`smit mkuser,chuser,lsuser,rmuser`	User accounts management
`$HOME/.login`	User login defaults
`$HOME/.profile`	User profile defaults
`$HOME/.<shell>rc`	Shell startup defaults

26

Process Management

26.1 Process Overview

A group of processes executing under AIX is analogous to the generations of a family tree. Child processes are begotten by parent processes.
Processes are born, live out their avocations, then pass away. Process
ID 1, init, is the great grandparent from which all process generations
owe their being. Like a loving grandparent, init takes in the orphan
processes that have lost their parents. Each process gets its turn to
execute on the CPU. Like little children, they require the guidance of
the scheduler so that everyone is ensured a fair share of the CPU. The
system administrator represents the grand overseer over the process
universe, wielding ultimate control over the lives of all processes. A
benevolent and all-seeing system administrator will learn the ways of
process life in the AIX world so that his may live in tranquility and
peace.

26.2 Process Attributes

A process is comprised of an executing program and its address space.
Each process is named by a positive integer number called the process
identifier (PID). The PID is a vector index in the kernel process table.
PIDs are unique and are allocated in a somewhat random fashion.
Process table entries point to per process kernel data structures. The
proc data structures define the attribute values associated with the
process. See /usr/include/sys/proc.h. The global AIX process table can
support up to 131,071 PIDs. Let's see you get that many running on one
machine!

Here is a small sampling of process attributes:

Process identifier

Process group identifier

Process parent identifier

Process owner

Effective and real user and group identifiers

Priority

Controlling terminal

Address space

Size in pages

Paging statistics

Resource utilization

Process state

26.2.1   Displaying process attributes

Active process attributes can be interrogated from the command line using the ps command. You can also use SMIT to invoke ps, but you may find that using ps from the command line to be faster. AIX supports two flavors of ps: SYSV and BSD. The SYSV personality is used when the command line arguments are preceded by the hyphen character; otherwise, the BSD format is used.

ps -elk   SYSV process display format

F	S	UID	PID	PPID	C	PRI	NI	ADDR	SZ	WCHAN	TTY	TIME	CMD
303	A	0	0	0	120	16	--	707	4		-	0:05	swapper
200003	A	0	1	0	0	60	20	505	220		-	0:07	init
303	A	0	516	0	120	127	--	808	0		-	113:17	kproc
303	A	0	774	0	0	36	--	606	8		-	0:00	kproc
303	A	0	1032	0	0	37	--	b0b	40	*	-	0:04	kproc
40201	A	0	1874	0	0	60	20	1b1b	8		-	0:00	kproc

ps auxw   BSD process display format

USER	PID	%CPU	%MEM	SZ	RSS	TTY	STAT	STIME	TIME	COMMAND
root	516	95.7	0.0	0	4	-	A	00:19:28	113:29	kproc
root	4992	0.3	0.0	8	12	-	A	00:22:10	0.19	kproc
root	1	0.1	0.0	220	180	-	A	00:19:58	0:07	/etc/init
root	0	0.1	0.0	4	8	-	A	00:19:28	0.05	swapper
root	1032	0.1	0.0	40	48	-	A	00:19:28	0:04	kproc

The COMMAND and CMD columns represent the program being run in the process address space. A special set of kernel processes, kprocs, are represented to collect accounting data for system overhead. You may notice that one kproc process collects very high amounts of CPU. There is no cause for alarm. This kproc entry collects the system wait and idle time and represents it in the CPU field.

26.2.2 Process Identifiers

Along with its PID, each process records the integer ID of its parent and its group membership, parent process identifier (PPID), and process group identifier (PGID). Process groups are collections of one or more processes. The group leader has a PGID equal to its PID, and each member has a PGID that matches the leader. Unless reset by a setpgrp() call, a process inherits the PGID of its parent. Process groups provide a mechanism for signaling all processes within the group using the PGID. This eliminates the need to know each member's PID. The PID, PPID, and PGID are the primary handles used by the system administrator for controlling process behavior.

There is a real nice public domain tool called pstree that will graphically map process relationships on the screen (see Fig. 26.1). It's available from aixpdslib.seas.ucla.edu (Appendix A).

```
# pstree
```

26.2.3 Effective and real UID and GID

Processes are associated with an owning user identifier (UID) and group identifier (GID). The UID and GID name space are maintained as part of the system account management and are recorded in the

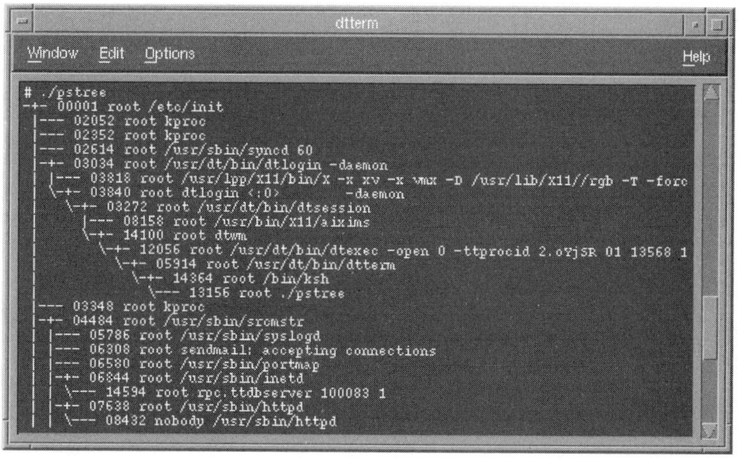

Figure 26.1 Pstree.

/etc/passwd and /etc/group files (see Chap. 28). The real UID and real GID numbers identify process owners for accounting and process control purposes. An effective UID (EUID) and effective GID (EGID) are assigned to each process and represent the permissions and privileges available to the process during its lifetime.

26.2.4   Controlling terminal

Processes other than system daemons are usually associated with a Control Terminal. The control terminal represents the default device for standard input, output, and error channels and for sending signals via keyboard control characters. The control character-to-signal mapping is user-customizable and recorded in the termio structure. See Chap. 12 for details on keyboard mapping. The controlling terminal is identified in the ps TTY column.

26.2.5   Resource utilization and priority

AIX uses a priority-based set of run queues to allocate CPU resources among active processes. Priorities values range from 0 to 127, each of which is represented by a run queue. Lower-numbered queues are scheduled more often than higher-numbered queues. Processes in a run queue level are scheduled in a round robin fashion. Each processes queue priority is calculated from the sum of its short-term CPU usage (0 to +100), its nice value (0 to 40), and the minimum user process level (40). The priority value increases for processes that execute frequently and decrease for those that are waiting for execution. Processes with a priority value exceeding 120 will execute only when no other process in the system requires CPU resources. Process short-term CPU usage, priority, and nice value are displayed in the PRI, C, and NI fields using the SYSV ps -1 option.

The nice value is an integer that represents coarse priorities between processes. AIX supports both the BSD nice value range of 20 to -20 and the SYSV range of 0 to 39. The larger the number, the lower the scheduling priority. The two value ranges are mapped such that BSD -20 corresponds to SYSV 0 for highest priority and BSD 20 to SYSV 39 for lowest priority.

New processes inherit the nice value of their parents. The nice value may be altered dynamically during the process lifetime. The owning UID for a process can lower the process nice value. Only the superuser can improve nice priority. The nice value can be set from the command line using the nice command.

```
# nice -n <value> <command>
```

Process owners and the superuser can modify existing process nice values by using the renice command.

```
# renice <value> -p <PID>
```

Be aware that the BSD #CPU field represents the percentage of CPU resources that a process has used in its lifetime. You may see short-lived processes shoot up to very high #CPU numbers. A better gauge for identifying CPU crunchers or runaway processes is the TIME column.

26.2.6 Process state

The scheduler parcels out CPU time slices at a frequency that makes it appear as if all processes are executing at the same time. In fact, they are being scheduled one at time, except in the case of multiprocessor systems. When a process isn't executing on the CPU, it may be waiting on a resource or lock, sleeping on an event, being suspended, or moving through some dispatch or scheduler state. The process state is maintained as part of the proc structure information. The process state is displayed by "ps" in the STAT column when the BSD "1" or SYSV "-1" flag is used (see Table 26.1). For processes that are flagged as waiting, the WCHAN column identifies the address of the event being waited on.

26.3 Parent Child Inheritance

A parent process creates a new child process by invoking the fork() system call. The kernel reserves a vacant PID for the child and copies the attribute data associated with the parent into the child's proc structure. The child is a clone of the parent until either the child, the parent, or a privileged authority modifies the child's attributes via a system call. The most common method of modifying a child's proc attributes is by invoking a new program via the exec() system call.

**TABLE 26.1 Process States
Displayed by "ps"**

A	Active
O	Nonexistent
S	Sleeping
W	Waiting
R	Running
I	Intermediate
Z	Cancelled
T	Stopped
K	Available kernel process
X	Growing

26.4   Controlling Processes

In Sec. 26.2.5, I talked about using the nice and renice commands to coarsely control the scheduling priorities between processes. What do you do when process management requires a heavier hand? You use the kill command!

The command name *kill* sounds much more ominous than in fact it is. What kill does is send a specified signal to a process. The signal does not necessarily cause process termination. Note that kill is a built-in command for some shells like /bin/csh, for example. The behavior of the shell version of kill and /bin/kill may be different.

```
# kill [-Signal] [PID PID PID …]
```

PID > 0	Send signal to specified PIDs
PID = 0	Send signal to PIDs that have PGIDs equal to the sender
PID = -1	Send signal to all PIDs with EUID equal to the sender
PID < -1	Send signal to all PIDs with a PGID equal to the absolute value of the specified PID

If you want to send a signal to all your processes except the sending process, use the killall command.

```
# killall [-signal]
```

To display the set of supported signals, use the -1 argument of kill:

```
# /bin/kill -l

NULL HUP INT QUIT ILL TRAP IOT EMT FPE KILL BUS SEGV SYS PIPE ALRM
TERM URG STOP TSTP CONT CHLD TTIN TTOU IO XCPU XFSZ MSG WINCH PWR
USR1 USR2 PROF DANGER VTALRM MIGRATE PRE GRANT RETRACT SOUND
SAK
```

AIX signals are based on the SYSV implementation; however, some BSD signals are mapped to their SYSV counterparts, and BSD signal system calls are available. When writing or porting programs that use BSD signals and calls, be aware that signals are not automatically reset after being caught. They must be specifically reset to the required behavior in the signal handler routine. See Tables 26.2 and 26.3.

26.4.1   Rules of thumb

It seems to be a common practice to use the KILL (9) signal to terminate a process. I recommend that you do this only as a last resort after first trying HUP (1) and ABRT (6). The latter two signals allow a

TABLE 26.2   Signal Names and Numbers

SIGHUP	1	Hang up at terminal disconnect
SIGINT	2	Interrupt
SIGQUIT	3	Quit
SIGILL	4	Illegal instruction
SIGTRAP	5	Trace trap
SIGABRT	6	Abort process and core dump
SIGEMT	7	EMT instruction
SIGFPE	8	Floating point exception
SIGKILL	9	Kill process; can't be caught or ignored
SIGBUS	10	Bus error
SIGSEGV	11	Segmentation violation
SIGSYS	12	System call, bad argument
SIGPIPE	13	Write on a pipe with no one reader
SIGALRM	14	Alarm clock timeout
SIGTERM	15	Termination signal
SIGURG	16	Urgent condition on I/O channel
SIGSTOP	17	Stop; can't be caught or ignored
SIGTSTP	18	Interactive stop
SIGCONT	19	Continue; can't be caught or ignored
SIGCHLD	20	Sent to parent on child stop or exit
SIGTTIN	21	Background read attempted from control terminal
SIGTTOU	22	Background write attempted to control terminal
SIGIO	23	I/O possible or completed
SIGXCPU	24	CPU time limit exceeded
SIGXFSZ	25	File size limit exceeded
SIGMSG	27	Input data is in the HFT ring buffer
SIGWINCH	28	Window size changed
SIGPWR	29	Power-fail restart
SIGUSR1	30	User-defined signal 1
SIGUSR2	31	User-defined signal 2
SIGPROF	32	Profiling time alarm
SIGDANGER	33	System crash imminent; free page space
SIGVTALRM	34	Virtual time alarm
SIGMIGRATE	35	Migrate process (Locus TCF)
SIGPRE	36	Programming exception
SIGVIRT	37	AIX virtual time alarm
SIGALRM	38	m:n condition variables
SIGWAITING	39	m:n scheduling
SIGGRANT	60	HFT monitor mode granted
SIGRETRACT	61	HFT monitor mode should be relinquished
SIGSOUND	62	HFT sound control has completed
SIGSAK	63	Secure attention key

process to terminate gracefully. In the case of ABRT, a core file is produced which may be used for debugging. The KILL signal basically attempts to yank the process out of the process table without permitting any cleanup activities.

```
# kill -1 <PID>     First try HUP
# kill -6 <PID>     Then try ABRT
# kill -9 <PID>     KILL if all else fails
```

TABLE 26.3   Signal Compatibility Mapping

SIGIOINT	SIGURG	Printer to backend error signal
SIGAIO	SIGIO	Base LAN I/O
SIGSIGPTY	SIGIO	PTY I/O
SIGSIGIOT	SIGABRT	Abort process
SIGSIGCLD	SIGCHLD	Death of child
SIGLOST	SIGIOT	BSD signal

Occasionally a user may try out some ingenious bit of C code that contains a statement along the lines of:

```
while(1) fork();
```

I'm not insinuating that this is done on purpose, but it can be a pain in the neck to stop. New processes are being created as fast as you can kill them. One little trick you can try is to kill them by PGID. Use the formatted output (-F) option with SYSV ps to display the PGID. Then send a signal to the negative PGID.

```
# ps -el -F pgid,runame=<procname>
# kill -6 -<pgid>
```

26.4.2   Ignoring hangup

A common problem is starting a command in the background or as a daemon from the command line of a login shell only to find that the command exits when you logout. This is because a hangup (HUP) signal is sent to the process when your terminal connection has been broken. You can specify that these commands are to ignore HUP by using the nohup command.

```
# nohup <command> &        Background process ignoring hangup
```

26.5   Scheduled Processes (cron)

The UNIX cron utility provides a basic means for scheduling jobs to be run at a particular time of the day or on a periodic basis. cron can be used to take care of regular system housecleaning tasks like synchronizing disk writes, cleaning out /tmp, and running accounting programs. These types of periodic tasks may be tailored through the use of crontabs. A crontab is a list of commands and scripts with designated runtimes that will be invoked by cron under the EUID of the owner. cron reports any errors or output information to the owning user after the commands are executed. cron logs errors to a log file, /var/adm/cron/log, and, if AIX auditing is enabled, produces audit records.

26.5.1   crontab

To create a crontab, use your favorite editor and create a table with the following format:

```
minutes hours day month weekday command
```

Each of the time-associated fields may be represented as a comma-separated list. An asterisk (*) may be used to represent all possible times. For example, if I wanted to display uptime statistics every half hour on the system console, I would add the following line to my crontab file.

```
0,30 * * * * /bin/uptime> /dev/console
```

Once you have your crontab file tailored to your liking, hand it off to cron by invoking the crontab command.

```
# crontab <YourCrontabFile>
```

All crontabs are stored in /var/adm/cron/crontabs under the owning user name.

```
User adm Crontab

# (C) COPYRIGHT International Business Machines Corp. 1989,1991
# All Rights Reserved
# Licensed Materials - Property of IBM
#==================================================================
# SYSTEM ACTIVITY REPORTS
# 8am-5pm activity reports every 20 mins during weekdays.
# activity reports every an hour on Saturday and Sunday.
# 6pm-7am activity reports every an hour during weekdays.
# Daily summary prepared at 18:05.
#==================================================================
# Daily summary prepared at 18:05.
#==================================================================
0 8-17 * * 1-5 /usr/lib/sa/sa1 1200 3 &
0 * * * 0,6 /usr/lib/sa/sa1 &
0 18-7 * * 1-5 /usr/lib/sa/sa1 &
5 18 * * 1-5 /usr/lib/sa/sa2 -s 8:00 -e 18:01 -i 3600 -ubcwyaqvm &
#==================================================================
# PROCESS ACCOUNTING:
runacct at 11:10 every night
# dodisk at 11:00 every night
```

```
# ckpacct every hour on the hour
# monthly accounting 4:15 the first of every month
#==================================================================
10 23 * * 0-6 /usr/lib/acct/runacct 2>/usr/adm/acct/nite/accterr>/dev/null
0 23 * * 0-6 /usr/lib/acct/dodisk>/dev/null 2>&1
* * * * /usr/lib/acct/ckpacct>/dev/null 2>&1
15 4 1 * * /usr/lib/acct/monacct > /dev/null 2>&1
#==================================================================
```

The system administrator can enforce access controls on who may use cron services by listing user names, one per line, in the /usr/adm/cron/{cron.allow,cron.deny} files. cron checks the authorization of these files before invoking a user's crontab file. The default is to allow access to all users.

26.5.2   Ad hoc jobs

Suppose you want to run a job off hours but don't want to create a crontab entry for it. It may be a one-time-only run. You can do this using the at and batch commands. Note that batch is just a script that invokes at. Execute at, specifying the time and the input stream of commands. The job stream is copied to the /usr/spool/cron/atjobs directory. cron then executes the job stream at the specified time. Authorization to run jobs with at is controlled like crontab by listing user names in the /usr/adm/cron/{at.allow,at.deny} file. The default is to allow access to all users.

```
# at <time> input <Ctrl-D>      Start a job at time
# at -r jobnumber                Remove a job
# atq <username>                 List scheduled jobs
```

If a more sophisticated batch scheduling system is required, see Chap. 33.

26.5.3   Managing cron activities

In active batch environments, you might want to place some limits on cron scheduling. The /usr/adm/cron/queuedefs file can be configured to limit the number of concurrent jobs by event type, set the default nice value, and set the retry limit. Event controls are listed one per line in the queuedefs file.

Queuedefs format is as follows:

```
e.[j#][n#][w#]
```

where   e = Event type (see Table 26.4)
        j = Maximum number of concurrent jobs
        n = Nice value
        w = Retry wait in seconds

The queuedefs file is shipped empty. Default values for all event types support 100 concurrent jobs at nice value 2 with a 60-second retry limit. Here is a sample queuedefs entry:

```
c.2j2n90v     2 crontab jobs, nice value 2, retry every 90 seconds
```

26.6   System Resource Controller

AIX provides a mechanism for controlling and managing sets of programs that function collectively as a unit. This mechanism is called the system resource controller (SRC). SRC provides simple command interfaces to display status, refresh, start, and stop system services as a single entity. These interfaces reduce the operation and administration complexity of managing all the daemons and programs that make up a particular service.

The collection of programs that comprises an SRC service unit are called subsystems. The daemons that make up a subsystem are known as subservers. Subsystems may be grouped by the overall service they provide and are identified as subsystem groups. For example, the ftpd daemon is a subserver of the inetd subsystem. The inetd subsystem is a group member of the TCPIP subsystem group. SRC allows the operator or administrator to operate on a service at the subserver, subsystem, or subsystem group level (see Fig. 26.2).

26.6.1   SRC components

Overall, SRC is provided by the srcmstr daemon. srcmstr is started at boot time by an entry in /etc/inittab.

```
srcmstr:2:respawn:/etc/srcmstr     # System resource controller
```

srcmstr identifies subsystem components from definition in ODM object classes /etc/objrepos/{SRCsubsys,SRCnotify. Subsystems and subserver configuration information is managed through the use of the

TABLE 26.4   Queuedefs Events Types

a	at events
b	batch events
c	crontab events
d	sync events
e	ksh events
f	csh events

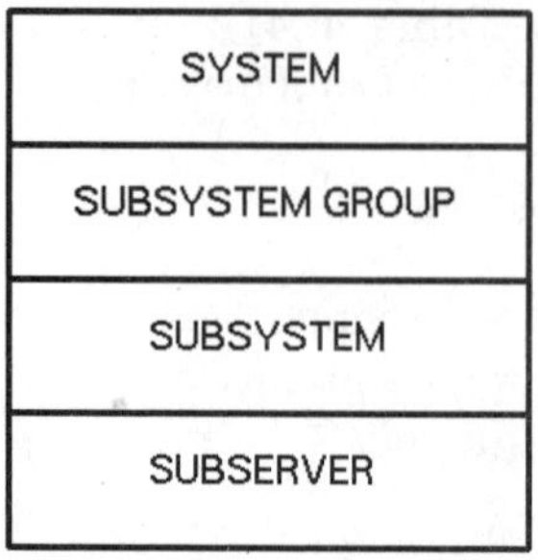

```
┌─────────────────────────┐
│         SYSTEM          │
├─────────────────────────┤
│    SUBSYSTEM GROUP      │
├─────────────────────────┤
│       SUBSYSTEM         │
├─────────────────────────┤
│       SUBSERVER         │
└─────────────────────────┘
```

Figure 26.2 SRC hierarchy.

{mk,ch,rm}server and {mk,ch,rm}ssys commands. In most cases, the subsystems and subservers are predefined for each product at installation time.

Once a subsystem group, subsystem, or subserver is configured into the ODM, it may be operated on using the following commands.

startsrc	Start a subsystem
stopsrc	Stop a subsystem
refresh	Restart or refresh a subsystem
trace{on,off}	Trace a subsystem
lssrc	Display subsystem status

Subsystems may be started at boot time following the srcmstr by invoking the startsrc command as part of a boot rc script or directly from /etc/inittab. Some SRC command examples:

# startsrc -g tcpip	Start the TCPIP subsystem group
# stopsrc -s qdaemon	Stop the qdaemon subsystem

To display the status of all defined subsystems, use the lssrc command. Note that subsystem control may also be invoked via the SMIT subsys and subserver FastPaths.

```
# lssrc -a

Subsystem      Group      PID      Status
syslogd        ras        4484     active
lpd            spooler    5511     active
routed         tcpip      6296     active
portmap        portmap    5820     active
inetd          tcpip      6091     active
biod           nfs        8417     active
nfsd           nfs        13324    active
rpc.mountd     nfs        15908    active
rpc.statd      nfs        12851    active
```

```
rpc.lockd    nfs         18499   active
qdaemon      spooler     12627   active
writesrv     spooler     13157   active
infod        infod       19063   active
iptrace      tcpip               inoperative
gated        tcpip               inoperative
named        tcpip               inoperative
rwhod        tcpip               inoperative
timed        tcpip               inoperative
sendmail     mail                inoperative
snmpd        tcpip               inoperative
keyserv      keyserv             inoperative
ypserv       yp                  inoperative
ypbind       yp                  inoperative
ypupdated    yp                  inoperative
yppasswdd    yp                  inoperative
llbd         ncs                 inoperative
nrglbd       ncs                 inoperative
```

26.7   InfoExporer Keywords

init	at
process	crontab
ps	batch
kproc	atjobs
setpgrp	atq
/etc/passwd	subsystems
/etc/group	subservers
termio	/etc/inittab
nice	srcmstr
renice	startsrc
kill	stopsrc
signal	lssrc
nohup	killall
cron	

26.8   QwikInfo

Process control:

```
/usr/include/sys/proc.h
```
Process attributes

```
ps -<options>
```
Display running process information
(SYSV)

`ps <options>`	Display running process information (BSD)
`nice`	Lower process priority
`renice`	BSD administration process control
`kill`	Send/process a signal
`kill -1`	List signals
`killall`	Kill all your processes
`nohup`	Ignore hangup signal

Batch support:

`cron`	System job scheduler
`/var/spool/cron/crontabs`	Cron job tables
`/usr/adm/cron/{cron.allow,cron.deny}`	Authorize cron use
`at`	Batch job support
`/usr/adm/cron/queuedefs`	cron job limits

Subsystems:

`srcmstr`	Subsystem master daemon
`startsrc,stopsrc,refresh`	Manage subsystems
`lssrc`	List subsystem state

27

System Accounting

27.1 Accounting Overview

Let's see . . . that's 22 minutes of CPU, 3 MB of disk space, and 9 hours of connect time. Will you be using credit card, cash, or check? Nothing in life is free! Especially computer resources.

Even if you don't chargeback for system resources, it's a good idea to regularly monitor utilization. By collecting accounting data you get a reasonable profile of how your system is being used. Who are the big resource hitters? How soon are you going to need that extra 2 GB of disk space? Maybe you need to justify the resources to a higher authority.

The AIX accounting system is very SYSV in flavor. For those of you with a BSD inclination, there is a set of the standard BSD accounting system management commands bolted onto the SYSV environment. Sites that write their own accounting programs and scripts will find that AIX provides the tools and accounting data formats that will facilitate porting an existing system from other UNIX environments. For the less adventurous, AIX supplies all the commands and scripts required to manage system accounting data. The accounting system is based on a set of three components:

- Data collection
- Management and reporting commands
- Periodic data management scripts

Data collection takes place automagically when accounting is enabled. Management and commands allow you to start and stop the accounting system, manage the data files, and generate reports. The data management scripts are invoked through CRON to automate closing out data and generating general summary information.

27.2   Data Collection

Data collection begins when system accounting is turned on and stops when it is turned off. AIX samples and records process utilization and session data for each user in the system. The collected information represents connect time, process resources, commands, disk usage, and print queuing utilization.

27.2.1   Connect time

Connect time data is accumulated in the /var/adm/wtmp and /etc/utmp files. Each time you login to AIX, the login process writes a record to wtmp and utmp. The data indicates the user name, date, time, port, and connecting address. A similar record is written by the init process when you exit the system. This data represents the duration time of your connection to the system.

Combinations of rsh and X11 clients make connection data a bit fuzzy in environments where there is heavy X11 usage. The xterm terminal emulation client provides a flag indicating whether or not an /etc/utmp record should be written. xterm also has a nasty habit of trashing the /etc/utmp file. You'll notice the latter problem when your uptime statistics look too good to be true. See Appendix F for example source code for cleaning up utmp records.

The acctwtmp command records system boot and shutdown times in the /var/adm/wtmp file. This data provides an audit trail concerning the comings and goings of users on your system.

27.2.2   Process resource usage

Resource utilization information for each process run by the operating system is recorded in the /var/adm/pacct file at process exit. The bad news is that no information is run for processes that don't exit! A process accounting record indicates the UID, GID, user name, elapsed wall clock time, CPU time, memory use, character I/O total, and disk block I/O totals.

27.2.3   Command usage

A nice side effect of process data is an audit trail of command and application usage. This data provides a profile of application use and may assist in tracking security problems. Be aware that experienced hackers tend to fix up accounting information before leaving the scene. See Chap. 28 for secure system auditing details.

27.2.4   Disk usage

You can periodically collect disk usage information for the system and store it in the /var/adm/dtmp file. Collecting disk usage data can cause a bit of a load on the system, so it's a good idea to run it during an off-hour shift. AIX assigns disk usage data to users based on the files they own in the file system and any links to files they may have created. The usage statistics for a file are distributed evenly between the users with links to the file.

It is also possible to track disk usage and regulate limits on usage by user and/or group. This is done through the disk quota system. See Chap. 25 concerning details on the disk quota system.

27.2.5   Print usage

Print queuing system utilization statistics are recorded by the enq command and the qdaemon process. enq writes a record for each print job it handles. The record indicates the print job owner, job number, and the file name. When the file is printed, qdaemon writes another record that includes this information plus the number of pages that were printed. There are public domain backends for postscript queues that will supply accounting records for postscript conversion and attributes.

27.2.6   Accounting files

Accounting records are stored in a set of files located in the /var/adm directory. They are as follows:

pacct	Active process data
Spacct.<mmdd>	Daily active process data (runacct)
qacct	Print usage data
ctmp	Connect session data
dtmp	Disk usage data
wtmp	Active process data

27.3   Accounting Configuration

To configure the accounting system, begin by creating file name stubs with the correct permissions for each of the data collection files. This must be done with adm authority. The file name stubs can be created by touching the file name or running the nulladm command. nulladm creates the file names supplied as arguments and sets the correct permissions. Make sure bos.acct has been installed.

27.3.1   Setup collection files

```
# touch /var/adm/{wtmp,pacct}
# chown adm /var/adm/{wtmp,pacct}
# chgrp adm /var/adm/{wtmp,pacct}
# chmod 644 /var/adm/{wtmp,pacct}

# /usr/sbin/acct/nulladm wtmp pacct
```

27.3.2   Identifying shifts

Configure the /etc/acct/holidays file to reflect your prime-time shift and scheduled holidays. The first line in the file indicates the year and the starting and ending times for prime shift. Subsequent lines indicate the data and description of each holiday scheduled over the year. Each holiday entry indicates:

Integer day of the year

Three-character month name

Integer day of the month

Text string holiday description

Your /etc/acct/holidays file might read something like this:

```
* (C) COPYRIGHT International Business Machines Corp. 1989
* All Rights Reserved
* Licensed Material - Property of IBM
*
* Prime/Nonprime Table for AIX Accounting System
*
* Curr Prime Non-Prime
* Year Start Start
*
   1990 0800  1700
*
   1       Jan 1      New Year's Day
   50      Feb 19     Washington's Birthday (Obsvd.)
   148     May 28     Memorial Day (Obsvd.)
   185     Jul 4      Independence Day
   246     Sep 3      Labor Day
   326     Nov 22     Thanksgiving Day
   327     Nov 23     Day after Thanksgiving
   359     Dec 25     Christmas Day
   365     Dec 31     New Years Eve
```

27.3.3   Disk accounting (/etc/filesystems)

If you will be collecting disk usage information, add an account=true entry in the stanza for each file system you intend to monitor in the /etc/filesystems table. Here is a sample filesystems entry:

```
/home:
dev      = /dev/hd1
vfs      = jfs
log      = /dev/hd8
mount    = true
```

```
check    = true
vol      = /home
free     = false
account  = true
```

27.3.4   Print accounting (/etc/qconfig)

Print usage records will be saved if an account file destination path is identified by the acctfile =file-name parameter for each queue stanza. An /etc/qconfig entry looks like this:

```
acctfile = /var/adm/qacct
```

Rebuild the /etc/qconfig.bin file by refreshing the qdaemon subsystem.

```
# refresh -s qdaemon
```

27.3.5   Report directories

Make sure the report summary subdirectories nite, fiscal, and sum exist with adm permissions in /var/adm/acct.

```
# cd /var/adm/acct
# mkdir nite fiscal sum
# chown adm nite fiscal sum
# chgrp adm nite fiscal sum
# chmod 644 nite fiscal sum
```

27.3.6   Crontab entries

Remove the comments from the adm and root crontab files. Edit the crontab files using crontab -e. adm crontab looks like this:

```
#=============================================================
#   PROCESS ACCOUNTING:
# runacct at 11:10 every night
# dodisk at 11:00 every night
# ckpacct every hour on the hour
# monthly accounting 4:15 the first of every month
#=============================================================
10 23 * * 0-6 /usr/lib/acct/runacct 2>/usr/adm/acct/nite/acc-
terr > /dev/null
0 23 * * 0-6 /usr/lib/acct/dodisk >/dev/null 2>&1
0 * * * * /usr/lib/acct/ckpacct > /dev/null 2>&1
15 4 1 * * /usr/lib/acct/monacct > /dev/null 2>&1
#=============================================================
```

27.3.7 Work unit fees

The chargefee command can be used to add work unit entries for each user on the system into the /var/adm/fee file. This data is later merged with other accounting files by acctmerg. chargefee can be incorporated into the system accounting scripts to implement a chargeback system.

27.4 Accounting Commands

As I mentioned in the introduction, AIX offers both SYSV and a subset of the BSD accounting commands. These commands allow you to display, manage, generate reports, and record charge fees from the collected accounting information.

27.4.1 Starting and stopping accounting.

Start the accounting system by invoking one of the startup, runacct, turnacct, or accton commands.

```
# startup
# runacct 2> /var/adm/acct/nite/accterr &
# turnacct on/off
# accton /var/adm/pacct
```

Stop system accounting by using the shutacct, turnacct, or accton commands.

```
# shutacct
# turnacct off
# accton
```

Add a command entry to the /etc/rc script to start accounting at boot time.

27.4.2 Displaying statistics

At any time you can take the pulse of your system or look back through accounting history from the command line. You can also create ad hoc reports by directing stdout to a file.

A general summary of data stored in the /var/adm/pacct can be displayed using the sa command. The sa command supports a number of flags that can be used to filter and restrict the output. Two of the most useful flags are the -m flag, which summarizes by user, and the -s flag, which summarizes by command. The -s flag can also be used to merge the summary with an existing history file.

```
# sa -m

root        1038     0.97cpu     8688904tio      9412563k*sec
daemon      34       0.06cpu     1005455tio      6494k*sec
uas         5        0.01cpu     194494tio       2626k*sec
info        1        0.00cpu     6tio            0k*sec
ops         212      30.65cpu    7768811tio      12002184533k*sec

# sa -s

2       2295.47re      28.11cpu    88544avio       41k     xhm
3       2069.41re      3.40cpu     92088832avio    106k    xlock
18      251.81re       2.17cpu     303992avio      65k     vi
4       115.28re       0.43cpu     234688avio      218k    aixterm
94      162.88re       0.24cpu     19148avio       1k      rsh
6       66.91re        0.21cpu     435008avio      30k     rn
343     0.26re         0.16cpu     2927avio        0k      mount
99      1.56re         0.15cpu     10412avio       3k      sendmai*
374     3553.89re      0.15cpu     152avio         0k      sh
21      12.79re        0.13cpu     23194avio       11k     csh
6       22.60re        0.12cpu     71467avio       46k     xterm
2       1480.58re      0.11cpu     221680avio      128k    twm
```

Connection histories can be displayed using the BSD ac and last commands or the SYSV acctcon1 and lastlog (SYSV) commands. The ac and acctcon1 commands can tally connection times by day or for the interval of time covered by the /var/adm/wtmp file. The last and lastlog commands can be used to display the login times for all users or an individual user.

```
# ac -p

duane       0.46
deroest     264.16
donn        487.54
noyd        9961.55
ops         1453.22
fox         5.45
root        0.09

# ac -d

Sep 01 total 269.68
Sep 02 total 613.75
Sep 03 total 914.32
Sep 04 total 1110.79
```

```
Sep 05 total 1103.98
Sep 06 total 1058.19
Sep 07 total 1060.23
Sep 08 total 933.98
Sep 09 total 944.53


# last -20


ops       pts/92 xtreme.sar.washi   Fri Sep 17 10:41 still logged in
donn      pts/86 xceed.bnn.washin   Fri Sep 17 10:07 still logged in
kenm      pts/75                    Fri Sep 17 10:00 - 10:22 (00:21)
davidw    pts/56 redy.aal.washing   Fri Sep 17 08:23 still logged in
```

Exhaustive command usage information can be generated using the BSD lastcomm command. Like sa this command supports a large number of flags to filter the output. Be aware that it will also use significant system resources when invoked!

```
# lastcomm


sh          S    root _        0.01 secs Fri Sep 17 10:58
umount      S    root _        0.02 secs Fri Sep 17 10:58
rlogin           deroest pts   0.02 secs Fri Sep 17 10:57
rlogin      F    deroest pts   0.01 secs Fri Sep 17 10:57
sendmail    F    root _        0.01 secs Fri Sep 17 10:58
sendit           csandahl _    0.08 secs Fri Sep 17 10:58
sendmail    F    root _        0.05 secs Fri Sep 17 10:58
sendmail    F    root _        0.11 secs Fri Sep 17 10:58
sendmail    F    root _        0.01 secs Fri Sep 17 10:58
sendmail    F    root _        0.03 secs Fri Sep 17 10:58
sendit           grcm _        0.16 secs Fri Sep 17 10:58
sh          S    root _        0.02 secs Fri Sep 17 10:58
sh          S    root _        0.02 secs Fri Sep 17 10:58
umount      S    root _        0.01 secs Fri Sep 17 10:58
nfsmnthe    S    root _        0.01 secs Fri Sep 17 10:58
```

27.4.3 Summary reports

A standard set of reports is produced at intervals by the runacct and monacct commands. These commands are run by the default adm and root crontabs. The summaries and reports are recorded in the following /var/adm subdirectories:

nite   Daily files used by runacct

sum   Daily summaries created by runacct

fiscal   Monthly summaries created by monacct

Reports and data files of interest include:

nite/lineuse	Line usage statistics for serial ports
nite/dacct	Daily disk accounting records
nite/reboots	List of system reboot times
sum/tacct	Total accounting summary
sum/cms	Command use summary
sum/loginlog	Last use time for user accounts
sum/rprt[mmdd]	Daily summary report
fiscal/cms[n]	Fiscal command summary
fiscal/tacct[n]	Fiscal total accounting summary

27.5   Periodic Housecleaning

Turning on system accounting is a little like opening the floodgates. On an active multiuser system, accounting can generate a large amount of data that must be filtered and archived as part of your regular house-cleaning activities. The default accounting procedures specified in the adm and root crontabs periodically close and rename accounting files to assist in managing the data. It is left up to the system administrator to implement procedures to archive and clean up the old data files. It is a good idea to restart the accounting system daily to keep accounting files from becoming too large to manage.

What information should be saved for posterity? You can take the conservative approach and save everything, reports and data files, or throw caution to the wind and delete the files on a daily basis. Moderation suggests that it might be wise to periodically compress and archive the summary files and keep a copy of the previous day's data files online for short-term history queries.

27.6   InfoExplorer Keywords

wtmp	ac	qdaemon
pacct	last	/etc/acct/holidays
nulladm	lastcomm	/etc/filesystems
startup	utmp	cron
runacct	init	crontab
turnacct	uptime	chargefee
accton	acctwtmp	/var/adm/fee
shutacct	dtmp	acctmerg
sa	enq	monacct

27.7 QwikInfo

Data collection and configuration files:

`/var/adm/wtmp`	User, system events
`/etc/utmp`	User access times
`/var/adm/pacct`	Process account file
`/var/adm/dtmp`	Disk usage
`/var/adm/Spacct.<mmdd>`	Daily active process data from runacct
`/var/adm/qacct`	Print usage data
`/var/adm/ctmp`	Connect session data
`/etc/holidays`	Define accounting shifts
`/var/adm/acct/{nite fiscal sum}`	Accounting summaries
`/var/spool/cron/crontabs/adm`	Accounting crontab

Collection and reporting:

`runacct, turnacct on, accton`	Start system accounting
`shutacct, turnacct off, acctoff`	Stop system accounting
`sa`	Filter account data
`ac, last, lastcom`	History data

Security

28

Auditing and Security

28.1 Security Overview

This age of worldwide communications is bringing us all closer together. Its also means a world of new and unsuspecting targets for the hacker community. It doesn't matter whether your system is stand-alone or tapped into a large network superhighway, it doesn't pay to leave the key under the mat. Sadly enough, this is true for friends as well as enemies. Loose lips sink ships! Corny but true!

Consider that the standard login security based solely on user name and password is in need of improvement. Password expiration is unpopular with users and is rarely enforced. Passwords are often easily guessable words that are quickly cracked given the processing speed that is widely available at a modest cost. In many cases it doesn't even require the use of sophisticated cracking programs. Users tend to write passwords down and share them with colleagues. In some cases, additional levels of security are required that are not easily compromised by user insensitivity to security.

Even if you don't think you have anything that someone would want, your system could be a stepping stone to others. Useful information to system hackers comes in forms like network address tables, E-mail addresses, and modem dialup numbers. Physical resources like tape, disk, and CPU time can be exploited to store information or crack passwords. System intruders may be curiosity seekers just poking around or they might be professionals up to serious mischief. Hackers make their way through the back roads of the network, exploiting numerous known security holes because administrators are not staying informed. What do you do?

28.2 Defining a Security Policy

Before you pack up your computer and store it in a bank vault, consider the benefits of defining and implementing a formal security policy. By setting down and enforcing some simple rules and implementing regular system auditing, you can protect yourself from the majority of attacks. It may not be perfect, but it can go a long way toward peace of mind.

When defining your security policy, keep in mind that there is a tradeoff between level of security and level of usability. Unless you're charged with securing national secrets, try to remember that AIX is an open system. That's *open* as in "ease of use" rather than "no locks supplied." Make sure that the policy is distributed to your user community and that they understand their responsibility is protecting resources. The policy should consider maintaining:

User privacy

System integrity

Authorized availability

Ease of use

Auditing and accountability

28.3 Passwords

What makes a good password? It has to be easy to remember, but it shouldn't be a plain text word or phrase like your mother's name or words from the dictionary. It must *not* be shared between users.

Who has access to privileged passwords like the root password? Who has access to the table of encrypted passwords? These are questions and policies that must be implemented to ensure a basic level of security. AIX provides tools that address some of these issues. Others simply require changes in the way we use the system. Sometimes old dogs have to learn new tricks or someone will take all the bones!

28.3.1 Shadow password files

One of the biggest problems with traditional UNIX password implementations is that the /etc/passwd contains the encrypted password for each user and it is world-readable. Although the passwd command uses one-way encryption, crack programs can encrypt common strings and compare the results against the encrypted password in /etc/passwd. In the 1960s, this was deemed to be an algorithm that would take hundreds or thousands of years of CPU time to compare all the possibilities. By using dictionaries and common password patterns, faster crypt() routines and higher speed processors available today, you can crack most common passwords in reasonable periods of time.

How do you fix this problem? You move the encrypted passwords into a secure table and directory and require the use of secure setuid subroutines to access the information. This is what IBM has implemented in AIX. A placeholder character, the exclamation point (!), is inserted in the passwd field of the /etc/passwd file. A secure shadow password file, /etc/security/passwd, contains the encrypted password for each user.

Here is /etc/passwd in mode 644:

```
root:!:0:0:Almighty Overseer:/:/bin/ksh
```

Here is /etc/security/passwd in mode 600:

```
root:
password = asldfi0237xa0
lastupdate = 728707306
flags =
```

28.3.2 Password rules and restrictions

Users are not inclined to use esoteric passwords, and they do not like to change their passwords more than once a lifetime. Unfortunately, this breaks the first law of account security. AIX allows the system administrator to remind them somewhat forcefully that it's time for a change and that they need to be somewhat imaginative in what they choose. You don't want to be a nag, so don't require changes too often and don't require them to be so cryptic that they have to write them down. Tailor password aging and character restrictions in the pw_restrictions stanza in the /etc/security/login.cfg file. Restrictions are applied systemwide. Once the maxage limit is passed, users are required to select a new password at next login. Password restrictions can be placed at the user level as well (Chap. 25).

The password restrictions found in /etc/security/login.cfg are as follows:

```
                   Def  Max  Rec
pw_restrictions:
       maxage =     0    52   8    Max weeks before update enforced
       minage =     0    52   1    Min weeks before update allowed
     minalpha =     0     8   4    Min number of alpha characters
     minother =     0     8   2    Min number of nonalpha characters
      mindiff =     0     8   3    Min chars different from old password
   maxrepeats =     8     8   1    Max number of repeats for any character
```

SMIT mkuser Password Fields

Days to WARN USER before password expires	Number days to warn user with message at login
Password CHECK METHODS	Rules for validating proper passwords
Password DICTIONARY FILES	Word dictionaries used to validate password
NUMBER OF PASSWORDS before reuse	How many passwords before reuse
WEEKS before password reuse	How long before reuse
Weeks between password	How long after expiration before restricting access
EXPIRATION and LOCKOUT	
Password MAX AGE	Maximum time before requiring a password change
Password MIN AGE	Minimum time before a password can be changed
Password MIN LENGTH	How short can a password be
Password MIN ALPHA	Minimum number of alphabetic characters
Password MIN OTHER	Minimum number of nonalpha characters
Password MAX REPEATED	Maximum repeated characters allowed
Password MIN DIFFERENT	Minimum number of different chars required
Password REGISTRY	Authentication mechanism

28.3.3 Resetting user passwords

It doesn't seem to matter whether a password is cryptic or a common word. Users always seem to forget them. A common complaint from system administrators is that AIX requires root's password to reset a user password. In fact, AIX does require root's password if you are not a member of the security group and if you don't use the pwdadm command or SMIT to update passwords. As a member of the security group, you are required to enter your own password to validate who you are.

```
# pwdadm sleepy

<your> Password:
Changing password for "sleepy"
sleepy's New password:
Re-enter sleepy's new password:
```

28.3.4 Superuser access

Care should be taken as to who has access to root's password and how it is used. Users with access to privileged accounts should login using their own nonprivileged account and use the su command to set uid to privileged accounts. The su command logs all invocations to the /var/adm/sulog file. This provides an audit trail on who, when, and success of access.

Shell aliases mapping su to the full path name /bin/su will limit the possibility of a trojan horse su command from being used on a compromised account. A trojan horse copy of su will usually act as you would expect, except that it will record passwords in a file monitored by the perpetrator.

AIX provides an additional level of su security by defining whether an account can be accessed via su and which groups are permitted access via su to the account. These restrictions are applied on a per-user basis in the /etc/security/user file:

```
robin:
    su = <true/false>        # Users may su to this account.
    sugroups = <ALL|list>    # Groups that may su to this account.
```

28.3.5 Auditing passwords

Even when you are enforcing password controls, it is a good idea to audit passwords on your system periodically. It is often a good idea to keep abreast of password cracking tools used by the hacker community. Check out anonymous ftp archives like wuarchive.wustl.edu and ftp.uu.net for password cracking tools like Crack and killer cracker.

The COPS package available from CERT and Satan contain various security tools along with password crackers for validating network security. These tools are available via anonymous ftp from cert.org.

AIX provides its own set of password validation tools. These tools are part of the larger security system called the Trusted Computing Base (TCB). An important piece of the TCB system are the table validation tools. These tools may be invoked individually or as part of the overall system validation from the tcbck command. Other TCB password validation commands are:

pwdck	Check consistency of the /etc/passwd and /etc/security/passwd files
grpck	Check consistency of the /etc/group and /etc/security/group files
usrck	Validate entries in the /etc/security/user file

28.3.6   Converting password files
from other sources

If you are moving a large user community from another UNIX platform onto AIX, fear not; AIX provides a means for converting standard UNIX /etc/passwd files into the various AIX password files. The same tools used to audit password file consistency can be used to convert password files from other systems.

First copy the password file into the AIX /etc/passwd path. Once the password file is available, execute the pwdck command to create /etc/security/passwd entries.

```
# pwdck -y ALL
```

Next create user stanza entries for each user in the /etc/security/limits file and /etc/security/user files using the usrck command.

```
# usrck
```

Finally update /etc/group with any GIDs and group members that existed on the old system. Once updates have been completed, execute the grpck command to create /etc/security/group entries.

```
# grpck
```

28.4   Trusted Computing Base

AIX V4 has an integrated security system called the Trusted Computing Base (TCB). TCB validates and audits both hardware and software components of the RISC System/6000 and AIX V4. TCB is made up of kernel interfaces, configuration tables, and trusted setuid/setgid programs that monitor system consistency.

28.4.1   tcbck command

The system administrator may add trusted applications to the TCB system using the tcbck command. It is the administrator's responsibility to guarantee the security of any new application added to TCB.

```
# tcbck -a <pathname> [attrib=value]
```
Mark application as trusted

```
# tcbck -d <pathname>
```
Remove trusted status

The attributes of trusted components of the TCB system are recorded in the /etc/security/sysck.cfg table. The tcbck command reads the information recorded in sysck.cfg when auditing the security state of the system. The tcbck command can be run periodically, using cron, or interactively from the command line. The latter is useful when you suspect the possibility of the system having been compromised.

```
# tcbck -p ALL
```

You can use tcbck to check the integrity of all file system files in the event that they may have been compromised. During a file system scan, tcbck validates that files with setuid root and administrative setgid bits pre-exist in the /etc/security/sysck.cfg file. If they do not exist, then the privileged bits are cleared. The same is true for device special files, links to trusted files, and files with the tcb attribute. Note that this can take a significant amount of time.

```
# tcbck -t tree    Invoke file system check
```

28.4.2   /etc/security/sysck.cfg

Trusted applications are identified by stanza entries in the /etc/security/sysck.cfg file bearing the path names. Each stanza is followed by a set of parameters defining the attributes of the trusted application (see Table 28.1). Here is an example:

```
/usr/bin/acledit:
        owner = bin
        group = bin
        mode = TCB,555
        type = FILE
        oldpath = /bin/acledit
        class = apply,inventory,bos.obj
        size = 5010
        checksum = "44904 5"
```

TABLE 28.1   TCB /etc/security/sysck.cfg Parameters

class	Identifier that is used to group a set of applications. Applications identified by a class may be checked as a unit by tcbck. Multiple class names may be specified for an application.
owner	File-owning username. Must match directory-owner value.
group	File group name. Must match directory group value.
mode	Specifies one of SUID, SGID, SVTX, or TCB followed by the file permissions. Permissions may be specified as an octal value (i.e., 644) or a nine-character value (i.e., rw-r--r--).
links	List of path names that are hard links to this file. Entries in the list are separated by commas.
symlinks	List of path names that are symbolic links to this file. Entries in the list are separated by commas.
program	Program path name and arguments that may be invoked to check the application.
acl	The access control list (ACL) value for the file. If the ACL value does not match that of the file, tcbck applies the value listed in stanza acl parameter. The value must be consistent with the SUID, SGID, and SVTX values listed in the mode parameter.
source	The source file name that is to be copied for checking.

28.4.3 Trusted communication path

For applications that require a secure interface between the application and the user's terminal, AIX provides the concept of a trusted communication path. Trusted communication paths allow only TCB-trusted programs and devices to interact with the user's terminal. This limits the possibility of trojan horse or eavesdropping applications from opening file descriptors associated with a TTY port.

A trusted communication path is invoked by pressing a secure attention key (SAK). The SAK key sequence, CTRL-X/CTRL-R is enabled by the system administrator in the /etc/security/login.cfg file. SAK support may be set for individual TTY ports.

A secure login session begins by pressing the SAK prior to typing in your username and password. After the SAK sequence has been entered, init revokes all previous opens on the port. A getty is started on the port, and a new login herald is displayed. After entering your user name and password, TTY port permissions are restricted to your account and the trusted shell (tsh) is invoked. The tsh shell is akin to the Korn shell (ksh) and will only allow execution of trusted applications (those marked with the TCH bit). It is a good idea to initiate a trusted path when working as root or setting passwords.

28.5 Access Control

Access control defines the who and how of access to system resources. Traditional UNIX access control is based on user and group ownership of a resource and associated mode bits that define read, write, execute, setuid, and setgid access. Read, write, and execute permissions are set individually for the resource owner, group, and other (everyone). The setuid mode bit indicates that when the resource is invoked the resulting process takes on the effective UID permissions of the resource owner. The setgid mode bit indicates that effective GID permissions will be enabled for the process.

The chown, chgrp, and chmod commands are used to set the owner, group, and mode for a resource. A three-digit octal mask called the umask may be set by each user to set the default mode bits automatically when new files are created.

```
# chown <user name> <path name>      Set user ownership
# chgrp <group name> <path name>     Set group ownership
# chmod <mode> <path name>           Set mode permissions
# umask <mask>                       Set creation mask
```

To list the ownership and mode permissions for a file, use the ls command.

```
# ls -alF /home/deroest

total 1152
drwxr-xr-x   4 deroest system   1024   Nov 14 04:45 ./
drwxr-xr-x   5 bin bin           512   Aug 08 16:08 ../
-rw-------   1 deroest system    150   Aug 12 04:56 .Xauthority
drwxr-xr-x   8 deroest system    512   Aug 12 04:56 .dt/
-rwxr-xr-x   1 deroest system   3970   Aug 12 04:56 .dtprofile*
-rwxr-----   1 deroest system    254   Aug 08 16:08 .profile*
-rw-------   1 deroest system     54   Sep 26 07:43 .sh_history
drwxr-xr-x   4 deroest system    512   Sep 26 07:42 info/
```

Using entries in /etc/group to support file sharing does not scale well in large multiuser environments. Discretionary access rights should be controlled by the owner of the resource and not require intervention by the system administrator.

28.5.1 Access control lists

To address the requirement for extra discretionary access privacy under user control, AIX V4 provides access control lists (ACL). ACLs have been used on a number of other operating systems for many years. ACLs work in conjunction with AIX groups and grouplists. They provide a finer granularity of control over access rights within groups. Note that JFS ACLs are not the same as DFS ACLs (Chap. 19).

ACLs are made up of a set of access control entries (ACE) that define the access rights to system objects. There are three sections to an ACL. The first defines the file attributes like SUID permission. The second section defines the traditional UNIX base permissions, owner, group, and other IDs and modes. The third section defines the extended permissions for the file. This section provides finer control over access rights to the file.

Here is an example ACL:

```
attributes:      SUID                              Section 1
base permissions                                   Section 2
      owner (gilbert):   rwx
      group (user):      r-x
      others:            ---
extended permissions                               Section 3
      enabled
      permit        r--    u:jill              ACE
      deny          -w-    g:staff             ACE
      specify       r-x    g:user, g:ops       ACE
```

Extended permission ACEs use the format action; access mode; users/groups. The ACE action field must be permit, deny, or specify. The permit and deny actions add to or remove the access mode from the standard mode value, while the specify action uses the exact access mode for the user/group set that follows. This overrides the standard modes defined for the file. Multiple user/group sets specified by u:user name and g:group name, respectively, indicate that a particular user must be identified by each value in the list before the access mode applies to the user.

Access rights or restrictions are based on the logical union of the representative ACEs for a particular user or group and the traditional UNIX access modes. You have to be very careful managing both ACLs and traditional UNIX permissions. AIX will resolve contradictions between multiple ACLs and standard permissions. Note that using the chmod command with octal permission arguments will remove any ACL associated with a file. This can be a problem if you're like me and prefer to use the numbers (sigh).

To create an ACL, use the acledit command. A default ACL is opened for update in the editor specified by the EDITOR environment variable. Tailor the ACL to fit the access rights you have in mind. Set the disabled field to "enabled" and save the file. The application will ask you whether you want to apply the ACL on exit.

```
# acledit
```

Use the aclget and aclput commands to display or apply ACL information for a file.

```
# aclput acl-name file-name      Apply an ACL to a file
# aclget file-name               Display ACL information
```

In cases where you want to define a set of ACLs that are to be applied to a set of files, use acledit to create and save the ACLs to generic file names. You can then use aclput to apply each ACL type to the desired files.

28.6   Authentication Methods

The designers of the AIX TCB system thought about these issues and provided an interface that allows you to add to, replace, and apply system authentication mechanisms on an individual basis. What's more, it doesn't require modifications to the default authentication code, /bin/login@ -> /usr/sbin/tsm, or alteration of the password file format as understood by the command set. Sound real nice? It *is* real nice!

The facility is simple to understand and easy to use. The TCB system passes the user name to be authenticated to your local application as an argument. Your code takes whatever action is appropriate to authenticate the user and returns 0 if authentication is successful or 1 if it has failed. Login processing will proceed or abort based on this return code.

28.6.1 Authentication tables

To define your authentication code to the system requires an entry in the /etc/security/login.cfg file. As a superuser using your favorite editor, edit the login.cfg file and look for the comment line that contains auth_method:. For each authentication program you want to add, enter a stanza of the form:

```
method_name:
      program=your_program
```

Example 28.1
```
TOKcheck:
      program=/usr/local/etc/validateTOK
```

The method name you choose will be used to identify the authentication program in the /etc/security/user file. Supply a stanza for each authentication method you intend to use.

Next you identify which user names will use these methods in the /etc/security/user file. As superuser, edit the user file. The user file header explains the use of the two authorization parameters auth1 and auth2. The auth1 stanza identifies the primary authentication methods to be employed for each user. If this method set fails, login is denied. The auth2 stanza defines a secondary set of methods that are invoked after the auth1 methods are run. If these methods fail, login is not denied. These secondary methods could be used to provide extra authorization to access secure system resources.

The format of the auth parameters is:

```
auth1=method[,method…][;username]
auth2=method[,method…][;username]
```

Supply each method name to be invoked delimited by commas. The default action is to pass the invoking user name to the method. You can override this by providing the user name to be used after the method list, delimited by a semicolon. The special method names SYSTEM and NONE specify that the standard password check or no authentication method is to be run, respectively.

To indicate that a method set is to be run for all users unless it is specifically overridden, use the default: stanza located after the header in the /etc/security/user file. In Ex. 28.2, the TOKcheck method that we identified earlier in the /etc/security/login.cfg file will be run after the standard password check for all users.

Example 28.2

```
default:
        admin = false
        login = true
        su = true
        daemon = true
        rlogin = true
        sugroups = ALL
        ttys = ALL
        auth1 = SYSTEM,TOKcheck
        auth2 = NONE
        tpath = nosak
        umask = 022
        expires = 0
```

In the case that we want to override the default authentication for a particular user, include local auth1 and auth2 parameters after the stanza identifying the user name.

Example 28.3

```
operator:
        auth1 = SYSTEM,TOKcheck
        auth2 = OPScheck;operator

ops1:
        auth1 = SYSTEM,TOKcheck
        auth2 = OPScheck;operator

ops2:
        auth1 = SYSTEM,TOKcheck
        auth2 = OPScheck;operator

opsmgr:
        auth1 = SYSTEM,TOKcheck
        auth2 = OPScheck;operator
```

In Ex. 28.3, we have identified a secondary method called OPScheck that might give access to a particular set of commands or resources to system operators. Note also that the user name "operator" is passed to the method program. This will allow the addition of new operator account names without having to identify each one explicitly in the OPScheck source code.

28.6.2   Smart card authentication

In the previous section the examples referred to a sample method called TOKcheck. This means that, in addition to requiring a user name and password for authorization, a token that uniquely identifies each user must be supplied. There are a number of smart cards and key cards on the market that can be used to provide unique authentication tokens. A token card is given to each user and is identified by a unique string that is stored with the user name in a secure central database.

An application called TOKcheck can now be installed to generate a random string and display it as output. The user keys the string into his or her personal token card. Then DES encrypts the string and outputs it to the card's display. The user types this encrypted string back into the TOKcheck application on the terminal. TOKcheck also encrypts the original string using the unique DES key associated with the user's token card in the database. It compares the result with that supplied by the user.

There are automated smart cards available that periodically cycle through encryption strings on both a server and the smart cards. The cards and the server are synchronized by clocks. Using automated smart cards, the user need only enter the current string displayed on the smart card display when the token is requested by an application.

This scheme ensures that the user must be in possession of the correct token card as well as the correct user name and password. What's more, the encryption string is only valid for a short period of time and cannot be reused by anyone eavesdropping on the wire.

28.6.3   Kerberos—trusted third party

Another authentication mechanism that is used in the Open Software Foundation's distributed computing environment (DCE) (Chap. 29) is the Kerberos V5 authentication system. Kerberos was originally developed at M.I.T. and is based on the trusted third party model. The original design is described in a series of papers presented at the 1988 USENIX Winter Conference.

Kerberos assumes that everything is untrustworthy except the authentication server itself. The authentication server acts as an intermediary between the client and the desired services (see Fig. 28.1). The client must authenticate itself to the Kerberos authentication server to gain a ticket that grants the rights to access distributed services. You only need to validate yourself once to the server rather than once for each service you wish to access. The access rights tickets are also valid for a given period of time. The Kerberos ticket mechanism eliminates the need to transmit passwords over network in clear text. Client and server passwords are known by the authentication server.

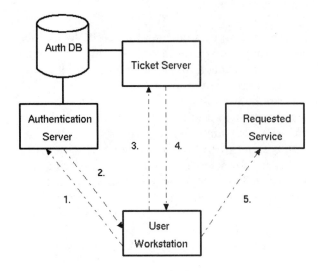

1. Request authentication for user and service.

2. Return TS session key and identifiers.

3. Request ticket using sealed authenticator.

4. Return ticket for requested service.

5. Connect to service with authenticator ticket.

Figure 28.1 Kerberos ticket flow.

Whenever access to services are requested by an unauthenticated client, a message is sent to the authentication server that contains the client name and the Kerberos ticket-granting service name. The authentication server looks up the names and obtains the encryption key for the client and the ticket server. The encryption key is known only to the owning agent and the authentication server. The encryption key can be a one-way DES-encrypted password. A message is constructed by the authentication server containing the client and ticket server names, address, and a random session key that it encrypts using the client's encryption key. The message is called a ticket and is sent to the client. The client uses its encryption key to decrypt the ticket and store it for the duration for which it is valid. The session key is used to encrypt ticket communication with the Kerberos ticket service to gain access to other services and resources.

When access to a service is requested, the ticket service provides a new session key along with a ticket encrypted with the services encryption key from the authentication server's database. The client uses the new session key to create an authenticator ticket for identification and sends it along with the encrypted service ticket to the new service. The service decrypts the ticket using its encryption key. The service ticket contains the session key, which is then used to decrypt the authenticator ticket. Now the client and service know about each other and real work can begin.

It may seem like a lot of mumbo jumbo to inhibit clear text passwords and authentication information from being broadcast over the network. On the other hand, it is extremely easy to eavesdrop on the wire. All this negotiation is taking place under the covers, so it is not visible to the end user. Kerberos won't restrict access to someone that has already compromised another user's login ID and password.

28.7 Network Security

AIX TCB also encompasses network interfaces and applications. The network component of TCB is called the Network Trusted Computing Base (NTCB). Security issues related to the various network interfaces and protocols are covered in detail in the chapters related to networking. Refer to these chapters for specific information.

28.8 System Auditing

When talking about security breaches, it is often not sufficient to check periodically to see if someone left the barn door open. It's much better to be informed when the door is opened. AIX TCB provides an auditing system that supports event detection, data collection, and report processing. TCB event-detection code is integrated in the kernel and trusted programs. Event detection may be enabled for the entire system or for local processes only.

28.8.1 Audit logging

The TCB event detection code reports event information to an audit logger. The audit logger constructs the audit trail for events. The audit trail includes the type of event, responsible UID, date, time, status, and any event-specific information. Audit logging can be done in either user state or kernel state. The audit records are logged in one of two types of log modes:

BIN   Audit information is logged to a series of files (bins). Data may be compressed and filtered.

STREAM   Audit records are written to a circular buffer that is read synchronously through a pseudo-device. STREAM mode provides realtime event monitoring.

28.8.2 Event types

The AIX audit system allows you to configure both event detection and audit trail recording. Event detection can be selected on a per-user basis. Care should be taken to audit those events that are of most interest for your environment. Auditing too many event types can cause significant threats to be lost in the noise. Too few event types may miss important events. Event selection may be per process or per object.

Event Types

Security policy events
    Subject events
        Process creation
        Process deletion
        Process attribute changes
    Object events
        Object creation
        Object deletion
        Object open
        Object close
        Object attribute changes
Import/export events
    Importing/exporting an object
Accountability events
    Updating password tables
    Updating group tables
    User login
    User logoff
    Updating use authentication data
    Updating trusted path configuration
    Authentication configuration
    Auditing configuration and updates
General system administration events
    Privilege use
    File system configuration
    Device configuration

System parameter configuration

Boot and shutdown

RAS configuration

Other system configuration

Security violation events

Access permission refusals

Privilege failures

Diagnostic detected system errors

Attempted alteration of TCB

28.8.3 Audit configuration

To configure the AIX TCB auditing system, begin by selecting the event types to be collected. Event types are defined in the /etc/security/audit/ events file. Using an editor, add or remove event types and the associated output formats.

Group related event types into audit classes. Audit classes are one of three types:

General   Alterations in the authentication and access controls of the system

System   Account modifications and installation

Init   Init process events, login, cron, etc.

Record each audit class in the /etc/security/audit/config file. If the audit class is to be assigned to individual users, add the class to the users stanza.

```
/etc/security/audit/config
start:
        binmode = on
        streammode = off

bin:
        trail = /audit/trail
        bin1 = /audit/bin1
        bin2 = /audit/bin2
        binsize = 10240
        cmds = /etc/security/audit/bincmds

stream:
        cmds = /etc/security/audit/streamcmds
```

```
classes:
        general = USER_SU,PASSWORD_Change,
                  FILE_Unlink,FILE_Link,FILE_Rename
        objects = S_ENVIRON_WRITE,
                  S_GROUP_WRITE,S_LIMITS_WRITE,S_LOGIN_WRITE,
                  S_PASSWD_READ,S_PASSWD_WRITE,
                  S_USER_WRITE,AUD_CONFIG_WR
        SRC     = SRC_Start,SRC_Stop,SRC_Addssys,SRC_Chssys,
                  SRC_Delssys,SRC_Addserver,SRC_Chserver,
                  ·SRC_Delserver
        kernel  = PROC_Create,PROC_Delete,PROC_Execute,
                  PROC_RealUID,PROC_AuditID,
                  PROC_RealGID,PROC_AuditState,PROC_AuditClass,
                  PROC_Environ,PROC_SetSignal,PROC_Limits,
                  PROC_SetPri,PROC_Setpri,PROC_Privilege
        files   = FILE_Open,FILE_Read,FILE_Write,FILE_Close,
                  FILE_Link,FILE_Unlink,FILE_Rename,
                  FILE_Owner,FILE_Mode,FILE_Acl,
                  FILE_Privilege,DEV_Create
        svipc   = MSG_Create,MSG_Read,MSG_Write,MSG_Delete,
                  MSG_Owner,MSG_Mode,SEM_Create,SEM_Op,
                  SEM_Delete,SEM_Owner,SEM_Mode,
                  SHM_Create,SHM_Open,SHM_Close,SHM_Owner,
                  SHM_Mode
        mail    =  SENDMAIL_Config, SENDMAIL_ToFile
        cron    =  AT_JobAdd,AT_JobRemove,CRON_JobAdd,
                  CRON_JobRemove
        tcpip   = TCPIP_config,TCPIP_host_id,TCPIP_route,
                  TCPIP_connect,TCPIP_data_out,TCPIP_data_in,
                  TCPIP_access,TCPIP_set_time,
                  TCPIP_kconfig,TCPIP_kroute,TCPIP_kconnect,
                  TCPIP_kdata_out,TCPIP_kdata_in,TCPIP_kcreate

users:
        root = general
```

Audit classes assigned to objects must be configured into the /etc/security/audit/objects file. Log mode, BIN, or STREAM is also defined in this file. Tailor the binmode or streammode stanzas to enable data collection. Any programs used to filter audit records must be defined in /etc/security/audit/{bincmds,streamcmds}.

```
/etc/security/audit/objects

        /etc/security/environ:
        w = "S_ENVIRON_WRITE"
```

```
/etc/security/group:
        w = "S_GROUP_WRITE"

/etc/security/limits:
        w = "S_LIMITS_WRITE"

/etc/security/login.cfg:
        w = "S_LOGIN_WRITE"

/etc/security/passwd:
        r = "S_PASSWD_READ"
        w = "S_PASSWD_WRITE"

/etc/security/user:
        w = "S_USER_WRITE"

/etc/security/audit/config:
        w = "AUD_CONFIG_WR"

/etc/security/audit/{bincmds,streamcmds}
            audit,auditpr,auditselect,auditstream
```

28.9   Security Tools and Information

I've talked about setting security policies, enforcing access controls, and auditing different aspects of system authentication and authorization. Is this enough to protect your system? The problem is that hackers are busy bees who won't stop prying and testing just because you have put a few access controls in place. You have to keep informed and continue looking for problem areas in the system.

28.9.1   virscan

AIX provides a virus-scanning application called virscan. The virscan command reads a set of known virus signatures from the /usr/lib/security/scan/{virsig.lst,addenda.lst} files. The signatures are familiar virus bit strings that may be found in system files and executables. You can add new signatures to the addenda.lst file. If virscan finds a signature in a file, the signature is recorded to the positive.vir file.

```
# virscan <PathName>     Invoke virscan on a directory tree
```

28.9.2   COPS

In the previous section concerning password cracking, I mentioned the COPS packages from the Computer Emergency Response Team (CERT) at Carnegie Mellon University. COPS will audit system files, look for setuid/setgid programs, writable device files, and the like. You can obtain a copy of the COPS package via anonymous ftp to cert.sei.cmu.edu.

28.9.3 Information sources

CERT regularly posts security advisory memos to the Usenet group comp.security.announce. The memos are also available in CERT's anonymous ftp archive. Report any security problems to CERT. They can be reached at:

Computer Emergency Response Team/Coordination Center
Software Engineering Institute
Carnegie Mellon University
Pittsburgh PA 15213-3890
(412)268-7090
cert@cert.org
anonymous ftp: cert.org

28.10 InfoExplorer Keywords

/etc/passwd	/etc/security/sysck.cfg
passwd	cron
crypt	ACL
/etc/security/passwd	SAK
/etc/security/login.cfg	tsh
pwdadm	chown
security	chgrp
su	chmod
/var/adm/sulog	umask
/etc/security/user	acledit
TCB	aclget
tcbck	aclput
pwdck	audit
grpck	auditpr
usrck	auditselect
/etc/group	auditstream
/etc/security/group	virscan

28.11 QwikInfo

User passwords:

/etc/security/passwd	Secure password file
/etc/security/login.cfg	Set password restrictions
pwdadm	Reset user passwords; should be a member of security group

Superuser access:

su	Set user command
/var/adm/sulog	Log of su activity
/etc/security/user	Set su restrictions

Password auditing:

pwdck	Check /etc/passwd,etc/security/passwd consistency
grpck	Check /etc/group, /etc/security/group consistency
usrck	Validate entries in /etc/security/user

System auditing:

tcbck	Manage auditing system
/etc/security/sysck.cfg	System audit configuration
/etc/security/audit/events	Audit event types
/etc/security/audit/config	Audit class configuration
/etc/security/audit/objects	Audit object configuration
audit, auditpr, auditselect, auditstream	Audit system

Authorization and access:

SAK	Secure attention key
tsh	Trusted shell
/etc/security/user: auth1 auth2	Define alternate login authorization routines
chown, chgrp, chmod	Set standard UNIX access permissions
umask <mask>	File creation mask
acledit	Edit access control lists
aclget, aclput	Assign ACLs

Virus detection:

virscan <PathName>	Invoke virscan
/usr/lib/security/scan/ {virsig.lst,addenda.lst}	Virus signatures
/usr/lib/security/scan/ positive.vir	Virus found log

29

Distributed Computing Environment

29.1 DCE Overview

Remember DCE? The Open Software Foundation's (OSF) distributed computing environment? Early on it looked like DCE would be the proverbial party where nobody came. I've attended a number of "DCE users experience" sessions at conferences over the last few years only to discover that the presenters were all still in the evaluation phase of their DCE experience. I've even participated in some of these sessions hoping that maybe one of the other speakers was further along with DCE than we were!

Times have changed and DCE sites are now springing up everywhere. DCE technology has matured over the last few years. Testimony to this fact is the pervasive use of DCE for open distributed security in most vendor operating systems. I believe DCE's newfound popularity stems from the infrastructure requirements of the highly distributed computing world we find ourselves in. DCE may not have all the answers, but it's the only game in town to bind legacy computing environments with newer distributed technologies under a single security and communication frame work.

In May of 1990, OSF announced the specification for DCE based on vendor technologies provided by DEC, HP, Siemens, MIT, Microsoft, Sun, and Transarc (see Table 29.1). DCE is basically a set of RPC hooks, routines, and servers that facilitate the development of distributed services across a network of heterogeneous systems. DCE provides the layer of glue to bind distributed applications onto the underlying operating system and network services.

At the top level, DCE defines a decentralized hierarchy of administrative domains called cells (see Fig. 29.1). Cells identify administrative domains of DCE services and objects for naming, security, and

TABLE 29.1   DCE Technology Selections

HP/DEC	RPC
DEC	Threads (CMA)
	Time services (DECDTS)
	Name services (DECDNS)
Siemens	X.500 (DIR-X)
MIT Project Athena	Security (Kerberos)
Microsoft/Sun/HP	PC integration services
Transarc	Distributed file system
Transarc/HP	Diskless services

management purposes. Cells are hierarchical in the global DCE name space and interoperate based on levels of trust (see Table 29.2).

29.1.1   DCE RPC

At the lowest level, DCE clients and servers communicate via remote procedure calls (RPC). An interface definition language (IDL) is provided to build DCE interfaces into applications, hiding the RPC intricacies and architecture dependencies from the programmer. The IDL compiler produces a language-dependent interface called a stub that can be incorporated into the target application client and server software. Stubs are uniquely identified in the name space and are responsible for maintaining client/server context and state information (see Fig. 29.2).

29.1.2   Cell directory service

Objects within and between cells are located and identified via queries to directory name services (DNS). DCE Global DNS is based on X.500

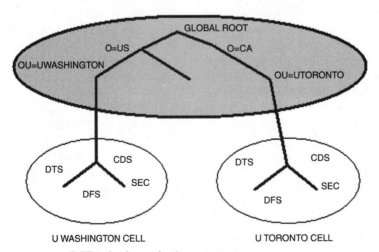

Figure 29.1   DCE technology selections.

TABLE 29.2   DCE Components

Remote procedure call	Routines for building distributed services
Directory services	Global and cell name service
Security service	Authentication, authorization, and access control services
Distributed time service	Cell time synchronization service
Thread services	POSIX thread service for multiplexing RPC interfaces
Distributed file system	Distributed file service based on AFS

and the X/Open Directory Service API (XDS). Name service with a cell is based on Internet DNS and the Cell Directory Service (CDS). DCE objects may include people, organizations, systems, resources, services, and so on. Directory services are hierarchical and decentralized to support worldwide and local cell name spaces. Replication and caching are used to guarantee local access performance levels.

Syntax for global directory service (GDS), cell directory service (CDS), and Internet domain name service (DNS) can be a bit confusing. The following syntax examples illustrate the naming convention used by GDS and DNS. The "/..." symbols represent the GDS and DNS root level. "/.../[CellName]" and "/.:" symbols represent the local cell root.

GDS X.500
```
C=[Country]/O=[Organization]/OU=[Org Unit]/
CN=[Common Name]
/.../C=US/O=University of Washington/ \
OU=Computing & Communications/CN=DeRoest
```
DNS
```
/.../[CellName]/[SubClass]
/.../cac.washington.edu/sec/principal/deroest
/.:/sec/principal/deroest
```

The real unit of binding within DCE directory service is a 128-bit number called a universal unique identifier (UUID). Each RPC inter-

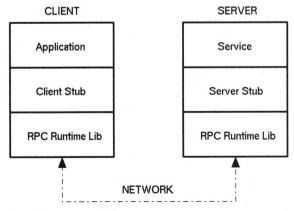

Figure 29.2   DCE stubs interface.

face in the name space is represented by a UUID. Directory services provide the mapping of object name to UUID for DCE applications. The uuidgen utility is used to create UUIDs for new interfaces.

29.1.3 Security service

DCE security service is based on Kerberos Version 5. The encryption mechanism uses private or secure keys versus public keys. The private key is the first level of authorization and authentication in the cell. Keys are generated for each account/password and are stored in a key table on the master server. The private key is checked by the master security server at dce_login time. Once the user is validated, the security server will issue session keys (tickets) for use with each service as it is requested by the client. Session keys are distributed by the security server using key-within-a-key encryption. A ticket may also include a privilege authorization certificate (PAC). PACs describe the client's authorization level for a particular service. The ticket exchange interaction can be quite confusing. Find a good description of Kerberos ticket passing (Chap. 28) and read it until you can recite it in your sleep.

Finer grained access control is provided using POSIX .6 Draft 12 access control lists (ACLs). ACLs may be associated with any object. They are similar to standard UNIX permissions but provide additional levels of access control. ACLs may be defined at the user or group level by both the end user and system administrator. The ACL is basically a list that says who can do what to an object. ACLs also represent another level of complexity beyond the initial security authorization and access control. You need to give some very careful thought into how ACLs and groups will be defined for your cell. The DCE administration groups are as follows:

sec_admin	Security service administration
cds_admin	Cell directory service administration
dts_admin	Distributed time service administration
dfs_admin	Distributed file system administration

29.1.4 Distributed time service

DCE distributed time service (DTS) is pretty straightforward. Time service is implemented as a hierarchy of servers that synchronize timing in the cell. At the top level, a time provider obtains standardized time from a standards body or hardware device. Global time servers distribute the time reference from the provider to the clients and servers in the cell. If the cell contains multiple LANs, each LAN will require a local time server. All nodes within the cell synchronize local system time via a time clerk. The clerks obtain the reference time from the servers via time couriers.

The DCE time standard is based on coordinated universal time (UTC). Like Greenwich mean time (GMT), UTC is based from 0 degrees longitude. Time zones are calculated by adding a positive or negative time differential factor (TDF) to the UTC time. UTC is formatted as a 128-bit time stamp with 100-nanosecond resolution. DTS protocol is interoperable with network time protocol (NTP). Clock correction routines manage skewing, communication delay, and leap seconds between machines and cells.

29.1.5 Threads

Posix 1003.4a compatible threads support parallelization and pipelining between DCE clients and servers. A thread can be thought of as a single task or flow of control. Threads share the process address space, so do not necessarily require special IPC mechanisms to share data. Facilities are available to implement synchronization and locking between process threads and to manage scheduling.

29.1.6 Distributed file service

Data sharing is facilitated by the distributed file system (DFS) (Chap. 19), which was derived from the Andrew file system (AFS) technology developed by Transarc and Carnegie Mellon University. The major differences between DFS and AFS involve the integration of DFS with the other DCE services and the underlying DCE local file system (LFS) architecture. LFS is a dynamic, log-based file system that is very similar to the AIX journaled file system (JFS). LFS structures also map quite closely to AFS constructs. For example, DFS file system trees are similar to AFS in that a common root is identified with the next level delimited by cell name. The DFS shared root is named "/..." and cell subdirectories follow as "/.../cellname/." Local and remote access transparency is maintained using a token passing mechanism and POSIX semantics to mediate updates and locking. A high level of file system availability is maintained through replication and local caching. DFS supports both scheduled and release file system replication. DFS can export any virtual file system (VFS) that has been enhanced to support DCE VFS (see Table 29.3).

29.1.7 DCE versions

The OSF released DCE V1.0 way back in 1991. Until recently, the third release of Version 1, DCE V1.0.3, was the basis of most vendor offer-

TABLE 29.3   Basic DCE Lingo

binding	Process through which a client establishes contact with a server
cell	Collection of nodes and resources to be administered as a unit
client	An entity that requests a service
clerk	Similar to a client but is autonomous; clerks are used for maintenance purposes
courier	Requests time information from a global server on behalf of a clerk
local DTS	Time server for a LAN within a cell
global DTS	Time server for a cell
provider DTS	Obtains standardized time information for DTS servers
principal	Any entity involved in a security interaction with the DCE security service
server	A service provider
UUID	Universal unique identifier; a bit string that uniquely identifies all DCE entities

ings, including AIX V3. DCE V1.1 hit the streets in November of 1994. DCE V1.1 is the code base used by AIXV4 and OS2 Warp. DCE V1.1 addressed many of the complaints levied by users of the previous code base. Specifically, V1.1 reduced much of the complexity in administering DCE. A single administrator interface, dcecp, was introduced; it simplifies the cumbersome command line interface. A DCE master daemon, dced, provides remote administration access to DCE services. Cell aliasing allows you to change or reference your cell by different names without requiring a complete rebuild. The beginnings of hierarchical cell administration are introduced, but you will need to wait for V1.2 to really capitalize on this feature. New programmatic features are added including extended registry attributes and generic security service application program interface (GSSAPI). Using extended registry attributes, you can map DCE and legacy security systems together to support single signon; for example, you can bind MVS RACF and DCE authentication.

DCE V1.2 will be coming soon to a vendor near you. This update includes new dcecp enhancements, DFS improvements, and IDL C++ support. C++ support in DCE begs the question, "Should you be using object or DCE technology?" Why not do both? Hewlett-Packard has already grafted DCE and objects in its object-oriented DCE (OODCE) offering. The OODCE technology has also been submitted to the OSF. If you're a CORBA crusader, then you can use the DCE interface in CORBA. Microsoft is reportedly using DCE RPC in its network OLE implementation. I believe network OLE is now called "COM."

29.2   AIX and DCE

The DCE layer between the application and the operating network is thicker than one might have thought! Do you really need all those services to support a distributed application? The answer is yes. However, you don't need the full set of DCE services on every node in a cell. IBM has packaged its DCE products such that you can make the DCE layer only as thick as required for each node. For example, each DCE client does not need the full set of directory services code. A client only needs the sufficient set of routines to contact a directory server.

AIX DCE V2.1 Products

DCE base services	Included in AIX base	dce.client*
		dce.doc*
		dce.msgs*
		dce.pthreads*
		dce.xdsxom*
DCE DFS	Included in AIX base	dce.dfs*
DCE for application developers	5765-532	dce.tools*
DCE security services	5765-533	dce.security*
DCE cell directory services	5765-534	dce.cds*
DCE enhanced distributed file system	5765-537	dce.edfs*
DCE user data masking and encryption	5765-538	dce.des*
DCE NFS to DFS authenticating gateway	5765-540	dce.dfsnfs*

The AIX DCE V2.1 base product, DCE Base Services for AIX, provides DCE client support for RPC, CDS, DTS, SS, and DFS functions. DCE base services are packaged with AIX and can be integrated into AIX authentication services. The DCE threads library, libc_r.a, is also part of the AIX base. Other components in the base include documentation, SMIT interface, X/Open directory service (XDS), and abstract data manipulation (XOM).

The AIX DCE Security Services product is a separate security service from standard AIX security features. The DCE security server secd and database management tools are included in the product. Authentication via the security server requires that client users invoke the DCE login facility dce_login. Authentication via the security server is required to create a DCE context used to gain access to other DCE services and satisfy ACL permissions in DFS. As mentioned in the DCE overview, these security features are based on the Kerberos third-party authentication algorithm.

DCE directory service is provided by the AIX DCE cell directory service. DCE DNS is interoperable with both Bind DNS and X.500 protocols. The server is comprised of a cell directory server (CDS) and a global directory agent (GDA). The CDS manages the database of resources within a cell. The GDA communicates between cells to access global resources. Note that AIX DCE V2.1 does not support GDS. The AIX DCE V2.1 GDA can be used to interact with an AIX DCE V1.0.3 GDS for intercell communication. AIX DCE V2.1 also does not support hierarchical cells or cell aliasing.

DCE LFS incorporates a number of enhancements to the facilities you are familiar with under the AIX Logical Volume Manager. AIX JFS and CD-ROM file systems may be exported to the DCE DFS file space, but you will need to manage them as separate entities. Standard AIX JFS commands cannot be used to manipulate DFS and LFS. AIX JFS ACLs and DFS ACLs are not interoperable. DFS will coexist with NFS and AFS. Access to NFS file systems are not authenticated under DCE, and SYSV locking is not supported. The AIX DCE NFS to DFS Authenticating Gateway Service can be used to manage DCE context for NFS clients. See Tables 29.4 and 29.5.

29.3   DCE Planning

It is critical that you carefully plan out your overall DCE cell topology before getting too far into the installation process. Once your configuration is in production, it is extremely difficult to change. For example, in the current release of AIX DCE V2.1, something as simple as the cell name is not easily changed. There is hope in coming releases with features like cell aliases.

29.3.1   Cell topology

Begin by projecting your expected population growth over the next couple of years. You should take into account increases in numbers of users, computers, applications, and administrative groups. If you expect rapid growth, it may be prudent to start with a number of cells that map to the administrative roles in your organization. Combine groups of users and systems that function as a unit, share resources, and exhibit a common authentication base. Keep in mind that the principal name space that identifies all users, computers, and services in a cell must be unique. Network topology might also dictate the boundaries chosen for a cell. Try to stay away from single points of failure and network bottlenecks between clients and critical services. Multiple cells may scale better over the longer term compared with putting

TABLE 29.4   AIX DCE Clients and Servers

SS	secd	Security server
	dced	Client security/rpc server
	dceunixd	DCE/AIX security integrator
CDS	cdsd	Cell directory server
	cdsadv	CDS advertiser—help clients access CDS
	cdsclerk	Interface between CDS client and server
	gdad	Global directory agent—intercell access
DTS	dtsd	DTS client/server
DFS	dfsd	See Chap. 19 for client/server list

TABLE 29.5   AIX DCE Administration Commands

mkdce	
lsdce	
rmdce	
dcecp	Security server administration
rpccp	RPC maps, profiles, and group administration
cdscp	CDS administration
dtscp	Time service administration
rgy_edit	Security server administration
uuidgen	Create principals
rmxcred	Remove stale credentials
chpesite	Update pe_site files
rc.dce	Start DCE services
dce_clean	Shut down DCE
passwd_import	Populate registry from AIX password files
passwd_export	Create AIX password files from registry
cdsbrowser	Motif CDS browser tool
cdsli	CDS recursive list
cdsdel	CDS recursive delete
sec_create_db	Initialize security database
dfs	See Chap. 19

everything in one cell. Cell hierarchies will assist in managing multiple cells; however, it's not supported in AIX DCE 2.1.

Once you have identified your cell layout, choose unique cell names that will assist in identifying your workgroups and simplify intercell communication. Keep in mind the formats used for intercell (X.500) and intracell (DNS) identification. If you already have existing Internet DNS domain names that represent departments in your organization, consider using these as cell names. Map each DNS domain level to an X.500 level. If you will be operating with existing cells outside your organization, you may need to follow cell naming conventions used in the external environment. Choose carefully! It's a real pain to change them later on.

29.3.2   Server topology

Now decide how you will distribute DCE servers in your cell. Decisions here are going to be based on computer and network hardware topology. Each server type can coexist with other DCE servers on the same computer or reside on a dedicated system. If you can afford the hardware, the latter is preferred. You should also consider replicating the servers for availability. There is a tradeoff to be made between availability and performance. More replicas mean more time spent in synchronizing and checkpointing all copies. DCE supports two kinds of name space replication between servers: immediate and skulk. Immediate replication occurs each time the master server is updated. Periodic updates are performed using skulk replication. You may also prioritize access to servers via profiles. A default and lan-profile profile are provided as part of the base installation. You can customize your own server profiles, but it means keying in UUID information by hand. Sorry, no tools. You should deploy an odd number of replicas to simplify server voting to determine master and slave roles.

A minimum DCE configuration requires the following three servers:

Security server

Cell directory server

Distributed time server

Use the hard key procedure for architecting your security server environment. This means dedicate a machine and lock it in a closet!

If you plan to use DFS for sharing data in your cell, refer to Chap. 19 for details on planning, installing, and administering DFS.

29.3.3 Principals and security

Every user, computer, and service in your cell is identified as a principal and associated with a UUID number. As the number of principals in your cell grows, it will be easier to identify roles if you allocate UUID ranges to each principal type. You should also consider defining additional groups to facilitate access control early on.

Before beginning the installation process, choose a cell administrator ID and password. This account will be used to administer the DCE security service and registry. You might also restrict use of the cell administrator account to a particular machine or secure subnet, the reason being that you must type in the administrator password to create context for administrative functions. Other solutions might include the use of smart cards and keytab files on a machine dedicated to cell administration.

You will also need to decide how to keep AIX and DCE security information synchronized. User password information must be added to the local AIX databases and also to the DCE security registry. Fortunately, tools are provided to assist in maintaining synchronization. The AUTHSTATE environment variable can be used to point at the local AIX password information or the DCE registry and honored when the passwd command is used. Note that DCE and UNIX (AIX) use a different crypt function so they can't share encrypted passwords.

```
AUTHSTATE=DCE        Update DCE security registry
AUTHSTATE=compat     Update AIX password data
```

To batch updates to either database, the passwd_export and passwd_import tools can be used. Invoke passwd_import to read your existing AIX password information and initialize your DCE registry after installing DCE. The passwd_export tool reads from the registry and creates AIX password files.

passwd_import   AIX password data to DCE registry

passwd_export   DCE registry to AIX password data

To more fully integrate DCE in the AIX authentication process at login time, use the dceunixd service. This will keep users from having specifically to invoke dce_login after logging into AIX.

The procedure is as follows:

1. Edit /etc/security/login.cfg and add the DCE authentication stanza.
   ```
   DCE:
   Program=/usr/lib/security/DCE
   ```

2. Edit /etc/security/user to set DCE allow/deny for your users.

3. Edit /opt/dcelocal/etc/passwd_override, group_override files to explicitly override registry entries for specific users.

4. Start the dceunixd daemon.

29.3.4   Test cell

It's a very good idea to set up a test cell for validating and stress testing your DCE configuration. A test cell is also an excellent learning tool for new DCE systems programmers, administrators, operators, and end users. If you can afford the machines, keep the test cell in place after deploying your production system. It will give you a chance to try out new configurations without disrupting production service and assist in tuning and debugging. Use the test cell for checking interoperability for phased migration and implementation.

29.4   DCE Installation and Configuration

Before starting the installation process, create a separate file system for /var/dce in a non-rootvg volume group. Nearly everything that DCE services creates is stored in the /opt/dcelocal directory, which is an AIX link to the /var/dce directory. Creating a separate /var/dce will cut down on grumbling later on when you start running out of space in rootvg. This should preferably be done before you install DCE components. The IBM texts recommend making /var/dce 30 MB. If you are running multiple DCE services on a machine, you should make /var/dce twice that size and monitor it carefully for possible expansion. You will regularly need to clean out expired credentials, logs, and audit files from this file system, so consider adding these housekeeping tasks to cron.

Refer to Chap. 6 for instructions on installing the AIX DCE V2.1 packages that will be used on each computer in the cell. Remember that DCE base services including client support are included in the AIX V4 operating system. Only install the DCE packages required for the services you intend to support on each machine.

Configure DCE in two steps. First configure and start the base cell services: master security server, cell directory server, and a time server. After these services have been configured and started, configure additional DCE services and replica servers. Use SMIT or mkdce to configure these services and register the cell name. Note that you will need to completely remove a service if a failure occurs during configuration or if you wish to make changes. You can remove a service by selecting the unconfigure option in SMIT or by invoking rmdce. Use the lsdce command to verify the configuration status (see Fig. 29.3).

# smit dce	SMIT DCE configuration
# mkdce [Options]	Create DCE clients and servers
# lsdce [Options]	List DCE services
# rmdce [Options]	Remove DCE services

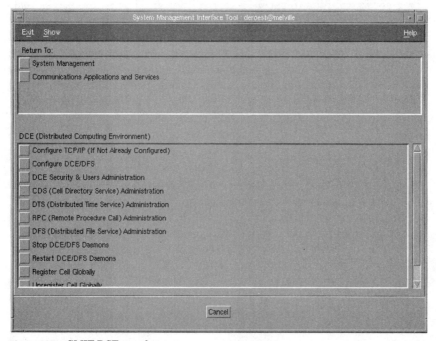

Figure 29.3 SMIT DCE panel.

29.4.1 Security service

You begin by defining the master security server using the SMIT Fast-Path smit mkdcesecsrv. Select "primary" from the list when prompted. You will be asked to define the cell name, security server host name, the cell administrator's account, and whether you wish to merge the existing AIX password and group files into DCE. Choose the starting and maximum UID range you will use for principals. Once completed, SMIT will start the dced and secd daemons on the machine (see Fig. 29.4).

> # smit mkdcesecsrv   Create security server

29.4.2 Directory service

Configure the master cell directory server by invoking SMIT mkcdssrv. You will be prompted for the cell name and security server name configured in the previous section. Verify that the other DCE fields are correct and select a host name for the CDS. Once completed, the master CDS server, a CDS clerk, and RPC services are started. SMIT will also create an initial clearinghouse for the CDS (see Fig. 29.5).

> # smit mkcdssrv   Create cell directory server

29.4.3 Distributed time service

Next create a distributed time server for the base cell by executing SMIT mkdtssrv. You will be prompted to select the DTS type for this machine. Note that a DTS server cannot coexist with another DTS server or client. If the DTS is on a separate subnet from the security

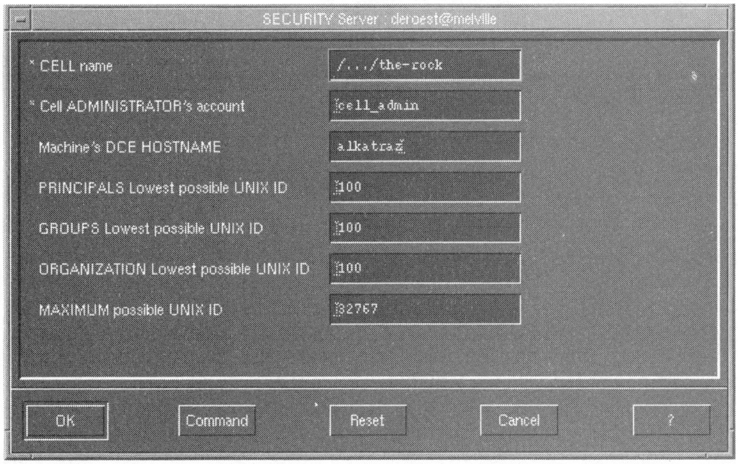

Figure 29.4 SMIT DCE security server panel.

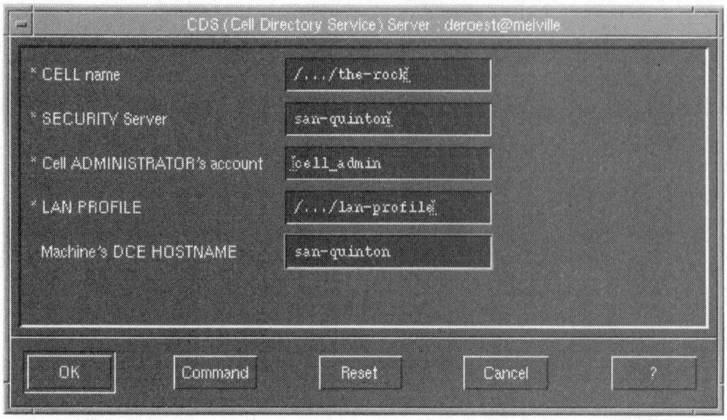

Figure 29.5   SMIT DCE CDS panel.

server which inhibits broadcasts, enter the security server host name. When competed, the system will be configured as a CDS client and DTS local or global time service will be started (see Fig. 29.6).

```
# smit mkdtssrv          Create distributed time server
```

29.4.4   Clients and servers

Now you are ready to configure additional server replicas, other DCE servers like DFS (Chap. 19), and DCE clients. Clients can be created such

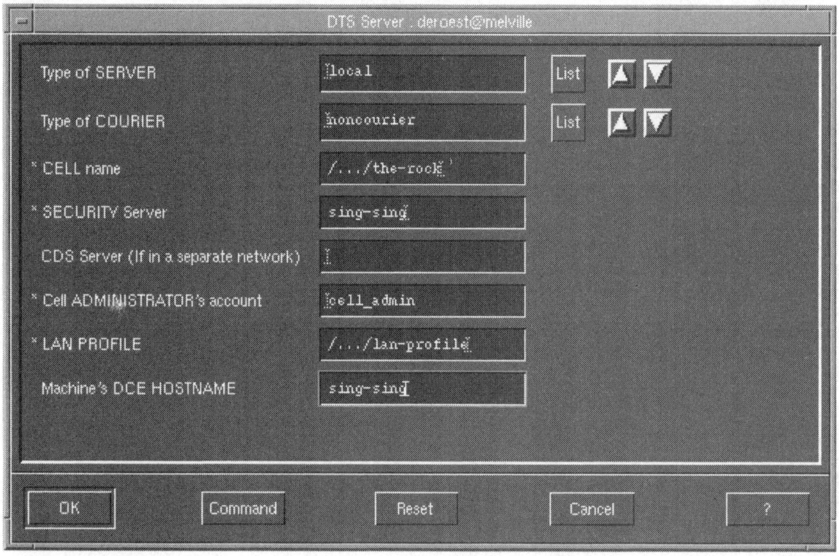

Figure 29.6   SMIT DCE DTS panel.

that they can gain full or local administrator access. In the latter case, the cell administrator does not have root access to the local client, and the local client does not have cell administrator access. In this case, DCE client setup is a two-step process. First, the admin portion is executed on a cell machine with cell administrator access. This is followed by the local portion on the local client machine. Both steps can be completed on the local machine if full access is selected. Invoke SMIT mkdceclient to create a DCE client. Note that one of the first clients you create should be the security server client process (see Figs. 29.7 and 29.8).

```
# smit mkdceclient      Create a DCE client
```

29.4.5 Verifying DCE configuration

After completing configuration of the DCE client and server machines, verify the configuration from each participating system. First look at the /etc/mkdce.data file to list the DCE services being run on the particular machine:

```
# cat /etc/mkdce.data

cds_cl     COMPLETE     CDS Clerk
cds_srv    COMPLETE     Initial CDS Server
dfs_cl     COMPLETE     DFS Client Machine
```

Figure 29.7 SMIT DCE client type list.

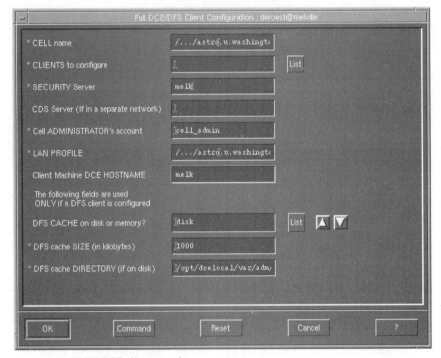

Figure 29.8 SMIT DCE client panel.

```
dts_local    COMPLETE    Local DTS Server
rpc          COMPLETE    RPC Endpoint Mapper
sec_cl       COMPLETE    Security Client
sec_srv      COMPLETE    Security Server
```

Run the lsdce command. This should list the same information.

```
# lsdce

Current state of DCE configuration:
cds_cl       COMPLETE CDS Clerk
cds_srv      COMPLETE Initial CDS Server
dts_local    COMPLETE Local DTS Server
rpc          COMPLETE RPC Endpoint Mapper
sec_cl       COMPLETE Security Client
sec_srv      COMPLETE Security Server (Master)
```

Use dcecp to list the hosts you have configured in the cell:

```
dcecp
dcecp> host catalog
```

```
/.../alcatraz.u.washington.edu/hosts/robocop
/.../alcatraz.u.washington.edu/hosts/warden
/.../alcatraz.u.washington.edu/hosts/nomad
/.../alcatraz.u.washington.edu/hosts/inmate
```

You can also use the dcecp catalog option to list other principals and resources configured in the cell.

29.5 DCE Implementation Considerations

If you're ready to build your first DCE cell or you are thinking of upgrading an existing cell, consider these tips from a few experienced DCE users. The first recommendation is that you use a vendor implementation that supports the DCE V1.1 code base for your servers. As I pointed out earlier, V1.1 administration is much simpler and the overall system is more robust and scalable. DCE V1.0.3 clients are compatible with V1.1 servers that will help in migrating existing DCE cells.

Next, when looking for a V1.1 implementation, remember that the vendor release numbers and names may differ from the OSF numbers. For example, the AIX implementation of OSF DCE V1.1 is AIX DCE V2.1. AIX and OS/2 directory and security services have also been repackaged as the distributed security service (DSS). The story is pretty much the same game for other vendor DCE offerings.

Carefully plan the name space size and the number of cells your server will deploy. There are a couple of "AIXpert" articles by Bob Russell of IBM that will lend assistance in determining the size and topology of the servers required to meet your name space needs (Appendix A). These articles are based on DCE V1.0.3, but most of the recommendations offered are still true for the current release.

In most cases, you will want to use replicated servers and dedicate separate machines for CDS and security servers. If your name space is large, say 100,000 principals or larger, you are going to need large memory spaces on these servers. Most of the server name space has to be held in virtual memory, so that means RAM and swap. You can reduce some of the memory hold on your primary servers by distributing the CDS name space between the replica servers. This way your primary CDS server won't get bogged down with infrequently accessed data. Resource consumption by the CDS and security servers grows linearly with the size of the name space. The good news is that the data access profiles are pretty much flat, even with large name spaces. The database size doesn't seem to adversely affect queries. Get the latest patches for AIX DCE if you are running an early AIX DCE V2.1 release. These patches will reduce the memory requirements for your CDS and security servers along with increasing the size limit of the name space.

When determining machine configurations for servers, remember that DCE randomly selects systems among replicas. This means your overall throughput is going to be affected by your slowest server. You also need to be aware of service interruptions during replica checkpoints. You can tune the frequency of checkpoints to limit service outages during prime time. Note that the CDS servers are cached but not validity-based. This means that data can become inconsistent between replicas. This isn't good for frequently changing data. You will need to remember this when determining checkpoint frequency and what information you decide to store in the CDS.

Try to limit the CDS lookup frequency when building applications and configuring your environment. The CDS is referenced each time an application requires the address of a service. For example, the location of a security server must be obtained at DCE login time. When coding an application, you might cache a server's address when feasible rather than doing a lookup for each access. You can also distribute a pe_site file to your DCE clients. This file lists the addresses of frequently used servers like the security servers. Clients will look up addresses in the site file before going to the CDS. This will reduce the load on your CDS server but will require that you keep the site files up to date.

If you wish to run a mix of Kerberos and DCE applications, you will find a fair amount of compatibility between Kerberos V5 and DCE. We've been experimenting with some of the Kerberos V5 patches that Doug Engert of Argonne National Laboratory has made available. Our experience has been pretty good in getting Kerberos V5 applications to work with DCE security service and DCE tickets. If you are interested in DCE and Kerberos interoperability, take a look at Authentication Task Force project on the ESnet Web page (Appendix A).

Over the last few years, we developed new distributed services using Network Computing System (NCS) RPCs. NCS RPCs are similar to DCE RPCs and provide a migration path for getting to DCE. This turned out to be time well spent. The test NCS clients ported easily to DCE. The NCS interfaces were redefined and compiled using DCE interface definition language (IDL). No other changes to the client application were required. The converted clients were able to interoperate with existing NCS-based servers. When binding your code, you need to be aware of possible problems with other libraries that are not threadsafe. This is especially tricky in shared library environments like AIX. A threadsafe C library, libc_r.a, is provided with the AIX V4 threads support that helps avoid most problems. You also need to be aware of thread scheduling and RPC timeouts when using debuggers like dbx. Finally, whenever possible, use explicit binding in your DCE applications. Partial or dynamic binding can result in a new binding for each RPC invoked by the application.

29.6   InfoExplorer Keywords

DCE	rgy_edit
secd	uuidgen
dced	rmxcred
dceunixd	credentials
CDS	cell
cdsd	chpesite
cdsadv	pe_site
cdsclerk	rc.dce
gdad	dce_clean
DTS	passwd_import
dtsd	passwd_export
dfsd	registry
DFS	cdsbrowser
clerk	cdsli
courier	cdsdel
mkdce	sec_create_db
lsdce	RPC
rmdce	threads
deecp	GDS
rpccp	GDA
cdscp	X.500
dtscp	DNS

29.7   QwikInfo

Components:

Cell	Administrative domain of management
SS	Security server
CDS	Cell directory server
DTS	Distributed time server
RPC	DCE remote procedure call
Threads	DCE posix threads
DFS	DCE distributed file service (Chap. 19)

Files and directories:

"/.../[CellName]", "/.:", "/:"	Cell root level
/var/dce, /opt/dcelocal	Config file, cache, logs, etc.
/etc/mkdce.data	Configured components
/usr/lpp/dce	DCE product set

Configuration:

smit dce	DCE configuration
smit mkdcesecsrv	Create security server
smit mkcdssrv	Create cell directory server
smit mkdtssrv	Create distributed time server
smit mkdceclient	Create a DCE client

Servers:

secd	Security server
dced	Client security/RPC server
dceunixd	DCE/AIX security integrator
cdsd	Cell directory server
cdsadv	CDS advertiser—help clients access CDS
cdsclerk	Interface between CDS client and server
gdad	Global directory agent—intercell access
dtsd	DTS client/server
dfsd	DFS server

System Recovery and Tuning

Backup and Copy Utilities

30.1 System Backups

How much is your time and your data worth to you? How many times have you erased what you thought was an unnecessary file only to discover a week later that it contained some vital piece of information? Even the most meticulously maintained system will be subject to disk failures. A regular schedule for system backups will significantly reduce the cost and frustration related to data loss problems. Believe me, you will rest easier each night!

30.2 Backup Strategies

When defining a backup strategy, tradeoffs must be made between the time and cost of performing the backups and the level of data recovery that is required. For single-user workstations, the workstation owner has a good idea when a backup should be made to protect critical data. Even in the single-user environment, it's a good idea to develop a discipline for performing regular backups. Large multiuser systems have very dynamic file update characteristics, which make it difficult to perform backups on an as-needed basis. Careful thought must be devoted to implementing backup policies that meet the needs of a large and diverse user base.

Here are some important backup policy considerations:

Which file systems are backed up and how often

Backup while file systems are mounted or unmounted

Full and incremental dump schedules

Size of file systems

Media types

Media rotation schedule

Backup verification schedule

Offsite storage

Bandwidth considerations for network based backups

Backup program and format to be used

Restore procedures

Data protection and privileges

30.2.1   What and when

With the price of storage at one dollar a megabyte and falling, it is awfully easy to keep throwing disk packs at storage bottlenecks. The problem is that you end up spending all your time backing up this proliferation of disks. Vendors don't want you to stop buying disks, so you need to take a harder look at which file systems actually need to be dumped.

Root file systems, like /usr and "/" tend to be static in nature and may be replicated on a number of machines. Thus, they may not require dumping as often as dynamic file systems like those containing user home directories and work areas.

30.2.2   Mounted or unmounted

To guarantee data integrity, a file system should be synched and unmounted during backup. Environments that require 24-hour by 7-day-a-week availability may find this procedure difficult to live with. You can perform dumps while a file system is mounted and in use; however, you run the risk of missing data block updates in progress during the dump. A number of shops, including my own, run dumps on live file systems. For the most part we have not experienced a large number of problems. As a rule, it is not a good practice to dump a live file system if you can avoid it. There are some commercial backup packages available that perform a checksum on each file during a live backup to ensure data integrity. Advanced file systems like DFS (Chap. 19) allow you to copy or mirror a file system, take the copy offline, and then back it up. High file system availability requirements mean that you either spend a little more money for duplicate storage or you cross your fingers and hope that a missed block isn't yours.

30.2.3   Sizing

Tune your file system sizes to match the backup media and time constraints. Very large file systems require frequent manual intervention to mount new media and thus more time to dump. It also means more media must be scanned when doing a restore. You know, the file you wanted restored is always the very last of one of a 20-reel backup set.

Consider using devices that provide hardware data compression or use a compression program like compress or pack to compact data on the media. Software compression will take additional time, but the additional time may be offset by media utilization costs.

30.2.4   Full and incremental dumps

Time and money always being the deciding factor, it's not practical to run a full file system dump every day. What you really want is to run a periodic full dump followed by daily incremental dumps of the changes made against the full dump. Most UNIX backup commands implement this feature using a set of dump levels, 0 through 9. A level-0 dump represents a full dump. Levels 1 through 9 are the incremental dumps that represent file system changes against the previous less-than or equal-to dump level.

Level 0   Full dump
Levels 1–9   Incremental dumps

30.2.5   Backup schedules and rotation

There are many strategies you can use to rotate between full and incremental dumps to optimize media utilization and dump wall clock time. The tradeoff here is media utilization and complexity. On the simple side, a weekly level-0 full dump can be followed by daily level-1 dumps. When a restore operation is requested, the level 0 is consulted followed by the most recent level 1. Simple, but not very elegant.

To optimize media utilization and dump time, one of the more complex rotation strategies like the "Towers of Hanoi" sequence may be used. I must admit I have always hated the Towers of Hanoi sequence after having to sweat over the algorithm in Computer Science 101. Never the less, it provides a very good rotation mechanism and saves on tapes.

The Towers of Hanoi sequence involves a new level 0 dump for each file system followed by five sequences of levels 1 through 9. Four sets of level-1 tapes are used for each file system. Tapes for levels 2 through 9 are reused, and it is assumed that levels 2 through 9 will fit on one tape.

Towers of Hanoi Dump Level Sequence

Dump type	Dump level number sequence
Full	1
Incremental	3 2 5 4 7 6 9 8

Complex dump sequences can be tracked through the use of the /etc/dumpdates file. The dumpdates file records the file system, dump level, and time stamp. The -u flag provided by the backup and rdump commands will update the time stamp each time a backup is run.

```
/etc/dumpdates

/dev/rhd1       1 Mon Aug 30 02:10:56 1993
/dev/rhd2       1 Mon Aug 30 02:04:25 1993
/dev/rhd1       0 Tue Aug 3 03:25:15 1993
/dev/rhd2       0 Sun Aug 1 03:23:12 1993
/dev/rhd4       0 Fri Aug 20 02:00:04 1993
/dev/rhd9var    0 Sat Aug 21 02:30:59 1993
/dev/rhd4       1 Mon Aug 30 02:00:04 1993
/dev/rhd9var    1 Mon Aug 30 02:09:33 1993
/dev/rlv00      0 Sun Aug 1 04:24:41 1993
/dev/rlv00      1 Mon Aug 30 02:17:25 1993
```

The sequence of dump levels can be automated using cron. The following is the backup level crontab:

```
02 * * 1 /etc/backup -0 -uf/dev/rmt0.1 /home
02 * * 2 /etc/backup -3 -uf/dev/rmt0.1 /home
02 * * 3 /etc/backup -2 -uf/dev/rmt0.1 /home
02 * * 4 /etc/backup -5 -uf/dev/rmt0.1 /home
02 * * 5 /etc/backup -4 -uf/dev/rmt0.1 /home
02 * * 6 /etc/backup -7 -uf/dev/rmt0.1 /home
02 * * 7 /etc/backup -6 -uf/dev/rmt0.1 /home
```

30.2.6 Disaster recovery and validation

It follows that, while you are safeguarding your file systems, you will also want to safeguard the backups themselves. First and foremost, you should periodically test your backup sets by performing a restore operation. Verify that the backup media is good and that the data is valid. This will eliminate the problem of backing up bad data.

Periodically rotate a full set of backup media off-site. Disasters can range from the file level to the building and city level.

Regularly cycle the media through a physical cleaning and validation check. This will include periodic maintenance and cleaning of the backup devices.

30.2.7 Backup media

Choose backup media that fits your environment. I think we all agree that it doesn't make much sense to backup 500 megabytes of file system space using diskettes. Careful consideration must be given weigh ing media cost, transfer rate, and storage capacity. Larger shops might opt for optical storage or robotic jukeboxes. See Chap. 7 for information on the various tape media characteristics.

30.3 Backing Up a File System

The AIX backup/restore commands are very similar to their BSD dump/restore counterparts. backup can be used to dump entire file systems as well as support a backup by name for dumping subdirectory trees. The following examples demonstrate a filesystem full dump and backing up a subdirectory tree by name:

```
# backup -0 -u -f/dev/rmt0.1 /usr
# find /usr/local -print | backup -i -f/dev/rmt0.1
```

30.4 Restoring Files and File Systems

The restore command options are similar to those used by backup. If you have problems remembering the path name of a particular file you wish to restore, you can use the -t flag to output an index of the files on the tape. You can also use the -i flag to run restore in an interactive mode for file system inode dumps. This allows you to move around the directories stored on the tape similar to the way you would with directories on a disk.

```
# restore -T -f/dev/rmt0.1          Display media index
# restore -r -f/dev/rmt0.1          Restore full file system
# restore -f/dev/rmt0.1 -xdv bin    Restore file in bin directory
# restore -i -f/dev/rmt0.1          Start interactive restore
```

30.5 Other Dump Utilities

The tar and cpio utilities can be used when portability is an issue. Both tar and cpio will allow you to copy files and directory trees between systems, preserving UIDs and permissions. In some cases, tar will not span multiple volumes. Use cpio on SYSV UNIX machines where tar is not available.

```
# tar -cvf /dev/rmt0.1 ./source     Copy to tape
# tar -xvf /dev/rmt0.1              Restore tar archive
# find . -print | cpio -ov > /dev/rmt0   Copy to tape
# cpio -ipdmv < /dev/rmt0.1          Restore cpio archive
```

If you have the disk space to spare, you can copy a logical volume using the cplv command. This mechanism could be used to create a file system copy for backup, leaving the primary copy online.

```
# cplv -e <ExistingLV> <SourceLV
```
Copy a logical volume

30.6 Operating System Dumps

To backup AIX rootvg file systems, consider using the mksysb command. mksysb creates a tar image of root file systems complete with file system descriptions that can be used to restore from the standalone maintenance system. Invoke the mkszfile to create a .fs.size table that describes the rootvg file systems. Edit .fs.size to include only those file systems to be used for restoration purposes. Run the mksysb command to create the backup image.

To create backup copy of root volume group:

```
# mkszfile
```
Create rootvg map

```
# chdev -l rmt0 -a block_size=512
```
Set correct block size

```
# tctl -f /dev/rmt0 rewind
```
Rewind tape

```
# mksysb /dev/rmt0
```
Create backup

```
# chdev -l rmt0 -a block_size=<blocksize>
```
Reset tape block size

30.7 Network Backups

What about using the network to backup remote workstations onto machines equipped with high-capacity tape drives? You can do this by using the rdump and rrestore commands. rdump and rrestore are very similar to the backup and restore commands described above. They share many of the same flags and parameters. The primary difference is that they use a remote_host:device argument to the -f flag, which designates the host name of the machine equipped with the backup device.

```
# rdump -u -0 -f daffy:/dev/rmt0.1 /home
# rrestore -x -f daffy:/dev/rmt0 /home
```

Another network-based option is to use the remote shell command rsh with one of the local backup or copy commands. You can use rsh with pipes and redirection to obtain results similar to rdump and rrestore.

```
tar cvf- ./home | rsh judy "dd of=/dev/rmt0 obs=1024"
rsh judy "dd if=/dev/rmt0 ibs=1024" | ( cd /home; tar xvf - )
```

In either of the above cases, if you do not wish to be prompted for a password on the remote system, create a .rhosts file in the $HOME directory of the remote user ID being used for the remote shell. On each line of the .rhosts file, enter the names of each machine and user ID that are allowed to connect without providing a password.

30.8 The Whole Nine Yards

The preceding information combined with tape information from Chap. 10 describes the traditional tools used to manage UNIX tapes and backups. These are a long way from the features supported by the mature proprietary backup packages available on other operating systems. The vendor community is quickly filling this gap. A number of very good packages are available, complete with features like label validation, multivolume support, and tape librarian interfaces. See *RS/Magazine,* "Taming the Backup Beast," vol. 2, no. 2, Feb. 1993 for details on a number of vendor packages that are supported under AIX.

30.9 InfoExplorer Keywords

compress	tctl
pack	rmt
/etc/dumpdates	tar
backup	cpio
rdump	cplv
cron	mksysb
restore	mkszfile
rrestore	.fs.size
find	rsh
rmt	.rhosts
mt	dd

30.10 QwikInfo

Backup and restore:

```
/etc/dumpdates
```
Set file system dump dates and levels

```
backup -[level] -u -f
[media] [file-system]
```
Back up file system, where level 0 = full dump and levels 1–9 = incremental dumps

```
find /usr/local -print |          Back up by name
backup -i -f [media]
restore -T -f <media>             Display media index
restore -r -f <media>             Restore file system
restore -f <media> -xdv <file|dir>  Restore file/directory
restore -i -f <media>             Interactive restore
tar,cpio                          Archive commands
cplv -e [ExistingLV] [SourceLV]   Copy a logical volume
```

RootVG backup:

```
mkszfile                          Create rootvg map file for
                                  mksysb

mksysb                            RootVG backup
```

Network backup:

```
rdump -u [level] -f [host]:[media]   Network dump
[file-sys]
rrestore -x -f [host]:[media]        Network restore
[file-sys]
```

31

System Monitoring and Tuning

31.1   Know Your Workload

You've heard that advice many times. Before you can begin to tune your system or recommend adding resources, you have to know what the workload profile is and what level of response is expected. You have to accurately define the performance goals in order to achieve them!

Begin with a good understanding of how the operating system manages its resources. Document the throughput limits of the physical resources (hardware, peripherals, network). Next, characterize the workload as needing a single-user workstation, a multiuser time sharing setup, or a batch/network server. Identify and prioritize critical applications and the resources they require. Look for areas of contention. It may be that partitioning workloads by shift or machine will solve particular resource bottlenecks. Now begin monitoring the system under real and modeled workloads. This requires some knowledge of the tools available and their characteristics. Gather and review all the data to determine where adjustments or additional resources are required. Sounds easy, doesn't it?

Since they're your workload, applications, resources, and performance expectations, I'll concentrate on AIX OS characteristics and the available tool sets. Hardware characteristics are described in chapters related to the particular devices.

31.2   AIX Operating System Characteristics

31.2.1   CPU scheduling

A good deal of CPU resources can be saved by painstakingly profiling and tuning application code. Even though you may not have the luxury of source code, the AIX tprof profiler can give you a very good idea of where the application is spending its time.

As described in Chap. 26, the AIX scheduler uses a set of 128 run queues to prioritize active processes. Lower-numbered queues are scheduled more often than those with higher numbers; thus, they receive a larger share of CPU resources. Processes in a common priority queue are scheduled round robin. After execution, the process returns to the end of the line.

Process priorities are based on the sum of the short-term CPU usage (0 to +100), process nice value (0 to 40), and the minimum user process level. At each reschedule time quantum, the short CPU usage is updated and new priorities computed for processes in the ready-to-run state. Processes burning higher CPU usage levels will have their priority number increased, dropping their relative priority to other processes. Any process with a priority value greater than 120 will only be run when no other process in the system requires the CPU.

Process rescheduling can occur at every clock tick. Unless a process is preempted, blocked, or terminated, it will consume its CPU quantum (up to 10 milliseconds) and be rescheduled at the next clock interrupt. Processes tend to spend their time in either the runnable or blocked state.

Because priorities tend to float up and down, the nice command doesn't provide an adequate hammer to control process priorities. Some degree of success can be accomplished by implementing a daemon that periodically checks CPU usage and scheduler priority, then renices jobs to favor critical applications. AIX also provides a setpri() system call that can be used to fix the priority level of a process. This is especially useful for real-time applications. Care must be taken in multiuser workloads that fixing a process priority above 60 (which will have a lower number) does not adversely affect interactive response.

The previous discussion is based on the standard AIX scheduler. AIX V4 offers three schedulers: SCHED_RR, SCHED_FIFO, and SCHED_OTHER. SCHED_RR enforces strict round robin scheduling. SCHED_FIFO uses a fixed priority, first-in, first-out ordering. SCHED_FIFO does not support preemption and is not time-sliced. A thread must either block or yield the processor when running under the SCHED_FIFO scheduler. The third option, SCHED_OTHER, represents the standard AIX scheduling algorithm where task priority degrades with CPU usage.

31.2.2 Virtual memory management

The job of the virtual memory manager (VMM) is to allocate memory for process active working sets and recover stale or unused memory pages. The latter requires that some process pages be moved from memory to secondary storage (paging space). Even in well-tuned systems, some amount of paging activity will usually be taking place.

The VMM in AIX 3.2 was enhanced with the addition of process swap support. AIX uses a lazy swapping technique that keeps the system from swapping processes when memory is not constrained. If a thrashing situation is detected, AIX suspends the processes that are responsible. The offending process pages become stale and are paged out. If thrashing continues, new processes are suspended as well. When the memory becomes available, the suspended processes are reactivated.

VMM enhancements also include the differentiation of computational memory and file memory. As you would expect, computational memory defines those pages that belong to a program's working set, and file memory makes up the rest. The VMM maintains a repage fault history for each of these memory types that is then used to determine if a thrashing condition exists. A repage fault represents a recently read page from disk that has been referenced and is not found in memory. The VMM looks at the computational and file repage rates to determine which type of page should be stolen in a constrained situation.

You may tune the following set of memory load parameters to represent your workloads computational and file memory requirements. An example: The application for tuning these parameters, called schedtune, is available in /usr/lpp/bos/samples. Care must be taken when modifying these parameters. Use schedtune in conjunction with rmss to model memory loading. The rmss command allows you to simulate real memory configurations on the running system.

h   Memory committment high-water mark

w   Wait time before reactivating suspended processes

p   Process memory high-water mark

m   Minimum active processes

e   Time exempt from suspension

Memory is overcommitted when:

$$\frac{\text{\# page writes in last second}}{\text{\# page steals in last second}} > \frac{1}{h}$$

A process is considered to be thrashing when:

$$\frac{\text{\# repages in last second}}{\text{\# page faults in last second}} > \frac{1}{p}$$

Make sure you have adequate paging space available. The actual amount required is going to depend on your workload. I generally use a 3-to-1 ratio of paging space to real memory. Paging space should be distributed across multiple volumes, if possible.

vmtune, a companion to schedtune, can also be used to tune page replacement and stealing. For more information on tuning VMM, see the InfoExplorer document "Performance Overview of the Virtual Memory Manager (VMM)."

31.2.3   Disk I/O

You may recognize the situation on many UNIX systems when a process creating large write queues holds up processes attempting to read. These large writes queues can exhaust the file system free lists and hold up the reads required to replenish the free list, making the problem worse. AIX provides a facility to control file output queue contention through the use of high- and low-water marks. When a process writing to a file hits its high-water mark, that process is suspended until the queue drops to or below the low-water mark. This facility is called I/O pacing. I/O pacing will allow you to manage the tradeoff between interactive response and I/O throughput. High- and low-watermark values of 0 disable I/O pacing. You can set these parameters using the SMIT chgsys FastPath (see Fig. 31.1).

```
# smit chgsys
```

The AIX asynchronous I/O facility can be used to improve I/O performance for applications that are heavily I/O-bound. Asynchronous I/O routines must be added to the application source code, and the application must be rebuilt. These routines allow the application to continue processing rather than being blocked during I/O operations. Notification of I/O completion is posted as an event back to the process. The application can poll for these events to keep track of data written to disk.

31.2.4   Network performance

If you have spent any time administering large networked multiuser or application server systems, doubtless you have experienced the dead-end situation of "no more mbufs." mbuf structures are used to store data moving between the network and the operating system. In most cases, when you hit the mbuf wall, you have to increase the kernel parameter for mbufs and/or mbclusters, rebuild the kernel, and reboot. This is real bad news for your uptime statistics.

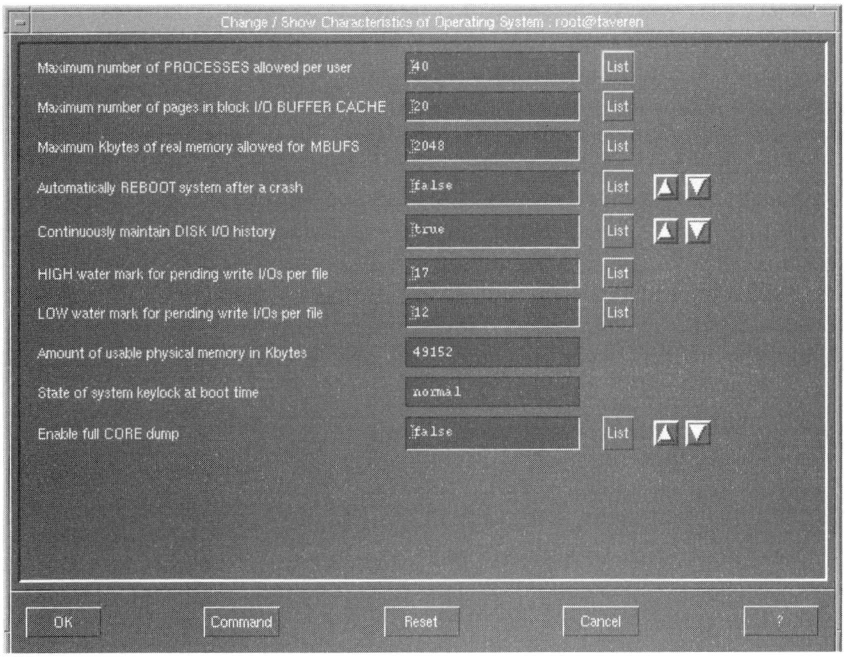

Figure 31.1 SMIT operating system parameters panel.

AIX provides an mbuf management facility that dynamically controls the allocation and use of mbufs and mbclusters. The default allocation is based on a low to medium packet rate and is somewhat dependent on the number of adapters. The mbuf management facility netm uses a set of parameters to control the minimum and maximum available free space in the pools and the maximum amount of memory that may be used for the pools. Note that the mbuf and mbcluster pools are pinned in memory. netm increases the pool sizes as network load increases. The mbcluster pool is reduced as load decreases; however, the mbuf pool is never decreased. Each mbuf is 256 bytes in size, and each mbcluster is 4,096 bytes. You don't want netm to be dispatched unnecessarily, and you don't want to overcommit memory to mbuf pools. What you need to do is monitor your packet rates under normal loads and adjust the mbuf parameters to pin as much memory as you will need and no more. Use the netstat command to check mbuf utilization during heavy traffic. If statistics indicate that mbuf requests are being denied, increase the value of thewall using the no command.

```
# netstat -m            Check MBUF utilization
# no -o thewall=[value]  Set new MBUF limit
```

Some network environments require modification of other kernel network parameters like "time to live" and "keep alive" values. The no command can be used to display and set a number of these kernel network parameters.

no -a   Query TCPIP network option settings

```
thewall = 8192
sb_max = 65536
somaxconn = 1024
net_malloc_police = 0
rto_low = 1
rto_high = 64
rto_limit = 7
rto_length = 13
arptab_bsiz = 7
arptab_nb = 25
tcp_ndebug = 100
ifsize = 8
arpqsize = 1
strmsgsz = 0
strctlsz = 1024
nstrpush = 8
strthresh = 85
psetimers = 20
psebufcalls = 20
strturncnt = 15
pseintrstack = 12288
lowthresh = 90
medthresh = 95
subnetsarelocal = 1
maxttl = 255
ipfragttl = 60
ipsendredirects = 1
ipforwarding = 0
udp_ttl = 30
tcp_ttl = 60
arpt_killc = 20
tcp_sendspace = 16384
tcp_recvspace = 16384
udp_sendspace = 9216
udp_recvspace = 41600
rfc1122addrchk = 0
nonlocsrcroute = 0
tcp_keepintvl = 150
tcp_keepidle = 14400
bcastping = 0
udpcksum = 1
```

```
tcp_mssdflt = 512
icmpaddressmask = 0
tcp_keepinit = 150
ie5_old_multicast_mapping = 0
rfc1323 = 0
ipqmaxlen = 100
directed_broadcast = 1<<t>>
```

```
# no -o [parameter]=[value]        Set TCPIP network option
```

31.3   AIX Monitoring and Tuning Tools

AIX V4 has repackaged a number of your favorite performance tools into separately installed filesets. These filesets make up two new performance monitoring and diagnostic systems called Performance Diagnostics Tool (PDT) and PerfPMR. Both systems are catchall monitoring tools for checking the pulse of your overall system. Support AIX monitoring tools are located in the performance toolbox (PTX) fileset.

`bos.perf.diag_tool`	Performance Diagnostics Tool
`/usr/sbin/perf/diag_tool`	PDT executables
`perfagent.tools`	PTX performance tools

Install bos.perf.diag_tool to gain access to PDT. PDT is a system monitoring tool that runs continuously and generates daily reports in /var/perf/tmp/PDT_REPORT. After installing PDT, you invoke pdt_config to configure and start the monitor. PDT resides in the /usr/sbin/perf/diag_tool directory.

The second package, perfpmr, is installed from the bos.perf.pmr fileset. perfpmr is designed to gather system statistics to assist in problem reporting and resolution. After installing the system, invoke perfpmr during your heaviest workload to create a baseline profile of your system. Run the system again when you have made a system change or suspect problems. The two performance datasets can be compared to gain insight into problem configurations. perfpmr resides in the /usr/sbin/perf/pmr directory and generates to /var/perf/tmp. When working a problem with IBM support, tar together the data from /var/perf/tmp and mail it to:

IBM Corporation, Mail Drop 2900
11400 Burnet Road
Austin TX, 78758
Attn: AIX Program Services V4DEFECT

To set the baseline profile for your system, invoke:

```
# perfpmr 3600
```

General configuration and interval sampled data from the monitor parameter will be written to the following files:

File	Command data
monitor.int	`ps -elk`, `ps gv` (before and after)
	`sar -A`
	`iostat`
	`vmstat`
monitor.sum	Averages from above commands
netstat.int	`netstat -v`
	`netstat -m`
	`netstat -rs`
	`netstat -s`
nfsstat.int	`nfsstat -csnr`
Pprof.stt, Pprof.flow	Process profile (PID, PPID, times, etc.)

If you like to monitor your system the old-fashioned way, you can run the commands used by PDT and PerfPMR individually. Performance monitoring tools available under AIX V4 are listed in the next two sections. You will have to install the PTX perfagent.tools fileset to gain access to some of the AIX-specific tools.

31.3.1 Traditional UNIX tools

`uptime, rup`	Provide system load averages and the current number of users. These are quick, one-stop commands to get a brief picture of system activity.
`ps`	Displays process table statistics. Don't underestimate the information you can get from ps. AIX supports both SYSV and BSD options. You can easily set up shell aliases with ps to get quick information on the top CPU and storage users on your system. Use ps to check for defunct processes that may be tying up memory.
`sar`	System Activity Recorder. Along with sadc, sa1, and sa2, it can be used to take snapshots of system activity for all or specific system resources at specified intervals. Use cron to regularly execute sar at specific times based on your workload profile, and the sa1, sa2 scripts to maintain a report history of system usage.
`vmstat`	Provides statistics on process queues, memory, paging, interrupts, and CPU usage. You can run vmstat at specified intervals and repetitions to take a quick look at memory and CPU usage.

iostat	Similar to vmstat in that it can be run for specified intervals and number of repetitions. Provides usage statistics on CPU and the I/O subsystem. Using the -d flag will display a snapshot of disk I/O activity.
pstat	Similar to crash in that it allows you to display the contents of various systems tables. Not interactive.
netstat	Provides various information on network activity. The -m flag can be used to review mbuf allocation. There are options to display routing tables and current connections statistics.
nfsstat	Displays information concerning NFS and RPC interfaces. You may distinguish between client and server information as well as NFS and RPC traffic.
acctcom, acctcms	Process and display system accounting information from the /usr/adm/pacct file—acctcom provides a detailed process chronology by user; acctcms combines identical process information to give you overall system totals.
gprof, time, timex	If you have tracked resource untilization problems down to a specific application, these tools provide a means of profiling and tuning the code. time and timex can be used to snapshot the user, system, and wall clock execution times. gprof will provide CPU usage by subroutine and a call graph profile of the application. Note that you must compile the code with the -pg option.

31.3.2 AIX specific tools

trace, trcrpt	Allow you to record and report on system events at a finer granularity than any of the other performance tools in this set. System events are time-stamped such that the sequence and context of execution is maintained. The trace facility does not cause significant additional overhead to the running system. System tracing is started and stopped using the trcon and trcstop commands.
rmap	No longer supported in AIX V4.
filemon	Also run against trace data to provide statistics on file system performance. Provides detailed information on the most active files, logical volumes, and physical volumes in the system.
fileplace	Maps the placement of file blocks within logical and physical volumes. Indicates the level of fragmentation for files in a file system.
rmss	Simulates reductions in available real memory on the RS/6000. This tool is quite useful when monitoring the behavior of an application in a memory-constrained situation.

svmon	Displays a snapshot of virtual memory. Note that it is not entirely accurate because it is run in user state with interrupts enabled.
netpmon	Also uses trace data to monitor network activity. netpmon is a new version of what was formally known as netmon in older versions of AIX. It gathers statistics on CPU usage; device driver queue lengths and utilization; socket calls; and NFS I/O calls.
lockstat	Provides statistics on kernel locks. Very helpful in diagnosing locking problems when running an MP kernel.
lslv, lvmake, lvedit, lvextend, reorgvg	Provide finer grained control over the definition and allocation of logical and physical volumes in the system. Quite useful when tuning the placement of databases.
tprof	Used like its predecessor gprof to profile CPU usage by subroutine in an application. Does not require that the application be recompiled but will provide additional information if the application is compiled with the -qlist option.

31.3.3 Graphical performance and monitoring tools

If you fancy performance tools that provide graphical modeling and reporting interfaces, then I would suggest you take a look at the following packages. They each have their merits and are best left to the end user to decide how well they map to a particular environment. Three of the best are:

IBM Performance Toolbox/6000

AIX Capacity Planner from BGS Systems

DEC Capacity Planner

31.3.4 Public domain monitor package

If you're on a budget, take a look at the public domain monitor package written by Jussi Maki. The package provides pseudo-real time statistics on CPU, memory, and I/O utilization and rates (see Fig. 31.2). An ASCII-based interface allows it to be used with most display types. The monitor system may be downloaded via anonymous FTP from aix-pdslib.seas.ucla.edu.

```
# monitor
```

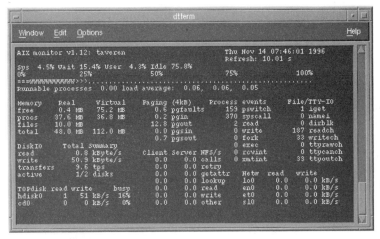

Figure 31.2   Monitor panel.

31.4   Additional Help and Documentation

Take a look at the *AIX Versions 3.2 and 4 Performance Monitoring and Tuning Guide,* SC23-2365. This document contains a wealth of information and examples. Your IBM SE can also assist in tuning and capacity-planning activities.

31.5   InfoExplorer Keywords

tprof	rup
nice	ps
renice	sar
setpri	sadc
schedtune	sa1
rmss	sa2
maxpout	vmstat
minpout	iostat
chgsys	pstat
no	netstat
ping	nfsstat
mbuf	acctcom
uptime	acctcms

gprof	lslv
time	lvmake
timex	lvedit
trace	lvextend
trcrpt	reorgvg
filemon	repage
fileplace	perfpmr
svmon	PDT
netpmon	PTX

31.6   QwikInfo

Kernel parameters:

`getpri(), setpri()`	Set/query process queue priority
`schedtune, vmtune`	VMM and kernel tuning
`smit chgsys`	Set kernel parameters
`no`	Display/set kernel network parameters
`PDT, bos.perf.diag_tool`	Performance Diagnostic Tool
`PerfPMR, bos.perf.pmr`	PMR performance collector
`PTX, perfagent.tools`	AIX performance tools

32

Problem Analysis and Recovery

32.1 When Things Go Bump in the Night

Do you ever wonder if there isn't a little gremlin lurking just behind the front cover of your RS/6000? From time to time you just catch a glimpse of two beady little eyes peering out of the diskette slot. You do a double take, and nothing is blinking except one of the tape or diskette lights. With a nervous shrug you go ahead and fire up that high-priority application you have put off until the very last minute. Just at the critical point in your timeline, you notice an eerie flickering in the room. With a sinking feeling in your stomach, you look at the front panel, and there it is: the dreaded flashing 888. Fingers trembling, you press the RESET button and stare at the play of glowing numbers after each touch. Your luck continues to fail as the dump LED reads 0c5. System dump attempted and failed. You power down, pause to wipe the sweat off your brow, and power-cycle back up. The numbers dance across the LED window. Is that a malevolent giggling you hear? It can't be. You tell yourself that it's only too many hours of overtime or one too many lattes. With bloodshot eyes you wince at the glare from the LEDs, and they pound into your head: 888, 888, 888 . . . Too bad you can't have the same fun with a PowerPC. No LEDs (sigh)!

Gruesome, isn't it? The only thing missing is "It was a dark and stormy night." Don't get me wrong; I'm not insinuating that system failures and panics are particularly commonplace on the POWER or PowerPC systems. Failures do happen however, and they usually occur at the most inopportune times. The trick is to make sure that you have your system logging and recovery homework done before the gremlins begin playing with your sanity.

32.2   Backups and Bootable Media

Backups. If you don't have them, then none of the rest of this information is going to do you much good. It's surprising how many calls I get from users who are hoping for a miracle, one that will recover a bad disk because they never took the time to do backups. See Chap. 24 for details on system backups.

Next, make sure you have multiple copies of stand-alone bootable media that reflect the new system's install and maintenance level. Notice I said *multiple copies*. I must admit that I have been bitten more than once by having only a single copy of some crucial bit of data. Create a backup image of the new rootvg on tape using the mksysb command. These tapes can be used to recover from a disk failure or be used to install additional machines. Begin by using the mkszfile command to create a /image.data file. This file contains descriptive information about the file systems in the rootvg. Edit this file so that it contains only those file systems you wish to include in your reference set. Use the following procedures to create the backup and bootable images. When booting from the stand-alone tape, the AIX Install/Maint shell is executed. This will guide you through the restoration process.

To create a backup copy of the root volume group:

`# mkszfile`	Create rootvg map
`# chdev -l rmt0 -a block_size=512`	Set correct block size
`# tctl -f/dev/rmt0 rewind`	Rewind tape
`# mksysb /dev/rmt0`	Create backup
`# chdev -l rmt0 -a` `  block_size=<blocksize>`	Reset tape block size

To create bootable media:

`# cp /var/adm/ras/bosinst.data` `  /bosinst.data`	Create bosinst.data
`# mkszfile`	Create rootvg map
`# chdev -l rmt0 -a block_size=512`	Set correct block size
`# tctl -f/dev/rmt0 rewind`	Rewind tape
`# bosboot -ad /dev/rmt0.1`	Create boot image
`# mkinsttape /dev/rmt0`	Create bos install/maintenance
`# chdev -l rmt0 -a block_size=<blocksize>`	Reset tape block size

Make certain that you test the media after creating it. It will bring you peace of mind and familiarize you with the stand-alone boot procedure:

1. Set system key in service position (if present).

2. Insert a CD-ROM or tape containing a boot image and power on the system.

3. When prompted, select the console display.

4. Select "Start Maintenance Mode for System Recovery."

5. Select "Access Advanced Maintenance Mode Functions."

32.3 LED Status Information

If you don't have LEDs on your computer front panel, go grab a cup of coffee and then skip down to Sec. 32.4, System Memory Dumps.

The story always begins with the dreaded flashing 888 on the LED front panel. Before deciding to punt and hitting the power switch, press the RESET button to cycle though the set of four halt status numbers. These numbers indicate the current system state, the reason for the halt, and the dump state. Write them down. You're going to need them later in the analysis processes. Here is the sequence:

```
888 - bbb - eee - ddd
```

The first number following 888 on the LED display, represented by bbb in the example, indicates the hardware built-in self-test (BIST) status. In most cases, the BIST status will read 102, which indicates that BIST has started following a system reset. Other values may indicate a hardware problem. The next number, represented by eee, indicates the cause of the system halt (see Table 32.1).

The last number in the sequence indicates the status of any dump associated with the failure (see Table 32.2).

TABLE 32.1   LED Halt Reason Code

20x	Machine checks
300	Storage interrupt: processor
32x	Storage interrupt: I/O channel controller
38x	Storage interrupt: Serial link adapter
400	Storage interrupt: instruction
500	External interrupt: DMA, bus error
52x	External interrupt: IOCC checks/time out
53x	External interrupt: IOCC time out
700	Program interrupt
800	Floating point unavailable

TABLE 32.2   LED Dump Status Codes

0C0	Dump successful
0C2	User dump in progress
0C4	Partial dump successful
0C5	Dump device not accessible
0C6	Prompt for secondary dump device
0C7	Remote dump in progress
0C8	No dump device defined
0C9	Dump in progress

32.4   System Memory Dumps

When a system fault occurs, an automatic dump of selected kernel address regions are recorded on the dump device as defined in the master dump table. The primary dump device is a dedicated storage area for holding dumps. A shared secondary device that requires operator intervention may be defined. The default primary dump device is /dev/hd6 and the secondary device is sysdumpnull by default. Dump devices are defined and managed using the sysdumpdev command or using the SMIT FastPath dump (see Figs. 32.1 and 32.2). Make certain

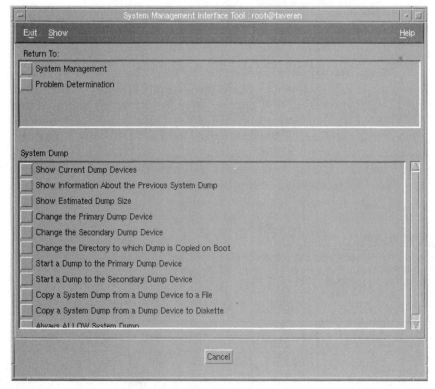

Figure 32.1   SMIT system "dump admin" panel.

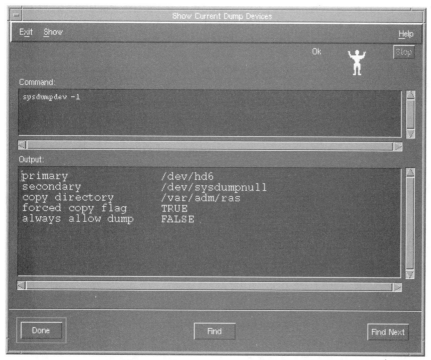

Figure 32.2   SMIT system "dump device" panel.

that your dump device is assigned and is large enough to contain at least one full dump.

```
# sysdumpdev -L    List current dump status
# sysdumpdev -l    List primary dump device location
# sysdumpdev -P    Assign dump device
# smit dump
```

Although it is acceptable to interrogate kernel dumps residing in the primary dump area, it's a good idea to copy them onto an AIX file system or removable media type. This will secure the data and free up the dump area for problems lurking in your future. Use snap to read from the raw dump device, or mount the dump device and use cp or backup to copy the dump to alternate storage. You can also manage dump files using SMIT.

```
# snap -gfkD -o /dev/<output-dev>
# mkdir /tmp/dumpdev
# mount /dev/<dump-device>/tmp/dumpdev
# cp /tmp/dump-dev/dump-name /tmp/dump-name
# ls /tmp/dumpdev | backup -ifv
```

You can force a system panic dump by using the sysdumpstart command, using SMIT, or by turning the key to the service position (if present) and pressing the LEFT-CNTRL+ALT+1 keys simultaneously.

32.5   System Logs

Now that your disaster recovery media is in place, it's always nice to be able to determine why you crashed in the first place. Start by looking at the system error log. The error log file /var/adm/ras/errlog is updated by /usr/lib/errdemon, which is executed at system startup. The error daemon reads system exception data from /dev/error and creates entries in the log file based on templates from /var/adm/ras/errtmplt and the message catalog /usr/lpp/msg/$LANG/codepoint.cat. You can produce a report of entries in the error log by running the errpt command or using smit errpt. Make sure that you save and clean out error log data periodically so that problem information doesn't get lost in the noise. You can accomplish both of these tasks by having cron regularly back up the error log and then clear out old information using the errclear command via the SMIT FastPath error. There are also commands that allow you to add your own error templates and messages to the system for custom applications (see Figs. 32.3 and 32.4).

errpt	Create error log report
errclear	Clear error log
errstop	Stop errdemon
errupdate	Update templates
errmsg	Add/display error message catalog

Individual events in the error log report are identified by error type labels. The labels are listed in the *AIX Problem Solving Guide and Reference,* SC23-2204. Each error event is time-stamped and listed with summary information by type. For example, suppose the LED halt rea-

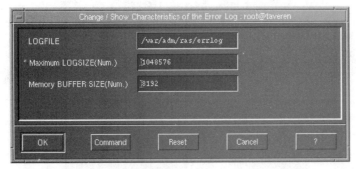

Figure 32.3   SMIT error log panel.

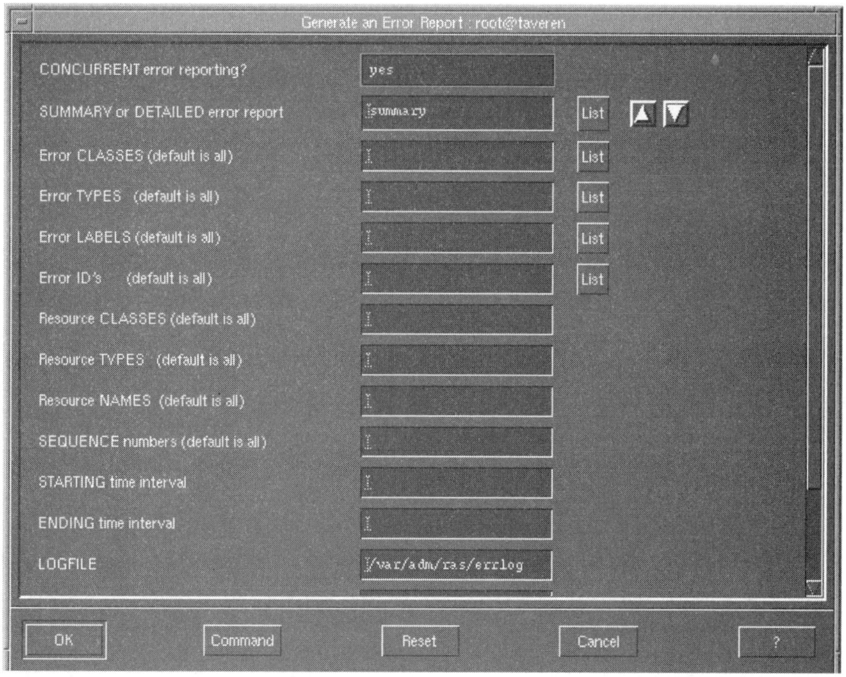

Figure 32.4   SMIT "generate error report" panel.

son code was 700, indicating that a program interrupt caused the crash. The error log should contain an entry labeled **PROGRAM_INT**, time-stamped with the date and time of the failure. The associated detail data lists the segment, status, and state registers (SRRs) entries that point to the subroutine and instruction involved in the failure. This information will be used when analyzing the dump.

Here is an example of an error log entry:

```
ERROR LABEL:        PROGRAM_INT
ERROR ID:           DD11B4AF

Date/Time:          Wed Dec 8 11:46:08
Sequence Number:    484128
Machine Id:         000015086600
Node Id:            mead
Class:              S
Type:               PERM
Resource Name:      SYSPROC
Error Description
Program Interrupt

Probable Causes
SOFTWARE PROGRAM
```

```
Failure Causes
SOFTWARE PROGRAM

Recommended Actions
IF PROBLEM PERSISTS THEN DO THE FOLLOWING
CONTACT APPROPRIATE SERVICE REPRESENTATIVE

Detail Data
Segment Register, SEGREG
0000 0000
Machine Status Save/Restore Register 0
0005 3AC4
Machine Status Save/Restore Register 1
0002 0000
Machine State Register, MSR
0002 90B0
```

The next place to look is at messages created by syslogd. The syslogd daemon receives messages via datagram sockets created by applications that use the syslog subroutine. syslogd directs the incoming messages to files or other systems as described by entries in the /etc/syslog.conf file. This file is read each time syslogd is started or receives a HUP signal. Due to the application-specific nature of syslogd, AIX provides an example /etc/syslog.conf template that must be configured to your application requirements. Each line in /etc/syslog.conf contains message selectors separated by semicolons followed by a field indicating where the message is to be sent. Incoming messages specify a facility code that represents one of the selectors. See /usr/include/sys/syslog.h for a list of codes and selectors. In the following example, mail messages are sent to a central repository on another system called daffy; all debug messages, to /var/adm/debug.log; kernel critical and emergency messages, to /var/adm/kernel.log; and alert messages, to the ops user ID.

```
/***********Example /etc/sys.log.conf*************/
mail                     @daffy
*.debug                  /var/adm/debug.log
kern.crit;kern.emerg     /var/adm/kernel.log
*.alert                  ops
```

Remember that for real-time debugging, you can always use the system trace for even finer detail.

```
trcon       Start trace
trcstop     Stop trace
trcrpt      Generate trace report
```

32.6   AIX Kernel Structure

With the error log and LED status information in hand, we are ready to examine the dump. First, let's lay a little groundwork concerning the characteristics of the AIX kernel. AIX is based on a preemptible kernel. The kernel is divided into pinned and pageable regions. The pinned low region of the kernel contains the interrupt handler, the kernel text and data areas, the process table, and the page map. Pageable kernel regions included the file table; vnode, gnode, and inode structures; and kernel extensions. It is important to remember that activities and services in the pageable kernel region are synchronous, whereas the pinned region activities are asynchronous. For example, an external I/O interrupt may be serviced by the pinned region long after the process initiating the request has completed its time slice and has been paged out.

Interrupts are divided into processor and external interrupt classes. All I/O type interrupts are multiplexed into one external interrupt. External interrupts include I/O bus and system board devices. External interrupts are the only interrupt class that can be masked. Processor interrupts include system reset, machine check, storage, program, alignment, floating point, and SVC interrupts.

Memory addresses are based on a 32-bit (POWER) or 64-bit (PowerPC) effective address and a 24-bit segment address. The first four most significant bits of the effective address represent one of sixteen segment registers. The remaining 28 bits of the effective address are used along with the 24-bit segment address to indicate a position in virtual memory (see Table 32.3).

Kernel and application address spaces are somewhat similar. For debugging purposes, it is important to understand the general layout of kernel regions. The exact addresses of kernel boundaries will be dependent on the AIX release you are running. Here are the kernel symbols and addresses for V3.2.5:

TABLE 32.3   AIX Address Segments

0	Kernel segment (data and extensions)
1	Text segment
2	Private process segment (data, u-block, and stack)
3-C	Available
B	VMM data
D	Shared libraries
E	Reserved
F	I/O support

Beginning of kernel	`0x00000000`
End of pinned kernel	`pin_obj_end`
Table of contents	`TOC`
End of kernel	`endcomm`
Process table offset	`0xe3000000`

It's a good idea to generate a complete listing of kernel symbols and addresses for use when analyzing a dump. Use the nm command on the kernel object file associated with the dump.

```
# nm -vfx /unix
```

32.7   Using crash

The crash command can be run in interactive or batch mode. Batch mode is useful when you need to send a formatted dump to IBM support. Use the crash -a option directed to a file to produce a formatted crash dump. For an interactive session, invoke crash, specifying the dump file or device and kernel file as arguments.

```
# crash /dev/hd6 /unix                              Interactive mode
# crash -a /dev/hd6 /unix > /tmp/crash.MMDD          Batch mode
```

Here are some useful crash subcommands:

p	Display process blocks of all processes or a particular process.
u	Display u-block or u-area. If no process ID is given, the running process at the time of the dump is displayed.
ds	Offset to the nearest kernel symbol.
nm	Display address of a symbol.
od	Display hexadecimal dump of memory.
trace	Display traceback of stack.
dump	Dump information.
?	Help.

Now you are ready to get down to business. Display the u-area of the process running at the time of the dump by entering the u subcommand without an argument (or nasty comments). A formatted display of the process private u-area is displayed. The first line of the display indicates the process name and process table address. Each process table entry on the RS/6000 is 0x100 bytes in length. Subtract the process table offset, 0xE3000000, from the process slot address. Ignore the lower two digits of the answer and you have the process slot number of the last running process. The u-block and process table data will provide you with the process state, executing program, open files, locks, controlling TTY, and so on. Use the following as an example:

```
# crash /dev/hd7

Using /unix as the default namelist file.
Reading in Symbols ......................

>u Display u-block

    USER AREA FOR xperfmon (ProcTable Address 0xE3001200)

Do the arithmetic ...............

Process slot address     0xE3001200

Process table offset      - 0xE3000000
                         =============
                          0x1200
Ignore lower 2 digits     0x12
Decimal Process Slot ID   18

>p - 18   Display Process Table Entry
```

The trace, nm, and ds subcommands are very helpful when diagnosing kernel problems. The trace subcommand provides a look backwards through the kernel stack. The nm and ds commands display the address for a symbol or the symbol associated with an address range, respectively. Error log and LED information may be more helpful with kernel problems than the current running process information. For example, in the case of exceptions caused by an interrupt, the process that requested the service related to the interrupt may have been paged out while the request was being serviced.

In the event of a system hang, you may not have error log or LED data to assist. The hang may be the result of a resource deadlock or a looping process. If a deadlock is suspected, check the proc_lock and kernel_lock symbols. Look at the RW values displayed by nm. A hexadecimal value of ffffffff indicates that the lock is free; otherwise, the value is the PID of the process holding the lock. If a high-priority process loop is responsible for the hang, then it is likely to be the last process executing (if you're lucky). For an addressing exception, use nm to locate the vmmerrlog structure. Check the vmm return code and fault address at offsets 0x20 and 0x1C, respectively. Next, use trace to display the failing routine, followed by ds to locate the offset within the failing routine. If the exception was in a kernel extension, you may have to walk the kernel load list, as kernel extensions are pageable.

Running down the culprit in a crash caused by an interrupt can be a bit tricky. As mentioned earlier, the requesting process may have been paged out. If segment register data was logged in the error log, the address in SRR0 will indicate the return address of the routine that caused or is waiting for a program interrupt to be serviced. External interrupt conditions will likely log the IOCC bus number and interrupt level.

32.8 Hardware Diagnostics

The RS/6000 is very good about checking its hardware during the built-in self-test (BIST) at power-up time. Keeping track of the LED information during system power-up will assist you in debugging hardware problems. If you suspect hardware problems or the system won't boot, use the diagnostic programs to assist in determining the failure. The diagnostic programs may be run in stand-alone mode from diskettes or in concurrent mode with AIX online using the diag command. For concurrent mode operation, as superuser enter the diag command and follow the menu instructions. Follow the procedure for booting to stand-alone mode in Sec. 32.2.

32.9 Calling for Help

Once you have determined that a software or hardware problem exists, collect all the pertinent log, dump, and LED information before contacting IBM support. You might also want to run the snap, lslpp -hBc > filename, and perfprm commands to snapshot the maintenance level and configuration of your system.

You can review the problem and service database yourself if you have network access to IBMLink or Support Line sites. If you don't have network access to these sites, IBM provides periodic snapshots of the IBMLink question and service databases on CD-ROM. Order AIX Technical Library/6000 CD-ROM. See Table 32.4 and Appendix A for additional information on AIX help sites and archives on the Internet. The more information you gather, the faster your problem is going to be resolved.

You are now ready to contact IBM support.

TABLE 32.4   AIX Support on the Internet

# telnet IBMLink.advantis.com	Remote login
http://service.software.ibm.com/aixsupport	Web sites
http://www.ibmlink.ibm.com/	
http://www.austin.ibm.com/services/	

IBM Support
1-800-237-5511

IBM AIX/6000 support offers a number of options for specialist assistance for installation, problem solving, and tuning. For general information, contact AIX support at:

AIX/6000 Support Family
40-B2-05
IBM Corporation
P.O. Box 9000
Roanoke, Texas 76262-9989

1-800-CALL-AIX
1-800-IBM-4FAX
call-aix@vnet.ibm.com

You can download patches and fixes over the Internet using IBM's FixDist tool kit. FixDist is an FTP interface that allows users to select and retrieve maintenance from anonymous FTP servers at the service.software.ibm.com site. You can select maintenance by PTF and APAR numbers. FixDist will take care of ensuring that all requisite fixes are included in the set. A companion tool called TapeGen can then be used to stack the fixes onto a tape that can be read by SMIT. This is handy if you are maintaining a large number of machines that don't have access to a network install service. These tools are available via anonymous FTP from service.software.ibm.com in the /aix/tools/fixdist directory.

```
# ftp service.software.ibm.com
   login: anonymous
   password:your-email@address.com
   ftp> bin
   ftp> cd/aix/tools/fixdist
   ftp> get fd.tar.Z     FixDist tool
   ftp> get fixdist.ps.ZPostScript users guide
   ftp> quit
```

After uncompressing and untarring FixDist into a directory on your workstation, you can invoke the tool by typing fixdistc for character mode or fixdistm for X-display (see Fig. 32.5). Tailor FixDist for your site. Configuration information will be stored in $HOME/.fixdist_home/.fixdistcfg. Download a copy of the current fix database fddb. You can now search and select fixes from the database for downloading from the FTP fix server (see Fig. 32.6).

If you have access to a Usenet news service, check out the comp.unix.aix discussion and archives. The best help information

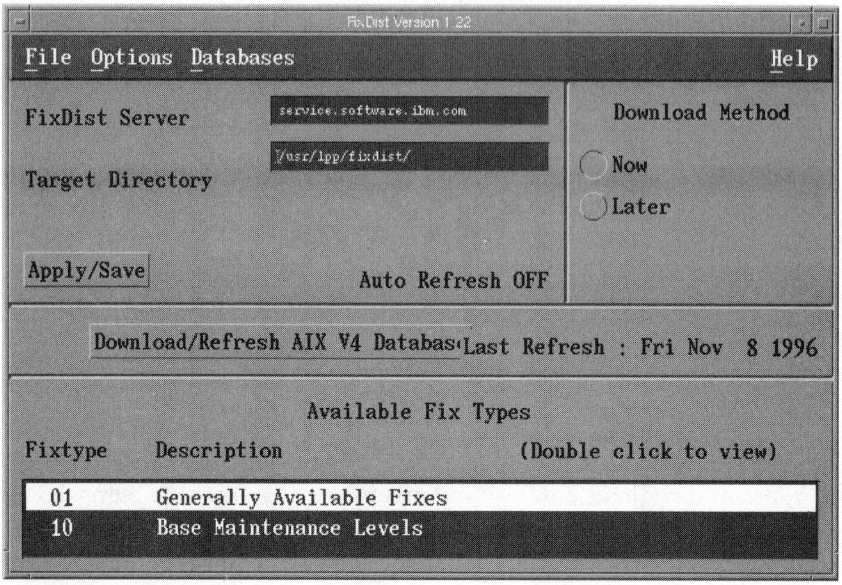

Figure 32.5 FixDist display.

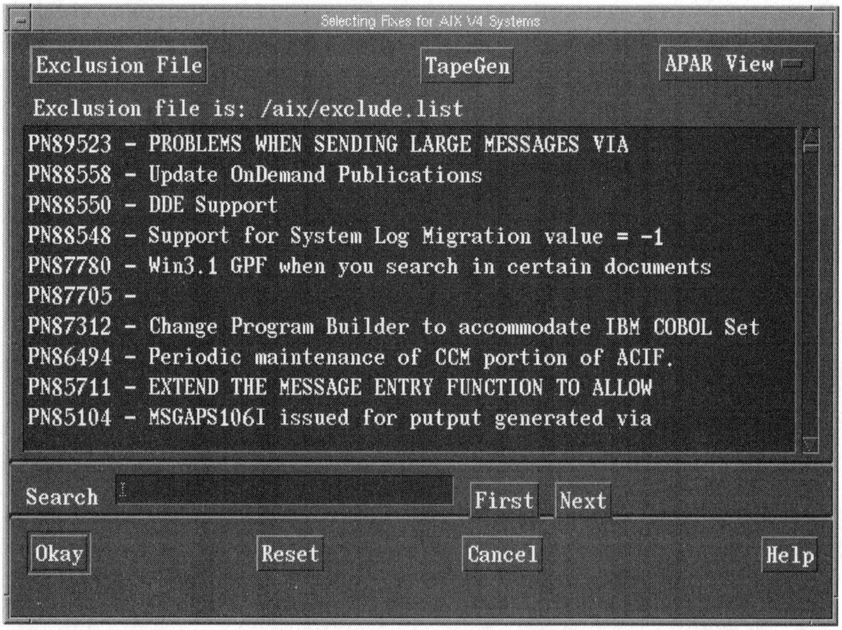

Figure 32.6 FixDist search and select.

comes from peers who are using AIX in the field. IBM support personnel and developers also watch these groups and may lend assistance.

It's always a good plan of action to read the required texts as part of the homework. Take a look at *RISC System / 6000 Diagnostic Programs: Operators Guide,* SA23-2631-05; *RISC System / 6000 Problem Solving Guide,* SC23-2204-02; and *AIX Version 3.2 for RISC System / 6000 Installation Guide,* SC23-2341-05.

32.10   InfoExplorer Keywords

bosboot	errpt	trcrpt
mkdispdskt	errclear	panic
mkextdskt	errstop	dump
mkinstdskt	errupdate	sysdumpstart
getrootfs	errmsg	dd
mksysb	errinstall	crash
mkszfile	syslogd	errdead
.fs.size	/etc/syslog.conf	nm
errdemon	trcon	diag
/var/adm/ras/errlog	trcstop	snap

32.11   QwikInfo

RootVG backup:

mkszfile	Create rootvg map for mksysb
mksysb <media>	Backup RootVG

System error logs:

errdemon	Error daemon
errpt	Error log report
errclear	Clear error log
errstop	Stop error daemon
errupdate, errmsg	Update error message catalogs and templates
/var/adm/ras/errtmplt	Error message templates

System trace:

trcon, trcstop	Start/stop tracing
trcrpt	Generate trace report

System dumps:

`sysdumpdev`	Set/display dump device
`sysdumpstart`	Force a panic dump
`errdead`	Retrieve /dev/error
`crash`	Format/review a dump
`nm`	Display symbol table

Advanced Distributed Architectures

33

Clustering

33.1 Cluster Overview

What do you get when you tie a bunch of RS/6000s together with a network? Answer: a loosely coupled multiprocessor capable of supporting batch, parallel, and multiuser workloads at a fraction of the cost of a high-end mainframe. RISC and Pentium workstations are already exceeding the CPU performance and addressing range of all but the techno-elite of mainframe engines. Innovations in networking bandwidth are rapidly approaching and surpassing I/O bandwidth of traditional storage devices. All that's required is the software smoke and mirrors to make the group function as a single system image.

Case in point: The IBM SP product line represents cluster complexes of 2 to 512 individual POWER, POWER2, or PowerPC nodes. An SP cluster can also include 2- to 8-way SMP nodes. Tie the SP complex together with a high speed switch operating at a hardware peak rate of 300 MB/sec, bidirectional, node-to-node, and you have a computer cluster that challenges the largest mainframe collosus. The Load Leveler queuing system and AIX cluster support work together to make an SP cluster function as a unit. Sure it's expensive, but we're talking top of the line here. You'd be amazed at what can be done with just a few Power-PCs and lower-speed networks like FDDI and Ethernet. Feature a cluster architecture of sixty 80-MHz RS/6000 250s with an Ethernet Front door network for interactive traffic and a FDDI back door network for data traffic. Partition work profiles in the cluster such that some of the nodes support interactive logins, some nodes provide file service, and others are dedicated to specific application services like electronic mail and Web support. Would you believe that this cluster can support 55,000 user accounts with 4,000 concurrent logins distributed across thirty machines? How about 1.4 million logins per month with peaks of

4,000 logins per hour? While all this is going on, the cluster supports password updates across all machines in seconds. Now add a half million mail messages per day. It's real. We built it here at the University of Washington. This cluster represents high-level system linking to enable a single system view of the cluster. No kernel hacking here. I'll use this architecture as an example of how clustering can be tailored to meet the requirements of specific application environments.

33.2 Rules of the Road

When we first embarked down the clustered highway years ago, there was little more than distributed batch software systems available in the marketplace. We wanted to expand the batch cluster concept to include interactive work and client/server applications. A number of interesting papers had been presented at various conferences on the topic, but most included some fairly heavy kernel work. We wanted to limit operating system and command modifications to ensure that we would be able to buy shrink-wrapped systems off the shelf and not find ourselves in an endless cycle of retrofitting kernel modifications. Kernel modification also assumes that you have source code! These are the criteria we used to define the project:

Single system image—one domain address per cluster

Minimized operating system and command modifications

Workload kept well within limits of hardware and software

Open systems and standard protocols

Heterogeneous architectures supported where sensible

System and network boundaries hidden from user base

With these goals in mind, we have been quite successful in implementing clusters for all our application sets. Early on, we found that, although we could throw hardware (processors, memory, network) at a problem, it was often an operating system or a system management problem that limited the size and scope of a cluster. We have been able to overcome most of these limitations by addressing four software subsystems: domain name service, the password system, software/configuration installation, and network file system. First, a word about cluster hardware topology.

33.3 Hardware Topology

The majority of the systems we use in our clusters are various flavors of RS/6000 and DEC computers. We also have a few HP systems. An important criterion for us when choosing a platform is support for UID spaces larger than 32,000. The cluster members are made up of compute servers, application servers, file servers, password servers, and a reference system. Access to the compute and application servers is provided via a front door Ethernet network. The compute and application servers communicate with the file and password servers via a back door FDDI network to isolate data I/O traffic from the user community (Fig. 33.1). The cluster file servers and back door networks are linked together using a set of crossbar switches. The switches are connected in turn to our backup and archive server system and STK tape silos. A dedicated switch is used to link a RAID disk farm to our research cluster. The consoles from all the cluster computers are connected to a set of terminal servers that reside on a secure subnet. A special-purpose server on this subnet is then used by operations and support staff to access the console of any machine using an X-terminal. Locally developed software monitors and logs the console data from each machine in the cluster. Authentication to the console server is provided via a SecurID card challenge.

The following are more detailed discussions of the cluster server types (see also Fig. 33.2):

Cluster HardwareTopology

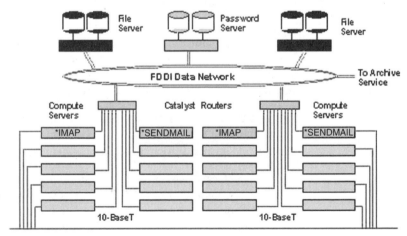

Figure 33.1   Cluster hardware topology.

Figure 33.2   RS/6000 250 cluster.

Compute servers	These are the machines onto which you log to read your mail or to do your work. They are usually what you think of when you refer to "the computer." Reference them using a single host name like "Homer." They are individually identified by adding numbers to the general computer name (such as Homer01, Homer 02, etc.). It does not matter which of these machines you connect to—they all perform the same functions and share access to the same user file systems.
File servers	Mail folders and other user files are made available to the compute servers by file servers using NFS, AFS, or DFS. In some instances, a set of file servers may support more than one cluster.
Password servers	Identity and authentication in a cluster is managed by a master password server. These servers make certain that the local copies of the password files on each of the cluster computers are kept in synchronization.
Application servers	If special application services are required that are not appropriate for execution on the compute servers, dedicated application servers are used to provide the service via a networked client/server software interface. Application servers are used to keep resource-intensive software partitioned away from general interactive processes to minimize contention.

Mail servers   The popularity and resource demands of electronic mail service has mandated that we treat it as a separate cluster component. Similar to the application servers, mail servers offload and isolate mail processing overhead away from the compute servers. The mail servers process incoming mail and manage user inboxes. They may also be used for outbound delivery.

33.4   Single System Image

What defines a single system image? Basically, the cluster of machines should present themselves as a single machine to the user community. Resources available on any individual machine must be accessible yet hide any notion of locale outside a single cluster domain name. Some level of process queuing must be available to distribute load evenly between the processors, a common view of file system resources available from any machine in the cluster. This includes a uniform UID and GID name space, uniform file permissions, and file locking. Lastly, the cluster must support centralized operations and administration. The list goes on, but you get the idea.

33.4.1   Cluster domain name

Standard TCP-based services provide the foundation base for building the cluster. Name service based on BSD bind can be modified to respond with any one of a set of IP addresses for a single cluster domain name. A time-to-live (TTL) value of 0 is passed back to the querying system with the chosen IP address. If the system making the query does not cache the information, then this IP address will be used for this query only. There is a feature in bind such that any TTL value less than 5 minutes is reset to 5 minutes by the resolver. In practice, this 5-minute window does not cause significant problems. Without resolver caching, each name service query to resolve the cluster domain name to an IP number will result in a new call to the nameservice daemon.

To cluster a group of computers under a single domain name, a hybrid name service must be used that will respond with one of the set of possible IP addresses for a single domain name. There are a number of DNS techniques available to select from a set of IP addresses. Enabling the Beecher Shuffle algorithm in the Berkeley bind software will return a random IP address from the set of possible addresses for a given domain name. In our implementation, we have added an algorithm to Berkeley bind V4.9.2 that responds to DNS queries with a subset of the cluster IP addresses ordered by increasing system load (see Fig. 33.3). This code is a derivation of the groupd software developed by UCLA. The first address in the list is the address of the least

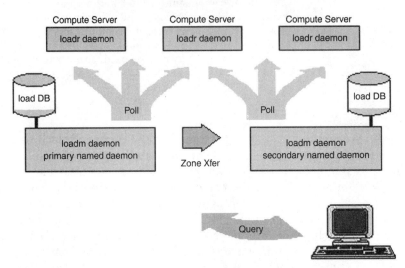

Figure 33.3   Load-based DNS.

busy machine in the cluster and thus should provide the best application response. This ordering is accomplished via information that is collected by the name service from load reporter daemons that run on each computer in the cluster. The load reporters can be tailored to collect application-specific load information. For example, you could build a load metric that included run queue load and number of logged-in users or the number of process instances of a particular application. A load manager associated with the name server records the load information in a database. This information is then used by the name server when responding to address queries. When a query is resolved, the load data is artificially incremented, assuming that a connection has been made to the cluster. The load data is then corrected at the next polling interval. This facility allows us to distribute workload evenly across the machines in a cluster. It also allows us to take machines out of service for maintenance, leaving the rest of the cluster available for service. If all the machines are down, the name server responds with the first set of addresses for the cluster.

33.4.2   Common file system

A single view of the cluster file system hierarchy from any machine in the cluster can be realized through the use of a remote file system like NFS or DCE. End user file systems are exported from a cluster NFS server to each machine. Each machine maintains a local copy of the operating system and application set based on a reference system. Note that you could use DFS replication rather than local copies. This allows each machine to function independently should the NFS server fail. The reliability of the server can be improved through the use of High-Availability Network File System/6000 (see Chap. 18).

In our implementation there are instances where the same file systems are mounted on clusters that represent different hardware and operating system architectures. The idea is to make the user's files available if it makes sense for the application profile that is supported by the cluster. When a user account is created, we set up login and shell rc files as the source default configuration files maintained in a central location. We can then modify these files and be reasonably sure that the updates will be referenced by the majority of our user community. One of the default commands run in this configuration is the arch command, which identifies the hardware and operating system architecture type. This information is then used to configure the $PATH variable to reference user and system binaries for the given architecture.

33.4.3 Scalable password service

Maintaining user credentials in a clustered environment is probably the greatest challenge when it comes to scaling clusters of machines. Until recently, many UNIX operating systems could not handle user communities larger than 32,000. As of this writing, our total user UID space across all clusters is approximately 65,000 and climbing. The scope of user name space scaling goes beyond limitations on a single architecture. Resource, security, and update information must be coordinated across hundreds of machines in a timely manner. Delays in update propagation cannot be allowed to impact simple commands and applications that rely on that data. This is especially critical at times when updates are high. As an example, we experience approximately 15,000 updates within the first week of our academic fall quarter.

The backbone of our user name space management comes from a series of servers that maintain an authentication database of all university faculty, staff, and students as well as their computing resource entitlement and mail forwarding information. These servers validate users when they run an automated utility to create accounts. Later, when a user is using his/her account, the servers answer requests from resource control managers running on each cluster computer to manage CPU and disk usage. These servers also provide mail forwarding information to the sendmail server cluster for each E-mail message arriving addressed to user@u.washington.edu (see Fig. 33.4). Although originally based on locally developed database engines, we are in the

Mail Delivery - Phase 1

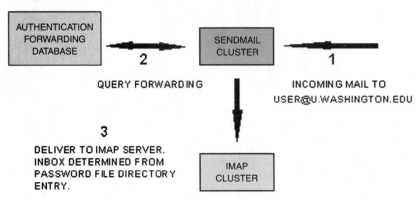

Figure 33.4   Mail flow via user information database.

process of moving this information to Informix. Benchmarking has shown that Informix servers can sustain 50 network transactions per second against our user database of 65,000. Our current environment sees about 5 transactions per second—that includes everything from mail forwarding queries to account creation and resource updates.

Once an account has been created, security information relating to the account name space must be coordinated between all the machines that make up the cluster. This is done via a master password server for each cluster (see Fig. 33.5). Updates to password information are passed to the master server via an encrypted socket session. The updates are processed by the master server using transaction semantics against an in-memory copy of the account database. These updates are then distributed to a synchronization daemon running on each computer in the cluster, which in turn updates a local copy of the password information in a dbm database. The updates to the dbm files are delta updates rather than entirely rebuilt dbm databases. The password management system is one instance where we have had to augment the vendor-supplied system in order to solve scaling problems and add security. If passwd file update levels are high, the master server will group the updates received and process them as a batch. In most cases, the individual synch daemons are notified within seconds that an update has occurred. If a cluster member has fallen too far behind in updates, it can request a full copy of the password file. We are currently in the process of augmenting this environment to include Kerberos 5 and DCE services.

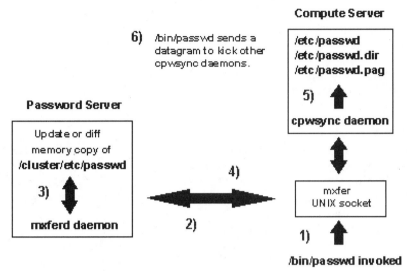

Figure 33.5   Password transaction service.

33.4.4   Configuration and installation management

A great deal of care must be taken to ensure application and configuration consistency when managing hundreds of computers. Different application profiles and configurations are required for each cluster and server. To facilitate updates and maintain uniformity, we use a locally developed tool called tulsa (Tom's User Local Source Administration) and the reference system mentioned earlier. The tulsa system maintains a profile database that describes each computer and cluster. Along with the machine profile information, tulsa manages source and binary product trees for all the application and configuration files currently in use. Once a week, tulsa checks the profiles and product sets against what is currently installed on the clusters. If an update or new product release has been added to its application tree, tulsa will install it on the system complete with error checking and logging. Tulsa also maintains a separate product tree that is used by the support staff for testing new products and configurations. Note that there are many vendor applications that provide the same kind of distributed configuration support. The only reason we haven't used them is because we were forced to develop tulsa before any of the vendor solutions were available in the market. We also need more functionality than what could be found in standard UNIX tools like rdist.

Operating system upgrades are managed under the reference system. The reference system is a computer that is configured to match the operating system profile of a cluster. Maintenance is validated on the reference system and then cloned to each of the cluster systems in turn. Installable copies of the reference systems are archived on a network install server should they be needed for recovery purposes.

33.4.5 Cluster batch queuing

To distribute batch work loads between cluster sites, you could implement a few scripts that take advantage of at, cron, rsh, and the like. However, there are packages available that perform this function with all the bells and whistles we have come to expect from more mature mainframe batch systems.

Most distributed UNIX batch queuing systems are loosely based on the Network Queuing System (NQS) model developed for the NASA Ames NPSN complex. A user submits a job to a master scheduler daemon, which in turn hands the job off to local or remote queues for execution. UNIX kernel limits like CPU time, stack and data size, working set size, and file size are used to govern the resources consumed by individual jobs. In most implementations, electronic-mail notification of job boundary status is available, as well as distributed spooling of job output.

One of the areas of primary interest and development is in the queuing scheduler. Early systems like NQS had no mechanism to load balance jobs between multiple batch queues. The result is that jobs end up waiting in busy queues while other queues stand empty. Load balancing schedulers were then introduced that would allocate jobs between queues based on a system load feedback mechanism. Jobs were evenly distributed between machines, but the single scheduler proved to be a single point of failure. The next stage in scheduler development involves redundant schedulers and the ability for schedulers to pass jobs between themselves. We originally used the distributed queuing system (DQS) developed by the folks at Florida State SCRI. DQS includes all the features present in NQS type systems. DQS also supports dedicated and nondedicated workstation queues and architecture queue classes. This means that you can distribute batch jobs to idle workstations or to specific architecture types. DQS includes a load-based scheduler, PVM support, Group Queues, NFS/AFS support, user access controls, interactive sessions, and an X11 and motif GUI. DQS is commercially available as a product called Codine.

In keeping with our desire to use shrink-wrapped code when possible, we have migrated our DQS system to IBM's Load Leveler. Load

Leveler is an enhanced version of the Condor distributed batch system designed by the University of Wisconsin. Load Leveler is similar to DQS. It also includes support for redundant schedulers and configuration of abstract resource types.

33.5 Summary

Clustered computing allows us to take a "divide and conquer" approach to a number of the scaling problems we encountered in the large-single-CPU world. Workloads are divided up across multiple computers such that the resource demands remain well within the limits that the operating system, application set, and hardware can provide.

Problems also exist in the interactions between mixed-application workloads on a single time-shared computer. Applications that consume large amounts of memory can bring smaller interactive work to a standstill. A runaway server program can cause other critical resources and applications to fail. Clustering allows us to isolate critical resources and applications on dedicated computers, keeping them away from other problem applications.

Using the client/server software architecture in a cluster has allowed us to mask the location of an application or resource. Client software invoked from the user's home system can access services anywhere in the network. In most cases, the interface is architecture-neutral, allowing us to provide an application service from a hardware platform on which it is most mature and robust. In the event that a vendor application has not been designed with client/server operation in mind, we provide a software wrapper that can mimic this behavior.

Multiple computers each running a copy of a particular service application provides a means for ensuring availability. A single machine in the cluster may fail or be taken down for maintenance without interrupting overall service. The remaining systems are still accessible. Cluster redundancy can be extended to disk, network interfaces, and other components.

The bottom line always shows up somewhere in design specifications. Clustered, low-cost workstations can provide the same CPU, memory, and disk resources previously only available on multimillion-dollar mainframe computers. Rather than upgrading an entire system to keep pace with growth, new machines can be added to a cluster incrementally to meet resource demands. The same is true of system components such as network adapters and disks. Technology upgrades can be added alongside existing equipment—you won't have to throw out the old mainframe engine for the next newer model. You don't have to do some of the custom development we have done to implement our cluster model. Many vendor packages are available that provide the same infrastructure. The point to this chapter is to get you thinking about computing in the network-centric world we are living in. Our experience has been that it hasn't taken additional staff to support a cluster of 300 systems versus a couple of large mainframes. Much of the savings in support has been due to concurrent availability of system management software like Tivoli's TME or HP OpenView.

34

Network Archiving

34.1 Storage Management

The information age credo is, "The one who holds the most data wins." Everybody's building a tower of data gold along with a Web page to show it off. Home pages on the "infobahn" are as dazzling as Vegas marquees on a starry desert night. "Movie clips, sound bites, reference data, mail archives, shareware . . . it's all here! Just step into my parlor. Sure, you may have seen some of my wares elsewhere on the Net, but have you ever seen a bigger collection or a better display? Browse and sample the merchandise. Download as much as you want. Did you see my rating on the 'Best of Web?' Be sure to tell your friends!"

If you thought it was tough coercing your users into cleaning their data houses in the past, you haven't seen anything yet. Everyone's cruising the Web and filling their pockets with data candy. The rules of the road are: "Keep a private copy" and "Don't throw anything away." Many of the information tidbits are multimedia-based, where multimegabyte data sizes are the norm. This activity only compounds the problem of managing legacy enterprise data. In most cases, you can't make value judgements as to the importance of your user community's storage requirements. You can't keep throwing disks at the problem, and you can't have your operations staff running backups 24 hours a day, 7 days a week.

The solution is to provide a reliable, automated, hierarchical, and scalable means of storage management. The solution must go beyond traditional backup support by automating file migration to low-cost storage based on aging and free space policies. Tools must be provided to allow the end user and support staff to exercise control over how files are staged and how they are accessed. Ultimately you should be able to operate on staged data sets in a manner similar to operating on local files. Enter mass storage systems. Once considered a tool for large supercomputing environments, mass storage management applications have evolved to meet the needs of mixed large-data and large-user-population shops. Before reviewing the facilities provided by a sampling of storage management systems, let's take a look at the model on which they are based.

34.2   IEEE Mass Storage Reference Model

The IEEE Mass Storage Systems Technology Committee (MSSTC) has been working for nearly two decades on refining a reference model for storage management systems. The model describes a modular system that addresses the needs of small to large, stand-alone and distributed heterogeneous environments. The model provides an excellent foundation for implementing software and hardware systems to solve the data management problems described above. The proposed user interface is defined to mask the complexity of storage architecture and hierarchy. It allows the end user to control which files require archiving, how long they should be retained, the number of copies, versions, and access security. It recommends a separation of data and control message paths but does not define a particular network protocol to ensure open connectivity. Rather than dictate a single access method for interacting with data storage, it describes three options that may be used to develop clients: operating system traps (similar to NFS trapping of I/O system calls), application level processes (FTP is an example), and an API for developing custom access mechanisms. It defines an open interface to support a wide range of storage mediums.

34.2.1   Components

In a nutshell, the components and interaction of the reference model are as follows (see Fig. 34.1). Files are called *bitfiles* and are represented as bit streams with an associated unique bitfile ID and header. There is no modification of the data itself. A name server maps the operating-system-dependent file names to the unique bitfile IDs. Bitfile servers manage bitfile attributes maintained in the headers. This includes things like file size, access control information, logical location, and so on. Bitfile movers are used to transfer bitfiles between client systems and the storage servers. The storage servers track the location of bitfiles on the physical volume repositories. There is also a migration manager that is responsible for maintaining free space on the storage media by migrating bitfiles between devices as needed. The modular nature of this model provides flexibility in distributing and replicating function between many nodes in a network environment.

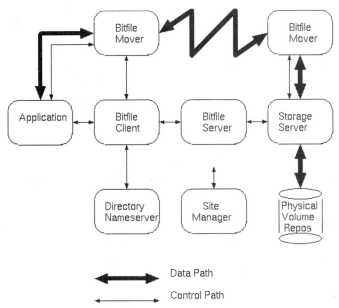

Figure 34.1   IEEE mass storage reference model.

A number of popular commercial storage management products are based on the IEEE model. Examples include ADSM, Epoch, AMass, Datatree, and Unitree. Many of these packages have their roots in implementations developed by programmers and scientists at the national labs. An MVS-based system called the Common File System developed at Los Alamos Lab and a UNIX-based system called LINCS from Lawrence Livermore National Laboratory were the precursors of the Datatree and Unitree products.

34.2.2   Development history

You may be familiar with a number of mass storage implementations that may or may not follow the IEEE reference model. Examples are IBM's MVS system managed storage (DFSMS) and VM Workstation data save facility (WDSF). The MVS-based Common File System developed by Los Alamos National Laboratory has been in production for over thirteen years and is now marketed by the DISCOS division of General Atomics under the name DataTree. Lawrence Livermore National Laboratory developed a UNIX-based mass storage system called LINCS and has been in production there since 1988. The Livermore Lab is a test bed for software and hardware integration under the IEEE reference model. The LINCS system is now marketed by many vendors as a product called Unitree. The Livermore National Storage Laboratory has since developed an enhanced version of Unitree called NSL-Unitree. NSL-Unitree moves further into the realm of distributed storage servers and storage hierarchies. Unitree has been ported to AIX and conforms to the IEEE mass storage reference model. For the sake of this discussion, I'll focus on Unitree, since it is representative of the IEEE reference model and is the most commonly known implementation.

34.3   ADSTAR Distributed Storage Manager (ADSM)

IBM's ADSM is an excellent example of a policy-based incremental backup and archive system. The product is a follow-on to the VM Work-station data save facility, and it has its roots in MVS DFSMS architecture. ADSM is especially useful in environments where you want to provide unattended scheduled backup services for workstation LANs to a central site. The server side of ADSM supports a hierarchy of raw or file-system-based storage pools to house incoming data. Migration and compaction algorithms are used to optimize utilization of storage media. Supported storage devices include disk, optical, tape, and robotic silos. A GUI-based client allows users to register workstations for backup and archive services. The client software is also used to access and manage data stored in the server. ADSM currently supports thirteen client platforms and seven server platforms. Clients include AIX, Solaris, HP-UX, SVR4, SCO, UNIX, SINIX, Ultrix, DOS, MS/Windows, Netware, Macintosh, OS/2, and AS/400. Server software is available for AIX, Solaris, HP-UX, MVS, VM, VSE, and OS/2. Network transport protocols between client and server include TCP/IP and various flavors of SNA.

34.4   Unitree

Unitree has long been the de facto standard when it comes to storage management for UNIX systems. In its most common incarnation, Unitree uses a two-tier storage hierarchy consisting of disk as a first-level archival staging area and tape as the second level. Users move files into and out of the storage system via NFS, FTP, or Unitree-provided DFTP clients. A migration process in the central server copies files from the disk staging area to tape after aging or to maintain free space. Eventually, the disk copy of the file may be purged. When a user accesses a particular file, Unitree will retrieve the data from the current level of storage on which it resides transparent to the user. This is where a robotic tape system comes in handy. You can easily run your operations staff ragged in a fairly active system without the use of some kind of robot.

There are few architectural limits in the Unitree system. There are no maximum limits in the code for number of files, number of directories, file size, or file names. Granted, there may be limits imposed by the operating system. A single file may span multiple physical volumes. Thus, terabyte files and file systems may be configured. Under the NFS interface, users operate on archived files using standard UNIX file system semantics and commands.

NSL-Unitree represents the most extensive and robust implementation of the Unitree architecture. Multiple dynamic storage hierarchies provide a means for tuning the storage system to provide different performance classes to meet user access requirements. A third-party data transfer capability allows applications direct access to lower levels of storage without requiring intermediate handling of the data by Unitree storage servers. Frequently accessed files can be collocated in the archive for quick access. NSL-Unitree also extends reporting and monitoring facilities.

34.5 High-Performance Storage System (HPSS)

HPSS represents the next generation of storage management systems. It is being developed as a joint project between IBM's Federal Systems division and the National Storage Labs. This system is designed to scale storage management an order of magnitude over existing architectures. Based on Version 5 of the IEEE reference model, HPSS provides a distributed mass storage environment capable of interoperating and sharing data between geographically distant locations. HPSS supports file name spaces exceeding billions of objects. Bitfile sizes scale to 2^{64}, enabling storage capacities in the multipetabyte range. That should be enough storage to hold a few GIF files! A striped API library provides application support for parallel I/O streams. By using parallel data streams, gigabyte per second transfer rates can be realized between multiple storage volumes and the client application.

HPSS employs OSF DCE services as its underlying architecture. The control network of the IEEE reference model is implemented using DCE RPC and DCE threads. This allows HPSS clients and servers to multitask multiple concurrent communication streams. Authentication, access control, and auditing are provided by the DCE security service and access control lists. Transarc's Encina is used to manage server transactions and ensure the integrity of file metadata. Mirroring of metadata and embedded reconnect logic are implemented for fault tolerance. The modular design of HPSS and the DCE service base make it very easy to layer new features and modules into the system to pace new technologies and requirements.

HPSS entities communicate over any network based on TCP/IP sockets or IPI-3. Plans are in the works to support Fibre Channel and ATM. The current set of client interfaces include FTP, parallel FTP, NFS, PFS, and an API library. Future development will add support for AFS, DFS, VFS, and NFS V3. The distributed file interfaces allow end users to operate on server-managed data as if it resided on local disk. For higher-speed access, FTP and parallel FTP clients are available. HPSS is configured and managed using an X11-based GUI. A toolset is provided to assist existing Unitree shops to migrate their data into HPSS. Although HPSS is designed to meet the storage demands of the next-generation grand-challenge applications, it will work equally well in smaller clustered or multiprocessor environments. For more information on HPSS, check out the HPSS home page at Oak Ridge National Lab.

```
http://gopher.ccs.ornl.gov/HPSS/HPSS.html
```

34.6   Choosing a Storage Management System

When evaluating a storage management product for your enterprise, take special care in weighing your requirements for backup, migration, and archive services. Features of the backup service might include access controls for user restore capabilities, multiple concurrent backup streams to the server, and catalog disaster recovery. Migration services are primarily used to control free space in local file systems automatically by moving low-activity files to remote storage. This can be very useful in workstation environments. An archive service may be combined with migration facilities, but it is essentially an end-user-controlled function. Files that are not currently required by the user are either moved to remote storage by the user or tagged by the user for scheduled staging. Other options worth consideration are how well the system scales in a number of files, file size limits, number of users, and catalog overhead. Does the system provide device striping or staged caching to improve transfer rates for large datasets? How well does the network file system implementation handle serial versus random file access?

The three storage management products described above are all IBM products or development projects. My intent was to illustrate the range of backup to archive services, user interfaces, and scaling capabilities provided by each system. There are a number of similar products marketed by other vendors, so shop around. Look for a feature set that meets your needs and pocketbook.

Unfortunately, I don't seem to be able to save this chapter to disk. Time to archive a few MPEG and sound files. Gee, I can't do without that Ren and Stimpy screen saver. Decisions . . . decisions . . .

Appendix

Who do you turn to when you can't decipher the configuration intricacies of the AIX Network Install Manager after reading all the manuals? Maybe you have heard about a new performance patch for AIX DCE but can't remember the APAR number. How are you going to find it? You've heard all this talk about the great public and shareware applications available for AIX on the Internet. Where are they? I'm not sure I know either, but over the years I've compiled a list of Internet sites that I use as references for these kinds of questions. What I have collected is a mixture of "official" sites blessed by IBM marketing and development organizations along with a number of user-supported archives. The corporate sites usually offer the best technical and product information. Discussion groups made up of peer users provide the most current product experiences and they always offer a supportive shoulder when things aren't going well around the shop.

Keeping current a list of information sites and repositories like these requires a bit of housekeeping. Sites come and go or are reorganized by their maintainers. New server and interface technologies debut, making all your access information obsolete. Large information providers like IBM often have the same problem. One organization in the company reworks an information archive while another either duplicates the effort or moves critical data that the first site was referencing. Just when you think you have assembled a complete set of information services, somebody makes a change and you spend another half day trying to find that crucial article you need to finish a project. So go the slings and arrows of information infrastructure. The good news is that the World Wide Web has at least made it easier to move around between the various information sources. You no longer have to rely on old conference crib notes scribbled on a paper napkin telling you how to subscribe to a particular E-mail list server or access an anonymous FTP site. Most Web browsers will handle these tasks for you. A good Web browser and a few directory and search engines will usually turn up what you're looking for. The following list of Web sites should help get you started poking around the world of AIX software and information archives. You won't find any recommendations on a good Web browser in the paragraphs that follow. That is a religious decision best left to the vendor faithful.

RS/6000 Welcome Center

If you have installed AIX V4, then you will have likely come across references to the RS/6000 Welcome Center. The Welcome Center is a tool that will take you on a whirlwind tour of the features and capabilities of AIX V4 and the POWER product line. There are multimedia demos, configuration and setup assistance displays, and even a game to soothe your furrowed brow during tedious AIX installations. AIX and Windows NT versions of Welcome Center are available to meet your desktop preference. The AIX version requires that you first install Ultimedia Services/6000 2.1.4.0 if you want to experience all the multimedia features of the tool. If you didn't install Welcome Center during AIX V4 installation, you can install it from the product media or download a copy from:

http://www.rs6000.ibm.com/support/welcome/

IBM Austin

For the latest information on POWER hardware and software products, check out the IBM Austin Web site. This is an actively maintained Web site that provides up-to-date news articles, product announcements, and pointers to other sites of interest. The Austin page is a good starting point for linking to some of the other sites I'll discuss below. You can also access the main IBM corporate home page if your interests include other IBM operating systems and product offerings. Use the IBM search engine at the bottom of each page if you're having a hard time finding particular product information or announcement letters.

http://www.austin.ibm.com/

IBM Direct

The IBM Direct Web page is your gateway to online product ordering. This page provides the same information available in the IBM Direct catalogs you receive in the mail. The site lists current product promotions and announcements. Product information can be located by using either the index or search interface. If you need assistance configuring your order, there is a helpful worksheet form that will step you through the configuration and ordering process. You can contact the IBM Direct order desk via E-mail if you need additional help.

http://ibm-direct.e-com.ibm.com/rsdirect/

AIX Customer Support

Check out the AIX Customer Support site for current maintenance and fix information. One of the first things you'll want to do is download a copy of fixdist and tapegen. fixdist is a tool that assists you in browsing APAR information and downloading maintenance sets. The companion tool, tapegen, stacks maintenance sets onto tape in backup format ready for installp. The AIX Customer Support page also has links to AIX related publications, trade show events, and user group information. There is a Q&A service that allows you to submit questions and browse online support information. Note that access to some services require that you have a Support Line contract and logon account.

```
http://service.software.ibm.com/aixsupport/
```

IBMLink

Most of you IBM mainframe folks will be familiar with IBMLink. IBMLink was one of the first online interfaces for accessing IBM product information over the Internet. Most of the features you may have come to know in the older telnet version of IBMLink are still available under the new IBMLink Web interface. These include InfoLink for announcements and press releases, OrderLink to configure and order products, and TalkLink for conferencing access to other customers and IBM support personnel. IBMLink requires a logon account to access all services.

```
http://www.ibmlink.ibm.com/
```

IBM Solution Developer Support

The IBM Solution Developer Support Web site maintains a large archive of information of interest to product developers and business partners. The site requires a logon account to gain access. Individual accounts are free. You can register online by following instructions on the home page. Even if you are not a developer, you will find a great deal of technical information that will be helpful in using and administering IBM systems. Technical documents include white papers, AIX-related publications, and development articles. Q&A and bulletin board services provide access to other AIX product developers and customers.

```
http://www.developer.ibm.com/
```

Team RS/6000

The Team RS/6000 Web site is a forum for organizing communication between customers and the IBM development labs. The site includes referral and resource information for contacting consultants and solution developers. Access to the RS/6000 development labs will be handled via a Lotus Notes interface called LabLink. Membership is open to anyone interested in RS/6000 issues for a fee. I'll refer you to the Web page for details.

```
http://www.teamrs6000.org/
```

RS/Magazine

How about access to information related to your favorite computer publication, *RS/Magazine?* Computer Publishing Group maintains a Web page that features the latest issues of *RS/Magazine, SunExpert,* and *WebServer* magazines. You'll also find product reviews and an editorial calendar at the site. Too bad they don't have back issues online (hint, hint).

```
http://www.cpg.com/
```

AIX FAQ

If you looking for the answer to a nagging AIX question, then check out one of the AIX FAQ sites. A FAQ (frequently asked questions) document is comprised of topical information gleaned from many AIX-related news groups. It provides answers to many common AIX questions and issues that plague all of us. The FAQ will also direct you to other AIX related publications, books, and information resources.

```
http://euch6h.chem.emory.edu/services/aix-faq/     Emory
http://www.cis.ohio-state.edu/hypertext/           Ohio State
faq/usenet/aix-faq/top.html
```

AIX Software Archive

A number of sites on the Net provide access to public domain software and shareware archives via anonymous FTP or Web pages. The sites listed below feature software that has been built and tested on AIX. The software repository maintained by UCLA provides both source code and compiled versions of products. Special care is taken at the UCLA site to ensure that the distributions install in the /usr/local tree. This keeps them from getting mixed in with other licensed products and keeps them out of the way of operating-system maintenance activities.

```
ftp://aixpdslib.seas.ucla.edu/        UCLA
http://aixport.sut.ac.jp/software/
http://www.support.ibm.com/download/
```

Newsgroups and Mail Lists

There are a number of newsgroups and mail lists that discuss AIX- and POWER-related topics. Some of the more prominent include comp.unix.aix, comp.sys.powerpc, and aix-l. IBM maintains a Web page that makes it very easy to subscribe to these public lists as well as IBM product and information mail lists. Web pages like this keep me from having to explain the details of getting on and off mail lists and newsgroups in this book. Speaking of newsgroups, there is an excellent search tool available on the Web called dejanews. The dejanews site makes it very easy to sift through multiple newsgroup archives when you are looking for particular gems of information. It keeps you from having to read every article.

```
http://www.rs6000.ibm.com/resource/       IBM mail list page
maillist.html

http://www.dejanews.com/                   News search engine
```

City of AIX

All you real AIX enthusiasts will definitely want to check out the City of AIX or Aix-en-Provence in France. Rumor has it that the very first POWER chip was found in a cabbage patch in one of the many gardens in the city. And you always thought RS/6000s were the result of years of design and development efforts.

```
http://www-eleves.int-evry.fr/~galland/Aix/Eng/index.html
```

Other Sites of Interest

DCE

```
http://www.osf.org/dce/                    OSF DCE

http://www.osf.org/www/dceweb/             OSF DCE Web

http://www.es.net/hypertext/               DCE and Kerberos
committees/auth.html
```

CDE

```
http://www.xopen.org/public/presents/          X/Open
uniforum/cde/tsld010.htm
```
```
XoPubs@xopen.org
```

Internet Security

```
http://www.ietf.org/                            Drafts and RFCs
```
```
http://www.ibm.com/Security                     IBM security
```
```
http://home.netscape.com/newsref/               Netscape
ref/netscape-security.htm                       security
```
```
http://www.rsa.com/rsalabs/faq/faq_misc.html    RSA PKCS
```

Pine, IMAP, IMSP

```
http://www.washington.edu/imap/                 IMAP
```
```
http://andrew2.andrew.cmu.edu/                  IMSP
cyrus/cyrus.html
```
```
http://www.cac.washington.edu/pine/             Pine
```

Bibliography

AIX Version 4 Desktop Handbook, GG24-4451-00.

AIX Installation Guide Version 4.2, SC23-1924-00.

AIX Version 4 System Management Guide, SC23-2525.

AIX Version 4 Problem Solving Guide and Reference, SC23-2606.

AIX Version 4 System User's Guide: Communication and Networks, SC23-2545.

AIX Version 4 System User's Guide: Operating System and Devices, SC23-2544.

AIX Version 4 System Management Guide: Communication and Networks, SC23-2526.

Prabhat K. Andleigh, *UNIX System Architecture,* New Jersey: Prentice Hall, 1990.

Dipto Chakravarty, *Power RISC System/6000: Concepts, Facilities, and Architecture,* New York: McGraw-Hill, Inc., 1994.

Dipto Chakravarty and Casey Cannon, *PowerPC: Concepts, Architecture and Design,* New York: McGraw-Hill, Inc., 1994.

Kevin Dowd, "Programming in Parallel," *RS/Magazine,* **2**(3), March 1993.

John Eargle, *Handbook of Recording Engineering,* New York: Van Nostrand Reinhold Company Inc., 1986.

Aeleen Frisch, "Boosting Performance on the RS/6000," *RS/Magazine,* **2**(5), May 1993.

Aeleen Frisch, *Essential System Administration,* O'Reilly & Associates, Inc., September 1995.

Aeleen Frisch, "Writing it Down," *RS/Magazine,* **2**(6), June 1993.

G. Benton Gibbs, "Demistifying the Object Data Manager" Part 1, */AIXtra,* **2**(2), April 1992.

G. Benton Gibbs, "Demistifying the Object Data Manager" Part 2, */AIXtra,* **2**(3), July 1992.

G. Benton Gibbs, "Demistifying the Object Data Manager" Part 3, */AIXtra,* **2**(4), October 1992.

Russel A. Heise, "Performance Tuning: A Continuing Series—The vmstat Tool," */AIXtra,* **3**(5), September/October 1993.

Robert S. Henson, "A New, Improved AIX—Version 4.2," */AIXtra,* September/October 1996.

"IBM RISC System/6000 Processor," *IBM Journal of Research and Development,* **34**(1), January 1990.

IBM RISC System/6000 Technology, SA23-2619.

Elizabeth Lewis, "Performance Tuning: Theory and Practice," */AIXtra,* **3**(2), March/April 1993.

David S. Linthicum, "NFS Explained," *RS/Magazine,* **2**(4), April 1993.

David S. Linthicum, "Using UUCP: The Basics," *RS/Magazine,* **1**(7), July 1993.

Harold W. Lockhart Jr., *OSF DCE,* New York: McGraw-Hill, Inc., 1994.

Mike Loukides, *System Performance Tuning,* O'Reilly & Associates, Inc., November 1990.

Jane Majkiewicz, "Taming the Backup Beast," *RS/Magazine,* **2**(2) February 1993.

Paul Martin and Dinah McNutt, "Customizing SMIT," *RS/Magazine,* **1**(5), May 1992.

Sape Mullender, *Distributed Systems,* Reading, MA: ACM Press, 1993.

Evi Nemeth, Garth Snyder, and Scott SeeBass, *UNIX System Administration Handbook,* New Jersey: Prentice Hall Software Series, 1989.

Jerry Peek, Mike Loukides, and Tim O'Reilly, *UNIX Power Tools,* Bantam Books, March 1993.

"Printing for Fun and Profit Under AIX V3," IBM International Technical Support Centers "Red Book", GG24-3570.

W. Richard Stevens, *Advanced Programming in the UNIX Environment,* Reading, MA: Addison-Wesley Publishing Company, Inc., 1992.

W. Richard Stevens, *UNIX Network Programming,* New Jersey: Prentice Hall Software Series, 1990.

Dawn C. Stokes, "A Comparison of DCE DFS and AFS," /*AIXtra,* **2**(4), October 1992.

Andrew S. Tanenbaum, *Computer Networks,* New Jersey: Prentice Hall, 1981.

"TCP/IP Tutorial and Technical Overview," IBM International Technical Support Centers "Red Book", GG24-3376.

Mary Vicknair Wise, "High Availability for Network File System," /*AIXtra,* **3**(1), January 1993.

Index

accounts. *See* user environment
accounting, 461–470
  accounting files, 463
  command usage, 462
  commands, 466
  configuration, 463–466
  connect time, 462
  crontab entries, 465
  data collection, 461–463
  disk usage, 462–463, 464–465
  /etc/utmp, 462
  house cleaning, 469
  overview, 461
  print usage, 463, 465
  process resource usage, 462
  reports, 465–469
  shifts, 464
  statistics, 466–468
  /var/adm/pacct, 462
  /var/adm/wtmp, 462
architecture, 25–34
  601, 29, 33, 34
  602, 29, 33, 34
  603, 29, 33, 34
  604, 29, 33, 34
  620, 29, 33, 34
  801 project, 26
  AMERICA, 26
  common hardware reference platform (CHRP), 29
  high performance switch (HPS), 32
  MCM and multichip module, 27
  POWER, 25, 26, 33, 34
  POWER2, 26, 27, 33, 34
  PowerPC, 28, 29, 33, 34
  RISC, 26
  RT, 26
  scalable POWER parallel (SP), 32
  symmetric multiprocessor (SMP), 29–30, 39–40
archiving, 567–572
  ADSTAR, 570
  choosing a system, 572

archiving (*Cont.*):
  components, 568–569
  high-performance storage system (HPSS), 571–572
  IEEE reference model, 568, 569
  storage management, 567–568
  Unitree, 570–571
auditing, 487–490
  audit logging, 487
  classes, 490
  configuration, 489
  /etc/security/audit/config, 489–490
  /etc/security/audit/objects, 490–491
  event types, 488
  objects, 490

backup and copy utilities, 517–524
  backup, 521
  backup strategies, 517–518
  disaster recovery, 520
  /etc/dumpdates, 520
  full and incremental dumps, 519
  media, 520–521
  mksysb, 81, 100, 175, 522
  mkszfile, 81, 100, 175, 522
  mounted or unmounted, 518
  network backups, 522–523
  OS dumps, 522
  rdump, 522
  restore, 521
  rrestore, 522
  schedules and rotation, 519–520
  sizing, 518–519
  utilities, 521–522
basic operating system (BOS), 62, 64, 71, 78
  bos.rte, 64, 74, 79, 80
bonus pak. *See* World Wide Web
boot:
  bffcreate, 76
  boot kernel, 105
  bootinfo, 40, 89
  bootlist, 99

boot (*Cont.*):
  bosboot, 89, 100
  built-in self test (BIST), 102, 539
  cfgmgr. *See* object data manager
  core sequence controller (CSC),
    103
  /etc/inittab, 111
  /etc/nologin, 69
  init, 110
  initial program load (IPL), 104
  initial sequence controller (ISC),
    103
  I/O channel controller (IOCC), 106
  ipl_varyon, 70
  media, 80, 100
  mkinsttape, 82, 100, 538
  mksysb, 81, 100, 175, 522, 538
  mkszfile, 81, 100, 175, 522, 538
  phase 1, 106
  phase 2, 109
  phase 3, 110
  POST Test, 103
  ROS init, 101
  runtime, 111
  shutdown, 112
  system state, 69
  telinit, 69
  troubleshooting, 112
  vital product data (VPD), 106

clustering, 555–565
  application server, 558
  batch queuing, 564
  cluster domain name service,
    559–560
  common file system, 560–561
  compute server, 558
  configuration and installation, 563
  file server, 558. *See also* Network
    File System
  hardware topology, 556–558
  mail server, 559
  password server, 558
  rules, 556
  scalable password service, 561–562
  single system image, 559
  summary, 565–566
Common Open Software Environ-
    ment (COSE), 4, 407
Common Desktop Environment
    (CDE), 4, 397, 406–414
  components, 408
  directories, 408, 409, 415

Common Desktop Environment
    (CDE) (*Cont.*):
  environment variables, 412
  file and application managers,
    411–412
  front panel, 411
  help manager, 413–414
  login manager, 409
  overview, 407
  session manager, 410
  style manager, 411
  summary, 414
  technologies, 407
  workspace manager, 412–413
  X11 and X Windows. *See* X11
    administration
  XDT to CDE conversion (xdt2cde),
    407–408

desktop file services, 343–349
  Columbia Appletalk Package
    (CAP), 349
  components, 345
  DAVE, 349
  directory shares, 346–347
  /etc/hosts. *See* Transmission Con-
    trol Protocol/Internet Protocol
  GatorBox, 349
  installation and configuration,
    343–347
  licensing, 348
  LMHOSTS, 345
  name service, 345–346
  NetBIOS, 343
  NFS and DFS compatibility, 348
  printer shares, 347–348
  Samba, 343–349
  SMB, 343
  smb.conf, 344–345, 346, 348
  WINS, 345
devices. *See* object data manager
disk, 149–154
  architecture, 151
  diag, 152
  diagnostics, 152
  hardware, 150
  installation, 152
  integrated drive electronics (IDE),
    150
  redundant array of independent
    disks (RAID), 150, 151
  serial storage architecture (SSA),
    150

disk (*Cont.*):
 SCSI. *See* small computer system
  interface
Distributed Computing Environment
  (DCE), 323, 394, 495–514
 ACLs, 498. *See also* auditing; distributed file system; security
 cell, 324, 502–503, 505
 cell directory service (CDS), 324,
  496–497, 501
 cell_admin, 332, 335
 clients, 502, 508
 commands, 503
 components, 497
 CORBA, 500
 DFS. *See* distributed file system
 directory name service (DNS),
  496–497, 507
 distributed time service (DTS),
  324, 498, 501, 507
 /etc/mkdce.data, 335, 509
 Generic Security Service API
  (GSSAPI), 395, 500
 global directory service (GDS), 324,
  496–497, 501
 implementation considerations,
  511–512
 installation and configuration,
  505–511
 Interface Definition Language
  (IDL), 496
 LFS. *See* distributed file system
 Network Time Protocol (NTP), 499
 object-oriented DCE (OODCE),
  500
 planning, 502
 principals, 504
 privilege authorization certificate
  (PAC), 498
 products, 501
 remote procedure call (RPC), 324,
  496
 security service (SS), 324, 498,
  504–505, 507
 servers, 502, 503, 508
 stubs, 497
 technologies, 496
 threads, 499
 time differential factor (TDF), 499
 versions, 499–500
 X.500, 496
 X/Open directory service (XDS),
  501

distributed file system (DFS),
  323–342, 499
 access control, 324–325
 Access Control Lists (ACL), 324,
  327, 338. *See also* auditing; Distributed Computing Environment; security
 acl_edit, 327, 334
 aggregate, 326, 329, 333–334
 Andrew File System (AFS),
  323–324
 backup, 339–340
 Backup Database Machine (BDM),
  328, 335
 bak, 340
 binary distribution machine, 328
 bosserver, 327
 clients, 329
 components, 327–329
 dfsexport, 334, 336
 exporting and mounting, 334
 file replicator machine, 328, 335
 file server machine, 328, 332
 fileset database (FLDB), 328, 332
 file system structure, 325–326
 filesets, 326, 329, 333–334
 fts, 336
 installation and configuration,
  329–336
 local file system (LFS), 323, 326,
  329, 502
 lsfldb, 336
 operation and administration,
  336–337
 /opt/dcelocal/var/dfs, 327
 replication, 338–339
 starting DFS, 337
 System Control Machine (SCM),
  327, 331
 Tape Coordinator Machine (TCM),
  328
 /var/dce/dfs, 327
 VFS. *See* Network File System
Distributed Management Environment (DME), 3
Distributed systems management,
  55–57
 DSMIT, 56–57
 Tivoli, 55

electronic mail, 353–371
 addressing and headers, 355
 aliases, 361–362

electronic mail (*Cont.*):
  Application Configuration Access
    Protocol (ACAP), 368
  comsat, 366
  /etc/aliases, 361, 362
  Internet message access protocol
    (IMAP), 367
  Internet message support protocol
    (IMSP), 368
  logs, 362–363
  MAIL, 365, 366
  mail transport agent (MTA), 353,
    354, 356
  Mail.rc and .mailrc, 354
  MAILMSG, 365, 366
  managing mail queues, 365
  multipurpose Internet mail exten-
    sions (MIME), 367, 370
  Pine, 354, 368–370
  POP and IMAP, 366–370
  post office protocol (POP), 367
  RFC 821 and RFC 822, 355
  sendmail configuration, 356–363
  sendmail tables, 356
  sendmail.cf, 357–360
  sendmail.nl, 360–361
  simple mail transfer protocol
    (SMTP), 355
  starting and stopping sendmail,
    363
  troubleshooting, 363–365
  user agent (UA), 353–354, 356
  /usr/lib/sendmail, 362, 363
  /var/spool/mail, 365, 366

file systems, 161
  data blocks, 164
  inodes, 162, 163, 303
  istat, 163
  JFS. *See* journaled file system
  super block, 161–162

InfoExplorer, 9–22
  ASCII interface, 13, 15
  bookmarks, 15
  fixed disk, 11
  history, 15
  hypertext links, 14
  merging notes, 17
  notes, 16
  over NFS, 12
  printing, 17
  searching, 14–15

InfoExplorer (*Cont.*):
  using, 12
  X11 interface, 12, 13
installation and maintenance, 61–96
  AIX Support Family, 65, 548–549
  APPLY, COMMIT, and REJECT,
    68
  /etc/nologin, 69
  fixdist, 66, 67, 549–550
  IBMLink, 65
  install steps, 72
  install type, 68
  installp, 68, 69, 72, 75, 79, 80, 85
  Licensed Program Product (LPP),
    72, 73
  lslpp, 64, 72, 79
  NIM. *See* Network Install Manager
  oslevel, 63
  packaging, 63
  planning, 62
  prereq and coreq, 78
  program temporary fix (PTF), 65
  reference system, 82
  tapegen, 66
  uname, 63

journaled file system (JFS), 161–173
  AIX V3 compatibility, 172
  compression, 165
  configuration, 167, 168
  crfs and crjfs, 168
  defragfs, 164
  df, 171
  /etc/filesystems, 12, 168–169, 308,
    312, 430
  fragments, 164
  fuser and lsof, 171
  large files, 166
  mount and umount, 170
  mounting, 170
  moving file systems, 175
  Number of Bytes per Inode (NBPI),
    163
  quotas. *See* user environment
  resizing file systems, 175
  rmfs and rmjfs, 168
  root file system, 171–172
  troubleshooting, 176

Kerberos. *See* security
kernel, 35–41
  bindprocessor, 39
  cpu_state, 39

kernel (*Cont.*):
  locks, 38
  lockstat, 38
  multiprocessor (MP), 39–40
  pthreads, 37
  scheduling and dispatching, 39,
    525–526
  signals, 37
  threads, 37
  uniprocessor (UP), 39–40
  Virtual Memory Manager (VMM),
    36, 105, 526

logical volume manager (LVM), 108,
    152–154, 157–159
  chpv, 157
  configuration, 154
  exportvg, 70, 80, 157
  extendvg, 155
  importvg, 70, 80, 157
  interdisk, 157
  intradisk, 158
  Logical Volume Group (LVG), 153
  lspv, 155
  lsvg, 71, 156
  mirrors, 151, 159, 160
  mkvg, 155
  physical volume identifier (PVID),
    108, 154
  quorum, 156
  root volume group (rootvg), 81,
    157, 160
  size, 157
  stripe, 151, 154
  troubleshooting, 176
  types, 157
  varyoffvg, 157
  varyonvg, 156
  volume group descriptor area
    (VGDA), 156, 157, 158
  volume group identifier (VGID),
    156
  volume group status area (VGSA),
    156, 158
  volume groups, 154

mail. *See* electronic mail
maintenance. *See* installation and
    maintenance
man pages, 18–21
  catman, 22
  man, 18
  MANPATH, 20

modems. *See* terminals and modems
monitoring and tuning, 525–536
  bos.perf, 531
  CPU scheduling, 39, 525–526
  disk, 528
  graphical tools, 534
  netstat, 271, 272, 529
  network, 528–529
  no, 272, 273, 530
  performance toolbox (PTX),
    531–532
  PerfPMR, 531–532
  public domain tools, 534–535
  rmss, 527
  schedtune, 527
  traditional tools, 532–534
  Virtual Memory Manager (VMM),
    36, 105, 526
  workload analysis, 525

network architecture, 227–232
  Advanced Mobile telePhone Sys-
    tem (AMPS), 230
  Advanced Radio Telephone System
    (ARTS), 230
  ARPANET, 228, 231
  asymmetric digital subscriber line
    (ADSL), 229
  BITNET, 229
  cable modem, 229
  cellular modems, 230
  Computer Science Network
    (CSNET), 229
  Corporation for Research and Edu-
    cation Network (CREN), 229
  Defense Advanced Research Proj-
    ect Agency (DARPA), 228
  Defense Research Internet (DRI),
    228
  International Mobile Station Iden-
    tity (IMSI), 230
  International Standards Organiza-
    tion (ISO), 227
  mobile IP, 231
  network job entry (NJE), 229
  NSFNET, 228–229
  Open Systems Interconnect (OSI),
    227, 233
  OSI model, 227–228, 233–234
  packet radio, 231
  personal digital assistant, 230
  plain old telephone service (POTS),
    229

network architecture (*Cont.*):
  SNA. *See* System Network Architecture
  TCP/IP. *See* Transmission Control Protocol/Internet Protocol
  terminal node controller (TNC), 231
  wireless networking, 230–232
Network File System (NFS), 303–321
  biod, 304, 306, 308
  configuring NFS, 304
  /etc/exports, 12, 304, 306–307, 312
  /etc/filesystems. *See* journaled file systems
  /etc/rc.nfs, 304
  /etc/vfs, 303, 305
  exporting file systems, 306–307
  external data representation (XDR), 304
  gnode, 303
  high-availability cluster multiprocessor (HACMP), 318
  high availability NFS (HANFS), 306, 317–318
  high-speed NFS, 319
  NFS clients, 307–309
  NFS server, 305–307
  NFS V3, 319
  nfsd, 304, 306
  nfsstat, 314
  nobody, 307
  portmap, 306, 308
  remote procedure call (RPC), 304
  rpc.lockd, 304, 306
  rpc.mountd, 305, 306
  rpc.statd, 304, 306
  secure NFS, 309
  showmount, 314
  troubleshooting, 314–316
  Virtual File System (VFS), 166, 303, 327
  vnode, 303
  vsops, 303
network information system (NIS), 309–314
  automounter, 313–314
  /bin/domainname, 310
  domain, 310
  /etc/netgroups, 310
  /etc/publickey, 312
  file classes, 311
  map files, 310

network information system (NIS) (*Cont.*):
  mkkeyserv, 312
  name space, 310
  netgroups, 310
  newkey, 312
  servers and clients, 311
  services, 313
  /var/yp/yppasswd, 311
  yellow pages (YP), 309, 310
  ypinit, 311
Network Install Manager (NIM), 83–96
  clients, 88–90
  commands, 84, 85
  /etc/niminfo, 85
  /export, 84
  IPL ROM emulation, 89–90
  master server, 84
  resources, 87–88
  routing, 86
  shared product object tree (SPOT), 62, 87, 88
  /tftpboot, 84
  utilities, 92
news, 373–378
  network news transfer protocol (NNTP), 374
  news readers, 375
  newsgroup classifications, 377
  newsgroups, 376–377
  .newsrc, 376
  NNTP commands, 374
  /usr/lib/news/nntp.access, 374, 375
  /var/spool/news, 374

object data manager (ODM), 125–137
  cfgmgr, 107
  components, 126
  configuration, 129
  customized (CuXX), 132
  devices, 131
  lsdev, 71
  objects, 127
  odmadd, 53
  ODMDIR, 126
  odme, 128–130
  odmget, 53
  odmshow, 53, 132
  predefined (PdXX), 132
  savebase and restbase, 134
  states, 134

paging space, 173–174
  commands, 174
  swapon, 174
passwords. *See* auditing; security;
  user environment
printers, 201–223
  administration, 217, 220
  ASCII printers, 220–221
  backend, 210–211
  banner, 212–214
  BSD, SYSV, 211
  custom, 212
  enq, 217, 218, 219, 220
  /etc/hosts.lpd, 217
  /etc/qconfig, 203, 204
  /etc/qconfig, 203, 204, 215–216
  local and remote, 210
  lpd, 203, 216–217
  lptest, 214
  lpx, 222
  mkpq, 210
  mkprt, 205, 206
  mkvirprt, 214, 221
  pass-through mode, 221
  postscript, 212
  print device, 203, 204–209
  print queue, 203, 209–210
  printer state, 219
  priority, 219
  qadm, 218
  qcan, 220
  qchk, 219
  qdaemon, 215
  qpri, 220
  qstatus, 219
  queue, 202, 203
  queue device, 202, 203
  queues and printers, 218
  splp, 208
  troubleshooting, 208, 214
  /usr/lpd/piobe, 211
  /usr/lpd/rembak, 211
  virtual printer, 202, 203
  VSM, 201–202
  X-station printers, 221–222
process management, 447–459
  ad hoc jobs, 456
  controlling processes, 452
  controlling terminal, 450
  CPU priority, 450
  cron and schedule process,
    454–457

process management (*Cont.*):
  crontab, 455–456
  effective GID (EGID), 449–450
  effective UID (EUID), 449–450
  hangup and nohup, 454
  kill, 452–454
  parent child inheritance, 451
  process attributes, 447, 448
  process group ID (PGID), 449
  process ID (PID), 447, 449
  process identifiers, 449
  process parent ID (PPID), 449
  process state, 451
  ps, 448
  pstree, 448
  queuedefs, 456–457
  run queue, 450
  signals, 452–454
  /usr/include/sys/proc.h, 447
problem analysis and recovery,
    537–552
  bootable media, 80, 100
  built-in self test (BIST), 102, 539
  crash, 546–547
  dumps, 122, 540–542
  errlog, 542, 122
  /etc/syslog.conf, 544
  fixdist, 66, 67, 549–550
  hardware diagnostics, 548
  IBM support, 65, 548–549
  kernel, 545. *See also* kernel
  LED status, 537, 539
  log commands, 542
  logs, 542–544
  mkinsttape, 82, 100, 538
  mksysb, 81, 100, 175, 522, 538
  mkszfile, 81, 100, 175, 522, 538
  nm, 546
  segments, 545
  syslog, 544
  trace, 544
  /var/adm/ras/errlog, 542

runtime configuration, 117–124
  Alog, 121
  console, 123
  dump devices, 122, 542
  errlog, 121, 542
  language environment, 118
  licensed users, 121
  max processes, 119–120
  OS characteristics, 118

runtime configuration (*Cont.*):
PTYs, 122
system logs, 121
time zone, 117, 118

security, 473–493
access control, 480. *See also* DCE
access control lists (ACL),
481–482
auditing passwords, 477
authentication tables, 483
authentication methods, 482–487
/bin/login and /usr/bin/tsm, 482
chgrp, 480
chown, 480
Computer Emergency Response
Team (CERT), 491–492
converting password files, 478
COPS, 491
DES encryption, 485
/etc/security/login.cfg, 484
/etc/security/passwd. *See* user environment
/etc/security/sysck.cfg, 479
Kerberos, 57, 324, 394, 486–487
password rules, 475–476
passwords, 474–478
policy, 474
resetting passwords, 476
secure attention key (SAK), 480
shadow password files, 474
smart card, 485
su, 477
super user and root, 477
tcbck, 478–479
trusted communication path, 480
Trusted Computing Base (TCB),
478–480
umask, 480
virscan, 491
shared product object tree (SPOT),
62, 87, 88
shell. *See* user environment
small computer system interface
(SCSI), 135, 150, 152
addressing, 136
differential, 135
single-ended, 135
System Management Interface Tool,
45–60
customizing, 52–53
display, 47

System Management Interface Tool
(*Cont.*):
fastpath, 51–52
smit.log, 49
smit.script, 51
smitty, 47
using, 46
System Network Architecture (SNA),
291–299
advanced program-to-program
communication (APPC), 292
interface, 294
logical unit (LU), 291, 292, 293
management, 297
Netview, 297
network addressable unit (NAU),
291, 292, 293
network definition, 294–295
physical unit (PU), 291, 292, 293
security, 296–297
SNA services/6000, 293
SNA subsystem, 295–296
SNMP. *See* Transmission Control
Protocol/Internet Protocol
system services control point
(SSCP), 292
Tivoli, 297
troubleshooting, 297
system resource controller (SRC),
457–459
commands, 458
components, 457
hierarchy, 458
subservers, 457
subsystems, 457

tapes, 139–147
block size, 141
characteristics, 139, 146–147
commands, 145
conversion, 142
dd, 141, 142
density, 143
device names, 142, 143
format, 140
ioctl mapping, 144
tctl, 144
tools, 145
terminals and modems, 179
AT&T style, 197
BSD style, 198
cabling, 180–183

terminals and modems (*Cont.*):
  code sets, 195
  commands, 193
  console, 196–197
  control characters, 188
  CRT, 179
  Data Communications Equipment
    (DCE), 181, 182
  data format, 186
  Data Terminal Equipment (DTE),
    181, 182
  DB25, 180–183
  DB9, 180–183
  display, 194
  EIA-CCITT, 181
  /etc/pse.conf, 179, 180
  /etc/termcap, 187
  fonts, 194–196
  high function terminal (HFT),
    193
  keyboard, 193–194
  line discipline, 188
  line signals, 191
  line speed and baud rate, 185
  login state, 190
  low function terminal (LFT), 192
  mktty, 184
  modem support, 190–192
  port addressing, 184
  pseudo-TTY (PTY), 179, 197–198
  RS-232C, 180–183
  serial port configuration, 184–190
  serial TTY, 180–190
  STREAMS, 179
  stty, 188, 189
  terminal type, 186
  troubleshooting, 192, 197
  tset, 187
  TTY, 179
  /usr/lib/terminfo, 187
Transmission Control Protocol/Inter-
    net Protocol (TCP/IP), 233–276
  anonymous FTP, 265–266
  ATM, 243–244
  bind, 247
  CERT, 268
  CMIP over TCP (CMOT), 268
  common management information
    protocol (CMIP), 268
  configuration, 244–266
  dedicated slip, 261–262
  domain address, 246

Transmission Control Protocol/Inter-
    net Protocol (TCP/IP) (*Cont.*):
  domain name service (DNS),
    246–251
  dynamic routes, 253
  /etc/hosts, 246, 310, 345
  /etc/hosts.equiv, 310
  /etc/inetd.conf, 257
  /etc/services, 257–259
  Ethernet, 235–238
  FDDI, 239–240
  File Transfer Protocol (FTP), 234
  hardware, 234–244
  hardware address, 244
  host table, 246
  ifconfig, 255
  inetd, 256–260
  interface, 254–255
  Internet Control Message Protocol
    (ICMP), 233
  Internet Protocol (IP), 233
  IP address, 244–246
  iptrace, 270–271
  Kerberos. *See* security
  link control protocol (LCP), 263
  mbufs, 119–120, 272
  message information block (MIB),
    268, 269
  named, 248
  netstat, 271, 272, 529
  network daemons, 259
  NFS. *See* Network File System
  network-managed stations, 268
  network management, 268–270
  no, 272, 273, 530
  nondedicated slip, 262–263
  nslookup, 272
  performance, 272–273
  ping, 271
  planning, 234
  point-to-point protocol (PPP), 260,
    263–265
  ppp authentication, 264–265
  pppap, 265
  pppdial, 265
  pppip, 264
  ppplcp, 264
  protocols, 252
  reachability, 271
  resolver, 251
  resource records, 250
  routed, 253

Transmission Control Protocol/Internet Protocol (TCP/IP) (*Cont.*):
routing, 251–254
security, 266–268
serial line internet protocol (SLIP), 260–263
servers, 271
simple mail transfer protocol (SMTP). *See* electronic mail
simple network management protocol (SNMP), 268, 269, 297
slattach, 261, 262
SLIP/PPP, 241–242
slipcall, 263
sliplogin, 262
sniffers, 270
snmpd, 270
SOCC, 242–243
SRC. *See* system resource controller
static routes, 252
subnets, 253–254
token ring, 238–239
Transmission Control Protocol (TCP), 233
troubleshooting, 270–272
trusted computing base (TCB), 267
User Datagram Protocol (UDP), 233

UNIX history, 5
UNIX to UNIX Copy Program (UUCP), 277–290, 373
addressing, 278
basic networking utilities (BNU), 277
commands, 287–288
configuration, 278–286
daemons, 286
devices, 282–283
dialcodes, 282, 285–286
dialers, 285
directories, 279–280
hardware, 287
HoneyDanBer, 277
login account, 279
logs, 286–287
permissions, 283
system, 281
tables, 280
troubleshooting, 288

UNIX to UNIX Copy Program (UUCP) (*Cont.*):
using, 277–278
uucheck, 284
uucico, 288
uucpadm, 280
uuname, 279
UUNET, 278
user environment, 423–445
account access rights, 431
account environment, 431–438
ACLs, 425. *See also* auditing; DFS; security
adding user accounts, 438–439
.cshrc, 437
environment variables, 432
/etc/environment, 432, 433
/etc/filesystems. *See* journaled file system
/etc/group, 425–426
/etc/passwd, 425, 442
/etc/profile, 432, 434–435
/etc/security/environ, 435
/etc/security/group, 425–426
/etc/security/limits, 427–428
/etc/security/login.cfg, 438
/etc/security/mkuser.default, 436, 440
/etc/security/passwd, 425, 443, 475
/etc/security/user, 443
file systems, 424
group commands, 426
Group ID (GID), 425
limits, 427–431
mkuser.sys, 436
policy, 423
quotas, 429–431
removing user accounts, 441
resources, 424
restricting account access, 442
UID space, 425
updating user accounts, 439

VFS. *See* Network File System: Virtual File System
visual system manager, 54, 201–202
commands, 54

World Wide Web (WWW), 379–395
access control, 386
Adobe Acrobat Reader, 381, 382

World Wide Web (WWW) (*Cont.*):
applet, 391
bonus pak, 381–385
browsers, 380
certificates and X.509, 394
creating HTML documents,
  388–390
Generic Security Service API
  (GSSAPI), 395, 500
httpd, 385
hypertext markup language
  (HTML), 380, 388, 389, 390
hypertext transport protocol
  (HTTP), 379, 380
Internet connection secure server,
  381, 385
IPSec, 395
Java, 381, 390–391
Java Development Kit (JDK), 391,
  392
JavaScript, 391–393
Kerberos. *See* security
lightweight directory access protocol (LDAP), 395
MIME. *See* electronic mail
Netscape Commerce Server, 381,
  384–385
Netscape Navigator, 381, 382
Public Key Cryptography Standard
  (PKCS), 393
Secure Socket Layer (SSL), 394
security, 393–395
server administration, 385–388
servers, 379–380
site structure, 387–388

World Wide Web (WWW) (*Cont.*):
Ultimedia Services for AIX, 381,
  383
uniform resource locator (URL),
  380–381

X/Open, 4, 397
X11 administration, 397–419
AIXWindows, 397, 398
AIXWindows Desktop (XDT), 407
application defaults, 399
CDE. *See* Common Desktop Environment
components, 398
configuration, 403
fonts, 400
fonts.alias, 400–402
fonts.dir, 400–401
mkfontdir, 400
Motif, 403–404
OPEN LOOK, 405
product filesets, 399
Project Athena, 398
resources, 403
window managers, 402–405
X-Consortium, 397–398
X-Windows Display Manager
  (XDM), 406
Xstation administration, 414–418
boot, 415–417
configuration, 415–417
overview, 407
printing. *See* printers
X11 and X-Windows. *See* X11
  administration

ABOUT THE AUTHOR

James W. DeRoest is Assistant Director of the Advanced Systems Technologies Group, University Computing Services, at the University of Washington. He writes the monthly "AIXtensions" column for *RS/Magazine* (now *SunExpert*), and is the author of the acclaimed *AIX RS/6000: System and Administration Guide* (also published by McGraw-Hill). Jim DeRoest earned his B.S. in computer science at the University of Oregon. He lives with his wife and five children in Bothell, Washington.